Fundamentals of Organizational Behavior

Fundamentals of Organizational Behavior

MANAGING PEOPLE AND ORGANIZATIONS

Ricky W. Griffin
TEXAS A&M UNIVERSITY

Gregory Moorhead
ARIZONA STATE UNIVERSITY

Houghton Mifflin Company   Boston   New York

*For Professor Gavril Ilizarov and Dr. Joseph Gugenheim
for "thinking outside the box"*
   —*Ricky Griffin*

*This book is dedicated to my fellow cancer survivors—Live
Strong!*
   —*Greg Moorhead*

V.P, Editor-in-Chief: *George Hoffman*
Senior Sponsoring Editor: *Lisé Johnson*
Associate Editor: *Julia Perez*
Senior Project Editor: *Fred Burns*
Editorial Assistant: *Brett Pasinella*
Senior Manufacturing Coordinator: *Marie Barnes*
Senior Art and Design Coordinator: *Jill Haber*
Senior Composition Buyer: *Sarah Ambrose*
Executive Marketing Manager: *Steven W. Mikels*
Marketing Associate: *Lisa E. Boden*
Cover image: ©Getty Images
Photo Credits: Page 8: ©Michael Grimm; p. 17: ©Katherine Lambert; p. 19: ©Russ
Quackenbush; p. 32: © Juliana Sohn/M.S. Logan Ltd.; p. 39: ©Greg Girard/Contact
Press Images; p. 43: ©Gene Puskar/AP/Wide World; p. 64: ©Peter Cosgrove/AP/Wide
World; p. 69: Courtesy Lockheed-Martin;. p. 76: ©France Ruffenach; p. 93: ©Alessandra
Sanguinetti; p. 97: ©Clive Brunskill/Getty Images; p. 101: ©Saureb Das/AP/Wide World;
p. 123: ©Peter M. Fisher/Corbis; p. 126: ©Taro Yamasak/People Weekly/Time, Inc.;
p. 133: ©Christina Caturano; p. 145: ©Dorothy Low; p. 154: ©Dennis Brack/
Bloomberg/Landov; p. 176: ©Robert Burroughs; p. 179: ©Robert Brenner/
PhotoEdit; p. 185: Chris Mueller/Redux Pictures; p. 201: ©John Russell/
AP/Wide World; p. 208: ©Barbel Schmidt; p. 214: ©Erica Berger/Corbis Outline;
p. 229: ©John R. Boehm; p. 236: © Thomas Broening; p. 240: © Pablol Bartholomew/
MediaWeb India; p. 262: Jose Azel/Aurora & Quanta Productions; p. 266:
©Michele Asselin; p. 268: ©Margaret Salmon; p. 281: ©Peter Serling. All Rights
Reserved; p. 284: ©Axel Koester; p. 286: AP/Wide World Press; p. 315:
©David McLean/Aurora & Quanta Productions; p. 321: ©Laura Pedrick/The New York
Times; p. 326: ©Corbis; p. 345: ©Robert Semeniuk; p. 350 (left): ©Robert Laberge/
Getty Images; p. 350 (right) ©AP; p. 359: ©Mark Richards; p. 371: ©Michael L.
Abramson; p. 379: ©Greg Miller; p. 381: ©Andrew Garn; p. 395: ©Mark Ralston/SCMP;
p. 402: ©Everett Collection; p. 409: ©Beth Claggett/Bloomberg/Landov

Printed in the U.S.A.

Library of Congress Control Number: 2004116804

ISBN: 0-618-49270-4

2 3 4 5 6 7 8 9—DOW—09 08 07 06 05

CONTENTS

Part Two   Individual Processes in Organizations   59

3   Foundations of Individual Behavior   60

Organization Development   399

Systemwide Organization Development 399   Task and Technological Organization Development 400   Group and Individual Organization Development 401

Resistance to Change   405

Organizational Sources of Resistance 405   Individual Sources of Resistance 407

Managing Successful Organization Change and Development   408

Take a Holistic View 408   Start Small 409   Secure Top Management Support 409 Encourage Participation 409   Foster Open Communication 409   Reward Contributors 409

Organizational Behavior Case for Discussion: *Change of Direction at Schwab*   **411**

Experiencing Organizational Behavior: *Planning a Change at the University*   **413**

Self-Assessment Exercise: *Support for Change*   **413**

OB Online   **414**

Building Managerial Skills   **414**

Part Five Video Case: *Organization Structure and Design*   **417**

PREFACE

Organizational behavior is the study of human behavior in organizations, of the interface between human behavior and the organization, and of the organization itself. Hence, it reflects an exciting but challenging part of every manager's work—dealing with people. As the field of organizational behavior has grown, however, so too has the length of survey textbooks traditionally used in organizational behavior courses.

As we prepared this first edition of *Fundamentals of Organizational Behavior*, we carefully considered what material could be viewed as "fundamental" in nature—that is, what material simply had to be discussed in any course in organizational behavior. We chose to provide detailed coverage of that material, but to not include other material that, while interesting and important, was not as essential.

This book reflects this differentiation between essential and non-essential material. Traditional survey books today tend to have twenty or more chapters; we have been able to cover the fundamental material from the field, though, in only fifteen chapters and far fewer pages than you might see in a comprehensive book. But that does not mean that the book is a superficial or "discount" treatment of the field. As you will see, our text covers the fundamentals in detail and is presented in a dynamic and contemporary fashion; it also makes full use of bold visual features such as color and photographs that are generally preferred by today's readers.

We believe that *Fundamentals of Organizational Behavior* will prepare and energize managers of the future for the complex and challenging tasks of the new century while preserving the past contributions of the classics. Even though this text focuses only on the fundamentals, it is comprehensive in its presentation of practical perspectives, backed by the research and teachings of the experts. We expect each reader to be inspired by the most exciting task of the new century: managing people in organizations.

Content and Organization

Part One discusses the managerial context of organizational behavior. In Chapter 1 we introduce the field of organizational behavior and relate it to the manager's job. Chapter 2 provides a thorough treatment of two increasingly important contextual perspectives on organizational behavior, global issues and workforce diversity.

Part Two includes four chapters that focus on key aspects of individual processes in organizations. Chapter 3 presents the foundations for understanding individual behavior in organizations by discussing the psychological nature of people, elements of personality, individual attitudes, perceptual processes, and creativity. Chapter 4 discusses employee motivation. Chapters 5 and 6 focus on specific methods, techniques, and strategies used by managers to affect individual performance in organizations.

In Part Three we move from the individual aspects of organizational behavior to the more interpersonal aspects of the field, including communication, groups, and teams. Chapter 7 describes the behavioral aspects of communication in organizations. Chapters 8 and 9 are a two-chapter sequence on groups and teams in organizations. We believe there is too much important material to just have one chapter on these topics. Therefore, we present the basics of understanding the dynamics of small group behavior in Chapter 8 and discuss the more applied material on teams in Chapter 9.

Part Four is devoted to leadership and decision making. We start by presenting leadership in a two-chapter sequence, examining models and concepts in Chapter 10 and influence processes in Chapter 11. The third chapter in Part Four, Chapter 12, is devoted to decision making and negotiation. This chapter also discusses group decision making.

In Part Five we address more macro and system-wide aspects of organizational behavior. Chapter 13 describes organization design. Chapter 14 moves on to the more elusive concept of organizational culture. The final chapter, Chapter 15, could really be the cornerstone of every chapter, because it presents the classical and contemporary views of organizational change. Due to the demands on organizations today, as stated earlier and by every management writer alive, change is the order of the day, the year, the decade, and the new century. Indeed, it might be argued that the only constant in organizations today is constant change.

Features of the Book

Fundamentals of Organizational Behavior is guided by our devotion to the preparation of the next generation of managers. This is reflected in four key elements of the book that we believe stem from this guiding principle: a strong student orientation; contemporary content; a real-world, applied approach; and effective pedagogy.

- *Student Orientation:* We have insured that students will find this book to be easy and even enjoyable to read with its direct and active style. We have tried to write in a style that is energetic and lively and geared to the student reader. We want students to enjoy reading the book while they learn from it.

- *Contemporary Content Coverage:* While focusing only on the fundamental concepts of the field of organizational behavior, our book also covers this material in a contemporary fashion. While we often describe the historical background of major topics, we also present the most modern management approaches as expressed in the popular press and the academic research.

- *Real-World, Applied Approach:* The organizations cited in the opening incidents, examples, cases, and boxed features throughout our book represent a blend of large, well-known and smaller, less well-known organizations so that students will see the applicability of the material in a variety of organizational settings. Each chapter opens and closes with concrete examples of relevant topics from the chapter. Each chapter also contains one box. Each box has a unique, identifying icon that distinguishes it and makes it easier for students to identify.

  - Each *"Mastering Change"* box shows an organization rethinking its methods of operation to respond to changes in the business climate.

  - Each *"Business of Ethics"* box explores an organization dealing with ethical issues.

■ Each *"World View"* box examines an issue an organization and the people in it face as the organization expands its global operations.

■ *Effective Pedagogy:* Our guiding intent has been to put together a package that enhances student learning. The package includes several features of the book, many of which have already been mentioned.

   ■ Each chapter begins with a Management Preview, including chapter objectives, and ends with a Synopsis.

   ■ "Discussion Questions" at the end of each chapter stimulate interaction among students and provide a guide to complete studying of the chapter concepts.

   ■ The end-of-chapter case, "Organizational Behavior Case for Discussion," offers a real-life scenario that shows a company or organization putting into practice concepts from the chapter.

   ■ An "Experiencing Organizational Behavior" exercise at the end of each chapter helps students make the transition from textbook learning to real-world application.

   ■ A "Self Assessment" activity at the end of each chapter gives students the opportunity to apply a concept from the chapter to a brief self-assessment or diagnostic activity.

   ■ The "OB Online" feature encourages students to reach beyond the text to find organizations or other resources on the Web that illustrate the issues discussed in the chapter.

   ■ The "Building Managerial Skills" activity provides an opportunity for students to "get their hands dirty" and really use something discussed in the chapter.

   ■ The "Test Prepper" appears at the end of each chapter and contains true/false and multiple-choice questions to gauge students' retention and comprehension of chapter material. The answers can be found at the end of the text, before the Index.

   ■ The "Part Video Cases" appear at the end of each of the five parts of the text. The cases can be used as stand-alone cases without showing the videos in class or can be used in conjunction with airing the video in class. Companies highlighted include: Southwest Airlines, Wheelworks, Denver Broncos, Bakers' Best, and General Mills.

A Complete Teaching and Learning Package

A complete package of teaching and learning support materials accompanies this edition.

For Instructors

The *Instructor's Resource Manual,* written by Sean Valentine (University of Wyoming), includes for each chapter a synopsis, chapter objectives, detailed lecture outline, suggested answers to the text questions and activities, a supplemental mini-lecture, and additional experiential exercises. Also included are a section on learning and teaching ideologies, suggested course outlines, and suggestions on how to use the mini-lectures.

The *Test Bank*, prepared by Margaret Hill, contains 120 questions consisting of true/false, multiple-choice, completion, matching, and essay. A text page reference, learning-level indicator, question type, and keyword accompany each question.

The *HMClassPrep/HMTesting Instructor CD* is designed to assist the instructor with in-class lectures. The CD offers Lecture Outlines, PowerPoint Slides, a Video Guide, and much more. The CD also contains electronic Test Bank items. This computerized Test Bank enables instructors to administer tests via a network system, modem, or personal computer, and it includes a grading function that lets them set up a new class, record grades from tests or assignments, and analyze grades to produce class and individual statistics.

The completely new password-protected *Instructor Web Site* provides several tools to help prepare and deliver lectures: downloadable files of the *Instructor's Resource Manual*; downloadable PowerPoint slides; suggested answers to the activities on the Student Web Site, and the Video Guide with video summaries, suggested uses, and questions for discussion.

A detailed set of *PowerPoint Slides*, available on both the *Instructor Web Site* and the *HM ClassPrep CD*, combines clear, concise text and art to create a complete lecture package with more than 20 slides per chapter. Instructors can use the slides as-is or edit them. Slides can also be printed for lecture notes and class distribution.

A *video program* is provided to enhance the teaching package. The five companies highlighted in the end-of-part Video Cases appear in the program, along with three other segments. Focusing on key topics of organizational behavior, the videos present additional material to help bring the concepts to life. Teaching notes and suggestions are also provided in the Video Guide.

Blackboard/ WebCT Course. Through Houghton Mifflin's partnership with Blackboard and WebCT, instructors can create and customize course materials for online/distance learning courses. Assets include links to website material, student quizzes, lecture aids, PowerPoint slides, video segments with talking points, glossaries, and much more.

For Students

The *Student Web Site* provides additional information, study aids, activities, and resources that help reinforce the concepts presented in the text. The site includes: learning objectives; brief chapter outlines; chapter summaries; ACE self-tests; a glossary of key terms; flash cards for reviewing the key terms; additional cases; convenient chapter links to the organizations highlighted in the text; and a resource center with links to various sites of general organizational behavior interest.

Acknowledgments

Although this book bears our two names, numerous people have contributed to it. Through the years we have had the good fortune to work with many fine professionals who helped us to sharpen our thinking about this complex field and to develop new and more effective ways of discussing it. Their contributions were essential to the development of this text. Any and all errors of omission, interpretation, and emphasis remain the responsibility of the authors.

Several advisory board members made essential contributions to the development of this textbook. We would like to express a special thanks to them for taking the time to provide us with their valuable assistance:

Chris Beloin, University of Wisconsin

Bryan Booth, Shippensburg University
Mark Butler, San Diego State University
Joseph DeFilippe, Suffolk Community College
Joseph Kavanaugh, Sam Houston State University
Bryan Kennedy, Athens State University
JR Minifie, Texas State University
Joelle Nisolle, Pittsburg State University
Elizabeth Ravlin, University of South Carolina
Robert Rubin, DePaul University
Terri Scandura, University of Miami

We would also like to acknowledge the outstanding team of professionals at Houghton Mifflin Company who helped us prepare this book. Julia Perez, Kristin Penta, and Fred Burns have done yeoman's work in pulling all of the parts of this book together and shepherding it through the process. George Hoffman was also a key player in planning the book and supplements package from start to finish.

Finally, we would like to acknowledge the essential role our families play in our lives. While family members are almost always thanked at the end of a preface, their influence in reality extends from the beginning of everything until its end. It pervades all of what we do, and is the foundation of our lives. Throughout our trials and tribulations, joys and triumphs, successes and failures, our families have stood by our sides and never questioned the value of our work while at the same time providing constant meaning to our lives.

Ricky W. Griffin
Gregory Moorhead

PART ONE

Introduction to Organizational Behavior

CHAPTER 1

An Overview of Organizational Behavior and Management

MANAGEMENT PREVIEW

Effectively managing organizational resources is one of the most critical activities of business in any complex society. Human behaviors, decisions, and actions, in turn, play vital and pervasive roles throughout every aspect of both management processes and organizations. Thus, understanding human behavior in organizational settings is a fundamental necessity for all managers, including both current practitioners and those who aspire to hold management positions in the future. In this opening chapter, we introduce you to the meaning of organizational behavior and trace its development from its earliest simple concepts through its evolution into a complex, multidisciplinary field capable of explaining many different forms of complex organizational phenomena. We conclude the chapter by presenting useful contextual perspectives that effectively link the field's theoretical concepts with the practical elements of organizational realities.

After you have studied this chapter, you should be able to:
- ☐ *Define and describe organizational behavior.*
- ☐ *Trace the historical roots of organizational behavior.*
- ☐ *Describe the emergence of organizational behavior.*
- ☐ *Characterize contemporary organizational behavior.*
- ☐ *Discuss the role of organizational behavior in management.*
- ☐ *Identify and discuss contemporary managerial challenges.*
- ☐ *Discuss the role of organizational behavior in managing for effectiveness.*

We begin by illustrating how one successful firm, Southwest Airlines, effectively uses an array of resources, including its employees, to remain at the forefront of its industry.

Would you love to work for a company that just lost its charismatic founder, replacing him with the company's lawyer and the CEO's one-time secretary? Would you jump at the chance for a job with a firm that pays one-half to two-thirds what its rivals pay, doubles their workload, and asks them to clean up their workplace to avoid hiring a cleaning service? Would you be thrilled to land a position in a business that offers only a stock ownership program, with no pension plan, whose stock recently declined 24 percent? As it turns out, many people would if the firm is Southwest Airlines. In one recent year, more than 200,000 people submitted applications and résumés for just 6,000 jobs. Positions with the firm are so coveted that Southwest can be more selective than Harvard.

Following the recent retirement of founder and long-time CEO Herb Kelleher, long-time corporate counsel Jim Parker assumed the CEO role and secretary-turned-human-resources-manager Colleen Barrett became president and COO. These two leaders have done an exemplary job of carrying on the carrier's tradition of success.

From the beginning, Southwest did not adopt the hub-and-spoke system, preferring a short-haul, point-to-point schedule instead. This keeps costs low. The carrier operates out of smaller, less expensive airports in many major markets, such as Long Island's Islip rather than New York's LaGuardia or Kennedy. The company flies only one type of jet, the Boeing 737, reducing its expenses in every area from purchasing to maintenance to training. Due to these early, smart decisions, Southwest "has long-term, systematic advantages the other carriers can likely never match," says pilot and industry consultant Vaughn Cordle.

Southwest derives its most significant advantages, however, from its people. Although highly unionized, the firm has never experienced a labor strike. Southwest management sits down personally to negotiate every union contract. "The biggest complaint in the industry is that management doesn't listen to employees," says Southwest pilot Brad Bartholomew. "But you can't say that at Southwest. The top guy is in the room." Among the benefits Southwest employees enjoy are extensive training, a no-layoffs policy, and generous profit sharing and stock ownership. Although currently there are few profits to share and stock price is down, employees are optimistic that situation won't last. At a time when other airlines have been reducing wages, Southwest has been giving pay hikes.

"We aren't in the 'airline business'; we are in the 'Customer Service business,' and we just happen to fly airplanes." —Colleen Barrett, president and COO, Southwest Airlines

Compare Southwest's position to that of other airlines. U.S. Airways filed for Chapter 11 bankruptcy and seems unlikely to remain in business. United Airlines' managers claim United, too, is headed for bankruptcy. Further, in the wake of September 11th, the major carriers laid off 100,000 employees, many of whom they have not replaced. Layoffs and pay cuts have contributed to low morale, which leads to low productivity, further hurting the traditional carriers. Analysts estimate that the major carriers would need to collectively reduce expenses by $18.6 billion, about 29 percent, to match Southwest's low-cost performance. Consultant Ron Kuhlmann says, "There's no easy way to [cut costs]. The problem is that major carriers are preserving their own model rather than paying attention to what customers are willing to pay for." Consultant Michael Boyd says, ". . . I'm very concerned over whether the airline industry can survive." "JetBlue may be the only [airline] out there that can compete head-to-head with Southwest," explains Daryl Jenkins, director of the Aviation Institute.

Every airline has adopted some of Southwest's pioneering concepts, such as eliminating meals. "Stepping up to the new reality is a healthy thing," says Gordon Bethune, retired CEO of Continental Airlines. "Only those companies that change with it will survive." However, to stay on top, Southwest must learn to compete with firms that are imitating its strategies. And it will have to grow, yet maintain the personalized service and customer loyalty associated with small size. Southwest president Barrett sums up the carrier's culture: "We aren't in the 'airline business'; we are in the 'Customer Service business,' and we just happen to fly airplanes."

The prevailing, optimistic view is pithily summed up by Michael O'Leary, CEO of Ryanair, a European-based carrier following Southwest's no-frills model. Evaluating the traditional carriers, O'Leary asserts, "They're basket cases. They're incredibly high-cost, very ineffective . . . These are stupid businesses for the amount of capital tied up in them. They never make any money . . . I think they'll limp along from crisis to crisis . . . [Airfares will continue to] decline for another 20, 30, 40 years." When asked for his opinion of Southwest, O'Leary replies, "If I were Southwest, I wouldn't be worried."

References: "Can Airlines Bring Costs Down to Earth?" *BusinessWeek*, October 23, 2002; "Full-Service Airlines are 'Basket Cases,'" *BusinessWeek*, September 12, 2002; Colleen Barrett, "The Southwest Difference," Southwest Airlines website; "The Airlines: Caught between a Hub and a Hard Place," *BusinessWeek*, August 5, 2002.

The success of Southwest Airlines has been based on a number of factors, including the skills of the firm's top managers and their understanding of the importance of other people. They clearly recognize the value of control and operational systems in a successful organization. But perhaps even more important, they see the value of people as a key determinant of success. Indeed, no manager can succeed without the assistance of others. Thus, any manager—whether responsible for an industrial giant like General Electric, Honda, IBM, or British Airways; the Boston Celtics basketball team; the Mayo Clinic; or a local Pizza Hut restaurant—must strive to understand the people who work in the organization. This book is about those people. It is also about the organization itself and the managers who operate it. The study of organizations and of the people who work in them constitutes the field of organizational behavior. We begin our exploration of this field with a more detailed discussion of its meaning and its importance to managers.

What Is Organizational Behavior?

LEARNING OBJECTIVE

Define and describe organizational behavior.

Organizational behavior (OB) is the study of human behavior in organizational settings, of the interface between human behavior and the organization, and of the organization itself.

Organizational behavior (OB) is the study of human behavior in organizational settings, of the interface between human behavior and the organization, and of the organization itself.[1] Although we can focus on any one of these three areas, we must remember that all three are ultimately necessary for a comprehensive understanding of organizational behavior. For example, we can study individual behavior (such as the behavior of Jim Parker or Colleen Barrett, or of one of their Southwest Airlines employees) without explicitly considering the organization. But because the organization influences and is influenced by the individual, we cannot fully understand the individual's behavior without learning something about the organization. Similarly, we can study organizations (such as Southwest Airlines itself) without focusing explicitly on the people within them. But again, we would be looking at only a portion of the puzzle. Eventually we must consider the other pieces as well as the whole.

Figure 1.1 illustrates this view of organizational behavior. It shows the linkages among human behavior in organizational settings, the individual-organization interface, the organization itself, and the environment surrounding the organization. Each individual brings to an organization a unique set of personal background and characteristics, as well as experiences from other organizations. In considering the people who work in organizations, therefore, a manager must look at the unique perspective each individual brings to the work setting. For example, suppose The Home Depot hires a consultant to investigate employee turnover. As a starting point, the consultant might analyze the types of people the company usually hires. The goal would be to learn as much as possible about the nature of the company's workforce as individuals: their expectations, their personal goals, and so forth.

But individuals do not work in isolation. They come in contact with other people and with the organization in a variety of ways. Points of contact include managers, coworkers, the organization's formal policies and procedures, and various

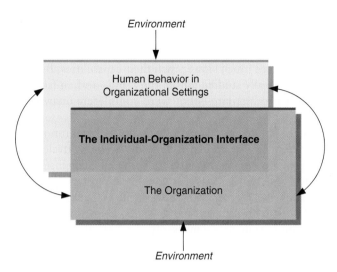

FIGURE 1.1

The Nature of Organizational Behavior

The field of organizational behavior attempts to understand human behavior in organizational settings, the organization itself, and the individual organization interface. As illustrated here, these areas are highly interrelated.

changes implemented by the organization. Over time, the individual changes too as a function both of personal experiences and maturity and of work experiences and the organization. The organization, in turn, is affected by the presence and eventual absence of the individual. Clearly, then, managers must also consider how the individual and the organization interact. Thus, the consultant studying turnover at The Home Depot might next look at the orientation procedures for newcomers to the organization. The goal of this phase of the study would be to understand some of the dynamics of how incoming individuals interact with the broader organizational context.

An organization, of course, exists before a particular person joins it and continues to exist after he or she leaves. Thus, the organization itself represents a crucial third perspective from which to view organizational behavior. For instance, the consultant studying turnover would also need to study the structure and culture of The Home Depot. An understanding of factors such as the performance evaluation and reward systems, the decision-making and communication patterns, and the design of the firm itself can provide added insight into why some people choose to leave a company and others elect to stay.

Thus, the field of organizational behavior is both exciting and complex. Myriad variables and concepts accompany the interactions just described, and together these factors greatly complicate the manager's ability to understand, appreciate, and manage others in the organization. They also provide unique and important opportunities to enhance personal and organizational effectiveness. Clearly, then, an understanding of organizational behavior can play a vital role in managerial work. To use the knowledge this field provides most effectively, however, managers must understand its various concepts, assumptions, and premises. To lay the groundwork for this understanding, we next examine the field's historical roots.

The Historical Roots of Organizational Behavior

LEARNING OBJECTIVE

Trace the historical roots of organizational behavior.

Many disciplines, such as physics and chemistry, are literally thousands of years old. Management has also been around in one form or another for centuries. For example, the writings of Aristotle and Plato abound with references to and examples of management concepts and practices. But because serious interest in the study of management did not emerge until around the turn of the twentieth century, the study of organizational behavior is only a few decades old.[2]

The Scientific Management Era

Scientific management, one of the first approaches to the study of management, focused on the efficiency of individual workers.

One of the first approaches to the study of management, popularized during the early 1900s, was scientific management. **Scientific management** focused primarily on the efficiency of individual workers. Several individuals helped develop and promote scientific management, including Frank and Lillian Gilbreth, Henry Gantt, and Harrington Emerson, but Frederick W. Taylor is most closely identified with this approach.[3] Early in his life, Taylor developed an interest in efficiency and productivity. While working as a foreman at Midvale Steel Company in Philadelphia from 1878 to 1890, he became aware of a phenomenon he called "soldiering": employees working at a pace much slower than their capabilities. Because most managers had never systematically studied jobs in the plant—and, in fact, had little idea how to gauge worker productivity—they were completely unaware of this practice.

To counteract the effects of soldiering, Taylor developed several innovative techniques. For example, he scientifically studied all the jobs in the Midvale plant and developed a standardized method for performing each one. He also installed a piece-rate pay system in which each worker was paid for the amount of work that individual completed during the workday rather than for the time spent on the job. (Taylor believed money was the only important motivational factor in the workplace.) These innovations boosted productivity markedly and form the foundation of scientific management.

After leaving Midvale, Taylor spent several years working as a management consultant for industrial firms. At Bethlehem Steel Company, he developed several efficient techniques for loading and unloading rail cars. At Simonds Rolling Machine Company, he redesigned jobs, introduced rest breaks to combat fatigue, and implemented a piece-rate pay system. In every case, Taylor claimed his ideas and methods greatly improved worker output. His book *Principles of Scientific Management*, published in 1911, was greeted with enthusiasm by practicing managers and quickly became a standard reference.

Scientific management soon became a mainstay of business practice. Among other things, it facilitated job specialization and mass production, profoundly influencing the U.S. business system.[4] It also demonstrated to managers the importance of enhancing performance and productivity, and confirmed their influence on these dimensions. For example, firms such as UPS and McDonald's still use some of the basic concepts introduced during the scientific management era in their efforts to become ever more efficient.

Taylor had his critics, however. Labor opposed scientific management because its explicit goal was to get more output from workers. Congress investigated Taylor's methods and ideas because some argued that his incentive system might dehumanize the workplace and reduce workers to little more than drones. Later theorists recognized that Taylor's views of employee motivation were inadequate and narrow. Others have alleged that Taylor falsified some of his research findings and paid someone to do his writing for him. Nevertheless, scientific management represents a key milestone in the development of management thought.[5]

Classical Organization Theory

During the same era, another perspective on management theory and practice was emerging. Generally referred to as **classical organization theory,** this perspective was concerned with structuring organizations effectively. Whereas scientific management studied how individual workers could be made more efficient, classical organization theory focused on how a large number of workers and managers could be organized most effectively into an overall structure. Interestingly, whereas scientific management was generally an American phenomenon, classical organization theory has a much more international heritage.

Max Weber, a German sociologist, is the most prominent contributor to classical organization theory (other notable pioneers in this area included Henri Fayol and Lyndall Urwick). Weber proposed a "bureaucratic" form of structure that he

Classical organization theory, another early approach to management, focused on how organizations can be structured most effectively to meet their goals

believed would work for all organizations.[6] Although today the term *bureaucracy* conjures up images of paperwork, red tape, and inflexibility, in Weber's model bureaucracy embraced logic, rationality, and efficiency. Weber assumed the bureaucratic structure would always be the most efficient approach. (Such a blanket prescription represents what is now called a universal approach.)

In contrast to Weber's views, contemporary organization theories recognize that different organization structures may be appropriate in different situations. However, like scientific management, classical organization theory played a key role in the development of management thought, and Weber's ideas and the concepts associated with his bureaucratic structure are still interesting and relevant today. (Chapter 13 discusses contemporary organization theory.)

The Emergence of Organizational Behavior

LEARNING OBJECTIVE

Describe the emergence of organizational behavior.

Rationality, efficiency, and standardization were the central themes of both scientific management and classical organization theory. The roles of individuals and groups in organizations were either ignored altogether or given only minimal attention. A few early writers and managers, however, recognized the importance of individual and social processes in organizations.

Precursors of Organizational Behavior

In the early nineteenth century, Robert Owen, a British industrialist, attempted to better the condition of industrial workers. He improved working conditions, raised minimum ages for hiring children, introduced meals for employees, and shortened working hours. In the early twentieth century, the noted German psychologist Hugo Münsterberg argued that the field of psychology could provide important insights into areas such as motivation and hiring of new employees. Another writer in the early 1900s, Mary Parker Follett, believed management should become more democratic in its dealings with employees. An expert in vocational guidance, Follett argued that organizations should strive harder to accommodate their employees' human needs.[7] Indeed, Follett's work, neglected in the years following her death, foreshadowed many of today's most popular and widely used management innovations.

Like Follett's perspective, the views of Owen and Münsterberg were not widely shared by practicing managers. Not until the 1930s did management's perception of the relationship between the individual and the workplace change significantly. At that time, a series of now classic research studies led to the emergence of organizational behavior as a field of study.

The Hawthorne Studies

The **Hawthorne studies,** conducted between 1927 and 1932, led to some of the first discoveries of the importance of human behavior in organizations.

The **Hawthorne studies** were conducted between 1927 and 1932 at Western Electric's Hawthorne plant near Chicago. (General Electric initially sponsored the research but withdrew its support after the first study was finished.) Several researchers were involved, the best known being William Dickson, chief of Hawthorne's Employee Relations Research Department, who initiated the research, and Elton Mayo and Fritz Roethlisberger, Harvard faculty members and consultants, who were called in after some of the more interesting findings began to surface.[8]

The first major experiment at Hawthorne investigated the effects of different levels of lighting on productivity. The researchers systematically manipulated the

The emergence of organizational behavior was characterized by the growing recognition of the importance of individual and social processes. For instance, the New York cancer center named for comedian Gilda Radner recently needed a facelift. Elaine Griffin, a noted Harlem-based interior designer took on the project. She started by interviewing people who used the space to find out what they wanted—what would make them feel good, help relax them, and so forth. Her goal then became to create space that would be warm and inviting to patients and their families.

lighting of the area in which a group of women worked. The group's productivity was measured and compared with that of another group (the control group), whose lighting was left unchanged. As lighting was increased for the experimental group, productivity went up—but, surprisingly, so did the productivity of the control group. Even when lighting was subsequently reduced, the productivity of both groups continued to increase. Not until the lighting had become almost as dim as moonlight did productivity start to decline. This result led the researchers to conclude that lighting had no relationship to productivity—and it was at this point that General Electric withdrew its sponsorship of the project!

In another major experiment, a piecework incentive system was established for a nine-person group that assembled terminal banks for telephone exchanges. Scientific management theory would have predicted that each individual would work as hard as he or she could to maximize personal income. But the Hawthorne researchers found instead that the group as a whole established an acceptable level of output for its members. Individuals who failed to meet this level were dubbed "chiselers," and those who exceeded it by too much were branded "rate busters." A worker who wanted to be accepted by the group could not produce at too high or too low a level. Thus, as a worker approached the accepted level each day, she or he slowed down to avoid overproducing.

After a follow-up interview program with several thousand workers, the Hawthorne researchers concluded that the human element in the workplace was considerably more important than previously believed. The lighting experiment, for example, suggested that productivity might increase simply because workers were singled out for special treatment and thus perhaps felt more valued. In the incentive system experiment, being accepted as a part of the group evidently meant more to the workers than earning extra money. Several other studies supported the overall conclusion that individual and social processes are too important to ignore.

Like the work of Taylor, unfortunately, the Hawthorne studies recently have been called into question. Critics cite deficiencies in research methods and alternative explanations of the findings. Again, however, these studies played a major role in the advancement of the field and are still among its most frequently cited works.[9]

The **human relations movement**, the beginning of organizational behavior, was based on the assumption that employee satisfaction is a key determinant of performance.

The Human Relations Movement

The Hawthorne studies created quite a stir among managers, providing the foundation for an entirely new approach to management known as the human relations movement. The basic premises underlying the **human relations movement** were that people respond to their social environment, motivation depends more on social needs than on economic needs, and satisfied employees work harder than unsatisfied employees. This perspective represented a fundamental shift away from the philosophy and values of scientific management and classical organization theory.

The works of Douglas McGregor and Abraham Maslow perhaps best exemplified the early values of the human relations approach to management.[10] McGregor is best known for his classic book *The Human Side of Enterprise*, in which he identified two opposing perspectives that he believed typified managerial views of employees. Some managers, McGregor said, subscribed to what he labeled Theory X. **Theory X** takes a pessimistic view of human nature and employee behavior. In many ways, it is consistent with the premises of scientific management. In contrast, McGregor's **Theory Y** takes a much more optimistic and positive view of employees. Theory Y, which is generally representative of the human relations perspective, was the approach McGregor himself advocated. Table 1.1 lists the basic assumptions of Theory X and Theory Y.

In 1943, Abraham Maslow published a pioneering theory of employee motivation that became well known and widely accepted among managers. Maslow's theory, which we describe in Chapter 4, assumes that motivation arises from a hierarchical series of needs. As the needs at each level are satisfied, the individual progresses to the next higher level.

The Hawthorne studies and the human relations movement played major roles in developing the foundations for the field of organizational behavior. Some of the early theorists' basic premises and assumptions were incorrect, however. For example, most human relationists believed that employee attitudes such as job satisfaction are the major causes of employee behaviors such as job performance. As we will see later, however, this usually is not the case. Also, many of the human relationists' views were unnecessarily limited and situation specific. Thus, there was still plenty of room for refinement and development in the emerging field of human behavior in organizations.

Theory X, described by Douglas McGregor, is an approach to management that takes a negative and pessimistic view of workers.

Theory Y, also described by McGregor, is an approach to management that offers a more positive and optimistic perspective on workers.

Toward Organizational Behavior: The Value of People

Organizational behavior began to emerge as a mature field of study in the late 1950s and early 1960s.[11] That period witnessed the field's evolution from the simple

As the field of organizational behavior began to emerge, managers came to better appreciate the importance of human behavior at work. This view does not imply, of course, that the social environment is the only thing that matters. If a manager took the approach reflected here, the firm probably would not survive very long. Enlightened managers should remember that a variety of factors, including technology, profitability, and the social environment, are all important. Successful organizations are usually those that optimize these and other imperatives in an effective manner.

"*You know what I think, folks? Improving technology isn't important. Increased profits aren't important. What's important is to be warm, decent human beings.*"

TABLE 1.1

Theory X and Theory Y

Theory X Assumptions	Theory Y Assumptions
1. People do not like work and try to avoid it.	1. People do not naturally dislike work; work is a natural part of their lives.
2. People do not like work, so managers have to control, direct, coerce, and threaten employees to get them to work toward organizational goals.	2. People are internally motivated to reach objectives to which they are committed.
3. People prefer to be directed, to avoid responsibility, to want security; they have little ambition.	3. People are committed to goals to the degree that they receive personal rewards when they reach their objectives.
	4. People will seek and accept responsibility under favorable conditions.
	5. People have the capacity to be innovative in solving organizational problems.
	6. People are bright, but under most organizational conditions, their potentials are underutilized.

Reference: Douglas McGregor, *The Human Side of Enterprise* (New York: McGraw-Hill, 1960), pp. 33–34, 47–48.

assumptions and behavioral models of the human relationists to the concepts and methodologies of a true scientific discipline. Since that time, organizational behavior as a scientific field of inquiry has made considerable strides, although there have been occasional steps backward as well. Overall, however, managers increasingly recognize the value of human resources and strive to better understand people and their roles in complex organizations and competitive business situations.[12] Many of the ideas discussed in this book have emerged over the past two or three decades. We turn now to contemporary organizational behavior.

Contemporary Organizational Behavior

LEARNING OBJECTIVE

Characterize contemporary organizational behavior.

Researchers and managers who use concepts and ideas from organizational behavior must recognize that the field has an interdisciplinary focus and a descriptive nature; that is, it draws from a variety of other fields and attempts to describe behavior (rather than examine how behavior can be changed in consistent and predictable ways). The central concepts of organizational behavior can be grouped into three basic categories: (1) individual processes, (2) interpersonal processes, and (3) organizational processes and characteristics. As Figure 1.2 shows, these categories provide the basic framework for this book.

Part Two of the book addresses individual processes, starting with foundations of individual behavior and then moving to popular motivational theories and techniques organizations use to increase the motivation of their employees. Part Three addresses such interpersonal processes as communication, groups, and teams. Part Four covers related interpersonal processes such as leadership, decision making, and negotiation. Finally, Part Five focuses on the organizational processes of organization design, culture, and change and development.

FIGURE 1.2

**The Framework for
Understanding
Organizational Behavior**

*Organizational behavior is an
exciting and complex field of
study. The specific concepts and
topics that constitute the field can
be grouped into three categories:
individual, interpersonal, and organizational processes and characteristics. Here these concepts
and classifications are used to
provide an overall framework for
the organization of this book.*

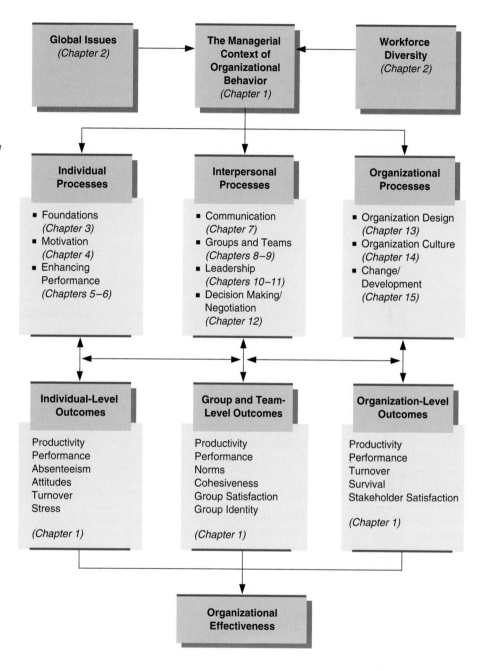

FIGURE 1.2

**The Framework for
Understanding
Organizational Behavior**

*Organizational behavior is an
exciting and complex field of
study. The specific concepts and
topics that constitute the field can
be grouped into three categories:
individual, interpersonal, and organizational processes and characteristics. Here these concepts
and classifications are used to
provide an overall framework for
the organization of this book.*

The Situational Perspective

The **situational perspective**
suggests that in most organizations, situations and
outcomes are contingent
on, or influenced by, other
variables.

One fundamental viewpoint essential for understanding behavior in organizations
comes from the **situational perspective.** In the earlier days of management studies, managers searched for universal answers to organizational questions. They
sought prescriptions, the "one best way" that could be used in any organization under any conditions—searching, for example, for forms of leadership behavior that
would always lead employees to be more satisfied and to work harder. Eventually,
however, researchers realized that the complexities of human behavior and organizational settings make universal conclusions virtually impossible. They discovered
that in organizations, most situations and outcomes are situational; that is, the

FIGURE 1.3

Universal Versus Situational Approach

Managers once believed they could identify the "one best way" to solve problems or react to situations. Here we illustrate a more realistic view, the situational approach. The situational approach suggests that approaches to problems and situations depend on elements of the situation.

Universal Approach

| Organizational problems or situations determine . . . | → | the one best way of responding. |

Situational Approach

| Organizational problems or situations must be evaluated in terms of . . . | → | elements of the situation, which then suggest . . . | → | contingent or situational ways of responding. |

relationship between any two variables is likely to be contingent on, or to depend on, other variables.[13]

Figure 1.3 distinguishes the universal and situational perspectives. The universal model, shown at the top of the figure, presumes a direct cause-and-effect linkage between variables. For example, it suggests that whenever a manager encounters a certain problem or situation (such as motivating employees to work harder), a universal approach is used (such as raising pay or increasing autonomy) that will lead to the desired outcome. The situational perspective, on the other hand, acknowledges that several other variables alter the direct relationship. In other words, the appropriate managerial action or behavior in any given situation depends on the elements of that situation. The field of organizational behavior gradually has shifted from a universal approach in the 1950s and early 1960s to a situational perspective today.

The **interactional perspective** suggests that individuals and situations interact continuously to determine individuals' behavior.

The Interactional Perspective

The **interactional perspective** is another useful way to better understand behavior in organizational settings. First presented in terms of interactional psychology, this view, illustrated in Figure 1.4, assumes individual behavior results from a continuous and multidirectional interaction between the characteristics of the person and the characteristics of the situation. More specifically, the interactional perspective attempts to explain how people select, interpret, and change various situations.[14]

The interactional view implies that simple cause-and-effect descriptions of organizational phenomena are not enough. For example, one set of research studies may suggest that job changes lead to improved employee attitudes, whereas another set may propose that attitudes influence how people perceive their jobs in the first place. Both positions are probably incomplete: Employee attitudes may influence job perceptions, but these perceptions may in turn influence future attitudes.

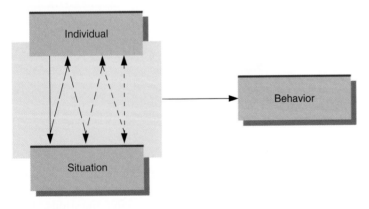

FIGURE 1.4

The Interactionist Perspective on Behavior in Organizations

When people enter an organization, their own behaviors and actions shape that organization in various ways. Similarly, the organization itself shapes the behaviors and actions of each individual who becomes a part of it. This interactionist perspective can be useful in explaining organizational behavior.

The Role of Organizational Behavior in Management

Virtually all organizations have managers with titles such as chief financial officer, marketing manager, director of public relations, vice president for human resources, and plant manager. But probably no organization has a position called "organizational behavior manager." The reason is simple: Organizational behavior is not a designated function or area; rather, an understanding of organizational behavior is a fundamental perspective or set of tools that all managers can use to carry out their jobs more effectively.[15]

An appreciation and understanding of organizational behavior help managers better recognize why others in the organization behave as they do.[16] For example, most managers in an organization are directly responsible for the work-related behaviors of a set of other people: their immediate subordinates. Typical managerial activities in this realm include motivating employees to work harder, ensuring that employees' jobs are properly designed, resolving conflicts, evaluating performance, and helping workers set goals to achieve rewards. The field of organizational behavior abounds with models and research relevant to each of these functions.[17]

Unless they happen to be chief executive officers (CEOs), managers also report to others in the organization (and even the CEO reports to the board of directors). In dealing with these individuals, an understanding of basic issues associated with leadership, power and political behavior, decision making, organization structure and design, and organization culture can be extremely beneficial. Again, the field of organizational behavior provides numerous valuable insights into these processes. Managers can also use their knowledge of organizational behavior to better understand their own needs, motives, behaviors, and feelings, which will help them improve their decision-making capabilities, control stress, communicate better, and comprehend how career dynamics unfold. The study of organizational behavior provides insights into all of these concepts and processes.

Managers interact with a variety of colleagues, peers, and coworkers inside the organization. An understanding of attitudinal processes, individual differences, group and intergroup dynamics, organization culture, and power and political behavior can help managers handle such interactions more effectively. Organizational behavior provides a variety of practical insights into these processes. Virtually all of the behavioral processes already mentioned are also valuable in interactions with people outside the organization: suppliers, customers, competitors, government officials, representatives of citizens' groups, union officials, and potential joint venture partners. In addition, a special understanding of the environment, technology, and global issues is valuable. Again, organizational behavior offers managers numerous insights into how and why things happen as they do. The Business of Ethics box provides an unfortunate illustration of how management and organizational behavior can also be related.

Finally, these patterns of interactions hold true regardless of the type of organization. Whether a business is large or small, domestic or international, growing or stagnating, its managers perform their work within a social context. The same can be said of managers in health care, education, government, and student organizations such as fraternities, sororities, and professional clubs. We can see, then, that it is essentially impossible to understand and practice management without considering the numerous areas of organizational behavior. Hence we now look at the nature of the manager's job in more detail. There are many different ways to conceptualize the job of a contemporary manager.[18] The most widely accepted approaches, however, are from the perspectives of basic managerial functions, common managerial roles, and fundamental managerial skills.[19]

BUSINESS OF ETHICS

Putting a Price on Talent Can Be a Slippery Slope

In 2003, American corporations paid their top managers more money than ever before in U.S. history and more than in any other nation. The high level of compensation can be partly explained by the nature of the job: Executives deserve large salaries because their jobs are difficult and require specialized skills. Another explanation is the economic principle of supply and demand: Because few individuals possess the experience and training necessary to head a major corporation, high demand for executive talent leads to high compensation.

For companies with financial difficulties or impending bankruptcies, however, there is a third explanation: the need to retain managerial talent. Top managers are likely to look for employment elsewhere when bankruptcy threatens, but companies in dire circumstances often hope to retain their most experienced managers to help them through the difficult period. Thus, troubled firms often rely on bonuses as additional compensation intended to discourage top managers from "jumping ship."

But what seems like a sound business policy can have severe negative consequences for other interested parties. For example, Enron reportedly paid more than $55 million in bonuses to about five hundred key personnel after beginning bankruptcy proceedings. That money could have been used instead to pay employees, retirees, investors, and suppliers of the failed firm. Investors and employees have often reacted to this practice by seeking to overthrow retention bonus plans in bankruptcy court before the compensation can be paid. This has happened

in cases involving steelmaker LTV; Polaroid, manufacturer of cameras and film; and clothing manufacturer Burlington Industries.

Groups opposed to the bonus plans claim that such bonuses reward the managers who are most directly responsible for the company's current problems. They also assert that such payments are unfair to lower-level employees, who are least able to find another job and have the fewest personal resources to sustain them through a period of unemployment. Personal finance advisers counsel employees of companies facing bankruptcy to seek other employment, demand a retention bonus, and even hire a lawyer. "By definition, bankruptcy is a world inhabited by companies that have trouble keeping promises. It's a world where promises aren't kept and there isn't enough to go around," says Stephen Bubo, a bankruptcy attorney with the Chicago law firm D'Ancono and Pflaum. Workers and investors of failed companies, who have been stripped of their jobs and billions of investment dollars, would surely agree.

> *"By definition, bankruptcy is a world inhabited by companies that have trouble keeping promises." —Stephen Bobo, bankruptcy attorney with the Chicago law firm D'Ancona & Pflaum*

References: "Use of Retention Bonuses Draws Fire: Select Few Get Cash While Others Face Financial Ruin," *USA Today*, February 14, 2002; Victoria Zunitch, "What If Your Company Fails?: Five Ways to Protect Your Finances and Career When Your Employer Goes Bankrupt," CNN/Money online, January 23, 2002, www.money.cnn.com on February 25, 2002; "Polaroid Retirees Lose Benefits," *USA Today*, January 14, 2002.

Fundamental Managerial Functions

Managers in all organizations engage in four basic functions, generally referred to as planning, organizing, leading, and controlling. All organizations also use four kinds of resources: human, financial, physical, and information. As Figure 1.5 illustrates, managers combine these resources through the four basic functions, with the ultimate purpose of efficiently and effectively attaining the goals of the organization. That is, the figure shows how managers apply the basic functions across resources to advance the organization toward its goals.

Planning is the process of determining an organization's desired future position and the best means of getting there.

Planning　**Planning,** the first managerial function, is the process of determining the organization's desired future position and deciding how best to get there. The planning process at Sears, for example, includes studying and analyzing the envi-

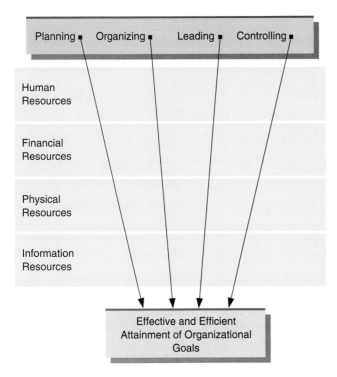

FIGURE 1.5

Basic Managerial Functions

Managers engage in the four basic functions of planning, organizing, leading, and controlling. These functions are applied to human, financial, physical, and information resources, with the ultimate purpose of attaining organizational goals efficiently and effectively.

Organizing is the process of designing jobs, grouping jobs into units, and establishing patterns of authority between jobs and units.

Leading is the process of getting the organization's members to work together toward achieving the organization's goals.

Controlling is the process of monitoring and correcting the actions of the organization and its members to keep them directed toward their goals.

ronment, deciding on appropriate goals, outlining strategies for achieving those goals, and developing tactics to help execute the strategies. Behavioral processes and characteristics pervade each of these activities. Perception, for instance, plays a major role in environmental scanning, and creativity and motivation influence how managers establish goals, strategies, and tactics for their organization. Larger corporations, such as General Electric and IBM, usually rely on their top management teams to handle most planning activities. In smaller firms, the owner usually takes care of planning.

Organizing   The second managerial function is **organizing,** the process of designing jobs, grouping jobs into manageable units, and establishing patterns of authority among jobs and groups of jobs. This process produces the basic structure, or framework, of the organization. For large organizations such as Sears, that structure can be extensive and complicated. Smaller firms can often function with a relatively simple and straightforward form of organization. As noted earlier, the processes and characteristics of the organization itself are a major theme of organizational behavior.

Leading   **Leading,** the third managerial function, is the process of motivating members of the organization to work together toward achieving the organization's goals. A Sears manager, for example, must hire people, train them, and motivate them. Major components of leading include motivating employees, managing group dynamics, and the actual process of leadership. These are all closely related to major areas of organizational behavior. All managers, whether they work in a huge multinational corporation or a small neighborhood business, must understand the importance of leading.

Controlling   The fourth managerial function, **controlling,** is the process of monitoring and correcting the actions of the organization and its people to keep them headed toward their goals. A Sears manager has to control costs, inventory, and so on. Again, behavioral processes and characteristics are a key part of this function. Performance evaluation, reward systems, and motivation, for example, all apply to control. Control is important to all businesses, but it may be especially critical to smaller ones. General Motors, for example, can withstand a loss of several thousand dollars due to poor control, but the same loss may be devastating to a small firm.

Basic Managerial Roles

In an organization, as in a play or a movie, a role is the part a person plays in a given situation. Managers often play a number of different roles. The traditional model of managerial roles, summarized in Table 1.2, identifies ten basic roles clustered into three general categories: interpersonal, informational, and decision-making roles.[20]

TABLE 1.2

Important Managerial Roles

Category	Role	Example
Interpersonal	Figurehead	Attend employee retirement ceremony
	Leader	Encourage workers to increase productivity
	Liaison	Coordinate activities of two committees
Informational	Monitor	Scan *BusinessWeek* for information about competition
	Disseminator	Send out memos outlining new policies
	Spokesperson	Hold press conference to announce new plant
Decision-making	Entrepreneur	Develop idea for new product and convince others of its merits
	Disturbance handler	Resolve dispute
	Resource allocator	Allocate budget requests
	Negotiator	Settle new labor contract

Key **interpersonal roles** are the figurehead, the leader, and the liaison.

Interpersonal Roles   **Interpersonal roles** are primarily social in nature; that is, they are roles in which the manager's main task is to relate to other people in certain ways. The manager sometimes may serve as a *figurehead* for the organization. Taking visitors to dinner and attending ribbon-cutting ceremonies are part of the figurehead role. In the role of *leader*, the manager works to hire, train, and motivate employees. Finally, the *liaison* role consists of relating to others outside the group or organization. For example, a manager at Intel might be responsible for handling all price negotiations with a key supplier of electronic circuit boards. Obviously each of these interpersonal roles involves behavioral processes.

Key **informational roles** are the monitor, the disseminator, and the spokesperson.

Informational Roles   The three **informational roles** involve some aspect of information processing. The *monitor* actively seeks information that might be of value to the organization in general or to specific managers. The manager who transmits this information to others is carrying out the role of *disseminator*. The *spokesperson* speaks for the organization to outsiders. A manager chosen by Dell Computer to appear at a press conference announcing a new-product launch or other major deal, such as a recent decision to undertake a joint venture with Microsoft, would be serving in this role. Again, behavioral processes are part of each of these roles because information is almost always exchanged between people.

Important **decision-making roles** are the entrepreneur, the disturbance handler, the resource allocator, and the negotiator.

Decision-Making Roles   Four **decision-making roles** exist. The *entrepreneur* voluntarily initiates change, such as innovations or new strategies, in the organization. The *disturbance handler* helps settle disputes between various parties, such as other managers and their subordinates. The *resource allocator* decides who will get what: how the organization's resources will be distributed among various individuals and groups. The *negotiator* represents the organization in reaching agreements with other organizations, such as when settling contracts between management and labor unions. Again, behavioral processes clearly are crucial in each of these decisional roles.

Critical Managerial Skills

Another important element of managerial work involves the skills necessary to carry out basic functions and fill fundamental roles. In general, most successful managers have a strong combination of technical, interpersonal, conceptual, and diagnostic skills.[21]

Technical skills are the skills necessary to accomplish specific tasks within the organization.

The manager uses **interpersonal skills** to communicate with, understand, and motivate individuals and groups.

The manager uses **conceptual skills** to think in the abstract.

The manager uses **diagnostic skills** to understand cause-and-effect relationships and to recognize the optimal solutions to problems.

Technical Skills   **Technical skills** are abilities necessary to accomplish specific tasks within the organization. Designing a new network card for IBM, developing a new formula for a frozen-food additive for Conagra, and writing a press release for Exxon require technical skills. Hence, these skills are generally associated with the operations the organization employs in its production processes. For example, Bill Hewlett and David Packard, founders of Hewlett-Packard, began their careers as engineers. They still work hard today to keep abreast of new technology; their technical skills are an important part of their success. Other examples of managers with strong technical skills include H. Lee Scott (president and CEO of Wal-Mart, who started his career as a store manager) and Gordon Bethune (retired CEO of Continental Airlines, a former pilot).

Interpersonal Skills   A manager uses **interpersonal skills** to communicate with, understand, and motivate individuals and groups. As we noted, managers spend a large portion of their time interacting with others, so clearly it is important that they get along with other people. During his tenure as CEO of Continental Airlines, Gordon Bethune became one of the most admired business leaders in America. Part of his success was attributable to how he dealt with people in the firm; he treated them with dignity and respect, and was always open and direct when he talked to them. For example, he referred to everyone in the firm, from baggage handlers to pilots to executives, as his coworkers, and he was candid when he had to relay bad news.

Management involves four basic functions, ten roles, and four fundamental skills. The work of Claire Fraser, president of the Institute for Genomic Research, clearly illustrates several of these. Her current challenges include supervising research leading to new scientific breakthroughs, managing the institute's most talented employees, keeping abreast of all current developments in her field, and managing several ongoing applied and basic research programs.

Conceptual Skills   **Conceptual skills** involve the manager's ability to think in the abstract. A manager with strong conceptual skills is able to see the "big picture"; that is, she or he can see opportunity where others perceive roadblocks or problems. For example, after Steve Wozniak and Steve Jobs built a small computer of their own design in a garage, Wozniak saw merely a new toy that could be tinkered with. Jobs, however, saw far more and convinced his partner that they should start a company to make and sell the computers. Thus was born Apple Computer.

Diagnostic Skills   Most successful managers also bring diagnostic skills to the organization. **Diagnostic skills** allow managers to better understand cause-and-effect relationships and to recognize the optimal solutions to problems. For example, when Gordon Bethune took over Continental, he immediately began searching for ways to turn the failing company around. It was his diagnostic skills that enabled him to first recognize the enormous costs incurred because of late departures and arrivals, then identify the reasons for this problem, and, finally, determine how to most effectively change things to solve the problem.

Contemporary Managerial Challenges

Organizational behavior has several implications for various organizational and managerial challenges. In this section, we identify some of the challenges and opportunities facing managers today and note their relevance to organizational behavior.

Workforce Rightsizing

Rightsizing is the process of optimizing the size of an organization's workforce through downsizing, expanding, and/or outsourcing.

One important challenge involves workforce **rightsizing,** achieving and maintaining the optimal workforce in terms of size and location. Since 1990 alone, for instance, many organizations have had to first reduce their workforces during the economic slowdown in the early 1990s, then expand by hiring new employees during the boom period of the late 1990s, and then reduce them once again as a result of another economic downturn that began in 2001. In 2004, hiring began to increase once again.

Downsizing   *Downsizing* means purposely becoming smaller by reducing the size of the workforce or by shedding entire divisions or businesses. Downsizing became common in the mid-1980s. For example, IBM and AT&T underwent major downsizing efforts involving thousands of employees. Because of declining sales of Western-style boots, Justin Industries closed two of its factories, putting 260 people out of work. Growing international competition recently compelled Kellogg Company to shut down much of its oldest factory, cutting 550 jobs. Organizations undergoing such downsizing must strive to manage the effects of these cutbacks, not only for those employees who are let go but also for those who continue—albeit with reduced security. Of course, downsizing sometimes has positive results. The firm that cuts staff presumably lowers its costs. But the people who leave may find they are happier as well. Many start their own businesses, and some find employment with companies that better meet their needs and goals. Unfortunately, others suffer the indignities of unemployment and financial insecurity.

Expansion   During boom periods, such as the late 1990s, downsizing gives way to *expansion*. Indeed, some sectors, especially those involving high-technology and intensive knowledge work, sometimes experience such severe labor shortages that firms may have to pay hefty signing bonuses and provide an array of benefits and perks. A clear understanding of organizational behavior can help managers in this situation in a variety of ways. These include attracting new workers in sufficient numbers and with necessary skills and abilities, retaining both newer and older workers in the face of alternative work options, and blending newer and older workers into a harmonious and effective workforce.

Simultaneously, even during the best of times, managers should be somewhat cautious to avoid expanding too quickly. If an organization hires more workers than it can sustain, managers may once again find themselves having to reduce their workforce as soon as economic growth slows or the firm's fortunes stall. To help buffer against this possibility, many firms, especially larger ones, rely on adding temporary workers to their workforce to meet expansion needs without incurring a substantial commitment to providing those workers with long-term job security. Here again, organizational behavior concepts help managers deal with issues arising from blending permanent and temporary workers in a single job setting.

Outsourcing A related element of rightsizing is *outsourcing*, contracting some organizational functions to other firms. This practice has been common for years. For instance, many larger firms routinely outsource such activities as office maintenance and food service operations to other firms specializing in those areas. By focusing its workforce on its essential activities, a business can presumably maintain a more stable workforce and be more competitive. In recent years, however, outsourcing has become more and more controversial as organizations have started sending more of their work to foreign firms. For instance, if a domestic manufacturing firm employing 10 people on its cleaning crew outsources that work to a domestic janitorial services firm, the manufacturing firm may eliminate 10 jobs but the janitorial services firm creates 10 new ones. In contrast, if the janitorial work is outsourced abroad, domestic jobs are eliminated with no corresponding increase in the foreign firm.

New Ways of Organizing

Another challenge today is dealing with the complex array of new ways to organize.[22] Recall from our earlier discussion that theorists such as Max Weber advocated "one best way" of organizing. These organizational prototypes generally resembled pyramids—tall structures with power controlled at the top and rigid policies and procedures governing most activities. Today, however, many organizations seek greater flexibility and the ability to respond more quickly to their environment by adopting flat structures. These structures are characterized by few levels of management; broad, wide spans of management; and fewer rules and regulations. The increased use of work teams also goes hand in hand with today's approach to organizing.

The modern competitive environment and globalization combine to make competition increasingly complex for today's managers. Harley-Davidson has faced increasingly stiff competition in recent years from BMW, Honda, and Kawasaki. While Harley has an almost cultlike following among its current owners, the firm must look to the future. Harley has initiated a new program called Rider's Edge, a two-and-a–half-day training program to introduce potential customers to motorcycle ownership. This first-time Harley rider is learning from Rider's Edge instructor Paul Lessard.

Globalization

The world economy is becoming increasingly global in character.[23] Managing in a global economy poses many different challenges and opportunities. For example, at a macro level, property ownership arrangements vary widely. So does the availability of natural resources and components of infrastructure, as well as the role of government in business. For our purposes, a very important consideration is how behavioral processes vary widely across cultural and national boundaries. Values, symbols, and beliefs differ sharply among cultures. Different work norms and the role work plays in a person's life influence patterns of both work-related behavior and attitudes toward work. They also affect the nature of supervisory relationships, decision-making styles and processes, and organizational configurations. Group and intergroup processes, responses to stress, and the nature of political behaviors also differ from culture to culture.

Ethics and Social Responsibility

Individual **ethics** are personal beliefs about what is right and wrong or good and bad.

An organization's **social responsibility** is its obligation to protect or contribute to the social environment in which it functions.

Another challenge that has taken on renewed importance concerns ethics and social responsibility. An individual's **ethics** are his or her beliefs about what is right and wrong or good and bad. **Social responsibility** is the organization's obligation to protect and contribute to the social environment in which it functions. Thus, the two concepts are related, but they are also distinct from each other.

Both ethics and social responsibility have taken on new significance in recent years. Scandals in organizations ranging from Royal Caribbean Cruise Lines (improper dumping of waste) to Tyco (improper use of company assets for the benefit of senior managers) to various Olympics committees (bribery of government officials) have made headlines around the world. The fallout from the Enron scandal will no doubt continue for years. From the social responsibility angle, pollution and the obligation of businesses to help clean up our environment, business contributions to social causes, and similar issues are receiving increasing attention.

Leadership, organization culture, and group norms—all important organizational behavior concepts—are relevant in managing these processes.[24] For example, Enron's collapse has been partly attributed to a work culture that promoted overly aggressive competition among the firm's own employees, group norms that made it acceptable to take risks that others would deem unacceptable, and top management leadership that continued to encourage questionable business practices.

Managing for Effectiveness

┌─ LEARNING OBJECTIVE ─┐

Discuss the role of organizational behavior in managing for effectiveness.

Earlier in this chapter, we noted that managers work toward various goals. We will now look at the nature of these goals in detail. In particular, as Figure 1.6 shows, goals, or outcomes, exist at three specific levels in an organization: individual-level, group-level, and organizational-level outcomes. Of course, it may sometimes be necessary to make tradeoffs among these three types of outcomes, but in general each is seen as a critical component of organizational effectiveness. The sections that follow elaborate on these levels in more detail.

FIGURE 1.6

Managing for Effectiveness

Managers work to optimize a variety of individual-level, group- and team-level, and organization-level outcomes. Sometimes it is necessary to make tradeoffs among the different types and levels of outcomes, but each is an important determinant of organizational effectiveness.

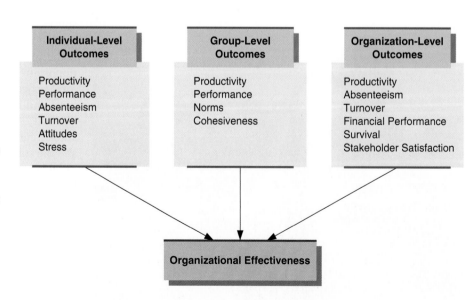

Individual-Level Outcomes

Several different outcomes at the individual level are important to managers. Given the focus of the field of organizational behavior, it should not be surprising that most of these outcomes are directly or indirectly addressed by various theories and models.

Individual Behaviors   First, several individual behaviors result from a person's participation in an organization. One important behavior is productivity. A person's productivity is an indicator of his or her efficiency and is measured in terms of the products or services created per unit of input. For example, if Bill makes 100 units of a product in a day and Sara makes only 90 units in a day, then, assuming that the units are of the same quality and that Bill and Sara earn the same wages, Bill is more productive than Sara.

Performance, another important individual-level outcome variable, is a somewhat broader concept. It is made up of all work-related behaviors. For example, even though Bill is highly productive, he may also refuse to work overtime, express negative opinions about the organization at every opportunity, and do nothing that does not fall precisely within the boundaries of his job. Sara, on the other hand, may always be willing to work overtime, is a positive representative of the organization, and goes out of her way to make as many contributions to the organization as possible. Based on the full array of behaviors, then, we might conclude that Sara actually is the better performer.

Two other important individual-level behaviors are absenteeism and turnover. Absenteeism is a measure of attendance. Although virtually everyone misses work occasionally, some people miss far more than others. Some look for excuses to miss work and call in sick regularly just for some time off; others miss work only when absolutely necessary. Turnover occurs when a person leaves the organization. If the departing individual is a good performer or if the organization has invested heavily in training the person, turnover can be costly.

Individual Attitudes and Stress   Another set of individual-level outcomes influenced by managers consists of individual attitudes. (We discuss attitudes more fully in Chapter 3.) Levels of job satisfaction or dissatisfaction, organizational commitment, and organizational involvement all play an important role in organizational behavior. Stress, also discussed in Chapter 3, is another important individual-level outcome variable. Given its costs, both personal and organizational, it is evident that stress is becoming an increasingly important topic for both researchers in organizational behavior and practicing managers.

Group- and Team-Level Outcomes

Another set of outcomes exists at the group and team level. Some of these outcomes parallel the individual-level outcomes just discussed. For example, if an organization makes extensive use of work teams, team productivity and performance are important outcome variables. On the other hand, even if all the people in a group or team have the same or similar attitudes toward their jobs, the attitudes themselves are individual-level phenomena. Individuals, not groups, have attitudes. But groups or teams can also have unique outcomes that individuals do not share. For example, as we will discuss in Chapter 8, groups develop norms that govern the behavior of individual group members. Groups also develop different levels of cohesiveness. Thus, managers need to assess both common and unique outcomes when considering the individual and group levels.

Organization-Level Outcomes

Finally, a set of outcome variables exists at the organization level. As before, some of these outcomes parallel those at the individual and group levels, but others are unique. For example, we can measure and compare organizational productivity. We can also develop organization-level indicators of absenteeism and turnover. Profitability, however, is generally assessed only at the organizational level. Organizations are also commonly assessed in terms of financial performance: stock price, return on investment, growth rates, and so on. They are also evaluated in terms of their ability to survive and the extent to which they satisfy important stakeholders such as investors, government regulators, employees, and unions.

Clearly, then, the manager must balance different outcomes across all three levels of analysis. In many cases, these outcomes appear to contradict one another. For example, paying workers high salaries can enhance satisfaction and reduce turnover, but it may also detract from bottom-line performance. Similarly, exerting strong pressure to increase individual performance may boost short-term profitability but increase turnover and job stress. Thus, the manager must look at the full array of outcomes and attempt to balance them in an optimal fashion. The manager's ability to do this is a major determinant of the organization's success.

Synopsis

Organizational behavior is the study of human behavior in organizational settings, of the interface between human behavior and the organization, and of the organization itself. The study of organizational behavior is important because organizations have a powerful influence over our lives. Serious interest in the study of management first developed around the beginning of the twentieth century. Two of the earliest approaches were scientific management (best represented by the work of Frederick Taylor) and classical organization theory (exemplified by the work of Max Weber).

Organizational behavior began to emerge as a scientific discipline as a result of the Hawthorne studies. Douglas McGregor and Abraham Maslow led the human relations movement that grew out of those studies. The basic concepts of the field fall into three categories: individual processes, interpersonal processes, and organizational processes and characteristics. Those categories form the framework for the organization of this book. Important contextual perspectives

on the field of organizational behavior are the situational and interactional perspectives.

By its very nature, management requires an understanding of human behavior to help managers better comprehend those at different levels in the organization, those at the same level, those in other organizations, and themselves. The manager's job can be characterized in terms of four functions, three sets of roles, and four skills. The basic managerial functions are planning, organizing, leading, and controlling. The roles consist of three interpersonal roles, three informational roles, and four decision-making roles. The four basic skills necessary for effective management are technical, interpersonal, conceptual, and diagnostic skills.

Several challenges confront managers today. Among the most important are workforce rightsizing, new ways of organizing, globalization, and ethics and social responsibility. Managing for effectiveness involves balancing a variety of individual-level, group- and team-level, and organization-level outcome variables.

Discussion Questions

1. Some people have suggested that understanding human behavior at work is the single most important requirement for managerial success. Do you agree or disagree with this statement? Why?

2. In what ways is organizational behavior comparable to functional areas such as finance, marketing,

and production? In what ways does it differ from these areas? Is it similar to statistics in any way?

3. Identify some managerial jobs that are highly affected by human behavior and others that are less affected. Which would you prefer? Why?

4. Besides those cited in the text, what reasons can you think of for the importance of organizational behavior?

5. Suppose you are hiring a new manager. One candidate has outstanding technical skills but poor interpersonal skills. The other has exactly the opposite mix of skills. Which would you hire? Why?

6. Some people believe individuals working in an organization have a basic human right to satisfaction with their work and to the opportunity to grow and develop. How would you defend this position? How would you argue against it?

7. Many universities offer a course in industrial or organizational psychology. The content of those courses is quite similar to the content of this course. Do you think behavioral material is better taught in a business or in a psychology program, or is it best to teach it in both?

8. Get a recent issue of a popular business magazine such as *BusinessWeek* or *Fortune*, and scan its major articles. Do any articles reflect concepts from organizational behavior? Describe.

9. The text identifies four basic managerial functions. Based on your own experiences or observations, provide examples of each function.

10. Which managerial skills do you think are among your strengths? Which are among your weaknesses? How might you improve the latter?

11. Are there any kinds of businesses that have not been affected by globalization? Explain.

12. What individual-level, group- or team-level, or organization-level outcome variables can you identify beyond those noted in the text?

Organizational Behavior Case for Discussion

Yellow Rules the Road

Since its founding in 1923, Yellow Corporation (formerly Yellow Freight Corporation) has led the transportation industry by using its trucks to haul large, heavy items between major shipping centers in the United States, Canada, and Mexico. For decades the firm focused on ways to increase its efficiency, such as ensuring that all trucks were full before they left the warehouse and using an inflexible delivery schedule to reduce last-minute changes. But Yellow was the victim of its own success: As operational efficiency increased, customer service received less attention, allowing newer and more responsive companies to lure away many of the firm's customers. Further, the customers most likely to seek a more service-oriented transportation provider were the very ones that were willing to pay premium prices for the extra service.

Bill Zollars, who assumed the role of chief executive officer (CEO) of Yellow in 1996, was intrigued by the opportunity to revitalize the carrier. James Welch, president and chief operating officer, recollects, "We were a defensive company—a follower, not a leader. We were yearning for leadership. This company was ready for change." Zollars understood that successful organizational transformation would need to be profound, altering the attitudes, behaviors, and performance of each of the firm's 30,000 employees.

Communication was one key to Zollars' management revolution at Yellow. The CEO spent eighteen months traveling to the company's several hundred locations to talk face to face with customers and employees at all levels. He repeatedly put forth his message of the need for enhanced customer service, but the meetings consisted of more than promises and motivational speeches. Zollars was the first Yellow manager to accurately report the true defect rate: the percentage of shipments that were late, wrong, or damaged. Yellow employees were stunned to learn that their defect rate was a whopping 40 percent, but that knowledge was necessary to provide motivation and a benchmark for improvement. Zollars also instituted the company's first ongoing program for surveying customer satisfaction and reporting the results openly throughout the company.

Zollars' leadership created a sense of motivation and pride among employees, which in turn led to continuing high levels of productivity and performance. He made a great effort to listen to his employees, entertain their suggestions, and give them additional authority to make decisions. He earned an enviable reputation for honesty and commitment, attempting to "walk the walk" as well as "talk the talk." Zollars asserts, "If people doing the work don't believe what's coming from the leadership, it doesn't get implemented. Period."

Technology also played an important role in Yellow's success. The firm implemented a variety of automated systems to improve customer service and satisfaction. The systems provide up-to-the-minute information about a shipment's progress via the Internet, maintain a customer database that enables faster scheduling, and develop truck-loading procedures and routes to ensure on-time delivery. However, the real technology success story at Yellow isn't merely the innovative and efficient use of technology but also the savvy application of those systems to support employees and customers.

Perhaps the most challenging yet most important change at Yellow was the re-envisioning of the company's mission from delivery of freight to customer service. When employees saw their primary goal as the efficient movement of cargo, the firm focused on one set of processes. Today, thanks to the efforts of Zollars and other managers, employees realize that supporting customers by meeting their delivery needs is their paramount task. This shift in perspective enables the firm to provide better service to its customers, develop innovative new products and services, improve its performance, and, ultimately, compete successfully in an increasingly tough industry. As Bill Zollars says in the firm's 2000 annual report, "Our business really isn't about moving freight. It's about earning the trust of the consumers of our services."

Case Questions

1. What role has organizational behavior played at Yellow?
2. Identify examples of management functions, roles, and skills as reflected by Bill Zollars' actions at Yellow.
3. What measures of effectiveness are most relevant for a firm like Yellow? How might behavioral processes affect each measure?

References: Matthew Boyle, "America's Most Admired Companies: The Right Stuff," *Fortune*, March 4, 2002, www.fortune.com on March 6, 2002; Chuck Salter, "Fresh Start 2002: On the Road Again," *Fast Company*, January 2002, pp. 50–58 (quotation on p. 57), www.fastcompany.com; "Yellow Corporation 2000 Annual Report," March 2001, www.yellowcorp.com on March 6, 2002.

Experiencing Organizational Behavior

Relating OB and Popular Culture

Purpose: This exercise will help you appreciate the importance and pervasiveness of organizational behavior concepts and processes in both contemporary organizational settings and popular culture.

Format: Your instructor will divide the class into groups of three to five. Each group will be assigned a specific television program to watch before the next class meeting.

Procedure: Arrange to watch the program as a group. Each person should have a pad of paper and a pencil handy. As you watch the show, jot down examples of individual behavior, interpersonal dynamics, organizational characteristics, and other concepts and processes relevant to organizational behavior. After the show, spend a few minutes comparing notes. Compile one list for the entire group. (It is advisable to turn off the television set during this discussion!)

During the next class meeting, have someone in the group summarize the plot of the show and list the concepts it illustrated. The following television shows are especially good for illustrating behavioral concepts in organizational settings:

Network Shows	Syndicated Shows
Survivor	*Seinfeld*
The West Wing	*Cheers*
N.Y.P.D. Blue	*Star Trek*
The Apprentice	*Home Improvement*
24	*L.A. Law*
CSI	*Gilligan's Island*

Follow-up Questions

1. What does this exercise illustrate about the pervasiveness of organizations in our contemporary society?
2. What recent or classic movies might provide similar kinds of examples?
3. Do you think television programs from countries other than the United States would provide more or fewer examples of shows set in organizations?

Self-Assessment Exercise
Assessing Your Own Theory X and Theory Y Tendencies

The following questions aim to provide insights into your tendencies toward Theory X or Theory Y management styles. Answer each question on the scale by circling the number that best reflects your feelings. For example, circle a 5 for a statement if you strongly agree with it or a 2 if you disagree with it.

1. Most employees today are lazy and have to be forced to work hard.
2. People in organizations are motivated only by extrinsic rewards such as pay and bonuses.
3. Most people do not like to work.
4. Most people today generally avoid responsibility.
5. Many employees in big companies today do not accept the company's goals but instead work only for their own welfare.
6. Most people are not innovative and are not interested in helping their employer solve problems.
7. Most people need someone else to tell them how to do their job.
8. Many people today have little ambition, preferring to stay where they are and not work hard for advancement.
9. Work is not a natural activity for most people; rather, it is something they feel they have to do.
10. Most employees today are not interested in utilizing their full potential and capabilities.

Instructions: Add up your responses. If you scored 40 or above, you have clear tendencies toward the Theory X view of management. If you scored 20 or below, you have clear tendencies toward the Theory Y view of management. If you scored between 20 and 40, your tendencies fall in between the extreme Theory X and Y viewpoints, and you have a more balanced approach. (*Note:* This brief instrument has not been scientifically validated and is to be used for classroom discussion purposes only.)

OB Online

1. Find a company website that stresses the firm's history. What role, if any, does that history seem to play in the way the firm is currently managed?
2. Do a web search using the key word *bureaucracy*. Based on a representative sample of sites identified by your search, what is the prevailing meaning most people seem to attach to this term?
3. Do a web search for the key term *Hawthorne studies*. What information beyond that provided in the chapter do these sites contain?
4. Visit Amazon.com or another Internet book retailer and identify the top ten best-selling business books today. What, if anything, do they seem to have in common?

Building Managerial Skills

Exercise Overview: Conceptual skills involve the ability to think in the abstract; diagnostic skills focus on responses to situations. Managers must frequently use these skills together to better understand the behavior of others in the organization, as this exercise illustates.

Exercise Background: Human behavior is a complex phenomenon in any setting, but is especially so in organizations. Understanding how and why people choose particular behaviors can be difficult and frustrating, but also very important. Consider the following scenario.

Sandra Buckley has worked in your department for several years. Until recently, she was a model employee. She always arrived on time, or even early, to work and stayed late whenever necessary to get her assignments done. She was upbeat and cheerful, and worked very hard. She frequently said the company was the best place she had ever worked and you were the perfect boss.

About six months ago, you began to notice changes in Sandra's behavior. She has come in late occasionally, and you cannot remember the last time she agreed to work past 5:00 P.M. She also complains a lot. Other workers have started to avoid her because she is so negative all the time. You also suspect she may be looking for a new job.

Exercise Task: Using the preceding scenario as background, do the following:

1. Assume you have done some background work to find out why Sandra's behavior has changed. Write a brief case that includes possible reasons for these changes (e.g., your case might include the fact that you recently promoted someone else to a position that Sandra may have expected to get). Make the case as descriptive as possible.

2. Relate elements of your case to the various behavioral concepts discussed in the chapter.

3. Decide whether or not you might be about to resolve things with Sandra to overcome whatever issues have arisen from your case. For example, if Sandra is upset because she was passed over for a promotion, how might you attempt to straighten things out?

4. Which behavioral process or concept discussed in the chapter is easiest to change? Which is the most difficult to change?

TEST PREPPER

ACE self-test

You have read the chapter and studied the key terms, and the exam is any day now. Think you're ready to ace it? Take this sample test to gauge your comprehension of chapter material. You can check your answers at the back of the book. Want more test questions? Visit the student website at http://college.hmco.com/business/students/ (select Griffin/Moorhead, Fundamentals of Organizational Behavior 1e) and take the ACE quizzes for more practice.

1. **T F** Southwest Airlines claims its most significant advantages come from its employees.

2. **T F** Fredrick Taylor developed ways for employees to work at a pace slower than their capabilities.

3. **T F** Scientific management, developed in the early 1900s, is no longer used today.

4. **T F** Sociologist Max Weber described "bureaucracies" as inefficient, inflexible organizations.

5. **T F** Hawthorne studies identified a strong relationship between lighting and employee productivity.

6. **T F** The human relations movement supported the idea that a satisfied employee will work harder than an unsatisfied employee.

7. **T F** "Universal" models suggest that certain management solutions will work in all situations.

8. **T F** An example of the controlling function is monitoring the actions of employees.

9. **T F** Jack manages a group of software programmers and is an excellent programmer himself. From this you know Jack has strong conceptual skills.

10. **T F** One of the main issues surrounding outsourcing is whether the net number of domestic jobs is decreased.

11. **T F** Managers who are interested in successfully achieving company goals should focus primarily on individual-level outcomes.

12. **T F** Performance is a broader outcome than productivity.

13. **T F** Attitudes can be measured at the group level.

14. **T F** Attempting to positively influence outcomes at the individual level can negatively influence outcomes at the organization level.

15. Jim is a manager who is taking a class in organizational behavior. Jim will likely learn about all of the following in his class except
    a. human behavior in organizational settings.
    b. some employees' decision to leave a company while others decide to stay.
    c. the interface between human behavior and the organization.
    d. competition and how it affects the stock prices of publicly held firms.
    e. organizations themselves.

16. At Quiktire, Inc., managers have determined the most efficient method for installing customers' tires. Employees are required to follow these methods and are paid based on the number of tires they install each day. Quicktire's technique is similar to which of these management approaches?
    a. Bureaucracy
    b. System 4 management
    c. Unionization
    d. Soldiering
    e. Scientific management

17. The primary difference between scientific management and classical organization theory is that
    a. scientific management focuses on profits rather than losses.
    b. scientific management emphasizes individual efficiency rather than organizational efficiency.
    c. scientific management was developed outside rather than within the United States.
    d. scientific management is a more recent approach.
    e. scientific management failed rather than succeeded.

18. Early writers suggested all of the following as ways to improve management practices except
    a. improve working conditions.
    b. become more democratic in dealing with employees.
    c. accommodate employee needs.
    d. adjust lighting to enhance employee interaction.
    e. use psychology to understand employee motivation.

19. Scientific management predicts that each individual will produce as much as possible to increase personal income, but the Hawthorne researchers discovered
    a. the work group as a whole may establish acceptable levels of output.
    b. employees work only as hard as their supervisors.
    c. employees' efforts decline over the course of the five-day workweek.
    d. employees' efforts increase over the course of the five-day workweek.
    e. managers produce as much as possible, but to satisfy their egos rather than earn more income.

20. One basic premise of the human relations movement was that
   a. Theory X management is more effective than Theory Y management.
   b. "chiseling" and "rate busting" are unavoidable facts of work life.
   c. singling out workers for special treatment may actually decrease productivity.
   d. most employees work better alone than in groups.
   e. a satisfied employee will work harder than an unsatisfied employee.

21. If you were a manager, would you try to increase employees' performance by increasing their satisfaction?
   a. Yes, because a more satisfied worker is a more productive worker.
   b. No, because job satisfaction is not a major influence on job performance.
   c. Yes, but only for new workers.
   d. No, because the cost of satisfying workers outweighs the benefits of higher performance.
   e. Yes, but once workers were satisfied, I would stop trying to satisfy them.

22. Which of the following best illustrates the situational perspective of management?
   a. Science can determine the "one best way" to manage under any conditions.
   b. Management principles are universal and therefore apply in all situations.
   c. The appropriate way to manage depends on the nature of the particular situation.
   d. Simple cause-and-effect linkages between two variables are common.
   e. A manager can easily fix a problem in one situation with a solution that has worked in another situation.

23. Organizational behavior concepts apply
   a. in domestic but not international companies.
   b. in large but not small companies.
   c. in growing but not stable companies.
   d. in for-profit but not nonprofit organizations.
   e. in virtually all organizations.

24. Recently the managers at Practicum Unlimited, a firm that develops educational materials, redesigned its jobs, established new reporting and authority relationships, and grouped jobs into different departments. Which

managerial function did they perform?
   a. Planning   d. Controlling
   b. Organizing   e. Decision making
   c. Leading

25. The president of a university regularly attends graduation ceremonies, but her role there is not to plan, organize, lead, or control. Rather, in handing out diplomas, she is acting as a
   a. figurehead.   d. monitor.
   b. resource allocator.   e. decision maker.
   c. disseminator.

26. If you were hiring a new manager to help you see the "big picture" of how your organization might become more effective, you would consider applicants with strong
   a. technical skills.   d. diagnostic skills.
   b. interpersonal skills.   e. decision-making
   c. conceptual skills.   skills.

27. Which is not a way to rightsize an organization?
   a. Downsizing
   b. Outsourcing
   c. Expansion
   d. Eliminating an entire division or business
   e. Retaining the full number of employees during economic slowdowns

28. Which of the following are you least likely to see in modern organizations?
   a. Flat, flexible structures
   b. Power centralized at the top
   c. Wide spans of management
   d. Fewer rules and regulations
   e. Increased teamwork

29. Productivity is defined as
   a. the number of products or services created per unit of input.
   b. the combination of all work-related behaviors.
   c. the time a person spends at work.
   d. the number of days an employee is not absent in a given period.
   e. the quality of the products or services an employee produces.

30. Profitability is generally assessed only at which level?
   a. Individual   d. Group
   b. Industry   e. Team
   c. Organization

CHAPTER 2

Managing Global and Workforce Diversity

MANAGEMENT PREVIEW

Both the world of business and the workforces in organizations are becoming increasingly global and diverse. These developments affect our lives as workers and managers and pose numerous challenges. In some organizations, increasing workforce diversity is due to changing demographics among the general population of society; in others, it is the result of the globalization of the organization's products, services, suppliers, customers, and employees. Regardless of the cause of workforce diversity management must deal with diversity and develop ways to manage it. In this chapter, we explore how to manage these cross-cultural issues. First, we examine the different types and sources of diversity affecting organizations today. We then trace the emergence of international management issues and describe the dimensions and complexities of organizational diversity. Next, we discuss the primary and secondary dimensions of diversity. We also examine cross-cultural factors that affect individual, interpersonal, and organizational issues. Finally, we look at managing multicultural and multinational organizations.

After you have studied this chapter, you should be able to:

☐ *Describe the nature of diversity in organizations.*
☐ *Discuss the emergence of international management.*
☐ *Identify and explain key dimensions of diversity.*
☐ *Describe the fundamental issues in managing the multicultural organization.*

We start by describing the diversity programs in operation at Procter & Gamble.

P rocter & Gamble (P&G) produces a wide variety of items, including such popular U.S. brand names as Tide, Crest, Always, Pampers, Cover Girl, Olay, Secret, Scope, Charmin, Ivory, Folgers, and Pringles. With more than 250 brands, P&G is the largest producer of products for the home, products that are purchased primarily by women. A recent survey by P&G found that women control 80 percent of family purchasing decisions. As a result, P&G, long known for its effective marketing campaigns, now focuses on attracting and retaining more women to match the diversity represented by its customers.

Managing this diversity was not always a priority at P&G. Many female employees were leaving the company, with few remaining to be promoted to top management ranks. Even meetings to discuss products such as a diaper or makeup brand often failed to include a single female participant. The solution was clear: find out why women were leaving the company and respond. Today some of the new initiatives at P&G include local task forces for each facility, diversity specialists in the human resources departments, flexible work arrangements, generous family leave policies, and sabbaticals. A companywide survey identified areas of concern among female employees, and another survey gathered insights from those who had recently quit. The "Careers" page of the company website lists "We show respect for all individuals" as the firm's number one principle, supported by the statements "We believe that all individuals can and want to contribute" and "We value differences."

One-third of P&G vice presidents today are women, up from 5 percent in 1992, and two members of its board of directors are female, up from none in 1992. Women head some of P&G's most important brands, including Tide, the firm's bestseller. P&G was recognized by *Business Ethics* as number five among the one hundred best corporate citizens, in part for its diversity programs. P&G's website states, "Of the approximately 700 firms [being evaluated for this distinction], P&G is the only company that has ranked within the top 5 for all years of this ranking."

Business Ethics found that companies on its "100 Best" list had significantly higher financial performance than did comparable firms not on the list. P&G management also equates diversity with success. "Our success as a global company is a direct result of our diverse and talented workforce. Our ability to develop new consumer insights and ideas and to execute in a superior way across the world is the best possible testimony to the power of diversity that any organization could ever have," says John E. Pepper, P&G chairman.

"Our success as a global company is a direct result of our diverse and talented workforce." —John Pepper, chairman, Procter & Gamble

References: "Careers," "Diversity," "Purpose, Values, Principles," Procter & Gamble websites, www.pg.com and www.pgcareers.com, on April 23, 2004; *2001 Annual 10-K Report*, Procter & Gamble, p. 38; Mary Miller, "The 100 Best Corporate Citizens for 2002," *Business Ethics*, March–April 2001, www.business-ethics.com on April 23, 2004; Tara Parker-Pope, "P&G Retools to Keep More Female Employees," *Cincinnati Post*, September 14, 1998, p. 7B.

More and more organizations are developing and expanding their internal and external programs in the areas of diversity, and most are finding that doing so makes good business sense. Organizations such as Procter & Gamble, AT&T, Denny's (Advantica), Ernst and Young, the Anderson School at UCLA, Pitney Bowes, and Pfizer are using innovative ways to manage an increasingly diverse workforce through various diversity initiatives, including roundtables and seminars on diversity, and diversity marketing to reach new employees, suppliers, and customers that make a difference on the bottom line. It is essential that managers be aware of the different aspects of diversity, the wide range of diversity programs in use, and the impact of diversity on corporate performance. We start this chapter with a more detailed discussion of the meaning and nature of diversity in organizations.

The Nature of Diversity in Organizations

You have no doubt heard the term *diversity* many times, but what does it mean in the workplace today? Usually when we speak of diversity, we think only of the gender, racial, and ethnic differences in the workforce. More broadly, the term refers to a mixture of items, objects, or people characterized by differences and similarities.[1] The similarities can be as important as the differences. After all, none of us are exactly alike. We may be similar but never the same. Thus, although two employees may have the same gender, ethnicity, and even university education, they are different individuals who may act differently and react differently to various management styles. Managers have to deal simultaneously with similarities and differences among people in organizations.[2] They must deal with diversity within their own organizations and in the organizations they encounter all over the world. The opportunities and difficulties inherent in managing multicultural organizations will be a key management challenge in the twenty-first century.

The increasing diversity of the workforce is due to four trends. First, as the job market changes in response to economic conditions, it becomes increasingly important to find the best workers and then utilize them to best serve the organization. Layoffs are costly, as are recruiting and hiring new employees. During economic downturns, companies such as Silicon Graphics struggle to ensure that no one group of employees is disproportionately affected by layoffs, for example.[3] Second, more companies are focusing their marketing efforts on the increasing buying power in the minority markets. A diverse, or segmented, marketing effort requires a marketing team that represents the markets being targeted. As an example, McDonald's, highly ranked on *Fortune*'s list of the fifty best companies for minorities, is diversifying what it buys as well as what it sells by buying $3 billion a year from minority-owned firms.[4] Third, more companies are seeking to expand their markets around the world, requiring more diverse thinking to effectively reach global markets. Finally, companies seeking to achieve a global presence via expansion, acquisitions, and mergers inevitably go through a period of consolidation to reduce duplication of efforts around the world and to capitalize on the synergies of cross-border operations. Typically, consolidation means grouping employees from around the world together into newly streamlined units, resulting in more diverse groups. These four trends, then, are the drivers behind the increasing diversity in the workforce.[5]

What Is Workforce Diversity?

Workforce diversity is the similarities and differences in such characteristics as age, gender, ethnic heritage, physical abilities and disabilities, race, and sexual orientation among the employees of organizations.

Workforce diversity refers to the similarities and differences in such characteristics as age, gender, ethnic heritage, physical abilities and disabilities, race, and sexual orientation among the employees of organizations. 3M defines its goals regarding workforce diversity as "valuing uniqueness, while respecting differences, maximizing individual potentials, and synergizing collective talents and experiences for the growth and success of 3M."[6] In a diverse workforce, managers are compelled to recognize and handle the similarities and differences among the organization's people.

Employees' conceptions of work, expectations of rewards from the organization, and practices in relating to others are all influenced by diversity.[7] Managers of diverse work groups need to understand how the social environment affects employees' beliefs about work, and they must have the communication skills to

Coca-Cola CEO Douglas Daft (second from left) is shown with some of the employees who represent the company's drive to diversify its workforce. At Coca-Cola, 40 percent of new hires are minorities. This comes after a racial discrimination suit in 2000 that cost the company $192 million. And minorities are not only at the lower levels of the organization; they now make up 30 percent of the executive committee of the board of directors.

develop confidence and self-esteem in members of diverse work groups. Many people tend to stereotype others in organizations. A **stereotype** is a generalization about a person or a group of people based on certain characteristics or traits. Many managers fall into the trap of stereotyping workers as being like themselves and sharing a managerial orientation toward work, rewards, and relating to coworkers. However, if workers do not share those views, values, and beliefs, problems can arise. A second situation involving stereotyping occurs when managers characterize workers according to a particular attribute, such as age, gender, race, or ethnic origin. It is often easier for managers to group people based on easily identifiable characteristics and treat those groups as "different." Managers who stereotype workers based on assumptions about the characteristics of the work group tend to ignore individual differences, which leads to making rigid judgments about others that do not take into account the specific person and the current situation.[8]

Stereotypes tend to become rigid judgments about others that ignore the specific person and the current situation. Acceptance of stereotypes can lead to the dangerous process of prejudice toward others.

Prejudices are judgments about others that reinforce beliefs about superiority and inferiority.

Stereotypes can lead to the even more dangerous process of prejudice toward others. **Prejudices** are judgments about others that reinforce beliefs about superiority and inferiority. They can lead to an exaggerated assessment of the worth of one group and a diminished assessment of the worth of other groups.[9] When managers prejudge employees, they make assumptions about the nature of those individuals that may or may not be true, and they manage them accordingly. In other words, managers build job descriptions, reward systems, performance appraisal systems, and management systems and policies that fit their stereotypes of employees.

Management systems built on stereotypes and prejudices do not meet the needs of a diverse workforce. An incentive system may offer rewards that people do not value, job descriptions that do not fit the jobs and the people who do them, and performance evaluation systems that measure the wrong things. In addition, managers who engage in prejudice and stereotyping fail to recognize employees' distinctive individual talents, which often leads to lower self-esteem and possibly lower levels of job satisfaction and performance among those employees. Stereotypes can also become self-fulfilling prophecies.[10] If we assume someone is incompetent and treat the person as such, over time the employee may begin to share the same belief. This can lead to reduced productivity, lower creativity, and lower morale.

Of course, managers caught in this counterproductive cycle can change. As a first step, they must recognize that diversity exists in organizations. Only then can they begin to manage it appropriately. Managers who do not recognize diversity may face an unhappy, disillusioned, and underutilized workforce.

Who Will Be the Workforce of the Future?

Employment statistics can help us understand just how different the workforce of the future will be. Figure 2.1 compares the workforce composition of 1990 to projections for 2010. All workforce segments will increase as a percentage of the total workforce except the white male segment, which will decline from 47.4 to 43.2 percent. This may not seem very dramatic, but it follows decades in which white males have dominated the workforce by well over 50 percent. When one considers that the total U.S. workforce is expected to be more than 150 million people in 2010, a 4 percent drop represents a significant decline.[11]

Figure 2.2 shows the percentage of the growth attributable to each segment from 2000 to 2010. Although the overall workforce growth is expected to be 12 percent, the growth rate for white males is expected to be only 6.7 percent. The number of females in the workforce is predicted to increase by 15.1 percent; thus, more than 62 percent of women in the United States are expected to be working in 2010.

Examining the age ranges of the workforce gives us another view of the changes. In contrast to its standing in earlier decades, the sixteen-to-twenty-four age group will grow more rapidly than the overall population—an increase of 3.4 million (14.8 percent) between 2000 and 2010. The number of workers in the twenty-five-to-fifty-four age group is expected to increase by 5 million (5.0 percent), and the number of workers in the fifty-five and older group is expected to rise by 8.5 million (46.6 percent).[12]

FIGURE 2.1

Workforce Composition: 1990–2010

In the period between 1990 and 2010, all workforce segments are expected to increase as a percentage of the total workforce except the white male segment, which will decline from 47.4 to 43.2 percent.

Reference: Bureau of Labor Statistics, *Monthly Labor Review,* November 2001.

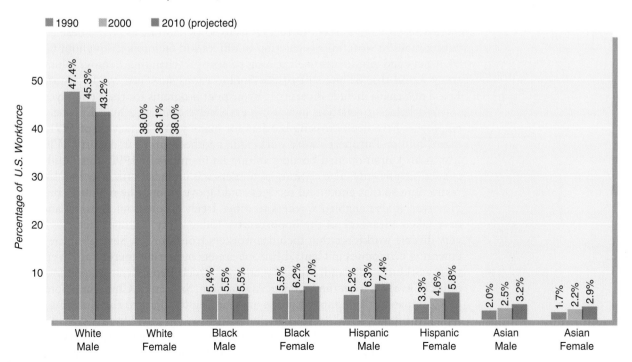

FIGURE 2.2

Expected Percentage of Growth in Workforce: 2000–2010

There is no question that the composition of the U.S. workforce is changing. For the period from 2000 to 2010, the growth rate in all segments is higher for women than for men and higher for non-whites than for whites.

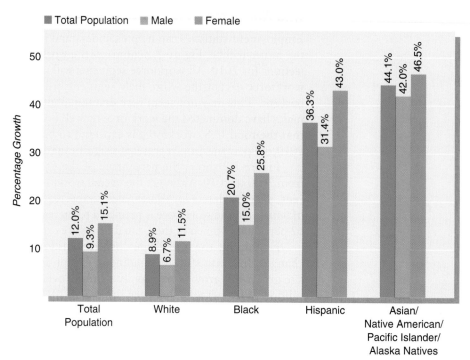

Reference: Bureau of Labor Statistics, *Monthly Labor Review,* November 2001.

Global Workforce Diversity

Diversity in the workforce is more than a U.S. phenomenon. Similar statistics on workforce diversity are found in other countries. In Canada, for instance, minorities are the fastest-growing segment of the population and the workforce. In addition, women make up two-thirds of the growth in the Canadian workforce, increasing from 35 percent in the 1970s to 45 percent in 1991.[13] These changes have initiated a workforce revolution in offices and factories throughout Canada. Managers and employees are learning to adapt to changing demographics. One study found that 81 percent of the organizations surveyed by the Conference Board of Canada include diversity management programs for their employees.[14]

Workplace diversity is increasing even more dramatically in Europe, where employees have been crossing borders for many years. In fact, as of 1991, more than 2 million Europeans were working in another European country. When the European Union opened borders among its members in 1992, this number increased significantly. The opening of borders was intended primarily to relax trade restrictions so that goods and services could move among the member countries. However, it also enabled workers to move freely throughout Europe, and they have taken advantage of the opportunity. Today many German factories have a very diverse workforce that includes workers from Turkey. Several of the newly emerging economies in Central Europe are encountering increasing diversity in their workforces. Poland, Hungary, and the Czech Republic are experiencing an influx of workers from the Ukraine, Afghanistan, Sri Lanka, China, and Somalia.[15]

Companies throughout Europe are learning to adjust to the changing workforce. Amadeus Global Travel Distribution serves the travel industry primarily in Europe, but its staff of 650 is composed of individuals from thirty-two countries. Amadeus developed a series of workshops to teach managers how to lead multicultural teams. Such seminars also teach them how to interact more effectively with peers, subordinates, and superiors who come from a variety of countries.[16] Other companies experiencing and responding to the same phenomenon in Europe include Mars, Hewlett-Packard Spain, Fujitsu in Spain, and BP. Companies in Asia are also encountering increasing diversity. In Thailand, where rapid industrialization and slow population growth have created a shortage of skilled and unskilled workers, demand for foreign workers to fill the gap is growing, creating problems integrating local and foreign workers.[17] Thus, the issues created by workforce diversity are prevalent throughout the globe. We discuss the emergence of international management in the next major section of this chapter. First, we need to look at why it is important to value diversity rather than just tolerate it.

The Value of Diversity

The United States has historically been seen as a "melting pot" of people from many different countries, cultures, and backgrounds. For centuries, it was assumed that people who came from other countries should assimilate themselves into the existing cultural context. Although equal employment opportunity and accompanying affirmative action legislation have had significant effects on diversifying workplaces, they sometimes focused on bringing into the workplace people from culturally different groups and fully assimilating them into the existing organization. In organizations, however, integration proved to be difficult. People were usually resistant to the change and slow to adopt it. Substantive career advancement opportunities rarely materialized for those who were "different."

Workforce diversity has become an increasingly important issue in the last few years as employees, managers, consultants, and the government finally recognize that the composition of the workforce affects organizational productivity. Today, instead of a melting pot, the U.S. workplace is regarded more as a "tossed salad" made up of a delightful mosaic of flavors, colors, and textures. Rather than trying to assimilate those who are different into a single organizational culture, the current view holds that organizations need to celebrate the differences and utilize the variety of talents, perspectives, and backgrounds of all employees.

Benefits of Valuing Diversity   **Valuing diversity** means giving up the assumption that everyone who is not a member of the dominant group must assimilate. This is not easily accomplished in most organizations. Truly valuing diversity is not merely giving lip service to an ideal, putting up with a necessary evil, promoting a level of tolerance for those who are different, or tapping into the latest fad. It is an opportunity to develop and utilize all of the human resources available to the organization for the benefit of the workers as well as the organization. Later in this chapter, we discuss the benefits of creating a multicultural organization.

Valuing diversity is not just the right thing to do for workers; it is the right thing to do for the organization, financially and economically. One of the most important benefits of diversity is the richness of ideas and perspectives it makes available to the organization. Rather than relying on one homogeneous dominant group for new ideas and alternative solutions to increasingly complex problems, companies that value diversity have access to more perspectives on a problem. These fresh perspectives may lead to development of new products, opening of new markets, or improving service to existing customers.

Overall, the organization wins when it truly values diversity. A worker whom the organization values is more creative and productive. Valued workers in diverse organizations experience less interpersonal conflict because employees understand

Valuing diversity means putting an end to the assumption that everyone who is not a member of the dominant group must assimilate.

one another. This understanding leads to a greater sense of teamwork, stronger identification with the team, and a deeper commitment to the organization and its goals.

Assimilation is the process through which members of a minority group are forced to learn the ways of the dominant group.

Assimilation **Assimilation** is the process through which members of a minority group are forced to learn the ways of the majority group. In organizations, this entails hiring people from diverse backgrounds and attempting to mold them to fit into the existing organizational culture. One way companies attempt to make people fit in is to require that employees speak only one language. In Chicago, Carlos Solero was fired three days after he refused to sign a work agreement that included a policy of English-only at a suburban manufacturing plant. Management said the intent of the English-only policy was to improve communication among workers at the plant. In response, Solero and seven other Spanish speakers filed lawsuits against the plant.[18] Attempts to assimilate diverse workers by imposing English-only rules can lead to a variety of organizational problems. Most organizations develop systems such as performance evaluation and incentive programs that reinforce the values of the dominant group. (Chapter 14 discusses organizational culture as a means of reinforcing organizational values and controlling workers' behavior.) By universally applying the values of the majority group throughout the organization, assimilation tends to perpetuate false stereotypes and prejudices. Workers who are different are expected to meet the standards for dominant-group members.[19]

Dominant groups tend to be self-perpetuating. Majority-group members may avoid people who are "different" simply because they find communication with them difficult. Moreover, informal discussions over coffee and lunch and during after-hours socializing tend to be limited to people in the dominant group. Those who are not in the dominant group miss out on informal communications regarding office politics, company policies, and other issues; as a result, they often do not understand more formal communications. For example, informal discussions may provide background and explanations; a subsequent formal memorandum may then be clear to those "in the know," but less clear to those not in the dominant group. The dominant group likewise remains unaware of opinions from "the outside."

Similarly, since the dominant group makes decisions based on their values and beliefs, the minority group has little say in decisions regarding compensation, facility location, benefit plans, performance standards, and other work issues that pertain directly to all workers. Workers who differ from the majority very quickly get the idea that to succeed in such a system, one must be like the dominant group in terms of values and beliefs, dress, and most other characteristics. Since success depends on assimilation, differences are driven underground.

Most organizations have a fairly predictable dominant group. Table 2.1 shows the results of interviews with members of several organizations who were asked to list the attributes reinforced by their organization's culture. Typically, white organization members view themselves as quite diverse. Others in the organization, however, view them as quite homogeneous, having attributes similar to those listed in the table. Also, dominant-group members tend to be less aware of the problems homogeneity can cause. Generally, those not in the dominant group feel the effects more keenly.

Failure to heed cultural diversity can be very costly to the organization. In addition to blocking minority involvement in communication and decision making, it can result in tensions among workers, lower productivity, rising costs due to increasing absenteeism, higher employee turnover, increased equal employment opportunity and harassment suits, and lower worker morale.[20]

TABLE 2.1

Attributes Reinforced by the Culture in Typical Organizations

- Rational, linear thinker
- Impersonal management style
- Married with children
- Quantitative
- Adversarial
- Careerist
- Individualistic
- Experience in competitive team sports
- In control
- Military veteran

- Age 35–49
- Competitive
- Protestant or Jewish
- College graduate
- Tall
- Heterosexual
- Predictable
- Excellent physical condition
- Willing to relocate

Reference: Marilyn Loden and Judy B. Rosener, *Workforce America! Managing Employee Diversity as a Vital Resource* (Homewood, IL: Business One Irwin, 1991), p. 43. Copyright © 1991 by Business One Irwin. Used with permission.

The Emergence of International Management

LEARNING OBJECTIVE

Discuss the emergence of international management.

A primary source of diversity in organizations is the increasing globalization of organizations and management. However, in many ways, international management is nothing new. Centuries ago, the Roman army was forced to develop a management system to deal with its widespread empire.[21] Likewise, the Olympic Games, the Red Cross, and many similar organizations have international roots. From a business standpoint, however, international management is relatively new, at least in the United States.

The Growth of International Business

In 2000, the volume of international trade in current dollars was almost forty times greater than the amount in 1960, and the figures are projected to continue escalating. What has led to this dramatic increase? As Figure 2.3 shows, four major factors account for much of the momentum.

First, communication and transportation have advanced dramatically over the past several decades. Telephone service has improved, communication networks span the globe and can interact via satellite, and once remote areas have become accessible. Telephone service in some developing countries is now based almost entirely on cellular phone technology rather than land-based wired telephone service. Fax machines and electronic mail allow managers to send documents around the world in seconds as opposed to the days it took in years past. In short, it is far easier to conduct international business today.

Second, businesses have expanded internationally to increase their markets. Companies in smaller countries, such as Nestlé in Switzerland, recognized long ago that their domestic markets were too small to sustain much growth and therefore moved into international activities. Many U.S. firms, on the other hand, had all the business they could handle until recently; hence, they are just beginning to consider international opportunities. As U.S. companies grow internationally, they confront many differences in the ways various countries conduct business. Differences in laws, local customs, tariffs, and exchange rates are only a few of these

FIGURE 2.3

Forces That Have Increased International Business

Movement along the continuum from domestic to international business is due to four forces. Businesses subject to these forces are becoming more international.

challenges. In spite of the Foreign Corrupt Practices Act in the United States, some companies are having difficulty finding legal ways to do business, and individuals are still getting into legal difficulties. For example, Saybolt, Inc., pled guilty to paying a $50,000 bribe to Panamanian government officials within the Panamanian Ministry of Commerce and Industries to obtain a government lease for a laboratory site adjacent to the Panama Canal. David H. Mean, then president of Saybolt, was convicted of conspiracy, violation of the Foreign Corrupt Practices Act, and interstate travel to promote bribery.[22] Companies in the tobacco industry that have significantly increased their global efforts are currently embroiled in a global controversy over the ethics of marketing tobacco products around the world.

Third, more and more firms are moving into the international realm to control costs, especially labor costs. Plans to cut costs in this way do not always work out as planned, but many firms are successfully using inexpensive labor in Asia and Mexico.[23] In searching for lower labor costs, some companies have discovered well-trained workers and built more efficient plants that are closer to international markets.[24]

Finally, many organizations have become international in response to competition. If an organization starts gaining strength in international markets, its competitors often must follow suit to avoid falling too far behind in sales and profitability. Exxon Mobil Corporation and Texaco realized they had to increase their international market share to keep pace with foreign competitors such as BP and Royal Dutch/Shell.

Trends in International Business

The most striking trend in international business is obvious: growth. More and more businesses are entering the international marketplace, including many smaller firms. We read a great deal about the threat of foreign companies. For example, for many years successful Japanese automobile firms such as Toyota and Nissan produced higher-quality cars for lower prices than did U.S. firms. What is often overlooked, however, is the success of U.S. firms abroad. Ford, for example, has long had a successful business in Europe and today employs less than half its total workforce on U.S. soil. Further, U.S. firms make dozens of products better than any other company in the world.[25] General Motors Europe has had strong sales in Europe since 1985, rising to a 13 percent market share, the second best in Europe, behind Volkswagen.[26] In addition, many foreign firms, such as BMW and Mercedes, are now producing their products in the United States because of the lower wage rates, more favorable tax rates, and improved quality.

Business transactions are also becoming increasingly blurred across national boundaries. Ford owns 25 percent of Mazda, General Motors and Toyota have a joint venture in California, Ford and Volkswagen have one in Argentina, and Honda and British Sterling have one worldwide. Mergers are also taking place all over the globe. Ford owns Jaguar and Volvo, Daimler-Benz merged with Chrysler to form DaimlerChrysler, and Renault and Nissan share ownership.

These workers in Alcatel's switch-making plant in Shanghai, China, exemplify the rapid changes in manufacturing in that country. Once known for inexpensive, low-skilled labor that made cheap trinkets, toys, textiles, and knock-offs of higher-quality goods, China has become a haven for high-tech manufacturing firms. Sophisticated electronic equipment, photonics, ceramic casings, liquid crystal display screens, digital switching systems, and much more are now among the goods being produced there. China's emergence is creating rapid shifts in investment around the world as manufacturers move to take advantage of the cheaper labor, high-quality workmanship, sophisticated engineering expertise, and proximity to the huge Chinese marketplace.

Indeed, several experts predict that some multinational firms will soon lose their national identity altogether and become truly global corporations. Events in other parts of the world are having major effects on business. The unification of Germany and the movement of the formerly communist-controlled countries in Central Europe toward free-market economies are providing many new opportunities and challenges to business. In many ways, then, we are becoming a truly global economy. No longer will a firm be able to insulate itself from foreign competitors or opportunities. Thus, it is imperative that every manager develop at least a rudimentary understanding of the dynamics of international management.[27]

Cross-Cultural Differences and Similarities

Since the primary concern of this discussion is human behavior in organizational settings, we now focus on differences and similarities in behavior across cultures. Because research in this area is still relatively new, many of the research findings we can draw on are preliminary at best.

General Cultural Issues Cultures and national boundaries do not necessarily coincide. Some areas of Switzerland are very much like Italy, other parts like France, and still other parts like Germany. Similarly, within the United States large cultural differences exist among southern California, Texas, and the East Coast.[28]

Given this basic assumption, one review of the literature on international management reached five basic conclusions.[29] First, behavior in organizational settings indeed varies across cultures. Thus, employees in companies based in Japan, the United States, and Germany are likely to have different attitudes and patterns of behavior that are pervasive throughout the organization.

Second, culture itself is one major cause of this variation. Culture is the set of shared values, often taken for granted, that help people in a group, an organization, or a society understand which actions are considered acceptable and which are deemed unacceptable (we use this same definition in our discussion of organizational culture in Chapter 14). Thus, although the behavioral differences just noted may result in part from different standards of living, different geographical conditions, and so forth, culture itself is a major factor apart from other considerations.

Third, although behavior within organizational settings (e.g., motivation and attitudes) remains quite diverse across cultures, organizations and the way they are structured appear to be increasingly similar. Hence, managerial practices at a general level may be more and more alike, but the people who work within organizations still differ markedly.

Fourth, the same manager behaves differently in different cultural settings. A manager may adopt one set of behaviors when working in one culture but change those behaviors when moved to a different culture. For example, Japanese executives who come to work in the United States slowly begin to act more like U.S. managers and less like Japanese managers. This is often a source of concern for them when they are transferred back to Japan.[30]

Finally, cultural diversity can be an important source of synergy in enhancing organizational effectiveness. More and more organizations are coming to appreciate the benefits of cultural diversity, but they still know surprisingly little about how to manage it.[31] Organizations that adopt a multinational strategy can, albeit with effort, become more than a sum of their parts. Operations in each culture can benefit from operations in other cultures through an enhanced understanding of how the world works.[32]

Specific Cultural Issues   Geert Hofstede, a Dutch researcher, studied workers and managers in sixty countries and found that attitudes and behaviors differed significantly along with the values and beliefs in those countries.[33] Table 2.2 shows how Hofstede's categories help us summarize differences for several countries.

Individualism is the extent to which people place primary value on themselves.

The two primary dimensions Hofstede found are the individualism/ collectivism continuum and power distance. **Individualism** exists to the extent that people in a culture define themselves as singular individuals rather than as part of one or more groups or organizations. At work, people from more individualistic cultures tend to be more concerned about themselves than about their work group, individual tasks are more important than relationships, and hiring and promotion are based on skills and rules. **Collectivism,** on the other hand, is characterized by tight social frameworks in which people tend to base their identities on the group or organization to which they belong. At work, employee-employer links are more

Collectivism is the extent to which people emphasize the good of the group or society.

TABLE 2.2

Work-Related Differences in Ten Countries

Country	Individualism/ Collectivism	Power Distance	Uncertainty Avoidance	Masculinity	Long-Term Orientation
Canada	H	M	M	M	L
Germany	M	M	M	M	M
Israel	M	L	M	M	(no data)
Italy	H	M	M	H	(no data)
Japan	M	M	H	H	H
Mexico	H	H	H	M	(no data)
Pakistan	L	M	M	M	L
Sweden	H	M	L	L	M
United States	H	M	M	M	L
Venezuela	L	H	M	H	(no data)

Note: H = high; M = moderate; L = low. These are only ten of the more than sixty countries that Hofstede and others have studied.
References: Adapted from Geert Hofstede and Michael Harris Bond, "The Confucius Connection: From Cultural Roots to Economic Growth," *Organizational Dynamics*, Spring 1998, pp. 5-21; Geert Hofstede, "Motivation, Leadership, and Organization: Do American Theories Apply Abroad?" *Organizational Dynamics*, Summer 1980, pp. 42–63.

like family relationships, relationships are more important than individuals or tasks, and hiring and promotion are based on group membership. In the United States, a highly individualistic culture, it is important to perform better than others and to stand out from the crowd. In Japan, a more collectivist culture, an individual tries to fit in with the group, strives for harmony, and prefers stability.

Power distance, also called **orientation to authority,** is the extent to which less powerful people accept the unequal distribution of power. In countries such as Mexico and Venezuela, for example, people prefer to be in a situation in which lines of authority are clearly understood and are never bypassed. On the other hand, in countries such as Israel and Denmark, authority is less highly respected and employees are comfortable circumventing lines of authority to accomplish something. People in the United States tend to fall somewhere in between, accepting authority in some situations but not in others.

Uncertainty avoidance, or **preference for stability,** is the extent to which people feel threatened by the unknown and prefer to be in unambiguous situations. People in Japan and Mexico prefer stability to uncertainty, whereas uncertainty is considered routine in Sweden, Hong Kong, and the United Kingdom. **Masculinity**, also called **assertiveness** or **materialism,** is the extent to which the dominant values in a society emphasize aggressiveness and the acquisition of money and things as opposed to concern for people, relationships among people, and overall quality of life. People in the United States are moderate on both the uncertainty avoidance and masculinity scales. Japan and Italy score high on the masculinity scale, whereas Sweden scores low.

Hofstede's framework has recently been expanded to include long-term versus short-term orientation. **Long-term** values include focusing on the future, working on projects that have a distant payoff, persistence, and thrift. **Short-term** values are oriented more toward the past and the present, and include respect for traditions and social obligations. Japan, Hong Kong, and China are highly long-term oriented; the Netherlands and Germany are moderately long-term oriented. The United States, Indonesia, West Africa, and Russia are more short-term oriented. Certain aspects of the culture of a specific country can change over time.

Hofstede's research presents only one of several ways to categorize differences across many countries and cultures. His system is, however, widely accepted and used by many companies. The important issue is that people from diverse cultures value things differently from one another and that all employees need to take these differences into account as they work.

Power distance (orientation to authority) is the extent to which less powerful individuals accept the unequal distribution of power.

Uncertainty avoidance (preference for stability) is the extent to which people prefer to be in unambiguous situations.

Masculinity (assertiveness or **materialism)** is the extent to which the dominant values in a society emphasize aggressiveness and the acquisition of money and material goods over concern for people, relationships among people, and the overall quality of life.

People with a **long-term orientation** focus on the future; people with a **short-term orientation** focus on the past or present.

Dimensions of Diversity

LEARNING OBJECTIVE

Identify and explain key dimensions of diversity.

People do not have to be from different countries to have different values. Within a single country significant differences exist in values, beliefs, and normally accepted ways of doing things. In the United States, race and gender were considered the primary dimensions of diversity during the past two decades. The earliest civil rights laws aimed to correct racial segregation. Other laws have dealt with discrimination on the basis of gender, age, and disability. However, diversity entails broader issues than these. In the largest sense, *workforce diversity* refers to all of the ways in which employees are similar and different. The importance of organizations' renewed interest in diversity is that it helps them reap the benefits of all the similarities and differences among workers. For discussion purposes, we have divided the many aspects of diversity into primary and secondary dimensions.

Primary Dimensions of Diversity

The **primary dimensions of diversity** are those factors that are either inborn or exert extraordinary influence on early socialization. These include age, race and ethnicity, gender, physical and mental abilities, and sexual orientation.[34] These factors make up the essence of who we are as human beings. They define us to others and, because of how others react to them, also define us to ourselves. These characteristics are enduring aspects of our human personality, and they sometimes present extremely complex problems to managers. In this section, we highlight a few issues surrounding the primary dimensions.

The **primary dimensions of diversity** are factors that are either inborn or exert extraordinary influence on early socialization: age, race and ethnicity, gender, physical and mental abilities, and sexual orientation.

Age   The age issue is multifaceted and very individualistic. As people age, they become more diverse in more ways. As the United States and the rest of the world's economy and labor productivity continue to grow, the demand for labor is expected to grow at 2 percent annually. At the same time, fewer people are entering the workforce, and the workforce is growing older overall as the baby boomers move into the over-fifty age range. The median age of the workforce increased from 36.6 years in 1990 to 39.3 years in 2000 and is expected to be 40.6 years by 2010.[35] In addition, the labor force participation rate for workers over sixty-five is expected to increase from 12.8 to 14.8 percent from 2000 to 2010.[36] This trend subsumes another: Workforce participation rates for women over age fifty are increasing faster than for men over fifty; thus, women constitute more of the increase in older workers.

Several aspects of these data require managerial attention. First, benefit packages may need to be changed to appeal to older workers. For example, for workers with no children at home, family benefit packages may be less attractive. Second, as the population ages, more people are living well into their eighties. A man who reaches age sixty-five is expected to live fourteen more years; a woman who reaches age sixty-five is expected to live another eighteen-and-a-half years. The over-eighty-five age group is the fastest-growing segment of the population.[37] Therefore, many children of this age group, themselves over fifty and still active in the workforce, are becoming primary caregivers for their elderly parents. These caregivers face increased stress, take more unscheduled days off, have more late arrivals to and early departures from work, and have above-average telephone use on the job.

Older workers may need additional and special training in new technologies and equipment to accommodate their distinctive needs. For example, consider how the eye functions. As people get older, the amount of light that reaches the retina falls by about 50 percent because of the gradual yellowing of the lens, distorting perceptions of blue, green, and gray. The average sixty-year-old needs two-and-a-half times as much light to read comfortably as the average twenty-year-old.[38] Differences also exist in manual dexterity, hearing, perception, cognition, strength, and agility. In the past, little allowance was made for workers unable to conform to the standard equipment and expectations of the workplace. Managers of today and the future will need to adjust physical facilities, equipment, and training methods to derive maximum productivity from the entire workforce.

Race and Ethnicity   Racial and ethnic differences may be more important than most managers initially realize because critical differences exist across cultures in attitudes toward, beliefs about, and values surrounding work. Data show that people of different racial and ethnic backgrounds are increasing in number and in percentage of the workforce. Although much has been accomplished in recent years, racial and ethnic minorities still believe that a significant barrier keeps them from the top executive positions in U.S. companies. One primary reason for turnover or attrition among minorities, as well as women, is the "glass ceiling" prevalent in U.S.

firms. The diversity director in one high-tech company estimates that the cost of recruiting and training one new worker to replace one who voluntarily leaves exceeds $112,000.[39] Another cost is lower morale and productivity among remaining workers. Companies today simply cannot afford to ignore the impact of racial and ethnic differences in the workforce. Yet in spite of years of progress and the recent emphasis on valuing diversity, the glass ceiling is still in place for minorities and women.

Gender   Women were one of the first groups to be emphasized in the early attempts to provide equal employment opportunity and affirmative action. Many organizations have always included at least some women, of course; the issue now is that women hold positions other than secretary, nurse, teacher, and receptionist. Xerox is among those firms that have learned the speed with which workforce composition can change. Between 1980 and today, the number of female managers at the firm grew from 10 to 45 percent, the number of female professionals increased from 18 to 48 percent, and the number of females in the sales force tripled from 22 to 66 percent.[40] After recognizing this trend, Xerox developed programs to help all employees work together in its newly diverse workforce.

Until recently, most managers assumed women should be treated the same way as men and that they react to issues in the same way. This is not always the case, however. Following an out-of-town sales meeting, for example, men often go to the hotel bar for relaxation and follow-up discussions. Female employees, however, often feel uncomfortable in the more social atmosphere of the bar and therefore are often excluded from the discussions. A similar situation arises when men leave a meeting to go to golf clubs, some of which still prohibit women. Situations such as these may exclude women from valuable socialization processes necessary for groups to coordinate activities and accomplish goals, and may have the unintended but systematic effect of excluding women from top management positions. Companies have found simple solutions to some of these situations by having sales meetings in conference centers and bringing refreshments into the meeting rooms after the meetings so all can participate in the follow-up sessions. Hosting dinners in the conference center can also help keep everyone involved after the formal meeting. The increasing number of women in the workforce means employees with different attitudes, backgrounds, and capabilities need to be utilized, possibly in different ways than were previously the norm in many organizations.

Akiro Iso became the National Football League's first female trainer in 2002. Although 47.9 percent of members of the National Athletic Trainer's Association are women, none had broken into the male-dominated professional level of the sport until Iso took the job with the Pittsburgh Steelers. Iso has a master's degree in the field and worked her way up in the industry. She has served at the university level, where she was involved with several sports, including football, and as a part-time summer intern with the Steelers. The Steelers maintained she was hired not because of her gender but because of her experience as an athletic trainer. The players like her work and claim she is a very good trainer.

The women's movement enabled women to make great strides toward true equality in society in general and in the workplace specifically. Such strides are also being made in Asia, as discussed in the World View box. Despite these advances, women's wages are still lower than men's, and the glass ceiling in most U.S. organizations excludes many women from upper-level positions. Moreover, beginning in the late 1980s, a form of backlash has occurred against the progress made by women. This backlash can take many forms. It may become apparent when men are asked about their views of women's advances in the workforce. When men are "passed over" for promotions, admission to some graduate schools, and other forms of advancement or opportunity, they often blame the "women's movement" as a force behind reverse discrimination. Some people blame myriad social ills on women's progress, including increases in crime, divorce, and stress levels at work.[41]

WORLD VIEW

Equality for Asian Women in the Workforce

Diversity consists of the similarities and differences in a workforce regarding age, gender, ethnicity, and other personal characteristics. Diversity, then, always is defined with regard to a specific group of workers and concerns different issues in different populations. Activists for equality for women in the U.S. workforce have tended to focus on issues such as child care, equal pay for equal work, and the "glass ceiling" effect. Female workers in Asia face the same issues, but with significant differences.

During the Cultural Revolution of the 1960s and 1970s, Chinese women were officially accorded equal social and political status with men—"Women can hold up half the sky," in the words of former chairman Mao Zedong. From that time forward, Chinese women experienced less hiring discrimination than did Western women, although they also suffered from the glass ceiling effect. Bonnie Furst, a PricewaterhouseCoopers human resources manager, says, "Many of my Chinese colleagues prefer to work in China where gender is less of an issue, all things considered . . . When I came to China ten years ago, my being a woman was less of an issue in everyday work life than it was in the [United States] and Japan, right up to the top levels."

However, in many Asian societies, women still struggle for respect and equality. Consider the case of female business managers in Japan. In the last ten years, the percentage of female managers has grown from a mere 0.04 percent to 8.9 percent. However, compare these numbers with the percentage of female managers in Hong Kong:

up from 16 to 22 percent. In addition, Japanese women are often guided into fields, such as human resources or services, in which pay and job security are typically lower than for manufacturing or technical positions.

"Many of my Chinese colleagues prefer to work in China where gender is less of an issue, all things considered."

—*Bonnie Furst, PricewaterhouseCoopers human resources manager*

Wiwam Tharahirunchote, a female finance company director in Thailand, claims, "Discrimination is gone." But she also believes women aren't suited to jobs in construction or engineering, explaining, "Women just don't have the physical strength to do that kind of thing." Doris Lau, HSBC bank vice president, notes that "The male executive I believe could work longer hours than the female;" she also maintains that women shouldn't enter into contract negotiations. Rochana Kosiyanon worked for DuPont in America for nine years before returning to Thailand to become managing director of a consulting firm. She asserts that gender discrimination was more of a problem in the United States than in her homeland. However, she also acknowledges, "[If a wife is successful in business], she may not be a wife for much longer. Asian male egos are fragile."

References: "Breaking Glass: Chinese Women on the Rise," *Business Beijing*, November 2001, pp. 26–31; Carol Hymowitz, "The Glass Ceiling's Jagged Edge—In a Slowing Economy, Women Who Achieved Now Face Sharper Scrutiny," *Asian Wall Street Journal*, March 16, 2001, p. W3; Samantha Marshall, "Women Stereotyping Women—Compounding Glass Ceiling, Some Women May Construct Their Own Workplace Barriers," *Asian Wall Street Journal*, May 21, 1999, p. 3.

In reality, extreme positions for or against women's advancements may be disruptive and hinder efforts to solve gender-based inequities. It is important for managers to recognize that strong feelings exist on both sides and that addressing tensions in the workplace over equality for all types of workers is paramount if managers and employees are to get their work done and reach organizational goals.

Different Abilities An often misunderstood group, and one that is more diverse than any other, is people whose abilities are in some way limited relative to those of the general population. Disabilities may take many different forms. Some individuals have missing or nonfunctioning limbs, some have sensory impairments, others have problems related to diseases such as multiple sclerosis, and still others have mental limitations of various kinds. The rights of these people are protected under the Americans with Disabilities Act and the Rehabilitation Act. Employers cannot discriminate in any way regarding employment of people with disabilities, and employers must make reasonable accommodations in the workplace to assist employees on the job. These workers are best referred to as "differently abled" or "physically or mentally challenged" to indicate respect for the abilities that make them unique and capable of making valuable contributions to the organization.[42]

Physically or mentally challenged people are just like everyone else except for their particular disability. Most are excellent employees in jobs appropriate for their skill types and levels. Reasonable workplace accommodations may include equipment purchase or modification, restructuring of jobs, reassignment to other jobs, making facilities accessible, modifying work schedules, and modifying examination and training materials.[43] Each case needs to be considered individually, and accommodations should be made for that specific case. One important accommodation is the reaction of coworkers to the hiring of a physically or mentally challenged person. It may take some training and personal accommodation for other members of the work group to adjust.

Many companies have attempted to appropriately accommodate differently challenged workers. Lotus Development has a hiring program that works in conjunction with Greater Boston Rehabilitation Services to hire differently abled workers in its assembly, packing, and shipping departments. Lotus provides a shuttle bus to the plant from the local train station and provides job coaches, special equipment, and new training programs to ensure the success of each worker. In addition, other Lotus employees participate in awareness programs to ease entry of new workers into the company. Eastman Kodak's warehouse in Oak Brook, Illinois, includes five employees who are both deaf and mute. The order-filling accuracy of these employees is more than 99 percent, exceeding that of other employees. Eastman Kodak accommodated these employees by placing them in an area that had no forklifts or other heavy equipment and adding special telephones that use a keyboard and screen for communication.[44]

Another primary dimension of diversity receiving increasing attention in organizations is sexual orientation. As in the population in general, an estimated 10 percent of the workforce is homosexual. Homosexuals work in all types of industries, including finance, insurance, science, engineering, and computers.[45] Although some homosexuals no longer try to hide their sexual preference, many still feel they must conceal it. A California judge ordered a Shell Oil subsidiary to pay $5.3 million in damages to a worker who was fired because of his homosexuality.[46] In contrast, companies such as Levi Strauss, Apple Computer, Boeing, DuPont, and Xerox have lesbian and gay groups that operate openly, holding meetings, orientation sessions, and special gay pride weeks. As open as some companies have become, however, many critics still assert that a glass ceiling exists for homosexual managers ready to advance to executive positions. Companies must also decide whether to extend dependent health coverage to gay and lesbian partners, as Kodak and IBM did recently.[47]

Secondary Dimensions of Diversity

Secondary dimensions of diversity include factors that are important to us as individuals and that to some extent define us to others but are less permanent and can be adapted or changed: educational background, geographical location, income, marital status, military experience, parental status, religious beliefs, and work experience.

Secondary dimensions of diversity include factors that matter to us as individuals and that to some extent define us to others but are less permanent than primary dimensions and can be adapted or changed. These dimensions include educational background, geographical location, income, marital status, military experience, parental status, religious beliefs, and work experience. These factors may influence our lives as much as the primary dimensions do. Many veterans of the wars in Afghanistan and Iraq, for example, were profoundly affected by their experience of serving in the military. The influence of religion and spirituality, two other secondary dimensions, is becoming more prevalent at work.

The impact of secondary dimensions may differ at various times in our lives. For example, moving to another part of the country or world may be traumatic for a parent with several children; a person with no close ties or dependents, on the other hand, may find it exciting. Family experiences may also influence a manager's degree of sympathy for the disruptions of work life that personal responsibilities sometimes create.

Employees enter the workforce with unique experiences and backgrounds that affect their perspectives of work rules, work expectations, and personal concerns. Although employees may have essentially the same work hours, job description, tenure with the company, and compensation, their reactions to the work situation may differ significantly because of differences in these primary and secondary dimensions of diversity.

Managing the Multicultural Organization

┌─────────────────────────┐
│ *LEARNING OBJECTIVE* │
└─────────────────────────┘
Describe the fundamental issues in managing the multicultural organization.

Reaping the rewards of workforce diversity poses difficult challenges, but it also presents new opportunities. Simply announcing that the organization values diversity is not enough. Management must work toward a *multicultural organization* in which employees of mixed backgrounds, experiences, and cultures can contribute and achieve their fullest potential to benefit both themselves and the organization. Management must plan to manage diversity throughout the organization and work hard to implement the plan.

Managerial Behavior Across Cultures

Some individual variations among people from different cultures shape the behavior of both managers and employees. Other differences are much more likely to influence managerial behavior.[48] In general, these differences relate to managers' beliefs about the role of authority and power in the organization. For example, managers in Indonesia, Italy, and Japan tend to believe the purpose of an organization structure is to let everyone know who his or her boss is (medium to high power distance). Managers in the United States, Germany, and Great Britain, in contrast, believe organization structure is intended to coordinate group behavior and effort (low power distance). On another dimension, Italian and German managers believe it is acceptable to bypass one's boss to get things done, but among Swedish and British managers, bypassing one's superior is strongly prohibited.

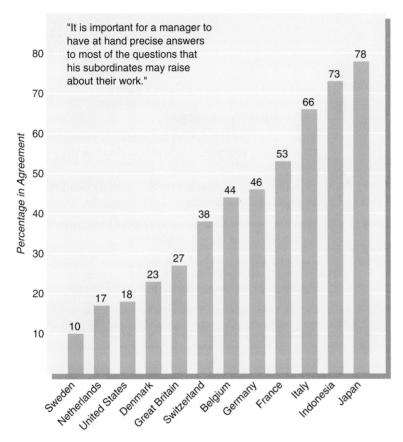

Figure 2.4 illustrates findings on another interesting point. Managers in Japan strongly believe a manager should be able to answer any question he or she is asked. Thus, they place a premium on expertise and experience. At the other extreme are Swedish managers, who are the least concerned about knowing all the answers. They view themselves as problem solvers and facilitators who make no claim to omnipotence.

Recent evidence suggests that managerial behavior is rapidly changing, at least among European managers. In general, these managers are becoming more career oriented, better educated, more willing to work cooperatively with labor, more willing to delegate, and more cosmopolitan.[49]

Multicultural Organization as Competitive Advantage

Movement toward more effective management of a diverse workforce usually begins for one or more of three reasons. Some companies, such as Xerox, were obligated to develop better management of a workforce made more diverse by affirmative action. Other companies, such as Hewlett-Packard, grew very quickly to remain competitive and then realized they had to work with multicultural constituencies. A third group of companies, which includes Avon Products, needed a diverse

FIGURE 2.4

Differences Across Cultures in Managers' Beliefs About Answering Questions from Subordinates

Managers in various cultures have different beliefs regarding the importance of their ability to provide definite, precise answers to questions from subordinates. Japan has the strongest expectations; Sweden has the weakest.

Reference: Reprinted from *International Studies of Management and Organization*, vol. XIII, no. 1–2, Spring–Summer 1983. Copyright © 1983 by M.E. Sharpe, Inc. Reprinted with permission.

workforce to match the diversity their target markets.[50] Companies of all three types need to manage their multicultural workforce more effectively to gain a competitive advantage in the marketplace. Business leaders, consultants, and academic scholars contend that having a multicultural organization can create a competitive advantage in the six ways shown in Table 2.3: cost, resource acquisition, marketing, creativity, problem solving, and system flexibility. Thus, a diverse workforce should be highly valued and managed well for reasons beyond the fact that doing so is socially responsible.[51]

As the workforce becomes increasingly diverse, the companies that value and integrate diverse employees most rapidly and most effectively will reap the greatest benefits. Lower personnel costs and improved quality of employees are two obvious benefits for such companies. In addition, access to diverse perspectives in problem solving, decision making, creativity, and product development and marketing activities is essential to creating a competitive advantage in the increasingly dynamic global marketplace.

TABLE 2.3

Six Ways Managing Diversity Can Create Competitive Advantage

Advantage	Contribution
Cost	Managing diversity well can trim the costs of integrating diverse workers.
Resource Acquisition	Companies that have the best reputation for managing diverse employees will have the best chance of hiring the best available diverse personnel.
Marketing	Increased insight and cultural sensitivity will improve the development and marketing of products and services for diverse segments of the population.
Creativity	Diversity of perspectives will improve levels of creativity throughout the organization.
Problem Solving	Problem solving and decision making will improve through groups with more diverse perspectives.
System Flexibility	Tolerance and valuing of diverse perspectives throughout the organization will make the organization more fluid, more flexible, and more responsive to environmental changes.

Reference: Adapted from Taylor Cox, Jr., and Stacy Blake, "Managing Cultural Diversity: Implications for Organizational Competitiveness," *Academy of Management Executive*, August 1991, pg. 47. Copyright © 1991 by ACADEMY of MANAGE-MENT. Reproduced with permission of ACADEMY of MANAGEMENT via Copyright Clearance Center.

Creating the Multicultural Organization

The **multicultural organization** has six characteristics: pluralism, full structural integration, full integration of informal networks, an absence of prejudice and discrimination, equal identification among employees with organizational goals for majority and minority groups, and low levels of intergroup conflict.

A **pluralistic organization** has diverse membership and takes steps to fully involve all people who differ from the dominant group.

A **multicultural organization** has six characteristics: pluralism, full structural integration, full integration of informal networks, an absence of prejudice and discrimination, equal identification with organizational goals for all groups, and low levels of intergroup conflict.[52] Developing the multicultural organization requires commitment from top management and a clear vision of the benefits of multiculturalism for the future of the organization. To achieve each of these characteristics requires specific activities.

A **pluralistic organization** has mixed membership and takes steps to fully involve all people who differ from the dominant group. Creating pluralism requires training and orientation programs that increase awareness of cultural differences and build skills for working together. Programs that describe how people of different ages and genders differ in some respects but are similar in others can be included in programs for new and existing employees. Language and culture training can help employees in the majority group better understand those from different cultures. Companies such as Motorola and Pace Foods offer language training on company time and at company expense.

Organizations have several ways to ensure that minority groups have input. First, minorities should be included in regular meetings at all levels. For example, *USA Today*'s daily news meetings include members of varied racial, ethnic, educational, and geographical groups.[53] Second, the organization must foster the development of minority advisory groups that meet regularly to discuss organizational issues and encourage top management to consult regularly with those groups. Organizations can also foster pluralism by explicitly stating in their mission statements and strategic policies that it is an integral part of the organization.

When an organization has minority group members serving at all levels, performing all functions, and participating in all work groups, it has achieved full

"As part of our commitment to cultural diversity, we've hired Ledyard, who has 8 earings on various portions of his anatomy..."

Creating the multicultural corporation requires commitment from top management and a clear vision of the benefits of multiculturalism for the future of the organization. Unfortunately, some organizations pretend they are working toward this ideal when in reality they are only engaging in tokenism. The people in this cartoon's company, for instance, are certain to see that the boss is more interested in the appearance rather than the substance of multiculturalism.

structural integration. This requires distributing education specialties and skill differences equally throughout the organization. Therefore, organizations must develop and support educational programs and skill building at all levels. They must also hire and promote minority group members into positions at all levels and jobs that perform all organizational functions.

Performance measurement and reward systems, discussed in Chapter 6, also need to be changed to promote pluralism. Organizations need to determine the extent to which managers incorporate multiculturalism into their work groups and whether they hire and promote with proper sensitivity to multicultural concerns. Desired changes need to be rewarded through formal incentives. Benefit plans and work schedules also need to be altered to accommodate differences in employees' family situations, needs, and values.

Mentoring programs, special social events, and support groups for minorities can foster integration in informal networks. Such incentives would seem to create more differences, but in practice they have the opposite effect: They give minority groups outlets to express their cultural identity and share part of themselves with dominant groups. Dominant-group members can then better understand the cultural heritages and traditions of minority members.

Several means can be used to create a bias-free organization. Equal-opportunity seminars have been used for some time to increase awareness among employees. In addition, organizations can conduct in-house focus groups to examine attitudes and beliefs about cultural differences and organizational practices. They can also sponsor bias reduction training programs, one- or two-day workshops designed to help employees identify and begin to modify negative attitudes toward people who are different. These programs usually include exercises and role-plays that expose stereotypes about minority-group members and help build the skills to eliminate those stereotypes. Another way to move toward a bias-free organization is to create task forces to monitor organizational policies and practices for evidence of inequities. Such task forces should consist of employees from every level and those who perform the full range of organizational functions to ensure that top management is committed. All minorities should be represented to ensure that the full spectrum of views is considered.

Employees develop a sense of identity with the organization's mission, goals, and strategies as a result of utilizing all the tools and techniques discussed. When members of different groups participate fully in determining the organization's direction and how to meet its goals, they better understand the organization and their place within it. Through training programs, mentoring programs, support groups, social events, and bias-free organizational practices, employees who are different from the dominant group can become an integral part of the organization.

Intergroup conflict can be minimized in several ways. As discussed in Chapter 8, some forms of conflict can be healthy if they stimulate creativity in problem solving and decision making. However, conflict based on cultural differences is usually unhealthy and detrimental to the multicultural organization. Survey feedback processes can be used to expose beliefs and attitudes toward others and to measure the success of the multicultural effort. Providing feedback to all relevant groups is important to ensure openness throughout the organization. Special training in conflict resolution has also been shown to help managers learn the skills of mediation and listening that are critical for managing conflict.

An integrated program involving activities such as those described here can help an organization become truly multicultural. The transition is not easy or quick, but once multiculturalism has been achieved, the organization will realize advantages in its efforts to compete successfully.

Synopsis

Workforce diversity is a function of the similarities and differences among employees in such characteristics as age, gender, racial and ethnic heritage, physical or mental ability or disability, and sexual orientation. Managers of diverse work groups need to understand how their members' social conditioning affects their beliefs about work and must have the communication skills to develop confidence and self-esteem in their employees.

Stereotypes can lead to prejudice toward others; prejudice consists of judgments concerning the superiority or inferiority of others and can lead to exaggerating the worth of one group while disparaging the worth of others. Management systems built on stereotypes and prejudices are inappropriate for a diverse workforce.

Employment statistics show that the future workforce will be radically different from the workforce of today. The goal of valuing diversity is to utilize all the differences among workers for the benefit of the workers and the organization.

International business has rapidly become an important part of almost every manager's life and is likely to become even more important in the future. Managers need to recognize that employees from different backgrounds are similar in some respects and different in others.

Diversity can be categorized as having primary and secondary dimensions. The primary dimensions of diversity are those that are either inborn or exert extraordinary influence on early socialization; dimensions of this type are age, race and ethnicity, gender, physical or mental abilities, and sexual orientation. Secondary dimensions of diversity include factors that are important to us as individuals and that to some extent define us to others but are less permanent and can be adapted or changed; such dimensions include educational background, geographical location, income, marital status, military experience, parental status, religious beliefs, and work experience.

A multicultural organization is one in which employees of different backgrounds, experiences, and cultures can contribute and achieve their fullest potential for the benefit of both themselves and the organization. Developing a multicultural organization is a significant step in managing a diverse workforce and may be crucial to sustaining a competitive advantage in the marketplace. A multicultural organization has six characteristics: pluralism, full structural integration, full integration of informal networks, an absence of prejudice and discrimination, equal identification with organizational goals among employees from both majority and minority groups, and low levels of intergroup conflict.

Discussion Questions

1. Why do organizations need to be concerned about managing diversity? Is it a legal or moral obligation, or does it have some other purpose?

2. Summarize in your own words what the statistics tell us about the workforce of the future.

3. What are the two major differences between the primary and secondary dimensions of diversity? Which particular dimension seems to be the most difficult to deal with in organizations?

4. Identify ways in which the internationalization of business affects businesses in your community.

5. All things considered, do you think people from diverse cultures are more alike or more different? Explain your answer.

6. What stereotypes exist about the motivational patterns of workers from other cultures?

7. What is the difference between assimilation of minority groups and valuing diversity in organizations?

8. Why does multiculturalism contribute to competitive advantage for an organization?

9. What are the characteristics of a multicultural organization?

10. Discuss three techniques that can contribute to the development of a multicultural organization.

Organizational Behavior Case for Discussion

UPS Delivers Diversity to a Diverse World

United Parcel Service (UPS) is a highly diverse organization and winner of the 2001 Ron Brown Award for Corporate Citizenship, the only presidential award for corporate leadership. The package delivery firm has appeared on *Fortune*'s "Best Companies for Minorities" list for several years. UPS's awards—slots on numerous "best" lists and dozens of diversity awards—are well deserved. Overall, one-third of UPS employees are ethnic or racial minority members and 20 percent are female. UPS human resources director Terri Champion explains, "We try to have our workforce reflect the community in which we work."

The company's commitment to diversity goes beyond merely hiring minorities and women to promoting these groups into managerial positions. UPS has 49,000 managers in the United States, of whom 25 percent are members of racial minorities and 25 percent are female. "At UPS, it's not where you're from or what you look like; it's how much you care and how good you are at your job," according to Hugo Parades. Parades, a Hispanic American who was originally hired as a package unloader, is now a UPS district manager who oversees 3,800 workers and millions of dollars in sales. The company hires women and minorities into traditionally white, male-dominated fields. Of its 4,000 information technology workers, 1,000 are minorities and 1,100 are women.

UPS also looks beyond the diversity elements of race and gender, hiring people with disabilities, non–English speakers, and senior citizens. Its Welfare to Work programs have moved more than 35,000 former welfare recipients into full-time jobs with benefits. In addition to its focus on workforce diversity, the delivery firm seeks to increase diversity among its suppliers and customers. UPS is partnered with more than 25,000 small minority- and woman-owned businesses in the United States, with a combined contract value of almost $600 million annually.

A true commitment to diversity requires that the firm take action and expend funds to support its values. UPS enrolls its senior managers in a community internship program in which managers spend one month working full time with diverse and disadvantaged populations such as residents of nursing homes, individuals with mental handicaps, and homeless people. These experiences give managers a better appreciation of the needs and talents of often overlooked groups. A program that provides education and internship opportunities for minority youth, developed in partnership with the NAACP, has helped hundreds of disadvantaged young people find jobs at UPS. The company has also given designated purchasing staff in each local office the responsibility to identify and encourage applications from minority-owned suppliers.

Today firms recognize that diversity in the workforce and supplier network is necessary to cope with increasing customer diversity. Virginia Clarke, cohead of the diversity practice at executive search firm Spencer Stuart, says, "There is a strong business case [for diversity] now. If you have any doubts about it, just look at the 2000 census figures. A third of all Americans belong to a minority group . . . [A] diverse workplace isn't a luxury—it's a necessity." UPS also sees its commitment to diversity as helping to attract and retain talented personnel, increase creativity, and give the firm a competitive advantage. On its website, the firm states, "We consider diversity a mindset of inclusiveness, respect and cooperation—a visible core value that helps drive the way we do business with our customers and suppliers—and strengthens our bonds with a multicultural community of friends and neighbors." The largest package delivery business in the world, UPS moves 13.6 million packages daily, with a net worth of 6 percent of the U.S. gross domestic product. Its service requires the efforts of more than 370,000 employees who operate in more than 200 countries around the world. With this level of operational complexity, diversity is a must.

Diversity remains a challenging issue for many firms. Nationwide, the number of minorities in senior positions is higher than ever, but 45 percent of minority executives have been the target of racial slurs or jokes, and this statistic includes only deliberate acts, not unintentional slights. In spite of the diversity programs at UPS, problem areas persist. For example, Bill Lewis, a UPS driver, confronted his boss about years of harassment only to have his boss reply, "I will never apologize to a black boy." Frustrated by senior managers' inaction, Lewis and others have filed class action lawsuits and made complaints to the Equal Employment Opportunity Commission. UPS executives point to the firm's excellent record on diversity while acknowledging that some individuals within the company may be prejudiced and engage in discrimination. Lea Soupata, senior vice president for human resources at UPS, says, "We're going to have [racial discrimination] cases, because . . . we have 300-and-something thousand people. We're not perfect. But to categorize the entire company as racist, . . . it's painful." The challenge for the firm lies in ensuring that its values of inclusion are communicated and implemented throughout the organization.

Case Questions

1. According to the case, which dimensions of diversity are present at UPS?
2. What steps has UPS taken to create a multicultural organization?
3. What actions could UPS take in the future to better manage its diverse workforce?

References: Jennifer Merritt, "Wanted: A Campus That Looks Like America," *BusinessWeek*, March 11, 2002; "The Ron Brown Award for Corporate Leadership," The Conference Board; "Helping People Succeed" and "Supplier Diversity," UPS company website (quotation), www.community.ups.com on February 23, 2002; "UPS Seeks Diverse Pros to Fuel Its Needs," *Diversity/Careers*, August–September 2001, www.Diversitycareers.com on February 23, 2002; Jeremy Kahn, "Best Companies for Minorities: Diversity Trumps the Downturn," *Fortune*, February 17, 2004; Stephanie N. Mehta, "Best Companies for Minorities: What Minority Employees Really Want," *Fortune*, July 10, 2000, www.fortune.com on March 28, 2002; John Koenig, "UPS Trains Its Managers by Putting Them in Shoes of Less Fortunate," *Orlando Sentinel*, July 6, 1998, p. 5.

Experiencing Organizational Behavior

Understanding Your Own Stereotypes and Attitudes Toward Others

Purpose: This exercise will help you better understand your own stereotypes and attitudes toward others.

Format: You will be asked to evaluate a situation and the assumptions you make in doing so. Then you will compare your results with those of the rest of the class.

Procedure

1. Read the following description of the situation to yourself, and decide who it is that is standing at your door and why you believe it to be that person. Make some notes that explain your rationale for eliminating the other possibilities and selecting that person. Then answer the questions that follow.
2. Working in small groups or with the class as a whole, discuss who might be standing at your door and why you believe it to be that person. Using the grid at the end of this exercise, record the responses of class members.

3. In class discussion, reflect on the stereotypes used to reach a decision and consider the following:
   a. How hard was it to let go of your original belief once you formed it?
   b. What implications do first impressions of people have concerning how you treat them, what you expect of them, and your assessment of whether they are likely to go beyond the initial stage?
   c. What are the implications of your responses to these questions concerning how you, as a manager, might treat a new employee? What will the impact be on that employee?
   d. What are the implications of your answers for yourself in terms of job hunting?

Situation: You have just checked into a hospital room for some minor surgery the next day. When you get to your room, you are told the following people will be coming to speak with you within the next several hours:

1. The surgeon who will do the operation
2. A nurse
3. The secretary for the department of surgery
4. A representative of the company that supplies televisions to the hospital rooms
5. A technician who does laboratory tests
6. A hospital business manager
7. The dietitian

You have never met any of these people before and do not know what to expect.

About half an hour after your arrival, a woman who seems to be of Asian ancestry appears at your door dressed in a straight red wool skirt, a pink-and-white-striped blouse with a bow at the neck, and red medium-high-heeled shoes that match the skirt. She is wearing gold earrings, a gold chain necklace, a gold wedding band, and a white hospital laboratory coat. She is carrying a clipboard.

Follow-up Questions

1. Of the seven people listed, who is standing at your door? How did you reach this conclusion?
2. If the woman had not been wearing a white hospital laboratory coat, how might your perceptions of her have differed? Why?
3. If you find out she is the surgeon who will be operating on you in the morning, and you initially thought she was someone else, how confident do you now feel in her ability as a surgeon? Why?

	Reasons	Number Who Made This Selection
Surgeon		
Nurse		
Secretary		
Television Representative		
Laboratory Technician		
Business Manager		
Dietitian		

Reference: Adapted from Janet W. Wohlberg and Scott Weighart, *OB in Action: Cases and Exercises.* Copyright © 1992 by Houghton Mifflin Company. Used by permission.

Self-Assessment Exercise
Cross-Cultural Awareness

The following questions are intended to provide insights into your awareness of other cultures. Indicate the best answers to the questions listed below. There is no passing or failing answer. Use the following scale, recording it in the space before each question.

1 = definitely no   2 = not likely   3 = not sure
4 = likely   5 = definitely yes

_____ 1. I can effectively conduct business in a language other than my native language.

_____ 2. I can read and write a language other than my native language with great ease.

_____ 3. I understand the proper protocol for conducting a business card exchange in at least two countries other than my own.

_____ 4. I understand the role of the *keiretsu* in Japan or the *chaebol* in Korea.

_____ 5. I understand the differences in manager-subordinate relationships in two countries other than my own.

_____ 6. I understand the differences in negotiation styles in at least two countries other than my own.

_____ 7. I understand the proper protocols for gift giving in at least three countries.

_____ 8. I understand how a country's characteristic preference for individualism versus collectivism can influence business practices.

_____ 9. I understand the nature and importance of demographic diversity in at least three countries.

_____ 10. I understand my own country's laws regarding giving gifts or favors while on international assignments.

_____ 11. I understand how cultural factors influence the sales, marketing, and distribution systems of different countries.

_____ 12. I understand how differences in male-female relationships influence business practices in at least three countries.

_____ 13. I have studied and understand the history of a country other than my native country.

_____ 14. I can identify the countries of the European Union without looking them up.

_____ 15. I know which gestures to avoid using overseas because of their obscene meanings.

_____ 16. I understand how the communication style practiced in specific countries can influence business practices.

_____ 17. I know in which countries I can use my first name with recent business acquaintances.

_____ 18. I understand the culture and business trends in major countries in which my organization conducts business.

_____ 19. I regularly receive and review news and information from and about overseas locations.

_____ 20. I have access to and utilize a cultural informant before conducting business at an overseas location.

_____ = Total Score

When you have finished, add up your score and compare it with those of others in your group. Discuss the areas of strengths and weaknesses of the group members. [Note: This brief instrument has not been scientifically validated and is to be used for classroom discussion purposes only.]

Reference: Neal R. Goodman, "Cross-Cultural Training for the Global Executive," in Richard W. Brislin and Tomoko Yoshida (eds.), *Improving Intercultural Interactions*, pp. 35–36, copyright © 1994 by Sage Publications, Inc. Reprinted by permission of Sage Publications, Inc.

OB Online

1. Use the Internet to research Denny's/Advantica to find out what Denny's has done to overcome charges of discrimination.

2. What characteristics of Denny's might have made it easier to change its culture? What characteristics might have made it more difficult?

3. Several Denny's executives have left the company to go to other organizations. Find news stories that describe who has left and determine why executives are leaving.

Building Managerial Skills

Exercise Overview: Conceptual skills involve a manager's ability to think in the abstract, while diagnostic skills focus on responses to situations. These skills must frequently be used together to better understand the behavior of others in an organization, as the following exercise illustrates.

Exercise Background: We often read about creating an organization in which diverse workers are welcomed and included in everyday work activities. However, working with a diverse workforce every day can be more difficult. Consider the following situation.

You are the office manager for a large call center in an urban area. You interview applicants, explain the type of work, and give them a quick, job-oriented test. At the call center, employees sit at a desk in front of a computer screen and answer calls and inquiries about the products of several companies. Employees must answer each call and determine the product; access the appropriate screen containing all the information about the product; and, if possible, complete the sale of the product and hopefully extend the purchase to related products. Employees must be able to use a computer and speak well. One day you interview a potential new employee, Sarah Jane. She completes the simple test that involves sitting at the desk, using the computer, and answering mock calls. Consequently, you hire Sarah Jane, who reports to work the following Monday.

About two weeks after her first day, Sarah Jane shows up with a large seeing-eye dog. Because the call stations are built to fit a normal-size person in a desk chair in front of a computer, there is no room for her dog. Sarah Jane requests a special accommodation for her dog. Other employees are concerned about having a large dog sitting underneath the workstations and complain to you about the situation.

Exercise Task: Using the preceding scenario as background, do the following:

1. You have to decide what to do and must write a report to your boss, as well as to Sarah Jane and the other employees. What do you decide? Do you fire Sarah Jane because she is legally blind? Do you fire Sarah Jane because her dog is bothering other employees just by sleeping underneath the workstations? Do you keep her and find her a separate, larger workstation to accommodate her dog without disturbing other employees?

2. Let's say that you fire her and, two weeks later, you get a call from her attorney, who is threatening to sue you for violation of the Americans with Disabilities Act (ADA). What resources could you contact to help you determine your alternatives? (Many states have offices to assist employers in complying with the ADA.) What are your responsibilities regarding the creation of accommodations for differently abled employees?

TEST PREPPER

ACE self-test

You have read the chapter and studied the key terms, and the exam is any day now. Think you're ready to ace it? Take this sample test to gauge your comprehension of chapter material. You can check your answers at the back of the book. Want more test questions? Visit the student website at http://college.hmco.com/business/students/ (select Griffin/Moorhead, Fundamentals of Organizational Behavior 1e) and take the ACE quizzes for more practice.

1. **T F** Companies on the "100 Best" list of publications such as *Business Ethics* had significantly higher financial performance than did comparable firms not on the list.

2. **T F** A diverse workforce helps companies benefit from the increased buying power of minority markets.

3. **T F** A stereotype is a judgment about others that reinforces beliefs about superiority and inferiority.

4. **T F** White males are projected to increase as a percentage of the total workforce in upcoming years.

5. **T F** Workforce diversity is an issue for companies in the United States, but not for companies in Europe.

6. **T F** The currently recommended approach to diversity in the U.S. workforce is assimilation.

7. **T F** Minority groups typically understand organizational communications better than dominant groups do.

8. **T F** Organizations are moving into the international realm to control costs, especially labor costs.

9. **T F** The behavior within a company is likely to be very consistent, regardless of the number of countries in which the company operates.

10. **T F** As older employees are exiting the workforce earlier, the average age of the workforce is getting younger.

11. **T F** Fortunately, the "glass ceiling" has all but been eliminated in the United States.

12. **T F** Managers should avoid hiring people with any disability because the disability will affect virtually every aspect of their performance.

13. **T F** A company becomes multicultural once it establishes operations in more than one country.

14. **T F** A pluralistic company involves all people who differ from the dominant group.

15. **T F** Allowing minority groups to express their cultural identity can help dominant-group members to better understand them.

16. **T F** Conflict that divides employees along cultural lines can stimulate creativity in problem solving.

17. Procter & Gamble's recent efforts to increase diversity in its workforce have focused on hiring and promoting
    a. women.
    b. minorities.
    c. younger employees.
    d. older employees.
    e. highly educated employees.

18. Which of the following is not a trend that has increased diversity in the workforce?
    a. Evolution of the job market, such as economic downturns
    b. Increased buying power of minorities
    c. Expansion into global markets
    d. Increased legislation mandating diversity
    e. Consolidation of duplicate efforts from operations around the world

19. Why are prejudicial views so counterproductive for managers?
    a. The organization's workforce may become too diverse.
    b. Distinctive individual talents may be overlooked.
    c. Competitors may imitate the company's strengths.
    d. Demand for the company's product or service may outpace supply.
    e. Self-esteem and job satisfaction may be too high.

20. The future workforce is projected to include an increased proportion of all of the following segments except
    a. White males.   d. Blacks.
    b. Hispanics.   e. White females.
    c. Asian women.

21. The employees Joan supervises include members of almost every culture and nationality in Europe. If Joan were to follow the current view of workforce diversity, she would
    a. try to assimilate those who are different into a single organizational culture.
    b. create a "melting pot" atmosphere to blend and eliminate differences.
    c. divide the workforce into smaller groups so people could work with others like themselves.

    d. celebrate the differences and utilize the variety of talents and perspectives.

    e. change hiring and promotion patterns to limit future excessive diversity.

22. Employees outside the dominant group tend to
    a. be relatively nondiverse.
    b. pay less attention to diversity than do employees in the dominant group.
    c. miss out on the informal communication that occurs in organizations.
    d. share the values and beliefs of the dominant group.
    e. generate most of the formal communication in the organization.

23. The most striking trend in international business is
    a. the absence of small companies.
    b. Spanish as the new language of business.
    c. growth.
    d. tax shelters.
    e. the elimination of labor costs.

24. Linda manages sales teams in Asia and the Middle East. Which of the following is most likely the case?
    a. Linda's employees in the two regions are likely to have the same attitudes.
    b. Linda will behave differently based on the cultures of the two regions.
    c. The structures of Linda's teams in the two regions will be very different.
    d. The diversity between the Asian and Middle Eastern teams will reduce the organization's effectiveness.
    e. The cultures of the two regions are irrelevant since both teams belong to the same organization.

25. Given the increasing average age of employees, managers should be prepared for all of the following except
    a. changed benefit packages.
    b. additional and special training.
    c. adjustments in physical facilities.
    d. increased unscheduled days off for primary caregiving.
    e. increased unionization of older employees.

26. What is one solution to the problem of women feeling excluded from informal follow-up discussions after formal meetings?
    a. Hold the discussions over drinks at a bar.
    b. Have the discussions at an exclusive golf club.
    c. Bring refreshments into the meeting rooms after the meeting.

    d. Avoid conversations in rooms with glass ceilings.
    e. Minimize the number of formal meetings.

27. What effect does the Americans with Disabilities Act have on employers?
    a. Employers are prohibited from hiring people with severe disabilities.
    b. Employers must promote people with disabilities at a preset rate.
    c. Physically challenged employees must be paid at a higher rate to compensate for their disability.
    d. Employers must make reasonable accommodations in the workplace to assist people with disabilities.
    e. Employers cannot discriminate against a physically challenged person unless that person is also mentally challenged.

28. All of these are primary dimensions of diversity except
    a. age.
    b. gender.
    c. race.
    d. marital status.
    e. physical disability.

29. How would you know whether your organization has achieved full structural integration?
    a. Your organization hires members of every available ethnic group.
    b. Your organization takes steps to fully involve all people who differ from the dominant group.
    c. Your organization makes reasonable accommodations for people with disabilities.
    d. Your organization has operations in many countries.
    e. Your organization has minority-group members serving at all levels.

30. Carlos is planning a special Hispanic social event for his company, since many employees are from Latin America. What outcome should Carlos expect?
    a. The minority employees will share part of themselves with the dominant group.
    b. The dominant group will understand the minority employees even less than before.
    c. The event will limit the usefulness of mentoring programs.
    d. The event alone will create a multicultural organization.
    e. The minority employees will feel even more removed from the dominant group.

PART ONE   VIDEO CASE

Karen Sand: A Manager in Action

Karen Sand is a manager for Southwest Airlines. Southwest, introduced in Chapter 1, is one of the few profitable airlines, largely as a result of the way its managers treat employees. Sand supervises the customer service representatives at an airport serviced by Southwest Airlines. She doesn't see herself as a supervisor or a boss, however. Instead, she sees herself as the "coach" of a talented group of employees who have an important job to do each day.

Sand's workday starts at 5:00 A.M. She is an "opening supervisor," meaning it is her job to see that everyone is in the right position to start Southwest Airline's day. Her initial tasks include checking sick call, making sure the airline is properly staffed, and ensuring the computers used by ticketing agents are up and running for the day. She knows that she leads by example and that everyone is watching her. Throughout the day, she schedules meetings, talks to customers, supervises the routine activities of the ticket agents, and troubleshoots problems that arise.

The video depicts the hectic nature of Sand's job and at the same time captures the upbeat manner in which she manages her day. Her most important challenge is to help Southwest get its planes off the ground on time. If a plane is late leaving the gate, it affects the timing of the whole system. To meet this challenge, Sand works closely with her ticket agents. She also communicates frequently, via a handheld radio, with baggage handlers, ramp agents, operations managers, and other Southwest employees. While she works hard to get planes off the ground on time, she tries to maintain a positive attitude and allow her employees to have fun. "You must motivate your people to try really hard to jump in there, work the flight, check in the customer, give them absolutely positively outrageous service, but still maintain that time frame," Sand says. "The planes must go on time—but you want [the ticket agents] to have fun while they are doing it." Maintaining a fun and positive atmosphere is the key in Sand's mind: "If your internal customer (which is what Sand calls her employees) is not having a good time, —they're not going to give you 100 percent," she says.

Another important role Sand plays is as an advocate for employees who often find themselves in the line of fire. An airline's front-line employees take a lot of heat from customers frustrated by flight delays and other problems. As a manager, Sand listens to her employee's experiences and provides them with suggestions for handling unhappy customers. She equips her customer service representatives with the authority to resolve problems by empowering them to make decisions, particularly when they have a customer right in front of them. This approach not only helps employees solve immediate problems but signals to them that they are an important link in the chain that makes the company thrive.

The final segment of the video focuses on communication, which Sand describes as a vital link between management and front-line employees. Southwest communicates with its customer service representatives via computer and memos, and through direct interaction between managers and employees. For example, if immediate training is needed, a manager will call employees aside in groups of two or three and train them in new procedures.

The overall mission of Southwest Airlines is to give the highest quality customer service while maintaining an atmosphere that's fun to work in. This objective is met through positive working relationships between managers and front-line employees.

Case Questions

1. List the positive steps Karen Sand takes to motivate and direct her employees. Do you think Sand is a good manager? Why or why not?

2. How does Karen Sand help her employees do their jobs effectively? Does Sand seem to appreciate the importance of the topics covered in Part I of this book? Cite several examples from the case to support your answer.

3. The roles managers perform can be divided into three categories: interpersonal roles, informational roles, and decision-making roles. Provide an example from the case of Karen Sand performing each of these roles. What would happen if Sand did not perform one or more of these roles well?

4. As Sand's workforce and customer base becomes more diverse, what type of training will she need to remain effective as a manager for Southwest Airlines?

References: Southwest Airlines home page, www.southwest.com on June 25, 2004; J. H. Gittell, *The Southwest Airlines Way* (New York: McGraw-Hill, 2003).

PART TWO

Individual Processes in Organizations

CHAPTER 3

Foundations of Individual Behavior

MANAGEMENT PREVIEW

Think about human behavior as a jigsaw puzzle. Puzzles consist of various pieces that fit together in precise ways. And, of course, no two puzzles are exactly alike. They have different numbers of pieces, the pieces are of different sizes and shapes, and the pieces fit together in different ways. The same can be said of human behavior and its determinants. Each of us is a whole picture, like a fully assembled jigsaw puzzle, but the puzzle pieces that define us and the way those pieces fit together are unique. Thus, every person in an organization is fundamentally different from everyone else. To be successful, managers must recognize that these differences exist and attempt to understand how they affect behavior. In this chapter, we explore some of the key characteristics that differentiate people from one another in organizations. First, we investigate the psychological nature of individuals in organizations. We then look at elements of people's personalities that can influence behavior and consider individual attitudes and their role in organizations. In subsequent sections we examine perception, stress, and creativity. Finally, we examine various kinds of workplace behaviors that affect organizational performance.

After you have studied this chapter, you should be able to:

- ☐ *Explain the nature of the individual-organization relationship.*
- ☐ *Define personality and describe personality attributes that affect behavior in organizations.*
- ☐ *Discuss individual attitudes in organizations and how they affect behavior.*
- ☐ *Describe basic perceptual processes and the role of attributions in organizations.*
- ☐ *Discuss the causes and consequences of stress and describe how stress can be managed.*
- ☐ *Describe creativity and its role in organizations.*
- ☐ *Explain how workplace behaviors can directly or indirectly influence organizational effectiveness.*

We begin by looking at healthy and unhealthy connections that people may develop within their workplace.

Y ou can love your job, but will it love you back? Psychologists and other experts who study job-related mental health report a disturbing trend: More and more workers say they prefer long hours. Many employees routinely put in 12-hour days or work from home every week-end. It's an ironic twist in a society where "formerly, personal success was evinced by the ability to not work, to be a part of a leisure class, to be idle," says psychotherapist and author Ilene Philipson. "Today, we measure our success by how *much* we work," she adds.

Philipson's book *Married to the Job: Why We Live to Work and What We Can Do About It* contains numerous examples. One high-performing manager fell out of favor after asking for a raise. The lack of subsequent praise caused deep depression and anxiety attacks. Philipson says this client is typical of the career-obsessed worker: "What [these workers] have done is to transfer all of their unmet emotional needs to the workplace." Many of these employees believe work is the most important thing in their life, to which Philipson responds, "Your boss is not your friend. Your colleagues are not your family. Workplaces are intensely political environments. If you bring your heart and soul there, you're likely setting yourself up for feeling betrayed."

Professor Benjamin Hunnicutt, an expert on work, claims, "Work has become how we define ourselves. It is now answering the traditional religious questions: Who am I? How do I find meaning and purpose? Work is no longer just about economics; it's about identity." Most of Philipson's patients have few social relationships outside of work. Many use work to help them through tough times. Yet the praise they receive at work is powerfully addictive, and that can also be dangerous. Yolanda Perry-Pastor, a patient of Philipson's, kept assuming more job duties until she suffered a nervous breakdown. She says, "I've been though a lot in my life," referring to domestic abuse and single parenthood, "but that was nothing compared with this."

Another contributing factor is companies that "ensnare" workers by offering a homelike environment, personal services, or just encouraging workers to consider their coworkers as family. For example, Houston-based BMC Software offers hammocks, a gym, sports leagues, a movie theater, live piano music, free gourmet meals, massages, banking, hairstyling services, oil changes and car washes, child care, elder care, pet care, medical exams, and even bedrooms for those who can't make it home. BMC's chief of human resources claims, "I know this is hard to believe, but . . . [i]t gives you a balanced life without having to leave." Psychologist Maynard Brusman disagrees: "The workplace has become [a workers'] community. They come to me anxious, and they don't know why. They've become caught up in the culture. The question is, 'Is that healthy?' From what I've seen, it isn't."

Workers who are obsessed with their careers find that work consumes all their passion and time, leaving nothing for other relationships. Perry-Pastor says of her two children during the time she was overworking, "They were never allowed to be sick. . . I would pay for baby-sitters, lessons, tutors, whatever they needed. I thought they were taken care of." Work relationships become more rewarding than relationships at home. Sociologist Arlie Hochschild theorizes that dual-income couples work long hours to escape their hectic home lives. "At home, you don't always get a pat on the back," says Karin Hanson, formerly of Microsoft. "In your office, you can hear, 'Hey, good work.'" Some managers may believe that an all-consuming interest in work is acceptable and even desirable, but the quality and quantity of work drop and incidences of absence, turnover, accidents, and workplace violence all increase with stress. Many workers drop out of the workforce entirely—a loss for families and for society.

Philipson claims that career-obsessed individuals are not weak or insecure. "These people are in the same boat with all of the rest of us who work longer hours, take fewer vacations, and wake up and go to sleep thinking about work," she asserts. So how can one avoid becoming over-involved in work? The psychotherapists recommend that you start by defining yourself and your worth in nonwork terms. Look to religion, family, or community for praise and comfort. Develop compelling interests and strong friendships outside of work. Take "real" nights, weekends, vacations—no work allowed. Focus less on praise, which can put you under someone else's control, and more on developing your own sense of self-worth. And, yes, miss work every now and then. Play hooky. Take an occasional day off and just relax.

"[F]ormerly, personal success was evinced by the ability to not work....Today, we measure our success by how much we work."—Psychotherapist and author Ilene Philipson

References: Andrea Sachs, "Wedded to Work," *Time*, September 2002, p. A21; Ilene Philipson,"Work Is Life," PsychotherapistResources.com website, April 22, 2004; Jerry Useem, "Welcome to the New Company Town," *Fortune*, February 13, 2004, pp. 76–84; Pamela Kruger, "Betrayed by Work," *Fast Company*, February 1, 2003.

People and the organizations where they work are continually defining and redefining their relationships. In much the same way, relationships between people evolve and change over time. To do so, they must assess how well their respective needs and capabilities match each other. As the opening vignette indicates, some people risk developing a dependence on their work. Others develop and maintain a healthy and productive relationship with their employer. A variety of unique characteristics possessed by each and every employee affects how these individuals feel about the organization, how they will alter their future attitudes about the firm, and how they perform their jobs. These characteristics reflect the basic elements of individual behavior in organizations.

Understanding Individuals in Organizations

LEARNING OBJECTIVE

Explain the nature of the individual-organization relationship.

As a starting point in understanding human behavior in the workplace, we consider the basic nature of the relationship between individuals and organizations. We also explore the nature of individual differences.

The Psychological Contract

Most people have a basic understanding of a contract. Whenever we buy a car or sell a house, for example, both buyer and seller sign a contract that specifies the terms of the agreement. A psychological contract is similar in some ways to a standard legal contract, but is less formal and clearly defined. In particular, a **psychological contract** is the overall set of expectations an individual holds with respect to what he or she will contribute to the organization and what the organization will provide in return.[1] Thus, a psychological contract is not written on paper, nor are all of its terms explicitly negotiated.

A **psychological contract** is a person's set of expectations regarding what he or she will contribute to the organization and what the organization will provide in return.

Figure 3.1 illustrates the essential nature of a psychological contract. The individual makes a variety of **contributions** to the organization: effort, skills, ability, time, loyalty, and so forth. These contributions presumably satisfy various needs and requirements of the organization. That is, since the organization may have hired the person because of her skills, it is reasonable for the organization to expect the employee to subsequently display those skills in performing her job.

An individual's **contributions** to an organization include such things as effort, skills, ability, time, and loyalty.

In return for these contributions, the organization provides **inducements** to the individual. Some inducements, such as pay and career opportunities, are tangible rewards. Others, such as job security and status, are more intangible. Just as the contributions the individual makes must satisfy the organization's needs, the inducements the organization offers must serve the individual's needs. That is, if a person accepts employment with an organization because he thinks he will earn an attractive salary and have an opportunity to advance, he will subsequently expect those rewards will actually be forthcoming.

Organizations provide **inducements** to individuals in the form of tangible and intangible rewards.

If both the individual and the organization perceive that the psychological contract is fair and equitable, they will be satisfied with the relationship and will likely continue it. On the other hand, if either party sees an imbalance or inequity

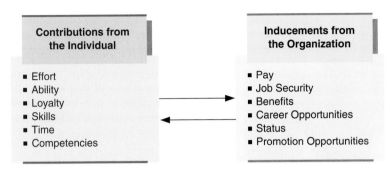

Contributions from the Individual	Inducements from the Organization
■ Effort ■ Ability ■ Loyalty ■ Skills ■ Time ■ Competencies	■ Pay ■ Job Security ■ Benefits ■ Career Opportunities ■ Status ■ Promotion Opportunities

FIGURE 3.1

The Psychological Contract

Psychological contracts govern the basic relationship between people and organizations. Individuals contribute such things as effort and loyalty. Organizations, in turn, offer such inducements as pay and job security.

in the contract, it may initiate a change. For example, the individual may request a pay raise or promotion, decrease her contributed effort, or look for a better job elsewhere. The organization can also initiate change by requesting that the individual improve his skills through training, transfer him to another job, or terminate his employment altogether.

A basic challenge the organization faces, then, is to manage psychological contracts. The organization must ensure that it is getting value from its employees. At the same time, it must ensure that it is providing employees with appropriate inducements. If the organization is underpaying its employees for their contributions, for example, they may perform poorly or leave for better jobs elsewhere. On the other hand, if they are being overpaid relative to their contributions, the organization is incurring unnecessary costs.[2]

The Person-Job Fit

Person-job fit is the extent to which the contributions the individual makes match the inducements the organization offers.

One specific aspect of managing psychological contracts is managing the person-job fit. **Person-job fit** is the extent to which the contributions the individual makes match the inducements the organization offers. In theory, each employee has a specific set of needs that he or she wants fulfilled and a set of job-related behaviors and abilities to contribute. Thus, if the organization can take perfect advantage of those behaviors and abilities and exactly fulfill the employee's needs, it will have achieved a perfect person-job fit.

Psychological contracts play an important role in the relationship between an organization and its employees. As long as both parties agree that the contributions an employee makes and the inducements the organization provides are balanced, both parties are satisfied and will likely maintain their relationship. But if a serious imbalance occurs, one or both parties may attempt to change the relationship. As illustrated here, an employee who is sufficiently dissatisfied may even resort to using company assets for his or her personal gain.

DILBERT reprinted by permission of United Feature Syndicate, Inc.

Understanding and managing person-job fit is an important element in effective psychological contracts. For example, consider the crew members for the *Atlantis* space shuttle. Each had demonstrated both the technical skills to perform in space and the emotional strength to withstand the rigors of space travel. Further, they have also demonstrated the ability to work together as a team both in training and in actual space missions. Clearly, then, each crew member has an advanced level of person-job fit.

Of course, such a precise level of person-job fit is seldom achieved. For one thing, organizational selection procedures are imperfect. Organizations can make approximations of employee skill levels when making hiring decisions and can improve them through training. But even simple performance dimensions are hard to measure objectively and validly. Second, as discussed in the Mastering Change box, both people and organizations change. An individual who finds a new job stimulating and exciting may find the same job boring and monotonous after a few years of performing it. Similarly, when the organization adopts new technology, it has changed the skills it needs from its employees. Third, each individual is unique. Measuring skills and performance is difficult enough; assessing needs, attitudes, and personality is far more complex. Therefore, each of these individual differences makes matching individuals with jobs a challenge.

The Nature of Individual Differences

Individual differences are personal attributes that vary from one person to another.

Individual differences are personal attributes that vary from one person to another. Individual differences may be physical, psychological, and emotional. Taken together, all of the individual differences that characterize any specific person serve to make that individual unique from everyone else. We devote much of the remainder of this chapter to individual differences. Before proceeding, however, we must note the importance of the situation in assessing the behavior of individuals.

Are specific differences that characterize a given individual good or bad? Do they contribute to or detract from performance? The answer, of course, is that it depends on the circumstances. One person may be very dissatisfied, withdrawn, and negative in one job setting but very satisfied, outgoing, and positive in another. Working conditions, coworkers, and leadership are all important ingredients.

Thus, whenever an organization attempts to assess or account for individual differences among its employees, it must also be sure to consider the situation in which behavior occurs. Individuals who are satisfied, productive workers in one context may prove to be dissatisfied, unproductive workers in another. Attempting to consider both individual differences and contributions in relation to inducements and contexts, then, is a major challenge for organizations as they attempt to establish effective psychological contracts with their employees and achieve optimal fits between people and jobs.

LEARNING OBJECTIVE

Define personality *and describe personality attributes that affect behavior in organizations.*

Personality and Individual Behavior

Personality traits represent some of the most fundamental sets of individual differences in organizations. **Personality** is the relatively stable set of psychological

MASTERING CHANGE

Changing the Way Companies Change

After many years of improving organizational technology and work processes, some managers are now concentrating on changing the way people think. For instance, many corporate leaders are coming to realize that internal mental processes such as attitudes, perception, and creativity are the fundamental sources of individual behavior. And the most thoughtful plans, the most remarkable innovations, and the most appealing products are worth very little without the support that comes from the sum of thousands of individual actions. "[W]hat I [previously] failed to recognize was that the way people think is far more important than the tools they use," says Dennis Pawley, a former Chrysler executive, now head of Lean Learning, a change consulting firm.

"Learning" has become the new corporate rallying cry. Corporations and consulting firms are developing training programs to teach workers how to learn. But many are finding that teaching people how to learn is much harder than teaching them specific skills. Peter Senge, a noted management expert, claims that organizations need to develop an increased sensitivity to human relationships at work. He explains, "[To change companies], we keep bringing in mechanics—when what we need are gardeners. We keep trying to drive change— when what we need to do is cultivate change." Senge agrees with a concept also articulated by Pawley: "The people who do the work should be the ones to improve the work." Senge asserts that in his extensive experience

as a management consultant, he has "never seen a successful organizational-learning program rolled out from the top [of the organization]. Not a single one."

So if change requires learning, and learning requires that organizations become more humane and experimen-

> *"We keep trying to drive change—when what we need to do is cultivate change."—Peter Senge, management expert*

tal, how exactly can training programs get workers to learn better? Most effective programs begin by selecting a motivated team, usually at the middle-management level. Then students receive training through a variety of media, including case studies, role playing, teaching, reading, and lectures. Next, students are asked to take their "book knowledge" and apply it in simulated environments. Lean Learning, for example, assigns students the task of reworking a toy-airplane assembly line to make it more efficient. To reinforce the lessons learned mentally and physically, students are asked to use journals and dialogues to express their feelings and reflections. Finally, students who have been transformed are themselves now ready to transform by spreading their learning throughout their organizations.

References: Lean Learning Center website, "How You Will Learn," www.leanlearningcenter.com on April 11, 2004; Fara Warner, "Think Lean," *Fast Company*, February 2003, pp. 40–42; Alan M. Webber, "Will Companies Ever Learn?," *Fast Company*, October 2002; Alan M. Webber, "Learning for a Change," *Fast Company*, May 1999 (quotation), www.fastcompany.com on April 11, 2002.

Personality is the relatively stable set of psychological attributes that distinguish one person from another.

attributes that distinguish one person from another.[3] Managers should strive to understand basic personality attributes and the ways they can affect people's behavior in organizational situations, as well as their perceptions of and attitudes toward the organization.

The "Big Five" Personality Traits

The **"big five" personality traits** are a set of fundamental traits that are especially relevant to organizations.

Psychologists have identified literally thousands of personality traits and dimensions that differentiate one person from another. But in recent years, researchers have identified five fundamental personality traits that are especially relevant to organizations. Because these five traits are so important and currently receive much attention, they are commonly referred to today as the **"big five" personality traits**.[4] Figure 3.2 illustrates these traits.

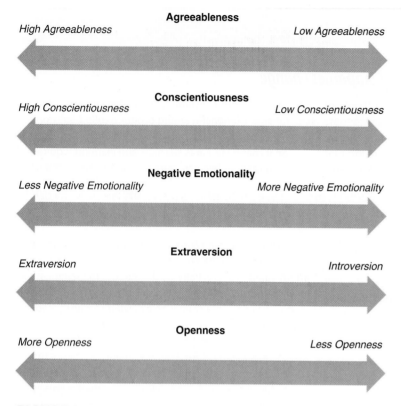

FIGURE 3.2

The "Big Five" Personality Framework

The "big five" personality framework is currently very popular among researchers and managers. These five dimensions represent fundamental personality traits presumed to be important in determining the behaviors of individuals in organizations. In general, experts agree that personality traits closer to the left end of each dimension are more positive in organizational settings, whereas traits closer to the right are less positive.

Agreeableness is the ability to get along with others.

Conscientiousness refers to the number of goals on which a person focuses.

Negative emotionality is characterized by moodiness and insecurity.

Extraversion is the quality of being comfortable with relationships; the opposite extreme, introversion, is characterized by more social discomfort.

Agreeableness is a person's ability to get along with others. Highly agreeable people tend to be gentle, cooperative, forgiving, understanding, and good-natured in their dealings with others. Disagreeable people are usually irritable, short-tempered, uncooperative, and generally antagonistic toward others. While research has not yet fully investigated the effects of agreeableness, it is likely that highly agreeable people are better able to develop good working relationships with coworkers, subordinates, and managers, whereas less agreeable people have less positive working relationships. The same pattern may extend to relationships with customers, suppliers, and other key organizational constituents.

Conscientiousness refers to the number of goals on which a person focuses. People who focus on relatively few goals at one time are likely to be organized, systematic, careful, thorough, responsible, and self-disciplined as they work to pursue those goals. Others tend to take on a wider array of goals and, as a result, to be more disorganized, careless, and irresponsible, as well as less thorough and self-disciplined. Research has found that more conscientious people tend to be higher performers than less conscientious people across a variety of jobs. This pattern seems logical, of course, since more conscientious people will take their jobs seriously and perform them in a responsible fashion.

Negative emotionality is characterized by moodiness and insecurity. People with less negative emotionality tend to be relatively poised, calm, resilient, and secure, whereas people with more negative emotionality are usually more excitable, insecure, reactive, and subject to extreme mood swings. People with less negative emotionality are better able to handle job stress, pressure, and tension. Their stability may also lead them to be seen as more reliable than their less stable counterparts.

Extraversion refers to a person's comfort level with relationships. People considered to be extraverts are sociable, talkative, assertive, and open to new relationships. In contrast, introverts are uncomfortable in social situations and less open to new relationships. Research suggests that extraverts tend to be higher overall job performers than introverts and are also more likely to be attracted to jobs based on personal relationships, such as sales and marketing positions.

Openness is the capacity to entertain new ideas and to change as a result of learning new information.

Finally, **openness** refers to a person's rigidity of beliefs and range of interests. People with high levels of openness are willing to listen to new ideas and change their own ideas, beliefs, and attitudes as a result of new information. They also tend to have broad interests and to be curious, imaginative, and creative. People with low levels of openness tend to be less receptive to new ideas and less willing to change their views, to have fewer and narrower interests, and to be less curious and creative. People with more openness are likely to be better performers, owing to their flexibility and their tendency to be better accepted by others in the organization. Openness may also encompass an individual's willingness to accept change. For example, people with high levels of openness are generally more receptive to change, whereas people with low levels of openness are more likely to resist change.

The "big five" framework continues to appeal to both researchers and managers. The potential value of this framework is that it encompasses an integrated set of traits that appear to be valid predictors of certain behaviors in particular situations. Thus, managers who can develop both an understanding of the framework and the ability to assess these traits in their employees will be in a good position to understand how and why employees behave as they do.[5] On the other hand, managers must also be careful not to overestimate their ability to assess the "big five" traits in others. Even assessment using the most rigorous and valid measures is likely to be somewhat imprecise. Another limitation of the "big five" framework is that it is based primarily on research conducted in the United States. Thus, questions about its generalizability to other cultures remain unanswered. Even within the United States, a variety of other factors and traits are also likely to affect behavior in organizations.

The Myers-Briggs Framework

Another interesting approach to understanding personalities in organizations is the Myers-Briggs framework. This framework, based on the classical work of Carl Jung, differentiates people in terms of four general dimensions, defined as follows:

- *Extroversion (E) Versus Introversion (I).* Extroverts get their energy from being around other people; Introverts feel worn out by others and need solitude to recharge their energy.
- *Sensing (S) Versus Intuition (N).* Sensing individuals prefer concrete ideas; Intuitives prefer abstract concepts.
- *Thinking (T) Versus Feeling (F).* Thinking individuals base their decisions more on logic and reason; Feeling individuals base their decisions more on feelings and emotions.
- *Judging (J) Versus Perceiving (P).* People who are the Judging type enjoy completion or being finished with tasks or activities; Perceiving individuals enjoy the process and open-ended situations.

To use this framework, the organization has people complete a questionnaire designed to measure their personalities on each dimension. Higher or lower scores on each dimension are used to classify people into one of sixteen different personality categories.

The Myers-Briggs Type Indicator (MBTI) is one popular questionnaire some organizations use to assess personality types. Indeed, it is among the most popular selection instruments used today, with as many as 2 million people participating each year. Research suggests that the MBTI is a useful method for determining communication styles and interaction preferences. In terms of personality attributes, however, questions exist about both the validity and the stability of the MBTI.

Other Personality Traits at Work

Besides the personality dimensions used in the "big five" and Myers-Briggs frameworks, several other personality traits influence behavior in organizations. Among the most important are locus of control, self-efficacy, authoritarianism, Machiavellianism, self-esteem, and risk propensity.

Locus of control is the extent to which people believe their behavior has a real effect on what happens to them.[6] Some people, for example, believe that if they work hard, they will succeed. They also may believe that people who fail do so because they lack ability or motivation. People who believe individuals are in control of their lives are said to have an *internal locus of control*. Other people think fate, chance, luck, or others' behavior determines what happens to them. For example, an employee who fails to get a promotion may attribute that failure to a politically motivated boss or just bad luck rather than to her or his own lack of skills or poor performance record. People who think forces beyond their control dictate what happens to them are said to have an *external locus of control*.

Self-efficacy is a related but subtly different personality characteristic. Self-efficacy is a person's beliefs about his or her capabilities to perform a task.[7] People with high self-efficacy believe they can perform well on a specific task, whereas people with low self-efficacy tend to doubt their ability to perform a particular task. While self-assessments of ability contribute to self-efficacy, so does the individual's personality. Some people simply have more self-confidence than others. As a result of their belief in their ability to perform a task effectively, they are more self-assured and better able to focus their attention on performance.

Another important personality characteristic is **authoritarianism,** the extent to which an individual believes power and status differences are appropriate within hierarchical social systems such as organizations.[8] A person who is highly authoritarian may accept directives or orders from someone with more authority purely because the other person is "the boss." On the other hand, while a person who is not highly authoritarian may still carry out appropriate and reasonable directives from the boss, she or he is also more likely to question things, express disagreement with the boss, and even refuse to carry out orders believed to be objectionable. A highly authoritarian manager may be autocratic and demanding, and highly authoritarian subordinates will be more likely to accept this behavior from their leader. On the other hand, a less authoritarian manager may allow subordinates a bigger role in making decisions, and less authoritarian subordinates will respond positively to this behavior.

Machiavellianism is another important personality trait, named after Niccolo Machiavelli, a sixteenth-century author. In his book *The Prince*, Machiavelli explained how the nobility could more easily gain and use power. Machiavellianism is now used to describe behavior directed at gaining power and controlling the behavior of others. Research suggests that Machiavellianism is a personality trait that varies from person to person. More Machiavellian individuals tend to be rational and nonemotional, may be willing to lie to attain personal goals, put little weight on loyalty and friendship, and enjoy manipulating others' behavior. Less Machiavellian individuals are more emotional, less willing to lie to succeed, value loyalty and friendship highly, and get little personal pleasure from manipulating others. By all accounts, Dennis Kozlowski, the indicted former CEO of Tyco International, had a high degree of Machiavellianism. He apparently came to believe his position of power in the company gave him the right to do just about anything he wanted with company resources.[9]

Locus of control is the extent to which people believe their circumstances are a function of either their own actions or external factors beyond their control.

Self-efficacy is a person's beliefs about his or her capabilities to perform a task.

Authoritarianism is the belief that power and status differences are appropriate within hierarchical social systems such as organizations.

People who possess the personality trait of **Machiavellianism** behave to gain power and control the behavior of others.

Self-esteem is the extent to which a person believes he or she is a worthwhile and deserving individual.

Self-esteem is the extent to which a person believes she or he is a worthwhile and deserving individual.[10] A person with high self-esteem is more likely to seek higher-status jobs, be more confident in his ability to achieve higher levels of performance, and derive greater intrinsic satisfaction from his accomplishments. A person with less self-esteem may be more content to remain in a lower-level job, be less confident of her abilities, and focus more on extrinsic rewards. Among the major personality dimensions, self-esteem has been the most widely studied in other countries. While more research is clearly needed, the published evidence suggests that self-esteem as a personality trait indeed exists in a variety of countries and that its role in organizations is reasonably important across different cultures.[11]

A person's **risk propensity** is the degree to which she or he is willing to take chances and make risky decisions.

Emotional intelligence (EQ) is the extent to which people are self-aware, can manage their emotions, can motivate themselves, express empathy for others, and possess social skills.

Risk propensity is the degree to which an individual is willing to take chances and make risky decisions. A manager with a high risk propensity, for example, might be expected to experiment with new ideas and gamble on new products. She may also lead the organization in new and different directions. This manager may also be a catalyst for innovation. On the other hand, the same individual could also jeopardize the continued well-being of the organization if her risky decisions prove to be bad ones. A manager with low risk propensity may lead to a stagnant and overly conservative organization. On the other hand, he may help the organization successfully weather turbulent times by maintaining stability and calm. Thus, the potential consequences of risk propensity to an organization depend heavily on that organization's environment.

Risk propensity is the degree to which a person is willing to take chances and make risky decisions. Top managers at Lockheed Martin demonstrated strong risk propensity in their quest to earn a $200 billion contract to build the Joint Strike Fighter shown here. No less than three times did they essentially risk the company's future to help it remain the leader in the bidding. Had they ultimately failed, Lockheed Martin would have suffered the consequences for years.

Emotional Intelligence

The concept of emotional intelligence has been identified in recent years and provides some interesting insights into personality. **Emotional intelligence, or EQ,** refers to the extent to which people are self-aware, can manage their emotions, can motivate themselves, express empathy for others, and possess social skills.[12] These various dimensions can be described as follows:

Self-awareness. This is the basis for the other components. It refers to one's capacity for being aware of how one is feeling. In general, greater self-awareness allows people to more effectively guide their own lives and behaviors.

Managing emotions. This refers to one's capacity to balance anxiety, fear, and anger so they do not overly interfere with getting things accomplished.

Motivating oneself. This dimension refers to the ability to remain optimistic and continue striving in the face of setbacks, barriers, and failure.

Empathy. Empathy is a person's ability to understand how others are feeling even without being explicitly told.

Social skill. This refers to a person's ability to get along with others and to establish positive relationships.

Preliminary research suggests that people with high EQs may perform better than others, especially in jobs that require a high degree of interpersonal interaction and involve influencing or directing the work of others. Moreover, EQ appears to be an attribute that isn't biologically based and therefore can be developed.[13]

Attitudes and Individual Behavior

┌─ *LEARNING OBJECTIVE* ─┐

Discuss individual attitudes in organizations and how they affect behavior.

Attitudes are a person's complexes of beliefs and feelings about specific ideas, situations, or other people.

Another important element of individual behavior in organizations is attitudes. **Attitudes** are complexes of beliefs and feelings that people have about specific ideas, situations, or other people. Attitudes are important because they are the mechanism through which most people express their feelings. An employee's statement that he feels underpaid by the organization reflects his feelings about his pay. Similarly, when a manager says she likes the new advertising campaign, she is expressing her feelings about the organization's marketing efforts.

Attitudes have three components. The *affective component* reflects feelings and emotions an individual has toward a situation. The *cognitive component* derives from knowledge an individual has about a situation. Note that cognition is subject to individual perceptions (discussed more fully later). Thus, one person may "know" that a certain political candidate is better than another, while someone else may "know" just the opposite. Finally, the *intentional component* of an attitude reflects how an individual expects to behave toward or in the situation.

To illustrate these three components, consider a manager who places an order for some supplies for his organization from a new office supply firm. Suppose many of the items he orders are out of stock, others are overpriced, and still others arrive damaged. When he calls someone at the supply firm for assistance, he is treated rudely and gets disconnected before his claim is resolved. When asked how he feels about the new office supply firm, he might respond, "I don't like that company [affective component]. They are the worst office supply firm I've ever used [cognitive component]. I'll never do business with them again [intentional component]."

Cognitive dissonance is the anxiety a person experiences when she or he simultaneously possesses two sets of knowledge or perceptions that are contradictory or incongruent.

People try to maintain consistency among the three components of their attitudes as well as among all their attitudes. However, circumstances sometimes arise that lead to conflicts. The conflict individuals experience among their own attitudes is called **cognitive dissonance**.[14] For example, an individual who has vowed never to work for a big, impersonal corporation intends instead to open her own business and be her own boss. Unfortunately, a series of financial setbacks leaves her with no choice but to give up her ambition and take a job with a large company. Thus, cognitive dissonance occurs: The affective and cognitive components of the individual's attitude conflict with her intended behavior. To reduce cognitive dissonance, which is usually an uncomfortable experience for most people, the individual might tell herself the situation is only temporary and she can go back out on her own in the near future. Or she might revise her cognitions and decide that working for a large company is more pleasant than she had expected.

Work-Related Attitudes

People in organizations form attitudes about many different things. For example, employees are likely to have attitudes about their salary, promotion possibilities, their boss, employee benefits, the food in the company cafeteria, and the color of the company softball team uniforms. Of course, some of these attitudes are more important than others. Especially important attitudes are job satisfaction or dissatisfaction and organizational commitment.[15]

Job satisfaction or **dissatisfaction** is the extent to which a person is gratified or fulfilled by his or her work.

Job Satisfaction or Dissatisfaction   **Job satisfaction** or **dissatisfaction** reflects the extent to which an individual is gratified by or fulfilled in his or her work. Extensive research conducted on job satisfaction indicates that personal factors such as an individual's needs and aspirations determine this attitude, along with group and organizational factors such as relationships with coworkers and supervisors, working conditions, work policies, and compensation.[16]

A satisfied employee also tends to be absent less often, to make positive contributions, and to stay with the organization.[17] In contrast, a dissatisfied employee may be absent more often, experience stress that disrupts coworkers, and be continually looking for another job. Contrary to what many managers believe, however, high levels of job satisfaction do not necessarily lead to higher levels of performance. One survey also indicates that contrary to popular opinion, Japanese workers are less satisfied with their jobs than their counterparts in the United States.[18]

Organizational commitment is a person's identification with and attachment to the organization.

Organizational Commitment   **Organizational commitment** reflects an individual's identification with and attachment to the organization itself. A person with a high level of commitment is likely to see herself as a true member of the organization (for example, referring to the organization in personal terms such as "we make high-quality products"), overlook minor sources of dissatisfaction with the organization, and see herself remaining a member of the organization. In contrast, a person with less organizational commitment is more likely to see himself as an outsider (for example, referring to the organization in less personal terms such as "they don't pay their employees very well"), express more dissatisfaction about work conditions, and see himself as a long-term member of the organization. Employees who feel committed to an organization have highly reliable habits, plan a long tenure with the organization, and muster more effort in performance. If managers treat employees fairly and provide reasonable rewards and job security, those employees will more likely be satisfied and committed. Allowing employees to have a say in how things are done can also promote positive attitudes.

Affect and Mood in Organizations

Researchers have recently started to focus renewed interest on the affective component of attitudes. Recall from our preceding discussion that the affective component of an attitude reflects our feelings and emotions. While managers once believed emotion and feelings vary among people from day to day, research now suggests that while some short-term fluctuation indeed occurs, there are also underlying stable predispositions toward fairly constant and predictable moods and emotional states.[19]

People who possess **positive affectivity** are upbeat and optimistic, have an overall sense of well-being, and see things in a positive light.

Some people, for example, tend to have a higher degree of **positive affectivity.** This means they are relatively upbeat and optimistic, have an overall sense of well-being, and usually see things in a positive light. Thus, they always seem to be in a good mood. Individuals with more **negative affectivity,** in contrast are generally downbeat and pessimistic, usually see things in a negative way, and seem to be in a bad mood most of the time.

People characterized by **negative affectivity** are generally downbeat and pessimistic, see things in a negative light, and seem to be perpetually in a bad mood.

Of course, as noted earlier, short-term variations can exist among even the most extreme types. People with a lot of positive affectivity, for example, may still be in a sour mood if they have just received some bad news—being passed over for a promotion, getting extremely negative performance feedback, or being laid off or fired, for instance. Similarly, those with negative affectivity may still be in a good mood—at least for a short time—if they have just been promoted, received very positive performance feedback, or had other good things befall them. After the initial impact of these events wears off, however, those with positive affectivity will generally return to their normal positive mood, and those with negative affectivity will gravitate back to their normal bad mood.

Perception and Individual Behavior

As noted earlier, an important element of an attitude is the individual's perception of the object about which the attitude is formed. Since perception plays a role in a variety of other workplace behaviors, managers need to have a general understanding of basic perceptual processes.[20] **Perception** is the set of processes by which an individual becomes aware of and interprets information about the environment. As Figure 3.3 shows, basic perceptual processes that are particularly relevant to organizations are selective perception and stereotyping.

Selective perception is the process of screening out information that we are uncomfortable with or that contradicts our beliefs. For example, suppose a manager is exceptionally fond of a particular worker, has a very positive attitude about the worker, and thinks he is a top performer. One day the manager notices the worker seems to be goofing off. Selective perception may cause the manager to quickly forget what he observed. Similarly, suppose a manager has formed a very negative image of a particular worker. She thinks this worker is a poor performer and never does a good job. When she happens to observe an example of high performance from the worker, she may not remember it for very long. In one sense, selective perception is beneficial because it allows us to disregard minor bits of information. Of course, this holds true only if our basic perception is accurate. If selective perception causes us to ignore important information, however, it can become quite detrimental.

Perception is the set of processes by which an individual becomes aware of and interprets information about the environment.

Selective perception is the process of screening out information that we are uncomfortable with or that contradicts our beliefs.

Stereotyping is the process of categorizing or labeling people on the basis of a single attribute.

Stereotyping is the process of categorizing or labeling people on the basis of a single attribute. Common attributes about which people often form stereotypes are race and gender. Of course, stereotypes along these lines are inaccurate and can be harmful. Suppose a manager forms the stereotype that women can perform only certain tasks and that men are best suited for other tasks. To the extent that this stereotyping affects the manager's hiring practices, the manager is (1) costing the organization valuable talent for both sets of jobs, (2) violating federal law, and (3) behaving unethically. On the other hand, certain forms of stereotyping can be useful and efficient. Suppose a manager believes that communication skills are important for a particular job and that speech communication majors tend to have exceptionally good communication skills. As a result, whenever he interviews candidates for jobs, he pays especially close attention to speech communication majors. To the extent that communication skills truly predict job performance and that majoring in speech communication does indeed provide those skills, this form of stereotyping can be beneficial.

FIGURE 3.3

Basic Perceptual Processes

Perception determines how we can become aware of information from our environment and how we interpret it. Selective perception and stereotyping are particularly important perceptual processes affecting behavior in organizations.

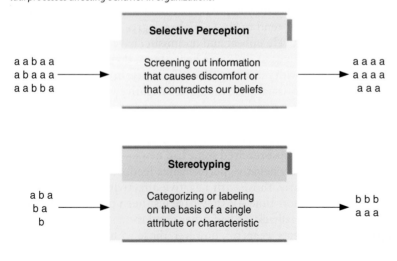

Stress and Individual Behavior

LEARNING OBJECTIVE

Discuss the causes and consequences of stress and describe how stress can be managed.

Stress is an individual's response to a strong stimulus.

A **stressor** is a strong stimulus that results in stress.

The **general adaptation syndrome (GAS)** is a cycle though which stress occurs: alarm, resistance, and exhaustion.

Type A individuals are extremely competitive, are very devoted to work, and have a strong sense of time urgency.

Another important element of behavior in organizations is stress. **Stress** is an individual's response to a strong stimulus called a **stressor.**[21] Stress generally follows a cycle referred to as the **general adaptation syndrome,** or **GAS,**[22] shown in Figure 3.4. According to this view, when an individual first encounters a stressor, the GAS is initiated and the first stage, alarm, is activated. The person may feel panic, may wonder how to cope, and may feel helpless. For example, suppose a manager is told to prepare a detailed evaluation of a plan by his firm to buy one of its competitors. His first reaction may be, "How will I ever get this done by tomorrow?"

If the stressor is too intense, the individual may feel unable to cope and never really try to respond to its demands. In most cases, however, after a short period of alarm, the individual gathers some strength and starts to resist the negative effects of the stressor. For example, the manager with the evaluation to write may calm down, call home to say he's working late, role up his sleeves, order out for coffee, and get to work. Thus, at stage 2 of the GAS, the person is resisting the effects of the stressor.

In many cases, the resistance phase may end the GAS. If the manager is able to complete the evaluation earlier than expected, he may drop it in his briefcase, smile to himself, and head home tired but satisfied. On the other hand, prolonged exposure to a stressor without resolution may bring on stage 3 of the GAS: exhaustion. At this stage, the individual literally gives up and can no longer resist the stressor. The manager, for example, might fall asleep at his desk at 3 A.M. and never finish the evaluation.

We should note that not all stress is bad. In the absence of stress, we may experience lethargy and stagnation. An optimal level of stress, on the other hand, can result in motivation and excitement. Too much stress, however, can have negative consequences. Excessive pressure, unreasonable demands on one's time, and bad news can all cause stress. Stress can also be caused by positive as well as negative events. For example receiving a bonus and then struggling to decide what to do with the money can be stressful. Likewise, receiving a promotion can make a person feel pressured to live up to the new job.

One important line of thinking about stress focuses on Type A and Type B personalities.[23] **Type A individuals** are extremely competitive, are very devoted to work, and have a strong sense of time urgency. They are likely to be aggressive, impatient, and very work oriented. They have a lot of drive and want to accomplish as much as possible as quickly as possible. **Type B individuals** are less competitive, are less devoted to work, and have a weaker sense of time urgency. Such individuals are less likely to experience conflict with other people and more likely to have a balanced,

FIGURE 3.4

The General Adaptation Syndrome

The general adaptation syndrome, or GAS, perspective describes three stages of the stress process. The initial stage is alarm. As illustrated here, a person's resistance often dips slightly below the normal level during this stage. Next comes actual resistance to the stressor, usually leading to an increase above the person's normal level of resistance. Finally, exhaustion may set in, dropping the person's resistance sharply below normal levels.

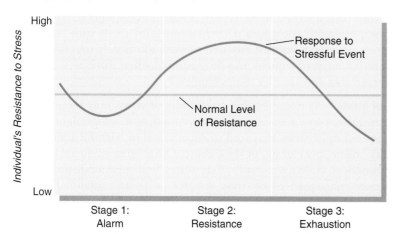

Type B individuals are less competitive, are less devoted to work, and have a weaker sense of time urgency.

relaxed approach to life. They are able to work at a constant pace without time urgency. Type B people are not necessarily more or less successful than Type A people. They are, however, less likely to experience stress.

Causes and Consequences of Stress

Stress is obviously not a simple phenomenon and has many different causes. While we focus on work-related stressors, we should keep in mind that stress can also result from personal circumstances.[24]

Causes of Stress   Work-related stressors fall into one of four categories: task, physical, role, and interpersonal demands. *Task demands* are associated with the task itself. Some occupations are inherently more stressful than others. Having to make fast decisions, decisions with less than complete information, or decisions that have relatively serious consequences can make some jobs stressful. The jobs of surgeon, airline pilot, and stockbroker are relatively more stressful than the jobs of general practitioner, airplane baggage loader, and office receptionist. While a general practitioner makes important decisions, he is also likely to have time to make a considered diagnosis and fully explore a number of different treatments. During surgery, in contrast, the surgeon must often make decisions quickly while realizing that the wrong one may endanger her patient's life.

Physical demands are stressors associated with the job setting. Working outdoors in extremely hot or cold temperatures, or even in an improperly heated or cooled office, can lead to stress. A poorly designed office, which makes it difficult for people to have privacy or promotes too little social interaction, can result in stress, as can poor lighting and inadequate work surfaces. Even more severe are actual threats to health. Examples include jobs such as coal mining, poultry processing, and toxic waste handling.

Role demands can also cause stress. A role is a set of expected behaviors associated with a position in a group or an organization. Stress can result from either role ambiguity or role conflict that people may experience in groups. For example, an employee whose boss is pressuring her to work longer hours or travel more while her family wants more time with her at home will almost certainly experience stress.[25] Similarly, a new employee experiencing role ambiguity because of poor orientation and training practices by the organization will also suffer stress.

Interpersonal demands are stressors associated with relationships that confront people in organizations. For example, group pressures regarding restriction of output and norm conformity can lead to stress. Leadership style may also cause stress. An employee who feels a strong need to participate in decision making may feel stress if his boss refuses to allow him participation. Individuals with conflicting personalities may experience stress if required to work too closely together. A person with an internal locus of control may be frustrated when working with someone who prefers to wait and "just let things happen."

Consequences of Stress   As noted earlier, the results of stress may be positive or negative. The negative consequences may be behavioral, psychological, or medical. Behaviorally, for example, stress may lead to detrimental or harmful actions, such as smoking, alcoholism, overeating, or drug abuse. Other stress-induced behaviors are accident proneness, violence toward self or others, and appetite disorders.

Psychological consequences of stress interfere with an individual's mental health and well-being. These outcomes include sleep disturbances, depression, family problems, and sexual dysfunction. Managers are especially prone to sleep disturbances when they experience stress at work.[26] Medical consequences of stress affect an individual's physiological well-being. Heart disease and stroke have been linked to stress, as have headaches, backaches, ulcers and related disorders, and skin conditions such as acne and hives.

Individual stress also has direct consequences for businesses. For an operating employee, stress may translate into poor-quality work and lower productivity. For a manager, it may mean faulty decision making and disruptions in working relationships. Withdrawal behaviors can also result from stress. People who are experiencing stress in their jobs are more likely to call in sick or to leave the organization. More subtle forms of withdrawal may also occur: A manager may start missing deadlines, for example, or taking longer lunch breaks. Employees may also withdraw by developing feelings of indifference. The irritation displayed by people under great stress can make them difficult to get along with. Job satisfaction, morale, commitment to the organization, and motivation to perform can all suffer as a result of excessive levels of stress.

Another consequence of stress is **burnout,** a feeling of exhaustion that develops when someone experiences too much stress for an extended period of time. Burnout results in constant fatigue, frustration, and helplessness. Increased rigidity follows, as does a loss of self-confidence and psychological withdrawal. The individual dreads going to work, often puts in longer hours but gets less accomplished than before, and exhibits mental and physical exhaustion. Because of the damaging effects of burnout, some firms are taking steps to prevent it. For example, British Airways provides all employees with training designed to help them recognize the symptoms of burnout and develop strategies for avoiding it.

Burnout is a sense of exhaustion that develops when someone experiences too much stress for an extended period of time.

Managing Stress

Given the potential consequences of stress, it follows that both people and organizations strive to limit its more damaging effects. Numerous ideas and approaches have been developed to help manage stress. Some are strategies for individuals, while others are strategies for organizations.[27]

One way people manage stress is through exercise. People who exercise regularly feel less tension and stress, are more self-confident, and are more optimistic. Their better physical condition also makes them less susceptible to many common illnesses. People who don't exercise regularly tend to feel more stress and are more likely to be depressed. Because of their physical condition, they are also more susceptible to heart problems and various illnesses. Another method people use to manage stress is relaxation. Relaxation allows individuals to adapt to, and therefore better deal with, their stress. Relaxation comes in many forms, such as taking regular vacations. A recent study found that people's attitudes toward a variety of workplace characteristics improved significantly following a vacation. People can also learn to relax while on their jobs. For example, some experts recommend that people take regular rest breaks during their normal workday.

People can also use time management to control stress. The idea behind time management is that many daily pressures can be reduced or eliminated if individuals manage their time more effectively. One approach to time management is to make a list every morning of the things to be done that day. The items on the list are then grouped into three categories: critical activities that must be performed, important activities that should be performed, and optional or trivial tasks that can be delegated or postponed. The individual performs the items on the list in their order of importance.

Organizations are also beginning to realize that they should be involved in helping employees cope with stress. One argument for this is that since the business is at least partially responsible for stress, it should also help relieve it. An-

Creativity is the ability to generate new ideas or conceive of new perspectives on existing ideas. For example, one of the most significant recent innovations in the food industry has been the "salad in a bag." We owe that innovation to Drew and Myra Goodman. The Goodmans were barely surviving farming a small plot of land; to save time, they pre-bagged salads for themselves every Sunday night. One day they decided to see if a San Francisco natural-food market was interested in selling the salads. The rest, as they say, is history: Today the Goodmans own Earthbound Farms and sell more than $200 million in packaged salads a year.

other is that stress-related insurance claims by employees can cost the organization considerable sums of money. Still another is that workers experiencing lower levels of detrimental stress will be able to function more effectively. AT&T has initiated a series of seminars and workshops to help its employees cope with the stress they face in their jobs. The firm was prompted to develop these seminars for all three reasons just noted.

A wellness program is a special part of the organization specifically created to help deal with stress. Organizations have adopted stress management programs, health promotion programs, and other initiatives for this purpose. The AT&T seminar program noted earlier is similar to this idea, but true wellness programs are ongoing activities that have a number of components. They commonly include exercise-related activities as well as classroom instruction programs dealing with smoking cessation, weight reduction, and general stress management.

Some companies are developing their own programs or using existing programs of this type. Johns-Manville, for example, has a gym at its corporate headquarters. Other firms negotiate discounted health club membership rates with local establishments. For the instructional part of the program, the organization can either sponsor its own training or jointly sponsor seminars with a local YMCA, civic organization, or church. Organization-based fitness programs facilitate employee exercise, a very positive consideration, but such programs are also quite costly. Still, more and more companies are developing fitness programs for employees.

Creativity in Organizations

Describe creativity and its role in organizations.

Creativity is the ability to generate new ideas or conceive of new perspectives on existing ideas.

Preparation, usually the first stage in the creative process, includes education and formal training.

Creativity is yet another important component of individual behavior in organizations. **Creativity** is the ability to generate new ideas or conceive of new perspectives on existing ideas. How does the creative process work? Although psychologists have not yet discovered complete answers to this question, examining a few general patterns can help us understand the sources of individual creativity within organizations.[28] Although creative people often report that ideas seem to come to them "in a flash," individual creative activity actually tends to progress through a series of stages. Figure 3.5 summarizes the major stages of the creative process. Not all creative activity follows these four stages, but much of it does.

The creative process normally begins with a period of **preparation.** Formal education and training are usually the most efficient ways to become familiar with this vast amount of research and knowledge. To make a creative contribution to business management or business services, individuals usually must receive formal training and education in business. This is one reason for the strong demand for undergraduate and master's-level business education. Formal business education

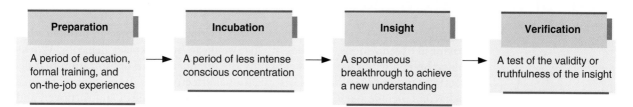

Preparation	Incubation	Insight	Verification
A period of education, formal training, and on-the-job experiences	A period of less intense conscious concentration	A spontaneous breakthrough to achieve a new understanding	A test of the validity or truthfulness of the insight

FIGURE 3.5

The Creative Process

The creative process generally follows the four steps illustrated here. Although exceptions exist, in most cases these steps capture the essence of the creative process.

Incubation is the stage of less intense conscious concentration, during which a creative person lets the knowledge and ideas acquired during preparation mature and develop.

Insight is the stage in the creative process when all the scattered thoughts and ideas that were maturing during incubation come together to produce a breakthrough.

In **verification**, the final stage of the creative process, the validity or truthfulness of the insight is determined.

can be an effective way for an individual to get "up to speed" and begin making creative contributions quickly. Experiences managers have on the job after completing their formal training can also contribute to the creative process. In an important sense, the education and training of creative people never really ends; it continues as long as they remain interested in the world and curious about the way things work. Bruce Roth earned a Ph.D. in chemistry and then spent years working in the pharmaceutical industry learning more and more about chemical compounds and how they work in human beings.

The second phase of the creative process is **incubation,** a period of less intense conscious concentration during which the knowledge and ideas acquired during preparation mature and develop. A curious aspect of incubation is that it is often helped along by pauses in concentrated rational thought. Some creative people rely on physical activity such as jogging or swimming to provide a "break" from thinking. Others read or listen to music. Sometimes sleep supplies the needed pause. Bruce Roth eventually joined Warner-Lambert, then an up-and-coming drug company, to help develop medication to lower cholesterol. In his spare time, Roth read mystery novels and hiked in the mountains. He later acknowledged that these "leisure" times were when he did his best thinking.

In the third phase of the creative process, **insight,** all the scattered thoughts and ideas that were maturing during incubation come together, producing a spontaneous breakthrough in which the person achieves a new understanding of the problem or situation. Insight may occur suddenly or develop slowly over time. Insight can be triggered by some external event, such as a new experience or an encounter with new data that forces the individual to think about old issues and problems in new ways, or it can be a completely internal event in which patterns of thought come to coalesce in ways that generate new understanding. One day Bruce Roth was reviewing data from some earlier studies that had found the new drug under development to be no more effective than other drugs already available. But this time he saw some statistical relationships that had not been identified previously. He knew then that he had a major breakthrough on his hands.

Once an insight has occurred, **verification** determines the validity or truthfulness of the insight. For many creative ideas, verification includes scientific experiments to determine whether or not the insight actually leads to the results expected. Verification may also include the development of a product or service prototype. A prototype is a single product or service, or a very small number, developed just to see if the ideas behind the new product actually work. Product prototypes are rarely sold to the public, but are very valuable in verifying the insights developed in the creative process. Once the new product or service is developed, verification in the marketplace is the ultimate test of the creative idea behind it. Bruce Roth and his colleagues set to work testing the new drug compound and eventually won FDA approval. The drug, Lipitor, is already the largest-selling pharmaceutical in history. And Pfizer, the firm that bought Warner-Lambert in a hostile takeover, is expected to soon earn more than $10 billion a year on the drug.[29]

Types of Workplace Behavior

Now that we have looked closely at how individual differences can influence behavior in organizations, let's look at what we mean by workplace behavior. **Workplace behavior** is a pattern of action by the members of an organization that directly or indirectly influences organizational effectiveness. Important workplace behaviors include performance and productivity, absenteeism and turnover, and organizational citizenship. Unfortunately, a variety of dysfunctional behaviors can also occur in organizational settings.

┌─*LEARNING OBJECTIVE*─┐
Explain how workplace behaviors can directly or indirectly influence organizational effectiveness.

Workplace behavior is a pattern of action by the members of an organization that directly or indirectly influences organizational effectiveness.

Performance behaviors are the total set of work-related behaviors that the organization expects the individual to display.

Performance Behaviors

Performance behaviors are the total set of work-related behaviors that the organization expects the individual to display. Thus, they derive from the psychological contract. For some jobs, performance behaviors can be narrowly defined and easily measured. For example, an assembly line worker who sits by a moving conveyor and attaches parts to a product as it passes by has relatively few performance behaviors. He is expected to remain at the workstation and correctly attach the parts. Performance can often be assessed quantitatively by counting the percentage of parts correctly attached.

For many other jobs, performance behaviors are more diverse and much more difficult to assess. For example, consider a research and development scientist at Merck. The scientist works in a lab trying to find new scientific breakthroughs that have commercial potential. The scientist must apply knowledge acquired in graduate school with experience gained from previous research. Intuition and creativity are also important elements. Further, the desired breakthrough may take months or even years to accomplish. Organizations rely on a number of different methods for evaluating performance. The key, of course, is to match the evaluation mechanism with the job being performed.

Withdrawal Behavior

Absenteeism occurs when an individual does not show up for work.

Another important type of work-related behavior results in withdrawal: absenteeism and turnover. **Absenteeism** occurs when an individual does not show up for work. The cause may be legitimate (illness, jury duty, death in the family, and so forth) or feigned (reported as legitimate but actually just an excuse to stay home). When an employee is absent, her or his work does not get done at all or a substitute must be hired to do it. In either case, the quantity or quality of actual output is likely to suffer. Obviously some absenteeism is expected. The key concern of organizations is to minimize feigned absenteeism and reduce legitimate absences as much as possible. High absenteeism may be a symptom of other problems as well, such as job dissatisfaction and low morale.

Turnover occurs when people quit their jobs.

Turnover occurs when people quit their jobs. An organization usually incurs costs in replacing individuals who have quit, and turnover among especially productive people is even more costly. Turnover can result from a number of factors, including certain aspects of the job, the organization, the individual, the labor market, and family influences. In general, a poor person-job fit is a likely cause of turnover. The current labor shortage is also resulting in higher turnover in many companies due to the abundance of more attractive alternative jobs available to highly qualified individuals.[30]

Efforts to directly manage turnover are frequently fraught with difficulty, even in organizations that concentrate on rewarding good performers. Of course, some turnover is inevitable and in some cases may even be desirable. For example, if the organization is trying to cut costs by reducing its staff, having people voluntarily choose to leave is preferable to having to terminate them. In addition, if the people who choose to leave are low performers or express high levels of job dissatisfaction, the organization may also benefit from turnover.

Dysfunctional Behaviors

Dysfunctional behaviors are work-related behaviors that detract from organiza-tional performance.

Dysfunctional behaviors are work-related behaviors that detract from rather than contribute to organizational performance. Absenteeism and turnover are among the more common types, but other forms of dysfunctional behavior may be even more costly for an organization. Theft and sabotage, for example, result in direct financial costs for an organization. Sexual and racial harassment also cost an orga-nization, both indirectly (by lowering morale, producing fear, and driving off valu-able employees) and directly (through financial liability if the organization responds inappropriately). So can politicized behavior, intentionally misleading others in the organization, spreading malicious rumors, and similar activities. Workplace vio-lence is also a growing concern in many organizations. Violence by disgruntled for-mer or existing workers results in dozens of deaths and injuries each year.[31]

Organizational Citizenship

A person's degree of **organi-zational citizenship** is the extent to which the individ-ual's behavior makes a positive overall contribution to the organization.

Organizational citizenship refers to the behavior of individuals that makes a pos-itive overall contribution to the organization.[32] Consider an employee who does work that is acceptable in terms of both quantity and quality. However, she refuses to work overtime, declines to help newcomers learn the ropes, and is generally un-willing to make any contribution to the organization beyond the strict perfor-mance of her job. While this person may be seen as a good performer, she is not likely to be considered a good organizational citizen.

Consider another employee who exhibits a comparable level of performance. In addition, he will always work late when the boss asks him to, takes time to help newcomers learn their way around, and is perceived as being helpful and commit-ted to the organization's success. While his level of performance may be seen as equal to that of the first worker, he is also likely to be considered a better organiza-tional citizen because of his other positive behaviors.

The determinant of organizational citizenship behaviors is likely to be a com-plex mosaic of individual, social, and organizational variables. For example, the in-dividual's personality, attitudes, and needs should be consistent with citizenship be-haviors. Similarly, the social context, or work group, in which the individual works will need to facilitate and promote such behaviors (we discuss group dynamics in Chapter 8). Further, the organization itself, especially its culture, must be capable of promoting, recognizing, and rewarding these types of behaviors if they are to be maintained. While the study of organizational citizenship is still in its infancy, preliminary research suggests that it may play a powerful role in organizational effectiveness.[33]

Synopsis

Understanding individuals in organizations is an im-portant consideration for all managers. A basic frame-work used to facilitate this understanding is the psy-chological contract, the set of expectations people hold with respect to what they will contribute to the organization and what they will get in return. Organi-zations strive to achieve an optimal person-job fit, but this process is complicated by the existence of individ-ual differences.

Personality is the relatively stable set of psychological and behavioral attributes that distinguish one person from another. The "big five" personality traits are agreeableness, conscientiousness, negative emotionality, extraversion, and openness. The Myers-Briggs framework can also be a useful mechanism for understanding personality. Other important traits are locus of control, self-efficacy, authoritarianism, Machiavellianism, self-esteem, and risk propensity. Emotional intelligence, a relatively recent concept, may shed additional insights into personality.

Attitudes are based on emotion, knowledge, and intended behavior. Some attitudes can be formed and changed easily, whereas others are more constant. Job satisfaction or dissatisfaction and organizational commitment are important work-related attitudes.

Perception is the set of processes by which an individual becomes aware of and interprets information about the environment. Basic perceptual processes include selective perception and stereotyping.

Stress is an individual's response to a strong stimulus. The general adaption syndrome (GAS) outlines the basic stress process. Stress can be caused by task, physical, role, and interpersonal demands. Consequences of stress include organizational and individual outcomes, as well as burnout. Individuals and organizations can both take steps to manage stress.

Creativity is the capacity to generate new ideas. The creative process includes preparation, incubation, insight, and verification.

Workplace behavior is a pattern of action by the members of an organization that directly or indirectly influences organizational effectiveness. Performance behaviors are the set of work-related behaviors the organization expects the individual to display to fulfill the psychological contract. Basic withdrawal behaviors are absenteeism and turnover. Dysfunctional behaviors can be very harmful to an organization. Organizational citizenship refers to behaviors that make a positive overall contribution to the organization.

Discussion Questions

1. What is a psychological contract? Why is it important? What psychological contracts do you currently have?

2. Sometimes people describe an individual as having "no personality." What is wrong with this statement? What does this statement actually mean?

3. Describe how the "big five" personality attributes might affect a manager's own behavior in dealing with subordinates.

4. What are the components of an individual's attitude?

5. Think of a person you know who seems to have positive affectivity. Think of another who has more negative affectivity. How constant are these individuals in their expressions of mood and attitude?

6. How does perception affect behavior?

7. What stereotypes have you formed about people? Are they positive or negative?

8. Recall a situation in which you experienced stress. Identify the factors that created this stress, and comment on how you responded.

9. Describe a situation in which you came up with a new idea by following the basic steps of the creative process described in the text.

10. Identify and describe several important workplace behaviors. As a manager, how would you go about trying to make someone a better organizational citizen?

Organizational Behavior Case for Discussion

Valuing Employees at the World's Largest Firm

In April 2004, *Fortune* magazine identified Wal-Mart as the world's largest company (based on sales) for the third year in a row. The discounter is the first service company ever to top that list. *Fortune* began publishing its list in 1955, before Wal-Mart was founded, and the largest firm that first year was General Motors. GM and Exxon have remained in the number one and two spots, respectively, until Wal-Mart's coup. The retailer's growth has been phenomenal since its 1962 founding. In 1979, Wal-Mart had annual sales of $1 billion; in 1993, $1 billion was just one week's sales and in 2001, just one day's. Today, however, like other American companies, Wal-Mart is facing the challenge of maintaining profitability in a tougher economy.

Wal-Mart CEO Lee Scott says, "We have not seen any marked increase in the level of consumer spending [in recent times]." In response, the retailer is aggressively adding new, larger stores that are open longer hours; 1,400 stores are open 24 hours. As a result, the firm's need for workers continues to grow rapidly. Also, through the 1990s, Wal-Mart sustained an 8 to 9 percent increase in sales annually and a 23 to 25 percent increase in profits. However, more recently Wal-Mart stores have experienced slower sales and profit growth. Although still much greater than competitors' growth, Wal-Mart's current growth is not rising to meet management expectations. Consequently, the company must continually reduce expenses to maintain target profit margins.

Wal-Mart has usually enjoyed a very harmonious relationship with its employees. The firm pays its hourly workers less than many competitors, but its corporate culture gives workers a sense that the company cares about them and their families. Wal-Mart's psychological contract is a product of founder Sam Walton's values. In his autobiography, Walton says, "If you're good to people, and fair with them, . . . they will eventually decide that you're on their side." During Walton's tenure as CEO, Wal-Mart employees had benefits and family-friendly policies such as time-and-a-half pay for working on Sunday, starting pay that was always above minimum wage, an internal promotion policy (70 percent of store managers were once hourly associates), and the opportunity for even low-wage workers to own stock and receive retirement benefits. Walton himself was a charismatic figure who truly listened to what workers had to say.

Unfortunately for workers, the constant pressures to reduce expenses, build ever-larger stores, and keep stores open 24 hours a day make it hard for Wal-Mart managers to maintain the personal touch that Walton employed so well. More and more Wal-Mart managers have come to believe that their contract with workers isn't being honored or just isn't working. Stan Fortune, former Wal-Mart manager, asserts, "My job was brainwashing. My job was to take you from your job across town and make you want to work for me, regardless of the pay. I'm almost embarrassed to say it, but that's what I did."

Of course, workers aren't living up to their end of the bargain, either. Having little personal contact with their managers, some workers miss work frequently or quit unexpectedly. "We had five call in and quit one day," says Stephanie Haynes, manager at the Madisonville, Texas, store. And Walton himself noted, as stores were being built in more urban areas, "We have

more trouble coming up with educated people who want to work in our industry, or with people of the right moral character and integrity." Workers in a Las Vegas store are considering unionizing, and if they choose to do so, they will be the first Wal-Mart employees to be represented by a union. And that could change the entire character of Wal-Mart's business.

Some signs indicate, however, that the retailing giant may be returning to more profitable times. Rival Kmart recently declared bankruptcy and continues to struggle, while Wal-Mart's stock price has started increasing once again. But the discounter still faces complex challenges, especially in managing its growing labor force. Wal-Mart's growth over the next several years will rely heavily on international markets. Stock analyst Jeff Klinefelter says, "I have no doubt they can [become the dominant retailer] globally. But it's going to change the profile of the company." Unhappy employees are less optimistic. At one time, every Wal-Mart employee wore a blue apron that read, "Our people make the difference." Today the apron slogan has been changed to "How may I help you?" For Wal-Mart workers, that change signals a shift in focus away from the worker and toward the customer. To ensure its success, Wal-Mart must find a way to provide what employees need, motivating them to continue to provide quality customer service. Unfortunately, a class-action suit against the retailer in mid-2004 alleging widespread sex discrimination may put a damper on the retailer's efforts!

Case Questions

1. According to the psychological contract previously observed in use at Wal-Mart, what were the employee contributions and the organizational inducements? In your opinion, was the contract fair and equitable? Why or why not?

2. According to the psychological contract currently in use at Wal-Mart, what are the employee contributions and the organizational inducements? Do you think the contract is fair and equitable? Why or why not?

3. What do you suggest Wal-Mart managers do to better manage their firm's organization culture as the company continues to grow? What effect is the lawsuit likely to have?

References: "The *Fortune* 500," *Fortune*, April 5, 2004; "Fourteen Top CEOs (and One President) Gauge the Year Ahead," *Fortune*, April 15, 2002; Brian O'Keefe, "The High Price of Being No. 1," *Fortune*, April 15, 2002; Cait Murphy, "Now That Wal-Mart Is America's Largest Corporation, the Service Economy Wears the Crown," *Fortune*, April 15, 2002; Mark Gimein, "Sam Walton Made Us a Promise," *Fortune*, March 18, 2002, pp. 120–130.

Experiencing Organizational Behavior

Matching Personalities and Jobs

Purpose: This exercise will give you insights into the importance of personality in the workplace and some of the difficulties associated with assessing personality traits.

Format: You will first try to determine which personality traits are most relevant to different jobs. You will then write a series of questions to help assess or measure those traits in prospective employees.

Procedure: First, read each of the following job descriptions.

Sales Representative—This position involves calling on existing customers to ensure they continue to be happy with your firm's products. The sales representative also works to get customers to buy more of your products and to attract new customers. A sales representative must be aggressive but not pushy.

Office Manager—The office manager oversees the work of a staff of twenty secretaries, receptionists, and clerks. The manager hires them, trains them, evaluates their performance, and sets their pay. The manager also schedules working hours and, when necessary, disciplines or fires workers.

Warehouse Worker—Warehouse workers unload trucks and carry shipments to shelves for storage. They also pull orders for customers from shelves and take products for packing. The job requires that workers follow orders precisely; there is little room for autonomy or interaction with others during work.

Working alone, think of a single personality trait that you think is especially important to enable a person to perform each job effectively. Next, write five questions that will help you assess how an applicant scores on that particular trait. These questions should be of the type that can be answered on a five-point scale (e.g., *strongly agree, agree, neither agree nor disagree, disagree, strongly disagree*). After completing your questions, exchange them with a classmate. Pretend you are an applicant for one of the jobs listed, and answer your partner's questions honestly. After you have both finished, discuss the traits each of you identified for each position and how well you think your classmate's questions actually measure those traits.

Follow-up Questions

1. How easy is it to measure personality?
2. How important do you believe it is for organizations to consider personality in hiring decisions?
3. Do perceptions and attitudes affect how people answer personality questions? Explain your answer.

Self-Assessment Exercise

Assessing Your Locus of Control

Read each pair of statements below and indicate whether you agree more with statement A or with statement B. There are no right or wrong answers. In some cases, you may agree somewhat with both statements; choose the one with which you agree more.

1. A. Making a lot of money is largely a matter of getting the right breaks.
   B. Promotions are earned through hard work and persistence.
2. A. There is usually a direct correlation between how hard I study and the grades I get.
   B. Many times the reactions of teachers seem haphazard to me.
3. A. The number of divorces suggests that more and more people are not trying to make their marriages work.
   B. Marriage is primarily a gamble.

4. A. It is silly to think you can really change another person's basic attitudes.
   B. When I am right, I can generally convince others.
5. A. Getting promoted is really a matter of being a little luckier than the next person.
   B. In our society, a person's future earning power is dependent upon her or his ability.
6. A. If one knows how to deal with people, they are really quite easily led.
   B. I have little influence over the way other people behave.
7. A. The grades I make are the result of my own efforts; luck has little or nothing to do with it.
   B. Sometimes I feel that I have little to do with the grades I get.

8. A. People like me can change the course of world affairs if we make ourselves heard.

   B. It is only wishful thinking to believe that one can readily influence what happens in our society at large.

9. A. A great deal that happens to me probably is a matter of chance.

   B. I am the master of my life.

10. A. Getting along with people is a skill that must be practiced.

   B. It is almost impossible to figure out how to please some people.

Give yourself 1 point each if you chose the following answers: 1B, 2A, 3A, 4B, 5B, 6A, 7A, 8A, 9B, 10A.

Sum your scores and interpret them as follows:

8–10 = high internal locus of control

 6–7 = moderate internal locus of control

   5 = mixed internal/external locus of control

 3–4 = moderate external locus of control

 1–2 = high external locus of control

(Note: This is an abbreviated version of a longer instrument. The scores obtained here are only an approximation of what your score might be on the complete instrument.)

Reference: Adapted from J. B. Rotter, "External Control and Internal Control," *Psychology Today*, June 1971, p. 42. Reprinted with permission from *Psychology Today Magazine*. Copyright © 1971 Sussex Publishers, Inc.

OB Online

1. Find an organization that seems to openly address the issue of person-job fit on its recruiting website. Look for such things as a discussion of what the organization expects from its employees and what it offers to them in return.

2. Pick six companies with which you are familiar and visit their websites. What examples illustrating perception can you identify?

3. Find a consulting firm on the Internet that offers services such as conducting attitude surveys. As a manager, how willing would you be to buy such services?

4. Search the Internet and find two or three recent high-profile examples of dysfunctional behavior, such as theft or violence, in an organization.

Building Managerial Skills

Exercise Overview: As discussed in Chapter 2, conceptual skills entail the ability to think in the abstract. This exercise will help you apply conceptual skills in a way designed to better understand the concepts of attitude formation and cognitive dissonance.

Exercise Task: Begin by considering the following situation. Assume a new restaurant has just opened near your house, apartment, or dorm. You decide to give it a try—and have one of the worst nights of your life. You wait 30 minutes to get seated and another 30 minutes before your server stops by. The menu you are handed is dirty, and a dead fly is floating in your water glass. Your food is served cold (unintentionally), the server spills food on you when clearing the table, the food is way overpriced, and when you return to your car you find it has been towed—all in all, not a pleasant experience. As a result, you vow never to set foot in that restaurant again.

Now suppose you have been trying to date a certain someone for months. While he or she seems to have an interest in you as well, circumstances have always kept the two of you apart. This person has just called you, however, and indicated a strong interest in going out with you next week—to that new restaurant you hate.

Using the situation above as background, answer the following questions:

1. Explain how your attitude about the restaurant was formed.

2. Explain how your attitude toward the other person was formed.

3. Describe what you would do when confronted with this choice.

4. Explain the role of cognitive dissonance in this situation.

TEST PREPPER

ACE self-test

You have read the chapter and studied the key terms, and the exam is any day now. Think you're ready to ace it? Take this sample test to gauge your comprehension of chapter material. You can check your answers at the back of the book. Want more test questions? Visit the student website at http://college.hmco.com/business/students/ (select Griffin/Moorhead, Fundamentals of Organizational Behavior 1e) and take the ACE quizzes for more practice.

1. **T F** Employers and employees must sign the psychological contract before work begins.

2. **T F** In exchange for employees' contributions, the organization offers inducements.

3. **T F** A precise person-job fit is easy to achieve if care is given in the hiring process.

4. **T F** The "big five" personality trait that refers to a person's comfort level with relationships is called *agreeableness.*

5. **T F** If John believes he can control his own destiny, he has an internal locus of control.

6. **T F** Someone with a high degree of Machiavellianism enjoys manipulating others.

7. **T F** Emotionally intelligent people can motivate themselves.

8. **T F** Attitudes have affective, cognitive, and intentional components.

9. **T F** A person with high positive affectivity can be in a temporary bad mood if he or she just received very bad news.

10. **T F** When a manager achieves "selective perception," she or he can recall all dimensions of an employee's performance.

11. **T F** The final stage of the general adaptation syndrome regarding stress is alarm.

12. **T F** Type A individuals are more competitive than Type B individuals.

13. **T F** Once a creative solution is identified, it should be verified.

14. **T F** Performance behaviors can be both easily defined and measured, and diverse and difficult to assess.

15. **T F** An organization usually incurs costs when a productive employee quits.

16. What seems to be the trend regarding employees' time at work?
    a. Employees typically take 3-day weekends.
    b. Most workers take an extended lunch.
    c. People work fewer hours but have more than one job.
    d. More and more workers say they prefer long hours.
    e. Off-work time, such as nights, weekends, and holidays, is more valued than ever.

17. Brandon expects to work 45 hours a week for his salary. He also believes if he works hard, he'll have a good chance of being promoted. This overall set of expectations represents Brandon's
    a. contributions.
    b. inducements.
    c. psychological contract.
    d. organizational behavior.
    e. person-job fit.

18. Managers have a difficult time achieving a precise level of person-job fit for all of the following reasons except
    a. organizational selection procedures are imperfect.
    b. people and organizations change over time.
    c. each individual is unique.
    d. the costs of achieving fit outweigh the benefits.
    e. All of these are reasons managers have a difficult time achieving precise fit.

19. Katie focuses on a few goals at once and systematically and carefully pursues those goals. Katie is also very organized. Which personality trait best describes Katie?
    a. High agreeableness
    b. High conscientiousness
    c. Low introversion
    d. High openness
    e. Low negative emotionality

20. The Myers-Briggs Type Indicator (MBTI) is a popular questionnaire. What is the best use of the MBTI?
    a. Developing struggling managers
    b. Determining communication styles and interaction preferences
    c. Assessing personality attributes
    d. Identifying outstanding performers
    e. Understanding consumer behavior

21. Laurie believes that if she works hard, she will be successful. Whitney believes that no matter how hard she works, her ultimate success is beyond her power. Laurie and Whitney differ in their
   a. conscientiousness.
   b. locus of control.
   c. negative emotionality.
   d. extroversion.
   e. authoritarianism.

22. Adam believes power and status differences among employees in his organization are appropriate. He follows the demands of his boss and thinks employees below him in the hierarchy ought to follow his orders. Which personality trait best describes Adam?
   a. Extroversion
   b. Negative emotionality
   c. Machiavellianism
   d. Self-efficacy
   e. Authoritarianism

23. Jeff doesn't feel especially worthwhile or deserving. Which of the following can Jeff's manager expect from him?
   a. Jeff will be relatively calm and resilient.
   b. Jeff will derive great intrinsic satisfaction from his accomplishments.
   c. Jeff will avoid extrinsic rewards.
   d. Jeff will be content to remain in a lower-level job.
   e. Jeff will be confident of his ability.

24. All of the following are dimensions of emotional intelligence except
   a. self-awareness.
   b. managing emotions.
   c. empathy.
   d. self-efficacy.
   e. social skills.

25. Managers who create high job satisfaction among their workers should expect all of the following outcomes except
   a. lower absenteeism.
   b. more positive contributions.
   c. less employee turnover.
   d. higher job performance.
   e. Managers can expect high job satisfaction to result in all of these outcomes.

26. Tesi is a relatively upbeat and optimistic employee. She has an overall sense of well-being and usually sees things in a positive light. Which of the following best describes Tesi?
   a. Positive affectivity
   b. Self-esteem
   c. Conscientiousness
   d. Machiavellianism
   e. Extroversion

27. A key competitor just introduced a product that may make Carlos' business obsolete. What state of the general adaptation syndrome is Carlos likely to experience first?
   a. Resistance
   b. Alarm
   c. Exhaustion
   d. Stress
   e. Stressor

28. Which of the following is not likely to cause work-related stress?
   a. A hot office
   b. A job with decisions that have serious consequences
   c. An uncertain set of expected behaviors
   d. Working with people with conflicting personalities
   e. All of these are likely to cause work-related stress.

29. Erik has been under high stress in his job for the last three years. Recently Erik has been putting in longer hours but getting less done. He dreads going to work and feels mentally and physically exhausted. Erik is experiencing
   a. an external locus of control.
   b. burnout.
   c. low conscientiousness.
   d. resistance.
   e. alarm.

30. Which of the following is not an effective way to manage stress?
   a. Exercise
   b. Relaxation
   c. Time management
   d. Alcohol
   e. Wellness programs

31. Erin has been struggling with a complex problem at work for the last two weeks. One night at dinner, she suddenly realizes the answer. What stage of the creative process has just occurred?
   a. Preparation
   b. Verification
   c. Insight
   d. Incubation
   e. Exhaustion

32. Kevin is an employee who makes a positive overall contribution to the organization. He is willing to help when needed and goes the extra mile to improve his company's performance. Kevin can be considered a good
   a. intrinsic motivator.
   b. authoritarian.
   c. person-job fit.
   d. psychological contract.
   e. organizational citizen.

CHAPTER 4

Motivation in Organizations

MANAGEMENT PREVIEW

Given the complex array of individual differences discussed in Chapter 3, it should be obvious that people work for a wide variety of reasons. Some people want money, some want challenge, and some want power. What people in an organization want from work and how they think they can achieve it plays an instrumental role in their motivation to work. As we see in this chapter, motivation is vital to all organizations. Indeed, the difference between highly effective organizations and less effective ones often lies in the motivation of their members. Thus, managers need to understand the nature of individual motivation, especially as it applies to work situations. In this chapter, we first explore various need-based perspectives on motivation. We then turn to the more sophisticated process-based perspectives. Finally, we focus on learning-based perspectives on motivation.

After you have studied this chapter, you should be able to:
- ☐ *Characterize the nature of motivation, including its importance and basic historical perspectives.*
- ☐ *Describe the need-based perspectives on motivation.*
- ☐ *Explain the major process-based perspectives on motivation.*
- ☐ *Describe learning-based perspectives on motivation.*

We begin with a description of the importance of employee motivation at Commerce Bancorp.

If you're like most people, it's been a while since you were inside your bank actually communicating face to face with an employee. Driven by cost concerns, many banks are actually discouraging customers from entering their building and instead are relying on drive-through windows, the Internet, or ATMs for many routine transactions. And when you do need to visit the bank's building, you probably often encounter those inconvenient "banker's hours." One firm, though, New Jersey–based Commerce Bancorp, is virtually alone in encouraging use of branches and staying open longer hours, including nights, weekends, and holidays. "Everyone else has given up on branches ... but people will always choose to bank in person. The problem with most banks is that they abuse their customers every day. We want to wow ours," says CEO Vernon Hill. The heart of the firm's customer service strategy is having high-performing employees who can make customers feel welcome, serve them efficiently, and build lasting personal relationships.

Hill, a former property locator for McDonald's, thinks of his business as retailing rather than banking. Says Dennis DiFlorio, chief retail officer, "The greatest insult you can give someone here is to say, 'You're thinking like a banker.'" To help employees shift their focus from money to providing customers with that "wow" service experience, new hires receive training at Commerce University. Hill tells the new managers, "We're asking you to forget the way you delivered your skills at other banks. In many ways, you have joined a service cult."

The "Kill a Stupid Rule" program pays $50 when workers identify a rule that interferes with great customer service. Even job applicants must have the right attitude. "This is not the job for someone who's interested in being cool or indifferent," says Wow Department vice president John Manning. After being carefully selected and trained, Commerce employees regularly earn rewards, ranging from $5,000 when a competing nearby branch bank closes to balloon bouquets, congratulatory notes, or pictures with Mr. C or Buzz, the company's mascots. Silliness and fun, two qualities that are rarely encouraged in the staid banking industry, prevail at Commerce. For example, the Wow Patrol routinely visits branches, rewarding high-performing staffers while singing songs, giving candy to customers, and leading group cheers.

Commerce's organization culture emphasizes rewarding high performers. Maintaining the consistency of rewards and using desirable rewards are also priorities. Mystery shoppers report on every detail of their experience, so having just one associate who gives incorrect information or fails to smile can keep the entire branch from getting a "wow" rating. Managers are competitive for the scarce rewards, says Jennifer Perrone, an assistant manager. "I don't want to give [the trophy] up. I'm obsessed with it. I leave notes for my tellers in the drive-through all the time to remind them to smile," she adds.

Having highly motivated employees seems to be paying off for Commerce. For example, Commerce holds market shares of up to 50 percent in some cities while paying below-average interest. Their high deposits give the company a larger and cheaper pool of money to lend. The high levels of customer satisfaction and profits have caught the attention of investors: Commerce stock value is increasing at a time when most bank stocks are declining. At Commerce, the motivation seems to be contagious.

References: "Branch Locations," Commerce Bancorp website, www.bank.commerceonline.com, on April 26, 2004; "Business Summary: Commerce Bancorp," "Analysts' Opinions," *BusinessWeek* website, www.research.businessweek.com, on April 28, 2004; Hoover's Online website, www.hoovnews.hoovers.com, on April 28, 2004; Chuck Salter, "Customer Service: Commerce Bank," *Fast Company*, Fifth Annual Best of the Business issue, May 2002, pp. 80–91 (quotation, p. 86).

Commerce Bancorp is clearly working to create a business model that is unique in its industry. The firm aims to instill high levels of motivation in all its employees, for example, and anticipates that this motivation will translate into higher earnings for the company itself. But rather than relying simply on bigger rewards, Commerce is trying to make motivation a fundamental business principle. This approach, in turn, provides interesting insights into how motivational processes work in organizations. Specifically, various theories and frameworks that address what motivates people and how motivational processes unfold can shed new light on how and why employees behave as they do and help managers structure rewards and other work-related outcomes to enhance employee motivation and performance.[1] We begin our discussion of these theories and frameworks by examining the nature of motivation.

The Nature of Motivation

Motivation is the set of
forces that leads people to
behave in particular ways.

Motivation is the set of forces that causes people to engage in one behavior
rather than some alternative behavior.[2] Students who stay up all night to ensure
their term papers are the best they can be, salespeople who work on Saturdays to
get ahead, and doctors who make follow-up phone calls to patients to check on
their conditions are all motivated people. Of course, students who avoid term papers by spending the day at the beach, salespeople who go home early to escape a
tedious sales call, and doctors who skip follow-up calls to have more time for golf
are also motivated, but their goals are different. From the manager's viewpoint,
the objective is to motivate people to behave in ways that are in the organization's
best interest.[3]

The Importance of Motivation

Managers strive to motivate the organization's people to perform at high levels.
This means getting them to work hard, come to work regularly, and make positive
contributions to the organization's mission. However, job performance depends on
ability and environment as well as on motivation. This relationship can be stated
as follows:

$$P = M + A + E$$

with P = performance, M = motivation, A = ability, and E = environment. To
reach high levels of performance, an employee must want to do the job well (motivation), must be able to do the job effectively (ability), and must have the materials,
resources, equipment, and information to do the job (environment). A deficiency
in any one of these areas hurts performance. A manager should thus strive to ensure that all three conditions are met.[4]

In most settings, motivation is the most difficult of these factors to manage. If
an employee lacks the ability to perform, she or he can be sent to training programs to learn new job skills. If the person cannot learn those skills, she or he can
be transferred to a simpler job and replaced with a more skilled worker. If an
employee lacks materials, resources, equipment, and/or information, the manager
can take steps to provide them. For example, if a worker cannot complete a project
without sales forecast data from marketing, the manager can contact marketing
and request that information. But if motivation is deficient, the manager faces the
more complex situation of determining what will motivate the employee to work
harder. This point is explored further in the Business of Ethics box.

The Motivational Framework

A **need** is anything an individual requires or wants.

We can start to understand motivation by looking at need deficiencies and goal-
directed behaviors. Figure 4.1 shows the basic motivational framework we use to
organize our discussion. A **need**—something an individual requires or wants—is
the starting point.[5] Motivated behavior usually begins when a person has one or
more important needs. Although a need that is already satisfied may also motivate
behavior (for example, the need to maintain a standard of living one has already
achieved), unmet needs usually result in more intense feelings and behavioral
changes. For example, if a person has yet to attain the standard of living he desires,
this unmet need may stimulate him to action.

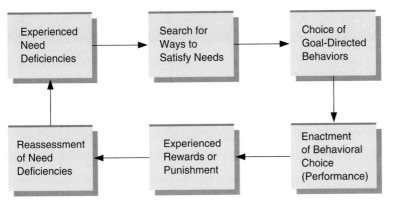

FIGURE 4.1

The Motivational Framework

This framework provides a useful way to see how motivated processes occur. When people experience a need deficiency, they seek ways to satisfy it, which results in a choice of goal-directed behaviors. After performing the behavior, the individual experiences rewards or punishments that affect the original need deficiency.

A need deficiency usually triggers a search for ways to satisfy it. Consider a person who believes her salary and position are deficient because she wants more income and because they do not reflect the importance to the organization of the work she does. She may think she has three options: to simply ask for a raise and a promotion, to work harder in the hope of earning a raise and a promotion, or to look for a new job with a higher salary and a more prestigious title.

Next comes a choice of goal-directed behaviors. Although a person might pursue more than one option at a time (such as working harder while also looking for another job), most effort is likely to be directed at one option. In the next phase, the person actually carries out the behavior chosen to satisfy the need. She will probably begin putting in longer hours, working harder, and so forth. Next, she will experience either rewards or punishment as a result of this choice. She may perceive her situation to be punishing if she ends up earning no additional recognition and not getting a promotion or pay raise. Alternatively, she may actually be rewarded by getting the raise and promotion because of her higher performance.

Finally, the person assesses the extent to which the outcome achieved fully addresses the original need deficiency. Suppose the employee wanted a 10 percent raise and a promotion to vice president. If she got both, she should be satisfied. On the other hand, if she got only a 7 percent raise and a promotion to associate vice president, she will have to decide whether to keep trying, to accept what she got, or to choose one of the other options considered earlier. (Sometimes, of course, a need may go unsatisfied altogether despite the person's best efforts.)

Historical Perspectives on Motivation

Historical views on motivation, although not always accurate, are of interest for several reasons. For one thing, they provide a foundation for contemporary thinking about motivation. For another, because they generally were based on common sense and intuition, an appreciation of their strengths and weaknesses can help managers gain useful insights into employee motivation in the workplace.

The Traditional Approach   As we noted in Chapter 1, Frederick Taylor, founder of the **scientific management approach,** assumed employees are economically motivated and work to earn as much money as they can.[6] Hence, he advocated incentive pay systems. Taylor believed that managers know more about the jobs being performed than do workers and that economic gain is the primary motivator for everyone. Other assumptions of the traditional approach were that work is inherently unpleasant for most people and that the money they earn is more important to employees than the nature of the job they are performing. Hence, people could be expected to perform any kind of job if they were paid enough. Although the role

The **scientific management approach** assumes that employees are motivated by money.

BUSINESS OF ETHICS

What Is the Price of Motivation?

Would you feel motivated if your boss gave you a pizza? What if she gave you a trip to the Super Bowl? Can the matter of motivation be reduced to a mere commercial transaction? As George Bernard Shaw asks, "Now that we have established what you are, madam, it is simply a matter of deciding on the price."

There is no doubt that companies benefit from increased worker motivation. Studies show that workers who report high motivation are more productive and innovative, have lower absenteeism and turnover, and provide better customer service. What has never been demonstrated is a sure method for achieving motivation and avoiding the sticky ethical issues that can arise.

Ethical concerns about giving rewards for performance include the following:

■ Workers may feel rewards trivialize their significant contributions. Some employees compare rewards to bribes, others to implicit threats.

■ It's hard to determine who deserves rewards. "The positive sometimes is negative because it seems unfair," according to motivational consultant Alex Heim.

■ Workers may become used to receiving rewards and expect them frequently, becoming unsatisfied and demanding if rewards don't arrive. "Downstream, the grand scheme doesn't always work. The fallout is disenchantment," says Joe Magliochetti, CEO of Dana, a supplier to the auto industry.

■ Rewards, which can cost hundreds of thousands of dollars, have no demonstrated relationship to a company's bottom line and may take funds away from other, more worthy programs.

> *"Downstream, the grand scheme doesn't always work. The fallout is disenchantment."—Joe Magliochetti, CEO of Dana Corporation*

Combine these concerns with the observation that increases in productivity due to rewards are fleeting, if they exist at all, and you will see why many companies are disillusioned. Nevertheless, motivation remains a critical issue: A recent poll found that one-fifth of workers are so negative that they poison others and that their employers would be better off without them.

This fact is not lost on such high-performing organizations as Microsoft, Sun Microsystems, and GE, which no longer try to motivate everyone. Former GE CEO Jack Welch claims, "A company that bets its future on its people must remove that lower 10 percent, and keep removing it every year." Welch's tough-love philosophy may be the most motivating message, in effect telling workers, "My way or the highway."

References: Michelle Conlin, "The Big Squeeze on Workers," *BusinessWeek*, May 13, 2002, www.businessweek.com on May 17, 2002; Nancy K. Austin, "Get Happy! Please," *Fortune*, May 1, 2002, www.fortune.com on May 17, 2002; Del Jones, "Firms Spend Billions to Fire Up Workers—With Little Luck," *USA Today*, May 10, 2001, p. 1A (quotation).

of money as a motivating factor cannot be dismissed, proponents of the scientific approach took too narrow a view of the role of monetary compensation and also failed to consider other motivational factors.

The human relations approach to motivation suggests that favorable employee attitudes result in motivation to work hard.

The Human Relations Approach   The **human relations approach,** also discussed in Chapter 1, assumed that employees want to feel useful and important, that employees have strong social needs, and that those needs are more important than money in motivating employees.[7] Advocates of the human relations approach advised managers to make workers feel important and allow them a modicum of self-direction and self-control in carrying out routine activities. The illusion of involvement and importance were expected to satisfy workers' basic social needs and result in higher motivation to perform. For example, a manager might allow a work group to participate in making a decision, even though he or she had already determined what the decision would be. The symbolic gesture of seeming to allow participation was expected to enhance motivation, even though no real participation took place.

The **human resource approach** to motivation assumes employees want and are able to make genuine contributions to the organization.

The Human Resource Approach   The **human resource approach** to motivation carries the concepts of needs and motivation one step further. Whereas the human relationists believed the illusion of contribution and participation would enhance motivation, the human resource view assumes the contributions themselves are valuable to both individuals and organizations. It asserts that people want to contribute and are able to make genuine contributions. Management's task, then, is to encourage participation and create a work environment that makes full use of the human resources available. This philosophy guides most contemporary thinking about employee motivation. At Ford, Westinghouse, Texas Instruments, and Hewlett-Packard, for example, work teams are being called on to solve a variety of problems and make substantive contributions to the organization.

Need-Based Perspectives on Motivation

LEARNING OBJECTIVE

Describe the need-based perspectives on motivation.

Need-based theories of motivation assume that need deficiencies cause behavior.

Maslow's **hierarchy of needs theory** assumes human needs are arranged in a hierarchy of importance.

Need-based perspectives represent the starting point for most contemporary thought on motivation, although these theories also attracted critics.[8] The basic premise of **need-based theories** and models, consistent with our motivation framework introduced earlier, is that humans are motivated primarily by deficiencies in one or more important needs or need categories. Need theorists have attempted to identify and categorize the needs that are most important to people. (Some observers call these *content theories* because they deal with the content, or substance, of what motivates behavior.) The best-known need theories are the hierarchy of needs, ERG, and dual-structure theories.

Hierarchy of Needs Theory

The **hierarchy of needs theory,** developed by psychologist Abraham Maslow in the 1940s, is the best-known need theory.[9] Influenced by the human relations school, Maslow argued that human beings are "wanting" animals: They have innate desires to satisfy a given set of needs. Furthermore, Maslow believed these needs are arranged in a hierarchy of importance, with the most basic needs at the foundation.

Figure 4.2 shows Maslow's hierarchy of needs. The three sets of needs at the bottom of the hierarchy are called *deficiency needs,* because they must be satisfied for the individual to be fundamentally comfortable. The top two sets of needs are termed *growth needs* because they focus on personal growth and development.

The most basic needs in the hierarchy are *physiological needs.* They include the needs for food, sex, and air. Next in the hierarchy are *security needs:* things that offer safety and security, such as adequate housing and clothing, and freedom from worry and anxiety. *Belongingness needs,* the third level in the hierarchy, are primarily social. Examples include the need for love and affection and the need to be accepted by peers. The fourth level, *esteem needs,* actually encompasses two slightly different kinds of needs: the need for a positive self-image and self-respect and the need to be respected by others. At the top of the hierarchy are *self-actualization needs.* These involve realizing one's full potential and becoming all that one can be.

Maslow believed each need level must be satisfied before the level above it can become important. Thus, once physiological needs have been satisfied, their importance diminishes, and security needs emerge as the primary sources of motivation. This escalation up the hierarchy continues until the self-actualization needs become the primary motivators. Suppose, for example, that Jennifer Wallace earns

FIGURE 4.2

The Hierarchy of Needs

Maslow's hierarchy of needs consists of five basic categories of needs. Of course, each individual has a wide variety of specific needs within each category.

all the money she needs and is very satisfied with her standard of living. Additional income may have little or no motivational impact on her behavior. Instead, Jennifer will strive to satisfy other needs, such as a desire for higher self-esteem.

However, if a previously satisfied lower-level set of needs becomes deficient again, the individual returns to that level. For example, suppose Jennifer unexpectedly loses her job. At first, she may not be too worried because she has savings and is confident she can find another good job. As her savings dwindle, however, she will become increasingly motivated to seek new income. Initially, she may seek a job that both pays well and satisfies her esteem needs. But as her financial situation grows increasingly grim, she may lower her expectations regarding esteem and instead focus almost exclusively on simply finding a job with a reliable paycheck.

In most businesses, physiological needs are probably the easiest to evaluate and to meet. Adequate wages, toilet facilities, ventilation, and comfortable temperatures and working conditions are measures taken to satisfy this most basic level of needs. Security needs in organizations can be satisfied by such things as job continuity (no layoffs), a grievance system (to protect against arbitrary supervisory actions), and an adequate insurance and retirement system (to guard against financial loss from illness and ensure retirement income).

Most employees' belongingness needs are satisfied by family ties and group relationships both inside and outside the organization. In the workplace, people usually develop friendships that provide a basis for social interaction and can play a major role in satisfying social needs. Managers can help satisfy these needs by fostering a sense of group identity and interaction among employees. At the same time, managers can be sensitive to the probable effects on employees (such as low performance and absenteeism) of family problems or lack of acceptance by coworkers. Esteem needs in the workplace are met at least partly by job titles, choice offices, merit pay increases, awards, and other forms of recognition. Of course, to be sources of long-term motivation, tangible rewards such as these must be distributed equitably and be based on performance.

Self-actualization needs are perhaps the hardest to understand and the most difficult to satisfy. For example, it is difficult to assess how many people completely meet their full potential. In most cases, people who are doing well on Maslow's hierarchy will have satisfied their esteem needs and will be moving toward self-actualization. Working toward self-actualization, rather than actually achieving it, may be the ultimate motivation for most people.

Research shows that the need hierarchy does not generalize very well to other countries. For example, in Greece and Japan, security needs may motivate employees more than self-actualization needs. Likewise, belongingness needs are especially important in Sweden, Norway, and Denmark. Research has also found differences in the relative importance of various needs in Mexico, India, Peru, Canada, Thailand, Turkey, and Puerto Rico.[10]

Maslow's need hierarchy makes a certain amount of intuitive sense. In addition, because it was the first motivation theory to become popular, it is also one of the best known among practicing managers. However, research has revealed a number of deficiencies in the theory. For example, five levels of needs are not always present, the actual hierarchy of needs does not always conform to Maslow's model, and need structures are more unstable and variable than the theory would lead us to believe.[11] Furthermore, managers' attempts to use a theory such as this one are often awkward or superficial. Thus, the theory's primary contribution seems to lie in providing a general framework for categorizing needs.

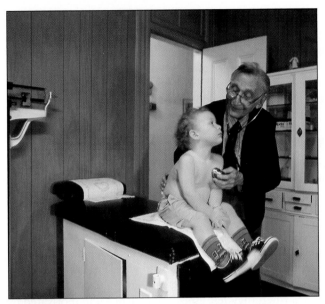

Need theories of motivation assume that need deficiencies cause behavior. Maslow's need hierarchy culminated with self-actualization needs, involving potential and fulfillment. For example, Dr. Salvator Altchek practiced medicine in Brooklyn for 67 years. For more than sixty of those years, he continued to make house calls and charged only $5 per visit for his services. Dr. Altchek clearly had all of the material possessions he needed and so chose to devote his life to helping others. Clearly, the needs that motivated this behavior had nothing to do with material things.

ERG Theory

ERG theory, developed by Yale psychologist Clayton Alderfer, is another historically important need theory of motivation.[12] In many respects, **ERG theory** extends and refines Maslow's needs hierarchy concept, although there are also several important differences between the two. The *E, R,* and *G* stand for three basic need categories: existence, relatedness, and growth. *Existence needs,* those necessary for basic human survival, roughly correspond to the physiological and security needs of Maslow's hierarchy. *Relatedness needs,* those involving the need to relate to others, are similar to Maslow's belongingness and esteem needs. Finally, *growth needs* are analogous to Maslow's needs for self-esteem and self-actualization.

ERG theory describes existence, relatedness, and growth needs.

In contrast to Maslow's approach, ERG theory suggests that more than one kind of need—for example, relatedness and growth needs—may motivate a person at the same time. A more important difference from Maslow's hierarchy is that ERG theory includes a satisfaction-progression component and a frustration-regression component. The satisfaction-progression concept suggests that after satisfying one category of needs, a person progresses to the next level. On this point, the need hierarchy and ERG theories agree. The need hierarchy model, however, assumes the individual remains at the next level until the needs at that level are satisfied. In contrast, the frustration-regression component of ERG theory suggests that a person who is frustrated by trying to satisfy a higher level of needs eventually will regress to the preceding level.[13]

Suppose Nick Hernandez has satisfied his basic needs at the relatedness level and now is trying to satisfy his growth needs. That is, he has many friends and social relationships, and now wants to learn new skills and advance in his career. For a variety of reasons, such as organizational constraints (few challenging jobs, a glass ceiling, etc.) and lack of opportunities to advance, he is unable to satisfy those needs. No matter how hard he tries, he seems stuck in his current position. According to ERG theory, frustration of his growth needs will cause Nick's relatedness needs to once again become dominant motivators. As a result, he will put renewed effort into making friends and developing social relationships.

Dual-Structure Theory

The **dual-structure theory** identifies motivation factors, which affect satisfaction, and hygiene factors, which determine dissatisfaction.

Another important need-based theory of motivation is the **dual-structure theory**, which in many ways is similar to the need theories just discussed. This theory was originally called the "two-factor theory," but the more contemporary name used here is more descriptive. Although few researchers today accept the theory, it has become widely known and accepted among practicing managers.

Development of the Theory   Frederick Herzberg and his associates developed the dual-structure theory in the late 1950s and early 1960s.[14] Herzberg began by interviewing approximately two hundred accountants and engineers in Pittsburgh. He asked them to recall times when they felt especially satisfied and motivated by their jobs and times when they felt particularly dissatisfied and unmotivated. He then asked them to describe what caused the positive and negative feelings. The responses to the questions were recorded by the interviewers and later subjected to content analysis. (In a content analysis, the words, phrases, and sentences respondents used are analyzed and categorized according to their meanings.)

To his surprise, Herzberg found that entirely different sets of factors were associated with the two kinds of feelings about work. For example, a person who indicated "low pay" as a source of dissatisfaction would not necessarily identify "high pay" as a source of satisfaction and motivation. Instead, people associated entirely different causes, such as recognition or achievement, with satisfaction and motivation. The findings led Herzberg to conclude that prevailing thinking about satisfaction and motivation was incorrect. As Figure 4.3 shows, at that time job satisfaction was viewed as a single construct ranging from satisfaction to dissatisfaction. If this were the case, Herzberg reasoned, one set of factors should influence movement back and forth along the continuum. But because his research had identified differential influences from two different sets of factors, Herzberg argued that two different dimensions must be involved. Thus, he saw motivation as a dual-structured phenomenon.

Figure 4.3 also illustrates the dual-structure concept that there is one dimension ranging from satisfaction to no satisfaction and another ranging from dissatisfaction to no dissatisfaction. The two dimensions presumably must be associated with the two sets of factors identified in the initial interviews. Thus, this theory proposed, employees might be either satisfied or not satisfied and, at the same time, dissatisfied or not dissatisfied.[15]

Motivation factors are intrinsic to the work itself and include factors such as achievement and recognition.

Hygiene factors are extrinsic to the work itself and include factors such as pay and job security.

In addition, Figure 4.3 lists the primary factors identified in Herzberg's interviews. **Motivation factors**, such as achievement and recognition, were often cited as primary causes of satisfaction and motivation. When present in a job, these factors apparently could cause satisfaction and motivation; when they were absent, the result was feelings of no satisfaction rather than dissatisfaction. The other set of factors, **hygiene factors**, came out in response to the question about dissatisfaction and lack of motivation. The respondents suggested that pay, job security, supervisors, and working conditions, if seen as inadequate, could lead to feelings of dissatisfaction. When these factors were considered acceptable, however, the person still was not

The Traditional View

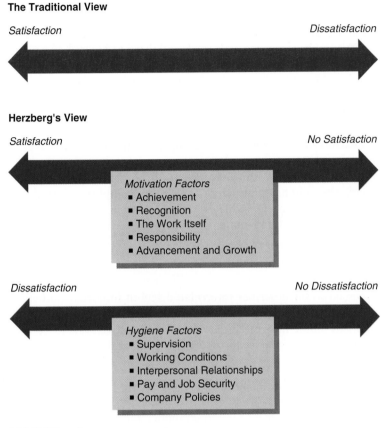

FIGURE 4.3

The Dual-Structure Theory of Motivation

The traditional view of satisfaction suggested that satisfaction and dissatisfaction are on opposite ends of a single dimension. Herzberg's dual-structure theory found evidence of a more complex view. In this theory, motivation factors affect one dimension, ranging from satisfaction to no satisfaction. Other workplace characteristics, called hygiene *factors, are assumed to affect another dimension, ranging from dissatisfaction to no dissatisfaction.*

necessarily satisfied; rather, he or she was simply not dissatisfied.[16]

To use the dual-structure theory in the workplace, Herzberg recommended a two-stage process. First, the manager should try to eliminate situations that cause dissatisfaction, which Herzberg assumed to be the more basic of the two dimensions. For example, suppose Susan Kowalski wants to use the dual-structure theory to enhance motivation in the group of seven technicians she supervises. Her first goal would be to achieve a state of no dissatisfaction by addressing hygiene factors. Imagine, for example, she discovers that their pay is a bit below market rates and a few are worried about job security. Her response would be to secure a pay raise for them and to allay their concerns about job security.

According to the theory, once a state of no dissatisfaction exists, trying to further improve motivation through hygiene factors is a waste of time.[17] At that point, the motivation factors enter the picture. Thus, when Susan is sure she has adequately dealt with hygiene issues, she should try to increase opportunities for achievement, recognition, responsibility, advancement, and growth. As a result, she would be helping her subordinates feel satisfied and motivated.

Unlike many other theorists, Herzberg described explicitly how managers could apply his theory. In particular, he developed and described a technique called *job enrichment* for structuring employee tasks.[18] (We discuss job enrichment in Chapter 5.) Herzberg tailored this technique to his key motivation factors. This unusual attention to application may explain the widespread popularity of the dual-structure theory among practicing managers.

Evaluation of the Theory   Because it gained popularity so quickly, the dual-structure theory has been scientifically scrutinized more closely than almost any other organizational behavior theory.[19] The results have been contradictory, to say the least. The initial study by Herzberg and his associates supported the basic premises of the theory, as did a few follow-up studies.[20] In general, studies that use the same methodology Herzberg did (content analysis of recalled incidents) tend to support the theory. However, this methodology has itself been criticized, and studies that use other methods to measure satisfaction and dissatisfaction frequently obtain results quite different from Herzberg's.[21] If the theory is "method bound," as it appears to be, its validity is therefore questionable.

Several other criticisms have been directed against the theory. Critics say the original sample of accountants and engineers likely does not represent the general working population. Furthermore, they maintain the theory fails to account for individual differences. Also, subsequent research has found that a factor such as pay may affect satisfaction in one sample and dissatisfaction in another, and that the effect of a given factor depends on the individual's age and organizational level. In addition, the theory does not define the relationship between satisfaction and motivation.

Research has also suggested that the dual-structure framework varies across cultures. Only limited studies have been conducted, but findings suggest that employees in New Zealand and Panama assess the impact of motivation and hygiene factors differently than U.S. workers.[22] It is not surprising, then, that the dual-structure theory is no longer held in high esteem by organizational behavior researchers. Indeed, the field has since adopted far more complex and valid conceptualizations of motivation, most of which we discuss later in this chapter. However, because of its initial popularity and its specific guidance for application, the dual-structure theory merits a special place in the history of motivation research.

Other Important Needs

Each theory discussed so far describes interrelated sets of important individual needs within specific frameworks. Several other key needs have been identified that are not allied with any single integrated theoretical perspective. The three most frequently mentioned needs are the needs for achievement, affiliation, and power.

The **need for achievement** is the desire to accomplish a task or goal more effectively than in the past.

The Need for Achievement   The **need for achievement** is most frequently associated with the work of David McClelland.[23] This need arises from an individual's desire to accomplish a goal or task more effectively than in the past. Individuals who have a high need for achievement tend to set moderately difficult goals and to make moderately risky decisions. Suppose Mark Cohen, a regional manager for a national retailer, sets a sales increase goal for his stores of either 1 percent or 50 percent. The first goal is probably too easy, and the second is probably impossible to reach; either would suggest a low need for achievement. But a mid-range goal of, say, 15 percent might present a reasonable challenge but also be within reach. Setting this goal may more accurately reflect a high need for achievement.

High-need achievers also want immediate, specific feedback on their performance. They want to know how well they did something as quickly after finishing it as possible. For this reason, high-need achievers frequently take jobs in sales, where they get almost immediate feedback from customers, and avoid jobs in areas such as research and development, where tangible progress is slower and feedback comes at longer intervals. If Mark Cohen asks his managers for their sales performance only on a periodic basis, he may not have a high need for achievement. But if he constantly calls each store manager in his territory to ask about their sales increases, this activity indicates a high need for achievement on his part.

Preoccupation with work is another characteristic of high-need achievers. They think about it on their way to the workplace, during lunch, and at home. They find it difficult to put their work aside, and they become frustrated when they must stop working on a partly completed project. If Mark Cohen seldom thinks about his business in the evening, he may not be a high-need achiever. However, if work is always on his mind, he may indeed be a high-need achiever.

Finally, high-need achievers tend to assume personal responsibility for getting things done. They often volunteer for extra duties and find it difficult to delegate part of a job to someone else. Accordingly, they derive a feeling of accomplishment

The need for achievement is the desire to accomplish a task or meet a goal more effectively than in the past. During the height of her tennis career, Martina Navratilova was the best and most feared player on earth. Her strong competitive drive recently prompted her to make a comeback at Wimbledon. Even though she did not fare well in her comeback attempt, her actions nevertheless reflect her strong need for achievement.

when they have done more work than their peers without the assistance of others. Suppose Mark Cohen visits a store one day and finds the merchandise is poorly displayed, the floor is dirty, and sales clerks don't seem motivated to help customers. If he has a low need for achievement, he may point the problems out to the store manager and then leave. But if his need for achievement is high, he may well stay in the store for a while, personally supervising the necessary changes.

Although high-need achievers tend to be successful, they often do not achieve top management posts. The most common explanation is that although high need for achievement helps these people advance quickly through the ranks, the traits associated with the need often conflict with the requirements of high-level management positions. Because of the amount of work they are expected to do, top executives must be able to delegate tasks to others. In addition, they seldom receive immediate feedback, and they often must make decisions that are either more or less risky than those with which a high-need achiever would be comfortable.[24] High-need achievers tend to do well as individual entrepreneurs with little or no group reinforcement. Steve Jobs, cofounder of Apple Computer, and Bill Gates, cofounder of Microsoft, are both recognized as being high-need achievers.

The **need for affiliation** is the need for human companionship.

The Need for Affiliation   Individuals also experience the **need for affiliation,** the need for human companionship.[25] Researchers recognize several ways in which people with a high need for affiliation differ from those with a lower need. Individuals with a high need tend to want reassurance and approval from others and usually are genuinely concerned about others' feelings. They are likely to act and think as they believe others want them to, especially those with whom they strongly identify and desire friendship. As we might expect, people with a strong need for affiliation most often work in jobs with a lot of interpersonal contact, such as sales and teaching positions.

Suppose Watanka Jackson is seeking a job as a petroleum field engineer, a job that will take her into remote areas for long periods of time with little interaction with coworkers. Aside from her academic training, one reason for the nature of her job search might be that she has a low need for affiliation. In contrast, a classmate of hers, William Pfeffer, may be seeking a job in the corporate headquarters of a petroleum company. His preferences might be dictated, at least in part, by a desire to be around other people in the workplace; he thus has a higher need for affiliation.

The **need for power** is the desire to control the resources in one's environment.

The Need for Power   A third major individual need is the **need for power,** the desire to control one's environment, including financial, material, informational, and human resources.[26] People vary greatly along this dimension. Some individuals spend much time and energy seeking power; others avoid power whenever possible. People with a high need for power can be successful managers if three conditions are met. First, they must seek power for the betterment of the organization rather than for their own interests. Second, they must have a fairly low need for affiliation, because fulfilling a personal need for power may alienate others in the workplace. Third, they need a great deal of self-control to curb their desire for power when it threatens to interfere with effective organizational or interpersonal relationships.[27]

Process-Based Perspectives on Motivation

Process-based perspectives on motivation deal with how motivation occurs. Rather than attempting to identify motivational stimuli, process perspectives focus on why people choose certain behavioral options to satisfy their needs and how they evaluate their satisfaction after they have attained those goals. Three useful process perspectives on motivation are the equity, expectancy, and goal-setting theories. We discuss the equity and expectancy theories here. Because of its much more applied focus, we cover goal-setting theory in Chapter 6.

Equity Theory of Motivation

The **equity theory** of motivation is based on the relatively simple premise that people in organizations want to be treated fairly.[28] The theory defines **equity** as the belief that one is being treated fairly in relation to others and *inequity* as the belief that one is being treated unfairly compared with others. Equity theory is just one of several theoretical formulations derived from social comparison processes. Social comparisons involve evaluating our own situation in terms of others' situations. In this chapter, we focus mainly on equity theory because it is the most highly developed of the social comparison approaches and the one that applies most directly to the work motivation of people in organizations.

Forming Equity Perceptions   People in organizations form perceptions about the equity of their treatment through a four-step process. First, they evaluate how they are being treated by the firm. Second, they assess how a "comparison-other" is being treated. The comparison-other might be a person in the same work group, someone in another part of the organization, or even a composite of several people throughout the organization.[29] Third, they compare their own circumstances with those of the comparison-other and use this comparison as the basis for forming an impression of either equity or inequity. Fourth, depending on the strength of this feeling, they may choose to pursue one or more of the alternatives discussed in the next section.

Equity theory describes the equity comparison process in terms of an input-to-outcome ratio. Inputs are an individual's contributions to the organization: such factors as education, experience, effort, and loyalty. Outcomes are what the person receives in return: pay, recognition, social relationships, intrinsic rewards, and similar things. In effect, then, this part of the equity process is essentially a personal assessment of one's psychological contract. A person's assessments of inputs and outcomes for both self and others are based partly on objective data (for example, the person's own salary) and partly on perceptions (such as the comparison-other's level of recognition). The equity comparison thus takes the following form:

$$\frac{\text{Outcome (self)}}{\text{Inputs (self)}} \text{ compared with } \frac{\text{Outcomes (other)}}{\text{Inputs (other)}}$$

If the two sides of this psychological equation are comparable, the person experiences a feeling of equity; if the two sides do not balance, a feeling of inequity results. We should stress, however, that a perception of equity does not require that the perceived outcomes and inputs be equal, only that their ratios be the same. A person may believe his comparison-other deserves to make more money because she works harder, thus making her higher ratio of outcome to input acceptable. Only if her outcomes seem disproportionate to her inputs does the comparison provoke a perception of inequity.

Responses to Equity and Inequity   Figure 4.4 summarizes the results of an equity comparison. If a person feels equitably treated, she is generally motivated to maintain the status quo. For example, she will continue to provide the same level of input to the organization as long as her outcomes do not change and the inputs and outcomes of the comparison-other do not change. But a person who is experiencing inequity, real or imagined, is motivated to reduce it. Moreover, the greater the inequity, the stronger the level of motivation.

There are six common methods to reduce inequity.[30] First, we may change our own inputs. Thus, we may put more or less effort into the job, depending on which way the inequity lies, as a way to alter our ratio. If we believe we are being underpaid, for example, we may decide not to work as hard.

Second, we may change our own outcomes. We might, for example, demand a pay raise, seek additional avenues for growth and development, or even resort to stealing as a way to "get more" from the organization. Or we might alter our perceptions of the value of our current outcomes, perhaps by deciding our present level of job security is greater and more valuable than we originally thought.

A third, more complex response is to alter our perceptions of ourselves and our behavior. After perceiving an inequity, for example, we may change our original self-assessment and decide we are really contributing less but receiving more than we originally believed. For example, we might decide we are not really working as many hours as we first thought—for instance, that some of our time spent in the office is really just socializing and not really contributing to the organization.

Fourth, we may alter our perception of the comparison-other's inputs or outcomes. After all, much of our assessment of other people is based on perceptions, and perceptions can be changed. For example, if we feel underrewarded, we may decide our comparison-other is working more hours than we originally believed—say, by coming in on weekends and taking work home at night.

Fifth, we may change the object of comparison. We might conclude, for instance, that the current comparison-other is the boss's personal favorite, is unusually lucky, or has special skills and abilities. A different person would thus provide a more valid basis for comparison. Indeed, we might change comparison-others fairly often.

FIGURE 4.4

Responses to Perceptions of Equity and Inequity

People form equity perceptions by comparing their situation with that of someone else. If they perceive equity, they are motivated to maintain the current situation. If they perceive inequity, they are motivated to use one or more of the strategies shown here to reduce the inequity.

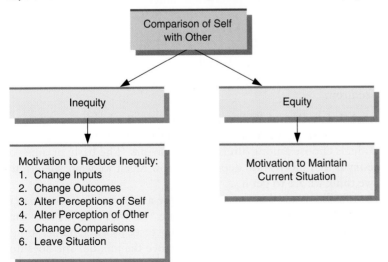

Finally, as a last resort, we may simply leave the situation; that is, we might decide that the only way to feel better about things is to be in a different situation altogether. Transferring to another department or seeking a new job may be the only way to reduce the inequity.

Evaluation and Implications   Most research on equity theory has been narrowly focused, dealing with only one ratio: between pay (hourly and piece-rate) and the quality or quantity of worker output given overpayment and underpayment.[31] Findings support the predictions of equity theory quite consistently, especially when the worker feels underpaid. When people being paid on a piece-rate basis experience inequity, they tend to reduce their inputs by decreasing quality and to increase their outcomes by producing more units. When a person paid by the hour experiences inequity, the theory predicts an increase in quality and quantity if he feels overpaid and a decrease in quality and quantity if he feels underpaid. Research provides stronger support for responses to underpayment than for responses to overpayment, but overall, most studies appear to uphold the basic premises of the theory. One interesting recent twist on equity theory suggests that some people are more sensitive than others to perceptions of inequity. That is, some people pay a good deal of attention to their relative standing within the organization. Others focus more on their own situation without considering others' situations.[32]

Social comparisons clearly are a powerful factor in the workplace. For managers, the most important implication of equity theory concerns organizational rewards and reward systems. Because "formal" organizational rewards (pay, task assignments, etc.) are more easily observable than "informal" rewards (intrinsic satisfaction, feelings of accomplishment, etc.), they are often central to a person's perceptions of equity.

Equity theory offers managers three messages. First, everyone in the organization needs to understand the basis for rewards. If people are to be rewarded more for high-quality work than for quantity of work, for instance, that fact needs to be clearly communicated to everyone. Second, people tend to take a multifaceted view of their rewards; they perceive and experience a variety of rewards, some tangible and others intangible. Finally, people base their actions on their perceptions of reality. If two people make exactly the same salary, but each thinks the other makes more, each will base his or her experience of equity on the perception, not the reality. Hence, even if a manager believes two employees are being fairly rewarded, the employees themselves may not necessarily agree if their perceptions differ from the manager's.

Expectancy Theory of Motivation

Expectancy theory is a more inclusive model of motivation than equity theory. Over the years since its original formulation, the theory's scope and complexity have continued to grow.

The Basic Expectancy Model   Victor Vroom is generally credited with first applying the theory to motivation in the workplace.[33] The theory attempts to determine how individuals choose among alternative behaviors. The basic premise of **expectancy theory** is that motivation depends on how much we want something and how likely we think we are to get it.

Expectancy theory suggests that people are motivated by how much they want something and the likelihood they perceive of getting it.

A simple example illustrates this premise. Suppose a recent college graduate is looking for her first managerial job. While scanning the want ads, she sees that Shell Oil is seeking a new executive vice president to oversee its foreign operations. The starting salary is $600,000. The student would love the job, but she does not

The expectancy theory of motivation suggests that people are motivated to pursue outcomes that they value and believe they have a reasonable chance to attain. Rock star Bono and Treasury Secretary Paul O'Neil toured impoverished areas of Africa together. The publicity generated by the odd couple—the anti-establishment rocker and the conservative government official—helped bring renewed attention to the poverty issue. In a nutshell, the two individuals saw a problem, decided how they could help address it, and then worked together to accomplish their goal.

bother to apply because she recognizes that she has no chance of getting it. Reading on, she sees a position that involves scraping bubble gum from underneath desks in college classrooms. The starting pay is $5.85 an hour, and no experience is necessary. Again, she is unlikely to apply; even though she assumes she could get the job, she does not want it.

Then she comes across an advertisement for a management training position with a large company known for being an excellent place to work. No experience is necessary, the primary requirement is a college degree, and the starting salary is $37,000. She will probably apply for this position because (1) she wants it and (2) she thinks she has a reasonable chance of getting it. (Of course, this simple example understates the true complexity of most choices. Job-seeking students may have strong geographic preferences, have other job opportunities, and also be considering graduate school. Most decisions of this type, in fact, are quite complex.)

Figure 4.5 summarizes the basic expectancy model. The model's general components are effort (the result of motivated behavior), performance, and outcomes. Expectancy theory emphasizes the linkages among these elements, which are described in terms of expectancies and valences.

Effort-to-performance expectancy is a person's perception of the probability that effort will lead to performance.

Effort-to-Performance Expectancy   **Effort-to-performance expectancy** is a person's perception of the probability that effort will lead to successful performance. If we believe our effort will lead to higher performance, this expectancy is very strong, perhaps approaching a probability of 1.0, where 1.0 equals absolute certainty that the outcome will occur. If we believe our performance will be the same

FIGURE 4.5

The Expectancy Theory of Motivation

The expectancy theory is the most complex model of employee motivation in organizations. As shown here, the key components of expectancy theory are effort-to-performance expectancy, performance-to-outcome expectancy, and outcomes, each of which has an associated valence. These components interact with effort, the environment, and the ability to determine an individual's performance.

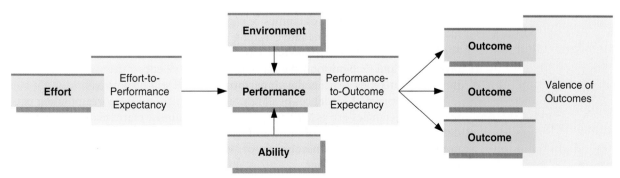

no matter how much effort we make, our expectancy is very low—perhaps as low as 0, meaning there is no probability that the outcome will occur. A person who thinks there is a moderate relationship between effort and subsequent performance—the normal circumstance—has an expectancy somewhere between 1.0 and 0. Mia Hamm, a star soccer player who believes she has a great chance of scoring higher than any opponent when she puts forth maximum effort, clearly sees a link between her effort and her performance.

Performance-to-Outcome Expectancy   **Performance-to-outcome expectancy** is a person's perception of the probability that performance will lead to certain other outcomes. If a person thinks a high performer is certain to get a pay raise, this expectancy is close to 1.0. At the other extreme, a person who believes raises are entirely independent of performance has an expectancy close to 0. Finally, if a person thinks performance has some bearing on the prospects for a pay raise, his or her expectancy is somewhere between 1.0 and 0. In a work setting, several performance-to-outcome expectancies are relevant because, as Figure 4.5 shows, several outcomes might logically result from performance. Each outcome, then, has its own expectancy. Green Bay quarterback Brett Favre may believe that if he plays aggressively all the time (performance), he has a great chance of leading his team to the playoffs. Playing aggressively may win him individual honors such as the Most Valuable Player award, but he may also experience more physical trauma and throw more interceptions. (All three anticipated results are outcomes.)

Outcomes and Valences   An **outcome** is anything that might potentially result from performance. High-level performance conceivably might produce such outcomes as a pay raise, a promotion, recognition from the boss—as well as fatigue, stress, or less break time—among others. The **valence** of an outcome is the relative attractiveness or unattractiveness—the value—of that outcome to the person. Pay raises, promotions, and recognition may all have positive valences, whereas fatigue, stress, and less break time may all have negative valences.

The strength of outcome valences varies from person to person. Work-related stress may be a significant negative factor for one person but only a slight annoyance to another. Similarly, a pay increase may have a strong positive valence for someone desperately in need of money; a slight positive valence for someone interested mostly in getting a promotion; or, for someone in an unfavorable tax position, even a negative valence!

The basic expectancy framework suggests that three conditions must be met before motivated behavior occurs. First, the effort-to-performance expectancy must be well above zero. That is, the worker must reasonably expect that exerting effort will produce high levels of performance. Second, the performance-to-outcome expectancies must be well above zero. Thus, the person must believe performance will realistically result in valued outcomes. Third, the sum of all the valences for the potential outcomes relevant to the person must be positive. One or more valences may be negative as long as the positives outweigh the negatives. For example, stress and fatigue may have moderately negative valences, but if pay, promotion, and recognition have very high positive valences, the overall valence of the set of outcomes associated with performance will still be positive.

Conceptually, the valences of all relevant outcomes and the corresponding pattern of expectancies are assumed to interact in an almost mathematical fashion to determine a person's level of motivation. Most people do assess likelihoods of and preferences for various consequences of behavior, but they seldom approach them in such a calculating manner.

Performance-to-outcome expectancy is an individual's perception of the probability that performance will lead to certain outcomes.

An **outcome** is anything that results from performing a particular behavior.

Valence is the degree of attractiveness or unattractiveness a particular outcome has for a person.

The Porter-Lawler Model   The original presentation of expectancy theory placed it squarely in the mainstream of contemporary motivation theory. Since then, the model has been refined and extended many times. Most modifications have focused on identifying and measuring outcomes and expectancies. An exception is the variation of expectancy theory developed by Lyman Porter and Edward Lawler. These researchers used expectancy theory to develop a novel view of the relationship between employee satisfaction and performance.[34] Although the conventional wisdom was that satisfaction leads to performance, Porter and Lawler argued the reverse: If rewards are adequate, high levels of performance may lead to satisfaction.

The Porter-Lawler model appears in Figure 4.6. Some of its features are quite different from the original version of expectancy theory. For example, the extended model includes abilities, traits, and role perceptions. At the beginning of the motivational cycle, effort is a function of the value of the potential reward for the employee (its valence) and the perceived effort-reward probability (an expectancy). Effort then combines with abilities, traits, and role perceptions to determine actual performance.

Performance results in two kinds of rewards. Intrinsic rewards are intangible: a feeling of accomplishment, a sense of achievement, and so forth. Extrinsic rewards are tangible outcomes such as pay and promotion. The individual judges the value of his or her performance to the organization and uses social comparison processes (as in equity theory) to form an impression of the equity of the rewards received. If the rewards are regarded as equitable, the employee feels satisfied. In subsequent cycles, satisfaction with rewards influences the value of the rewards anticipated, and actual performance following effort influences future perceived effort-reward probabilities.

FIGURE 4.6

The Porter-Lawler Model

The Porter-Lawler expectancy model predicts that satisfaction is determined by the perceived equity of intrinsic and extrinsic rewards for performance. That is, rather than satisfaction causing performance, which many people might predict, this model argues that it is actually performance that eventually leads to satisfaction.

REFERENCE: Figure from Porter, Lyman W., and Edward E. Lawler, *Managerial Attitudes and Performance*. Copyright © 1968. Reproduced by permission of Edward E. Lawler III.

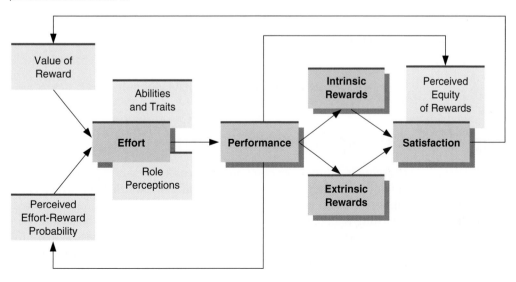

Evaluation and Implications   Expectancy theory has been tested by many researchers in a variety of settings and using a variety of methods.[35] As noted earlier, the complexity of the theory has been both a blessing and a curse.[36] Nowhere is this double-edged quality more apparent than in the research undertaken to evaluate the theory. Several studies have supported various parts of the theory. For example, both kinds of expectancy and valence have been found to be associated with effort and performance in the workplace.[37] Research has also confirmed expectancy theory's claims that people will not engage in motivated behavior unless they (1) value the expected rewards, (2) believe their efforts will lead to performance, and (3) believe their performance will result in the desired rewards.[38]

However, expectancy theory is so complicated that researchers have found it difficult to test. In particular, the measures of various parts of the model may lack validity, and the procedures for investigating relationships among the variables have often been less scientific than researchers would like. Moreover, people are seldom as rational and objective in choosing behaviors as expectancy theory implies. Still, the logic of the model, combined with the consistent, albeit modest, research support for it, suggests the theory has much to offer.

Research also suggests that expectancy theory is more likely to explain motivation in the United States than in other countries. People in the United States tend to be very goal oriented and to believe they can influence their own success. Thus, under the right combinations of expectancies, valences, and outcomes, they will be highly motivated. Different patterns may exist in other countries. For example, many people from Moslem countries believe God determines the outcome of every behavior; thus, the concept of expectancy is not applicable.[39]

Because expectancy theory is so complex, it is difficult to apply directly in the workplace. A manager would need to figure out what rewards each employee wants and how valuable those rewards are to each person, measure the various expectancies, and finally adjust the relationships to create motivation. Nevertheless, expectancy theory offers several important guidelines for the practicing manager. Following are some of the more fundamental guidelines:

1. Determine the primary outcomes each employee wants.
2. Decide what levels and kinds of performance are needed to meet organizational goals.
3. Make sure the desired levels of performance are possible.
4. Link desired outcomes and desired performance.
5. Analyze the situation for conflicting expectancies.
6. Make sure the rewards are large enough.
7. Make sure the overall system is equitable for everyone.[40]

Learning-Based Perspectives on Motivation

Learning is another key component in employee motivation. In any organization, employees quickly learn which behaviors are rewarded and which are ignored or punished. Thus, learning plays a critical role in maintaining motivated behavior. **Learning** is a relatively permanent change in behavior or behavioral potential that results from direct or indirect experience. For example, we can learn to use a new software application program by practicing and experimenting with its various functions and options.

Learning is a relatively permanent change in behavior or behavioral potential resulting from direct or indirect experience.

How Learning Occurs

Our understanding of how learning occurs has evolved from a simple and straightforward process to a much richer and more sophisticated one. The former is best represented by the traditional view, also called classical conditioning, while the latter is reflected in the contemporary view of learning as a cognitive process.

The Traditional View: Classical Conditioning   The most influential historical approach to learning is classical conditioning, developed by Ivan Pavlov in his famous experiments with dogs.[41] **Classical conditioning** is a simple form of learning that links a conditioned response with an unconditioned stimulus. In organizations, however, only simple behaviors and responses can be learned in this manner. For example, suppose an employee receives bad news one day from his boss. The employee could come to associate, say, the color of the boss's suit on that day with bad news. Thus, the next time the boss wears that suit to the office, the employee may experience dread.

This form of learning, however, is obviously simplistic and not directly relevant to motivation. Learning theorists soon recognized that although classical conditioning offered some interesting insights into the learning process, it was inadequate as an explanation of human learning. For one thing, classical conditioning relies on simple cause-and-effect relationships between one stimulus and one response; it cannot deal with the more complex forms of learned behavior that typify human beings. For another, classical conditioning ignores the concept of choice; it assumes behavior is reflexive, or involuntary. Therefore, this perspective cannot explain situations in which people consciously and rationally choose one course of action from among many. Because of these shortcomings of classical conditioning, theorists eventually moved on to other approaches that seemed more useful in explaining the processes associated with complex learning.

Classical conditioning is a simple form of learning that links a conditioned response with an unconditioned stimulus.

The Contemporary View: Learning as a Cognitive Process   Although not tied to a single theory or model, contemporary learning theory generally views learning as a cognitive process; that is, it assumes people are conscious, active participants in how they learn.[42]

First, the cognitive view suggests that people draw on their experiences and use past learning as a basis for their present behavior. These experiences represent knowledge, or cognitions. For example, an employee faced with a choice of job assignments will use previous experiences in deciding which one to accept. Second, people make choices about their behavior. The employee recognizes that she has two alternatives and chooses one. Third, people recognize the consequences of their choices. Thus, when the employee finds the job assignment rewarding and fulfilling, she will recognize that the choice was a good one and will understand why. Finally, people evaluate those consequences and add them to prior learning, which affects future choices. Faced with the same job choices next year, the employee will probably be motivated to choose the same one. As implied earlier, several perspectives on learning take a cognitive view. Perhaps foremost among them is reinforcement theory. Although reinforcement theory per se is not really new, it has been applied to organizational settings only in the last few years.

Reinforcement Theory and Learning

Reinforcement theory is based on the idea that behavior is a function of its consequences.

Reinforcement theory (also called *operant conditioning*) is generally associated with the work of B. F. Skinner.[43] In its simplest form, **reinforcement theory** suggests that behavior is a function of its consequences.[44] Behavior that results in pleasant consequences is more likely to be repeated (the employee will be motivated to repeat the current behavior), and behavior that results in unpleasant consequences is less likely to be repeated (the employee will be motivated to engage in different behaviors). Reinforcement theory also suggests that in any given situation, people explore a variety of possible behaviors. Future behavioral choices are affected by the consequences of earlier behaviors. Cognitions, as already noted, also play an important role. Therefore, rather than assuming the mechanical stimulus-response linkage suggested by the traditional classical view of learning, contemporary theorists believe people consciously explore different behaviors and systematically choose those that result in the most desirable outcomes.

Suppose a new employee at Monsanto in St. Louis wants to learn the best way to get along with his boss. At first, the employee is very friendly and informal, but the boss responds by acting aloof and, at times, annoyed. Because the boss does not react positively, the employee is unlikely to continue this behavior. In fact, he then starts acting more formal and professional, and finds the boss much more receptive to this posture. The employee will probably continue this new set of behaviors because they have resulted in positive consequences.

Types of Reinforcement in Organizations

Reinforcement is the consequences of behavior.

Positive reinforcement is a reward or other desirable consequence that a person receives after exhibiting behavior.

The consequences of behavior are called **reinforcement.** Managers can use various kinds of reinforcement to affect employee behavior. There are four basic forms of reinforcement: positive reinforcement, avoidance, extinction, and punishment.

Positive reinforcement is a reward or other desirable consequence that follows behavior. Providing positive reinforcement after a particular behavior motivates employees to maintain or increase the frequency of that behavior. A compliment from the boss after an employee has completed a difficult job and a salary increase following a worker's period of high performance are examples of positive reinforcement. This type of reinforcement has been used at Corning's ceramics factory in Virginia, where workers receive bonuses for pulling blemished materials from assembly lines before they go into more expensive stages of production.[45]

Avoidance, or negative reinforcement, is the opportunity to avoid or escape from an unpleasant circumstance after exhibiting behavior.

Avoidance, also known as **negative reinforcement,** is another means of increasing the frequency of desirable behavior. Rather than receiving a reward following a desirable behavior, the person is given the opportunity to avoid an unpleasant consequence. For example, suppose a boss habitually criticizes employees who dress casually. To avoid criticism, an employee may routinely dress to suit the supervisor's tastes. The employee is thus motivated to engage in desirable behavior (at least from the supervisor's viewpoint) to avoid an unpleasant, or aversive, consequence.

Extinction decreases the frequency of behavior by eliminating a reward or desirable consequence that follows that behavior.

Extinction decreases the frequency of behavior, especially behavior that was previously rewarded. If rewards are withdrawn for behaviors that were previously reinforced, the behaviors will probably become less frequent and eventually die out. For example, a manager with a small staff may encourage frequent visits from subordinates as a way to keep in touch with what is going on. Positive reinforcement might include cordial conversation, attention to subordinates' concerns, and encouragement to come in again soon. As the staff grows, however, the manager may find that such unstructured conversations make it difficult to get her own job done. She then might begin to brush off casual conversation and reward only to-the-point, "business" conversations. Withdrawing the rewards for casual chatting will probably extinguish that behavior. We should also note that if managers, inadvertently or otherwise, stop rewarding valuable behaviors such as good performance, those behaviors also may become extinct.

Positive reinforcement can be a powerful force in organizations and can help sustain motivated behaviors. But to really work, reinforcement must be of value to the individual and should conform to one of the five schedules, as discussed in the text. However, if someone is truly desperate for a pat on the back, a simple device such as the one shown here may have some hidden market potential.

© Harley L. Schwadron

Punishment is an unpleasant, or aversive, consequence that results from behavior.

Punishment, like extinction, also tends to decrease the frequency of undesirable behaviors. Punishment is an unpleasant, or aversive, consequence of a behavior.[46] Examples of punishment are verbal or written reprimands, pay cuts, loss of privileges, layoffs, and termination. Many experts question the value of punishment and believe managers use it too often and use it inappropriately. In some situations, however, punishment may be an appropriate tool for altering behavior. Many instances of life's unpleasantness teach us what to do by means of punishment. Falling off a bike, drinking too much, or going out in the rain without an umbrella all lead to punishing consequences (getting bruised, suffering a hangover, and getting soaked), and people often learn to change their behavior as a result. Furthermore, certain types of undesirable behavior may have far-reaching negative effects if they go unpunished. For instance, an employee who sexually harasses a coworker, a clerk who steals money from the petty cash account, and an executive who engages in illegal stock transactions all deserve punishment.

Schedules of reinforcement indicate when or how often managers should reinforce certain behaviors.

Schedules of Reinforcement in Organizations   Should the manager try to reward every instance of desirable behavior and punish every instance of undesirable behavior? Or is it better to apply reinforcement according to some plan or schedule? As you might expect, it depends on the situation. Table 4.1 summarizes five basic **schedules of reinforcement** managers can use.

With **continuous reinforcement**, behavior is rewarded every time it occurs.

Continuous reinforcement rewards behavior every time it occurs. Continuous reinforcement is a very effective motivator of desirable behaviors, especially in the early stages of learning. When reinforcement is withdrawn, however, extinction sets in very quickly. However, continuous reinforcement poses serious difficulties because the manager must monitor every behavior of an employee and provide effective reinforcement. This approach, then, is of little practical value to managers. Offering partial reinforcement according to one of the other four schedules is much more typical.

TABLE 4.1

Schedules of Reinforcement

Schedule of Reinforcement	Nature of Reinforcement
Continuous	Behavior is reinforced every time it occurs.
Fixed-Interval	Behavior is reinforced according to some predetermined, constant schedule based on time.
Variable-Interval	Behavior is reinforced after periods of time, but the time span varies from one time to the next.
Fixed-Ratio	Behavior is reinforced according to the number of behaviors exhibited, with the number of behaviors needed to gain reinforcement held constant.
Variable-Ratio	Behavior is reinforced according to the number of behaviors exhibited, but the number of behaviors needed to gain reinforcement varies from one time to the next.

Fixed-interval reinforcement provides reinforcement on a fixed time schedule.

Fixed-interval reinforcement is reinforcement provided on a predetermined, constant schedule. The Friday-afternoon paycheck is a good example of a fixed-interval reinforcement. Unfortunately, in many situations the fixed-interval schedule does not necessarily maintain high performance levels. If employees know the boss will drop by to check on them every day at 1:00 P.M., they may be motivated to work hard at that time, hoping to gain praise and recognition or to avoid the boss's wrath. At other times of the day, employees probably will not work as hard because they have learned reinforcement is unlikely except during the boss's daily visit.

Variable-interval reinforcement varies the amount of time between reinforcements.

Variable-interval reinforcement also uses time as the basis for applying reinforcement, but it varies the interval between reinforcements. This schedule is inappropriate for paying wages, but it can work well for other types of positive reinforcement, such as praise and recognition, and for avoidance. Consider the group of employees just described. Suppose that instead of coming by at exactly 1:00 P.M. every day, the boss visits at a different time each day: 9:30 A.M. on Monday, 2:00 P.M. on Tuesday, 11:00 A.M. on Wednesday, and so on. The following week, the times change. Because the employees do not know exactly when to expect the boss, they may be motivated to work hard for a longer period—until her visit. Afterward, though, they may drop back to lower levels because they have learned she will not be back until the next day.

Fixed-ratio reinforcement provides reinforcement after a fixed number of behaviors.

The fixed- and variable-ratio schedules gear reinforcement to the number of desirable or undesirable behaviors rather than to blocks of time. With **fixed-ratio reinforcement,** the number of behaviors needed to obtain reinforcement is constant. Assume a work group enters its cumulative performance totals into the firm's computer network every hour. The manager of the group uses the network to monitor its activities. He might adopt a practice of dropping by to praise the group every time it reaches a performance level of 500 units. Thus, if the group does this three times on Monday, he stops by each time; if it reaches the mark only once on Tuesday, he stops by only once. The fixed-ratio schedule can be fairly effective in maintaining desirable behavior. Employees may acquire a sense of what it takes to be reinforced and may be motivated to maintain their performance.

Variable-ratio reinforcement varies the number of behaviors between reinforcements.

With **variable-ratio reinforcement,** the number of behaviors required for reinforcement varies over time. An employee performing under a variable-ratio schedule is motivated to work hard because each successful behavior increases the probability that the next one will result in reinforcement. With this schedule, the exact number of behaviors needed to obtain reinforcement is not crucial; what is important is that the intervals between reinforcement not be so long that the worker gets discouraged and stops trying. The supervisor in the fixed-ratio example could reinforce his work group after it reaches performance levels of, say, 325, 525, 450, 600, and so on. A variable-ratio schedule can be quite effective, but it is difficult and cumbersome to use when formal organizational rewards, such as pay increases and promotions, are the reinforcers. A fixed-interval system is the best way to administer these rewards.

Social Learning in Organizations

In recent years, managers have begun to recognize the power of social learning. **Social learning** occurs when people observe the behaviors of others, recognize the consequences of those behaviors, and alter their own behaviors as a result. A person can learn to do a new job by observing others or by watching videotapes, or an employee may learn to avoid being late by seeing the boss chew out tardy coworkers. Social learning theory, then, suggests that individual behavior is determined by a person's cognitions and social environment. More specifically, people are presumed to learn behaviors and attitudes at least partly in response to what others expect of them.

> **Social learning** occurs when people observe the behaviors of others, recognize the consequences, and alter their own behaviors as a result.

Several conditions must be met to produce an appropriate environment for social learning. First, the behavior being observed and imitated must be relatively simple. Although we can learn by watching someone else how to push three or four buttons to set specifications on a machine or turn on a computer, we probably cannot learn a complicated sequence of operations for the machine or how to run a complex software package without also practicing the various steps ourselves. Second, social learning usually involves observed and imitated behavior that is concrete rather than intellectual. We can learn by watching others how to respond to the different behaviors of a particular manager or how to assemble a few component parts into a final assembled product. But we probably cannot learn through simple observation how to write computer software, how to write rich prose, how to conceptualize, or how to think abstractly. Finally, for social learning to occur, we must possess the physical ability to imitate the behavior observed. Most of us, even if we watch televised baseball games or tennis matches every weekend, cannot hit a fastball like Jason Giambi or execute a backhand like Venus Williams.

Social learning influences motivation in a variety of ways. Many of the behaviors we exhibit in our daily work lives are learned from others. Suppose a new employee joins an existing work group. She already has some basis for knowing how to behave from her education and previous experience. However, the group provides a set of very specific cues she can use to tailor her behavior to fit her new situation. The group may indicate how the organization expects its members to dress, how people are "supposed" to feel about the boss, and so forth. Hence, the employee learns how to behave in the new situation partly in response to what she already knows and partly in response to what others suggest and demonstrate.

Organizational Behavior Modification

Learning theory alone has important implications for managers, but organizational behavior modification has even more practical applications. Organizational behavior modification is an important application of reinforcement theory some managers use to enhance motivation and performance.

Organizational behavior modification, or **OB mod**, is the application of reinforcement theory to people in organizational settings.

Behavior Modification in Organizations   Organizational behavior modification, or OB mod, is the application of reinforcement theory to people in organizational settings.[47] Reinforcement theory says that we can increase the frequency of desirable behaviors by linking those behaviors with positive consequences and decrease undesirable behaviors by linking them with negative consequences. OB mod characteristically uses positive reinforcement to encourage desirable behaviors in employees. Figure 4.7 illustrates the basic steps in OB mod.

FIGURE 4.7

Steps in Organizational Behavior Modification

Organizational behavior modification involves using reinforcement theory to motivate employee behavior. By using the steps shown here, managers can often isolate behaviors they value and then link specific rewards to those behaviors. As a result, employees will be more likely to engage in those behaviors in the future.

Reference: "Steps in Organizational Behavior Modification," from *Personnel,* July–August 1974. Copyright ©1974 American Management Association. Reproduced with permission of American Management Association via Copyright Clearance Center.

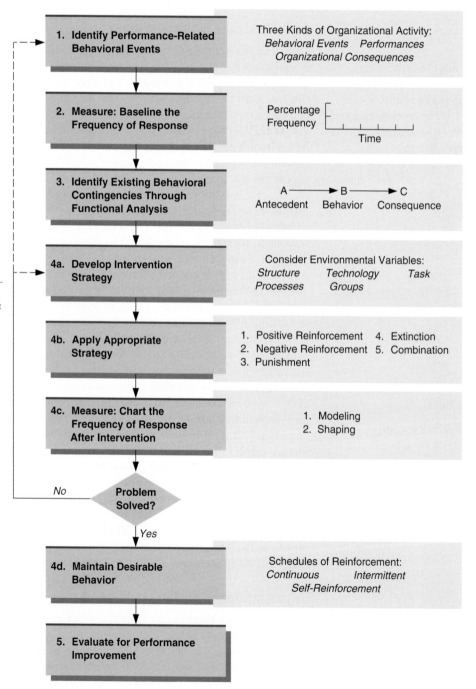

The first step is to identify performance-related behavioral events, that is, desirable and undesirable behaviors. A manager of an electronics store might decide that the most important behavior for salespeople working on commission is to greet customers warmly and show them the exact merchandise they came in to see. Note in Figure 4.7 that three kinds of organizational activity are associated with this behavior: the behavioral event itself, the performance that results, and the organizational consequences that befall the individual.

Next, the manager measures baseline performance, the existing level of performance for each individual. This is usually stated in terms of a percentage frequency across different time intervals. For example, the electronics store manager may observe that a particular salesperson presently is greeting around 40 percent of the customers each day as desired. Performance management techniques, described in Chapter 6, are used for this purpose.

The third step is to identify the existing behavioral contingencies, or consequences, of performance; that is, what happens now to employees who perform at various levels? If an employee works hard, does he or she get a reward or just get tired? The electronics store manager may observe that when customers are greeted warmly and assisted competently, they buy something 40 percent of the time, whereas customers who are not properly greeted and assisted make a purchase only 20 percent of the time.

At this point, the manager develops and applies an appropriate intervention strategy. In other words, some element of the performance-reward linkage—structure, process, technology, groups, or task—is changed to make high-level performance more rewarding. Various kinds of positive reinforcement are used to guide employee behavior in desired directions. The electronics store manager might offer a sales commission plan whereby salespeople earn a percentage of the dollar amount taken in by each sale. The manager might also compliment salespeople who give appropriate greetings and ignore those who do not. This reinforcement helps shape the salespeople's behavior. In addition, an individual salesperson who does not get reinforced may imitate the behavior of more successful salespeople. In general, this step relies on the reward system in the organization, as discussed previously.

After the intervention step, the manager again measures performance to determine whether the desired effect has been achieved. If not, the manager must redesign the intervention strategy or repeat the entire process. For instance, if the salespeople in the electronics store are still not greeting customers properly, the manager may need to look for other forms of positive reinforcement: perhaps a higher commission.

If performance has increased, the manager must try to maintain the desirable behavior through some schedule of positive reinforcement. For example, higher commissions might be granted for every other sale, for sales over a certain dollar amount, and so forth. (As we saw earlier, a reinforcement schedule defines the interval at which reinforcement is given.)

Finally, the manager looks for improvements in individual employees' behavior. Here the emphasis is on offering significant longer-term rewards, such as promotions and salary adjustments, to sustain ongoing efforts to improve performance.

The Effectiveness of OB Mod   Since the OB mod approach is relatively simple, many types of organizations have used it, with varying levels of success.[48] A program at Emery Air Freight prompted much of the initial enthusiasm for OB mod, and other success stories have caught the attention of practicing managers.[49] B. F. Goodrich increased productivity more than 300 percent, and Weyerhaeuser increased productivity by at least 8 percent in three different work groups.[50] These results suggest that OB mod is a valuable method for improving employee motivation in many situations.

OB mod also has certain drawbacks. For one thing, not all applications have worked. A program at Standard Oil of Ohio was discontinued because it failed to meet its objectives; another program at Michigan Bell was only modestly successful. In addition, managers frequently have only limited means for providing meaningful reinforcement for their employees. Furthermore, much of the research testing OB mod has gone on in laboratories and thus is hard to generalize to the real world. And even if OB mod works for a while, the impact of the positive reinforcement may wane once the novelty has worn off, and employees may come to view it as a routine part of the compensation system.[51]

The Ethics of OB Mod   Although OB mod has considerable potential to enhance motivated behavior in organizations, critics raise ethical issues about its use. The primary ethical argument is that use of OB mod compromises individual freedom of choice. Managers may tend to select reinforcement contingencies that produce advantages for the organization with little or no regard for what is best for the individual employee. Thus, workers may be rewarded for working hard, producing high-quality products, and so forth, while behaviors that promote their own personal growth and development or reduce their level of personal stress go unrewarded.

OB mod also involves an element of manipulation. Indeed, its very purpose is to shape the behaviors of others. Thus, rather than giving employees an array of behaviors from which to choose, managers may continually funnel employee efforts through an increasingly narrow array of behavioral options so that eventually workers have little choice but to select the limited set behaviors approved by managers.

These ethical issues are, of course, real concerns that should not be ignored. At the same time, many other methods and approaches used by managers have the same goal of shaping behavior. Thus, OB mod is not really unique in its potential for misuse or misrepresentation. The keys are for managers to recognize and not abuse their ability to alter subordinates' behavior and for employees to maintain control of their own work environment to the point where they are fully cognizant of the behavioral choices they are making.

Synopsis

Motivation is the set of forces that causes people to behave as they do. Motivation starts with a need. People search for ways to satisfy their needs and then behave accordingly. Their behavior results in rewards or punishment. To varying degrees, an outcome may satisfy the original need.

Scientific management asserted that money is the primary human motivator in the workplace. The human relations view suggested that social factors are primary motivators.

According to Abraham Maslow, human needs are arranged in a hierarchy of importance, from physiological to security to belongingness to esteem and, finally, to self-actualization. ERG theory is a refinement of Maslow's original hierarchy that includes

a frustration-regression component. In Herzberg's dual-structure theory, satisfaction and dissatisfaction are two distinct dimensions instead of opposite ends of the same dimension. Motivation factors are presumed to affect satisfaction and hygiene factors to affect dissatisfaction. Herzberg's theory is well known among managers but has several deficiencies. Other important individual needs include the needs for achievement, affiliation, and power.

The equity theory of motivation assumes that people want to be treated fairly. It hypothesizes that people compare their own input-to-outcome ratio in the organization with the ratio of a comparison-other. If they perceive their treatment has been inequitable, they take steps to reduce the inequity. Expectancy theory, a somewhat more complicated model, follows from the assumption that people are motivated to work toward a goal if they want it and think they have a reasonable chance to achieve it. Effort-to-performance expectancy is the belief that effort will lead to performance. Performance-to-outcome expectancy is the belief that performance will lead to certain outcomes. Valence is the desirability to the individual of the various possible outcomes of performance. The Porter-Lawler version of expectancy theory provides useful insights into the relationship between satisfaction and performance. This model suggests that performance may lead to a variety of intrinsic and extrinsic rewards. When perceived as equitable, these rewards lead to satisfaction.

Learning also plays a role in employee motivation. Various kinds of reinforcement provided according to different schedules can increase or decrease motivated behavior. People are affected by social learning processes. Organizational behavior modification is a strategy for using learning and reinforcement principles to enhance employee motivation and performance. This strategy relies heavily on the effective measurement of performance and the provision of rewards to employees after they perform at a high level.

Discussion Questions

1. Is it possible for someone to be unmotivated, or is all behavior motivated?

2. When has your level of performance been directly affected by your motivation? By your ability? By the environment?

3. Identify examples from your own experience that support, and others that refute, Maslow's hierarchy of needs theory.

4. Do you agree or disagree with the basic assumptions of Herzberg's dual-structure theory? Why?

5. How do you evaluate yourself in terms of your needs for achievement, affiliation, and power?

6. Have you ever experienced inequity in a job or a class? How did it affect you?

7. Which is likely to be a more serious problem: perceptions of being underrewarded or perceptions of being overrewarded? Explain.

8. What are some managerial implications of equity theory beyond those discussed in the chapter?

9. Do you think expectancy theory is too complex for direct use in organizational settings? Why or why not?

10. Do the relationships between performance and satisfaction suggested by Porter and Lawler seem valid? Cite examples that both support and refute the model.

11. Think of occasions on which you experienced each of the four types of reinforcement.

12. Identify the types of reinforcement you receive most often. On what schedule do you receive each type?

13. What is your opinion about the ethics of organizational behavior modification?

Organizational Behavior Case for Discussion

When Employees Are Owners

What do W. L. Gore (maker of Goretex), SAIC (a San Diego–based engineering firm), and Springfield Remanufacturing (an engine rebuilder created as a spin-off from International Harvester) have in common? One fundamental similarity is that each firm is owned by its employees. Unlike corporations with many public stockholders or most private firms, which are owned by one or a few individuals, employee-owned firms are private firms in which employees are the primary owners.

Employee ownership is not a new concept in the United States, where cooperatives have owned businesses since Revolutionary War times. During the early twentieth century, labor unions made such tremendous strides forward in improving working conditions and pay that there was little interest in employee ownership. In the 1970s, however, interest in employee ownership reemerged at least in part from the creation of employee stock ownership plans, which contribute company stock to retirement accounts. Twelve percent of the U.S. workforce—about 15 million individuals—have some company ownership, while the proportion of ownership ranges from less than 1 percent to 100 percent. Most employee-owned firms were previously profitable divisions of larger corporations that were sold to employees during a divestiture.

Publix Super Markets is a success story: It's the largest employee-owned firm in the United States, with 121,534 employees, 700 store locations in the Southeast, and annual sales of $15.9 billion. The firm has appeared on *Fortune*'s "100 Best Companies to Work For" list for the last seven years, is one of *Fortune*'s "Most Admired Companies," wins awards for supporting diversity and families, and, in 2002, ranked first in customer satisfaction in its industry. The firm attributes this remarkable success to the fact that it is 88 percent owned by employees. When the United Food and Commercial Workers Union (UFCW) recently tried to organize Publix workers, fewer than 20 percent voted in favor. "On their own time and at their own expense, our [employees] have campaigned against the UFCW . . . Their voices have now been heard," says Publix spokesperson Lee Brunson.

Employee ownership better aligns the interests of individual workers with the interests of the firm. Ownership also gives workers a sense of loyalty and commitment that is rare in today's uncertain corporate environments. According to Louise Brown, a Gore employee, "Nobody's afraid to jump in. Whenever you need to get the job done, people are always ready to do it." Other benefits of employee ownership include greater job security—Publix has never laid off an employee—and higher creativity. Worker loyalty translates into lower costs because productivity tends to be higher and turnover lower at employee-owned firms.

But there are some inherent risks in employee ownership as well. One potential problem is highlighted by the difficulties at United Airlines, which is 55 percent owned by employees. The company has had continuing struggles with labor unions, especially the powerful pilots' union. Recently, for example, the union's contract remained expired for more than a year before an agreement could be reached. Distrust and resentment from both management and labor continue at United in spite of employee ownership. United's experience contrasts sharply with that of Southwest Airlines, a firm known for its strong company loyalty, high productivity, and low turnover. The company is only 13 percent employee owned, but the organization culture motivates employees to feel a pride in ownership, which is greater than that felt by United's workers.

At Springfield Remanufacturing, managers found it important to educate workers about financial information. CEO Jack Stack organized weekly "huddles" in which all workers in the firm, from top managers to hourly wage earners, meet to discuss company data. "It's about truly understanding the business," says Stack. Workers learned to make use of cost data when making choices such as whether to repair or replace an engine part. Within three years, the firm's stock price soared from $0.10 to $13.60 per share, and 82 percent of that increase was owned by employees.

Virginia Vanderslice of Praxis Consulting claims that employee-owned firms can be high-performing organizations if the organization culture is participative and empowering. According to Vanderslice, neither participation nor ownership alone creates high performance; rather, the two must be used together. "At some point, employees in companies that have participation without ownership begin asking themselves: 'Why should I participate? What's in it for me?'" Corey Rosen, executive director of the National Center for Employee Ownership, says it's critical to give workers a meaningful stake in the company, whether it is ownership of shares or the opportunity to participate in decision making. Rosen advises workers, "What's really important is to have an influence on the way you do your day-to-day job."

Case Questions

1. Would employee ownership be considered a motivation factor or a hygiene factor according to Herzberg's dual-structure theory? Why?
2. What equity issues would relate to employee ownership?
3. Discuss the implications of expectancy theory for employee ownership.

References: "Awards," "Careers," "Facts and Figures," "News Room," Publix Super Markets website, www.publix.com on April 30, 2004; "History," The Worker-Ownership Institute website, www.workerownership.org, on April 30, 2004; Virginia Vanderslice, "Creating Ownership When You Already Have Participation," National Center for Employee Ownership website, www.nceo.org on April 29, 2004; Wendy Zellner, "We're All the Boss," *Time*, April 8, 2002, Inside Business Bonus pages (quotation).

Experiencing Organizational Behavior
Understanding the Dynamics of Expectancy Theory

Purpose: This exercise will help you recognize both the potential value and the complexity of expectancy theory.

Format: Working alone, you will be asked to identify the various aspects of expectancy theory that are pertinent to your class. You will then share your thoughts and results with some classmates.

Procedure: Considering your class as a workplace and your effort in the class as a surrogate for a job, do the following:

1. Identify six or seven things that might happen as a result of good performance in your class (for example, getting a good grade or a recommendation from your instructor). Your list must include at least one undesirable outcome (for example, a loss of free time).
2. Using a value of 10 for "extremely desirable," 210 for "extremely undesirable," and 0 for "complete neutrality," assign a valence to each outcome. In other words, the valence you assign to each outcome should be somewhere between 10 and 210, inclusive.
3. Assume you are a high performer. On that basis, estimate the probability of each potential outcome. Express this probability as a percentage.

4. Multiply each valence by its associated probability, and add the results. This total is your overall valence for high performance.
5. Assess the probability that if you exert effort, you will be a high performer. Express that probability as a percentage.
6. Multiply this probability by the overall valence for high performance calculated in step 4. This score reflects your motivational force—that is, your motivation to exert strong effort.

Now form groups of three or four. Compare your scores on motivational force. Discuss why some scores differ widely. Also, note whether any group members had similar force scores but different combinations of factors leading to those scores.

Follow-up Questions

1. What does this exercise tell you about the strengths and limitations of expectancy theory?
2. Would this exercise be useful for a manager to run with a group of subordinates? Why or why not?

Self-Assessment Exercise
Assessing Your Equity Sensitivity

The questions that follow are intended to help you better understand your equity sensitivity. Answer each question on the scales by circling the number that best reflects your personal feelings.

1. I think it is important for everyone to be treated fairly.
2. I pay a lot of attention to how I am treated in comparison to how others are treated.
3. I get really angry if I think I'm being treated unfairly.
4. It makes me uncomfortable if I think someone else is not being treated fairly.
5. If I thought I were being treated unfairly, I would be very motivated to change things.
6. It doesn't really bother me if someone else gets a better deal than I do.

7. It is impossible for everyone to be treated fairly all the time.
8. When I'm a manager, I'll make sure that all of my employees are treated fairly.
9. I would quit my job if I thought I was being treated unfairly.
10. Short-term inequities are okay because things all even out in the long run.

Instructions: Add up your total points (note that some items have a "reversed" numbering arrangement). If you scored 35 or higher, you are highly sensitive to equity and fairness; if 15 or lower, you have very little sensitivity to equity and fairness; if between 35 and 15, you have moderate equity sensitivity.

OB Online

1. Use a search engine to locate websites that deal with such topics as human needs and motivation. Then discuss how the information you found relates to this chapter.

2. Find two websites that discuss Frederick Taylor and his work. Then explain how they relate to the discussion in this chapter.

3. Find a website that discusses Herzberg's theory. Determine whether the site presents a positive, negative, or balanced assessment.

4. Use a search engine to find more information about the need for achievement, affiliation, or power. Then discuss how the information you found relates to this chapter.

Building Managerial Skills

Exercise Overview: Interpersonal skills—the ability to understand and motivate individuals and groups—are especially critical when managers attempt to deal with issues regarding equity and justice in the workplace. This exercise will help you gain insights into how these skills may be used.

Exercise Background: You are the manager of a group of professional employees in the electronics industry. One of your employees, David Brown, has asked to meet with you. You think you know what David wants to discuss, and you are unsure about how to proceed.

You hired David about ten years ago. During his time in your group, he has been a solid, but not an outstanding, employee. His performance, for example, has been satisfactory in every respect, but seldom outstanding. As a result, he has consistently received average performance evaluations, pay increases, and so forth. Indeed, he actually makes a somewhat lower salary today than do a few people in the group with less tenure but stronger performance records.

The company has just announced an opening for a team leader position in your group, and you know

David wants the job. He believes he has earned the opportunity to get the job on the basis of his consistent efforts. Unfortunately, you see things a bit differently. You really want to appoint another individual, Becky Thomas, to the job. Becky has worked for the firm for only six years, but she is your top performer. You want to reward her performance and think she will do an excellent job. On the other hand, you do not want to lose David because he is a solid member of the group.

Exercise Task: Using the previous information, answer the following questions:

1. Using equity theory as a framework, how do you think David and Becky are likely to see the situation?

2. Outline a conversation with David in which you will convey your decision to him.

3. What advice might you offer Becky in her new job? About interacting with David?

4. What other rewards might you offer David to keep him motivated?

TEST PREPPER

ACE self-test

You have read the chapter and studied the key terms, and the exam is any day now. Think you're ready to ace it? Take this sample test to gauge your comprehension of chapter material. You can check your answers at the back of the book. Want more test questions? Visit the student website at http://college.hmco.com/business/students/ (select Griffin/Moorhead, Fundamentals of Organizational Behavior 1e) and take the ACE quizzes for more practice.

1. **T F** Motivation is a person's belief system regarding what is right and wrong.

2. **T F** Performance depends on motivation, ability, and the environment.

3. **T F** Frederick Taylor, the founder of scientific management, thought money is the only thing that motivates people.

4. **T F** According to Maslow's hierarchy of needs, people will attempt to fulfill self-actualization needs before they will attempt to fulfill belongingness needs.

5. **T F** According to dual-structure theory, managers should first attempt to satisfy hygiene factors before trying to increase motivating factors.

6. **T F** Elaine is preoccupied with work, makes moderately risky decisions, and tries to accomplish goals more effectively than in the past. Elaine has a high need for power.

7. **T F** Cheryl wants reassurance and approval from others and is genuinely concerned about others' feelings. Cheryl has a high need for affiliation.

8. **T F** When people make an equity comparison, the other person with whom they compare themselves is always a coworker.

9. **T F** Inequity may prompt lower or higher effort on the job.

10. **T F** The basic premise of expectancy theory is that our motivation depends on how much we want something and how likely we think we are to get it.

11. **T F** If Pam believes she can reach a high level of performance and knows rewards are attached to that level of performance, she will be motivated to perform even if she finds the rewards unattractive.

12. **T F** Threatening to punish a person for poor performance in the hope that it will motivate him or her to perform well is an example of negative reinforcement.

13. **T F** When a software firm introduced a new version of its program, it stopped paying employees to answer customers' questions about the prior version. This is an example of extinction.

14. **T F** Continuous reinforcement is fairly uncommon in organizations.

15. **T F** In a fixed-ratio schedule of reinforcement, employees are rewarded after they have reached a preset quantity of performance.

16. **T F** Social learning works for behaviors employees cannot actually see.

17. **T F** Organizational behavior modification is based on a combination of expectancy and equity theories.

18. Frank manages a group of employees who are highly motivated. He has created a work environment in which his employees have all the materials, equipment, and information to do their jobs. Still, his employees' performance is rather low. Which of the following would most likely ensure higher performance?
    - a. Greater challenge
    - b. Better benefits
    - c. Shorter working hours
    - d. Higher employee ability
    - e. Increased wages

19. Which management approach assumes people want to contribute and are able to make genuine contributions?
    - a. Traditional approach (i.e., scientific management)
    - b. Human relations approach
    - c. Human resource approach
    - d. Hierarchy of needs approach
    - e. Self-actualization approach

20. Anna earns enough in her job to take care of her basic needs, such as rent and groceries. She also feels relatively safe in her job and expects to work at the company for at least the immediate future. According to Maslow's hierarchy of needs, which of the following need will Anna next attempt to satisfy?
    - a. Becoming all that she can be
    - b. Improving her self-image
    - c. Being respected by others
    - d. Feeling accepted by her peers
    - e. Increasing her self-respect

21. If you wanted to implement Herzberg's dual-structure theory at work, which of the following would you do first?
    a. Add elements to increase employee satisfaction
    b. Remove elements that cause employee dissatisfaction
    c. Increase employees' abilities
    d. Create effective work environments
    e. Develop a persuasive motivational style

22. Which type of worker will set moderately difficult goals, want immediate, specific feedback on performance, and accept personal responsibility for getting things done?
    a. An employee with a high need for affiliation
    b. An employee with a high need for power
    c. An employee with a high need for achievement
    d. An employee with a high need for security
    e. An employee with a high need for self-actualization

23. Mike has a bachelor's degree in management and has worked in his current position for three years. An intern who has not yet graduated from college is working at Mike's company for the summer and is paid an hourly wage near Mike's. Mike, of course, feels unfairly treated. According to equity theory, what is Mike's most likely course of action?
    a. Mike will quit.
    b. Mike will decide his inputs are more valuable.
    c. Mike will decide the inputs of the intern are less valuable.
    d. Mike won't work as hard.
    e. Mike will focus on the intern as his sole object of comparison.

24. According to expectancy theory, a person's motivation will be based on all of the following except
    a. the person's perception that effort will lead to successful performance.
    b. the person's perception that performance will lead to certain outcomes.
    c. the outcomes that are linked to performance are attractive.
    d. the person's perception that the process for determining rewards is fair.
    e. All of the above are the basis for motivation in expectancy theory.

25. The premise that behavior is a function of its consequences forms the basis of
    a. reinforcement theory.
    b. Maslow's hierarchy of needs.
    c. equity theory.
    d. classical conditioning.
    e. expectancy theory.

26. Every time Joan tells a joke during a staff meeting, everyone laughs. After several weeks, Joan's supervisor decides the joke telling has become distracting and asks the staff to avoid laughing at Joan's jokes. Joan's supervisor is using which form of reinforcement?
    a. positive
    b. negative
    c. extinction
    d. punishment
    e. classical

27. If you were trying to motivate an employee to perform a new, desirable behavior, which schedule of reinforcement might you use initially?
    a. Continuous
    b. Fixed-interval
    c. Variable-interval
    d. Fixed-ratio
    e. Variable-ratio

28. What is the disadvantage of rewards given on a fixed-interval schedule of reinforcement?
    a. Employees do not know when the rewards will be given.
    b. Fixed-interval schedules do not necessarily maintain high performance levels.
    c. Employees may not understand the frequency of the rewards.
    d. Such rewards are difficult for organizations to administer.
    e. Fixed-interval schedules are the most expensive form of reinforcement.

29. Which of the following behaviors would most likely be acquired by social learning?
    a. Writing the program for a new software package
    b. Troubleshooting a faulty aircraft engine
    c. Solving a complex math problem
    d. Arriving to meetings on time
    e. Mastering public speaking

30. It is important to measure the existing level of performance of an employee to accurately implement which technique?
    a. Hierarchy of needs
    b. Need for power
    c. Expectancy theory
    d. Social learning
    e. Organizational behavior modification

31. What ethical issue is related to OB mod?
    a. OB mod is not effective.
    b. The cost of OB mod outweighs the benefits.
    c. Unions prohibit the use of OB mod.
    d. An element of manipulation is involved in OB mod.
    e. Most managers refuse to use OB mod.

CHAPTER 5

Job Design and Work Structures

MANAGEMENT PREVIEW

Managers determine what jobs will be performed in their organizations and how those jobs will be performed. Managers must also determine how to motivate people and how to optimize their performance. The long-term key to success in business is to create jobs that optimize the organization's requirements for productivity and efficiency while simultaneously motivating and satisfying the employees who perform those jobs. As people and organizations change, and as we continue to learn more about management, it is important to look back occasionally at those jobs and make whatever changes are necessary to improve them. This chapter is the first of two that address the strategies managers use to optimize employees' performance. We begin with a discussion of job design, starting with a look at historical approaches to job design. Then we discuss an important contemporary perspective on jobs, the job characteristics theory. Next, we review the importance of employee participation and empowerment. Finally, we discuss alternative work arrangements that can be used to enhance motivation and performance.

After you have studied this chapter, you should be able to:

☐ *Explain the relationship between motivation and employee performance.*
☐ *Discuss job design, including its evolution and alternative approaches.*
☐ *Describe the relationship among participation, empowerment, and motivation.*
☐ *Identify and describe key alternative work arrangements.*

We first look at some contemporary approaches to changing jobs to improve organizational flexibility.

Firms in today's economy face myriad challenges, including mergers and acquisitions, layoffs, plant closures, outsourcing, and globalization. Manufacturing firms have been especially hard hit by the changes, losing 1.9 million jobs in the United States between 1999 to 2003. In this volatile environment, companies must reduce expenses, but they also recognize that repeated cycles of hiring and firing drive workers out of the industry, costing firms more in the long run. "It's important to have a skill base and good, loyal people who already know the company," says Richard Dillard, director of public affairs at Milliken & Company. To cope with hiring uncertainty, many firms are adapting by increasing job flexibility.

Each business must develop a customized approach to implementing job flexibility that best fits its needs. For example, the South Carolina Nestlé plant keeps a roster of part-time workers who can be called into work on a daily basis. Lincoln Electric, a Cleveland-based maker of welding equipment, moves workers between manufacturing positions and even into clerical jobs, paying different rates for each assignment. When Lincoln's sales declined in 2001, production supervisors moved into desk jobs. John Stropki, Lincoln's president of North American operations, says, "We pay [workers] for the job they are doing, not the job they used to do." Crown Mold and Machine transfers workers between day and night shifts at its Ohio fiberglass-mold factory. A & R Welding of Atlanta sends younger, unmarried welders to out-of-state projects when local demand is slack. The Ohio plant of Blackhawk Automotive Plastics cross-trains employees to operate any of its plastic-forming machinery. "We're continually re-fining the process and reallocating people," explains Clifford Croley, a Blackhawk owner. When Milliken & Company closed a textile factory, laying off 190 employees in South Carolina, it re-hired about 70 for nearby locations.

Employers appreciate the benefits of flexible job arrangements, including lower costs, less need for rehiring and retraining after a downsizing, and greater ease in scheduling staff. For workers, however, the reality is not always positive. Employees appreciate having more time to spend with family and benefits continuity, but fear loss of seniority or pay. Rick Willard, a thirty-year Lincoln veteran, made $20 an hour until his plant was sold. Today Lincoln is train-ing him for a new job, and he is working longer while earning 40 percent less. Willard says, "Some people resent being moved. I was just worried [about] what type of job I would have. [Retraining is] good for the company. Sometimes it's good for the employees." It remains un-clear whether internal flexibility works for all firms, but it seems to work best in manufactur-ing organizations. Economists Peter Cappelli and David Neumark, working with the National Bureau of Economic Research in 1999, found that only in manufacturing firms did the use of job flexibility reduce turnover.

Companies will no doubt continue to look for ways to increase their adaptability to change, and that could be a good thing for workers. E. Jeffrey Hill, research associate for Brigham Young University's Family Studies Department, takes a positive approach: "As compa-nies offer flexibility, . . . and more individuals use that flexibility, the work-family imbalance that was problematic for employees in the twilight of the twentieth century can become the bal-ance so many seek in the twenty-first century."

"It's important to have a skill base and good loyal people who already know the company."—Richard Dillard, director of public affairs, Milliken & Company

References: E. Jeffrey Hill, "Flexible Schedules Help Employees Work More Without Complaint," Brigham Young University, May 19, 2001, www.newswise.com on May 5, 2002; Clare Ansberry, "In the New Workplace, Jobs Morph to Suit Rapid Pace of Change," *Wall Street Journal*, March 22, 2002, pp. A1–A7; Peter Cappelli and David Neumark, "External Job Churning and Internal Job Flexibility," National Bureau of Economic Research, Working Paper No. w8111, February 2001, www.papers.nber.org on May 2, 2002.

Not all jobs are suitable for cross-training and frequent rotations in assign-ments, and certainly many workers have mixed feelings about such arrange-ments. But the very fact that some businesses are using this strategy under-scores the growing need for flexibility in the workplace. In the discussion that follows, we explore many of these problems and issues in more detail. First, we will examine a general framework that can guide managers as they attempt to put into practice the various need- and process-based theories of motivation.

Motivation and Employee Performance

Chapter 4 described a variety of perspectives on motivation. However, no single theory or model completely explains motivation; each covers only some of the factors that actually result in motivated behavior. Moreover, even if one theory were applicable in a particular situation, a manager might still need to translate that theory into operational terms. Thus, while using the actual theories as tools, managers need to understand various operational procedures, systems, and methods for enhancing motivation and performance.

Figure 5.1 illustrates a basic framework for relating various theories of motivation to potential and actual motivation and to operational methods for translating this potential and actual motivation into performance. The left side of the figure illustrates that motivated behavior can be induced by need-based or process-based circumstances. That is, people may be motivated to satisfy various specific needs or through various processes such as perceptions of inequity, expectancy relationships, and reinforcement contingencies.

These need-, process-, and learning-based concepts result in the situation illustrated in the center of the figure: A certain potential exists for motivated behavior directed at enhanced performance. For example, suppose an employee wants more social relationships; that is, he wants to satisfy belongingness, relatedness, or affiliation needs. This means there is potential for the employee to want to

FIGURE 5.1

Enhancing Performance in Organizations

Managers can use a variety of methods to enhance organizational performance. The need- and process-based perspectives on motivation explain some of the factors involved in increasing the potential for motivated behavior directed at enhanced performance. Managers can then use such means as goal setting, job design, alternative work arrangements, performance management, rewards, and organizational behavior modification to help translate this potential into actual enhanced performance.

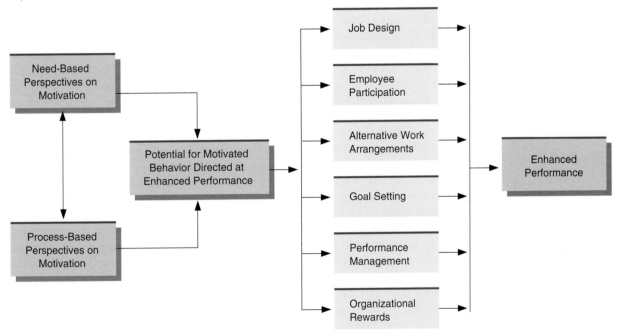

perform at a higher level if he thinks higher performance will satisfy those social needs. Likewise, if an employee's high performance in the past was followed by strong positive reinforcement, a potential exists for motivation directed at enhanced performance.

Managers may need to take certain steps to translate the potential for motivation directed at enhanced performance into real motivation and real enhanced performance. In some cases, these steps may be tied to the specific need or process that created the existing potential. For example, providing more opportunities for social interaction contingent on improved performance might capitalize on an employee's social needs. More typically, however, a manager needs to go further to help translate potential into real performance.

The right side of Figure 5.1 names some of the more common methods used to enhance performance. This chapter covers the first three: job design, employee participation and empowerment, and alternative work arrangements. The other three—goal setting, performance management, and organizational rewards—are discussed in Chapter 6.

Job Design in Organizations

Job design is how organizations define and structure jobs.

Job specialization, as advocated by scientific management, can help improve efficiency, but it can also promote monotony and boredom.

Job design is an important method managers can use to enhance employee performance.[1] **Job design** is how organizations define and structure jobs. As we will see, properly designed jobs can have a positive impact on the motivation, performance, and job satisfaction of those who perform them. On the other hand, poorly designed jobs can impair motivation, performance, and job satisfaction. The first widespread model of job design was job specialization.

Job Specialization

Frederick W. Taylor, the chief proponent of **job specialization,** argued that jobs should be scientifically studied, broken down into small component tasks, and then standardized across all workers doing those jobs.[2] Taylor's view grew from the historical writings about division of labor advocated by Scottish economist Adam Smith. In practice, job specialization generally brought most, if not all, of the advantages its advocates claimed. Specialization paved the way for large-scale assembly lines and was at least partly responsible for the dramatic gains in output U.S. industry achieved for several decades after the turn of the century.

On the surface, job specialization appears to be a rational and efficient way to structure jobs. The jobs in many factories, for instance, are highly specialized and are often designed to maximize productivity. In practice, however, performing those jobs can cause problems, particularly the extreme monotony of highly specialized tasks. Consider the job of assembling toasters. A person who does the entire assembly may find the job complex and challenging, albeit inefficient. If the job is specialized so that the worker simply inserts a heating coil into the toaster as it passes along on an assembly line, the process may be efficient, but it is unlikely to interest or challenge the worker. A worker numbed by boredom and monotony may be less motivated to work hard and more inclined to do poor-quality work or complain about the job. For these reasons, managers began to search for job design alternatives to specialization.

One primary catalyst for this search was a famous study of jobs in the automobile industry. The purpose of this study was to assess how satisfied automobile workers were with various aspects of their jobs.[3] The workers indicated they were

Job specialization is still a cornerstone of work design in many sectors of the economy. While traditionally found in assembly line production settings such as automobile plants, the service sector has also found uses for job specialization. Most call centers, such as this one, rely heavily on specialization. When calling an airline for reservations, for example, most consumers first select from an automated menu of services such as domestic flights, international flights, frequent-flyer reward travel, and so forth. The caller is then routed to the specialist in that area.

reasonably satisfied with their pay, working conditions, and the quality of their supervision. However, they expressed extreme dissatisfaction with the actual work they did. The plants were very noisy, and the moving assembly line dictated a rigid, grueling pace. Jobs were highly specialized and standardized.

The workers complained about six facets of their jobs: mechanical pacing by an assembly line, repetitiveness, low skill requirements, involvement with only a portion of the total production cycle, limited social interaction with others in the workplace, and lack of control over the tools and techniques used in the job. These sources of dissatisfaction were a consequence of the job design prescriptions of scientific management. Thus, managers began to recognize that although job specialization might lead to efficiency, it would have a number of negative consequences if carried too far.[4]

Early Alternatives to Job Specialization

In response to the automobile plant study, other reported problems with job specialization, and a general desire to explore ways to create less monotonous jobs, managers began to seek alternative methods to design jobs. Managers initially formulated two alternative approaches: job rotation and job enlargement.

Job rotation involves systematically moving workers from one job to another to minimize monotony and boredom.

Job Rotation   **Job rotation** involves systematically shifting workers from one job to another to sustain their motivation and interest. Under specialization, each task is broken down into small parts. For example, assembling prestige writing pens, such as those made by Mont Blanc or Cross, might involve four discrete steps: testing the ink cartridge, inserting the cartridge into the barrel of the pen, screwing the cap onto the barrel, and inserting the assembled pen into a box. One worker might perform step 1, another step 2, and so forth. When job rotation is introduced, the tasks themselves stay the same but the workers who perform them are systematically rotated across the various tasks. Jones, for example, starts out with task 1 (testing ink cartridges). On a regular basis—perhaps weekly or monthly—she is systematically rotated to task 2, to task 3, to task 4, and back to task 1. Gonzalez, who starts out on task 2 (inserting cartridges into barrels), rotates ahead of Jones to tasks 3, 4, 1, and back to 2. Numerous firms have used job rotation, including American Cyanamid, Baker Hughes, Ford, and Prudential Insurance.

Job rotation did not entirely live up to its expectations, however.[5] The problem again was narrowly defined, routine jobs. If a rotation cycle takes workers through the same old jobs, the workers simply experience several routine and boring jobs instead of just one. Although a worker may begin each job shift with a bit of renewed interest, the effect usually is short-lived. Job rotation may also decrease efficiency. For example, it clearly sacrifices the proficiency and expertise that grow from specialization.

At the same time, job rotation is an effective training technique because a worker rotated through a variety of related jobs acquires a larger set of job skills. Thus, there is increased flexibility in transferring workers to new jobs. Many U.S. firms now use job rotation for training or other purposes, but few rely on it to motivate workers. Pilgrim's Pride, one of the largest chicken-processing firms in the United States, uses job rotation, but not for motivation. Because workers in a chicken-processing plant are subject to cumulative trauma injuries such as carpel tunnel syndrome, managers at Pilgrim's believe that rotating workers across different jobs can reduce these injuries.[6]

Job enlargement involves giving workers more tasks to perform.

Job Enlargement   **Job enlargement,** or *horizontal job loading*, entails expanding a worker's job to include tasks previously performed by other workers. For instance, if job enlargement were introduced at a Cross pen plant, the four tasks noted earlier might be combined into two "larger" ones. Hence, one set of workers might each test cartridges and then insert them into barrels (old steps 1 and 2); another set of workers might then attach caps to the barrels and put the pens into boxes (old steps 3 and 4). The logic behind this change is that the increased number of tasks in each job reduces monotony and boredom.

Maytag was one of the first companies to use job enlargement.[7] In the assembly of washing machine water pumps, for example, jobs done sequentially by six workers at a conveyor belt were modified so that each worker completed an entire pump alone. Other organizations that implemented job enlargement include AT&T, the U.S. Civil Service, and Colonial Life Insurance Company.

Unfortunately, job enlargement also failed to have the desired effects. Generally, if the entire production sequence consisted of simple, easy-to-master tasks, merely doing more of them did not significantly change the worker's job. If the task of putting two bolts on a piece of machinery was "enlarged" to putting on three bolts and connecting two wires, for example, the monotony of the original job essentially remained.

Job Enrichment

Job rotation and job enlargement seemed promising, but eventually disappointed managers seeking to counter the ill effects of extreme specialization. They failed partly because they were intuitive, narrow approaches rather than fully developed, theory-driven methods. Consequently a new, more complex approach to task design, job enrichment, was developed. Job enrichment is based on the dual-structure theory of motivation, discussed in Chapter 4. That theory contends that employees can be motivated by positive job-related experiences such as feelings of achievement, responsibility, and recognition. To achieve these, **job enrichment** relies on vertical job loading: not only adding more tasks to a job, as in horizontal loading, but also giving the employee more control over those tasks.[8]

Job enrichment entails giving workers more tasks to perform and more control over how to perform them.

AT&T, Texas Instruments, IBM, and General Foods have all used job enrichment. For example, AT&T utilized job enrichment in a group of eight typists who were responsible for preparing service orders. Managers believed turnover in the group was too high and performance too low. Analysis revealed several deficiencies in the work. The typists worked in relative isolation, and any service representative could ask them to type work orders. As a result, they had little client contact or responsibility, and they received scant feedback on their job performance. The job enrichment program focused on creating a typing team. Each member of the team was paired with a service representative, and the tasks were restructured: Ten discrete steps were replaced with three more complex ones. In addition, the typists began to get specific feedback on performance, and their job titles were changed to reflect their greater responsibility and status. As a result of these changes, the number of orders delivered on time increased from 27 to 90 percent, accuracy improved, and turnover decreased significantly.[9]

One of the first published reports on job enrichment related how Texas Instruments used this technique to improve janitorial jobs. The company gave janitors more control over their schedules and let them sequence their own cleaning jobs and purchase their own supplies. As a direct result, turnover dropped, cleanliness improved, and the company reported estimated cost savings of approximately $103,000.[10]

At the same time, many job enrichment programs have failed. Some companies have found job enrichment to be cost ineffective, and others believe it simply did not produce the expected results.[11] Several programs at Prudential Insurance, for example, were abandoned because managers believed they were benefiting neither employees nor the firm. Some of the criticism is associated with the dual-structure theory of motivation, on which job enrichment is based: The theory confuses employee satisfaction with motivation, is fraught with methodological flaws, ignores situational factors, and is not convincingly supported by research.

Because of these and other problems, job enrichment recently has fallen into disfavor among managers. Yet some valuable aspects of the concept can be salvaged. The efforts of managers and academic theorists ultimately have led to more complex and sophisticated viewpoints. Many of these advances are evident in the job characteristics theory, which we consider next.

Job Characteristics Theory

The **job characteristics theory** identifies five motivational properties of tasks and three critical psychological states of people.

The **job characteristics theory** focuses on the specific motivational properties of jobs. The theory, diagrammed in Figure 5.2, was developed by J. Richard Hackman and Greg Oldham.[12] At the core of the theory is the idea of critical psychological states that are presumed to determine the extent to which characteristics of the job enhance employee responses to the task. The three critical psychological states are

1. *Experienced meaningfulness of the work*—the degree to which individuals experience their jobs as generally meaningful, valuable, and worthwhile
2. *Experienced responsibility for work outcomes*—the degree to which individuals feel personally accountable and responsible for the results of their work
3. *Knowledge of results*—the degree to which individuals continuously understand how effectively they are performing the job

If employees experience these states at a sufficiently high level, they are likely to feel good about themselves and respond favorably to their jobs. Hackman and Oldham suggest that the three critical psychological states are triggered by the following five characteristics of the job, or core job dimensions:

1. *Skill variety*—the degree to which the job requires a variety of activities that involve different skills and talents
2. *Task identity*—the degree to which the job requires completion of a "whole" and an identifiable piece of work; that is, the extent to which a job has a beginning and an end with a tangible outcome
3. *Task significance*—the degree to which the job affects the lives or work of other people, both in the immediate organization and in the external environment

FIGURE 5.2

The Job Characteristics Theory

The job characteristics theory is an important contemporary model of how to design jobs. By using five core job characteristics, managers can enhance three critical psychological states. These states, in turn, can improve a variety of personal and work outcomes. Individual differences also affect how the job characteristics affect people.

Reference: J. R. Hackman and G. R. Oldham, "Motivation Through the Design of Work: Test of Theory," in *Organizational Behavior and Human Performance,* Volume 16, 250–279. Copyright © 1976, with permission from Elsevier.

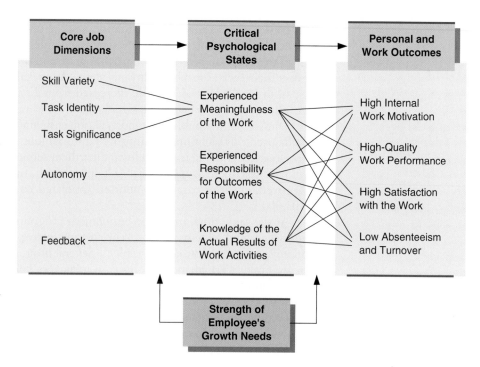

The experienced meaningfulness of the work, experienced responsibility for work outcomes, and knowledge of results are critical psychological states that affect how people respond to their jobs. Dr. Carolyn Stern was driven to become a doctor for just those reasons. Because she is deaf, it was very difficult for her to complete medical school. But today her disability enables her to effectively relate to her patients.

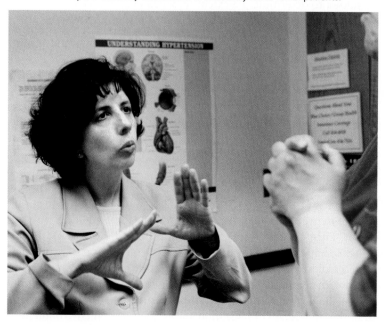

4. *Autonomy*—the degree to which the job allows the individual substantial freedom, independence, and discretion to schedule the work and determine the procedures for carrying it out

5. *Feedback*—the degree to which the job activities give the individual direct and clear information about the effectiveness of his or her performance

Figure 5.2 shows that these five job characteristics, operating through the critical psychological states, affect a variety of personal and work outcomes: high internal work motivation (that is, intrinsic motivation), high-quality work performance, high satisfaction with the work, and low absenteeism and turnover. The figure also suggests that individual differences play a role in job design. People with strong needs for personal growth and development will be especially motivated by the five core job characteristics. On the other hand, people with weaker needs for personal growth and development are less likely to be motivated by the core job characteristics.

Figure 5.3 expands the basic job characteristics theory by incorporating general guidelines to help managers implement it.[13] Managers can use such means as forming natural work units (that is, grouping similar tasks together), combining existing tasks into more complex ones, establishing direct relationships between workers and clients, increasing worker autonomy through vertical job loading, and opening feedback channels. Theoretically, such actions should enhance the motivational properties of each task. Using these guidelines, sometimes in adapted form, several firms, including 3M, Volvo, AT&T, Xerox, Texas Instruments, and Motorola, have successfully implemented job design changes.[14]

Much research has been devoted to this approach to job design.[15] This research has generally supported the theory, although performance has seldom been found to correlate with job characteristics.[16] Several apparent weaknesses in the theory have also come to light. First, the measures used to test the theory are not always as valid and reliable as they should be. Further, research has frequently failed to support the role of individual differences. Finally, guidelines for implementation are not specific; hence, managers usually must tailor them to their own particular circumstances. Still, the theory remains a popular perspective on studying and changing jobs.[17]

FIGURE 5.3

Implementing the Job Characteristics Theory

Managers should use a set of implementation guidelines when applying the job characteristics theory to their organizations. This figure shows some of these guidelines. For example, managers combine tasks, form natural work units, establish client relationships, vertically load jobs, and open feedback channels.

Source: J. R. Hackman, G. R. Oldham, R. Janson, and K. Purdy. "A New Stage for Job Enrichment." which appears in *The California Management Review*, vol. 17, no. 4. Copyright © 1975, by The Regents of the University of California. By permission of The Regents.

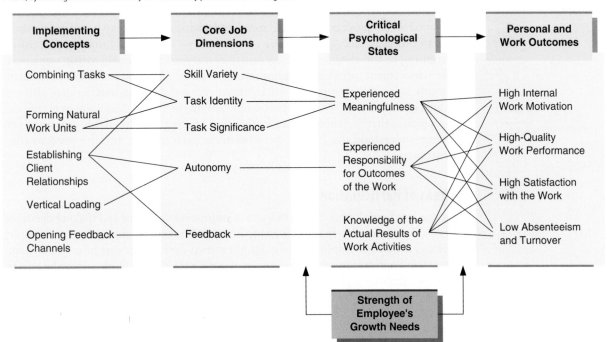

Participation, Empowerment, and Motivation

Participation entails giving employees a voice in making decisions about their own work.

Empowerment is the process of enabling workers to set their own work goals, make decisions, and solve problems within their sphere of responsibility and authority.

Participative management and empowerment are two more important methods managers can use to enhance employee motivation. In a sense, participation and empowerment are extensions of job design because each fundamentally alters how employees in an organization perform their jobs. **Participation** occurs when employees have a voice in decisions about their own work. (One important model that helps managers determine the optimal level of employee participation, the Vroom-Yetton-Jago model, is discussed in Chapter 10.) **Empowerment** is the process of enabling workers to set their own work goals, make decisions, and solve problems within their spheres of responsibility and authority. Thus, empowerment is a somewhat broader concept that promotes participation in a wide variety of areas, including but not limited to the work itself, the work context, and the work environment.[18]

Early Perspectives on Participation and Empowerment

The human relations movement in vogue from the 1930s through the 1950s (see Chapter 1) assumed employees who are happy and satisfied will work harder. This view stimulated management interest in having workers participate in a variety of organizational activities. Managers hoped that if employees had a chance to participate in decision making concerning their work environment, they would be satisfied, and this satisfaction would supposedly result in improved performance. However, managers tended to see employee participation merely as a way to increase satisfaction rather than as a source of potentially valuable input. Eventually managers began to recognize that employee input was useful in itself, apart from its presumed effect on satisfaction. In other words, they came to see employees as valued human resources who can contribute to organizational effectiveness.[19]

The role of participation and empowerment in motivation can be expressed in terms of both the need-based perspectives and the expectancy theory discussed in Chapter 4. Employees who participate in decision making may be more committed to executing decisions properly. Furthermore, successfully making a decision, executing it, and then seeing the positive consequences can help satisfy one's need for achievement, provide recognition and responsibility, and enhance self-esteem. Simply being asked to participate in organizational decision making may also enhance an employee's self-esteem. In addition, participation should help clarify expectancies; that is, participating in decision making should enable employees to better understand the linkage between their performance and the rewards they want most.

Areas of Participation

At one level, employees can participate in addressing questions and making decisions about their own jobs. Instead of just telling them how to do their jobs, for example, managers can ask employees to make their own decisions about how to do them. Based on their own expertise and experience with their tasks, workers may be able to improve their own productivity. In many situations, they may also be well qualified to make decisions about what materials to use, what tools to use, and so forth.

Managers might also let workers make decisions about administrative matters, such as work schedules. If jobs are relatively independent of one another, employees might decide when to change shifts, take breaks, go to lunch, and so forth. A

"DON'T FORGET TO EMPTY THE SUGGESTION BOX."

Participation and empowerment can play powerful roles in motivating employees. But for these benefits to have any hope of fruition, managers must ensure their efforts to involve employees in decision making are sincere. For example, if employees sense that their manager is asking for their opinion only for symbolic purposes and has already made a decision, things can backfire in unfortunate ways.

©Harley Schwadron.

work group or team might also be able to schedule vacations and days off for all its members. Furthermore, employees are getting increasing opportunities to participate in broader issues of product quality. Participation of this type has become a hallmark of successful Japanese and other international firms, and many U.S. companies have followed suit.[20]

Techniques and Issues in Empowerment

In recent years, many organizations have actively sought ways to extend participation beyond the traditional areas. Simple techniques such as suggestion boxes and question-and-answer meetings allow a certain degree of participation, for example. The basic motive has been to better capitalize on the assets and capabilities inherent in all employees. Thus, many managers today prefer the term *empowerment* to *participation* because it implies a more comprehensive involvement.

One method some firms use to empower their workers is the use of work teams. This method grew out of early attempts to use what Japanese firms call *quality circles*. A quality circle is a group of employees who voluntarily meet regularly to identify and propose solutions to problems related to quality. This use of quality circles quickly grew to encompass a wider array of work groups, now generally called *work teams*. These teams are groups of employees empowered to plan, organize, direct, and control their own work. Their supervisor plays the role of a "coach" rather than a traditional "boss." We discuss work teams more fully in Chapter 9.

Another method some organizations use to facilitate empowerment is to change their overall method of organizing. The basic pattern is for an organization to eliminate layers from its hierarchy, thereby becoming much more decentralized. Power, responsibility, and authority are delegated as far down the organization as possible, putting control of work squarely in the hands of those who actually do it.

Regardless of the specific technique used, however, empowerment enhances organizational effectiveness only if certain conditions exist. First, the organization must be sincere in its efforts to spread power and autonomy to lower levels; token efforts to promote participation in just a few areas are unlikely to succeed. This point is clearly illustrated in the cartoon. Second, the organization must be committed to maintaining participation and empowerment. Workers will be resentful if they are given more control only to later have it reduced or taken away altogether. Third, the organization must be systematic and patient in its efforts to empower workers. Turning over too much control too quickly can spell disaster. Finally, the organization must be prepared to increase its commitment to training. Employees receiving more freedom concerning how they work are likely to need additional training to help them exercise that freedom most effectively.

Alternative Work Arrangements

Beyond the actual redesigning of jobs and the use of participation and empowerment, many organizations today are experimenting with a variety of alternative work arrangements. These arrangements are generally intended to enhance employee motivation and performance by giving workers more flexibility regarding how and when they work. Among the more popular alternative work arrangements are variable work schedules, flexible work schedules, job sharing, and telecommuting.[21] As the Business of Ethics box points out, adopting any of these techniques is not necessarily a straightforward decision.

BUSINESS OF ETHICS

Safety Starts at Home

It's an interesting convergence of legal and social trends. Under pressure from both workers and employers, the Occupational Safety and Health Administration (OSHA) recently changed the way it protects workers who work for their employers at home.

Prior to the new ruling, employers who asked workers to work from home—for example, by telecommuting or doing home manufacturing—were legally liable for ensuring that employees had a safe and hazard-free working environment at all times. That meant employers had to inspect workers' homes to ensure that all safety requirements were being met. For example, the employer had to verify that there were two external exits, no lead paint had been used on the walls, the employee's chairs were ergonomically sound, and the indoor air quality met OSHA standards. This stipulation led to somewhat absurd decisions, such as corporations allowing employees to use home telephones but not home computers if the employees' monitors did not meet low-radiation requirements. An employer could also be held accountable for employees' unsafe behaviors, such as plugging too many electrical devices into one power outlet or standing on a chair rather than on a ladder to change a light bulb.

The OSHA ruling was very broad, requiring employers to take a proactive stance on home safety. "Even when the workplace is in a designated area in an employee's home, the employer retains some degree of control over the conditions of the 'work at home' agreement. Employers should exercise reasonable diligence to identify in advance the possible hazards associated with particular home work assignments... [This] may necessitate an on-site examination of the working environment by the employer," according to a 1999 OSHA publication for employers. Employers found the requirements burdensome, especially as more workers began telecommuting. Employees, too, thought the requirements were too intrusive, invading the privacy of their homes.

> *"If you would be liable for your employees on-site, then you wouldn't be less liable just because you have someone working off-site."*—Nicole Goluboff, attorney and specialist in the legal implications of telecommuting

Consequently, in 2000, OSHA backed down from its position on requirements, and the new policy became law in January 2001. However, it's still not clear how much responsibility a company has if a worker is injured at home. And a new area of growing concern has emerged: cybercrime. Is a company liable if a client's confidential information is stolen because an employee's home computer didn't have hacker protection? What if the employee uses a home computer for business and also peddles online pornography? Nicole Goluboff, an attorney specializing in the legal implications of telecommuting, says, "If you would be liable for your employees on-site, then you wouldn't be less liable just because you have someone working off-site." Who knows where all this will lead? Only time—and the courts, no doubt—will tell.

References: Jeremy Quittner, "OSHA Won't Come Knockin' on the Home Office Door," *BusinessWeek*, March 3, 2000, pp. 96–98; "Occupational Injury and Illness Recording and Reporting Requirements," Occupational Health and Safety Administration website, January 19, 2001, www.osha.gov on May 6, 2004; Chris Sandlund, "Telecommuting: A Legal Primer," *BusinessWeek*, March 20, 2000 (quotation), pp. 42–43.

Variable Work Schedules

Many exceptions exist, of course, but the traditional work schedule in the United States has long been days that start at 8:00 or 9:00 in the morning and end at 5:00 in the evening, five days a week (and, of course, managers often work many additional hours outside of this time period). Although exact starting and ending times vary, most companies in other countries have also used a well-defined work schedule. Such a schedule, however, makes it difficult for workers to attend to routine personal business: going to the bank, seeing a doctor or dentist for a checkup, attending a parent-teacher conference, getting an automobile serviced, and so forth. Employees locked into this work schedule may find they need to take a sick day or vacation day to handle these activities. On a more psychological level, some people may feel so powerless and constrained by their job schedules that they grow resentful and frustrated.

To help counter these problems, one alternative some businesses use is a compressed workweek schedule.[22] An employee following a **compressed workweek schedule** works a full forty-hour week in fewer than the traditional five days. Typically this schedule involves working ten hours a day for four days, leaving an extra day off. Another alternative is for employees to work slightly less than ten hours a day but complete the forty hours by lunchtime on Friday. A few firms have tried having employees work twelve hours a day for three days, followed by four days off. Firms that have used these forms of compressed workweeks include John Hancock, ARCO, and R. J. Reynolds. One problem with this schedule is that if everyone in the organization is off at the same time, the firm may have no one on duty to handle problems or deal with outsiders on the off day. On the other hand, if a company staggers days off across the workforce, people who don't get the more desirable days off (Monday and Friday, for most people) may be jealous or resentful. Another problem is that when employees put in too much time in a single day, they tend to tire and perform at a lower level later in the day.

A popular schedule some organizations are beginning to use is called a "nine-eighty" schedule. Under this arrangement, an employee works a traditional schedule one week and a compressed schedule the next, getting every other Friday off. That is, the employee works eighty hours (the equivalent of two weeks of full-time work) in nine days. By alternating the regular and compressed schedules across half of its workforce, the organization is staffed at all times but still gives employees two additional full days off each month. Shell Oil and Amoco Chemicals currently use this schedule.

> In a **compressed workweek**, employees work a full forty-hour week in fewer than the traditional five days.

Flexible Work Schedules

Another promising alternative work arrangement is **flexible work schedules,** sometimes called **flextime.** With the compressed workweek schedules previously discussed, employees get time off during normal working hours, but they must still follow a regular and defined schedule on the days they do work. Although flextime usually gives employees less say about what days they work, it also allows them more personal control over the times when they work on those days.[23]

Figure 5.4 illustrates how flextime works. The workday is broken down into two categories: flexible time and core time. All employees must be at their workstations during core time, but they can choose their own schedules during flexible time. Thus, one employee may choose to start work early in the morning and leave in mid-afternoon, another to start in the late morning and work until late afternoon, and a third to start early in the morning, take a long lunch break, and work until late afternoon.

> **Flexible work schedules,** or **flextime,** give employees more personal control over the hours they work each day.

6:00 A.M.	9:00 A.M. – 11:00 A.M.		1:00 P.M. – 3:00 P.M.	6:00 P.M.
Flexible Time	Core Time	Flexible Time	Core Time	Flexible Time

FIGURE 5.4

Flexible Work Schedules

Flexible work schedules are an important new work arrangement used in some organizations today. All employees must be at work during "core time." In the hypothetical example shown here, core time is from 9 to 11 A.M. and 1 to 3 P.M. The other time, then, is flexible: Employees can come and go as they please during that time, as long as the total time spent at work meets organizational expectations.

The major advantage of this approach, as already noted, is that workers get to tailor their workday to fit their personal needs. A person who needs to visit the dentist in the late afternoon can just start work early; a person who stays out late one night can start work late the next day; and an employee who needs to run some errands during lunch can take a longer midday break. On the other hand, flextime is more difficult to manage because others in the organization may not be sure when a person will be available for meetings other than during the core time. Expenses such as utilities will also be higher since the organization must remain open for a longer period each day.

Some organizations have experimented with a plan in which workers set their own hours but then must follow that schedule each day. Others allow workers to modify their own schedule each day. Organizations that have used the flexible work schedule method include Control Data Corporation, DuPont, Metropolitan Life, Chevron Texaco, and some offices of the U.S. government.

Job Sharing

In **job sharing**, two or more part-time employees share one full-time job.

Yet another potentially useful alternative work arrangement is job sharing. In **job sharing,** two part-time employees share one full-time job. Job sharing may be desirable for people who want to work only part-time or when job markets are tight. For its part, the organization can accommodate the preferences of a broader range of employees and may benefit from the talents of more people. Perhaps the simplest job-sharing arrangement to visualize is that of a receptionist. To share this job, one worker would staff the receptionist's desk from, say, 8:00 A.M. to noon each day, the office might close from noon to 1:00 P.M., and a second worker would staff the desk from 1:00 P.M. until 5:00 P.M. To the casual observer or visitor to the office, the fact that two people serve in one job is essentially irrelevant. The responsibilities of the job in the morning and the afternoon are not likely to be interdependent. Thus, the position can easily be broken down into two or perhaps even more components.

Organizations sometimes offer job sharing to entice more workers to the organization. If a particular kind of job is difficult to fill, a job-sharing arrangement may make it more attractive to more people. There are also cost benefits for the organization. Since the employees may be working only part-time, the organization does not have to give them the same benefits that full-time employees receive. The organization can also tap into a wider array of skills when it provides job-sharing arrangements. The firm gets the advantage of the two sets of skills from one job.

Job sharing is an alternative work arrangement in which two part-time employees share one full-time job. Amy Frank (left) and Denise Brown share the job of vice president of fixed-income sales at Fleet Boston. Frank works all day Monday and Tuesday, and Wednesday morning; Brown works Wednesday afternoon and all day Thursday and Friday. This arrangement allows each to pursue a career, earn a reasonable income, and spend time at home with their children.

Some workers like job sharing because it gives them flexibility and freedom. Certain workers, for example, may want only part-time work. Stepping into a shared job may also give them a chance to work in an organization that otherwise wants to hire only full-time employees. When the job sharer isn't working, she or he may attend school, take care of the family, or simply enjoy leisure time.

Job sharing does not work for every organization, and it isn't attractive to all workers, but it has produced enough success stories to suggest it will be around for a long time. Among the organizations particularly committed to job-sharing programs are the Bank of Montreal, United Airlines, and the National School Board Association. Each of these organizations, and dozens more, reports that job sharing has become a critical part of its human resource system. Although job sharing has not been scientifically evaluated, it appears to be a useful alternative to traditional work scheduling.

Telecommuting

Telecommuting is a work arrangement in which employees spend part of their time working off-site.

A relatively new approach to alternative work arrangements is **telecommuting,** in which employees spend part of their time working off-site, usually at home. By using email, computer networks, and other technology, many employees can maintain close contact with their organizations and do as much work at home as they could in their offices. The increased power and sophistication of modern communication technology is making telecommuting easier and easier.

Many employees like telecommuting because it gives them added flexibility. By spending one or two days a week at home, for instance, they have the same kind of flexibility to manage personal activities as by flextime or compressed schedules allow. Some employees also believe they get more work done at home because they are less likely to be interrupted. Organizations may benefit for several reasons as well: They can reduce absenteeism and turnover since employees will need to take less "formal" time off, and they can save on facilities such as parking spaces because fewer people will be at work on any given day.

On the other hand, many employees do not thrive under this arrangement. Some feel isolated and miss the social interaction of the workplace. Others simply lack the self-control and discipline to walk from the breakfast table to their desk and start work. As noted in the Business of Ethics box on page 130, another concern for some organizations is the safety and health of their employees who work at home. Managers may also encounter coordination difficulties in scheduling meetings and other activities that require face-to-face contact. Still, given the boom in communication technology and the pressures for flexibility, many more organizations will no doubt use telecommuting in the years to come.[24]

Synopsis

Managers seek to enhance employee performance by capitalizing on the potential for motivated behavior to improve performance. Methods often used to translate motivation into performance involve job design, employee participation and empowerment, alternative work arrangements, performance management, goal setting, and rewards.

Job design is how organizations define and structure jobs. Historically there was a general trend toward increasingly specialized jobs, but more recently the movement has consistently been away from extreme specialization. Two early alternatives to specialization were job rotation and job enlargement. Job enrichment approaches stimulated considerable interest in job design.

The job characteristics theory grew from early work on job enrichment. One basic premise of this theory is that jobs can be described in terms of a specific set of motivational characteristics. Another is that managers should work to enhance the presence of those motivational characteristics in jobs but also take individual differences into account.

Participative management and empowerment can help improve employee motivation in many business settings. New management practices, such as the use of various kinds of work teams and of flatter, more decentralized methods of organizing, are intended to empower employees throughout the organization. Organizations that want to empower their employees need to understand a variety of issues as they implement participation.

Alternative work arrangements are commonly used today to enhance motivated job performance. Among the more popular alternative arrangements are compressed workweeks, flexible work schedules, job sharing, and telecommuting.

Discussion Questions

1. What are the primary advantages and disadvantages of job specialization? Were they the same in the early days of mass production?

2. Under what circumstances might job enlargement be especially effective? Especially ineffective? What about job rotation?

3. What trends today might suggest a return to job specialization?

4. What are the strengths and weaknesses of job enrichment? When might this approach be useful?

5. Do you agree or disagree that individual differences affect how people respond to their jobs? Explain.

6. What are the primary similarities and differences between job enrichment and the job characteristics approach?

7. What are the motivational consequences of participative management from the perspective of expectancy and equity theories?

8. What motivational problems might result from an organization's attempt to set up work teams?

9. Which form of alternative work schedule might you prefer?

10. Do you think you would like telecommuting? Why or why not?

Organizational Behavior Case for Discussion

Employee Participation at Chaparral Steel

Chaparral Steel enjoys a stellar reputation as one of the most effective firms in the steel industry. Chaparral was founded in 1973 in a small town near Dallas and today enjoys annual sales of more than $500 million. In earlier times, most steel companies, such as U.S. Steel (now USX) and Bethlehem Steel, were large, bureaucratic operations. However, increased competition from low-cost foreign steel firms, especially in Japan and Korea, has caused major problems for these manufacturers with their high overhead costs and inflexible modes of operation.

These competitive pressures, in turn, have also led to the formation of so-called minimills such as Chaparral. These minimills are consciously designed to be much smaller and more flexible than the traditional steel giants. Because of their size, technology, and flexibility, these firms are able to maintain much lower production costs and respond more quickly to customer requests. Today Chaparral is recognized as one of the best of this new breed of steel companies. For example, whereas most mills produce 1 ton of steel with an average of 3 to 5 hours of labor, Chaparral produces a ton with fewer than 1.2 hours of labor. Chaparral has also successfully avoided all efforts to unionize its employees.

Since its inception, Chaparral has been led by Gordon Forward. Forward knew that if Chaparral was going to succeed with what was then a new strategic orientation in the industry, it would also need to be managed in new and different ways. One of the first things he decided to do as part of his new approach was to systematically avoid the traditional barriers that tend to arise between management and labor, especially in older industries such as steel. For example, he mandated that there would be neither reserved parking spaces in the parking lot nor a separate dining area inside the plant for managers. Today everyone dresses casually at the work site, and people throughout the firm are on a first-name basis with one another. Workers take their lunch and coffee breaks whenever they choose, and coffee is provided free for everyone.

Forward also insisted that all employees be paid on a salary basis—no time clocks or time sheets for anyone, from the president down to the custodians. Workers are organized into teams, and each team selects its own "leader." The teams also interview and select new members as needed and are responsible for planning their own work, setting their own work schedules, and even allocating vacation days among themselves. Teams are also responsible for implementing any necessary disciplinary actions toward a member. Finally, no one has a monotonous, narrowly defined job to be performed on a continuous basis. Instead, each team is responsible for an array of tasks and functions; the teams themselves are encouraged to ensure that all members know how to perform all the assigned tasks and functions and to rotate people across them regularly.

Forward clearly believes in trusting everyone in the organization. For example, when the firm recently needed a new rolling mill lathe, it budgeted $1 million for its purchase, then put the purchase decision in the hands of an operating machinist. The machinist, in turn, investigated various options, visited other mills in Japan and Europe, and then recommended an alternative piece of machinery costing less than half of the budgeted amount. Forward also helped pioneer an innovative concept called "open-book management": Any employee at Chaparral can see any document, record, or other piece of information at any time and for any reason.

Chaparral also recognizes the importance of investing in and rewarding people. Continuous education is an integral part of the firm's culture, with a variety of classes offered all the time. For example, one recent slate of classes included metallurgy, electronics, finance, and English. The classes are intended to benefit both individual workers and the organization as a whole. The classes are scheduled on-site and in the evening. Some include community college credit (tuition is charged for these classes, although the company pays for half the costs), while others are noncredit only (there are no charges for these classes). Forward has a goal that at any given time, at least 85 percent of Chaparral's employees will be enrolled in at least one class.

Everyone also participates in the good—and the bad—times at Chaparral. For example, all workers have a guaranteed base salary that is adequate but, by itself, is below the standard market rate. However, in addition to their base pay, employees get pay-for-performance bonuses based on their individual achievements. Finally, companywide bonuses are paid to everyone on a quarterly basis. These bonuses are tied to overall company performance. The typical bonuses increase an employee's total compensation to a level well above the standard market rate. Thus, hard work and dedication on everyone's part means all employees can benefit.

Case Questions

1. Describe how managers at Chaparral Steel appear to be implementing various need- and process-based theories of motivation.
2. Discuss the apparent role and nature of job design at Chaparral.
3. Describe how Chaparral uses participation and empowerment to motivate its workers.

References: "Chaparral Steel," Foundation for Enterprise Development website (reporting the U.S. Department of Labor, Office of the American Workplace, "best practices" winners), www.fed.org on April 27, 2004; John Case, "HR Learns How to Open the Books," *HRMagazine*, May 1998, pp. 70–76; John Case, "Opening the Books," *Harvard Business Review*, March–April 1997, pp. 118–129; Brian Dumaine, "Chaparral Steel: Unleash Workers and Cut Costs," *Fortune*, May 18, 1992, p. 88.

Experiencing Organizational Behavior

Learning About Job Design

Purpose: This exercise will help you assess the processes involved in designing jobs to make them more motivating.

Format: Working in small groups, you will diagnose the motivating potential of an existing job, compare its motivating potential to that of other jobs, suggest ways to redesign the job, and then assess the effects of your redesign suggestions on other aspects of the workplace.

Procedure: Your instructor will divide the class into groups of three or four. In assessing the characteristics of jobs, use a scale value of 1 ("very little") to 7 ("very high").

1. Using the scale values, assign scores on each core job dimension used in the job characteristics theory (see page 125) to the following jobs: secretary, professor, food server, auto mechanic, lawyer, short-order cook, department store clerk, construction worker, and newspaper reporter.

2. Researchers often assess the motivational properties of jobs by calculating their motivating potential score (MPS). The usual formula for MPS is

$$(\text{Variety} + \text{Identity} + \text{Significance})/3 \\ \times \text{Autonomy} \times \text{Feedback}$$

Use this formula to calculate the MPS for each job in step 1.

3. Your instructor will now assign your group one of the jobs from the list. Discuss how you might reasonably go about enriching the job.

4. Calculate the new MPS score for the redesigned job, and check its new position in the rank ordering.

5. Discuss the feasibility of your redesign suggestions. In particular, look at how your recommended changes might necessitate changes in other jobs, in the reward system, and in the selection criteria used to hire people for the job.

6. Briefly discuss your observations with the rest of the class.

Follow-up Questions

1. How might your own preexisting attitudes explain some of your own perceptions in this exercise?

2. Are some jobs simply impossible to redesign? Explain.

Self-Assessment Exercise

The Job Characteristics Inventory

The questionnaire below was developed to measure the central concepts of the job characteristics theory. Answer the questions in relation to the job you currently hold or the job you most recently held.

Characteristics from Hackman and Oldham's Job Diagnostic Survey

Reference: *Work Design* by Hackman/Oldham, © Adapted by permission of Pearson Education, Inc., Upper Saddle River, NJ.

Skill Variety

1. How much *variety* is there in your job? That is, to what extent does the job require you to do many different things at work, using a variety of your skills and talents?

1	**2**	**3**	**4**	**5**	**6**	**7**
Very little; the job requires me to do the same routine things over and over again.			Moderate variety			Very much; the job requires me to do many different things, using a number of different skills and talents.

2. The job requires me to use a number of complex or high-level skills.

How accurate is the statement in describing your job?

1	**2**	**3**	**4**	**5**	**6**	**7**
Very inaccurate	Mostly inaccurate	Slightly inaccurate	Uncertain	Slightly accurate	Mostly accurate	Very accurate

3. The job is quite simple and repetitive.*

How accurate is the statement in describing your job?

1	2	3	4	5	6	7
Very inaccurate	Mostly inaccurate	Slightly inaccurate	Uncertain	Slightly accurate	Mostly accurate	Very accurate

Task Identity

1. To what extent does your job involve doing a *"whole" and identifiable piece of work*? That is, is the job a complete piece of work that has an obvious beginning and end? Or is it only a small *part* of the overall piece of work, which is finished by other people or by automatic machines?

1	2	3	4	5	6	7
My job is only a tiny part of the overall piece of work; the results of my activities cannot be seen in the final product or service.			My job is a moderate-sized "chunk" of the overall piece of work; my own contribution can be seen in the final outcome.			My job involves doing the whole piece of work, from start to finish; the results of my activities are easily seen in the final product or service.

2. The job provides me a chance to completely finish the pieces of work I begin.

How accurate is the statement in describing your job?

1	2	3	4	5	6	7
Very inaccurate	Mostly inaccurate	Slightly inaccurate	Uncertain	Slightly accurate	Mostly accurate	Very accurate

3. The job is arranged so that I do *not* have the chance to do an entire piece of work from beginning to end.*

How accurate is the statement in describing your job?

1	2	3	4	5	6	7
Very inaccurate	Mostly inaccurate	Slightly inaccurate	Uncertain	Slightly accurate	Mostly accurate	Very accurate

Task Significance

1. In general, how significant or important is your job? That is, are the results of your work likely to significantly affect the lives or well-being of other people?

1	2	3	4	5	6	7
Not very significant; the outcomes of my work are *not* likely to have important effects on other people.			Moderately significant			Highly significant; the outcomes of my work can affect other people in very important ways.

2. This job is one in which a lot of people can be affected by how well the work gets done.

How accurate is the statement in describing your job?

1	2	3	4	5	6	7
Very inaccurate	Mostly inaccurate	Slightly inaccurate	Uncertain	Slightly accurate	Mostly accurate	Very accurate

3. The job itself is *not* very significant or important in the broader scheme of things.*

How accurate is the statement in describing your job?

1	2	3	4	5	6	7
Very inaccurate	Mostly inaccurate	Slightly inaccurate	Uncertain	Slightly accurate	Mostly accurate	Very accurate

Autonomy

1. How much *autonomy* is there in your job? That is, to what extent does your job permit you to decide *on your own* how to go about doing your work?

1	2	3	4	5	6	7
Very little; the job gives me almost no personal "say" about how and when the work is done.			Moderate autonomy; many things are standardized and not under my control, but I can make some decisions about the work.			Very much; the job gives me almost complete responsibility for deciding how and when the work is done.

2. The job gives me considerable opportunity for independence and freedom in how I do the work.

How accurate is the statement in describing your job?

1	2	3	4	5	6	7
Very inaccurate	Mostly inaccurate	Slightly inaccurate	Uncertain	Slightly accurate	Mostly accurate	Very accurate

3. The job denies me any chance to use my personal initiative or judgment in carrying out the work.*

How accurate is the statement in describing your job?

1	2	3	4	5	6	7
Very inaccurate	Mostly inaccurate	Slightly inaccurate	Uncertain	Slightly accurate	Mostly accurate	Very accurate

Feedback

1. To what extent does *doing the job itself* provide you with information about your work performance? That is, does the actual *work itself* provide clues about how well you are doing—aside from any "feedback" coworkers or supervisors may provide?

1	2	3	4	5	6	7
Very little; the job itself is set up so I could work forever without finding out how well I am doing.			Moderately; sometimes doing the job provides "feedback" to me; sometimes it does not.			Very much; the job is set up so that I get almost constant "feedback" as I work about how well I am doing.

2. Just doing the work required by the job provides many chances for me to figure out how well I am doing.

How accurate is the statement in describing your job?

1	2	3	4	5	6	7
Very inaccurate	Mostly inaccurate	Slightly inaccurate	Uncertain	Slightly accurate	Mostly accurate	Very accurate

3. The job itself provides very few clues about whether or not I am performing well.*

How accurate is the statement in describing your job?

1	2	3	4	5	6	7
Very inaccurate	Mostly inaccurate	Slightly inaccurate	Uncertain	Slightly accurate	Mostly accurate	Very accurate

Scoring: Responses to the three items for each core characteristic are averaged to yield an overall score for that characteristic. Items marked with an asterisk (*) should be scored as follows: $1 = 7$; $2 = 6$; $3 = 5$; $6 = 2$; $7 = 1$

$$\text{Motivating potential score} \times \left(\frac{\text{Skill variety} \times \text{Task identity} \times \text{Task significance}}{3} \right) \times \text{Autonomy} \times \text{Feedback}$$

OB Online

1. Find the website of a company that appears to promote job flexibility.

2. Visit the websites of the companies listed in the text that have used alternative approaches to job design, and try to find evidence of what job design practices, if any, they are promoting now.

3. Develop a framework that illustrates how the Internet might affect participation in the work-place. Use the Internet to find some evidence to support your framework.

4. Find the websites of at least four companies that discuss alternative work arrangements as part of their human resources recruiting process.

Building Managerial Skills

Exercise Overview: Conceptual skills involve a person's ability to think in the abstract. This exercise will help you develop your conceptual skills as they relate to designing jobs.

Exercise Background: Begin by thinking of three different jobs: one that appears to have virtually no enrichment, one that seems to have moderate enrichment, and one that appears to have a great deal of enrichment. These might be jobs you have personally held or jobs you have observed and about which you can make some educated or informed judgments.

Evaluate each job along the five dimensions described in the job characteristics theory. Next, see if you can identify ways to improve each dimension for each job; that is, try to determine how to enrich the jobs using the job characteristics theory as a framework.

Finally, meet with a classmate and share results. See if you can improve your job enrichment strategy based on the critique your classmate offers.

Exercise Task: Using the background information about the three jobs you examined as context, answer the following questions.

1. What job qualities make some jobs easier to enrich than others?
2. Can all jobs be enriched? Why or why not?
3. Even if a particular job can be enriched, does that always mean it *should* be enriched?
4. Under what circumstances might an individual prefer to have a routine and unenriched job?

TEST PREPPER

ACE self-test

You have read the chapter and studied the key terms, and the exam is any day now. Think you're ready to ace it? Take this sample test to gauge your comprehension of chapter material. You can check your answers at the back of the book. Want more test questions? Visit the student website at http://college.hmco.com/business/students/ (select Griffin/Moorhead, Fundamentals of Organizational Behavior 1e) and take the ACE quizzes for more practice.

1. **T F** Job flexibility can help employees reduce an imbalance between their work and their families.

2. **T F** Unmet employee needs typically translate into increased job performance without management intervention.

3. **T F** In job specialization, employees become skilled at as many tasks as possible.

4. **T F** The greatest problems with job specialization are employee boredom and monotony.

5. **T F** In job rotation, the employee searches for new ways to complete the same task.

6. **T F** Job enlargement is also known as horizontal job loading.

7. **T F** Giving employees control over their tasks is called vertical loading.

8. **T F** Virtually all job enrichment programs have failed to increase productivity.

9. **T F** According to job characteristics theory, one critical psychological state employees must experience to feel good about themselves and respond favorably to their jobs is experienced meaningfulness of the work.

10. **T F** Employees with the lowest need for personal growth and development will be the most easily motivated by the five core job dimensions.

11. **T F** A quality circle is defined by the links between the customer and the organization.

12. **T F** Efforts at increasing empowerment seem to work best if the organization is committed to maintaining participation and empowerment.

13. **T F** In a compressed workweek, all employees work on the same days and the business closes one extra day each week.

14. **T F** Employees on a "nine-eighty" schedule take one extra day off every two weeks.

15. **T F** One cost benefit to the organization of job sharing is that two part-time employees may not receive full-time benefits.

16. **T F** Organizations that use telecommuting save money on facilities such as parking spaces because fewer people are at work on any given day.

17. **T F** Telecommuting seems to be decreasing in popularity among many organizations.

18. To cope with the uncertainty accompanying today's economy, many firms have increased their
   a. job flexibility.
   b. long-term debt.
   c. hiring quotas.
   d. union membership.
   e. capital expenses.

19. Lower costs, less need for rehiring and retraining after a downsizing, and greater ease in scheduling staff are all benefits of
   a. equal employment opportunity.
   b. self-employment.
   c. regulated competition.
   d. flexible job arrangements.
   e. the baby boomer generation.

20. The framework in this chapter for linking motivation theories and operational methods is based on the idea that motivated behavior can be induced by _____ or _____ circumstances.
   a. specific, general
   b. need-based, process-based
   c. new, old
   d. individual, collective
   e. work-related, family-related

21. Megan likes to set up her subordinates' jobs by scientifically studying the work, breaking it down into small component tasks, and then standardizing the procedures for completing those tasks across all workers. Megan follows which approach to job design?
   a. Job rotation
   b. Job enlargement
   c. Job specialization
   d. Job enrichment
   e. Job characteristics

22. Kyle works in a machine shop. Every two weeks he moves to a different machine. Two weeks ago, he was stationed at the drill press; for the next two weeks, he

will work at the lathe; and two weeks from now, he will operate the metal press. Kyle's job is based on

a. rotation.
b. enlargement.
c. specialization.
d. enrichment.
e. facets.

23. According to the job characteristics theory, employees are most highly motivated when they achieve critical psychological states. Which of the following is not one of these critical psychological states?

a. Experienced meaningfulness of the work
b. Experienced satisfaction with pay for the work
c. Experienced responsibility for work outcomes
d. Knowledge of results
e. All of the above are critical psychological states in the job characteristics theory.

24. Bill is a general automotive mechanic. He fixes virtually every aspect of cars, from body work to engine repairs to interior and electronics. According to the job characteristics theory, Bill's job entails a high level of

a. autonomy.
b. feedback.
c. job specialization.
d. job rotation.
e. skill variety.

25. Job characteristics theory can be put into practice by implementing all of the following except

a. forming natural work units.
b. combining existing tasks into more complex ones.
c. establishing direct relationships between workers and clients.
d. increasing worker autonomy through vertical loading.
e. eliminating open feedback channels.

26. During the human relations movement (1930s–1950s), managers tended to view participation primarily as a way to

a. reduce employee theft.
b. increase job satisfaction.
c. eliminate unions.
d. close feedback channels.
e. reduce managers' workloads.

27. Which of the following best illustrates the relationship between participation and expectancy theory?

a. Employees who participate in making decisions will perceive they are being treated fairly.
b. Employees who participate in making decisions will better understand the linkage between their performance and the rewards they want most.

c. Employees who participate in making decisions will be absent less often.
d. Employees who participate in making decisions will be less likely to join unions.
e. Employees who participate in making decisions will be more committed to the organization.

28. Using work teams is a fairly common way to

a. build power for managers.
b. enlarge jobs.
c. empower workers.
d. increase job specialization.
e. limit participation.

29. For empowerment to enhance organizational effectiveness, all of the following conditions must exist except

a. the organization must be sincere in its efforts to spread power and autonomy.
b. the organization must be committed to maintaining participation and empowerment.
c. The organization must be systematic and patient in its efforts to empower workers.
d. The organization must be well established and engage in free-market practices.
e. All of the above are necessary conditions for empowerment to enhance organizational effectiveness.

30. Madison and Kennedy both want to work at The Fundamentals Group, a consulting firm that is looking to hire a new receptionist. However, neither wants to work a full forty-hour week. Which of the following alternative work schedules might solve this problem?

a. Flextime
b. Core time
c. Job sharing
d. Compressed workweek
e. Job enrichment

31. Organizations are increasingly using telecommuting because

a. telecommuters can be paid less.
b. telecommuters arrive at work when there is less traffic.
c. telecommuters need less training.
d. telecommuters require less empowerment.
e. telecommuters don't need to take as much "formal" time off.

CHAPTER 6

Goal Setting, Performance Management, and Rewards

MANAGEMENT PREVIEW

This chapter continues our discussion of how managers can use various strategies and techniques to enhance employee motivation and performance. Essentially, this chapter follows a logical progression of discrete activities that, taken together, provide an integrated, systematic approach to motivating employee performance. This sequence involves setting goals, evaluating performance, and providing rewards. We begin by examining the role of goal setting in employee motivation. Next, we look at performance management and measurement. Then we discuss in more detail how a good performance management system contributes to total quality management. We subsequently turn to reward systems and their role in motivation. Finally, we identify important types of rewards and explore perspectives on managing reward systems.

After you have studied this chapter, you should be able to:

☐ *Describe goal setting and relate it to motivation.*
☐ *Discuss performance management in organizations.*
☐ *Identify the key elements in an effective organizational reward system.*
☐ *Describe the issues and processes involved in managing reward systems.*

We begin by describing how Honda is using access to training as a meaningful reward for employees.

Employees often welcome the chance to obtain additional training, particularly if their employer is willing to foot the bill. Training is legitimately viewed as a means to increase workers' skills; these new skills, in turn, can lead to enhanced opportunities for promotion and advancement. Training also provides some protection against job loss because skilled workers can more easily find new employment if their current jobs are eliminated. Employers also appreciate the benefit training offers them: a more skilled and flexible workforce.

But have you ever heard of a company paying to train employees *before* they are hired? That's exactly what's happening at Honda's new minivan factory in Lincoln, Alabama. The automaker has built a $10 million pretraining facility, which includes replicas of Honda production equipment and multimedia classrooms. Andy Ritter, a Honda human resources manager, was chosen to lead the innovative project. He explains, "I knew I would need to find and train about 1,500 employees … The clock was ticking." Ritter brought a staff of experienced Honda managers to the new facility. Jim Willman became part of Ritter's training team. Willman says, "Everything in Ohio [Honda's first U.S. plant], I had inherited. The systems were in place; anyone could have done it. Andy [Ritter] gave me license to come down here and do it my way. He said, 'If it worked well in Ohio, we'll take it, but we don't have to use anything we're not comfortable with.'" Ken Pyo, who became the quality manager, maintains, "I saw an opportunity to live out a vision in quality that I had. It would have been very difficult for me to change things in Ohio because they're so instilled." As a result of Ritter's team effort, the Alabama plant opened six months earlier than scheduled.

In the program, applicants for production work are screened for education, experience, and residency requirements. Those who pass the screening then participate in a six-week training course that meets in the evenings. Trainees learn many different types of information about working at Honda, including viewing a video of a Honda assembly line and discussing how to get along with Japanese coworkers. Hands-on training requires applicants to perform basic production tasks while a team of assessors grades their performance.

During the training, "[Honda explains everything] up front, so there's no surprise. About 15 percent drop out," according to Lee Hammett, training project manager for Alabama Industrial Development Training. Even after applicants successfully complete the training course, there is no job guarantee, just the chance to apply for open positions. Furthermore, applicants may even have to risk their current jobs to take the training; some local businesses reportedly have fired employees who sign up for the sessions. Hammett says, "99 percent of the people who participate in the training have full-time jobs. They commit to the time and effort of the program with no guarantees. If they survive until the end, it tells Honda something special about them." Thus far, 2,600 trainees have completed the course, with another 1,400 waiting. Feedback about the program has been positive. Wendy Curvin, now a quality administrator, explains, "They taught you how to do things over and over so you'd see what it was like, and I'm using things I learned in the classroom … every day."

"[Applicants] commit to … the program with no guarantees. If they survive until the end, it tells Honda something special about them."—Lee Hammett, training manager, Alabama Industrial Development Training

References: Hiroyuki Yoshino, "Remarks: 2003 Year-End Press Conference," Honda website, www.hondanews.com on April 29, 2004; Robert J. Grossman, "Made from Scratch," *HR Magazine*, April 2002, pp. 44–48 (quotation, p. 48); "The Top 25 Managers of the Year: Hiroyuki Yoshino of Honda Motor," *BusinessWeek*, January 14, 2002.

For years, management experts have advocated the importance of providing meaningful rewards for employees. But until recently, most firms focused primarily on pay as the basic reward offered to employees. As the opening case illustrates, however, some forward-looking companies are realizing the benefit of offering new and innovative reward opportunities, including valuable job skills training. Of course, both the companies and the employees they seek to reward have important goals they hope to achieve. Goals, then, play an important foundational role in motivating employee behavior. As you will see, goals provide context and direction for assessing performance and allocating rewards.[1]

Goal Setting and Motivation

┌─ *LEARNING OBJECTIVE* ─┐

Describe goal setting and relate it to motivation.

A **goal** is a desirable objective.

Self-efficacy is the extent to which people believe they can accomplish their goals even if they failed to do so in the past.

Goal difficulty is the extent to which a goal is challenging and requires effort.

Goal setting is a very useful method of enhancing employee performance. From a motivational perspective, a **goal** is a desirable objective. Goals are used for two purposes in most organizations. First, they provide a useful framework for managing motivation. Managers and employees can set goals for themselves and then work toward them. Thus, if the organization's goal is to increase sales by 10 percent, a manager can use individual goals to help attain the overall goal. Second, goals are an effective control device; control is the monitoring by management of how well the organization is performing. Comparing people's short-term performances with their goals can be an effective way to monitor the organization's long-run performance.

Social learning theory perhaps best describes the role of goal setting in organizations.[2] This perspective suggests that feelings of pride or shame about performance are a function of the extent to which people achieve their goals. A person who achieves a goal will be proud of having done so, whereas a person who fails to achieve a goal will feel personal disappointment and perhaps even shame. Individuals' degree of pride or disappointment is affected by their **self-efficacy,** the extent to which they believe they can still meet their goals even if they failed to do so in the past.

Goal-Setting Theory

Social learning theory provides insights into why and how goals can motivate behavior. It also helps us understand how different people cope with failure to reach their goals. The research of Edwin Locke and his associates most clearly established the utility of goal-setting theory in a motivational context.[3]

Locke's goal-setting theory of motivation assumes behavior is a result of conscious goals and intentions. Therefore, by setting goals for people in the organization, a manager should be able to influence their behavior. Given this premise, the challenge is to develop a thorough understanding of the processes by which people set goals and then work to reach them. In the original version of goal-setting theory, two specific goal characteristics, goal difficulty and goal specificity, were expected to shape performance.

Goal Difficulty   **Goal difficulty** is the extent to which a goal is challenging and requires effort. If people work to achieve goals, it is reasonable to assume they will work harder to achieve more difficult goals. However, a goal must not be so difficult that it is unattainable. If a new manager asks her sales force to increase sales by 300 percent, the group may actually ignore her charge because they regard it as impossible to reach. A more realistic but still difficult goal—perhaps a 20 percent increase in sales—would probably be a better incentive. A substantial body of research supports the importance of goal difficulty.[4] In one study, managers at Weyerhaeuser set difficult goals for truck drivers hauling loads of timber from cutting sites to wood yards. Over a nine-month period, the drivers increased the quantity of wood they delivered by an amount that would have required $250,000 worth of new trucks at the previous per-truck average load.[5] Reinforcement also fosters motivation toward difficult goals. A person who is rewarded for achieving a difficult goal will be more inclined to strive toward the next difficult goal than will someone who received no reward for reaching the first goal.

Goals, or desirable objectives, play two important roles in organizations: They provide a framework for managing motivation, and they are effective control devices. Dr. Taryn Rose started her career as an orthopedic surgeon. But since one of her earliest interests was fashion, she was motivated to create fashionable women's footwear that was comfortable and less damaging to feet than traditional designer shoes. Motivated by her sense of style and her understanding of bone structures, she launched a line of designer shoes in 1997. Today the pricey shoes are sold in her two boutiques (in Beverly Hills and New York City), as well as in more than 200 other retail outlets, such as Neiman Marcus and Nordstrom. She still practices medicine, but spends most of her time running her growing shoe empire.

Goal specificity is the clarity and precision of a goal.

Goal acceptance is the extent to which a person accepts a goal as his or her own.

Goal commitment is the extent to which an individual is personally interested in reaching a goal.

Goal Specificity   **Goal specificity** is the clarity and precision of a goal. A goal of "increasing productivity" is not very specific; a goal of "increasing productivity by 3 percent in the next six months" is quite specific. Some goals, such as those involving costs, output, profitability, and growth, can easily be stated in clear, precise terms. Other goals, such as improving employee job satisfaction and morale, company image and reputation, ethical behavior, and social responsibility, are much harder to state in specific terms.

Like difficulty, specificity has been shown to be consistently related to performance. The study of timber truck drivers previously mentioned also examined goal specificity. The initial loads the truck drivers were carrying were found to be 60 percent of the maximum weight each truck could haul. The managers set a new goal for drivers of 94 percent, which the drivers were soon able to reach. Thus, the goal was quite specific as well as difficult.

Locke's theory attracted much widespread interest and support from both researchers and managers. Thus, Locke, together with Gary Latham, eventually proposed an expanded model of the goal-setting process. The expanded model, shown in Figure 6.1, attempts to capture more fully the complexities of goal setting in organizations.

The expanded theory argues that goal-directed effort is a function of four goal attributes: difficulty and specificity (which we already discussed), acceptance, and commitment. **Goal acceptance** is the extent to which a person accepts a goal as his or her own. **Goal commitment** is the extent to which an individual is personally interested in reaching the goal. The manager who vows to take whatever steps are necessary to cut costs by 10 percent has made a commitment to achieving the goal. Factors that can foster goal acceptance and commitment include participating in the goal-setting process, making goals challenging but realistic, and believing that goal achievement will lead to valued rewards.[6]

The interaction of goal-directed effort, organizational support, and individual abilities and traits determines actual performance. Organizational support is everything the organization does to help or hinder performance. Positive support might mean providing whatever resources are needed to meet the goal; negative support might mean failing to provide such resources, perhaps due to cost considerations or staff reductions. Individual abilities and traits are the skills and other personal

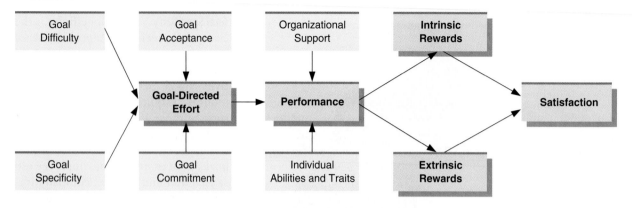

FIGURE 6.1

The Goal-Setting Theory

*The goal-setting theory of motivation provides an important means of enhancing employees' motivation. As illustrated here, appropriate goal diffi-
culty, specificity, acceptance, and commitment contribute to goal-directed effort. This effort, in turn, has a direct impact on performance.*

Source: From *Organizational Dynamics*, Vol. 8, No. 2, Gary P. Latham et al., "Goal Setting—A Motivational Technique That Works," pp. 68–80, 1979, with permission from Elsevier.

characteristics necessary to do a job. As a result of performance, a person receives various intrinsic and extrinsic rewards that, in turn, influence satisfaction. Note that the latter stages of this model are quite similar to those of the Porter-Lawler expectancy model discussed in Chapter 4.

Broader Perspectives on Goal Setting

Management by objectives (MBO) is a collaborative goal-setting process through which organizational goals cascade down throughout the organization.

Some organizations undertake goal setting from the somewhat broader perspective of **management by objectives,** or **MBO.** MBO is essentially a collaborative goal-setting process through which organizational goals systematically cascade down through the organization. Our discussion describes a generic approach, but many organizations adapt MBO to suit their own purposes.

A successful MBO program starts with top managers establishing overall goals for the organization. After these goals have been set, managers and employees throughout the organization collaborate to set subsidiary goals. First, the overall goals are communicated to everyone. Then each manager meets with each subordinate. During these meetings, the manager explains the unit goals to the subordinate, and the two together determine how the subordinate can contribute to the goals most effectively. The manager acts as a counselor and helps ensure that the subordinate develops goals that are verifiable. For example, a goal of "cutting costs by 5 percent" is verifiable, whereas a goal of "doing my best" is not. Finally, manager and subordinate ensure that the subordinate has the resources needed to reach his or her goals. The entire process spirals downward as each subordinate meets with his or her own subordinates to develop their goals. Thus, as we noted earlier, the initial goals set at the top cascade down through the entire organization.

During the time frame set for goal attainment (usually one year), the manager periodically meets with each subordinate to check progress. It may be necessary to modify goals in light of new information, provide additional resources, or take some other action. At the end of the specified time period, managers hold a final evaluation meeting with each subordinate. At this meeting, manager and subordinate assess how well goals were met and discuss why. This meeting often serves as the annual performance review as well, determining salary adjustments and other rewards based on reaching goals. This meeting may also serve as the initial goal-setting meeting for the next year's cycle.

Evaluation and Implications

Goal-setting theory has been widely tested in a variety of settings. Research has demonstrated fairly consistently that goal difficulty and specificity are closely associated with performance. Other elements of the theory, such as acceptance and commitment, have been studied less frequently. A few studies have shown the importance of acceptance and commitment, but little is currently known about how people accept and become committed to goals. Goal-setting theory may also focus too heavily on the short run at the expense of long-term considerations. Despite these questions, however, goal setting is clearly an important way for managers to convert motivation into actual improved performance.

From the broader perspective, MBO remains a very popular technique. Alcoa, Tenneco, Black & Decker, General Foods, and Du Pont, for example, have used versions of MBO with widespread success. The technique's popularity stems in part from its many strengths. For one thing, MBO clearly has the potential to motivate employees because it helps implement goal-setting theory on a systematic basis throughout the organization. It also clarifies the basis for rewards, and it can stimulate communication. Performance appraisals are easier and more clear-cut under MBO. Further, managers can use the system for control purposes.

However, using MBO also presents pitfalls, especially if a firm takes too many shortcuts or inadvertently undermines how the process is supposed to work. Sometimes, for instance, top managers do not really participate; that is, the goals are actually established at the middle levels of the organization and may not reflect the real goals of top management. If employees believe this situation to be true, they may become cynical, interpreting the lack of participation by top management as a sign that the goals are not important and their own involvement is therefore a waste of time. MBO also has a tendency to overemphasize quantitative goals to enhance verifiability. Another potential liability is that an MBO system requires a great deal of paperwork and recordkeeping, since every goal must be documented. Finally, some managers do not really let subordinates participate in goal setting but instead merely assign goals and order subordinates to accept them.

On balance, MBO is often an effective and useful system for managing goal setting and enhancing performance in organizations. Research suggests that it can actually do many of the things its advocates claim, but must also be handled carefully. In particular, most organizations need to tailor MBO to their own unique circumstances. When properly used, MBO can also be an effective approach to managing an organization's reward system. It requires, however, one-on-one interactions between each supervisor and each employee, which are often difficult because of the time they take and the likelihood that at least some of these interactions will involve critical assessments of unacceptable performance.

Performance Management in Organizations

LEARNING OBJECTIVE

Discuss performance management in organizations.

As described earlier, most goals are oriented toward some element of performance. Managers can do a variety of things to enhance employee motivation and performance, including redesigning jobs, allowing greater participation, creating alternative work arrangements, and setting goals. They may also fail to take steps that might have improved motivation and performance, and they may even inadvertently do things that reduce motivation and performance. Thus, it is clearly important that performance be approached as something that can and should be managed.

The Nature of Performance Management

The core of performance management is the actual measurement of the performance of an individual or a group. **Performance measurement,** or **performance appraisal,** is the process by which a manager (1) evaluates an employee's work behaviors by measurement and comparison with previously established standards, (2) documents the results, and (3) communicates the results to the employee.[7] A **performance management system (PMS)** comprises the processes and activities involved in performance appraisals, as shown in Figure 6.2.

Simple performance appraisal involves a manager and an employee, whereas a PMS incorporates the total quality management context along with the organizational policies, procedures, and resources that support the activity being approved. The timing and frequency of evaluations, choice of who appraises whom, measurement procedures, methods of recording the evaluations, and storage and distribution of information are all aspects of the PMS.

Purposes of Performance Measurement

Performance measurement may serve many purposes. The ability to provide valuable feedback is one critical purpose. Feedback, in turn, tells the employee where she or he stands in the eyes of the organization. Appraisal results, of course, are also used to decide and justify reward allocations. Performance evaluations may be used as a starting point for discussions of training, development, and improvement. Finally, the data produced by the performance appraisal system can be used to forecast fu-

Performance measurement, or **performance appraisal,** is the process by which a manager (1) evaluates an employee's work behaviors by measurement and comparison with previously established standards, (2) documents the results, and (3) communicates the results to the employee.

A **performance management system (PMS)** comprises the processes and activities involved in performance appraisals.

FIGURE 6.2

The Performance Management System

An organization's performance management system plays an important role in determining its overall level of effectiveness. This is especially true when the organization is attempting to employ total quality management. Key elements of a performance management system, as shown here, include timing and frequency of evaluations, choice of who does the evaluation, choice of measurement procedures, storage and distribution of performance information, and recording methods. These elements are used by managers and employees in most organizations.

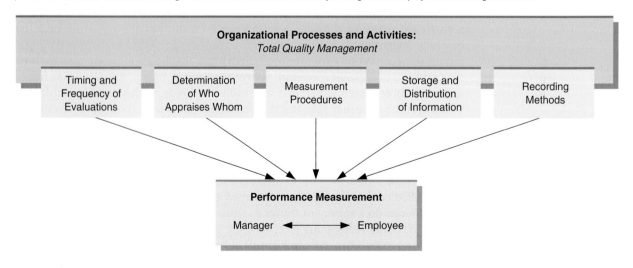

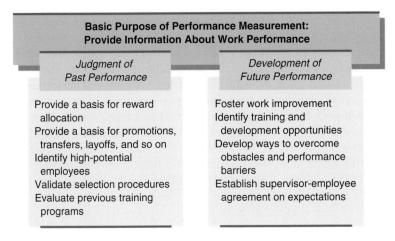

Basic Purpose of Performance Measurement:
Provide Information About Work Performance

Judgment of Past Performance	*Development of Future Performance*
Provide a basis for reward allocation Provide a basis for promotions, transfers, layoffs, and so on Identify high-potential employees Validate selection procedures Evaluate previous training programs	Foster work improvement Identify training and development opportunities Develop ways to overcome obstacles and performance barriers Establish supervisor-employee agreement on expectations

FIGURE 6.3

Purposes of Performance Measurement

Performance measurement plays a variety of roles in most organizations. This figure illustrates that these roles can help managers judge an employee's past performance and help managers and employees improve future performance.

ture human resource needs, plan management succession, and guide other human resource activities such as recruiting, training, and development programs.

Providing job performance feedback is the primary use of appraisal information. Performance appraisal information can indicate that an employee is ready for promotion or that he or she needs additional training to gain experience in another area of company operations. It may also show that a person lacks the skills for a certain job and that another person should be recruited to fill that particular role. Other purposes of performance appraisal can be grouped into two broad categories, judgment and development, as shown in Figure 6.3.

Performance appraisals with a judgmental orientation focus on past performance and deal mainly with measuring and comparing performance and with the uses of the information generated. Appraisals with a developmental orientation focus on the future and use information from evaluations to improve performance. If improved future performance is the intent of the appraisal process, the manager may focus on goals or targets for the employee, on eliminating obstacles or problems that hinder performance, and on future training needs.

Performance Measurement Basics

Employee appraisals are common in every type of organization, but how they are performed may vary. Many issues must be considered in determining how to conduct an appraisal. Three important issues are who does the appraisals, how often they are conducted, and how performance is measured.

The Appraiser   In most appraisal systems, the employee's primary evaluator is the supervisor. This stems from the obvious fact that the supervisor is presumably in the best position to be aware of the employee's day-to-day performance. Further, it is the supervisor who has traditionally provided performance feedback to employees and determined performance-based rewards and sanctions. Problems often arise, however, if the supervisor has incomplete or distorted information about the employee's performance. For example, the supervisor may have little firsthand knowledge of the performance of an employee who works alone outside the company premises, such as a salesperson who makes solo calls on clients or a maintenance person who handles equipment problems in the field. Similar problems may arise when the supervisor has a limited understanding of the technical knowledge involved in an employee's job.

One solution to these problems is a multiple-rater system that incorporates the ratings of several people familiar with the employee's performance. One alternative is to use the employee as an evaluator. Although they may not actually do so, most employees are actually very capable of evaluating themselves in an unbiased manner.

360-degree feedback is a performance management system in which people receive performance feedback from those on all sides of them in the organization: their boss, their colleagues and peers, and their own subordinates.

One of the more interesting approaches being used in many companies today is **360-degree feedback,** a performance management system in which people receive performance feedback from those on all sides of them in the organization: their boss, their colleagues and peers, and their own subordinates. Thus, the feedback comes from all around them, or from 360 degrees. This form of performance evaluation can be very beneficial to managers because it typically gives them a much wider range of performance-related feedback than a traditional evaluation provides. That is, rather than focusing narrowly on objective performance, such as sales increases or productivity gains, 360 feedback often focuses on such factors as interpersonal relations and style. For example, one person may learn that she stands too close to other people when she talks, another that he has a bad temper. These are the kinds of things a supervisor may not even be aware of, much less report as part of a performance appraisal. Subordinates or peers are much more willing to provide this sort of feedback.

Of course, to benefit from 360-degree feedback, a manager must have a thick skin. The manager is likely to hear some personal comments on sensitive topics, which may be threatening. Thus, a 360-feedback system must be carefully managed so that its focus remains on constructive rather than destructive criticism.[8] Because of its potential advantages and despite its potential shortcomings, many companies today are using this approach to performance feedback. AT&T, Nestlé, Pitney Bowes, and Chase Manhattan Bank are just a few major companies using 360-degree feedback to help managers improve a wide variety of performance-related behaviors.[9]

Frequency of the Appraisal   Another important issue is the frequency of appraisals. Regardless of the employee's level of performance, the type of task, or the employee's need for information on performance, the organization usually conducts performance appraisals on a regular basis, typically once a year. Annual performance appraisals are convenient for administrative purposes such as recordkeeping and scheduling. Some organizations also conduct appraisals semiannually.[10] Several systems for monitoring employee performance on an as-needed basis have been proposed as an alternative to the traditional annual system.

Managers in international settings must take care to incorporate cultural factors in their performance appraisal strategies. For example, in highly individualistic cultures such as the United States, appraising performance at the individual level is both common and accepted. In collectivistic cultures such as Japan, however, performance appraisals almost always need to focus more on group performance and feedback. In countries where people put a lot of faith in destiny, fate, or some form of divine control, employees may be strongly unreceptive to performance feedback, believing their actions are irrelevant to the results that follow.

Measuring Performance   The cornerstone of a good PMS is the method for measuring performance. Detailed descriptions of the many different methods for measuring performance are beyond the scope of this book; they are more appropriately covered in a course in human resource management or a specialized course in performance appraisal. However, we present a few general comments about how to measure performance. The Mastering Change box provides some useful insights into recent approaches to measuring performance.

The measurement method provides the information managers use to make decisions about salary adjustment, promotion, transfer, training, and discipline. The courts and Equal Employment Opportunity Commission guidelines have

MASTERING CHANGE

High-Tech Performance Measurement: Workers' Friend or Foe?

Advances in technology have enabled companies to gather, analyze, report, and use information in ways that would have been impossible a decade ago. One area in great need of improved accuracy and objectivity is worker performance measurement. "[W]hat was once a smushy, subjective effort by finger-in-the-wind managers is hitting new levels of scientific precision," says *BusinessWeek* writer Michelle Conlin. British Airways manager Steven Pruneau claims that the productivity of his airline's physical and financial capital can be measured precisely with indicators such as the hours planes spend in the air versus on the ground, but he explains, "[We don't have] a fraction of that kind of information about the productivity of our other assets—our human capital."

Consider the effects of the technology revolution on performance measurement at household goods retailer Pier 1 Imports. In the past, daily sales reports could be calculated only at the end of the day; thus, employees didn't know how well they were doing until it was too late to do anything about it. Now Pier 1 Imports uses information technology to tabulate sales continuously. In cities where Pier 1 has multiple stores, the same technology pits one store against the others because employees see their store's results as well as those of other stores. Employees check the sales performance data regularly and set improvement goals that enable the firm to boost sales and employees to increase their bonuses.

> *"[Worker performance measurement] was once a smushy, subjective effort by finger-in-the-wind managers, [but now it] is hitting new levels of scientific precision."—Michelle Conlin, writer for* BusinessWeek

At British Airways, software monitors employees' every action, ensuring their time in the break room or on a personal phone call doesn't get charged to the company. Progress toward corporate goals such as increased ticket sales and complaint resolutions is also tracked. Workers have instant access to their performance scores and can see the impact of incentive compensation on their daily pay.

Some firms are employing even more intrusive technologies, such as recording entry card data to determine what time workers arrive and leave and using security cameras—sometimes without notifying employees of their presence—in cubicles, hallways, and even restrooms. Software now enables managers to receive reports of every website their workers have accessed and also records employees' keystrokes. Many workers see the benefits of accurate and objective performance measurement, but others claim the systems invade workers' privacy. As technology continues to evolve, this debate is sure to persist.

References: James C. Cooper and Kathleen Madigan, "The Surprise Economy," *BusinessWeek*, March 18, 2002; "The Software Says You're Just Average," *BusinessWeek*, February 25, 2002 (quotation); "Making Performance Reviews Pay Off," *BusinessWeek*, February 6, 2002; Eric Wahlgren, "Have Investors Missed the Boat on Pier 1?" *BusinessWeek*, December 21, 2001.

mandated that performance measurements be based on job-related criteria rather than on some other factor such as age, sex, religion, or national origin. In addition, to provide useful information for the decision maker, performance appraisals must be valid, reliable, and free of bias. They must not produce ratings that are consistently too lenient, too severe, or clustered in the middle. They must also be free of perceptual and timing errors.

Some of the most popular methods for evaluating individual performance are graphic rating scales, checklists, essays or diaries, behaviorally anchored rating scales, and forced-choice systems. These systems are easy to use and familiar to most managers. However, two major problems are common to all individual methods: a tendency to rate most individuals at about the same level and the inability to discriminate among variable levels of performance.

Comparative methods evaluate two or more employees by comparing them with each other on various performance dimensions. The most popular comparative methods are ranking, forced distribution, paired comparisons, and the use of multiple raters. Comparative methods, however, are more difficult to use than the individual methods, are unfamiliar to many managers, and may require sophisticated development procedures and a computerized analytical system to extract usable information.

Individual Rewards in Organizations

As noted earlier, a primary purpose of performance management is to provide a basis for rewarding employees. We now turn to rewards and their impact on employee motivation and performance. The **reward system** consists of all organizational components—including people, processes, rules and procedures, and decision-making activities—involved in allocating compensation and benefits to employees in exchange for their contributions to the organization.[11] As we examine organizational reward systems, it is important to keep in mind their role in psychological contracts (discussed in Chapter 3) and employee motivation (discussed in Chapter 4). Rewards constitute many of the inducements organizations provide to employees as their part of the psychological contract, for example. Rewards also satisfy some of the needs employees attempt to meet through their choice of work-related behaviors.

Roles, Purposes, and Meanings of Rewards

The purpose of the reward system in most organizations is to attract, retain, and motivate qualified employees. The organization's compensation structure must be equitable and consistent to ensure equality of treatment and compliance with the law. Compensation should also be a fair reward for the individual's contributions to the organization, although in most cases these contributions are difficult, if not impossible, to measure objectively. Given this limitation, managers should be as fair and equitable as possible. Finally, the system must be competitive in the external labor market so the organization can attract and retain competent workers in appropriate fields.[12]

Beyond these broad considerations, an organization must develop its philosophy of compensation based on its own conditions and needs, and this philosophy must be defined and built into the actual reward system. For example, Wal-Mart has a policy that none of its employees will be paid the minimum wage. Even though it may pay some people only slightly more than this minimum, the firm nevertheless attempts to communicate to all workers that it places a higher value on their contributions than just having to pay them the lowest wage possible.

The organization needs to decide what types of behaviors or performance it wants to encourage with a reward system, because what is rewarded tends to recur. Possible behaviors include performance, longevity, attendance, loyalty, contributions to the "bottom line," responsibility, and conformity. Performance measurement, as described earlier, assesses these behaviors, but the choice of which behaviors to reward is a function of the compensation system. A reward system must also take into account volatile economic issues such as inflation, market conditions, technology, labor union activities, and so forth.

The **surface value of a reward** to an employee is its objective meaning or worth.

The **symbolic value of a reward** to an employee is its subjective and personal meaning or worth.

It is also important for the organization to recognize that organizational rewards have many meanings for employees. Intrinsic and extrinsic rewards carry both surface and symbolic value. The **surface value** of a reward to an employee is its objective meaning or worth. A salary increase of 5 percent, for example, means an individual has 5 percent more spending power than before, whereas a promotion, on the surface, means new duties and responsibilities. Managers must recognize that rewards also carry **symbolic value.** If a person gets a 3 percent salary increase when everyone else gets 5 percent, one plausible meaning is that the organization values other employees more. But if the same person gets 3 percent and all others get only 1 percent, the meaning may be just the opposite: the individual is seen as the most valuable employee. Thus, rewards convey to people not only how much the organization values them but also their importance relative to others. Managers need to tune in to the many meanings rewards can convey—not only to the surface messages but to the symbolic messages as well.

Types of Rewards

Most organizations use several types of rewards. The most common forms are base pay (wages or salary), incentive systems, benefits, perquisites, and awards. These rewards are combined to create an individual's **compensation package.**

An individual's **compensation package** is the total array of money (wages, salary, or commission), incentives, benefits, perquisites, and awards provided by the organization.

Base Pay   For most people, the most important reward for work is the pay they receive. Obviously money is important because of the things it can buy, but as we just noted, it can also symbolize an employee's worth. Pay is very important to an organization for a variety of reasons. For one thing, an effectively planned and managed pay system can improve motivation and performance. For another, employee compensation is a major cost of doing business—as much as 50 to 60 percent in many organizations; thus, a poorly designed system can be an expensive proposition. Finally, since pay is considered a major source of employee dissatisfaction, a poorly designed system can result in problems in other areas, such as turnover and low morale.

An **incentive system** is a plan in which employees can earn additional compensation in return for certain types of performance.

Incentive Systems   **Incentive systems** are plans that allow employees to earn additional compensation in return for certain types of performance. Examples of incentive programs include the following:

1. *Piecework programs,* which tie a worker's earnings to the number of units produced
2. *Gain-sharing programs,* which grant additional earnings to employees or work groups for cost reduction ideas
3. *Bonus systems,* which provide managers with lump-sum payments from a special fund based on the financial performance of the organization or a unit
4. *Long-term compensation,* which gives managers additional income based on stock price performance, earnings per share, or return on equity
5. *Merit pay plans,* which base pay raises on the employee's performance
6. *Profit-sharing plans,* which distribute a portion of the firm's profits to all employees at a predetermined rate
7. *Employee stock option plans,* which set aside stock in the company for employees to purchase at a reduced rate

Plans oriented mainly toward individual employees may cause increased competition for the rewards and some possibly disruptive behaviors, such as sabotaging a coworker's performance, sacrificing quality for quantity, or competing for

Anne Mulcahy is CEO of Xerox. Her compensation includes a combination of base salary plus incentives. Mulcahy's base salary is $2.5 million. However, she can also earn a considerable bonus plus receive potentially lucrative stock options if the firm meets and then exceeds the performance expectations of its board of directors.

customers. A group incentive plan, on the other hand, requires employees to trust one another and work together. Of course, incentive systems have advantages and disadvantages.

Long-term compensation for executives is particularly controversial because of the large sums of money involved and the basis for the payments. Indeed, executive compensation is one of the most controversial issues to challenge U.S. businesses in recent years. News reports and the popular press are quick to report stories about how this or that executive just received a huge windfall from his or her organization. Clearly, successful top managers deserve significant rewards. The job of a senior executive, especially a CEO, is grueling and stressful, and takes talent and decades of hard work to reach. Only a small handful of managers ever attain a top position in a major corporation. The question is whether some companies are overrewarding such managers for their contributions to the organization.[13]

When a firm is growing rapidly, and its profits are also growing rapidly, few would object to paying the CEO well. However, objections arise when an organization is laying off workers, its financial performance is less than expected, and the CEO is still earning a huge amount of money. Such a situation dictates that the company's board of directors take a close look at the appropriateness of its actions.[14]

Indirect Compensation   Another major component of the compensation package is **indirect compensation,** also commonly referred to as the *employee benefits plan.* Typical benefits provided by businesses include the following:

Indirect compensation, or *benefits,* refers to non wage or salary compensation such as paid time off and insurance coverage.

1. *Payment for time not worked,* both on and off the job. On-the-job free time includes lunch, rest, coffee breaks, and wash-up or get-ready time. Off-the-job time not worked includes vacation, sick leave, holidays, and personal days.
2. *Social security contributions.* The employer contributes half the money paid into the system established under the Federal Insurance Contributions Act (FICA). The employee pays the other half.
3. *Unemployment compensation.* People who have lost their jobs or are temporarily laid off get a percentage of their wages from an insurance-like program.
4. *Disability and workers' compensation benefits.* Employers contribute funds to help workers who cannot work due to occupational injury or ailment.
5. *Life and health insurance programs.* Most organizations offer insurance at a cost far below what individuals would pay to buy insurance on their own.
6. *Pension or retirement plans.* Most organizations offer plans to provide supplementary income to employees after they retire.

A company's social security, unemployment, and workers' compensation contributions are set by law. How much to contribute for other kinds of benefits is up to each company. Some organizations contribute more to the cost of these benefits than others. Some companies pay the entire cost; others pay a percentage of the cost of certain benefits, such as health insurance, and bear the entire cost of other benefits. Offering benefits beyond wages became a standard component of compensation during World War II as a way to increase employee compensation when wage controls were in effect. Since then, competition for employees and employee demands (expressed, for instance, in union bargaining) have caused companies to increase these benefits. In many organizations today, benefits account for 30 to 40 percent of the payroll.

The burden of providing employee benefits is growing heavier for firms in the United States than for organizations in other countries, especially among unionized firms. For example, consider the problem General Motors faces. Workers at GM's brake factory in Dayton, Ohio, earn an average of $27 an hour in wages. They also earn another $16 an hour in benefits, including full health care coverage with no deductibles, full pension benefits after thirty years of service, life and disability insurance, and legal services. Thus, GM's total labor costs per worker at the factory average $43 an hour. Meanwhile a German rival, Robert Bosch GmbH, has a nonunionized brake plant in South Carolina. It pays its workers an average of $18 an hour in wages, and its hourly benefit cost is around $5. Bosch's benefits include medical coverage with a $2,000 deductible, 401-K retirement plans with employee participation, and life and disability coverage. Bosch's total hourly labor costs per worker, therefore, are only $23. Toyota, Nissan, and Honda buy most of their brakes for their U.S. factories from Bosch, whereas General Motors must use its own factory to supply brakes. Thus, foreign competitors realize considerable cost advantages over GM in the brakes they use, and this pattern runs across a variety of other component parts as well.[15]

Perquisites are special privileges awarded to selected members of an organization, usually top managers.

Perquisites   **Perquisites** are special privileges awarded to selected members of an organization, usually top managers. For years, the top executives of many businesses were allowed privileges such as unlimited use of the company jet, motor home, vacation home, and executive dining room. In Japan, a popular perquisite is a paid membership in an exclusive golf club; a common perquisite in England is first-class travel. In the United States, the Internal Revenue Service has recently ruled that some "perks" constitute a form of income and thus can be taxed. This decision has substantially changed the nature of these benefits, but they have not entirely disappeared, nor are they likely to. Today, however, many perks tend to be more job related. For example, popular perks currently include a car and driver (so the executive can conduct business while being transported to and from work) and cellular telephones (so the executive can conduct business anywhere). More than anything else, though, perquisites seem to add to their recipients' status and thus may increase job satisfaction and reduce turnover.[16]

Awards   At many companies, employees receive awards for everything from seniority to perfect attendance, from zero defects (quality work) to cost reduction suggestions. Award programs can be costly in the time required to run them and in money if cash awards are given. But award systems can improve performance under the right conditions. In one medium-size manufacturing company, careless work habits were pushing up the costs of scrap and rework (the cost of scrapping defective parts or reworking them to meet standards). Management instituted a zero-defects program to recognize employees who did perfect or near-perfect work. During the first month, two workers in shipping caused only one defect in more than two thousand parts handled. Division management called a meeting in the lunchroom and recognized each worker with a plaque and a

Organizations often seek to recognize, reward, and motivate their best employees by giving them various awards. One long-standing tradition is to provide awards to long-term employees at key anniversary dates to reward their loyalty and dedication and to recognize their value or seniority. For such programs to be effective, the awards and prizes themselves must have value to the employees being recognized. For example, as illustrated here, although some employees might regard extra time with their boss as a reward, others clearly see it a different way.
DILBERT reprinted by permission of United Feature Syndicate, Inc.

ribbon. The next month, the same two workers had two defects, so there was no award. The following month, the two workers had zero defects, and once again top management called a meeting to give out plaques and ribbons. Elsewhere in the plant, defects, scrap, and rework decreased dramatically as workers evidently sought recognition for quality work. What succeeded in this particular plant may or may not work in others. And, of course, as the cartoon illustrates, managers and workers sometimes have very different perceptions of the value of different awards!

Managing Reward Systems

Much of our discussion on reward systems has focused on general issues. As Table 6.1 shows, however, the organization must address other issues when developing organizational reward systems. The organization must consider its ability to pay employees at certain levels, economic and labor market conditions, and the impact of the pay system on organizational financial performance. In addition, the organization must consider the relationship between performance and rewards, as well as the issues of reward system flexibility, employee participation in the reward system, pay secrecy, and expatriate compensation.

Linking Performance and Rewards

For managers to take full advantage of the symbolic value of pay, employees must perceive that their rewards are linked to their performance. For example, if everyone in an organization starts working for the same hourly rate and then receives a predetermined wage increase every six months or year, there is clearly no relationship between performance and rewards. Instead, the organization is indicating that all entry-level employees are worth the same amount, and pay increases are tied solely to the length of time worked in the organization. This holds true whether the employee is a top, average, or mediocre employee. The only requirement is that the employee works well enough to avoid being fired.

TABLE 6.1

Issues to Consider in Developing Reward Systems

Issue	Important Examples
Pay Secrecy	■ Open, closed, partial ■ Link with performance appraisal ■ Equity perceptions
Employee Participation	■ By human resource department ■ By joint employee/management committee
Flexible System	■ Cafeteria-style benefits ■ Annual lump sum or monthly bonus ■ Salary versus benefits
Ability to Pay	■ Organization's financial performance ■ Expected future earnings
Economic and Labor Market Factors	■ Inflation rate ■ Industry pay standards ■ Unemployment rate
Impact on Organizational Performance	■ Increase in costs ■ Impact on performance
Expatriate Compensation	■ Cost of living differentials ■ Managing related equity issues

At the other extreme, an organization might attempt to tie all compensation to actual performance. Thus, each new employee might start at a different wage as determined by his or her experience, education, skills, and other job-related factors. After joining the organization, the individual then receives rewards based on actual performance. One employee, for example, may start at $15 an hour because she has ten years of experience and a good performance record at her previous employer. Another may start the same job at a rate of $10.50 an hour because he has only four years' experience and an adequate but not outstanding performance record. If the first employee performs up to expectations, she may also get several pay increases, bonuses, and awards throughout the year, whereas the second employee may get only one or two small increases and no other rewards. Of course, organizations must ensure that pay differences are based strictly on performance-related factors (including seniority), not on factors unrelated to performance (such as gender, ethnicity, or other discriminatory factors).

In reality, most organizations attempt to develop a reward strategy somewhere between these two extremes. Because in reality it is difficult to differentiate all employees, most firms use some basic compensation level for everyone. For example, they may start all workers performing a specific job at the same rate, regardless of experience. They may also work to provide reasonable incentives and other inducements for high performers while taking care not to ignore the "average" employees. The key fact for managers to remember is simply that if they expect rewards to motivate performance, employees must see a clear, direct link between their own job-related behaviors and the attainment of those rewards.[17]

Flexible Reward Systems

A **flexible reward system** allows employees to choose the combination of benefits that best suits their needs.

Flexible, or cafeteria-style, reward systems are a recent and increasingly popular variation on the standard compensation system. A **flexible reward system** allows employees, within specified ranges, to choose the combination of benefits that best suits their needs. For example, a younger worker just starting out might prefer to have especially strong health care coverage with few deductibles, a worker with a few years of experience more child care benefits, a mid-career employee with greater financial security more time off with pay, and an older worker more rewards concentrated into his or her retirement plans.

Some organizations are starting to apply the flexible approach to pay. For example, employees sometimes have the option to take an annual salary increase in one lump sum rather than in monthly increments. General Electric recently implemented such a system for some of its managers. UNUM Corporation, a large insurance firm, allows all its employees the option to draw a full third of their annual compensation in the month of January. This makes it easier for them to handle such major expenses as purchasing a new automobile, buying a home, or covering college education costs for children. Obviously the administrative costs of providing this level of flexibility are greater, but many employees value this flexibility and may develop strong loyalty and attachment to an employer that offers such a compensation package.

Participative Pay Systems

In keeping with the current trend toward involving workers in organizational decision making, employee participation in the pay process is also increasing. A participative pay system may involve employees in the system's design, administration, or both. A pay system can be designed by staff members of the organization's human resources department, a committee of managers within the organization, an outside consultant, employees, or a combination of these sources. Organizations that have used a joint management employee task force to design the compensation system have generally succeeded in implementing a plan that is useful to managers and equitable to employees. Employee participation in administering the pay system is a natural extension of having employees participate in its design. Examples of companies that have involved employees in the administration of the pay system include Romac Industries, where employees vote on the pay of other employees; Graphic Controls, where each manager's pay is determined by a group of peers; and Friedman-Jacobs Company, where employees set their own wages based on their perceptions of their performance.[18]

Pay Secrecy

When a company has a policy of open salary information, the exact salary amounts for employees are public knowledge. State governments, for instance, make public the salaries of everyone on their payrolls. A policy of complete secrecy means no information is available to employees regarding other employees' salaries, average or percentage raises, or salary ranges. The National Labor Relations Board recently upheld an earlier ruling that an employer starting or enforcing a rule that forbids employees from discussing their salaries constitutes interference, restraint, and coercion of protected employee rights under the National Labor Relations Act. Although a few organizations have completely public or completely secret systems, most have systems somewhere in the middle.

Expatriate Compensation

Expatriate compensation is yet another important issue in managing reward systems.[19] Consider a manager living and working in Houston currently making $250,000 a year. That income allows the manager to live in a certain kind of home, drive a certain kind of car, have access to certain levels of medical care, and live a certain kind of lifestyle. Now suppose the manager is asked to accept a transfer to Tokyo, Geneva, or London, cities where the cost of living is considerably higher than in Houston. The same salary cannot begin to support a comparable lifestyle in those cities. Consequently, the employer is almost certain to redesign the manager's compensation package so the employee's lifestyle in the new location will be comparable to that in the former one.

Now suppose the same manager is asked to accept a transfer to an underdeveloped nation. The cost of living in this nation may be quite low by U.S. standards. But there may also be relatively few choices in housing, poorer schools and medical care, a harsh climate, greater personal danger, or similar unattractive characteristics. The firm will probably have to pay the manager some level of additional compensation to offset the decrement in quality of lifestyle. Thus, developing rewards for expatriates is a complicated process.

Figure 6.4 illustrates the approach to expatriate compensation used by one major multinational corporation. The left side of the figure shows how a U.S.

FIGURE 6.4

The Expatriate Compensation Balance Sheet

Organizations that ask employees to accept assignments in foreign locations usually must adjust their compensation levels to account for differences in cost of living and similar factors. Amoco used the system shown here. The employee's domestic base salary is first broken down into the three categories shown on the left. Then adjustments are made by adding compensation to the categories on the right until an appropriate, equitable level of compensation is achieved.

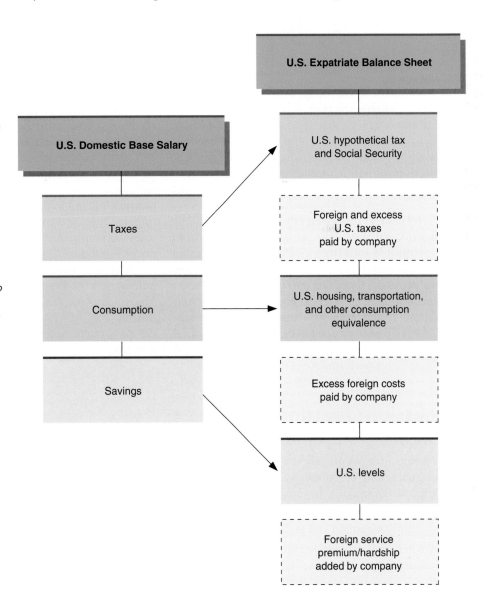

employee currently uses her or his salary: Part of it goes for taxes, part is saved, and the rest is consumed. When a person is asked to move abroad, a human resource manager works with the employee to develop an equitable balance sheet for the new compensation package. As shown on the right side of the figure, the individual's compensation package will potentially consist of six components. First, the individual will receive income to cover what his or her taxes and social security payments in the United States would have been. The employee may also have to pay foreign taxes and additional U.S. taxes as a result of the move, so the company covers these as well.

Next, the firm pays an amount adequate for the employee's current consumption levels in the United States. If the cost of living is greater in the foreign location than at home, the firm pays the excess foreign costs. The employee also receives income for saving comparable to what she or he is currently saving. Finally, if the employee faces a hardship because of the assignment, the firm provides an additional foreign service premium or hardship allowance. Not surprisingly, then, expatriate compensation packages can be very expensive for an organization and must be carefully developed and managed.[20]

Synopsis

A goal is a desirable objective. The goal-setting theory of motivation suggests that appropriate goal difficulty, specificity, acceptance, and commitment will result in higher levels of motivated performance. Management by objectives, or MBO, extends goal setting throughout an organization by cascading goals down from the top to the bottom of the hierarchy.

Performance measurement is the process by which work behaviors are measured and compared with established standards and the results recorded and communicated. Its purposes are to evaluate employees' work performance and provide information for organizational uses such as compensation, personnel planning, and employee training and development. Three primary issues in performance appraisal are who does the appraisals, how often they are conducted, and how performance is measured.

The purpose of the reward system is to attract, retain, and motivate qualified employees and to maintain a pay structure that is internally equitable and externally competitive. Rewards have both surface and symbolic value. Rewards take the form of monetary incentives, indirect compensation or benefits, perquisites, and awards. Factors such as motivational impact, cost, and fit with the organizational system must be considered when designing or evaluating a reward system.

Effective management of a reward system requires that performance be linked with rewards. Managing rewards entails dealing with issues such as flexible reward systems, employee participation in the pay system, secrecy of pay systems, and expatriate rewards.

Discussion Questions

1. Critique the goal-setting theory of motivation.
2. Develop a framework whereby an instructor could use goal setting in running a class such as this one.
3. Why are employees not simply left alone to do their jobs instead of having their performance constantly measured and evaluated?
4. In what ways is your performance as a student evaluated?
5. How is the performance of your instructor measured? What are the limitations of this method?
6. Can performance on some jobs simply not be measured? Why or why not?
7. What conditions make it easier for an organization to achieve continuous improvement in performance? What conditions make it more difficult?

8. As a student in this class, what "rewards" do you receive in exchange for your time and effort? What are the rewards for the professor who teaches this class? How do your contributions and rewards differ from those of one of your classmates?

9. Do you expect to obtain the rewards you discussed in question 8 on the basis of your intelligence, your hard work, the number of hours you spend in the library, your height, your good looks, your work experience, or some other personal factor?

10. What rewards are easiest for managers to control? What rewards are more difficult to control?

11. Institutions in federal and state governments often give the same percentage pay raise to all their employees. What do you think is the effect of this type of pay raise on employee motivation?

Organizational Behavior Case for Discussion

Rewarding the Hourly Worker

Hourly workers, people who are paid a set dollar amount for each hour they work, have long been the backbone of the U.S. economy. But times are changing, and with them the lot of the hourly worker. As with most employment conditions, organizations are able to take a wider variety of approaches to managing compensation for hourly workers. And nowhere are these differences more apparent than in the contrasting conditions for hourly workers at General Motors and Wal-Mart.

General Motors is an old, traditional industrial company that until recently was the nation's largest employer. For decades, its hourly workers have been protected by strong labor unions such as the United Auto Workers (UAW). These unions, in turn, have forged contracts and established working conditions that seem almost archaic in today's economy. Consider the employment conditions of Tim Philbrick, a forty-two-year-old plant worker and union member at the firm's Fairfax plant near Kansas City who has worked for GM for twenty-three years. Philbrick makes almost $20 an hour in base pay. With a little overtime, his annual earnings top $60,000. But even then, he is far from the highest-paid factory worker at GM. Skilled-trade workers such as electricians and toolmakers make $2.00 to $2.50 an hour more and, with greater overtime opportunities often make $100,000 or more per year. Philbrick also gets a no-deductible health insurance policy that allows him to see any doctor he wants. He gets four weeks of vacation per year, plus two weeks off at Christmas and at least another week off in July. He gets two paid twenty-three-minute breaks and a paid thirty-minute lunch break per day. He also has the option to retire after thirty years with full benefits.

GM estimates that, with benefits, its average worker makes more than $43 an hour. Perhaps not surprisingly, then, the firm is always looking for opportunities to reduce its workforce through attrition and cutbacks, with the goal of replacing production capacity with lower-cost labor abroad. The UAW, of course, is staunchly opposed to further workforce reductions and cutbacks. And long-standing work rules strictly dictate who gets overtime, who can be laid off and who can't, and myriad other employment conditions for Tim Philbrick and his coworkers.

The situation at Wal-Mart differs sharply in many ways from those at GM. Along many different dimensions, Wal-Mart is slowly but surely supplanting General Motors as the quintessential U.S. corporation. For example, it is growing rapidly, is becoming more and more ingrained in the American lifestyle, and now employs more people than GM did in its heyday. But the hourly worker at Wal-Mart has a much different experience than the hourly worker at GM. Consider Nancy Handley, a twenty-seven-year-old Wal-Mart employee who oversees the men's department at a big store in St. Louis. Jobs like Handley's pay between $9 and $11 an hour, or about $20,000 a year. About $100 a month is deducted from Handley's paycheck to help cover the costs of benefits. Her health insurance has a $250 deductible; she then pays 20 percent of her health care costs as long as she uses a set of approved physicians. During her typical workday, Handley gets two 15-minute breaks and an hour for lunch, which are unpaid. Some believe the compensation plan is inadequate. Barbara Ehrenreich, author of *Nickel and Dimed: On (Not) Getting By in America*, worked at a Wal-Mart while researching her book and now says, "Why would anybody put up with the wages we were paid?"

But Nancy Handley doesn't feel mistreated by Wal-Mart. Far from it—she says she is appropriately compensated for what she does. She has received three merit raises in the last seven years and has ample job security. Moreover, if she decides to try for advancement, Wal-Mart seems to offer considerable potential, promoting thousands of hourly workers a year to the ranks of management. And Handley clearly isn't unique in her views: Wal-Mart employees have routinely rejected most overtures from labor unions.

In the twenty-first century, the gap between "Old Economy" and "New Economy" workers, between unionized manufacturing workers and nonunion or service workers, may be shrinking. Unions are losing their power in the auto industry, for example, as foreign-owned plants within the United States give carmakers such as Toyota and BMW, which are nonunion, a cost advantage over the "big three" U.S. automakers. U.S. firms are telling the UAW and other unions, "We're becoming noncompetitive, and unless you organize the [foreign-owned firms], we're going to have to modify the proposals we make to you." At the same time, Wal-Mart is facing lawsuits from employees who claim the retailer forced them to work unpaid overtime, among other charges. And a recent class-action lawsuit charges that the retailer has discriminated against women in hundreds of different settings. At a Las Vegas store, the firm faces its first union election. In a world where Wal-Mart now employs three times as many workers as GM, it may be inevitable that the retailer's labor will organize. On the other hand, will labor unions continue to lose their power to determine working conditions for America's workforce?

Case Questions

1. Compare and contrast hourly working conditions at General Motors and Wal-Mart.
2. Describe the most likely role the hourly compensation at these two companies plays in motivating employees.
3. Discuss how goal setting might be used for each of the two jobs profiled in this case.

References: Joann Muller, "Can the UAW Stay in the Game?" *BusinessWeek*, June 10, 2002; Mark Gimein, "Sam Walton Made Us a Promise," *Fortune*, March 18, 2002; Barbara Ehrenreich, *Nickel and Dimed: On (Not) Getting By in America* (New York: Metropolitan Books, 2001); "I'm Proud of What I've Made Myself Into—What I've Created," *Wall Street Journal*, August 28, 1997, pp. B1, B5; "That's Why I Like My Job . . . I Have an Impact on Quality," *Wall Street Journal*, August 28, 1997, pp. B1, B8.

Experiencing Organizational Behavior
Using Compensation to Motivate Workers

Purpose: The purpose of this exercise is to illustrate how compensation can be used to motivate employees.

Format: You will be asked to review eight managers and make salary adjustments for each.

Procedure: Listed below are your notes on the performance of eight managers who work for you. You (either individually or as a group, depending on your instructor's choice) have to recommend salary increases for eight managers who have just completed their first year with the company and are now to be considered for their first annual raise. Keep in mind that you may be setting precedents and that you need to keep salary costs down. However, there are no formal company restrictions on the kind of raises you can give. Indicate the sizes of the raise that you would like to give each manager by writing a percentage next to each name.

Variations: The instructor might alter the situation in one of several ways. One way is to assume that all of the eight managers entered the company at the same salary, say $30,000, which gives a total salary expense of $240,000. If upper management has allowed a salary raise pool of 10 percent of the current salary expenses, then you as the manager have $24,000 to give out as raises. In this variation, students can deal with actual dollar amounts rather than just percentages for the raises. Another interesting variation is to assume that all of the managers entered the company at different salaries, averaging $30,000. (The instructor can create many interesting possibilities for how these salaries might vary.) Then, the students can suggest salaries for the different managers.

_____ % Abraham McGowan. Abe is not, as far as you can tell, a good performer. You have checked your view with others, and they do not feel that he is effective either. However, you happen to know he has one of the toughest work groups to manage. His subordinates have low skill levels, and the work is dirty and hard. If you lose him, you are not sure whom you could find to replace him.

_____ % Benjy Berger. Benjy is single and seems to live the life of a carefree bachelor. In general, you feel that his job performance is not up to par, and some of his "goofs" are well known to his fellow employees.

_____ % Clyde Clod. You consider Clyde to be one of your best subordinates. However, it is obvious that other people do not consider him to be an effective manager. Clyde has married a rich wife, and as far as you know, he does not need additional money.

_____ % David Doodle. You happen to know from your personal relationship with "Doodles" that he badly needs more money because of certain personal problems he is having. As far as you are concerned, he also happens to be one of the best of your subordinates. For some reason, your enthusiasm is not shared by your other subordinates, and you have heard them make joking remarks about his performance.

_____ % Ellie Ellesberg. Ellie has been very successful so far in the tasks she has undertaken. You are particularly impressed by this since she has a hard job. She needs money more than many of the other people, and you are sure that they respect her because of her good performance.

_____ % Fred Foster. Fred has turned out to be a very pleasant surprise to you. He has done an excellent job and it is generally accepted among the others that he is one of the best people. This surprises you because he is generally frivolous and does not seem to care very much about money and promotion.

_____ % Greta Goslow. Your opinion is that Greta is just not cutting the mustard. Surprisingly enough, however, when you check to see how others feel about her, you discover that her work is very highly regarded. You also know that she badly needs a raise. She was just recently widowed and is finding it extremely difficult to support her household and her young family of four.

_____ % Harry Hummer. You know Harry personally, and he just seems to squander his money continually. He has a fairly easy job assignment, and your view is that he does not do it particularly well. You are, therefore, quite surprised to find that several of the other new managers think that he is the best of the new group.

After you have made the assignments for the eight people, you will have a chance to discuss them either in groups or in the larger class.

Follow-up Questions

1. Is there a clear difference between the highest and lowest performer? Why or why not?
2. Did you notice differences in the types of information that you had available to make the raise decisions? How did you use the different sources of information?
3. In what ways did your assignment of raises reflect different views of motivation?

Source: By Edward E. Lawler III. Reprinted by permission of the author.

Self-Assessment Exercise
Diagnosing Poor Performance and Enhancing Motivation

Introduction: Formal performance appraisal and feedback are part of assuring proper performance in an organization. The following assessment is designed to help you understand how to detect poor performance and overcome it.

Procedure: Please respond to the following statements by writing a number from the following rating scale in the left-hand column. Your answers should reflect your attitudes and behaviors as they are _now_.

Strongly agree   = 6
Agree   = 5
Slightly agree   = 4

Slightly disagree = 3
Disagree   = 2
Strongly disagree = 1

When another person needs to be motivated,

_____ 1. I always approach a performance problem by first establishing whether it is caused by a lack of motivation or ability.
_____ 2. I always establish a clear standard of expected performance.
_____ 3. I always offer to provide training and information, without offering to do the task myself.

_____ 4. I am honest and straightforward in providing feedback on performance and assessing advancement opportunities.

_____ 5. I use a variety of rewards to reinforce exceptional performance.

_____ 6. When discipline is required, I identify the problem, describe its consequences, and explain how it should be corrected.

_____ 7. I design task assignments to make them interesting and challenging.

_____ 8. I determine what rewards are valued by the person and strive to make those available.

_____ 9. I make sure that the person feels fairly and equitably treated.

_____ 10. I make sure that the person gets timely feedback from those affected by task performance.

_____ 11. I carefully diagnose the causes of poor performance before taking any remedial or disciplinary actions.

_____ 12. I always help the person establish performance goals that are challenging, specific, and time-bound.

_____ 13. Only as a last resort do I attempt to reassign or release a poorly performing individual.

_____ 14. Whenever possible, I make sure that valued rewards are linked to high performance.

_____ 15. I consistently discipline when effort is below expectations and capabilities.

_____ 16. I try to combine or rotate assignments so that the person can use a variety of skills.

_____ 17. I try to arrange for the person to work with others in a team, for the mutual support of all.

_____ 18. I make sure that the person is using realistic standards for measuring fairness.

_____ 19. I provide immediate compliments and other forms of recognition for meaningful accomplishments.

_____ 20. I always determine if the person has the necessary resources and support to succeed in the task.

Source: From David A. Whetten and Kim S. Cameron, *Developing Management Skills.* 5th ed. Copyright © 2002. Reprinted by permission of Pearson Education, Inc., Upper Saddle River, NJ.

OB Online

1. Locate the website of a firm that indicates it uses goal setting and/or MBO for its employees. How similar or different is the process described on the website compared with the approaches discussed in this chapter?

2. Find five company websites that stress the importance of quality to the firm's mission and strategy. Identify the role of performance management in each firm's quality program.

3. Search for information on the Internet about 360-degree feedback. What kind of information is most widely available and accessible?

4. Find five company websites that provide some information about the rewards the firm makes available to employees. Relate each case to the discussion in this chapter.

Building Managerial Skills

Exercise Overview: All managers must be able to communicate effectively with others in the organization. Communication is especially important when dealing with employment-related issues.

Exercise Background: As noted in the chapter, many companies provide various benefits to their workers. These benefits may include pay for time not worked, insurance coverage, pension plans, and so forth. These benefits are often very costly to the organization, often equal to one-third or more of what employees are paid in wages and salaries. In some countries, such as Germany, the figures are even higher.

However, many employees often fail to appreciate the actual value of the benefits their employers provide. For example, they frequently underestimate the dollar value of their benefits. In addition, when comparing their incomes with those of others or comparing alternative job offers, many people focus almost entirely on direct compensation—wages and salaries directly paid to the individual.

For example, consider a college graduate who has two job offers. One offer is for $40,000 a year, and the other is for $42,000. The individual is likely to see the second offer as more desirable, even though the first offer may have sufficiently more attractive benefits to make the two total compensation packages equivalent.

Exercise Task: With this information as context, respond to the following questions:

1. Why do you think most people focus on pay when assessing their compensation?
2. If you were the human resource manager for a firm, how would you go about communicating benefit values to your employees?
3. Suppose an employee comes to you and says he is thinking about leaving for a "better job." You then learn he is defining "better" only in terms of higher pay. How might you go about helping him compare the total compensation (including benefits) package of his current job and of the "better" job?
4. Some firms today are cutting their benefits. How would you go about communicating a benefit cut to your employees?

TEST PREPPER

ACE self-test

You have read the chapter and studied the key terms, and the exam is any day now. Think you're ready to ace it? Take this sample test to gauge your comprehension of chapter material. You can check your answers at the back of the book. Want more test questions? Visit the student website at http://college.hmco.com/business/students/ (select Griffin/Moorhead, Fundamentals of Organizational Behavior 1e) and take the ACE quizzes for more practice.

1. **T F** Goals are used to motivate and control.

2. **T F** According to goal-setting theory, most goals are unconscious decisions.

3. **T F** The best goals set performance expectations just out of reach of most employees.

4. **T F** Allowing employees to participate in setting goals will likely increase goal commitment and acceptance.

5. **T F** Management by objectives (MBO) is an effective way to reduce the paperwork associated with goal setting.

6. **T F** Performance appraisals with a developmental orientation focus on ways to improve performance.

7. **T F** A 360-degree feedback system may provide managers with sensitive and potentially threatening feedback.

8. **T F** The Equal Employment Opportunity Commission requires that performance measurement include factors such as age, religion, and national origin.

9. **T F** Managers would do well to keep in mind the role of psychological contracts as they develop organizational reward systems.

10. **T F** Bobby has a higher level of performance than all other employees at his level in his organization. If his organization used a merit pay plan, Bobby would receive the highest pay.

11. **T F** In many organizations today, benefits account for 30 to 40 percent of the payroll.

12. **T F** Perquisites for senior managers seem to add to their status in the organization.

13. **T F** To take full advantage of the symbolic value of pay, managers must keep rewards separate from employees' performance levels.

14. **T F** A flexible reward system allows employees, within specified ranges, to choose the combination of benefits that best suits their needs.

15. **T F** Most organizations have a policy of complete pay secrecy.

16. **T F** An expatriate's compensation package may include a hardship allowance for facing special challenges in the assignment.

17. Most organizations use goals to _____ and to _____.
    - a. motivate, control
    - b. control, organize
    - c. organize, plan
    - d. plan, lead
    - e. lead, motivate

18. John failed to meet his sales goal last quarter, but he is highly confident he can reach his goal this quarter. John has high
    - a. turnover.
    - b. self-efficacy.
    - c. social learning.
    - d. job satisfaction.
    - e. expectancy.

19. The most effective goals are _____ and _____.
    - a. general, easy to reach
    - b. new, exciting
    - c. difficult, specific
    - d. self-set, flexible
    - e. rigid, distant

20. Michelle accepts the goals set in the organization as her own, but she isn't personally interested in reaching them. Michelle lacks
    - a. self-efficacy.
    - b. goal acceptance.
    - c. goal difficulty.
    - d. goal commitment.
    - e. goal specificity.

21. A collaborative goal-setting process through which organizational goals systematically cascade down through the organization is known as
    - a. goal-setting theory.
    - b. goal specificity.
    - c. goal commitment.
    - d. management by walking around.
    - e. management by objectives.

22. A lack of top management participation, an overemphasis on quantitative goals, and an abundance of paperwork and recordkeeping are all pitfalls of
    - a. goal-setting theory.
    - b. goal specificity.
    - c. goal commitment.
    - d. management by walking around.
    - e. management by objectives.

23. The basic process of performance management includes all of the following activities except
    a. measuring an employee's work behaviors.
    b. comparing the employee's measured work behaviors with previously established standards.
    c. documenting the results of the measurement and comparison.
    d. communicating the results to the employee.
    e. All of the above are steps in the performance management process.

24. As Sam completes his employees' performance appraisal, he focuses on their past performance and uses the results to determine organizational rewards. Sam is taking a(n) _____ approach to performance appraisal.
    a. instrumental
    b. acceptance
    c. commitment
    d. judgmental
    e. developmental

25. If a supervisor has incomplete information about an employee's performance or has a limited understanding of the technical knowledge involved in the employee's job, a better option for performance appraisal might involve
    a. dual-structure theory.
    b. management by objectives.
    c. a multi-rater system.
    d. empowerment.
    e. participative decision making.

26. James receives performance feedback from his subordinates, superiors, and peers. This approach to performance management is called
    a. management by objectives.
    b. 360-degree feedback.
    c. benefits feedback.

    d. OB mod.
    e. developmental appraisal.

27. Which of the following is a problem common to all individual methods of performance evaluation?
    a. A tendency to rate most individuals at about the same level
    b. The inability to maintain accurate records of performance
    c. The overwhelming amount of paperwork
    d. The lack of top management support
    e. A tendency to rate individuals based on organization-level success or failure

28. The purposes of reward systems in most organizations are to do all of the following except
    a. attract qualified employees.
    b. retain qualified employees.
    c. punish unqualified employees.
    d. motivate qualified employees.
    e. All of the above are purposes of reward systems in most organizations.

29. Stacey just received a large raise, but none of her coworkers doing the same work received any raise. Aside from the actual value of the raise, this reward has _____ for Stacey.
    a. symbolic value
    b. objective value
    c. surface value
    d. organizational value
    e. managerial value

30. In Pete's organization, employees and work groups receive additional earnings for effective cost reduction ideas. This program is called
    a. piecework.
    b. gain sharing.
    c. profit sharing.

    d. merit pay.
    e. stock options.

31. Julia is a senior manager at her company. She and a few other selected members of the organization have access to the company jet and the executive dining room. These rewards are examples of
    a. long-term compensation.
    b. bonus systems.
    c. merit pay.
    d. indirect compensation.
    e. perquisites.

32. How did the National Labor Relations Board rule regarding pay secrecy?
    a. Pay secrecy is legal for all companies.
    b. Pay secrecy is legal for public but not private companies.
    c. Pay secrecy violates the National Labor Relations Act.
    d. A pay secrecy policy must be passed by the organization's shareholders.
    e. A pay secrecy policy must apply to all individuals in the organization.

33. Expatriate compensation packages are
    a. illegal by rule of the National Labor Relations Board.
    b. offered to all of an organization's employees.
    c. offered only to new employees.
    d. part of a flexible benefits package.
    e. complicated to develop.

PART TWO   VIDEO CASE

Motivating the Salesforce at Wheelworks

Wheelworks, located near Boston, is one of the largest bicycle stores in the United States. With more than 8,000 square feet of showroom, the selection of bicycles and cycling-related products is second to none. The store sells about 10,000 units, ranging from a tricycle to a tandem bike, annually. The store's annual revenue is in the $10.5 million range.

Wheelworks was launched in 1977 by Peter Mooney and Clint Paige. Since its inception, customer service has been the company's lifeblood. Wheelworks wants to sell bikes, but it also wants each of its customers to get the bike that best fits them and to have a good experience with their purchase. The last thing the company wants is for a customer to buy a bike, use it for a month or so, and then park it in the garage or hang it in the basement and never use it again. To prevent this, Wheelworks works hard to find and motivate employees who are passionate about cycling and committed to helping customers.

Wheelworks employs 45 people on a full-time basis, and supplements that number with 25 full-time seasonal employees and 30 seasonal part-time employees. To illustrate the importance the company places on finding the right employees and motivating them to do good work, founder Clint Paige remarks, "My primary role is personnel selection—personnel encouragement—I spend a lot of time acting as a cheerleader and a coach." Paige notes that most of Wheelworks' employees make somewhat of a sacrifice to work in retail sales. These employees are highly educated and could be doing other things, but they choose to work for Wheelworks because they are passionate about cycling and want to share their passion with others.

To maintain an upbeat, positive atmosphere, Wheelworks keeps employees focused on the excitement of helping people recognize the enjoyment that comes with cycling. Its salesforce isn't paid on commission. Instead, the company has a wage, profit-sharing, and benefit package that is generous by retail store standards. This approach allows Wheelworks salespeople to focus on fitting customers with the best bike for them rather than trying to sell the most expensive models. Employees also have a lot of freedom in how they go about their jobs. One employee comments, "We [don't follow] a scripted sales pitch here—everyone can really be themselves—this is a rich environment for actually communicating with our customers."

To maintain the company's success, Wheelworks' managers recognize that employee selection and motivation are ongoing activities. "Our biggest challenge is recruiting, maintaining, and keeping the environment exciting and lively for the young adults that we employ," Paige says. One way the company does this is by providing continuing education to employees on a consistent basis. Three to five times a month, the company has a vendor or manufacturer's representative come into its store to conduct a clinic on some aspect of cycling or bicycle repair for Wheelworks employees. Most employees enjoy these clinics because they have a personal interest in cycling.

In recognition of its efforts, Wheelworks was recently voted the best bicycle shop in the United States by the Bicycle Trade Organization. More information on Wheelworks is available at the company's website at www.wheelworks.com. Of particular interest is the portion of the site labeled "employee spotlight." Here the company features individual employees and talks about how they became passionate about cycling. The descriptions provide insight into why each employee is a good fit for Wheelworks' unique approach to motivation and job design.

Case Questions

1. What techniques does Wheelworks use to motivate its employees? Do these techniques seem to be effective? Provide evidence from the case to support your conclusion.
2. Of the approaches to motivation discussed in Chapter 4, which seems most evident in the way managers at Wheelworks motivate their employees? Do you think Wheelworks' managers have chosen the best approach for their environment? Why or why not?
3. Do you think Wheelworks has designed its salespeople's jobs effectively? How does the design of salespeople's jobs affect their level of motivation and performance?
4. Do you think Wheelworks' compensation system is in or out of sync with the overall philosophy of its business and how it motivates its employees?

Reference: Wheelworks website, www.wheelworks.com on June 25, 2004.

PART THREE

Interpersonal Processes in Organizations

CHAPTER 7

Communication in Organizations

MANAGEMENT PREVIEW

Communication is something most of us take for granted. We have been communicating for so long that we pay little attention to the actual process. Even at work, we often focus primarily on doing our jobs and rarely consider how we communicate about those jobs. However, since methods of communication so profoundly affect behavior in organizations, we need to pay more attention to the processes that effectively link what we do to others in the organization. In this chapter, we focus on the important processes of interpersonal communication and information processing. First, we discuss the importance of communication in organizations and some important aspects of international communication. Next, we describe methods of organizational communication and examine the basic communication process. Then we look at the potential effects of computerized information technology and telecommunications. Next, we explore the development of communication networks in organizations. Finally, we discuss several common problems of organizational communication and methods of managing communication.

After you have studied this chapter, you should be able to:
- [ ] *Discuss the nature of communication in organizations.*
- [ ] *Describe the primary methods of communication.*
- [ ] *Describe the communication process.*
- [ ] *Explain how information technology affects communication.*
- [ ] *Describe the basic kinds of communication networks.*
- [ ] *Discuss how communication can be managed in organizations.*

We begin by describing how telecommunications are changing the way Reuters Group conducts its business.

The past 150 years have brought extraordinary change to Reuters Group, the British news firm. Founded in the 1850s, the company relied on carrier pigeons as its fastest and most dependable means of communication. The company was one of the first to invest heavily in that "new" technology, the telegraph, during the 1860s and 1870s. In fact, the firm was the first to report to Europe the news of Abraham Lincoln's assassination and described the end of the Boer War to the British two days ahead of the official report. The firm also established a huge non-news business based primarily on delivering financial quotes to customers through a proprietary network.

As new communication technologies, including satellites, cell phones, and the Internet, have been introduced, Reuters has struggled to keep up with the new demands placed on it by increasingly technology-savvy customers. Tom Glocer, who became CEO of Reuters in July 2001, has faced the task of transforming the company's communication strategy to fit today's communications environment. Glocer's vision of an Internet-based firm prevailed in the end. "What Tom did was to articulate the urgency of it," according to Devin Wenig, president of Reuters Information subsidiary. Glocer himself says modestly, "I was the dirt in the oyster."

Glocer is finding that changing the way Reuters communicates with customers affects everything the firm does. The new technology requires more technical know-how and places less emphasis on Reuters' traditional strength in news reporting. The cost structure has changed, too: As the proprietary network is replaced by Internet-accessible information, subscription fees grow while hardware and labor costs shrink. Glocer fears Internet sales will cannibalize the more profitable proprietary sales and the firm will have to charge less for its Internet offerings. Even Glocer himself, a lawyer and self-described "computer geek," is a symbol of change within the firm because he is the first nonjournalist and the first American to head the company. One former Reuters executive says Glocer was "not part of the old boys' network," and Reuters' chairman calls Glocer's appointment "a generational shift in leadership."

Meanwhile Reuters is reaping the benefits of adopting the newest technologies. Its customer base is expanding to include buyers who want only a small slice of the financial news, such as reports about currency trading in Brazilian reals or South African rand. Reuters' new system enables the firm to deliver customized portions of the news at a lower cost. While competitors such as Bloomberg continue to offer their traditional proprietary networks and to move into areas such as the financial cable network Bloomberg Television, Reuters is aggressively expanding into online services, including Instinet, an online financial trading subsidiary. Referring to Reuters' plan to invest in new technology, Derek Brown, an analyst with Robertson Stephens, says, "This is an example of a bricks-and-mortar media company adopting what I believe is a very sensible strategy." The giant firm is changing to keep up with the times, and it now remains to be seen whether Glocer and Reuters can make this "very sensible" strategy pay off.

"I was the dirt in the oyster"—Tom Glocer, CEO of Reuters Group

References: "Famous Reuters' People" and "Reuters Media Statement," Reuters' corporate website, www.reuters.com on May 7, 2004; "Instinet: How Not to Run a Trading Company," *BusinessWeek*, April 22, 2002; Mark Gimein, "The Other Bloomberg: Bloomberg Television Trails CNBC," *Fortune*, April 1, 2002; Katrina Brooker, "London Calling," *Fortune*, April 2, 2001, pp. 131–136 (quotation, p. 136); Amey Stone, "Now Comes the Real Test for Reuters' E-Strategy," Business Week Online, February 17, 2000.

Advances in electronic communication technology have greatly changed how businesses and people communicate. Indeed, our very lives have changed because we can now communicate instantaneously with almost anyone anywhere on the globe. In many cases, managers today do not even have to go to the office. Less than a generation ago, not going to the office was commonly considered slacking off; now, however, it may actually signal greater performance as managers move freely among work sites and interact with various stakeholders. Regardless of the technology involved, the basics of interpersonal communication remain important. Communication is critical in all phases of organizational behavior, but it is especially crucial in decision making, performance appraisal, motivation, and ensuring that the organization functions effectively. We begin our discussion of the role communication plays in organizational behavior by examining the most basic elements of communication.

The Nature of Communication in Organizations

LEARNING OBJECTIVE

Discuss the nature of communication in organizations.

Communication is the social process in which two or more parties exchange information and share meaning.

Communication is the social process in which two or more parties exchange information and share meaning. Communication has been studied from many perspectives. In this section, we provide an overview of the complex and dynamic communication process and discuss some important issues relating to international communication in organizations.

Purposes of Communication in Organizations

Communication among individuals and groups is vital in all organizations. Figure 7.1 shows some of the purposes of organizational communication. The primary purpose is to achieve coordinated action.[1] Just as the human nervous system responds to stimuli and coordinates responses by sending messages to the various parts of the body, communication coordinates the actions of the parts of an organization. Without communication, an organization would be merely a collection of individual workers doing separate tasks. Organizational action would lack coordination and be oriented toward individual rather than organizational goals.

A second purpose of communication is information sharing. The most important information relates to organizational goals, which give members a sense of purpose and direction. Another information-sharing function of communication is to give specific task directions to individuals. Whereas information about organizational goals gives employees a sense of how their activities fit into the overall picture, task communication tells them what their job duties are and are not. Employees must also receive information on the results of their efforts, as they do in performance appraisals.

Communication is essential to the decision-making process as well, as we discuss in Chapter 12. Information and information sharing are needed to define problems, generate and evaluate alternatives, implement decisions, and control and evaluate results.

Finally, communication expresses feelings and emotions. Organizational communication is far from merely a collection of facts and figures. People in organizations, like people anywhere else, often need to communicate emotions such as happiness, anger, displeasure, confidence, and fear.

Communication Across Cultures

Communication is an element of interpersonal relations that obviously is affected by the international environment, partly because of language issues and partly due to coordination issues.

FIGURE 7.1

Three Purposes of Organizational Communication

Achieving coordinated action is the primary purpose of communication in organizations. Sharing information properly and expressing emotions helps achieve coordinated action.

Language   Differences in language are compounded by the fact that the same word can mean different things in different cultures. For example, *Coca-Cola* meant "bite the head of a dead tadpole" in the first Chinese characters used in the product's advertising. The company had to quickly find other Chinese characters to use in its advertising in China. Chevrolet once tried to export a line of cars to Latin America that it called the Nova in the United States, but then learned that *no va* means "doesn't go" in Spanish—not the best name for an automobile!

Elements of nonverbal communication also vary across cultures. Colors and body language can convey quite a different message from one culture to another. For example, the American sign for *OK* (making a loop with thumb and first finger) is considered rude in Spain and vulgar in Brazil. Managers should be forewarned that they can take nothing for granted in dealing with people from other cultures. They must take the time to become as fully acquainted as possible with the verbal and nonverbal languages of a culture. And indeed, as the Mastering Change box illustrates, modern forms of communication technology, such as email, are actually changing language itself.

MASTERING CHANGE

Email's Effect on the English Language

With the widespread use of personal computers, the Internet, and email, it's clear that communication technology is rapidly changing. What may be less obvious are the ways in which email technology is changing English language usage.

Email messages consist of written words and simple pictures, and therein lies the trouble. People want to use email to express complex ideas that involve emotions, subtlety, irony, and other elements that are difficult to express in writing. New uses of English are transforming "flat" written emails into three-dimensional, meaningful messages. These enhanced messages attempt to mimic human speech and face-to-face dialogues by using written words and symbols to convey nuances of meaning, body language, and even tone of voice.

Online acronyms express subtle aspects of messages and also save time in typing repetitive phrases. Common acronyms used today include BTW ("by the way") and FYI, ("for your information"). Other, more recently coined acronyms are IMHO ("in my humble opinion"); LOL ("I laughed out loud"); TIA ("thanks in advance"); B2B ("business to business," referring to communication between two firms); and *2* to replace the word *too,* as in the acronym U2 (you, too).

Email technology has also created new meanings for many older words. For example, *spam* is the name for un-

wanted mass commercial solicitations, and *bounce* refers to email messages that are returned to the sender. A *flame* is an email message that is unreservedly hostile; *flame* is also used as a verb: "His joke wasn't funny, so he really got flamed!"

> *"The most difficult thing to convey in email is emotion."*
> —*Kaitlin Duck Sherwood, author of* Overcome Email Overload

According to Kaitlin Duck Sherwood, author of *Overcome Email Overload,* "the most difficult thing to convey in email is emotion." Users can express emphasis or changes in tone of voice by using asterisks for emphasis: "You *are* wrong." To convey hesitation or thoughtfulness, words can be typed with white space or repeated letters: "Www..eeee..llllll". Body language is expressed simply with <L> for laughing and <Y> for yawning. An *emoticon* uses an icon or a simple graphic to express emotions. Some typical emoticons include :-) for "happy," :-(for "sad," :-| for "skeptical," ;-) for "winking," :-O for "surprised," and :-P for "laughing." Having said all this, it's TTFN ("ta-ta for now")!

References: "High-Tech Dictionary," ComputerUser.com website, www.computeruser.com/resources/dictionary/emoticons.html on May 12, 2004; Kaitlin Duck Sherwood, *A Beginner's Guide to Effective Email,* World Wide Webfoot Press website (quotation), www.webfoot.com on April 30, 2002; Virginia Shea, *Netiquette* (Albion Press, 1994), www.netiquette.com.

Coordination   International communication is closely related to issues of coordination. For example, an American manager who wants to speak with his or her counterpart in Hong Kong, Singapore, Rome, or London must contend not only with language differences but also with a time difference of many hours. When the U.S. manager needs to conduct business on the telephone, the Hong Kong executive may be home asleep. Consequently, organizations are employing increasingly innovative methods for coordinating their activities in scattered parts of the globe. Merrill Lynch, for example, has its own satellite-based telephone network to monitor and participate in the worldwide money and financial markets.[2]

Methods of Communication

LEARNING OBJECTIVE

Describe the primary methods of communication.

The three primary methods of communicating in organizations are written, oral, and nonverbal. Often the methods are combined. Considerations that affect the choice of method include the audience (whether it is physically present), the nature of the message (its urgency or secrecy), and the costs of transmission. Figure 7.2 shows various forms each method can take.

Written Communication

Organizations typically produce a great deal of written communication of many kinds. A letter is a formal means of communicating with an individual, generally someone outside the organization. Probably the most common form of written communication in organizations is the office memorandum, or memo. Memos usually are addressed to a person or group inside the organization. They tend to deal with a single topic and are more impersonal (as they often are destined to reach more than one person) but less formal than letters. Most email is similar to the traditional memo and even less formal.

Other common forms of written communication include reports, manuals, and forms. Reports generally summarize the progress or results of a project and often provide information to be used in decision making. Manuals perform various functions in organizations. Instruction manuals tell employees how to operate machines; policy and procedures manuals inform them of organizational rules; operations manuals describe how to perform tasks and respond to work-related problems. Forms are standardized documents on which to report information. As such, they represent attempts to make communication more efficient and information more accessible. A performance

FIGURE 7.2

Methods of Communication in Organizations

The three methods of communication in organizations are related to one another. Each method supplements the others, although each can also stand alone.

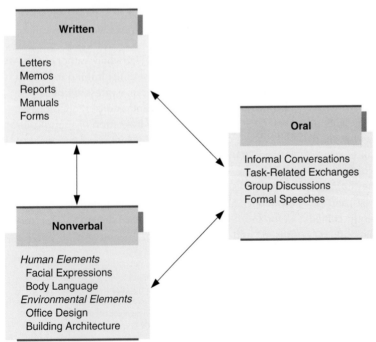

appraisal form is an example. Many of these forms of written communication historically have been used in a paper-based environment, but today they are increasingly being used on websites and intranets in many larger companies.

Oral Communication

The most prevalent form of organizational communication is oral. Oral communication takes place everywhere—in informal conversations, in the process of doing work, in meetings of groups and task forces, and in formal speeches and presentations. Recent studies identified oral communication skills as the number one criterion for hiring new college graduates.[3] Business school leaders have also been urged by industry to develop better communication skills in their graduates.[4] Even in Europe, employers have complained that the number one problem with current graduates is the lack of oral communication skills, citing cultural factors and changes in the educational process as primary causes.[5]

Oral forms of communication are particularly powerful because they include not only speakers' words but also changes in their tone, pitch, speed, and volume. Listeners, for their part, use all of these cues to understand oral messages. Try this example with a friend or work colleague. Say this sentence several times, each time placing the emphasis on a different word: "The boss gave Joe a raise." See how the meaning changes depending on the emphasis. Moreover, receivers interpret oral messages in the context of previous communications and, perhaps, the reactions of other receivers. (Try saying another sentence before saying the phrase about the boss, such as "Joe is so lazy" or "Joe is such a good worker.") Often the organization's top management sets the tone for oral communication throughout the organization.

Voicemail, the oral counterpart to email, has all the characteristics of traditional verbal communication except that no feedback occurs. The sender simply leaves a message on the machine or network and receives no confirmation that the message was, or will be, received. With no confirmation, the sender does not know for sure whether the message was or will be received as intended. Therefore, it is wise for the receiver of a voicemail to quickly leave a message on the sender's voicemail confirming receipt of the original message. However, the result could be voicemail "phone tag." At worst, the receiver then has an excuse if something goes wrong later and can claim that she or he left a return message on the sender's voicemail! The receiver could also pass the blame by saying that no such voice message was received. The lack of confirmation, or two-way communication, can lead to several problems, as we will discuss in later sections of this chapter.

Nonverbal Communication

Nonverbal communication includes all the elements associated with human communication that are not expressed orally or in writing. Sometimes nonverbal communication conveys more meaning than words do. Human elements of nonverbal communication include facial expressions and physical movements, both conscious and unconscious. Facial expressions have been categorized as (1) interest-excitement, (2) enjoyment-joy, (3) surprise-startle, (4) distress-anguish, (5) fear-terror, (6) shame-humiliation, (7) contempt-disgust, and (8) anger-rage.[6] The eyes are the most expressive component of the face.

Physical movements and "body language" are also highly expressive human elements. Body language includes both actual movement and body positions during communication. The handshake is a common form of body language. Other examples include making eye contact, which expresses a willingness to

Nonverbal communication involves the use of facial expressions, physical movements, and environmental elements to convey meaning. These trainers use hand signals to guide dolphins to vocalize and jump. In much the same way, people use their eyes and faces, body language, and office arrangements to convey meaning to others. A facial expression of disinterest, sitting back in a chair with folded arms, and frequent glances at the clock will clearly convey to someone that you are not interested in what she or he has to say.

communicate; sitting on the edge of a chair, which may indicate nervousness or anxiety; and sitting back with arms folded, which may convey an unwillingness to continue the discussion.

Environmental elements such as buildings, office space, and furniture can also convey messages. A spacious office, expensive draperies, plush carpeting, and elegant furniture can combine to remind employees or visitors that they are in the office of the firm's president or CEO. On the other hand, the small metal desk set in the middle of the shop floor accurately communicates the organizational rank of a first-line supervisor. Thus, office arrangements convey status, power, and prestige, and create an atmosphere for doing business. The physical setting can also be instrumental in the development of communication networks, because a centrally located person can more easily control the flow of task-related information.

The Communication Process

As defined earlier, communication is a social process in which two or more parties exchange information and share meaning. The process is social because it involves two or more people. It is a two-way process and takes place over time rather than instantaneously. The communication process illustrated in Figure 7.3 shows a loop between the source and the receiver.[7] Note the importance of the feedback portion of the loop; on receiving the message, the receiver responds with a message to the source to verify the communication. Each element of the basic communication process is important. If one part is faulty, the message may not be communicated as intended. Consider a simple organizational example: A manager attempts to give direction to an employee regarding the order in which to perform two tasks. (We refer to this example again in later discussions.) The manager wants to send a message and have the employee understand precisely the meaning she intends. Each part of the communication process is described next.

LEARNING OBJECTIVE

Describe the communication process.

Source

The **source** is the individual, group, or organization interested in communicating something to another party.

The **source** is the individual, group, or organization interested in communicating something to another party. In group or organizational communication, an individual may send the message on behalf of the organization. The source is responsible for preparing the message, encoding it, and entering it into the transmission medium. In some cases, the receiver chooses the source of information, as when a decision maker seeks information from trusted and knowledgeable individuals.[8] The source in organizational communication is often the manager giving directions to employees.

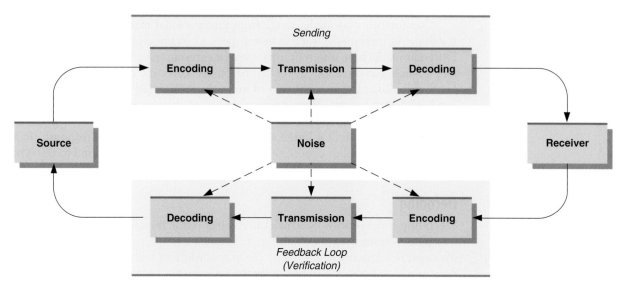

FIGURE 7.3

The Communication Process

The communication process is a loop that connects the sender and the receiver and operates in both directions. Communication is not complete until the original sender knows the receiver understands the message.

Encoding

Encoding is the process by which the message is translated from an idea or a thought into transmittable symbols.

Encoding is the process by which the message is translated from an idea or a thought into symbols that can be transmitted. The symbols may be words, numbers, pictures, sounds, or physical gestures and movements. In our simple example, the manager may use words in English as the symbols, usually spoken or written. The source must encode the message in symbols the receiver can decode properly; that is, source and receiver must attach the same meaning to the symbols. When we use the symbols of a common language, we assume those symbols have the same meaning to everyone who uses them. However, the inherent ambiguity of symbol systems can lead to decoding errors. In verbal communication, for example, some words have different meanings for different people. Parents and children often use the same word, but the differences in their positions and ages may lead them to interpret words quite differently. If a manager speaks only Spanish and an employee speaks only German, the message is unlikely to be understood. The meanings of words the sender uses may differ depending on the nonverbal cues, such as facial expression, that the sender transmits along with them.

Transmission

Transmission is the process through which the symbols that represent the message are sent to the receiver.

The **medium** is the channel, or path, through which the message is transmitted.

Transmission is the process through which the symbols that carry the message are sent to the receiver. The **medium** is the channel, or path, of transmission. The medium for face-to-face conversation is sound waves. The same conversation conducted over the telephone involves not only sound waves but also electrical impulses and the lines that connect the two phones. To tell the employee in what order to perform tasks, the manager could tell him face to face or use the telephone, a memo, email, or voicemail.

Communications media range from interpersonal media, such as talking or touching, to mass media, such as newspapers, magazines, or television broadcasts. Different media have different capacities for carrying information. For example, a face-to-face conversation generally has more carrying capacity than a letter because it allows the transmission of more than words. In addition, the medium can help determine the effect the message has on the receiver. Calling a prospective client on the telephone to make a business proposal is a more personal approach than sending a letter and is likely to elicit a different response. It is important that a sender choose the medium most likely to correspond to the type of message that needs to be sent and understood.

Decoding

Decoding is the process by which the receiver of the message interprets its meaning.

Decoding is the process by which the receiver of the message interprets its meaning. The receiver uses knowledge and experience to interpret the symbols of the message; in some situations, he or she may consult an authority such as a dictionary or a code book. Up to this point the receiver has been relatively inactive, but the receiver becomes more active in the decoding phase. The meaning the receiver attaches to the symbols may be the same as or different from the meaning intended by the source. If the meanings differ, of course, communication breaks down, and misunderstanding is likely. In our example, if the employee does not understand the language or a particular word, he will not comprehend the meaning intended by the sender (manager) and may do the tasks in the wrong order or not do them at all.

Receiver

The **receiver** is the individual, group, or organization that perceives the encoded symbols; the receiver may or may not decode them to try to understand the intended message.

The **receiver** of the message may be an individual, a group, an organization, or an individual acting as the representative of a group. The receiver decides whether to decode the message, whether to make an effort to understand it, and whether to respond. Moreover, the intended receiver may not get the message at all, whereas an unintended receiver may, depending on the medium, the symbols used by the source, and the attention level of potential receivers. An employee may share the same language (know the symbols) the manager uses but may not want to get the sender's meaning. For instance, the manager may be talking about impending financial cutbacks, but because the employee knows that this actually means some of her coworkers will lose their jobs, she chooses to not engage in further discussion because of the discomfort that has been created.

The key skill for proper reception of the message is good listening. If the receiver does not concentrate on the sender, the message, or the medium, the message is likely to get lost. Listening is an active process that requires as much concentration and effort from the receiver as sending the message does for the sender. The expression of emotions by sender and receiver enters into the communication process at several points. First, the emotions may be part of the message, entering into the encoding process. For example, if the manager's directions are encoded with a sense of emotional urgency—for example, given in a high-pitched or loud voice—the employee may move quickly to follow the directions. However, if the message is urgent but the manager's tone of voice is low and does not convey urgency, the employee may not act quickly. Second, as the message is decoded, the receiver may let his or her emotions perceive it differently from what the sender intended. Third, emotion-filled feedback from the intended receiver can cause the sender to modify her or his subsequent message.

Noise is any disturbance in the communication process that interferes with or distorts communication. Take this busy scene in New York City. Anyone attempting to have a quiet conversation or place a cell phone call would have difficulty hearing and being heard due to traffic and large numbers of passers-by. While most work settings are likely to have fewer sources of noise than this, people in organizations must still contend with other people talking, equipment noises, and similar distractions.

Feedback

Feedback is the receiver's response to the message. Feedback verifies the message by telling the source whether the receiver received and understood the message. The feedback may be as simple as a phone call from the prospective client expressing interest in the business proposal or as complex as a written brief on a complicated point of law sent from an attorney to a judge. In our example, the employee can respond to the manager's directions with a verbal or written response indicating he does or does not understand the message. Feedback can also be nonverbal, for example, if the employee does not perform either task. With typical voicemail, the feedback loop is missing, which can lead to many communication problems.

Noise

Noise is any disturbance in the communication process that interferes with or distorts communication. Noise can be introduced at virtually any point in the communication process. The principal type, called **channel noise,** is associated with the medium.[9] Radio static and "ghost" images on television are examples of channel noise, as is an email virus. When noise interferes in the encoding and decoding processes, poor encoding and decoding can result. Emotions that interfere with an intended communication are also considered a type of noise. In our example, the employee may not hear the directions given by the manager due to noisy machinery on the shop floor or competing input from other people.

Effective communication occurs when at least two people have shared information or meaning. Therefore, communication must include the response from the receiver back to the sender. The sender cannot know if the message was conveyed as intended if there is no feedback from the receiver, such as when leaving voicemail. Both parties are responsible for the effectiveness of the communication. As we will see in the next section, advances in technology in recent years have created both benefits and problems in the communication process.

Feedback is the process in which the receiver returns a message to the sender indicating receipt and understanding of the message.

Noise is any disturbance in the communication process that interferes with or distorts communication.

Channel noise is a disturbance in communication that is primarily a function of the medium.

Electronic Information Processing and Telecommunications

Changes in the workplace are occurring at an astonishing rate. Many innovations are based on new technologies: computerized information processing systems, new types of telecommunication systems, the Internet, organizational intranets, and various combinations of these technologies. Experts have estimated that performance of new information technology (at the same cost) doubles every eighteen months.[10] Managers can now send and receive memos and other documents to and from individuals or groups scattered around the world from their computers using the Internet, from cellular phones in their cars, or via their notebook computers on the commuter train. Soon they may be doing the same thing via their wrist-watches. Employees are now telecommuting from home rather than going to the office every day. Moreover, whole new industries are developing around information storage, transmission, and retrieval, advances that were not even dreamed of a decade ago.

The "office of the future" is here, but it may not be in a typical office building. Every office now has a facsimile (fax) machine, a copier, and personal computers, many of them linked into a single integrated system and to numerous databases and electronic mail systems. Automobile companies advertise that their cars and trucks have equipment for cellular telephones, laptop computers, and fax machines. The electronic office links managers, clerical employees, professional workers, sales personnel, and often suppliers and customers in a worldwide communication network that uses a combination of computerized data storage, retrieval, and transmission systems.

In fact, the computer-integrated organization is becoming commonplace. Ingersol Milling Machine of Rockford, Illinois, boasts a totally computer-integrated operation in which all major functions—sales, marketing, finance, distribution, and manufacturing—exchange operating information quickly and continuously via computers. For example, product designers can send specifications directly to machines on the factory floor, and accounting personnel receive online information about sales, purchases, and prices instantaneously. The computer system parallels and greatly speeds up the entire process.

Computers are facilitating the increase in telecommuting across the United States and reducing the number of trips people make to the office to get work done. More than ten years ago IBM provided many of its employees with notebook computers and told them not to come to the office but instead to use the computers to do the work out in the field and send it in electronically.[11] Other companies, such as Motorola and AT&T, have also encouraged telecommuting by employees. Employees report increased productivity, reduced fatigue and expenses caused by commuting, and increased personal freedom. In addition, telecommuting may reduce air pollution and overcrowding. Some employees have reported, however, that they miss the social interaction of the office. Some managers have also expressed concerns about the quantity and quality of the work telecommuting employees do when away from the office.

Research conducted among office workers using a new electronic office system indicated that attitudes toward the system were generally favorable. On the other hand, reduction of face-to-face meetings may depersonalize the office. Some observers are also concerned that companies are installing electronic systems with little consideration for the social structures of the office. As departments adopt computerized information systems, the activities of work groups throughout the organization are likely to become more interdependent, a situation that may alter power relationships among the groups. Most employees quickly learn the system of power, politics, authority, and responsibility in the office. A radical change in work and personal relationships caused by new office technology may disrupt normal ways of accomplishing tasks, thereby reducing productivity. Other potential problems include information overload, loss of records in a "paperless" office, and the dehumanizing consequences of using electronic equipment. In effect, new information processing and transmission technologies mean new media, symbols, message transmission methods, and networks for organizational communication.

The real increases in organizational productivity due to information technology may come from the ability to communicate in new and different ways rather than from simply speeding up existing communication patterns. For example, to remain competitive in a highly challenging global marketplace, companies will need to be able to generate, disseminate, and implement new ideas more effectively. In effect, organizations will become "knowledge-based" learning organizations that continually generate new ideas to improve themselves. This can occur only when expert knowledge is communicated and available throughout the organization.

One relatively recent way of communicating is idea sharing, or knowledge sharing, by sharing information on what practices work best. A computer-based system is necessary to store, organize, and then make available to others the best practices from throughout the company.[12] For example, Eli Lilly, a large pharmaceutical company, has developed a companywide intranet for all of its sixteen thousand employees. This system makes available internal email, corporate policies, and directories, and enables information sharing throughout the organization.[13] Electronic information technology is therefore speeding up existing communication and developing new types of organizational communication processes with potential new benefits—and problems—for managers.

Communication Networks

LEARNING OBJECTIVE

Describe the basic kinds of communication networks.

In a **wheel network**, information flows between the person at the end of each spoke and the person in the middle.

In a **chain network**, each member communicates with the person above and below, except for the individuals on each end, who communicate with only one person.

In a **circle network**, each member communicates with the people on both sides but with no one else.

In an **all-channel network**, all members communicate with all other members.

Communication links individuals and groups in a social system. Initially, task-related communication links develop in an organization so employees can get the information they need to do their jobs and coordinate their work with that of others in the system. Over a long period, these communication relationships become a sophisticated social system composed of both small-group communication networks and a larger organizational network. These networks structure both the flow and the content of communication, and support the organizational structure.[14] The pattern and content of communication also support the culture, beliefs, and value systems that enable the organization to operate.

Small-Group Networks

To examine interpersonal communication in a small group, we can observe the patterns that emerge as the group's work proceeds and information flows from some people in the group to others.[15] Four such patterns appear in Figure 7.4. The lines identify the communication links most frequently used in the groups.

In a **wheel network,** information flows between the person at the end of each spoke and the person in the middle. Those at the ends of the spokes do not directly communicate with each other. The wheel network is a feature of the typical work group, in which the primary communication occurs between the members and the group manager. In a **chain network,** each member communicates with the person above and below, except for the individuals on each end, who communicate with only one person. The chain network is typical of communication in a vertical hierarchy, in which most communication travels up and down the chain of command. Each person in a **circle network** communicates with the people on both sides but not with anyone else. The circle network is often found in task forces and committees. Finally, in an **all-channel network,** all members communicate with all other members. The all-channel network

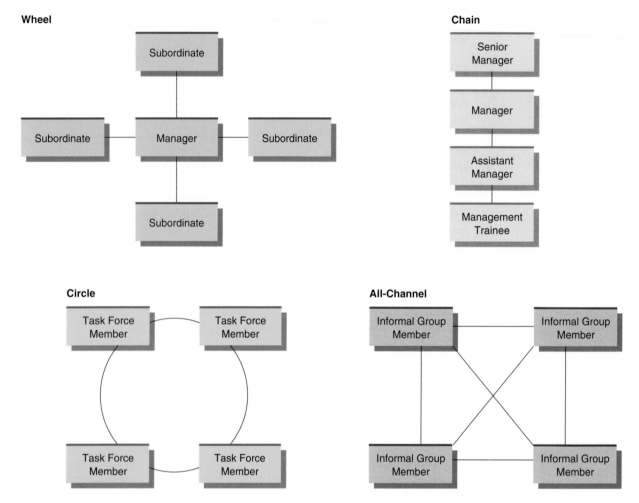

FIGURE 7.4

Small-Group Communication Networks

These four types of communication networks are the most common in organizations. The lines represent the most frequently used communication links in small groups.

often occurs with informal groups that have no formal structure, leader, or task to accomplish.

Communication may be more easily distorted by noise when much is being communicated or when the communication must travel a great distance. Improvements in electronic communication technology, such as computerized mail systems and intranets, are reducing this effect. A relatively central position gives a person an opportunity to communicate with all the other members; hence, a member in a relatively central position can control the information flow and may become a leader of the group. This leadership position is distinct from the formal group structure, although a central person in a group may also emerge as a formal group leader over a long period.

Communication networks form spontaneously and naturally as interactions among workers continue. They are rarely permanent since they change as the tasks, interactions, and memberships change. The task is crucial in determining the pattern of the network. If the group's primary task is decision making, an all-channel network may develop to provide the information needed to evaluate all possible alternatives. If, however, the group's task involves mainly the sequential execution of individual tasks, a chain or wheel network is more likely because communication among members may not be important to completion of the tasks.

The environment (the type of room in which the group works or meets, the seating arrangement, the placement of chairs and tables, the geographical dispersion, and other aspects of the group's setting) can affect the frequency and types of interactions among members. For example, if most members work on the same floor of an office building, the members who work three floors down may be considered outsiders and develop weaker communication ties to the group. They may even form a separate communication network.

Personal factors also influence the development of the communication network. These include technical expertise, openness, speaking ability, and the degree to which members are acquainted with one another. For example, in a group concerned mainly with highly technical problems, the person with the most expertise may dominate the communication flow during a meeting.

The group performance factors that influence the communication network include composition, size, norms, and cohesiveness. For example, group norms in one organization may encourage open communication across different levels and functional units, whereas the norms in another organization may discourage such lateral and diagonal communication. These performance factors are discussed in Chapter 8.

Because the outcome of the group's efforts depends on the coordinated action of its members, the communication network strongly influences group effectiveness. Thus, to develop effective working relationships in the organization, managers need to make a special effort to manage the flow of information and the development of communication networks. Managers can, for example, arrange offices and work spaces to foster communication among certain employees. Managers may also attempt to involve members who typically contribute little during discussions by asking them direct questions such as "What do you think, Tom?" or "Maria, tell us how this problem is handled in your district." Methods such as the nominal group technique, discussed in Chapter 12, can also encourage participation.

Another factor that is becoming increasingly important in the development of communication networks is the advent of electronic groups fostered by electronic distribution lists, chat rooms, discussion boards, and other computer networking systems. This form of communication results in a network of people who may have little or no face-to-face communication but still be considered a group communication network. For example, your professor is probably a member of an electronic group of other professors who share an interest in the topic of this course. Through the electronic group, they keep up with new ideas in the field.

Organizational Communication Networks

An organization chart shows reporting relationships from the line worker up to the CEO of the firm. The lines of an organization chart may also represent channels of communication through which information flows; however, communication may also follow paths that cross traditional reporting lines. Information moves not only from the top down—from CEO to group members—but also upward from group members to the CEO. In fact, a good flow of information to the CEO is an important determinant of the organization's success.

Several companies have realized that the key to their continuing success was improved internal communication. General Motors was known for its extremely formal, top-down communication system. In the mid-1980s, however, the formality of its system came under fire from virtually all of its stakeholders. GM's response was to embark on a massive communication improvement program that included sending employees to public-speaking workshops, improving the more than 350 publications the firm sends out, providing videotapes of management meetings to employees, and using satellite links between headquarters and field operations to establish two-way conversations around the world.

Downward communication generally provides directions, whereas upward communication provides feedback to top management. Communication that flows horizontally or crosses traditional reporting lines is usually related to task performance. For example, a design engineer, a manufacturing engineer, and a quality engineer may communicate about the details of a particular product design, thus making it easy to manufacture and inspect. Horizontal communication often travels faster than vertical communication because it need not follow organizational protocols and procedures.

Organizational communication networks may diverge from reporting relationships as employees seek better information with which to do their jobs. Employees often find that the easiest way to get their jobs done or obtain the necessary information is to go directly to employees in other departments rather than through the formal channels shown on the organization chart. Figure 7.5 shows a simple organization chart and the organization's real communication network. The communication network links the individuals who most frequently

FIGURE 7.5

Comparison of an Organization Chart and the Organization's Communication Network

A formal organization chart compared with actual communication patterns reflect different patterns from the reporting relationships shown in the organization chart.

Organization Chart

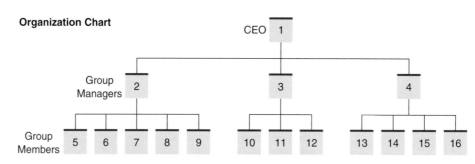

Communication Network of Most Frequent Communications for the Same Organization

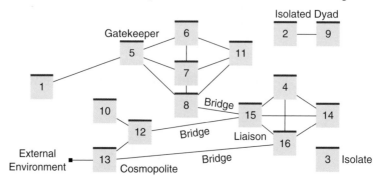

The **gatekeeper** has a strategic position in the network that allows him or her to control information moving in either direction through a channel.

The **liaison** serves as a bridge between groups, tying groups together and facilitating the communication flow needed to integrate group activities.

The **cosmopolite** links the organization to the external environment and may also be an opinion leader in the group.

communicate with one another; the firm's CEO, for example, communicates most often with employee 5. (This does not mean individuals not linked in the communication network never communicate; rather, their communications are relatively infrequent.) Perhaps the CEO and the employee interact frequently outside of work, in church, in service organizations such as Kiwanis, or at sporting events. Such interactions may lead to close friendships that carry over into business relationships. The figure also shows that the group managers do not have important roles in the communication network, contrary to commonsense expectations.

The roles people play in organizational communication networks can be analyzed in terms of their contribution to the functioning of the network.[16] The most important roles are labeled in the bottom portion of Figure 7.5. A **gatekeeper** (employee 5) has a strategic position in the network that allows him or her to control information moving in either direction through a channel. A **liaison** (employee 15) serves as a bridge between groups, tying groups together and facilitating the communication flow needed to integrate group activities. Employee 13 performs the interesting function of **cosmopolite,** who links the organization to the external environment by, for instance, attending conventions and trade shows, keeping up with outside technological innovations, and having more frequent contact with sources outside the organization. This person may also be an opinion leader in the group. Finally, the **isolate** (employee 3) and the **isolated dyad** (employees 2 and 9) tend to work alone and to interact and communicate little with others.

Each of these roles and functions plays an important part in the overall functioning of the communication network and in the organization as a whole. Understanding these roles can help both managers and group members facilitate communication. For instance, the manager who wants to ensure that the CEO receives certain information is well advised to go through the gatekeeper. If the employee who has the technical knowledge necessary for a particular project is an isolate, the manager can take special steps to integrate the employee into the communication network for the duration of the project.

Recent research indicates some possible negative impacts of communication networks. Employee turnover has been shown to occur in clusters related to employee communication networks.[17] That is, employees who communicate regularly in a network may share feelings about the organization and thus influence one another's intentions to stay or quit. Communication networks therefore may have both positive and negative consequences.

As we discuss in Chapter 13, a primary function of organizational structure is to coordinate the activities of many people doing specialized tasks. Organizational communication networks provide

Communication networks are a common element in organizations. Some firms ignore them, a few try to get rid of them, but some successful firms capitalize on their advantages. Techline, a custom furniture manufacturer, actively seeks to create communication networks among groups such as this one, in order to expedite the diffusion of information and enhance overall organizational performance.

The **isolate** and the **isolated dyad** tend to work alone and to interact and communicate little with others.

this much-needed integration. In fact, in some ways communication patterns influence organizational structure. Some companies are finding that the need for better communication forces them to create smaller divisions. The fewer managerial levels and improved team spirit of these divisions tend to enhance communication flows.

Managing Communication

Communication fidelity is the degree of correspondence between the message intended by the source and the message understood by the receiver.

As simple as the process of communication may seem, messages are not always understood. The degree of correspondence between the message intended by the source and the message understood by the receiver is called **communication fidelity.** Fidelity can be diminished anywhere in the communication process, from the source to the feedback. Moreover, organizations may have characteristics that impede the flow of information.

Improving the Communication Process

To improve organizational communication, one must understand potential problems. Using the basic communication process, we can identify several ways to overcome typical problems.

Source   The source may intentionally withhold or filter information on the assumption that the receiver does not need it to understand the communication. Withholding information, however, may render the message meaningless or cause an erroneous interpretation. For example, during a performance appraisal interview, a manager may not tell the employee all the sources of information being used to make the evaluation, thinking the employee does not need to know them. If the employee knew, however, he or she might be able to explain certain behaviors or otherwise alter the manager's perspective of the evaluation and thereby make it more accurate. Filtering may be more likely to occur in electronic communication such as email or voicemail, since they usually call for brevity and conciseness. Selective filtering may cause a breakdown in communication that cannot be repaired, even with good follow-up communication.

To avoid filtering, the communicator needs to understand why it occurs. Filtering can result from a lack of understanding of the receiver's position, from the sender's need to protect his or her own power by limiting the receiver's access to information, or from doubts about what the receiver might do with the information. The sender's primary concern, however, should be the message. In essence, the sender must determine exactly what message he or she wants the receiver to understand, send the receiver enough information to understand the message but not enough to create an overload, and trust the receiver to use the information properly.

Encoding and Decoding   Encoding and decoding problems occur as the message is translated into or from the symbols used in transmission. Such problems can relate to the meanings of the symbols or to the transmission itself. Encoding and decoding problems include lack of common experience between source and receiver, problems related to semantics and the use of jargon, and difficulties with the medium. The cartoon illustrates another potential problem.

Clearly the source and the receiver must share a common experience with the symbols that express the message if they are to encode and decode them in exactly the same way. People who speak different languages or come from different cultural

"I thought you said I should take the ball and slowly meander around with it."

Encoding and decoding are critical parts of the communication process. But all too often, errors and mistakes in one or both of these processes can lead to problems. For instance, in the situation shown here the boss apparently meant for his subordinate to "take the ball and run with it." But the subordinate heard something else altogether!

Semantics is the study of language forms.

Jargon is the specialized or technical language of a trade, field, profession, or social group.

backgrounds may experience problems of this sort. However, even people who speak the same language can misunderstand each other.

Semantics is the study of language forms, and semantic problems occur when people attribute different meanings to the same words or language forms. For example, J. Edgar Hoover, the legendary former director of the FBI, once jotted "watch the borders" on a memo he had received and sent it back to the senior agency manager who had written it. Only after dispatching several dozen agents to guard the border between the United States and Mexico did the agency manager learn what Hoover had actually meant: The margins on the memo were too narrow! Similarly, suppose that when discussing a problem employee, a division head tells her assistant, "We need to get rid of this problem." The division head means the employee should be scheduled for more training or transferred to another division. However, the assistant may interpret the statement differently and fire the employee.

Jargon is the specialized or technical language of a trade, field, profession, or social group. Jargon may be a hybrid of standard language and specialized language. For example, experts in the computer field use terms, such as *gigs*, *megs*, *RAM*, and *bandwidth*, that have little or no meaning to those unfamiliar with computers. The use of jargon makes communication within a close group of colleagues more efficient and meaningful, but outside the group it has the opposite effect. Sometimes a source person comfortable with jargon inadvertently uses it while communicating with a receiver who does not understand it; the result is a communication breakdown. In other cases, the source may use jargon intentionally to obscure meaning or to show outsiders that he or she belongs to the group that uses the language.

The use of jargon is acceptable if the receiver is familiar with it; otherwise, it should be avoided. Repeating a jargon-filled message in clearer terms should help the receiver understand it. In general, both source and receiver should clarify the set of symbols to be used before they communicate. Also, the receiver can ask questions frequently and, if necessary, ask the source to repeat all or part of the message. The source must send the message through a medium appropriate for the message itself and for the intended receiver. For example, a commercial run on an AM radio station will miss its intended effect if the people in the desired market segment listen only to FM radio.

Largely influenced by the Enron debacle, investors are increasingly beginning to scrutinize the financial reporting systems of larger companies. Coca-Cola, for instance, recently saw its own accounting practices criticized in the media. These critics contend that the firm is using increasingly complex reporting methods to make its earnings seem higher than if simpler and more straightforward accounting practices had been used.[18]

Receiver Several communication problems originate in the receiver, including problems with selective attention, value judgments, source credibility, and overload. Selective attention exists when the receiver attends only to selected parts of a message—a frequent occurrence with oral communication. For example, in a college class, some students may hear only part of the professor's lecture as their minds wander to other topics. To focus receivers' attention on the message, senders often engage in attention-getting behaviors such as varying the volume, repeating the message, and offering rewards.

Value judgments are influenced by the degree to which a message reinforces or challenges the receiver's basic personal beliefs. If a message reinforces the receiver's beliefs, she may pay close attention and believe it completely, without examination. On the other hand, if the message challenges those beliefs, the receiver may entirely discount it. Thus, if a firm's sales manager predicts that the demand for new baby-care products will increase substantially over the next two years, he may ignore reports that the birthrate is declining.

The receiver may also judge the credibility of the source of the message. If the source is perceived to be an expert in the field, the listener may pay close attention to the message and believe it. Conversely, if the receiver has little respect for the source, he or she may disregard the message. The receiver considers both the message and the source in making value judgments and determining credibility. An expert in nuclear physics may be viewed as a credible source if the issue is building a nuclear power plant; however, the same person's evaluation of the birthrate may be disregarded, perhaps correctly. This is one reason trial lawyers ask expert witnesses about their education and experience at the beginning of their testimony: to establish credibility.

A receiver experiencing communication overload is receiving more information than she or he can process. In organizations, this can happen very easily; a receiver can be bombarded with computer-generated reports and messages from superiors, peers, and sources outside the organization. It is not unusual for middle managers or telecommuters to receive one hundred email messages per day. Unable to take in all the messages, decode them, understand them, and act on them, the receiver may use selective attention and value judgments to focus on the messages that seem most important. Although this type of selective attention is necessary for survival in an information-glutted environment, the result may be that vital information is lost or overlooked.[19]

Verification is the feedback portion of communication in which the receiver sends a message to the source indicating receipt of the message and the degree to which he or she understood it.

Feedback   The purpose of feedback is **verification,** in which the receiver sends a message to the source indicating receipt of the message and the degree to which it was understood. Lack of feedback can cause at least two problems. First, the source may need to send another message that depends on the response to the first; if the source receives no feedback, he may not send the second message or may be forced to send the original message again. Second, the receiver may act on the unverified message; if she misunderstood the message, the resulting act may be inappropriate.

Because feedback is so important, the source must actively seek it and the receiver must supply it. Often it is appropriate for the receiver to repeat the original message as an introduction to the response, although the medium or symbols used may be different. Nonverbal cues can provide instantaneous feedback. These include body language and facial expressions such as anger and disbelief.

The source needs to be concerned with the message, the symbols, the medium, and the feedback from the receiver. Of course, the receiver is concerned with these things too, but from a different point of view. In general, the receiver

Focus	Source		Receiver	
	Question	**Corrective Action**	**Question**	**Corrective Action**
Message	What idea or thought are you trying to get across?	Give more information. Give less information. Give entire message.	What idea or thought does the sender want you to understand?	Listen carefully to the entire message, not just to part of it.
Symbols	Does the receiver use the same symbols, words, jargon?	Say it another way. Employ repetition. Use receiver's language or jargon. Before sending, clarify symbols to be used.	What symbols are being used—for example, foreign language, technical jargon?	Clarify symbols before communication begins. Ask questions. Ask sender to repeat message.
Medium	Is this a channel that the receiver monitors regularly? Sometimes? Never?	Use multiple media. Change medium. Increase volume (loudness).	What medium or media is the sender using?	Monitor several media.
Feedback	What is the receiver's reaction to your message?	Pay attention to the feedback, especially nonverbal cues. Ask questions.	Did you correctly interpret the message?	Repeat message.

TABLE 7.1

Improving the Communication Process

needs to be source oriented just as the source needs to be receiver oriented. Table 7.1 gives specific suggestions for improving the communication process.

Improving Organizational Factors in Communication

Organizational factors that can create communication breakdowns or barriers include noise, status differences, time pressures, and overload. As previously stated, disturbances anywhere in the organization can distort or interrupt meaningful communication. Thus, the noise created by a rumored takeover can disrupt the orderly flow of task-related information. Kmart's stock recently dropped precipitously based on rumors that the company planned to file bankruptcy. Although the retailer did eventually take this step, rumor alone caused great damage to the company in the eyes of the investment community.[20]

Status differences between source and receiver can cause some of the communication problems just discussed. For example, a firm's chief executive officer may pay little attention to communications from employees far lower on the organization chart, and employees may pay little attention to communications from the CEO. Both are instances of selective attention prompted by the organization's status system. Time pressures and communication overloads are also detrimental to communication. When the receiver is not allowed enough time to understand incoming messages, or when there are too many messages, he or she may misunderstand or ignore some of them. Effective organizational communication provides the right information to the right person at the right time and in the right form.

The **grapevine** is an informal system of communication that coexists with the formal system.

Reduce Noise   Noise is a primary barrier to effective organizational communication. A common form of noise is the rumor **grapevine,** an informal system of communication that coexists with the formal system. The grapevine usually transmits information faster than official channels do. Because the accuracy of this information is often quite low, however, the grapevine can distort organizational communication. Management can reduce the effects of the distortion by using the grapevine as an additional channel for disseminating information and constantly monitoring it for accuracy.

Foster Informal Communication   Communication in well-run companies was once described as "a vast network of informal, open communications."[21] Informal communication fosters mutual trust, which minimizes the effects of status differences. Open communication can also contribute to better understanding between diverse groups in an organization. Monsanto Company created fifteen-member teams in its Agricultural Group, the primary objective being to increase communication and awareness among various diverse groups. Its Chemical Group set up diversity pairs of one supervisor and one worker to increase communication and awareness. In both cases, Monsanto found that increasing communication between people who were different paid handsomely for the organization.[22] Open communication also allows information to be communicated when it is needed rather than when the formal information system allows it to emerge. Thomas Peters and Robert Waterman further describe communication in effective companies as chaotic and intense, supported by the reward structure and the physical arrangement of the facilities. This means the performance appraisal and reward system, offices, meeting rooms, and work areas are designed to encourage frequent, unscheduled, and unstructured communication throughout the organization.

Develop a Balanced Information Network   Many large organizations have developed elaborate formal information networks to cope with the potential problems of information overload and time pressures. In many cases, however, the networks have created problems instead of solving them. Often they produce more information than managers and decision makers can comprehend and use in their jobs. The networks also often use only formal communication channels and ignore various informal lines of communication. Furthermore, they frequently provide whatever information the computer is set up to provide—information that may not apply to the most pressing problem at hand. The result of all these drawbacks is loss of communication effectiveness.

Organizations need to balance information load and information processing capabilities. In other words, they must take care not to generate more information than people can handle. It is useless to produce sophisticated statistical reports that managers have no time to read. Furthermore, the new technologies that are making more information available to managers and decision makers must be unified to produce usable information. Information production, storage, and processing capabilities must be compatible with one another and, equally important, with the needs of the organization.

Some companies—for example, General Electric, Anheuser-Busch, and McDonald's—have formalized an upward communication system that uses a corporate "ombudsperson" position. A highly placed executive who is available outside the formal chain of command to hear employees' complaints usually holds this position. The system provides an opportunity for disgruntled employees to complain without fear of losing their jobs and may help some companies achieve a balanced communication system.

Synopsis

Communication is the process by which two parties exchange information and share meaning. It plays a role in every organizational activity. The purposes of communication in organizations are to achieve coordinated action, share information, and express feelings and emotions.

People in organizations communicate through written, oral, and nonverbal means. Written communications include letters, memos, email, reports, and the like. Oral communication is the type most commonly used. Personal elements, such as facial expressions and body language, and environmental elements, such as office design, are forms of nonverbal communication.

Communication among individuals, groups, or organizations is a process in which a source sends a message and a receiver responds. The source encodes a message into symbols and transmits it through a medium to the receiver, who decodes the symbols. The receiver then responds with feedback, an attempt to verify the meaning of the original message. Noise—anything that distorts or interrupts communication—may interfere in virtually any stage of the process.

The fully integrated communication-information office system—the electronic office—links personnel in a communication network through a combination of computers and electronic transmission systems. The full range of effects of such systems has yet to be fully realized.

Communication networks are systems of information exchange within organizations. Patterns of communication emerge as information flows from person to person in a group. Typical small-group communication networks include the wheel, chain, circle, and all-channel networks. The organizational communication network, which constitutes the real communication links in an organization, usually differs from the arrangement on an organization chart. Roles in organizational communication networks include those of gatekeeper, liaison, cosmopolite, and isolate or isolated dyad.

Managing communication in organizations involves understanding the numerous problems that can interfere with effective communication. Problems may arise from the communication process itself and from organizational factors such as status differences, time pressures, and information overload.

Discussion Questions

1. How is communication in organizations an individual process as well as an organizational process?

2. Discuss the three primary purposes of organizational communication.

3. Describe a situation in which you tried to carry on a conversation when no one was listening. Were any messages sent during the "conversation"?

4. A college classroom is a forum for a typical attempt at communication as the professor tries to communicate the subject to students. Describe classroom communication in terms of the basic communication process outlined in the chapter.

5. Is there a communication network (other than professor-to-student) in the class in which you are using this book? If so, identify the specific roles people play in the network. If not, why has no network developed? What would be the benefits of having a communication network in this class?

6. Why might educators typically focus most communication training on written and oral methods and pay little attention to nonverbal methods? Do you think more training emphasis should be placed on nonverbal communication? Why or why not?

7. Is the typical classroom means of transferring information from professor to student an effective form of communication? If not, where does it break down? What are the communication problems in the college classroom?

8. Who is responsible for solving classroom communication problems: the students, the professors, or the administrations?

9. Have you ever worked in an organization in which communication was a problem? If so, what were some causes of the problem?

10. What methods were used, or should have been used, to improve communication in the situation you described in question 9?

11. Would the use of advanced computer information processing or telecommunications have helped solve the communications problem you described in question 9?

12. What types of communication problems are new telecommunications methods expected to help solve? Why?

13. What types of communications would *not* be appropriate to send by email? By voicemail?

14. Which steps in the communication process are usually left out, or at least poorly done, when email and voicemail are used for communication?

Organizational Behavior Case for Discussion

A Tale of Two Companies

To quote Charles Dickens's *A Tale of Two Cities*, "It was the best of times[;] it was the worst of times." With apologies to Dickens, this description handily sums up the current state of affairs in the communications industry. Firms that are able to take advantage of technological developments prosper, whereas firms that have remained in traditional markets are losing sales and profits. Agilent, an electronics component manufacturer, described the situation in its 2001 annual report: "The dramatic slowdown in the communications and semiconductor markets defined Agilent's second year as an independent company. After very strong growth in 1999 and 2000, the decline in demand in these markets was unprecedented in its speed and severity . . . The downturn worsened as we moved through 2001."

EchoMail provides software that automatically processes, responds, stores, and tracks email correspondence, reducing the time users spend on these chores. Founded by MIT scientists and headquartered in Cambridge, Massachusetts, home of Harvard and MIT, EchoMail's clients include many large organizations such as AT&T, Compaq, Nike, and the U.S. Senate. EchoMail was used to create the controversial Calvin Klein advertisements that allowed consumers to email the "characters" in television or print ads and receive customized, scripted emails in response. EchoMail is the oldest firm (at seven years) in the intelligent-email response industry, which is predicted to grow to $500 million in sales by 2005. Thus, the firm is poised to take advantage of the expected flood of intelligent software users over the next decade, and it recently hired sales and technical professionals.

Agilent, in contrast, was created as a spinoff from Hewlett-Packard (HP) when that company refocused its businesses on computing and printing. The November 1999 initial public offering was the largest in Silicon Valley history, valued at $2.1 billion. With 43,000 employees in 40 countries, Agilent is a leader in developing and manufacturing electrical components and testing equipment, as well as in

installation and maintenance services for its equipment. Agilent customers compete in a wide variety of industries, including agricultural chemicals; pharmaceuticals; petrochemicals; semiconductors; wireless communications; PCs; foods; appliances; and automotive, aerospace, and consumer products. Therefore, Agilent is vulnerable to economic downturns in which manufacturers reduce their purchases of equipment and services. Agilent has instituted pay cuts; in 2001 the firm laid off 4,000 workers. Since then another 4,000 jobs have been eliminated.

Although Agilent seems to be facing a host of problems because of its dependence on a currently lackluster segment of the communications industry, there is also a bright side. Agilent considers itself the true heir of Hewlett-Packard founders Dave Packard and Bill Hewlett, who used participatory management, open-door policies, and decision making by consensus to keep HP employees working together as a team. Agilent, which carefully built on the foundation of HP's culture, also carefully worked to maintain its culture when things got tough. Initially the company tried everything within its power to avoid layoffs: cost cutting, hiring freezes, and even pay cuts. Then, when layoffs became inevitable, CEO Ned Barnholt asked each manager to choose from among the employees known personally to them and insisted that workers be told face to face. Barnholt made the announcement himself, ensuring that employees heard the news from him and not from reporters. He described exactly how employees would be evaluated and how the layoffs would occur. In a rough, emotional tone of voice, he intoned, "This is the toughest decision of my career, but we've run out of alternatives."

As a result of his honest and sincere communication, most Agilent employees did not blame the firm or their supervisors. "I knew that this isn't the HP Way, and it's not what Bill and Dave [Hewlett and Packard] would have wanted, but if they were faced with the same situation, they would have had to do the exact same thing. I know Ned [CEO Barnholt] probably lost a lot [of sleep] having to get up there in front of everybody and make this announcement and have to let go people in his family," said Benjamin Steers, an Agilent employee.

While EchoMail is prospering as its new technology enables the firm to increase sales, profitability, and personnel, Agilent is facing declining markets for many of its traditional products. Its hope for the future depends on its ability to innovate and develop new products. However, as Agilent is demonstrating, appropriate communication, especially of bad news, can be key to building a culture of responsibility, loyalty, and empathy.

Case Questions

1. How did Agilent's communication choices lead to an effective employee response to the firm's downsizing?

2. Both Agilent and EchoMail are international firms, with production and sales locations in multiple countries. What are some potential problems or challenges that these firms' international involvement present?

3. Communication is described as reflecting the organization culture and as having the power to change the culture. How does the communication taking place in your Management classroom reflect your school's culture? Has communication at your school changed its culture? If so, how?

References: "About Agilent," "History," "Industries," "2003 Annual Report," Agilent corporate website, www.agilent.com on May 10, 2004; "About EchoMail," corporate website; Daniel Roth, "How to Cut Pay, Lay Off 8,000 People, and Still Have Workers Who Love You. It's Easy: Just Follow the Agilent Way," *Fortune*, February 4, 2002; Erin Allday, "Agilent Cuts 600 More Local Jobs," *Press Democrat* (Santa Rosa, CA), December 11, 2001, p. A1; John Evan Frook, "Technology Leads Prospects to Sales," *BtoB Magazine*, October 10, 2002; Deborah Shapley, "Dr. E-Mail Will See You Now," *Technology Review*, January–February 2000, pp. 42–47; Roberta Fusaro, "E-Mail Adds Aura to Calvin Klein Campaign," *Computerworld*, November 30, 1998, p. 103.

Experiencing Organizational Behavior

The Importance of Feedback in Oral Communication

Purpose: This exercise demonstrates the importance of feedback in oral communication.

Format: You will be an observer or play the role of either a manager or an assistant manager trying to tell a coworker where a package of important materials is to be picked up. The observer's role is to make sure the other two participants follow the rules and to observe and record any interesting occurrences.

Procedure: The instructor will divide the class into groups of three. (Any extra members can be roving observers.) The three people in each group will take the roles of manager, assistant manager, and observer. In the second trial, the manager and the assistant manager will switch roles.

Trial 1: The manager and assistant manager should turn their backs to each other so that neither can see the other. Here is the situation: The manager is in another city that he or she is not familiar with but the assistant manager knows quite well. The manager needs to find the office of a supplier to pick up drawings of a critical component of the company's main product. The supplier will be closing for the day in a few minutes; the drawings must be picked up before closing time. The manager has called the assistant manager to

get directions to the office. However, the connection is faulty; the manager can hear the assistant manager, but the assistant manager can hear only enough to know the manager is on the line. The manager has redialed once, but the connection was still poor. Now there is no time to lose. The manager has decided to get the directions from the assistant without asking questions.

Just before the exercise begins, the instructor will give the assistant manager a detailed map of the city that shows the locations of the supplier's office and the manager. The map will include a number of turns, stops, stoplights, intersections, and shopping centers between these locations. The assistant manager can study it for no longer than a minute or two. When the instructor gives the direction to start, the assistant manager describes to the manager how to get from his or her present location to the supplier's office. As the assistant manager gives the directions, the manager draws the map on a piece of paper.

The observer makes sure no questions are asked, records the beginning and ending times, and notes how the assistant manager tries to communicate particularly difficult points (including points about which the manager obviously wants to ask questions) and any other noteworthy occurrences.

After all pairs have finished, each observer "grades" the quality of the manager's map by comparing it with the original and counting the number of obvious mistakes. The instructor will ask a few managers who believe they have drawn good maps to tell the rest of the class how to get to the supplier's office.

Trial 2: In trial 2, the manager and assistant manager switch roles, and a second map is given to the new assistant managers. The situation is the same as in the first trial except the telephones are working properly and the manager can ask questions of the assistant manager. The observer's role is the same as in trial 1: recording the beginning and ending times, the methods of communication, and other noteworthy occurrences.

After all pairs have finished, the observers grade the maps, just as in the first trial. The instructor then selects a few managers to tell the rest of the class how to get to the supplier's office. The subsequent class discussion should center on the experiences of the class members and the follow-up questions.

Follow-up Questions

1. Which trial resulted in more accurate maps? Why?
2. Which trial took longer? Why?
3. How did you feel when a question needed to be asked but could not be asked in trial 1? Was your confidence in the final result affected differently in the two trials?

Self-Assessment Exercise
Diagnosing Your Listening Skills

Introduction: Good listening skills are essential for effective communication and are often overlooked when communication is analyzed. This self-assessment questionnaire examines your ability to listen effectively.

Instructions: Go through the following statements, checking "Yes" or "No" next to each one. Mark each question as truthfully as you can in light of your behavior in the last few meetings or gatherings you attended.

Yes　No

1. I frequently attempt to listen to several conversations at the same time.
2. I like people to give me only the facts and then let me make my own interpretation.
3. I sometimes pretend to pay attention to people.
4. I consider myself a good judge of nonverbal communications.
5. I usually know what another person is going to say before he or she says it.
6. I usually end conversations that don't interest me by diverting my attention from the speaker.
7. I frequently nod, frown, or in some other way let the speaker know how I feel about what he or she is saying.
8. I usually respond immediately when someone has finished talking.

9. I evaluate what is being said while it is being said.
10. I usually formulate a response while the other person is still talking.
11. The speaker's "delivery" style frequently keeps me from listening to content.
12. I usually ask people to clarify what they have said rather than guess at the meaning.
13. I make a concerted effort to understand other people's point of view.
14. I frequently hear what I expect to hear rather than what is said.
15. Most people feel that I have understood their point of view when we disagree.

Scoring

The correct answers according to communication theory are as follows:

No for statements 1, 2, 3, 5, 6, 7, 8, 9, 10, 11, 14.
Yes for statements 4, 12, 13, 15.

If you missed only one or two responses, you strongly approve of your own listening habits, and you are on the right track to becoming an effective listener in your role as manager. If you missed three or four responses, you have uncovered some doubts about your listening effectiveness, and your knowledge of how to listen has some gaps. If you missed five or more responses, you probably are not satisfied with the way you listen, and your friends and coworkers may not feel you are a good listener, either. Work on improving your active listening skills.

Reference: "Diagnosing Your Listening Skills," from Ethel C. Glenn and Elliott A. Pond, "Listening Self-Inventory," *Supervisory Management*, January 1989, pp. 12–15. Copyright © 1989 by American Management Association. Reproduced with permission of American Management Association in the format Textbook via Copyright Clearance Center.

OB Online

1. Find the country-specific websites of a single large company, such as Coca-Cola, IBM, or Toyota, for at least three different countries. Then identify the similarities and differences among the websites.

2. Compare electronic communication with the three basic methods of communication. For example, can nonverbal messages be sent via email?

3. Identify how several attributes of electronic communication can serve as noise. For example, cell phone static may make it difficult for the receiver to hear the sender.

4. Use the Internet to research the most frequently used methods of communicating in organizations.

Building Managerial Skills

Exercise Overview: Communication skills involve a manager's ability both to convey ideas and information effectively to others and to receive ideas and information effectively from others. This exercise focuses on communication skills in deciding how to best convey information.

Exercise Background: Assume you are a middle manager for a large electronics firm. People in your organization generally use one of three means for communicating with one another. The most common way is oral communication, accomplished either face to face or by telephone. Electronic mail is also widely used. Finally, a surprisingly large amount of communication is still done on paper, such as through memos, reports, and letters.

During the course of a typical day, you receive and send a variety of messages and other communications. You generally use some combination of all the communication methods previously noted during the day. The things you need to communicate today include the following:

1. You need to schedule a meeting with five subordinates.
2. You need to congratulate a coworker who just had a baby.
3. You need to reprimand a staff assistant who has been coming to work late for the last several days.

4. You need to inform the warehouse staff that several customers have recently complained because their shipments were not properly packed.
5. You need to schedule a meeting with your boss.
6. You need to announce two promotions.
7. You need to fire someone who has been performing poorly for some time.
8. You need to inform several individuals about a set of new government regulations that will soon affect them.
9. You need to inform a supplier that your company will soon be cutting back on its purchases because a competing supplier has lowered its prices, and you plan to shift more of your business to that supplier.
10. You need to resolve a disagreement between two subordinates who want to take their vacation at the same time.

Exercise Task: Using the information just presented, do the following:

1. Indicate which methods of communication would be appropriate for each situation.
2. Rank-order the methods for each communication situation from best to worst.
3. Compare your rankings with those of a classmate, and discuss any differences

TEST PREPPER

ACE self-test

You have read the chapter and studied the key terms, and the exam is any day now. Think you're ready to ace it? Take this sample test to gauge your comprehension of chapter material. You can check your answers at the back of the book. Want more test questions? Visit the student website at http://college.hmco.com/business/students/ (select Griffin/Moorhead, Fundamentals of Organizational Behavior 1e) and take the ACE quizzes for more practice.

1. T F Gestures and facial expressions usually mean the same things across cultures.

2. T F The most common form of organizational written communication is the annual report.

3. T F The mouth is the most expressive component of the face.

4. T F The arrangement and nature of furniture in an office is a form of communication.

5. T F When a receiver gets a message from a source, he or she must encode it.

6. T F A face-to-face communication has a greater carrying capacity than does an email.

7. T F Feedback occurs when a message doesn't reach its destination and cycles back to the sender.

8. T F Telecommuting may increase productivity, personal freedom, and social interactions in the office.

9. T F The real increases in organizational productivity due to information technology may come from the ability to communicate in new and different ways rather than from simply speeding up existing communication patterns.

10. T F Roger works in an informal group without a designated leader. He is likely to be part of a chain communication network.

11. T F Latisha has a strategic position in the organization because she can control information moving in either direction through a channel. Latisha occupies a gatekeeper role.

12. T F Filtering is more likely to occur in electronic communication, such as email, than in face-to-face interactions.

13. T F Jargon can make the communication of a close group of colleagues more efficient.

14. T F Communication overload exists when a sender transmits more information than he or she is allowed to.

15. T F To establish the most effective communication, the source should actively seek feedback and the receiver should actively send it.

16. T F Information transmitted through the grapevine is often more accurate than information transmitted through official channels.

17. The primary purpose of organizational communication is to
   a. manage uncertainty.
   b. identify low performers.
   c. reward high performers.
   d. achieve coordinated action.
   e. make a profit.

18. Which of the following statements best captures the issues regarding communication across cultures?
   a. Colors and body language have universal meanings across nearly all cultures.
   b. Direct translations of messages ensure the clearest communication across cultures.
   c. Technology has overcome most of the problems involved in communicating across cultures.
   d. Managers should avoid attempting to communicate across cultures.
   e. Verbal and nonverbal messages may have different meanings in different cultures.

19. The most common form of written communications is the
   a. termination slip.
   b. application form.
   c. paycheck.
   d. work schedule.
   e. memo.

20. The most prevalent form of organizational communication is
   a. oral.
   b. nonverbal.
   c. written.
   d. body language.
   e. colors and symbols.

21. Which of the following is not an example of nonverbal communication?
   a. Eye contact
   b. Sitting on the edge of a chair during a discussion
   c. Facial expressions
   d. Office furniture
   e. Email

22. During the complete communication process, the receiver responds with a message to the source to verify the communication. This portion of the communication process is known as
    a. decoding.
    b. transmission.
    c. the medium of communication.
    d. the feedback loop.
    e. noise control.

23. Ronald has an idea he wants to communicate to his boss, so he writes it down on a piece of paper. Ronald has just completed which portion of the communication process?
    a. Source
    b. Encoding
    c. Medium
    d. Feedback
    e. Transmission

24. Which medium has the largest carrying capacity?
    a. Voicemail
    b. Email
    c. Letter
    d. Telephone
    e. Face-to-face conversation

25. After Josh received a letter communicating a job offer, he responded immediately by sending a letter indicating his acceptance. Josh's response is an example of which portion of the communication process?
    a. Noise reduction
    b. Decoding
    c. Feedback
    d. Receiver
    e. Verbal communication

26. Effective communication occurs when
    a. the sender encodes the message.
    b. the receiver decodes the message.
    c. the sender and the receiver share the same meaning.
    d. all noise has been eliminated.
    e. the appropriate transmission medium is used.

27. Which of the following is a disadvantage of telecommuting?
    a. Reduced personal freedom
    b. Decreased productivity
    c. Reduced social interactions
    d. Increased air pollution
    e. Increased fatigue

28. Electronic information technology not only speeds up existing communication but also
    a. eliminates obsolete communications.
    b. reduces unnecessary social interactions.
    c. reduces personal freedom.
    d. forces managers to spend more time at work.
    e. allows for communication in new and different ways.

29. An organization structured as a narrow vertical hierarchy likely follows which communication pattern?
    a. Wheel
    b. Chain
    c. Circle
    d. All-channel
    e. Spiral

30. Randy's work position requires him to relay information to many of his coworkers. This position is likely to affect which of the following for Randy?
    a. His level in the organizational hierarchy
    b. His organizing skills
    c. His technical skills
    d. His organizational commitment
    e. His opportunity for informal leadership

31. Which of the following generally provides directions rather than feedback to top management?
    a. Upward communication
    b. Downward communication
    c. Horizontal communication
    d. Lateral communication
    e. Informal communication

32. Lisa serves as the communication "go-between" for two manufacturing groups in the organization. Which communication role is she filling?
    a. Gatekeeper
    b. Liaison
    c. Cosmopolite
    d. Isolate
    e. Dyad

33. Carlos frequently leaves very short instructions for his subordinates because he believes they do not need to understand the extra information to complete their tasks. Carlos would improve his communications if he stopped
    a. encoding.
    b. decoding.
    c. sourcing.
    d. isolating.
    e. filtering.

34. Tammy heard about the company layoffs from James, who heard about them from Vince, who heard about them even before the official plans were announced by the company president. This is an example of the speed of
    a. dyadic interchanges.
    b. selective perception.
    c. vertical communication.
    d. the grapevine.
    e. a wheel network.

CHAPTER 8

Group Dynamics

MANAGEMENT PREVIEW

Just about everyone can identify several groups to which she or he belongs. Some groups are based on friendships and personal relationships; others are more formally established and may be part of a larger organization. All organizations have numerous groups that do some part of the organization's work. The performance and productivity of an organization is the total of the output and productivity of all of the individuals and groups that work within it. Large companies around the world are restructuring their organizations around work groups and teams to increase productivity and innovation and to improve customer service.

This chapter is the first of a two-chapter sequence on groups and teams in organizations: groups such as the traditional work groups to which most people belong in their work organizations, pit crews at stock-car races, the Zebra teams that reenergized the black-and-white photo processing unit at Eastman Kodak, a football team, an engineering work group, or a group of nurses working the night shift at a local hospital. In this chapter, we cover the basics of group dynamics: the reasons for group formation, the types of groups in organizations, group performance factors, and the potential for conflict in groups. In Chapter 9, we consider how today's organizations are using teams.

We begin this chapter by defining *group* and summarizing the importance of groups in organizations. We then describe different types of groups and discuss the stages in which they evolve from newly formed groups into mature, high-performing units. Next, we identify four key factors that affect group performance. We then move to a discussion of how groups interact with other groups in organizations and examine conflict among groups in organizations. Finally, we identify the important elements in managing groups in organizations.

After you have studied this chapter, you should be able to:

- [ ] *Define a group.*
- [ ] *Discuss the types of groups commonly found in organizations.*
- [ ] *Describe the general stages of group development.*

- ☐ *Discuss the major group performance factors.*
- ☐ *Describe intergroup dynamics.*
- ☐ *Explain conflict in organizations.*
- ☐ *Discuss methods for managing group and intergroup dynamics.*

We start with some examples that underscore the importance of groups to the successful performance of a variety of businesses today.

At one time, many observers feared that recent advances in communications marked the end of face-to-face dialogues, collaboration, teamwork, and other human interactions. Instead companies today are finding technology can enhance and extend the use of traditional team interactions. "There's an opportunity for a whole new level of business-performance improvements in the collaborative redesign of processes, using the Internet," according to James A. Champy, chairman of consulting at Perot Systems.

Lockheed Martin uses a system of ninety web software tools to coordinate a $200 billion project for building the next-generation stealth fighters. The manufacturer brings together 40,000 users, 80 subcontractors, and 187 locations around the world. Lockheed uses the Web to exchange documents and designs and to monitor project progress. "We're getting the best people, applying the best designs, from wherever we need them," says Mark Peden, Lockheed information systems vice president.

At General Motors, web collaboration helps engineers and external parts suppliers work together on product design. Complex designs might involve fourteen worldwide sites in addition to the dozens of partner firms that create components and subsystems. By saving time, the engineers are able to complete three or four alternative designs instead of just one and still finish weeks sooner.

Prospective students at Yale University use an Internet-based system to investigate the school, complete an application, and apply for financial aid. Admissions staff around the country then share information about applicants, with online discussion and comments posted to documents. Nevertheless, James Stevens, director of admissions, still notifies accepted applicants with a phone call. He explains, "[They will] hear from me personally. It is very important to us for people to understand how personal the experience is here."

General Electric holds virtual company meetings, with speeches webcast to all of its locations simultaneously. Management shares financial results with all employees via the Internet. "There are no secrets. The whole organization has everything," says former CEO Jack Welch. He claims the shared data facilitate building employees' trust and allow everyone to have the same information, thereby improving teamwork.

"Without meaningful personal interaction …, it's hard to build understanding and accountability."—Jon Katzenbach, consultant and author of The Discipline of Teams

The Children's Hospital at Montefiore has integrated a patient information system throughout the facility. Patients and family members use smart cards for customized access to information about illnesses and treatments, video games or movies on demand, and the Internet. "It's about the patient's ability to control [his or her] environment," says Jeb Weisman, software designer. David Rockwell, a lead designer of the system, says the intent is "to provide information, insight, and a sense of wonder and delight." Patients and their families thus become team members in their own treatment.

The technology is helpful, but it doesn't manage itself. Paul R. Gudonis, chairman and CEO of Genuity, Inc., says that although managers have made a good start in encouraging teams to use technology, "[t]hey've now found that it's going to take more effort offline to integrate

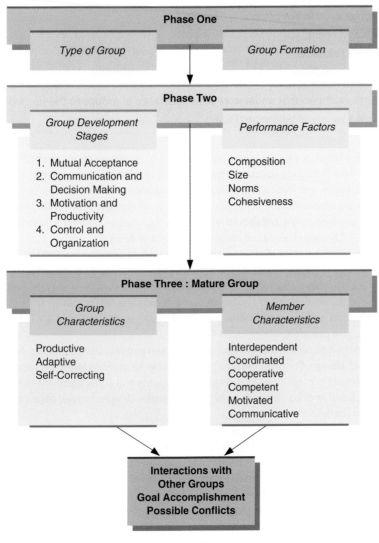

FIGURE 8.1

A General Model of Group Dynamics

This model serves as the framework for this chapter. In phase one, the reasons for group formation determine what type of group it will be. In the second phase, groups evolve through four stages under the influence of four performance factors. Finally, a mature group emerges that interacts with other groups and can pursue organizational goals; conflicts with other groups sometimes occur.

offline and online processes to get the kind of changed behavior and benefits that they're looking for." Jon Katzenbach, consultant and author of *The Discipline of Teams,* claims, "Without meaningful personal interaction and doing 'real' work together, it's hard to build understanding and accountability," reminding leaders of the continuing value of hands-on management and face-to-face meetings.

References: "Paul Gudonis, Chairman and CEO, Genuity, Inc." *Fast Company,* May 2002; Polly LaBarre, "Strategic Innovation: The Children's Hospital at Montefiore," *Fast Company,* May 2002; "The New Teamwork," *BusinessWeek,* February 18, 2002; Anne Fisher, "Virtual Teams and Long-Distance Meetings: More on Staying Grounded," *Fortune,* October 15, 2001 (quotation); "Giants Can Be Nimble," *BusinessWeek Biz,* September 18, 2000; "Meet Yale's Admissions Director," *BusinessWeek,* December 15, 1999.

Understanding how and why people interact with one another is a complex process, whether the interaction occurs in a sports team, a work group, or a school committee. This is especially true when those individuals are members of the same group. Figure 8.1 presents a three-phase model of group dynamics. In the first phase, the reasons for forming the group determine what type of group it will be. A four-step process of group development occurs during the second stage; the precise nature of these steps depends on four primary group performance factors. In the final phase, a mature, productive, adaptive group has evolved. As the model shows, mature groups interact with other groups, meet goals, and sometimes have conflicts with other groups. This model serves as the framework for our discussion of groups in this chapter.

The Nature of Groups

LEARNING OBJECTIVE

Define a group.

Definitions of *group* are as abundant as studies of groups. Groups can be defined in terms of perceptions, motivation, organization, interdependencies, and interactions. We define a **group** as two or more people who interact with one another such that each person influences and is influenced by each other person.[1] Two people who are physically near each other are not a group unless they interact and

A **group** is two or more people who interact with one another such that each person influences and is influenced by each other person.

have some influence on each other. Coworkers may work side by side on related tasks, but if they do not interact, they are not a group.

Although groups often have goals, our definition does not state that group members must share a goal or motivation. This omission implies that members of a group may identify little or not at all with the group's goal. People can be a part of a group and enjoy the benefits of group membership without wanting to pursue any group goal. Members may satisfy needs just by being members, without pursuing anything. Of course, the quality of the interactions and the group's performance may be affected by members' lack of interest in the group goal. Our definition also suggests a limit on group size. A collection of people so large that its members cannot interact with and influence one another does not meet this definition. Furthermore, in reality, the dynamics of large assemblies of people usually differ significantly from those of small groups. Our focus in this chapter is on small groups in which the members interact with and influence one another.

Understanding the behavior of people in organizations requires that we understand the forces that affect individuals as well as how individuals affect the organization. The behavior of individuals both affects and is affected by the group. The accomplishments of groups are strongly influenced by the behavior of their individual members. For example, adding one key all-star player to a basketball team may make the difference between a losing season and a league championship. At the same time, groups have profound effects on the behaviors of their members. Group pressure, for instance, is often cited as a reason for lying or cheating, activities members claim they would not have chosen on their own.

From a managerial perspective, the work group is the primary means by which managers coordinate individuals' behavior to achieve organizational goals. Managers direct the activities of individuals, but they also direct and coordinate interactions within groups. For example, efforts to boost salespeople's performance have been shown to have both individual and group effects.[2] Therefore, the manager must pay attention to both the individual and the group when trying to improve employee performance. Managers must be aware of individual needs and interpersonal dynamics to manage groups effectively and efficiently because the behavior of individuals is key to the group's success or failure.[3] The Mastering Change box underscores this point, showing how creating Innovation Teams made up of employees from various divisions, levels, and geographical regions has helped boost innovation at Whirlpool.

Groups form to meet individual and organizational needs. For example, each year the National Black MBA Association holds a meeting for its members. Attendees make contacts, get acquainted with their peers, and form numerous groups in response to similar goals, aspirations, interests, and experiences. Both the overall organization and the various groups formed help satisfy a variety of needs and offer networking and other support for their members.

MASTERING CHANGE

Ongoing Innovation at Whirlpool

The appliance industry has long been considered one of the most predictable areas of business, with the same types of products—refrigerators, dishwashers, washers, and dryers—sold to the same types of consumers. Competitors such as Whirlpool, General Electric, and Maytag have always competed by offering lower-cost and higher-quality products while reducing manufacturing and distribution costs. However, managers at Whirlpool found that using that proven strategy left the company stagnant, with little room to grow and change, so the company adopted a new strategy.

Today Whirlpool uses its own employees, as well as consumers, to supply new, innovative ideas built around current lifestyles. Nancy Snyder, a Whirlpool vice president, says, "We had this internal market of people we weren't tapping into. We wanted to get rid of the 'great man' theory that only one person . . . is responsible for innovation." To encourage creativity, the firm created a seventy-five-member Innovation Team of employees from every division, level, and geographical region to search the company for new ideas.

The change has been dramatic. One employee suggestion led to the creation of Whirlpool's Inspired Chef division. The business uses home-based parties that feature chefs cooking gourmet meals for paying guests in the hope of selling them the kitchenware used to prepare the meals. A pilot program, with sixty chefs in six states, was a success, and a national rollout began in 2002. Listening to customers and workers has led to innovations such as a juicer that rotates more slowly to reduce frothing and

"[T]his time, it feels like innovation has become a part of us . . . "—Nancy Snyder, Whirlpool vice president for Strategic Competency Creation

an oven that cooks from the top and bottom simultaneously to enhance baking results. Other employee suggestions have resulted in the development of specialized washing machines for international customers, such as a washer that specializes in cleaning white clothes for the Indian market, in which whiteness is associated with good hygiene and purity.

Whirlpool's challenge is to sustain such creative efforts over the long term. J. D. Rapp, an Innovation Team leader, says, "With the constant pressure to innovate and change, creative ideas can end up being one-hit wonders." Nancy Snyder believes the firm can extend its creative streak:" [T]his time, it feels like innovation has become a part of us, that it's bigger than a specific project."

References: "Whirlpool's 2003 Annual Report: Chairman's Letter," "Whirlpool North America," Whirlpool website, www.whirlpool.com on May 20, 2004; Fara Warner, "Recipe for Growth," *Fast Company*, October 2001, pp. 40–41 (quotation, p. 41); "Whirlpool Announces First Stage of Global Restructuring," *Appliance Manufacturer*, February 26, 2001.

Types of Groups

┌─ *LEARNING OBJECTIVE* ─┐

Discuss the types of groups commonly found in organizations.

Our first task in understanding group processes is to develop a typology of groups that provides insight into their dynamics. Groups may be loosely categorized according to their degree of formalization (formal or informal) and permanence (relatively permanent or relatively temporary).

Formal Groups

A **formal group** is formed by an organization to do its work.

Formal groups are established by the organization to do its work. Formal groups include command (or functional) groups, task groups, and affinity groups. A **command** group is relatively permanent and is characterized by functional reporting relationships, such as a group manager and those who report to the manager. Command groups are usually included in the organization chart. A **task,** or **special-project, group** is created to perform a specific task, such as solving a

A **command group** is a relatively permanent, formal group with functional reporting relationships and is usually included in the organization chart.

A **task,** or **special-project, group** is a relatively temporary, formal group established to do a specific task.

An **affinity group** is a collection of employees from the same level in the organization who meet on a regular basis to share information, capture emerging opportunities, and solve problems.

particular quality problem, and is relatively temporary. An **affinity group** is a relatively permanent collection of employees from the same level in the organization who meet on a regular basis to share information, capture emerging opportunities, and solve problems.[4]

In business organizations, most employees work in command groups, as typically specified on an official organization chart. The size, shape, and organization of a company's command groups can vary considerably. Typical command groups in organizations include the quality assurance department, the industrial engineering department, the cost accounting department, and the personnel department. Other types of command groups include work teams organized as in the Japanese style of management, in which subsections of manufacturing and assembly processes are each assigned to a team of workers. The team members decide among themselves who will perform each task.

Teams are becoming widespread in automobile manufacturing. For instance, General Motors has organized most of its highly automated assembly lines into work teams of five to twenty workers. Although participative teams are becoming more popular, command groups, whether entire departments or sophisticated work teams, are the dominant type of work group in organizations. Federal Express organizes its clerical workers into teams that manage themselves.

Task groups are typically temporary and are often established to solve a particular problem. The group usually dissolves once it solves the problem or makes recommendations. People typically remain members of their command groups, or functional departments, while simultaneously serving in a task group and continuing to carry out their normal job duties. Members' command group duties may be temporarily reduced if the task group requires a great deal of time and effort. Task groups exist in all types of organizations around the world. For example, the Pope once established a special task force of cardinals to study the financial condition of the Vatican and develop new ways to raise money.[5]

Affinity groups are a special type of formal group: They are set up by the organization, yet are not part of the formal organization structure. They are not really command groups because they are not part of the organizational hierarchy, and they are not task groups because they endure longer than any one task. Affinity groups are groups of employees who share roles, responsibilities, duties, and interests, and represent horizontal slices of the normal organizational hierarchy. Because members share important characteristics such as roles, duties, and levels, they are said to have an affinity for one another. Members of affinity groups usually have very similar job titles and similar duties, but work in different divisions or departments within the organization.

Affinity groups meet regularly, and members have assigned roles such as recorder, reporter, facilitator, and meeting organizer. Members follow simple rules such as communicating openly and honestly, listening actively, respecting confidentiality, honoring time agreements, being prepared, staying focused, being individually accountable, and being supportive of one another and of the group. The greatest benefits of affinity groups are that they cross existing organizational boundaries and facilitate better communication among diverse departments and divisions across the organization.

Informal Groups

An **informal group** is established by its members.

Whereas formal groups are established by the organization, **informal groups** are formed by their members and consist of friendship groups, which are relatively

TABLE 8.1

Classification Scheme for Types of Groups

	Relatively Permanent	Relatively Temporary	
Formal	**Command Groups**	**Task Groups**	**Affinity Groups**
	Quality-assurance department Cost-accounting group	Search committee for a new school superintendent Task force on new-product quality	New product development group
Informal	**Friendship Groups**	**Interest Groups**	
	Friends who do many activities together (attend the theater, play games, travel)	Bowling group Women's network	

A **friendship group** is relatively permanent and informal, and draws its benefits from the social relationships among its members.

An **interest group** is relatively temporary and informal, and is organized around an activity or interest shared by its members.

permanent, and interest groups, which may be shorter lived. **Friendship groups** arise out of the cordial relationships among members and the enjoyment they get from being together. **Interest groups** are organized around a common activity or interest, although friendships may develop among members.

Good examples of interest groups are the recently developed networks of working women. Many of these groups began as informal social gatherings of women who wanted to meet with other women working in male-dominated organizations, but they soon developed into interest groups whose benefits went far beyond their initial social purposes. The networks became information systems for career counseling, job placement, and management training. Some networks were eventually established as formal, permanent associations; some remained informal groups based more on social relationships than on any specific interest; others were dissolved. These groups may be partly responsible for the dramatic increase in the percentage of women in managerial and administrative jobs.

Table 8.1 provides examples of the various formal and informal groups in organizations.

Stages of Group Development

In the **mutual acceptance stage** of group development, members share information about themselves and get to know one another.

Groups are not static; they typically develop through a four-stage process: (1) mutual acceptance, (2) communication and decision making, (3) motivation and productivity, and (4) control and organization.[6] Figure 8.2 shows the stages and the activities that typify them. We treat the stages as separate and distinct. It is difficult to pinpoint exactly when a group moves from one stage to another, however, because the activities in each phase tend to overlap.

Mutual Acceptance

In the **mutual acceptance** stage of group development, the group forms and members get to know one another by sharing information about themselves. They often test one another's opinions by discussing subjects that have little to do with

Communication and decision making are key stages of group development, but it looks like this team may have skipped an early stage like mutual acceptance. Groups need to openly discuss and agree on their goals, motivations, and individual roles before they can successfully accomplish tasks. It is essential that groups go through all four stages of development to become a mature, productive group.

Copyright 2001 by Randy Glasbergen.
www.glasbergen.com

**"My team is having trouble thinking outside the box.
We can't agree on the size of the box, what materials
the box should be constructed from, a reasonable
budget for the box, or our first choice of box vendors."**

Although these stages are not separate and distinct in all groups, many groups make fairly predictable transitions in activities at about the midpoint of the period available to complete a task.[13] A group may begin with its own distinctive approach to the problem and maintain it until about halfway through the allotted time. The midpoint transition is often accompanied by a burst of concentrated activity, reexamination of assumptions, dropping old patterns of activity, adopting new perspectives on the work, and making dramatic progress. Following these midpoint activities, the new patterns of activity may be maintained until close to the end of the period allotted for the task. Another transition may occur just before the deadline. At this point, groups often go into the completion stage, launching a final burst of activity to finish the job.

Group Performance Factors

Group performance factors—composition, size, norms, and cohesiveness—affect the success of the group in fulfilling its goals.

Group composition is the degree of similarity or difference among group members on factors important to the group's work.

The performance of any group is affected by several factors other than the group's reasons for forming and the stages of its development. In a high-performing group, a group synergy often develops in which the group's performance is more than the sum of its members' individual contributions. Several additional factors may account for this accelerated performance.[14] The four basic **group performance factors** are composition, size, norms, and cohesiveness.

Composition

The composition of a group plays an important role in group productivity.[15] **Group composition** is most often described in terms of the homogeneity or heterogeneity of the members. A group is *homogeneous* if members are similar in one or several ways that are critical to the work of the group, such as in age, work experience, education, technical specialty, or cultural background. In *heterogeneous* groups, members differ in one or more ways critical to the group's work. Homogeneous groups are often created when people are assigned to command groups

Group composition is an important factor in understanding group dynamics. These women attended a Women in Business seminar for women holding key executive positions in major corporations. The fact that they are all female gave them a shared frame of reference and common perspectives from which to identify key issues that will help shape the future of their respective businesses.

based on a similar technical specialty. Although the people who work in such command groups may differ in some ways, such as in age or work experience, they are homogeneous in terms of a critical work performance variable: technical specialty.

Much research has explored the relationship between a group's composition and its productivity. The group's heterogeneity in terms of age and tenure with the group has been shown to be related to turnover: Groups with members of different ages and experiences with the group tend to undergo frequent changes in membership.[16] Table 8.2 summarizes task variables that make a homogeneous or heterogeneous group more effective. A homogeneous group is likely to be more productive when the group task is simple, cooperation is necessary, group tasks are sequential, or quick action is required. A heterogeneous group is more likely to be productive when the task is complex, requires a collective effort (that is, each member performs a different task, and the sum of these efforts constitutes the group output), and demands creativity, and when speed is less important than thorough deliberations. For example, a group asked to generate ideas for marketing a new product probably needs to be heterogeneous to develop as many different ideas as possible.

The link between group composition and type of task is explained by the interactions typical of homogeneous and heterogeneous groups. A homogeneous group tends to have less conflict, fewer differences of opinion, smoother communication, and more interactions. When a task requires cooperation and speed, a homogeneous group is therefore more desirable. If, however, the task requires complex analysis of information and creativity to arrive at the best possible solution, a heterogeneous group may be more appropriate because it generates a wide range of viewpoints. More discussion and more conflict are likely, both of which can enhance the group's decision making.

TABLE 8.2

Task Variable and Group Composition

A homogeneous group is more useful for:	A heterogeneous group is more useful for:
Simple tasks	Complex tasks
Sequential tasks	Collective tasks
Tasks that require cooperation	Tasks that require creativity
Tasks that must be done quickly	Tasks that need not be done quickly

Reference: Based on discussion in Bernard M. Bass and Edward C. Ryterband, *Organizational Psychology,* 2nd ed. (Allyn & Bacon, 1979). Reprinted by permission.

Group composition becomes especially important as organizations become increasingly diverse.[17] Cultures differ in the importance they place on group membership and in how they view authority, uncertainty, and other important factors. Increasing attention is being focused on how to deal with groups made up of people from different cultures.[18] In general, a manager in charge of a culturally diverse group can expect several things. First, members will probably distrust one another. Stereotyping will also present a problem, and communication difficulties are almost certain to arise. Thus, the manager needs to recognize that such groups will seldom function smoothly, at least at first. Managers may therefore need to spend more time helping a culturally diverse group through the rough spots as it matures, and they should allow a longer-than-normal time before expecting it to carry out its assigned task.

Many organizations are creating joint ventures and other types of alliances with organizations from other countries. Joint ventures have become common in the automobile and electronics industries, for example. However, managers from the United States tend to exhibit individualistic behaviors in a group setting, whereas managers from more collectivistic countries, such as the People's Republic of China, tend to exhibit more group-oriented behaviors. Thus, when these two different types of managers work together in a joint venture, they must be trained to be cautious and understanding in their interactions and in the types of behaviors they exhibit.

Size

Group size is the number of members of the group; group size affects the number of resources available to perform the task.

A group can have as few as two members or as many members as can interact and influence one another. **Group size** can have an important effect on performance. A group with many members has more resources available and may be able to complete a large number of relatively independent tasks. In groups established to generate ideas, those with more members tend to produce more ideas, although the rate of increase in the number of ideas diminishes rapidly as the group grows.[19] Beyond a certain point, the greater complexity of interactions and communication may make it more difficult for a large group to achieve agreement.

Interactions and communication are much more likely to be formalized in larger groups. Large groups tend to set agendas for meetings and to follow a protocol or parliamentary procedure to control discussion. As a result, some time that otherwise would be available to work on tasks is taken up in administrative duties such as organizing and structuring the interactions and communications within the group. Also, the large size may inhibit participation by some members and increase absenteeism; some people may stop trying to make a meaningful contribution and may even stop coming to group meetings if their repeated attempts to contribute are thwarted by the sheer number of similar efforts by other members. Furthermore, large groups present more opportunities for interpersonal attraction, leading to more social interactions and fewer task interactions. **Social loafing** is the tendency of some members of groups not to put forth as much effort in a group situation as they would working alone. Social loafing often results from the assumption by some members that if they do not work hard, other members will pick up the slack. How serious this situation becomes depends on the nature of the task, the characteristics of the people involved, and the ability of the group leadership to recognize the potential problem and do something about it.

Social loafing is the tendency of some members of groups to put forth less effort in a group than they would when working alone.

The most effective group size, therefore, is determined by the group members' ability to interact and influence one another effectively. The need for interaction is affected by the maturity of the group, the group's tasks, the maturity of individual members, and the ability of the group leader or manager to manage the communication, potential conflicts, and task activities. In some situations, the most effective group size is three or four; other groups can function effectively with fifteen or more members.

Norms

A **norm** is a standard against which the appropriateness of a behavior is judged.

A **norm** is a standard against which the appropriateness of a behavior is judged. Thus, norms determine the behavior expected in a certain situation. Group norms are usually established during the second stage of group development (communication and decision making) and carried forward into the maturity stage. By providing a basis for predicting others' behaviors, norms enable people to behave in a manner consistent with and acceptable to the group. Without norms, the activities in a group would be chaotic.

Norms result from the combination of members' personality characteristics, the situation, the task, and the historical traditions of the group.[20] Lack of conformity to group norms may result in verbal abuse, physical threats, ostracism, or ejection from the group. Group norms are enforced, however, only for actions that are important to group members. For example, if the office norm is for employees to wear suits to convey a professional image to clients, a staff member who wears blue jeans and a sweatshirt violates the group norm and will hear about it quickly. But if the norm is that dress is unimportant because little contact with clients occurs in the office, the fact that someone wears blue jeans may not even be noticed.

Norms serve four purposes in organizations. First, they help the group survive. Groups tend to reject deviant behavior that does not help meet group goals or contribute to the group's survival if it is threatened. Accordingly, a successful group that is not under threat may be more tolerant of deviant behavior. Second, norms simplify and make more predictable the behaviors expected of group members. Because they are familiar with norms, members do not have to analyze each behavior and decide on a response; they can anticipate the actions of others on the basis of group norms, usually resulting in increased productivity and goal attainment. Third, norms help the group avoid embarrassing situations. Group members often want to avoid damaging other members' self-images and are likely to avoid certain subjects that might hurt a member's feelings. Finally, norms express the central values of the group and identify the group to others. Certain clothes, mannerisms, or behaviors in particular situations may be a rallying point for members and may signify to others the nature of the group.[21]

Cohesiveness

Group cohesiveness is the extent to which a group is committed to staying together.

Group cohesiveness is the extent to which a group is committed to remaining together; it results from forces acting on the members to remain in the group. The forces that create cohesiveness are attraction to the group, resistance to leaving the group, and motivation to remain a member.[22] As Figure 8.3 shows, group cohesiveness is related to many aspects of group dynamics that we have already discussed: maturity, homogeneity, manageable size, and frequency of interactions.

The figure also shows that group cohesiveness can be increased by competition or by the presence of an external threat. Either factor can focus members' attention on a clearly defined goal and increase their willingness to work together. Finally, successfully reaching goals often increases the cohesiveness of a group because people are proud to be identified with a winner and to be thought of as com-

group members and the key characteristics of the group can help managers monitor intergroup interactions. Second, the organizational setting in which the groups interact can have a powerful influence on intergroup interactions. The organization's structure, rules and procedures, decision-making processes, and goals and reward systems all affect interactions. For example, organizations in which frequent interactions occur and strong ties among groups exist are usually characterized as low-conflict organizations.[26] Third, the task and situational bases of interactions focus attention on the working relationships among the interacting groups and on the reasons for the interactions.

As Figure 8.5 shows, five factors affect intergroup interactions: location, resources, time and goal interdependence, task uncertainty, and task interdependence. These factors both create the interactions and determine their characteristics, such as the frequency of interaction, the volume of information exchange among groups, and the type of coordination the groups need to interact and function. For example, if two groups depend heavily on each other to perform a task about which much uncertainty exists, they need a great deal of information from each other to define and perform the task.

Conflict in Groups and Organizations

LEARNING OBJECTIVE

Explain conflict in organizations.

Conflict is disagreement among parties.

Conflict often occurs when groups interact in organizations. In its simplest form, **conflict** is disagreement among parties. When people, groups, or organizations disagree over significant issues, conflict often results. Frequently political behavior or battles over limited resources generate conflict among groups. In particular, conflict frequently occurs when a person or group believes its attempts to achieve its goal are being blocked by another person or group. For example, conflict may arise over financial resources, the number of authorized positions in work groups, or the number of laptop computers to be purchased for departments. Conflict may also result from anticipating trouble. For example, a person may behave antagonistically toward another person whom he or she expects to pose obstacles to goal achievement.[27]

Although conflict is often considered harmful and thus something to avoid, it can also have some benefits. A total absence of conflict can lead to apathy and lethargy. A moderate degree of focused conflict, on the other hand, can stimulate new ideas, promote healthy competition, and energize behavior. In some organizations, especially profit-oriented ones, many managers believe conflict is dysfunctional. On the other hand, many managers in not-for-profit organizations view conflict as beneficial and conducive to higher-quality decision making.[28]

Competition occurs when groups strive for the same goal, have little or no antagonism toward one another, and behave according to rules and procedures. In conflict, on the other hand, one group's goals jeopardize the others', open antagonism exists among the groups, and few rules and procedures regulate behavior. When this happens, the goals become extremely important, the antagonism increases, rules and procedures are violated, and conflict occurs.[29] We discuss competition in more detail later in this section.

Reactions to Conflict

The most common reactions to conflict are avoidance, accommodation, competition, collaboration, and compromise.[30] Whenever conflict occurs between groups or organizations, it is really the people who are in conflict. In many cases, however, people are acting as representatives of the groups to which they belong. In effect, they

Conflict results from disagreements among parties (people and/or organizations). Dylan Lauren and her business partner, Jeff Rubin, have a unique way to resolve their conflicts. Each takes a piece of gum, takes three steps, and then blows a bubble. Whoever holds the bubble longest wins and gets to decide how to do things. Lauren, for example, won the contest to determine the name of the candy store they opened on Manhattan's Upper East Side. The name? What else but Dylan's Candy Bar!

work together, representing their group as they strive to do their part in helping the group achieve its goals. Thus, whether the conflict is between people acting as individuals or people acting as representatives of groups, the five types of interactions can be analyzed in terms of relationships among the goals of the people or the groups they represent.

As Figure 8.6 shows, reactions to conflict can be differentiated along two dimensions: how important each party's goals are to that party and how compatible the goals are. The importance of reaching a goal may range from very high to very low. The degree of **goal compatibility** is the extent to which the goals of more than one person or group can be achieved simultaneously. In other words, the goals are compatible if one party can meet its goals without preventing the other from meeting its goals. The goals are incompatible if one party's meeting its goals prevents the other party from meeting its goals. The goals of different groups may be highly compatible, completely incompatible, or somewhere in between.

Goal compatibility is the extent to which the goals of more than one person or group can be achieved at the same time.

Avoidance occurs when the interacting parties' goals are incompatible and the interaction among groups is relatively unimportant to the attainment of the goals.

Accommodation occurs when the parties' goals are compatible and the interaction among groups is relatively unimportant to the goals' attainment.

Competition occurs when the parties' goals are incompatible and the interactions among groups are important to meeting goals.

Avoidance   **Avoidance** occurs when an interaction is relatively unimportant to either party's goals and the goals are incompatible, as in the bottom left corner of Figure 8.6. Because the parties to the conflict are not striving toward compatible goals and the issues in question seem unimportant, the parties simply try to avoid interacting with one another. For example, one state agency may merely ignore another agency's requests for information. The requesting agency can then practice its own form of avoidance by not following up on the requests.

Accommodation   **Accommodation** occurs when the parties' goals are compatible but the interactions are not considered important to overall goal attainment, as in the bottom right corner of Figure 8.6. Interactions of this type may involve discussions of how the parties can accomplish their interdependent tasks with the least expenditure of time and effort. This type of interaction tends to be very friendly. For example, during a college's course scheduling period, potential conflict may exist between the marketing and management departments. Both departments offer morning classes. Which department is allocated the 9:00 A.M. time slot and which the 10:00 A.M. time slot is not that important to either group. Their overall goal is that the classes be scheduled so that students will be able to take courses.

Competition   **Competition** occurs when the goals are incompatible and the interactions are important to each party's meeting its goals, as in the top left corner of Figure 8.6. If all parties are striving for a goal but only one can reach the goal, the parties will be in competition. As we noted earlier, if a competitive situ-

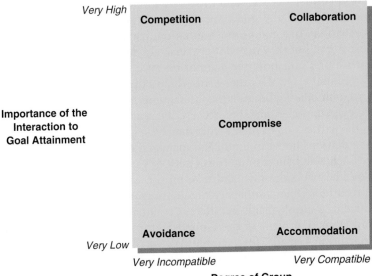

FIGURE 8.6

Five Types of Reactions to Conflict

The five types of reactions to conflict stem from the relative importance of interaction to goal attainment and the degree of goal compatibility.

Reference: Adapted from Kenneth Thomas, "Conflict and Conflict Management," in Marvin Dunnette, ed., *Handbook of Industrial and Organizational Psychology* (Chicago: Rand McNally, 1976), pp.889–935. Reprinted by permission of Marvin Dunnette.

ation gets out of control, such as when overt antagonism occurs, and there are no rules or procedures to follow, competition can result in conflict. Thus, competition may lead to conflict. In contrast, conflict can change to competition if the conflicting parties agree on rules to guide the interaction and agree not to be hostile toward one another.

In one freight warehouse and storage firm, the first, second, and third shifts each sought to win the weekly productivity prize by posting the highest productivity record. Workers on the winning shift received recognition in the company newspaper. Because the issue was important to each group and the groups' interests were incompatible, the result was competition. On the other hand, the competition encouraged each shift to produce more per week, which increased the company's output and eventually improved its overall welfare (and thus the welfare of each group). Both the company and the groups benefited from the competition because it fostered innovative and creative work methods, which further boosted productivity. After about three months, however, the competition got out of control and the groups started to sabotage other shifts and inflate records. Competitiveness became dominant, open antagonism resulted, rules were ignored, and the competition changed to open conflict. The result was decreases in overall work performance.[31]

Collaboration occurs when the interaction among groups is very important to goal attainment and the goals are compatible.

Collaboration   Collaboration occurs when the interaction among groups is very important to goal attainment and the goals are compatible, as in the top right corner of Figure 8.6. In the class scheduling situation mentioned earlier, conflict may arise over which courses to teach in the first semester and which ones in the second. Both departments would like to offer specific courses in the fall. However, by discussing the issue and refocusing their overall goals to match students' needs, the marketing and management departments can collaborate on developing a proper sequence of courses. At first glance, this may seem to be simple interaction in which the parties participate jointly in activities to accomplish goals after agreeing on the goals and their importance. In many situations, however, it is no easy matter to agree on goals, their importance, and especially the means for achieving them. In a collaborative interaction, goals may differ but be compatible. Parties to a conflict may initially have difficulty working out the ways in which all can achieve their goals. However, because the interactions are important to goal attainment, the parties are willing to continue to work together to achieve the goals. Collaborative relationships can lead to new, innovative ideas and solutions to differences among the parties.

Compromise occurs when the interaction is moderately important to meeting goals, and the goals are neither completely compatible nor completely incompatible.

Compromise   **Compromise** occurs when the interactions are moderately important to goal attainment and the goals are neither completely compatible nor completely incompatible. In a compromise situation, parties interact with others striving to achieve goals, but they may not aggressively pursue goal attainment in either a competitive or a collaborative manner because the interactions are not critical to goal attainment. On the other hand, the parties may neither avoid one another nor be accommodating because the interactions are somewhat important. Often each party gives up something, but because the interactions are only moderately important, the parties do not regret what they have given up.

Contract negotiations between union and management are usually examples of compromise. Each side brings numerous issues of varying importance to the bargaining table. The two sides give and take on the issues through rounds of offers and counteroffers. The complexity of such negotiations is increasing as negotiations spread to multiple plants in different countries. Agreements between management and labor in a plant in the United States may be unacceptable to either or both parties in Canada, for example. Weeks of negotiations ending in numerous compromises usually result in a contract agreement between the union and management.

Managing Conflict

Managers must know when to resolve conflict and when to stimulate it to avoid its potentially disruptive effects.[32] When a potentially harmful conflict situation exists, a manager needs to engage in **conflict resolution.** Conflict needs to be resolved when it causes major disruptions in the organization and absorbs time and effort that could be used more productively. Conflict should also be resolved when its focus is on the group's internal goals rather than on organizational goals. We look at the principal conflict-handling strategies later in this section.

Conflict resolution occurs when a manager resolves a conflict that has become harmful or serious.

Sometimes a manager should be concerned about the absence of conflict. An absence of conflict may indicate that the organization is stagnant and employees are content with the status quo. It may also suggest that work groups are not motivated to challenge traditional and well-accepted ideas. **Conflict stimulation** is the creation and constructive use of conflict by a manager. Its purpose is to bring about situations in which differences of opinion are exposed for examination by all. For example, if competing organizations are making significant changes in products, markets, or technologies, it may be time for a manager to stimulate innovation and creativity by challenging the status quo. Conflict may give employees the motivation and opportunity to reveal differences of opinion that they previously kept to themselves. When all parties to the conflict are interested enough in an issue to challenge other groups, they often expose their hidden doubts or opinions. These, in turn, allow the parties to get to the heart of the matter and often to develop unique solutions to the problem. Indeed, the interactions may lead the groups to recognize that a problem in fact exists. Conflict, then, can be a catalyst for creativity and change in an organization.

Conflict stimulation is the creation and constructive use of conflict by a manager.

Several methods can be used to stimulate conflict under controlled conditions. These include altering the physical location of groups to generate more interactions, forcing more resource sharing, and implementing other changes in relationships among groups. In addition, training programs can help increase employee awareness of potential problems in group decision making and group interactions. Adopting the role of "devil's advocate" in discussion sessions is another way to stimulate conflict among groups. In this role, a manager challenges the prevailing consensus to ensure that all alternatives have been critically appraised and analyzed. Although this role is often unpopular, employing it is a good way to stimulate constructive conflict.

Of course, too much conflict is also a concern. If conflict becomes excessive or destructive, the manager needs to adopt a strategy to reduce or resolve it. The manager should first attempt to determine the source of the conflict. If the source of destructive conflict is one or two individuals, it may be appropriate to alter the membership of one or both groups. If the conflict is due to differences in goals, perceptions of the difficulty of goal attainment, or the importance of the goals to the conflicting parties, the manager can attempt to move the conflicting parties into one of the five types of reactions to conflict, depending on the nature of the conflicting parties.

To foster collaboration, the manager can try to help people see that their goals are really not as different as they seem. The manager can help groups view their goals as part of a superordinate goal to which the goals of both conflicting parties can contribute. A **superordinate goal** is a goal of the overall organization and is more important to the well-being of the organization and its members than the more specific goals of the conflicting parties. If the goals are not really important and are very incompatible, the manager may need to develop ways to help the conflicting parties avoid each other. Similarly, accommodation, competition, or compromise might be appropriate for the conflicting parties.

> A **superordinate goal** is an organizational goal that is more important to the well-being of the organization and its members than the more specific goals of interacting parties.

Managing Group and Intergroup Dynamics in Organizations

┌─*LEARNING OBJECTIVE*─┐

Discuss methods for managing group and intergroup dynamics.

Managing groups in organizations is both important and complicated. Managers must know what types of groups—command or task, formal or informal—exist in the organization. If a certain command group is very large, there will probably be several informal subgroups to manage. A manager might take advantage of existing informal groups, "formalizing" some of them into command or task groups based on a subset of the tasks to be performed. Other informal groups might be broken up to make task assignment easier. In assigning tasks to people and subgroups, the manager must also consider individual motivations for joining groups and the composition of the groups.

Often a manager can help ensure a group develops into a productive unit by nurturing its activities in each stage of development. Helpful steps include encouraging open communication and trust among the members, stimulating discussion of important issues and providing task-relevant information at appropriate times, and helping the group analyze external factors such as competition and external threats and opportunities. Managers might also encourage development of norms and roles within the group to help its development.

In managing a group, managers must consider both the goals of individual members and the goals of the group as a whole. Developing a reward structure that lets people reach their own goals by working toward those of the group can result in a very productive group. A manager may also be able to improve group cohesiveness, for example, by stimulating competition, identifying an external threat to the group, establishing a goal-setting system, or employing participative approaches.

Managers must carefully choose strategies for dealing with interactions among groups after thorough examination and analysis of the groups, their goals, their unique characteristics, and the organizational setting in which the interactions occur. Managers can use a variety of strategies to increase the efficiency of

A **linking role** is a position for a person or group that coordinates the activities of two or more organizational groups.

intergroup interactions. One common mechanism is to encourage groups to focus on a superordinate goal, as mentioned earlier. In other situations, management might use a **linking role,** a position for a person or group that coordinates the activities of two or more organizational groups.[33] This approach may add a layer of management, but in very important situations it may be worthwhile. Finally, management may need to change reporting relationships, decision-making priorities, and rules and procedures to properly manage group interactions.

In summary, managers must be aware of the implications—organizational and social—of their attempts to manage people in groups. Groups affect how their members behave, and it is member behavior that adds up to total group performance. Groups are so prevalent in our society that managers must strive to work with them more effectively.

Synopsis

A group is two or more people who interact to influence one another. It is important to study groups because they can profoundly affect individuals' behavior, which is key to the group's success or failure. The work group is the primary means by which managers coordinate individual behavior to achieve organizational goals. Individuals form or join groups because they expect to satisfy personal needs.

Groups may be differentiated on the bases of relative permanence and degree of formality. The three types of formal groups are command, task, and affinity groups. Command groups are relatively permanent work groups established by the organization and are usually specified on an organization chart. Task groups, also established by the organization, are relatively temporary and exist only until the specific task is accomplished. Affinity groups are formed by the organization, consist of employees at the same level and doing similar jobs, and come together regularly to share information and discuss organizational issues. The major types of informal groups are friendship and interest groups. In friendship groups, the affiliation among members arises from close social relationships and the enjoyment that comes from being together. The common bond in interest groups is the activity in which the members engage.

Groups develop in four stages: mutual acceptance, communication and decision making, motivation and productivity, and control and organization. Although the stages are sequential, they may overlap. A group that does not fully develop within each stage will not fully mature as a group, resulting in lower group performance.

Four additional factors affect group performance: composition, size, norms, and cohesiveness.

The homogeneity of group members affects the interactions that occur and the group's productivity. The effect of increasing the size of the group depends on the nature of the group's tasks and the people in the group. Norms help people function and relate to one another in predictable and efficient ways. They facilitate group survival, simplify and make more predictable the behaviors of group members, help the group avoid embarrassing situations, express the central values of the group, and identify the group to others.

To comprehend intergroup dynamics, managers must understand the key characteristics of groups: that each group is unique, the specific organizational setting influences the group, and the group's task and setting affect group behavior. The five bases of intergroup interactions determine the characteristics of the interactions among groups, including their frequency, how much information is exchanged, and what type of interaction occurs.

Interactions among work groups involve some of the most complex relationships in organizations. They are based on five factors: location, resources, time and goal interdependence, task uncertainty, and task interdependence. Being physically near one another naturally increases groups' opportunities for interactions. If groups use the same or similar resources, or if one group can affect the availability of the resources another group needs, the potential for frequent interactions increases. The nature of the tasks groups perform, including time and goal orientation, the uncertainties of group tasks, and group interdependencies, influences how groups interact.

Conflict is disagreement among parties; it is a common cause of stress in organizations. Five types of reactions to conflict are avoidance, accommodation, competition, collaboration, and compromise. The types of interactions are determined by the compatibility of goals and the importance of the interaction to group goal attainment. Managers should recognize that conflict can be beneficial as well as harmful.

Managers must be aware of the many factors that affect group performance and understand both the individual and group issues. Groups influence how their members behave as individuals, and individual behavior helps define group performance. Since both individual and group behavior are common in organizations, managers need to understand how they affect each other.

Discussion Questions

1. Why is it useful for a manager to understand group behavior? Why is it useful for an employee?

2. Our definition of a group is somewhat broad. Would you classify each of the following collections of people as a group? Explain why.
   a. Seventy thousand people at a football game
   b. Students taking this course
   c. People in an elevator
   d. People on an escalator
   e. Employees of IBM
   f. Employees of your local college bookstore

3. List four groups to which you belong. Identify each as formal or informal.

4. Explain why each group you listed in question 3 formed. Why did you join each group? Why might others have decided to join each group?

5. In which stage of development is each of the four groups listed in question 3? Did any group move too quickly through any of the stages? Explain.

6. Analyze the composition of two of the groups to which you belong. How are they similar in composition? How do they differ?

7. Are any of the groups to which you belong too large or too small to get their work done? If so, what can the leader or the members do to alleviate the problem?

8. List two norms each for two of the groups to which you belong. How are these norms enforced?

9. Discuss the following statement: "Group cohesiveness is the good, warm feeling we get from working in groups and is something that all group leaders should strive to develop in the groups they lead."

10. Consider one of the groups to which you belong and describe the interactions between that group and another group.

11. Do you agree or disagree with the assertion that conflict can be both harmful and beneficial? Cite examples of both cases.

Organizational Behavior Case for Discussion

Using Groups to Get Things Done

After years of difficulties and many attempts to change, a Myerstown, Pennsylvania, pharmaceutical plant, part of the Consumer Care Division of German-owned Bayer Corporation, instituted a teams-based change program. The facility had been sold several times in recent years and operated under various organizations. The fifty-year-old factory was staffed at less than 50 percent when Bayer purchased it. There had been no plant manager for almost a year, and morale was at an all-time low. Worse yet, the factory was losing money, and the remaining em-ployees feared a shutdown. The outlook was bleak, but in the absence of leadership from the top level, the human resources department, under the guidance of director John Danchisko, decided the employees themselves could turn the low-performing facility around.

First, ninety-three employees were selected at random to participate in seven focus groups. At the meetings, workers brainstormed the answers to open-ended questions such as "Why do people work here?" and "Why do people leave here?" Their answers were compiled and sent to every employee for comments and input. Employees were impressed; they liked the new proactive and collaborative management style. Rick Higley, a pharmaceutical operator, says, "The thing I really appreciated about the process was that the managers listened to what everyone had to say, treated us as equals, and really valued our opinions."

Next, an eighteen-member cross-functional team was formed to recommend and help implement improvements. The team approach was clearly popular because fifty people volunteered for those eighteen slots. The team focused on five key priorities:

1. *Define site goals and strategy, and communicate them in interactive employee conferences.* Job security concerns and a need to see how shorter-term goals fit into the long-term strategy were important to employees.
2. *Develop a site communication process.* Employees believed their best option for getting information was no better than a "rumor mill," while supervisors often weren't given critical information. Having consistency of information from the top to the bottom of the organization benefited everyone.
3. *Develop hourly employee and supervisory role definitions and competency profiles.* Changing ownership had led to too many abandoned programs, and training had been inconsistent. Decision-making authority, span of control, and management roles were just a few areas of confusion.
4. *Identify areas of perceived inconsistencies in site practices and policies, and determine appropriate actions.* Employees wanted to ensure that any system used at the facility would be used consistently and that all workers would be treated the same.
5. *Develop a performance measurement process (a performance scorecard system).* Without some type of measurement system, workers and supervisors were unsure whether goals were being reached.

One of the biggest obstacles to change was the factory's past history of failed changes. An employee noted, "It would be nice if [managers] were really sincere in this, but we've all been through this before. I think this is going to be another flavor of the month." Employee skepticism began to change as the teams focused on what really mattered to the hourly workers. Employees began by asking, "What's in it for me?," but the teams proposed a pay-for-performance sys-

tem, with employees earning up to an additional 8 percent on top of their base pay when profitability was above target.

In its first year, the facility reached four of its five financial goals and became profitable earlier than expected. Employee satisfaction is now up, and accidents are down. On-time completion of weekly production quotas has risen from 53 percent (about average for this industry) to 85 percent. In 2000, the plant received *Workforce* magazine's Optimas award for excellence in human resources. Management was so pleased with the program's results that the teams have become permanent, with rotating membership. Danchisko says, "When we first started this, we didn't realize how big it would actually become for our site. Here we are, a few years down the road, and we're still heavily into this." The site's teams process has become a model for other Bayer facilities.

Werner Wenning, the new chairman of Bayer, has taken control of the firm at a difficult time. The stock price is declining, new products are slow to reach market, and the company is restructuring its divisional organization. Wenning admits that Bayer was too slow in its response to changing market conditions, noting, "In the future, we have to act more quickly." Perhaps the CEO ought to consider the team-based methods developed by his own employees at the Myerstown facility.

Case Questions

1. What type of group are the focus groups initially formed at Bayer's Myerstown facility? What type is the current eighteen-member, permanent group? Explain your answers.
2. Based on group performance factors, what do you predict will be the likely performance of the eighteen-member cross-functional team?
3. Initially workers at the Myerstown plant were skeptical about the use of teams and resisted the change. What conflict resolution approach was used to address this problem? Is that the approach you would recommend for a similar situation? Why or why not?

References: "About the Awards," *Workforce* website, www.workforce.com on May 20, 2004; "2003 Bayer Annual Report," Bayer website, www.bayer.com on May 20, 2004; "Bayer's Big Headache," *BusinessWeek*, May 6, 2002; John Danchisko, "Five Initiatives for Growth," *Workforce*, March 2000, pp. 37-45; Jennifer Koch Laabs, "Paving the Way to Profitability," *Workforce*, March 2000 (quotation), www.workforce.com on April 30, 2002; "Role Expectations for Supervisors at Bayer," *Workforce*, March 2000, www.workforce.com on May 21, 2002.

Experiencing Organizational Behavior

Learning the Benefits of a Group

Purpose: This exercise demonstrates the benefits a group can bring to a task.

Format: You will be asked to do the same task both individually and as part of a group.

Procedure: You will need a pen or pencil and an 8.5″ by 11″ sheet of paper. Working alone, do the following:

Part 1

1. Write the letters of the alphabet in a vertical column down the left side of the paper: A–Z.
2. Your instructor will randomly select a sentence from any written document and read out loud the first twenty-six letters in that sentence. Write these letters in a vertical column immediately to the right of the alphabet column. Everyone should have an identical set of twenty-six two-letter combinations.
3. Working alone, think of a famous person whose initials correspond to each pair of letters, and write the name next to the letters—for example, "MT Mark Twain." You will have ten minutes. Only one name per set is allowed. One point is awarded for each legitimate name, so the maximum score is twenty-six points.
4. After time expires, exchange your paper with another member of the class and score each other's work. Disputes about the legitimacy of names will be settled by the instructor. Keep your score for use later in the exercise.

Part 2

Your instructor will divide the class into groups of five to ten people. All groups should have approximately the same number of members. Each group now follows the procedure given in part 1. Again write the letters of the alphabet down the left side of the sheet of paper, this time in reverse order: Z–A. Your instructor will dictate a new set of letters for the second column. The time limit and scoring procedure are the same. The only difference is that the groups will generate the names.

Part 3

Each team identifies the group member who came up with the most names. The instructor places these "best" students into one group. Then all groups repeat part 2, but this time the letters from the reading will be in the first column and the alphabet letters will be in the second column.

Part 4

Each team calculates the average individual score of its members on part 1 and compares it with the team score from parts 2 and 3, kept separately. Your instructor will put the average individual score and team scores from each part of each group on the board.

Follow-up Questions

1. Are there differences in the average individual scores and the team scores? What are the reasons for the differences, if any?
2. Although the team scores in this exercise usually are higher than the average individual scores, under what conditions might individual averages exceed group scores?

Reference: Adapted from *The Handbook for Group Facilitators*, pp. 19–20, by John E. Jones and J. William Pfeiffer (eds.), Copyright © 1979 Pfeiffer. Reprinted with permission of John Wiley & Sons, Inc.

Self-Assessment Exercise

Group Cohesiveness

Introduction: You are probably a member of many different groups: study groups for school, work groups, friendship groups within a social club such as a fraternity or sorority, and interest groups. You probably have some feel for how tightly knit or cohesive each of those groups is. This exercise will help you diagnose the cohesiveness of one of those groups.

Instructions: First, pick one of the small groups to which you belong for analysis. Be sure that it is a small group, say between three and eight people. Next, rate on the following scale of 1 (poorly) to 5 (very well) how well you feel the group works together.

How well does this group work together?

Now answer the following six questions about the group. Put a check in the blank next to the answer that best describes how you feel about each question.

1. How many of the people in your group are friendly toward each other?
   ____ (5) All of them
   ____ (4) Most of them
   ____ (3) Some of them
   ____ (2) A few of them
   ____ (1) None of them

2. How much trust is there among members of your group?
   ____ (1) Distrust
   ____ (2) Little trust
   ____ (3) Average trust
   ____ (4) Considerable trust
   ____ (5) A great deal of trust

3. How much loyalty and sense of belonging is there among group members?
   ____ (1) No group loyalty or sense of belonging
   ____ (2) A little loyalty and sense of belonging
   ____ (3) An average sense of belonging
   ____ (4) An above-average sense of belonging
   ____ (5) A strong sense of belonging

4. Do you feel that you are really a valuable part of your group?
   ____ (5) I am really a part of my group.
   ____ (4) I am included in most ways.
   ____ (3) I am included in some ways but not others.
   ____ (2) I am included in a few ways but not many.
   ____ (1) I do not feel I really belong.

5. How friendly are your fellow group members toward each other?
   ____ (1) Not friendly
   ____ (2) Somewhat friendly
   ____ (3) Friendly to an average degree
   ____ (4) Friendlier than average
   ____ (5) Very friendly

6. If you had a chance to work with a different group of people doing the same task, how would you feel about moving to another group?
   ____ (1) I would want very much to move.
   ____ (2) I would rather move than stay where I am.
   ____ (3) It would make no difference to me.
   ____ (4) I would rather stay where I am than move.
   ____ (5) I would want very much to stay where I am.

Now add up the numbers you chose for all six questions and divide by 6. Total from all six questions = _____ / 6 = _____. This is the group cohesiveness score for your group.

Compare this number with the one you checked on the scale at the beginning of this exercise about how well you feel this group works together. Are they about the same, or are they quite different? If they are about the same, then you have a pretty good feel for the group and how it works. If they are quite different, then you probably need to analyze what aspects of the group functioning you misunderstood. (This is only part of a much longer instrument; it has not been scientifically validated in this form and is to be used for class discussion purposes only.)

Reference: The six questions were taken from John R. Montanari and Gregory Moorhead, "Development of the Groupthink Assessment Inventory," *Educational and Psychological Measurement*, 1989, vol. 39, pp. 209–219. Reprinted by permission of Gregory Moorhead.

OB Online

1. Can a virtual group (i.e., one whose members interact electronically) be a group in the same way that a traditional face-to-face group can? Why or why not?

2. Use a search engine to find information about each of the types of groups identified in the chapter. Try to locate information about other types of groups.

3. In what ways might electronic interaction affect the stages of group development discussed in the chapter?

4. Describe the roles the Internet and email might play in conflict. That is, in what ways might new forms of communication technologies both increase and decrease conflict in organizations?

Building Managerial Skills

Exercise Overview: A manager's interpersonal skills are her or his ability to understand how to motivate individuals and groups. Clearly, then, interpersonal skills play a major role in determining how well a manager can interact with others in a group setting. This exercise allows you to practice your interpersonal skills in relation to just such a setting.

Exercise Background: You have just been transferred to a new position supervising a group of five employees. The business you work for is fairly small and has few rules and regulations. Unfortunately, the lack of rules and regulations is creating a problem you must now address. Specifically, two of the group members are nonsmokers. They are becoming increasingly vocal about the fact that two other members of the group smoke at work. These two workers believe the secondary smoke in the workplace is endangering their health and want to establish a no-smoking policy such as those of many large businesses today.

The two smokers counter that since the firm did not have such a policy when they started working there, it would be unfair to impose such a policy now. One of them claims he turned down an attractive job with another company because he wanted to work in a place where he could smoke. The fifth worker is also a nonsmoker, but says she doesn't care if others smoke. Her husband smokes at home anyway, so she is used to being around smokers.

You suspect that if the two vocal nonsmokers are not appeased, they may leave. At the same time, you think the two smokers will leave if you mandate a no-smoking policy. All five do good work, and you don't want any of them to leave.

Exercise Task: With this information as context, do the following:

1. Explain the nature of the conflict in this work group.
2. Develop a course of action for dealing with the situation.

TEST PREPPER

ACE self-test

You have read the chapter and studied the key terms, and the exam is any day now. Think you're ready to ace it? Take this sample test to gauge your comprehension of chapter material. You can check your answers at the back of the book. Want more test questions? Visit the student website at http://college.hmco.com/business/students/ (select Griffin/Moorhead, Fundamentals of Organizational Behavior 1e) and take the ACE quizzes for more practice.

1. **T F** In a true group, all members share the same goals.

2. **T F** A group formed to complete a specific task is called an affinity group.

3. **T F** The marketing department in a company is an example of a command group.

4. **T F** Informal groups, such as interest groups and friendship groups, have little impact on organizations.

5. **T F** At this point in Daniel's group, members mostly discuss issues irrelevant to the group's task. Daniel's group is likely in the mutual acceptance stage of group development.

6. **T F** In mature groups, members' activities are relatively spontaneous rather than subject to rigid structural constraints.

7. **T F** Edward is worried because his group hasn't shown a lot of progress yet. Edward might benefit from knowing that at about the halfway point to the project deadline, his group will engage in a burst of activity.

8. **T F** Groups with a higher degree of heterogeneity experience higher member turnover.

9. **T F** Every time a manager places an additional member in a group, the quantity of new ideas presented in the group will increase by the same amount.

10. **T F** Greg works hard in a group of five members but less hard in a group of ten members. This tendency is called social loafing.

11. **T F** Without group norms, group activities would be chaotic.

12. **T F** Highly cohesive groups are the most productive groups, even if their goals are incompatible with organizational goals.

13. **T F** Goal compatibility means the goals of two groups are nearly identical.

14. **T F** Harold simply ignores Kristen's request for information because their respective groups have conflicting goals. Harold has used an avoiding style to deal with the conflict.

15. **T F** A compromise solution to conflict means both parties lose something.

16. **T F** Sometimes managers need to stimulate conflict in their companies.

17. **T F** A "devil's advocate" is a group member who is interested primarily in individual gains, not in group success.

18. **T F** A useful way to reach collaboration between two groups in conflict is to focus on a superordinate goal.

19. Which of the following is not an essential part of the definition of groups?
    a. Two or more people
    b. A shared goal
    c. Interaction
    d. Mutual influence among members
    e. All of the above are essential parts of the definition of groups.

20. Jay is the manager of the marketing department in his company. His department includes an assistant manager and four marketing specialists. Jay's department is a(n) _____ group.
    a. command
    b. task
    c. affinity
    d. interest
    e. friendship

21. A recently passed law makes it necessary for Ginger's firm to upgrade its safety devices. Ginger and three other employees have been asked to perform this specific job over the next three months. Ginger's group is a(n) _____ group.
    a. command
    b. task
    c. affinity
    d. interest
    e. friendship

22. Once a month, the line managers at a large manufacturer get together to discuss common problems and explore creative solutions. This group is a(n) _____ group
    a. command
    b. task
    c. affinity
    d. interest
    e. friendship

23. Once group members get to know and accept one another, the next step in their development includes
    a. agreeing on goals and assigning roles and tasks.
    b. high motivation and creative task completion.
    c. spontaneity and flexibility in performing work.
    d. self-correction and individual rewards.
    e. a shift away from personal concerns to activities that will benefit the group.

24. What happens at about the midpoint of the allotted time a group has to complete its task?
    a. The group's progress stalls.
    b. Low-performing members are dismissed.
    c. A new leader is elected.
    d. An intense level of interpersonal conflict erupts among the members, followed by a general reconciliation.
    e. A burst of concentrated activity, reexamination of assumptions, and dramatic progress occur.

25. Research has shown which of the following to be higher in heterogeneous groups than in homogeneous groups?
    a. Productivity in simple tasks
    b. Cohesiveness
    c. Average age of group members
    d. Turnover
    e. Average education of group members

26. Sam belongs to a relatively homogeneous group. His friend Pam is part of a heterogeneous group. Which group will likely experience more conflict?
    a. Sam's group
    b. Pam's group
    c. Sam's group, if all its members are men
    d. Pam's group, if all its members are women
    e. The level of conflict will likely be the same in both groups.

27. Which of the following is likely to happen as a group grows larger?
    a. Group productivity is likely to decline.
    b. The average age of group members is likely to be older.
    c. The average age of group members is likely to be younger.
    d. The complexity of interactions is likely to decrease.
    e. Interactions and communication are much more likely to be formalized.

28. The tendency of some members of groups not to put forth as much effort in a group situation as they would working alone is called
    a. homogeneity.
    b. heterogeneity.
    c. social loafing.
    d. formalization.
    e. centralization.

29. Group norms serve all of the following purposes except
    a. they help the group survive.
    b. they ensure the group will be successful in task performance.
    c. they help the group avoid embarrassing situations.
    d. they express the central values of the group and identify the group to others.
    e. they simplify and make more predictable the behaviors expected of group members.

30. In Melanie's work group, conflict is never allowed to surface. Which of the following is most likely true?
    a. Melanie's group will perform at a higher level than groups with conflict.
    b. Melanie's group will suffer from apathy and lethargy.
    c. Melanie's group will remain in the storming stage of group development.
    d. Melanie's group will meet infrequently.
    e. Melanie's group will have lower cohesiveness than groups with conflict.

31. When the goals of two groups are compatible but intergroup interactions are not considered important to overall goal attainment, the groups may look for solutions that allow each group to accomplish their independent tasks with the least expenditure of time and effort. This approach to conflict resolution is called
    a. avoiding.
    b. competing.
    c. accommodating.
    d. collaborating.
    e. compromising.

32. Robert believes his group doesn't sufficiently explore alternatives before making a choice, so he adopts a strategy to occasionally take the "other" side during group discussions. Robert's approach is called
    a. collaboration.
    b. compromise.
    c. groupthink.
    d. cohesiveness stimulation.
    e. devil's advocate.

33. In Brandon's most recent position as a manager, he coordinates the work shared by two separate production teams. Brandon's new position is a(n)
    a. conflict stimulation role.
    b. linking role.
    c. devil's advocate role.
    d. accommodating role.
    e. mutual influence role.

CHAPTER 9

Using Teams in Organizations

MANAGEMENT PREVIEW

Teams are an integral part of the management process in many organizations today. The notion of using teams as a way of organizing work is not new, however, nor is it an American or Japanese innovation. One of the earliest uses and analyses of teams was the work of the Tavistock Institute in the United Kingdom in the late 1940s.[1] Major companies such as Hewlett-Packard, Xerox, Procter & Gamble, General Motors, and General Mills have been using teams as a primary means of accomplishing tasks for many years. The popular business press, such as *Fortune, BusinessWeek, Forbes,* and *The Wall Street Journal,* regularly reports on the use of teams in businesses around the world. Managers and experts agree that using teams can be the key to organizing and managing successfully in the twenty-first century.

This chapter outlines several current issues involving teams in organizations. First, we define team and differentiate teams from normal work groups. We then discuss the rationale for using teams, including the benefits and the costs. Next, we describe six types of teams in use in organizations today. Then we present the steps involved in implementing teams. Finally, we look briefly at two essential issues surrounding the use of teams.

After you have studied this chapter, you should be able to:
- ☐ *Differentiate teams from groups.*
- ☐ *Discuss the benefits and costs of teams in organizations.*
- ☐ *Describe various types of teams.*
- ☐ *Explain how organizations implement the use of teams.*
- ☐ *Discuss other essential team issues.*

We first look at teams as they are used in one unconventional work setting.

For many of us, the creation of art is an individual achievement, one person's expression of his or her unique perspective. Imagine the painter alone behind the canvas with a personal vision. Or consider the solitary sculptor chipping away at a stone block. However, glass blowing, an ancient art in which the production methods, tools, and team organization have remained the same for 2,000 years, depends on the cooperation of a team of artists.

A glass-blowing team consists of a starter, a glass master, and assistants. The starter gathers molten glass from a 2,300-degree furnace into a glob on the tip of a hollow metal pipe and rotates the glob through molds to form the rough shape of the piece. The glass master then directs the starter and assistants as they blow, shape, cool, heat, cut, bend, color, and fuse blobs of white-hot liquid glass to create the finished item.

The process resembles a ballet, with each performer moving around the central piece. Correct timing and coordination are essential. At Cloud Cap Glass in Montana, a four-person team has been working for an hour to create a stemmed goblet when something goes suddenly wrong. The worker gathering the small blob to "glue" the stem to the cup hesitates for a second, and as a result, the cup fuses to the metal tool gripping it. Silently the team throws the ruined pieces into the waste can. Rich Langley, the glass master, says, "It's my fault. I've been practicing these goblets for two years. They're very complicated. But what it boils down to is that [this] was the first piece of the day. Later in the day, after we've worked on them for awhile, everybody's timing is in synch."

Dale Chihuly of Seattle, the best-known American glass artist, runs his glass-blowing school based on techniques he learned from visits to international glassworks, especially the traditional schools on the island of Murano in Venice, Italy. While there, Chihuly witnessed the workings of hierarchical production teams in which each worker is given a specific role. His teachings have had a tremendous influence on American glass blowing; nearly every studio today uses the team techniques that he brought back to this country. Chihuly acts much like the director in a film production: He sets the stage, creates the concept, begins the action, and then allows each artist to fulfill his or her role with spontaneity. To inspire workers, he often plays music or hires a chef to prepare an elegant meal in the workspace. One of his artists claims Chihuly's ideas become an integrated part of every worker. "When I work for Dale, I almost become him," says Flora Mace.

American teams tend to be more democratic than Italian teams, and Langley emphasizes the importance of every worker: "This is a unique art form. It's not like painting, where it's just you and the canvas. It's a team effort." At first glance, glass blowing seems to be very different from business tasks, but corporate managers could learn much about creating cooperation and integration by observing the team approach used in this fascinating industry.

"This is a unique art form. It's not like painting, where it's just you and the canvas. It's a team effort."—Rich Langley, glass blower, Cloud Cap Glass

References: "The Art of Making Glass," Bendheim Glass Studios website, www.bendheim.com on May 24, 2004; Karen Chambers, "With the Team," Dale Chihuly website, www.chihuly.com on May 24, 2004; "Matthew's Biography," Thames Glass website, www.thamesglass.com on May 24, 2004; Daryl Gadbow, "'Blow Hard': Teamwork and Timing Are Essentials at Florence Glass-Blowing Studio," *Missoulian* (Missoula, Montana), February 3, 2002 (quotation); see www.missoulian.com.

Glass blowing clearly requires an advanced level of teamwork. The same is true of many organizations' tasks and responsibilities today. This chapter describes some techniques for making the best use of teams in organizations.

Differentiating Teams from Groups

LEARNING OBJECTIVE

Differentiate teams from groups.

Teams have been used, written about, and studied under many names and organizational programs: self-directed teams, self-managing teams, autonomous work groups, participative management, and many others. Groups and teams are not the same thing, although the two words are often used interchangeably in popular usage. *Group* usually refers to an assemblage of people or objects gathered together, whereas *team* typically refers to people or animals organized to work together. Thus, a team places more emphasis on concerted action than a group does. In everyday usage, however, *committee, group, team,* and *task force* are often used interchangeably.

In organizations, teams and groups are quite different. As we noted in Chapter 8, a group is two or more people who interact with one another such that each person influences and is influenced by each other person. We specifically noted that individuals interacting and influencing one another need not have a common goal. The collection of people who happen to report to the same supervisor or manager can be called a "work group." Group members may be satisfying their own needs in the group and have little concern for a common objective. This is where a team and a group differ. In a team, all members are committed to a common goal.

We could therefore say that a team is a group with a common goal, but teams differ from groups in other ways, too. Specifically, a **team** is a small number of people with complementary skills who are committed to a common purpose, performance goals, and approach for which they hold themselves mutually accountable.[2] Several facets of this definition need further explanation. A team includes few people, much like the small group described in Chapter 8, because the interaction and influence processes the team needs to function can occur only when the number of members is small. When many people are involved, they have difficulty interacting and influencing one another, utilizing their complementary skills, meeting goals, and holding themselves accountable. Regardless of the name, by our definition mature, fully developed teams are self-directing, self-managing, and autonomous. If they are not, someone from outside the group must be giving directions; hence, such a group cannot be considered a true team.[3]

Teams include people with a mix of skills appropriate to the tasks to be done. Three types of skills are usually required in a team. First, the team must have members with the technical or functional skills to do the jobs. Some types of engineering, scientific, technological, legal, or business skills may be necessary. Second, some team members need to have problem-solving and decision-making skills to help the team identify problems, determine priorities, evaluate alternatives, analyze tradeoffs, and make decisions about the direction of the team. Third, members need interpersonal skills to manage communication flow, resolve conflict, direct questions and discussion, provide support, and recognize the interests of all team members. Not all members will have all the required skills, especially when the team first convenes; each member will have different skills. However, as the team matures, team members will come to have more of the necessary skills.[4]

Having a common purpose and shared performance goals sets the tone and direction of the team. Unlike a work group, in which members merely report to the same supervisor or work in the same department, a team comes together to take action to pursue a goal. The purpose becomes the focus of the team, which makes all decisions and takes all actions in pursuit of the goal. Teams often spend days or weeks establishing the reason for their existence, an activity that builds strong identification and fosters commitment to the team. This process also helps team members develop trust in one another.[5] Usually the defining purpose comes first, followed by development of specific performance goals.

For example, a team of local citizens, teachers, and parents may come together for the purpose of making the local schools the best in the state. Then the team establishes specific performance goals to serve as guides for decision making, maintain the focus on action, differentiate the team from other groups working to

A **team** is a small number of people with complementary skills who are committed to a common purpose, common performance goals, and an approach for which they hold themselves mutually accountable.

Teams have become an increasingly important mechanism for organizations to get things done. For example, some large companies are beginning to suggest that small suppliers work together as partners to win major contracts. To facilitate such partnerships, each supplier generally provides one or more team members who work together to coordinate their efforts. Woodrow Hall, owner of a plastic packaging business, Film Fabrications, Inc., and Robert Johnson, owner of Johnson-Bryce Corporation, a plastic bag manufacturer and printer, worked together as a team in pursuit of a major contract from Proctor & Gamble.

improve schools, and challenge people to commit themselves to the team. Jon Katzenbach and Douglas Smith studied more than thirty teams and found that demanding, high-performance goals often challenge members to create a real team—as opposed to being merely a group—because when goals are truly demanding, members must pull together, find resources within themselves, develop and use the appropriate skills, and take a common approach to reach the goals.[6]

Agreeing on a common approach is especially important for teams because it is often the approach that differentiates one team from others. The team's approach usually covers how work will be done, social norms regarding dress, attendance at meetings, tardiness, norms of fairness and ethical behavior, and what will and will not be included in team activities.

Finally, the definition states that teams hold themselves mutually accountable for results rather than merely meeting a manager's demands for results, as in the traditional approach. If the members translate accountability to an external manager into internal, or mutual, accountability, the group moves toward acting as a team. Mutual accountability is essentially a promise members make to one another to do everything possible to achieve their goals, and it requires the commitment and trust of all members. It is the promise of each member to take personal responsibility for the team's goals that earns that individual the right to express her or his views and expect them to get a fair and constructive hearing. With this promise, members maintain and strengthen the trust essential for the team to succeed. The clearly stated high-performance goals and the common approach serve as the standards to which the team holds itself. Because teams are mutually accountable for meeting performance goals, three other differences between groups and teams become important: job categories, authority, and reward systems. Table 9.1 summarizes these differences.

Job Categories

The work of conventional groups is usually described in terms of highly specialized jobs that require minimal training and moderate effort. Tens or even hundreds of people may have similar job descriptions and see little relationship between their effort and the end result or finished product. In teams, on the other hand, members have many different skills that fit into one or two broad job categories. Neither workers nor managers worry about who does what job as long as the team puts out the finished product or service and meets its performance goals.[7]

TABLE 9.1

**Differences Between
Teams and Traditional
Work Groups**

Issue	Conventional Work Groups	Teams
Job Categories	Many narrow categories	One or two broad categories
Authority	Supervisor directly controls daily activities	Team controls daily activities
Reward System	Depends on the type of job, individual performance, and seniority	Based on team performance and individual breadth of skills

Reference: Adapted from Jack D. Osburn, Linda Moran, and Ed Musselwhite, with Craig Perrin, *Self-Directed Work Teams: The New American Challenge* (Homewood, Ill.: Business One Irwin, 1990), p. 11.

Authority

As Table 9.1 shows, in conventional work groups the supervisor directly controls workers' daily activities. In teams, members discuss what activities need to be done and determine who has the necessary skills and who will do each task. The team, rather than the supervisor, makes the decisions. If a "supervisor" remains on the team, the person's role usually changes to that of coach, facilitator, or one who helps the team make decisions rather than the traditional role of decision maker and controller.

Reward Systems

How employees are rewarded is vital to the long-term success of an organization. The traditional reward and compensation systems suitable for individual motivation (discussed in Chapter 4) are not appropriate in a team-based organization. In conventional settings, employees are usually rewarded on the basis of their individual performance, seniority, or job classification. In a team-based situation, team members are rewarded for mastering a range of skills needed to meet team performance goals, and rewards are sometimes based on team performance. Such a pay system tends to promote the flexibility teams need to be responsive to changing environmental factors. Three types of reward systems are common in a team environment: skill-based pay, gain-sharing systems, and team bonus plans.

Skill-Based Pay   Skill-based pay systems require team members to acquire a set of the core skills needed for their particular team plus additional special skills, depending on career tracks or team needs. Some programs require all members to acquire the core skills before any member receives additional pay. Usually employees can increase their base compensation by some fixed amount—say, $0.30 per hour for each additional skill acquired—up to some fixed maximum. Companies using skill-based pay systems include Eastman Chemical Company, Colgate-Palmolive Company, and Pfizer.

Gain-Sharing Systems   Gain-sharing systems usually reward all team members from all teams based on the performance of the organization, division, or plant. Such a system requires a baseline performance that team members must exceed to receive some share of the gain over the baseline measure. Westinghouse gives equal one-time, lump-sum bonuses to everyone in the plant based on improvements in productivity, cost, and quality. Employee reaction is usually positive because when employees work harder to help the company, they share in the profits they helped generate. On the other hand, when business conditions or other factors beyond their control make it impossible to generate improvements over the preset baseline, employees may feel disappointed and even disillusioned with the process.

Team Bonus Plans Team bonus plans are similar to gain-sharing plans except that the unit of performance and pay is the team rather than a plant, a division, or the entire organization. For the plan to be effective, each team must have specific performance targets or baseline measures that it considers realistic. Companies using team bonus plans include Milwaukee Insurance Company, Colgate-Palmolive, and Harris Corporation.

Changes in an organizational compensation system can be traumatic and threatening to most employees. However, matching the reward system to the way work is organized and accomplished can have very positive benefits. The three types of team-based reward systems presented can be used in isolation for simplicity or in some combination to address different types of issues for each organization.

Benefits and Costs of Teams in Organizations

LEARNING OBJECTIVE

Discuss the benefits and costs of teams in organizations.

Given the increasing use of teams worldwide, some organizations may be starting to use teams simply because everyone else is doing it, which is obviously the wrong reason. The reason for creating teams should be that teams make sense for that particular organization. The best reason to start teams in any organization is to recap the potential benefits of a team-based environment: enhanced performance, employee benefits, reduced costs, and organizational enhancements. Table 9.2 shows four categories of benefits and examples of each.

Enhanced Performance

Enhanced performance can take many forms, including improved productivity, quality, and customer service. Working in teams enables workers to avoid wasted effort, reduce errors, and respond better to customers, resulting in more output for each unit of employee input.

Such enhancements result from pooling individual efforts in new ways and continuously striving to improve for the benefit of the team. For example, a General Electric plant in North Carolina experienced a 20 percent increase in productivity after team implementation.[8] K Shoes reported a 19 percent increase in productivity and significant reductions in rejects in the manufacturing process. The Mastering Change box discusses how technological advances mandated that scientists at Roche Group begin working in collaborative groups to best utilize their new knowledge.

Employee Benefits

Employees tend to benefit as much as organizations in a team environment. Much attention has focused on the differences between the baby boom generation and the "postboomers" in their attitudes toward work, its importance to their lives, and what they want from it. In general, younger workers tend to be less satisfied with their work and the organization, to have lower respect for authority and supervision, and to want more than a paycheck every week. Teams can provide the sense of self-control, human dignity, identification with work, and sense of self-worth and self-fulfillment for which current workers seem to strive. Rather than relying

TABLE 9.2

Benefits of Teams in Organizations

Type of Benefit	Specific Benefit	Organizational Examples
Enhanced Performance	• Increased productivity • Improved quality • Improved customer service	Ampex: On-time customer delivery rose 98%. K Shoes: Rejects per million dropped from 5,000 to 250. Eastman: Productivity rose 70%.
Employee Benefits	• Quality of work life • Lower stress	Milwaukee Mutual: Employee assistance program usage dropped to 40% below industry average.
Reduced Costs	• Lower turnover, absenteeism • Fewer injuries	Kodak: Reduced turnover to one-half the industry average. Texas Instruments: Reduced costs more than 50%. Westinghouse: Costs down 60%.
Organizational Enhancements	• Increased innovation, flexibility	IDS Mutual Fund Operations: Improved flexibility to handle fluctuations in market activity. Hewlett-Packard: Innovative order-processing system.

References: Adapted from Richard S. Wellins, William C. Byham, and George R. Dixon, *Inside Teams* (San Francisco: Jossey-Bass, 1994); Charles C. Manz and Henry P. Sims Jr., *Business Without Bosses* (New York: Wiley, 1993).

on the traditional, hierarchical, manager-based system, teams give employees the freedom to grow and to gain respect and dignity by managing themselves, making decisions about their work, and making a genuine difference in the world around them.[9] As a result, employees have a better work life, face less stress at work, and make less use of employee assistance programs.

Reduced Costs

As empowered teams reduce scrap, make fewer errors, file fewer worker compensation claims, and reduce absenteeism and turnover, organizations based on teams are showing significant cost reductions. Team members believe they have a stake in the outcomes, want to make contributions because they are valued, and do not want to let their team down. Wilson Sporting Goods reported saving $10 million per year for five years thanks to its teams. Colgate-Palmolive reported that technician turnover was extremely low—more than 90 percent of technicians were retained after five years—once it changed to a team-based approach.

Organizational Enhancements

Other improvements in organizations that result from moving from a hierarchically based, directive culture to a team-based culture include increased innovation, creativity, and flexibility.[10] Use of teams can eliminate redundant layers of bureaucracy and flatten the hierarchy in large organizations. Employees feel closer and more in

MASTERING CHANGE

Technology Changes the Culture at Roche

Conducting 1 million genomics* experiments a day? Testing more than 3 million new compounds annually? It sounds impossible, but it's the new reality for pharmaceutical firms. Of the myriad technological developments and applications of the last fifteen years, perhaps none are as rapid in their evolution or startling in their outcomes as the recent advances in bioengineering. Industries as diverse as agriculture and petrochemicals are feeling the impact as the pharmaceutical industry is experiencing an unprecedented upheaval.

The technological revolution began with the decoding of human DNA. Innovative equipment now uses that knowledge to match compounds with their affected genes. Promising compounds are then tested to ensure their effectiveness against cancer-causing genes and determine whether they have adverse effects on other body organs.

Before these advances, Swiss drug manufacturer Roche Group had a competitive culture that pitted development teams against one another. The system worked when the firm was occupied with finding ideas for new blockbuster drugs. However, breakthroughs in technology made that culture obsolete, pushing the firm to adopt a more collaborative team approach. One incentive for more teamwork is to reduce the number of experiments given their cost in computer capacity and researcher time. One Roche scientist explains, "Back when we were work-

ing on one gene, we could do fishing experiments. [However, w]hen you get [information] from 12,000 genes, you need to be careful … If it isn't useful, you can waste a lot of time looking at it." Teams found they needed members from all parts of the organization to access specialized knowledge. Roche researcher Barry Goggin recalls, "We'd just get together in the corridors and design all sorts of small projects." At first, team members had trouble communicating, but they learned how to share information effectively. "It was almost as if two different languages were being spoken by the geneticists and the oncologists," Goggin says. "We had to bridge the gap."

Although the increase in collaboration and cross-specialty communication is good for the firm, some workers are suffering. The changing technology and increased capacity of robotic equipment have caused Roche to lay off some R&D staff. Although this move will reduce costs, Roche must proceed cautiously to avoid upsetting its new and effective collaborative organization culture.

*Genomics is the study of DNA nucleotide sequences.

References: "Roche in the Sciences and Medicine," "Innovative R & D," Roche website, www.roche.com on May 24, 2004; Jesse Eisinger, "Roche's Planned Job Cuts Look Desperate, Not Smart," *Wall Street Journal,* June 1, 2001; interactive.wsj.com/archive on May 11, 2002; George Anders, "Roche's New Scientific Method," *Fast Company,* January 2002, pp. 60–67 (quotation p. 64).

touch with top management. Employees who think their efforts are important are more likely to make significant contributions. In addition, the team environment constantly challenges teams to innovate and solve problems creatively. If the "same old way" does not work, empowered teams are free to throw it out and develop a new way. With increasing global competition, organizations must constantly adapt to keep abreast of changes. Teams provide the flexibility to react quickly. One of Motorola's earliest teams challenged a long-standing top-management policy regarding supplier inspections to reduce cycle times and improve delivery of crucial parts.[11] After several attempts, management finally allowed the team to change the system and consequently reaped the expected benefits.

Costs of Teams

The costs of teams are usually expressed in terms of the difficulty of changing to a team-based organization. Managers have expressed frustration and confusion about their new roles as coaches and facilitators, especially if they developed their managerial skills under the traditional hierarchical management philosophy. Some managers have felt they were working themselves out of a job as they turned over more and more of their old directing duties to a team.[12]

Employees may also feel like losers during the change to a team culture. Some traditional staff groups, such as technical advisory staffs, may fear their jobs are in jeopardy as teams do more and more of the technical work formerly done by technicians. New roles and pay scales may need to be developed for the technical staff in these situations. Often technical people have been assigned to a team or a small group of teams and become members who fully participate in team activities.

Another cost associated with teams is the slowness of the process of full team development. As discussed earlier, it takes a long time for teams to go through the full development cycle and become mature, efficient, and effective. If top management balks at the slow progress, teams may be disbanded, returning the organization to its original hierarchical form with significant losses for employees, managers, and the organization.

Probably the most dangerous cost is premature abandonment of the change to a team-based organization. If top management gets impatient with the team change process and cuts it short, never allowing teams to develop fully and realize benefits, all the hard work of employees, middle managers, and supervisors is lost. As a result, employee confidence in management in general and in the decision makers in particular may suffer for a long time.[13] The losses in productivity and efficiency will be very difficult to recoup. Management must therefore be fully committed before initiating a change to a team-based organization.

Types of Teams

LEARNING OBJECTIVE

Describe various types of teams.

Many different types of teams exist in organizations today. Some evolved naturally in organizations that permit various types of participative and empowering management programs. Others were formally created at the suggestion of enlightened management. One easy way to classify teams is by what they do; for example, some teams make or do things, some teams recommend things, and some teams run things. The most common types of teams are quality circles, work teams, and problem-solving teams; management teams are also quite common.

Quality Circles

Quality circles (QCs) are small groups of employees from the same work area who regularly meet to discuss and recommend solutions to workplace problems.

Quality circles (QCs) are small groups of employees from the same work area who meet regularly (usually weekly or monthly) to discuss and recommend solutions to workplace problems.[14] QCs were the first type of team created in U.S. organizations, becoming most popular during the 1980s in response to growing Japanese competition. QCs had some success in reducing rework and cutting defects on the shop floors of many manufacturing plants. Some attempts have been made to use QCs in offices and service operations. They exist alongside the traditional management structure and are relatively permanent. The role of QCs is to investigate a variety of quality problems that might come up in the workplace. They do not replace the work group or make decisions about how the work is done. Interest in QCs has dropped somewhat, although many companies still have them.[15] QCs are teams that make recommendations.

Work Teams

Work teams include all the people working in an area, are relatively permanent, and do the daily work, making decisions regarding how the team's work is done.

Like quality circles, **work teams** tend to be permanent, but they, rather than auxiliary committees, are the teams that do the daily work.[16] The nurses, orderlies, and various technicians responsible for all patients on a floor or wing in a hospital comprise a work team. Rather than investigate a specific problem, evaluate alternatives, and recommend a solution or change, a work team does the actual daily work of the unit. The difference between a traditional work group of nurses and the patient care team is that the latter has the authority to decide how the work is done, in what order, and by whom; the entire team is responsible for all patient care. When the team decides how the work is to be organized or performed, it becomes a self-managing team that accrues all of the benefits described in this chapter. Work teams are teams that make or do things.

Problem-Solving Teams

Problem-solving teams are temporary teams established to attack specific problems in the workplace.

Problem-solving teams are temporary teams established to tackle specific problems in the workplace. Teams can use any number of methods to solve the problem, as discussed in Chapter 12. After solving the problem, the team is usually disbanded, allowing members to return to their normal work. One survey found that 91 percent of U.S. companies utilize problem-solving teams regularly.[17] High-performing problem-solving teams are often cross-functional, meaning team members come from many different functional areas. Crisis teams are problem-solving teams created only for the duration of an organizational crisis and are usually composed of people from many different areas. Problem-solving teams are teams that make recommendations for others to implement.

Management Teams

Management teams consist of managers from various areas and coordinate work teams.

Management teams consist of managers from various areas and coordinate work teams. They are relatively permanent because their work does not end with the completion of a particular project or resolution of a problem. Management teams must concentrate on the teams that have the most impact on overall corporate performance. The primary job of management teams is to coach and counsel other teams to be self-managing by making decisions within the team. The second most important task of management teams is to coordinate work between work teams that are interdependent in some manner. Digital Equipment Corporation abandoned its team matrix structure because the matrix of teams was poorly organized and coordinated. Team members at all levels reported spending endless hours in meetings trying to coordinate among teams, leaving too little time to get the real work done.[18]

Top-management teams may have special problems. First, the work of the top-management team may not be conducive to teamwork. Vice presidents or heads of divisions may be in charge of different sets of operations that are unrelated and do not need to be coordinated. Forcing that type of top-management group to be a team may be inappropriate. Second, top managers often have reached high levels in the organization because they have certain characteristics or abilities to get things done. For successful managers to alter their style, pool resources, and sacrifice their independence and individuality can be very difficult.[19]

Product Development Teams

Product development teams are combinations of work teams and problem-solving teams that create new designs for products or services that will satisfy customer needs.

Product development teams are combinations of work teams and problem-solving teams that create new designs for products or services that will satisfy customer needs. They are similar to problem-solving teams in that when the product is fully developed and in production, the team may be disbanded. As global com-

Product development teams are commonly used in organizations today. Apple hardware chief Jon Rubenstein and industrial designer Jonathan Ive worked with a group of other specialists to help create the Apple iPod. The team designed the product and got it into production in just eight months.

petition and electronic information storage, processing, and retrieving capabilities increase, companies in almost every industry are struggling to cut product development times. The primary organizational means of accomplishing this important task is the "blue-ribbon" cross-functional team. Boeing's team that developed the 777 commercial airplane and the platform teams at Chrysler are typical examples.

The rush to market with new designs can lead to numerous problems for product development teams. The primary problems of poor communication and coordination of typical product development processes can be rectified by creating self-managing cross-functional product development teams.[20]

Virtual Teams

Virtual teams may never actually meet together in the same room; their activities take place on the computer via teleconferencing and other electronic information systems. Engineers in the United States can directly connect audibly and visually with their counterparts around the globe, sharing files via Internet, electronic mail, and other communication utilities. All participants can look at the same drawing, print, or specification; hence, decisions are made much faster. With electronic communication systems, team members can move in or out of a team or a team discussion as the issues warrant.

Implementing Teams in Organizations

Implementing teams in organizations is not easy; it takes a lot of hard work, time, training, and patience. Changing from a traditional organizational structure to a team-based structure is much like other organizational changes (which we discuss in Chapter 15). It is a complete cultural change for the organization. Typically the organization is hierarchically designed to provide clear direction and control. However, many organizations need to be able to react quickly to a dynamic environment. Team procedures artificially imposed on existing processes are a recipe for disaster. In this section, we look at several essential elements specific to an organizational change to a team-based situation.

Virtual teams work together via computer and other electronic communication utilities; members move in and out of meetings and the team itself as the situation dictates.

Planning the Change

The change to a team-based organization requires a great deal of analysis and planning before it is implemented; the decision cannot be made overnight. It is such a drastic departure from the traditional hierarchy and authority-and-control orientation that significant planning, preparation, and training are prerequisites. The plan-

Organizations planning to implement teams are generally advised to follow a clear plan. Of course, too much bureaucracy in the process can quickly derail any effort. For instance, Dilbert's boss is making the implementation of his idea so onerous that he is likely to think twice before making future suggestions.

DILBERT reprinted by permission of United Feature Syndicate, Inc.

ning takes place in two phases, the first leading to the decision about whether to move to a team-based approach and the second while preparing for implementation.

Making the Decision   Prior to making the decision, top management needs to establish the leadership for the change, develop a steering committee, conduct a feasibility study, and then make the go/no-go decision. Top management must be sure the team culture is consistent with its strategy, as we discuss in Chapter 14. Often the leadership for the change is the chief executive officer, the chief operating officer, or another prominent person in top management. Regardless of the position, the person leading the change must (1) have a strong belief that employees want to be responsible for their own work, (2) be able to demonstrate the team philosophy, (3) articulate a coherent vision of the team environment, and (4) have the creativity and authority to overcome obstacles as they surface.

The leader of the change needs to put together a steering committee to help explore the organization's readiness for the team environment and lead it through the planning and preparation for the change. The steering committee can be of any workable size, from two to ten people who are influential and know the work and the organization. Members may include plant or division managers, union representatives, human resource department representatives, and operational-level employees. The work of the steering committee includes visits to sites that might be candidates for utilizing work teams, visits to currently successful work teams, data gathering and analysis, low-key general discussions, and deliberating and deciding whether to use a consultant during the change process.

A feasibility study is critical before making the decision to use teams. The steering committee needs to know if the work processes are conducive to team use, if the employees are willing and able to work in a team environment, if the managers in the unit to be converted are willing to learn and apply the hands-off managerial style necessary to make teams work, if the organization's structure and culture are ready to accommodate a team-based organization, if the market for the unit's products or services is growing or at least stable enough to absorb the increased productive capacity the teams will be putting out, and if the community will support the transition teams. Without answers to these questions, management is merely guessing and hoping that teams will work, and may be destined for many surprises that could doom the effort.

After the leadership has been established, the steering committee set up, and a feasibility study conducted, the go/no-go decision can be made. The committee and top management will need to decide jointly to go ahead if conditions are right. On the other hand, if the feasibility study indicates that the organizational unit's readiness is questionable, the committee can decide to postpone implementation while changes are made in personnel, organizational structure, organizational policies, or market conditions. The committee may also decide to implement training and acculturation for employees and managers in the unit in preparation for later implementation.

Preparing for Implementation   Once the decision is made to change to a team-based organization, much needs to be done before implementation can begin. Preparation consists of the following five steps: clarifying the mission, selecting the site for the first work teams, preparing the design team, planning the transfer of authority, and drafting the preliminary plan.

The mission statement is simply an expression of purpose that summarizes the long-range benefits the company hopes to gain by moving to a team environment. It must be consistent with the organization's strategy as it establishes a common set of assumptions for executives, middle managers, support staff, and the teams. In addition, it sets the parameters or boundaries within which the change will take place. It may identify which divisions or plants will be involved or what levels will be converted to teams. The mission statement attempts to stimulate and focus the energy of those people who will be involved in the change. The mission can focus on continuous improvement, employee involvement, increasing performance, competition, customer satisfaction, and contributions to society. The steering committee should involve many people from several areas of the company to foster fuller involvement in the change.

Once the mission is established, the steering committee needs to decide where teams will be implemented first. Selection of the first site is crucial because it sets the tone for the success of the total program. The best initial site is one that includes workers from multiple job categories, where improving performance or reaching the targets set in the mission is feasible, and where workers accept the idea of using teams. Also valuable are a tradition or history of success and a staff that is receptive to training, especially training in interpersonal skills. One manufacturing company based its choice of sites for initial teams not on criteria such as these but on the desire to reward the managers of successful divisions or to "fix" areas performing poorly. Consequently team implementation in that company was very slow and not very successful.[21] Initial sites must also have a local "champion" of the team concept.

Once the initial sites have been identified, the steering committee needs to set up the team that will design the other teams. The design team is a select group of employees, supervisors, and managers who will work out the staffing and operational details to make the teams perform well. The design team selects the initial team members, prepares members and managers for teams, changes work processes for use with the team design, and plans the transition from the current state to the new self-managed team structure. The design team usually spends the first three months learning from the steering committee, visiting sites where teams are being used successfully, and spending a significant amount of time in classroom training. Considering the composition of the teams is one of the most important decisions the design team has to make.

Planning the transfer of authority from management to teams is the most important phase of planning the implementation. It is also the most distinctive and difficult part of moving to a team-based organization. The planning is a gradual process, taking from two to five years in most situations. Teams must learn new skills and make new decisions related to their work, all of which take time. It is, essentially, a cultural change for the organization.

The last stage of planning the implementation is to write the tentative plan for the initial work teams. The draft plan combines the work of the steering and design committees and becomes the primary working document that guides the continuing work of the design teams and the first work teams. The draft plan (1) recommends a process for selecting the people who will be on the first teams; (2) describes roles and responsibilities for all those who will be affected (team members, team leaders, facilitators, support teams, managers, and top management); (3) explains what training the various groups will need; (4) identifies specifically which work processes will be involved; (5) describes what other organizational systems will be affected; and (6) lays out a preliminary master schedule for the next two to three years. Once the steering committee and top management approve the preliminary plan, the organization is ready to start the implementation.

Phases of Implementation

As we just noted, implementation of self-managing work teams is a long and difficult process, often taking two to five years. During this period, the teams go through a number of phases (see Figure 9.1); these phases are not, however, readily apparent at the times the team is going through them.

Phase 1: Start-Up   In phase 1, team members are selected and prepared to work in teams so the teams have the best possible chance of success. Much of the initial training is informational or "awareness" training sending the message that top management is firmly committed to teams and teams are not experimental. The steering committee usually starts the training at the top, and the training and information are passed down the chain to the team members. Training covers the rationale for moving to a team-based organization, how teams were selected, how they work, their roles and responsibilities, compensation, and job security. In general, training covers the technical skills necessary to do the team's work, the administrative skills the team needs to function within the organization, and the interpersonal skills necessary to work with people in the team and throughout the organization. Sometimes the interpersonal skills are important. Perhaps most important is establishing the idea that teams are not "unmanaged" but "differently managed." The difference is that the new teams manage themselves. Team

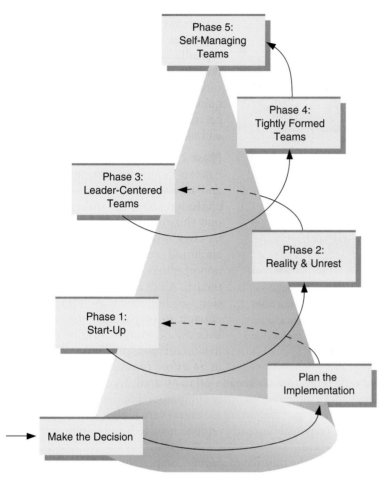

FIGURE 9.1

Phases of Team Implementation

Implementation of teams in organizations is a long, arduous process. After the decision is made to initiate teams, the steering committee develops plans for the design team, which plans the entire process. The goal is for teams to become self-managing. The time each stage takes varies with the organization.

Implementing teams in organizations is a complex and multistep process. But if done well, the payoffs can be dramatic. India's Wipro Technologies moved to a team organization to compete more effectively with other international software solution companies such as EDS and IBM Global Solutions. Wipro's teams helped the firm win a major contract from Home Depot.

boundaries are also identified, and the preliminary plan is adjusted to fit the particular team situations. Employees typically sense that much is changing during the first few months, enthusiasm runs high, and employees' anticipation is quite positive. Performance by teams increases at start-up because of this initial enthusiasm for the change.

Phase 2: Reality and Unrest   After perhaps six to nine months, team members and managers report frustration and confusion about the ambiguities of the new situation. For employees, unfamiliar tasks, more responsibility, and worry about job security replace hope for the opportunities presented by the new approach. All of the training and preparation, as important as it is, is never enough to prepare for the storm and backlash. Cummins Engine Company held numerous "prediction workshops" in an effort to prepare employees and managers for the difficulties that lay ahead—all to no avail. Its employees reported the same problems that employees of other companies did. The best advice is to perform phase 1 effectively and then make managers very visible, continue to work to clarify the roles and responsibilities of everyone involved, and reinforce the positive behaviors that do occur.

Some managers make the mistake of staying completely away from the newly formed teams, thinking the whole idea is to let teams manage themselves. In reality, managers need to be highly visible to provide encouragement, monitor team performance, act as intermediaries between teams, help teams acquire needed resources, foster the right type of communication, and, sometimes, protect teams from those who want to see them fail. Managers, too, feel the unrest and confusion. The change they supported results in more work for them. In addition, there is the real threat, at least initially, that work will not get done, projects will not get finished, or orders will not get shipped on time and that they will be blamed for these problems.[22] Managers also report that they still have to intervene and solve problems for the teams because the teams do not know what they are doing.

Phase 3: Leader-Centered Teams   As the discomfort and frustrations of the previous phase peak, teams usually long for a system that resembles the old manager-centered organizational structure (see Figure 9.1). However, members are learning about self-direction and leadership from within the team and usually start to focus on a single member as the team leader. In addition, the team begins to think of itself as a unit as members learn to manage themselves. Managers begin to appreciate the potential benefits of organizing in teams and to withdraw slowly from the units' daily operations and begin focusing on standards, regulations, systems, and resources for the team.[23] This phase is not a setback to team development, although it may seem like one because development of and reliance on one internal leader is a move away from focusing on the old hierarchy and traditional lines of authority.

The design and steering committees need to be sure that two things happen during this phase. First, they need to encourage the rise of strong internal team leaders. The new leaders can be either company appointed or team appointed. Top managers sometimes prefer the additional control they get from appointing the team leaders, assuming production will continue through the team transition. On the other hand, if the company-appointed leaders are the former managers, team members have trouble believing that anything has really changed. Team-appointed leaders can be a problem if the leaders are not trained properly and oriented toward team goals.

If the team-appointed leader is ineffective, the team usually recognizes the problem and makes the adjustments necessary to get the team back on track. Another possibility for team leadership is a rotating system in which the position changes every quarter, month, week, or even day. A rotating system fosters professional growth of all members of the team and reinforces the strength of the team's self-management.

The second important issue for this phase is to help each team develop its own sense of identity. Visits to observe mature teams in action can be a good step for newly formed teams. Recognizing teams and individuals for good performance is always powerful, especially when the teams choose the recipients. Continued training in problem-solving steps, tools, and techniques is imperative. Managers need to push as many problem-solving opportunities as possible down to the team level. Finally, as team identity develops, teams develop social activities and display T-shirts, team names, logos, and other items that show off their identity. All of these events are a sure sign that the team is moving into phase 4.

Phase 4: Tightly Formed Teams   In the fourth phase of team implementation, teams become tightly formed to the point that their internal focus can become detrimental to other teams and to the organization as a whole. Such teams are usually extremely confident of their ability to do everything. They are solving problems, managing their schedule and resources, and resolving internal conflicts. However, communication with external teams begins to diminish, the team covers up for underperforming members, and interteam rivalries can turn sour, leading to unhealthy competition.

To avoid the dangers of the intense team loyalty and isolation inherent in phase 4, managers need to ensure that teams continue to do the things that have enabled them to prosper thus far. First, teams need to keep the communication channels with other teams open through councils of rotating team representatives who meet regularly to discuss what works and what does not; teams that communicate and cooperate with other teams should be rewarded. At the Digital Equipment plant in Connecticut, team representatives meet weekly to share successes and failures so that all can avoid problems and improve the ways their teams operate.[24] Second, management needs to provide performance feedback, either through computer terminals in the work area that give up-to-date information on performance or via regular feedback meetings. At TRW plants, management introduced peer performance appraisal at this stage of the team implementation process. It found that in phase 4, teams were ready to take on this administrative task but needed significant training in how to perform and communicate appraisals. Third, teams need to follow the previously developed plan to transfer authority and responsibility to the teams and ensure that all team members have followed the plan to get training in all of the skills necessary to do the team's work. By the end of phase 4, the team should be ready to take responsibility for managing itself.

Phase 5: Self-Managing Teams   Phase 5 is the end result of the months or years of planning and implementation. Mature teams are meeting or exceeding their performance goals. Team members are taking responsibility for team-related leadership functions. Managers and supervisors have withdrawn from the daily operations, and are planning and providing counseling for teams. Probably most important, mature teams are flexible—taking on new ideas for improvement; making changes as needed to membership, roles, and tasks; and doing whatever it takes to meet the organization's strategic objectives. Although the teams are mature and functioning well, several things need to be done to keep them on track. First and foremost, individuals and teams need to continue their training in job skills and in team and interpersonal skills. Second, support systems need to be constantly improved to facilitate team development and productivity. Third, teams always need to improve their internal customer and supplier relationships within the organization. Partnerships among teams throughout the organization can help the internal teams continue to meet the needs of external customers.

Essential Team Issues

┌─*LEARNING OBJECTIVE*─┐

*Discuss other essential team
issues.*

This chapter has described the many benefits of teams and the process of changing to a team-based organization. Teams can be utilized in small and large organizations, on the shop floor and in offices, and in countries around the world. Teams must be initiated for performance-based business reasons, and proper planning and implementation strategies must be used. In this section, we discuss two additional issues organizations face as they move to a team-based setup: team performance and starting at the top.

Team Performance

Organizations typically expect too much too soon when they implement teams. In fact, things often get worse before they get better.[25] Figure 9.2 shows how, shortly after implementation, team performance often declines and then rebounds to rise to the original levels and above. Management at Investors Diversified Services, the financial services giant in Minneapolis, expected planning for team start-up to take three or four months; the process took eight-and-a-half months.[26] It often takes a year or more before performance returns to at least before-team levels. If teams are implemented without proper planning, their performance may never return to prior levels. The long lead time for improving performance can be discouraging to managers who jumped on the team "bandwagon" and expected immediate returns.

The phases of implementation discussed in the previous sections correspond to key points on the team performance curve. At start-up, performance is at its normal levels, although sometimes the anticipation of and enthusiasm for teams cause a slight increase in performance. In phase 2, reality and unrest, teams are often confused and frustrated with the training and lack of direction from top management to the point that actual performance may decline. In phase 3, leader-centered teams become more comfortable with the team idea and refocus on the team's work. They once again have established leadership, although now with an internal leader rather than an external manager or supervisor. Thus, their performance usually returns to at least their former levels. In phase 4, teams are beginning to experience the real potential of teamwork and are producing above their prior levels. Finally, in phase 5, self-managing teams are mature, flexible, and usually setting new records for performance.

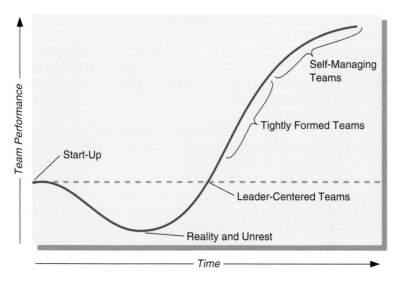

FIGURE 9.2

Performance and Implementation of Teams

The team performance curve shows that performance initially drops as reality sets in and team members experience frustration and unrest. However, performance soon increases and rises to record levels as the teams mature and become self-managing.

Reference: Reprinted by permission of Harvard Business School Publishing. From *The Wisdom of Teams: Creating the High Performance Organization* by Jon R. Katzenbach and Douglas K Smith. Boston, MA, 1993, p. 84. Copyright ©1993 McKinley & Company, Inc. All rights reserved.

Organizations changing to a team-based arrangement need to recognize the time and effort involved in making such a change. Hopes for immediate, positive results can lead to disappointment. The most rapid increases in performance occur between the leader-centered phase and the team-centered phase because teams have managed to get past the difficult, low-performance stages, have had a lot of training, and are ready to utilize their independence and freedom to make decisions about their own work. Team members are deeply committed to one another and to the success of the team. In phase 5, management needs to make sure teams are focused on the strategic goals of the organization.

Start at the Top

The question of where to start in team implementation is really not an issue. Change starts at the top in every successful team implementation. Top management has three important roles to play. First, top management must decide to go to a team-based organization for sound, business performance–related reasons. A major cultural change cannot be made simply because it is the fad, because the boss went to a seminar on teams, or because a quick fix is needed. Second, top management is instrumental in communicating the reasons for the change to the rest of the organization. Third, top management must support the change effort during the difficult periods. As discussed previously, performance usually goes down in the early phases of team implementation. Top-management support may involve verbal encouragement of team members, but organizational support systems for the teams are also needed. Examples of support systems for teams include more efficient inventory and scheduling systems, better hiring and selection systems, improved information systems, and appropriate compensation systems.

Synopsis

Teams are much different from work groups. A team is a small number of people with complementary skills who are committed to a common purpose, shared performance goals, and a common approach for which they hold themselves mutually accountable. Teams differ from traditional work groups in their job categories, authority, and reward systems.

Teams are used because they make sense for a specific organization. Organizational benefits include enhanced performance, employee benefits, and reduced costs, among others.

Many types of teams exist in organizations. Quality circles are small groups of employees from the same work area who meet regularly to discuss and recommend solutions to workplace problems. Work teams perform the daily operations of the organization and make decisions about how to do the work. Problem-solving teams are temporarily established to solve a particular problem. Management teams consist of managers from various areas; these teams are relatively permanent and coach and counsel the new teams. Product development teams are responsible for developing a new product or service for the organization. Members of virtual teams usually meet via teleconferencing, may never actually sit in the same room together, and often have a fluid membership.

Planning the change to a team-based organization entails all the activities leading to the decision to utilize teams and then preparing the organization for the initiation of teams. Essential steps include establishing leadership for the change, creating a steering committee, conducting a feasibility study, and making the go/no-go decision. After the decision to use teams has been made, preparations include clarifying the mission of the change, selecting the site for the first teams, preparing the design team, planning the trans-

fer of authority, and drafting the preliminary implementation plan.

Implementation includes five phases: start-up, reality and unrest, leader-centered teams, tightly formed teams, and self-managing teams. Implementation of teams is essentially a cultural change for the organization.

For teams to succeed, the change must start with top management, who must decide why the change is needed, communicate the need for the change, and support the change. Management must not expect too much too soon because team performance tends to decrease before it returns to prior levels and then increases to record levels.

Discussion Questions

1. Why is it important to make a distinction between *group* and *team*? How might they differ in terms of behaviors?

2. Other than the obvious example of the strong presence of teams, what other organizational characteristics are different for a team-based organization?

3. Some say that changing to a team-based arrangement "just makes sense" for organizations. What are the four primary reasons this might be so?

4. If employees are happy working in a traditional hierarchical organization, why should management even consider changing to a team-based organization?

5. How are the six types of teams related to one another?

6. Under what circumstances is a cross-functional team useful in an organization?

7. Which type of team is the most common in organizations? Why?

8. Why is planning the change to a team-based structure important in the implementation process?

9. What can happen if an organization prematurely starts building a team-based organization by clarifying the mission and then selecting the site for the first work teams?

10. What are two primary issues facing team-based organizations?

Organizational Behavior Case for Discussion

None of Us Is as Smart as All of Us

Are you unhappy about your recent encounters with the medical profession? Do you think doctors are too rushed and impersonal, insurance companies have too much control, fees are too high, and procedures and tests are inadequately explained? If you do, you're not alone; national consumer surveys show a low level of satisfaction with health care. But at the Mayo Clinic in Rochester, Minnesota, patient satisfaction soars above the average. At the same time, costs are lower and the staff is happier than those at most other hospitals. Teamwork is the key to the clinic's remarkable success.

The Mayo Clinic was founded by Dr. William W. Mayo, a Minnesota physician, and his two sons,

William J. and Charles, also physicians. After a catastrophic tornado in 1883, the doctors joined forces with nurses from the Sisters of St. Francis, and the arrangement was made permanent with the opening of St. Mary's Hospital in 1889. The Mayo brothers recruited more physicians, hiring technicians and business managers and creating one of the first group medical practices. The closeness of the two brothers, coupled with advances in medicine, helped guide the development of Mayo's team-based culture. Harry Harwick, its first business manager, claims, "The first and perhaps greatest lesson I learned from the Mayos was that of teamwork. For 'my brother and I' was no mere convenient term of reference, but rather the expression of a basic, indivisible philosophy of life." Dr. William J. Mayo said, "It has become necessary to develop medicine as a cooperative science; the clinician, the specialist, and the laboratory workers uniting for the good of the patient. Individualism in medicine can no longer exist."

The team approach permeates the culture of the entire organization. It begins with staff and physician recruiting. Mayo runs its own medical school and residency programs, and hires many of its own graduates. The clinic selects only those with the "right" attitude, the ones who are willing to put patients' needs first. All clinic medical staff, including doctors, nurses, and technicians, call one another "consultants," a term that emphasizes collaboration and reduces status barriers, enabling all workers to participate as equals in patient care decisions. The CEO is a physician; every committee is headed by medical personnel, with business staffers working as advisers only. The Mayo brothers turned their life savings into the Mayo Foundation, which funds the clinic's operation as well as medical education and research. Doctors at Mayo are employees, not owners, so they receive a salary, ensuring they will make decisions in the best interests of their patients rather than for personal gain. Without worries about turf battles, collaboration is the norm. Oncologist Lynn Hartman explains, "I take great comfort in the proximity of expertise. I feel much more confident in the accuracy of my diagnosis because I've got some very, very smart people next to me who have expertise that I don't have."

A typical patient's experience at Mayo goes something like this: A cancer patient would have multiple professionals involved in his or her care, from oncologists to nurses to radiologists to surgeons to social workers, and the group would meet as a team with the patient to work out a joint strategy for treatment. Cancer patients typically feel they have little control, but Mayo doctors know that getting patients actively involved in their own care dramatically increases the odds of successful treatment. Hartman claims, "Most patients today want a more interactive style . . . so [that] they can be part of the decision. They're on the Internet; they're doing their own research. What they're looking for is someone who can help them sort through that information." With help from the professionals, patients can work out a treatment that makes sense for their particular circumstances. When a patient's needs or questions change, the team adapts. "We work in teams, and each team is driven by the medical problems involved in a case and by the patient's preferences. Sometimes that means that a team must be expanded—or taken apart and reassembled," says Hartman.

Part of Mayo's success comes from past successes—for example, when its medical school graduates refer patients to the clinic. The foresight of William and Charlie Mayo in providing financially for the clinic is another factor. Mayo's reputation also creates opportunities, such as Mayo physician Donald D. Hensrud's recurring column for *Fortune* readers and the award-winning website mayoclinic.com. But most of Mayo's success is due to the passion for teamwork expressed in the founders' philosophy: "No one is big enough to be independent of others. None of us is as smart as all of us."

Case Questions

1. Would you consider the patient care groups at the Mayo Clinic to be teams? Explain your answer in terms of job categories, authority, and reward system. (Hint: See Table 9.1 for guidance.)
2. What team-related benefits does this case describe? What are the possible team-related costs?
3. What type of team are the patient care teams? Explain your answer.

References: 2003 Mayo Foundation Annual Report, www.mayoclinic.org on May 23, 2004; "History," "Mayo's Mission," "The Tradition," Mayo clinic website (quotation from "History"), www.mayoclinic.org on May 23, 2004; Paul Roberts, "The Agenda—Total Teamwork," *Fast Company*, April 1999.

Experiencing Organizational Behavior

Using Teams

Introduction: The use of groups and teams is becoming more common in organizations throughout the world. The following assessment surveys your beliefs about the effective use of teams in work organizations.

Instructions: You will agree with some of the statements and disagree with others. In some cases, you may find making a decision difficult, but you should force a choice. Record your answers next to each statement according to the following scale:

4 = Agree Strongly
3 = Agree Somewhat
2 = Disagree Somewhat
1 = Disagree Strongly

_____ 1. Each individual in a work team should have a clear assignment so that individual accountability can be maintained.

_____ 2. For a team to function effectively, the team must be given complete authority over all aspects of the task.

_____ 3. One way to get teams to work is to simply assemble a group of people, tell them in general what needs to be done, and let them work out the details.

_____ 4. Once a team "gets going," management can turn its attention to other matters.

_____ 5. To ensure that a team develops into a cohesive working unit, managers should be especially careful not to intervene in any way during the initial start-up period.

_____ 6. Training is not critical to a team because the team will develop any needed skills on its own.

_____ 7. It's easy to provide teams with the support they need because they are basically self-motivating.

_____ 8. Teams need little or no structure to function effectively.

_____ 9. Teams should set their own direction, with managers determining the means to the selected end.

_____ 10. Teams can be used in any organization.

For interpretation, see the Interpretation Guide in the *Instructor's Resource Manual.*

Reference: Adapted from J. Richard Hackman (ed.), *Groups That Work (and Those That Don't)*, pp. 493–504. Copyright © 1990. Reprinted with permission of John Wiley & Sons, Inc.

Self-Assessment Exercise

Understanding the Benefits of Teams

Purpose: This exercise will help you understand some of the benefits of teamwork.

Format: Your instructor will divide the group into teams of four to six people. (These could be previously formed teams or new teams.) Teams should arrange their desks or chairs so that they can interact and communicate well with each other.

Procedure: Consider that your team is an engineering design team assigned to work out this difficult problem whose solution would be the key to getting a major purchase contract from a large influential buyer. The task seems simple, but working out such tasks (at different levels of complexity) can be very important to organizations.

1. It is important for your team to work together to develop your solution.
2. Look at the following figure. Your task is to create a single square by making only two straight-line cuts and then reassembling the pieces so that all material is used in the final product.

The Figure:

3. It might be easier to trace the design onto stiff paper or cardboard to facilitate working with the pieces.
4. Your instructor has access to the correct answer key from the *Instructor's Resource Manual.*

Follow-up Questions

1. How did the other members of your team help or hinder your ability to solve the problem?
2. Did your team have a leader throughout the exercise? If so, can you identify why that person emerged as the leader?

OB Online

1. Identify an example of a team that interests you, and find as much as you can about it on the Internet. An example might be your favorite sports team or performing arts company.
2. In what ways might the Internet reshape organizational thinking about teams?

Building Managerial Skills

Exercise Overview: Teams are becoming increasingly important in organizations. This exercise will allow you to practice your conceptual skills as they apply to work teams in organizations.

Exercise Background: A variety of highly effective groups exists outside the boundaries of typical business organizations. For example, each of the following represents a team:

1. A basketball team
2. An elite military squadron
3. A government policy group such as the presidential cabinet
4. A student planning committee

3. What type of training would have helped your team solve the problem better or faster?

Reference: From John W. Newstrom and Edward E. Scannell, *Games Trainers Play: Experiential Learning Exercises*, p. 259. Copyright © 1980 by McGraw-Hill Companies. Reproduced with permission of The McGraw-Hill Companies.

3. Which do you think would result in a more effective team: one that is first formed electronically and then begins to work together face to face, or vice versa? Why?
4. Use the Internet to find one example of each type of teams identified in the chapter.

Exercise Task

1. Identify an example of a real team, such as one just listed. Choose one (1) that is not part of a normal business and (2) that you can argue is highly effective.
2. Determine the reasons for the team's effectiveness.
3. Determine how a manager could learn from this particular team and use its success determinants in a business setting.

TEST PREPPER

ACE self-test

You have read the chapter and studied the key terms, and the exam is any day now. Think you're ready to ace it? Take this sample test to gauge your comprehension of chapter material. You can check your answers at the back of the book. Want more test questions? Visit the student website at http://college.hmco.com/business/students/ (select Griffin/Moorhead, Fundamentals of Organizational Behavior 1e) and take the ACE quizzes for more practice.

1. **T F**   The use of teams is a new way to manipulate workers into producing more.

2. **T F**   A team is a group with a common goal.

3. **T F**   Even in teams, an outside supervisor controls the daily activities of employees.

4. **T F**   A sound reason to adopt teams is that so many other companies are using teams.

5. **T F**   Today's employees benefit from teams because in general they like making decisions about their work.

6. **T F**   A quality circle focuses on creating new product designs to meet customer needs.

7. **T F**   The teams that do the daily work of the organization are called management teams.

8. **T F**   Teams are almost always appropriate for the work of the top-management group.

9. **T F**   Virtual teams may never actually meet together in the same room.

10. **T F**   A study to assess the feasibility of teams should be conducted before top managers make the decision whether to adopt a team-based organization.

11. **T F**   The best initial site for implementing teams is one in which existing managers deserve to be rewarded for good performance.

12. **T F**   Occasionally the switch to teams takes a long time, but in most organizations it can be successfully accomplished in six to nine months.

13. **T F**   A major purpose of initial training during the switch to teams is to make team members aware of top management's support.

14. **T F**   It is important for team members to recognize they will be unmanaged in their new roles.

15. **T F**   During the reality and unrest phase of team implementation, the best strategy for managers is to stay completely away from the new teams and let them manage themselves.

16. **T F**   When teams have become highly confident of their abilities, communicate less with other teams, and engage in high levels of interteam competition, the implementation of a team-based structure is a success.

17. **T F**   Managers can usually expect an initial decrease in performance when switching to a team-based organization.

18. What is the difference between a *group* and a *team*?
    a. A team places more emphasis on concerted action.
    b. A group's task is more interdependent.
    c. The members of a group are more committed.
    d. The members of a team have fewer personal differences.
    e. A group and a team are the same thing.

19. Which of the following best describes the nature of job categories with regard to teams?
    a. The work is divided into highly specialized jobs.
    b. Jobs in teams require minimal training.
    c. Team members have may different skills that fit into one or two broad job categories.
    d. Managers make a great effort to ensure each member does his or her own job.
    e. Members see little relationship between their effort and the end result.

20. In a gain-sharing system,
    a. team members are rewarded when baseline performance is exceeded.
    b. team members acquire a set of core skills plus additional special skills.
    c. supervisors receive the same rewards as team members.
    d. employees are placed in teams if the organization makes a profit.
    e. two or more teams share a reward that originally belonged to one of the teams.

21. The best reasons to start teams in any organizations include all of the following except
    a. enhanced performance.
    b. employee benefits.
    c. the fact that many other organizations are using teams.
    d. reduced costs.
    e. organizational enhancements.

22. "Postboomers," people born after the baby boom generation, benefit from teams because teams give them

248

a. a chance to participate in a traditional, manager-based system.

b. a clear position in the organizational hierarchy.

c. a chance to file more worker compensation claims.

d. fewer penalties for missing work and arriving late to work.

e. freedom to grow and gain respect by managing themselves.

23. What effect do teams have on the organizational hierarchy?

   a. Teams increase the height of the organizational hierarchy.

   b. Teams successfully add a measure of separation between employees and top management.

   c. Teams often disrupt the organizational hierarchy.

   d. Teams can eliminate redundant layers of bureaucracy.

   e. Teams make the organizational hierarchy more resistant to change.

24. Anna is part of a team that meets regularly to discuss and recommend solutions to workplace problems. Anna is part of a _____ team.

   a. management

   b. quality circle

   c. problem-solving

   d. work

   e. product development

25. Carl is part of a management team. His primary job is to

   a. do the actual daily work of the organization.

   b. attack specific problems in the workplace.

   c. discuss and recommend solutions to workplace problems.

   d. coach and counsel other teams to be self-managing.

   e. eliminate low performers from work teams.

26. A virtual team is

   a. a "dream team" top mangers seek to assemble.

   b. an ideal team that exists in theory, but not in real organizations.

   c. a team with members who place the team's interests before their own.

   d. a team charged with planning the future of the organization.

   e. a team that interacts electronically rather than in person.

27. What is the role of a steering committee in a company's change to a team-based organization?

   a. The steering committee explores the organization's readiness for the team environment.

   b. The steering committee acts as a "devil's advocate" and presents reasons not to change to a team-based organization.

c. The steering committee keeps an eye on competitors while the change to teams takes place.

d. The steering committee finds new positions for employees who oppose the change to a team-based organization.

e. The steering committee has a role in the change only once top managers decide to make the change to a team-based organization.

28. The best initial site for team implementation is one in which all of the following features exist except

   a. a desire to "fix" areas performing poorly.

   b. workers from multiple job categories.

   c. potential to improve performance.

   d. workers' acceptance of the idea of using teams.

   e. The best initial site for team implementation includes all of the above features.

29. Which of the following is not in the tentative plan for team implementation (i.e., the "draft plan")?

   a. Roles and responsibilities for all who will be affected

   b. Which work processes will be involved

   c. The master schedule for the next two to three years

   d. Plans for a feasibility study

   e. Recommendations for a process to select the first team members

30. Ryan first implemented teams in his organization about six months ago. As the initial start-up phase comes to an end, what can Ryan expect from team members?

   a. Heightened excitement about teams

   b. Frustration and confusion

   c. Complete abandonment of the implementation

   d. Up to a doubling in organizational performance

   e. A general change in all employee's attitudes to view teams more favorably

31. Why is sustained top-management support so critical in switching to a team-based organization?

   a. Teams are usually highly critical of top managers.

   b. Such support will increase employees' confidence in top managers.

   c. A positive attitude will make up for deficiencies in the implementation of teams.

   d. Performance usually goes down in the early phases of team implementation.

   e. Teams will improve performance, so managers need to be supportive initially to receive credit in the end.

PART THREE   VIDEO CASE

Denver Broncos: Teamwork in Action

To its fans, the Denver Broncos is a football team. But the Broncos, like other professional sports teams, is run like a business, with departments that focus on marketing, finance, accounting, and other activities, along with football operations. Much of the work the functional departments do involves teamwork.

Specifically, the Denver Broncos' marketing department is made up of employees who work together to meet their individual and departmental goals. These employees enjoy their jobs and the collaborative nature of their work environment. They also take pride in the fact that they work for one of the best teams in the NFL and in the unique nature of their jobs. One marketing employee remarks, "What's cool about our jobs, that someone who's not in the sports industry would envy, is that it's our job to come in here and talk about sports." Along with 'talking about sports' comes a healthy sense of what the organization's overriding mission is: to encourage everyone to view the Denver Broncos as a first-class organization.

To get the public to feel this way about the organization, the internal message of teamwork and working toward a common goal must be reinforced. Broncos' employees share a strong sense of camaraderie. One employee remarks, "We have such a good group—we get along so well—that's what makes it so fun." This type of atmosphere promotes collaboration. Employees often pitch in to help one another complete projects. This type of help is reciprocated, and the end result is a team whose members don't hesitate to call on one another when necessary.

With regard to decision making, the fact that the employees within the marketing department work well together doesn't mean they always agree. Sometimes when employees bounce ideas off one another informally or in meetings, heated debate ensues regarding the merits of a particular idea. One employee comments, "We debate back and forth and sometimes it gets pretty heated, but it's never a personal thing. We get all sides on the table, [so] everyone feels comfortable with the decision once the decision is made." To further illustrate the nature of these debates, one employee explains that even though people have their own agendas, at the end of the day what invariably

emerges from their discussions is that the course of action to be taken should involve what is best for the department as a whole. Recounting a time when his idea was not met with praise, one employee recalls, "I may have to bite the bullet this time, but that helps me out with cooperation in the future." He acknowledged that though he thought his idea was a good one, he needed to compromise and back down to maintain the integrity of the team mission.

Occasionally employees in the marketing department get to interact with coaches and players. Camaraderie and teamwork are not exclusive to separate groups within the organization. Specifically, on one occasion several marketing department employees accompanied the Broncos players on a trip to Boston to play the New England Patriots. On the return bus trip to the airport, the bus was involved in a minor traffic accident. The team was stalled in traffic for about 45 minutes. To kill time, the players started telling jokes and laughing among one another. One of the star players spotted an employee from the marketing department and asked who he was. The employee introduced himself as the "new guy" in the department. The player promptly stood up and announced to the entire bus that the "new guy" was going to start telling the jokes. After a few nervous seconds, the employee was let off the hook, but not before everyone on the bus got to see who he was and shared a good laugh.

Teamwork is vital to every facet of the Denver Bronco organization—from the marketing team, to the players on the field, to upper management. This facet of the organization helps the Broncos win not only on the field but in every department of their organization.

Case Questions

1. What type of group is the Denver Broncos' marketing department? On a scale of 1 to 5 (5 is highest), how effective does the group seem to be? Provide evidence from the case to support your conclusion.

2. What type of group norms is present in the Denver Broncos' marketing department? Describe

how these norms enhance or detract from the group's effectiveness..

3. Would you characterize the Denver Broncos' marketing department as a cohesive group? If so, how does the group avoid the negative potential aspects of group cohesiveness, such as groupthink?

4. Do you consider the Denver Broncos' marketing department to be a group or a team? Explain your answer.

References: Denver Broncos website, www.denverbroncos.com on June 25, 2004; M. Shanahan, *Think Like a Champion: Building Success One Victory at a Time* (New York: HarperBusiness, 2000).

PART FOUR

Leadership and Decision-Making Processes in Organizations

CHAPTER 10

Leadership Models and Concepts

MANAGEMENT PREVIEW

The mystique of leadership makes it one of the most widely debated, studied, and sought-after commodities of organizational life. Managers talk about the characteristics that make an effective leader, and organizational scientists have extensively studied leadership and myriad related phenomena. We begin this chapter, the first of two devoted to leadership, with a discussion of the meaning of leadership, including its definition and the distinctions between leadership and management. Then we turn to historical views of leadership, focusing on the trait and behavioral approaches. Next, we examine three contemporary leadership theories that have formed the basis for most leadership research: the LPC theory developed by Fiedler, the path-goal theory, and Vroom's decision tree approach to leadership. Finally, we look at two other popular models of leadership. In the next chapter we explore other elements of leadership, focusing more specifically on influence processes in organizations.

After you have studied this chapter, you should be able to:

- ☐ *Characterize the nature of leadership.*
- ☐ *Trace the early approaches to leadership.*
- ☐ *Describe the LPC theory of leadership.*
- ☐ *Discuss the path-goal theory of leadership.*
- ☐ *Describe Vroom's decision tree approach to leadership.*
- ☐ *Discuss two other contemporary approaches to leadership.*

First, we examine the odyssey of one leader and his amazing transformation.

Andrall (Andy) Pearson, founding chairperson of YUM! Brands, a Pepsi spinoff that owns Pizza Hut, Taco Bell, and KFC (Kentucky Fried Chicken), first ruled his businesses through fear and punishment, but eventually learned to govern with respect—and even love—for his workers. Pearson's evolution from feared dictator to beloved guru was quite a journey.

A snapshot of the "old" Andy: A graduate of USC and armed with a Harvard MBA, Pearson sums up the first fifty years of his career as follows: "I proved that I was smart by finding fault with other people's ideas." He began at the strategic consulting firm McKinsey & Company, rising to become senior director in charge of the firm's marketing practice. During his fourteen-year stint as president and COO of PepsiCo, he was known for being abrasive, numbers oriented, and hard to please. His favorite phrase was "So what?" *Fortune* named him one of the top ten toughest bosses in 1980, in part because he often drove employees to tears or to quitting if they failed to meet his expectations. In fact, he routinely helped people out the door: His policy was to fire the lowest-performing 10 to 20 percent of all employees each year.

As a tenured professor at the Harvard Business School, Pearson contributed articles to the prestigious *Harvard Business Review* with titles such as "Tough-Minded Ways to Get Innovative." He was invited to join the PepsiCo spinoff (originally named Tricon) by CEO David Novak, who saw that Pearson's no-nonsense style would complement his own people-oriented approach. When Pearson first came to Tricon, "he was brutal," according to Aylwin Lewis, Tricon's COO. "One time he told us, 'A room full of monkeys could do better than this!'"

Now a picture of the "new Andy": Employees still weep, but this time it's with gratitude for praise from Pearson. Managers who are mentored by Pearson tell him the experience is life changing. Pearson says, "I get letters that would just bring tears to your eyes." Pearson is greeted with loud cheers when he tells a crowd, "My experience at Tricon represents the capstone of my career." At the beginning, Novak told Pearson, "We can learn from each other," and when Pearson arrived at headquarters, hundreds of employees were cheering and a band was playing. "All the time I was at Pepsi, nothing remotely like this had ever happened. It was overwhelming," says Pearson. "I knew something was going on that was fundamentally very powerful. If we could learn how to harness that spirit with something systematic, then we would have something unique."

Pearson was first softened and then transformed. When he says, "If I could only unleash the power of everybody in the organization, instead of just a few people, ... we'd be a much better company," he seems to truly care about employees. His thinking about leadership has matured as well: "Great leaders find a balance between getting results and how they get them. A lot of people make the mistake of thinking that getting results is all there is to a job ... Your real job is to get results and to do it in a way that makes your organization a great place to work."

"Great leaders find a balance between getting results and how they get them."
—*Andy Pearson, founding chairperson, YUM! Brands*

References: "Our Vision," YUM! website www.yum.com on May 24, 2004; "America's Most Admired Companies: 2002 All-Stars: Food Service," *Fortune*, March 4, 2002; "Tricon's Fast-Food Smorgasbord," *BusinessWeek*, February 11, 2002; Brian O'Keefe, "The New Future: Global Brands," *Fortune*, November 26, 2001; David Dorsey, "Andy Pearson Finds Love," *Fast Company*, August 2001, pp. 78–86 (quotation, p. 84); *Hoover's Handbook of American Business 2004* (Austin: Hoover's Business Press, 2004), pp. 898–899.

Andy Pearson represents two extremes of leadership: the harsh, brutal autocrat and the caring, considerate, supportive leader. As we will see in this chapter, each approach is necessary in certain situations. In addition, some leaders appear to be capable of using either approach, whereas other leaders are unable to change their behavior. In some organizational settings, leaders make the difference between enormous success and overwhelming failure; in others, leaders appear to have no significant effect on the organization. Some leaders are effective in one organization but not in others, and some succeed no matter where they are. Despite hundreds of studies on leadership, researchers have found no simple way to account for these inconsistencies. Why, then, should we study leadership? First, leadership has great practical importance for organizations. Second, researchers have isolated and verified some key variables that influence leadership effectiveness.[1]

The Nature Of Leadership

Because *leadership* is a term often used in everyday conversation, you may assume it has a common accepted meaning. In fact, the opposite is true: Like several other key organizational behavior terms, such as *personality* and *motivation*, *leadership* is used in a variety of ways. Thus, we first clarify its meaning as used in this book.

The Meaning of Leadership

Leadership is both a process and a property. As a process, leadership involves the use of noncoercive influence. As a property, leadership is the set of characteristics attributed to someone who is perceived to use influence successfully.

We define **leadership** in terms of both process and property.[2] As a process, leadership is the use of noncoercive influence to direct and coordinate the activities of group members to meet a goal. As a property, leadership is the set of characteristics attributed to those who are perceived to use such influence successfully.[3] From an organizational viewpoint, leadership is vital because it has such a powerful influence on individual and group behavior.[4] Moreover, because the goal toward which the group directs its efforts is often the desired goal of the leader, it may or may not mesh with organizational goals.

Leadership involves neither force nor coercion. A manager who relies solely on force and formal authority to direct the behavior of subordinates is not exercising leadership. Thus, as discussed more fully in the next section, a manager or supervisor may or may not also be a leader. Furthermore, a leader may actually possess the characteristics attributed to him or her or merely be perceived as possessing them.

Leadership Versus Management

From these definitions, it should be clear that leadership and management are related but are not the same. A person can be a manager, a leader, both, or neither.[5] Table 10.1 summarizes some of the basic distinctions between management and leadership. On the left side of the table are four elements that differentiate leadership from management. The two columns show how each element differs when considered from a management and a leadership point of view. For example, when executing plans, managers focus on monitoring results, comparing them with goals, and correcting deviations. In contrast, leaders focus on energizing people to overcome bureaucratic hurdles to help reach goals. Thus, when Andy Pearson monitors the performance of his YUM! employees, he is playing the role of manager. When he inspires them to work harder at achieving their goals, he is playing the role of leader.

To further underscore the differences, consider the various roles managers and leaders might assme in a hospital setting. The chief of staff of a large hospital is clearly a manager by virtue of the position itself. At the same time, this individual may not be respected or trusted by others and may have to rely solely on the authority vested in the position to get people to do things. However, an emergency room nurse with no formal authority may be fully capable of taking charge of a chaotic situation and directing others in how to deal with specific patient problems. Other emergency room staff respond because they trust the nurse's judgment and have confidence in his decision-making skills. The head of pediatrics, supervising a staff of twenty other doctors, nurses, and attendants, may also enjoy the staff's complete respect, confidence, and trust. They readily take her advice and follow directives without question, and often go far beyond what is necessary to help carry out the unit's mission. Thus, being a manager does not ensure that a person is also a leader; any given manager may or may not also be a leader.

Activity	Management	Leadership
Creating an Agenda	**Planning and budgeting.** Establishing detailed steps and timetables for achieving needed results; allocating the resources necessary to make those needed results happen	**Establishing direction.** Developing a vision of the future, often the distant future, and strategies for producing the changes needed to achieve that vision
Developing a Human Network for Achieving the Agenda	**Organizing and staffing.** Establishing some structure for accomplishing plan requirements, staffing that structure with individuals, delegating responsibility and authority for carrying out the plan, providing policies and procedures to help guide people, and creating methods or systems to monitor implementation	**Aligning people.** Communicating the direction by words and deeds to all those whose cooperation may be needed to influence the creation of teams and coalitions that understand the vision and strategies and accept their validity
Executing Plans	**Controlling and problem solving.** Monitoring results vs. plan in some detail, identifying deviations, and then planning and organizing to solve these problems	**Motivating and inspiring.** Energizing people to overcome major political, bureaucratic, and resource barriers to change by satisfying very basic, but often unfulfilled, human needs
Outcomes	Produces a degree of predictability and order and has the potential to consistently produce major results expected by various stakeholders (e.g., for customers, always being on time; for stockholders, being on budget)	Produces change, often to a dramatic degree, and has the potential to produce extremely useful change (e.g., new products that customers want, new approaches to labor relations that help make a firm more competitive)

Reference: Reprinted with the permission of the Free Press, a Division of Simon & Schuster Adult Publishing Group, from *A Force for Change: How Leadership Differs from Management*, by John P. Kotter, 1990. All rights reserved. Copyright © 1990 by John P. Kotter, Inc.

TABLE 10.1

Distinctions Between Management and Leadership

Similarly, a leadership position can also be formal, as when someone appointed to head a group has leadership qualities, or informal, as when a leader emerges from the ranks of the group according to a consensus of the members. The chief of staff described earlier is a manager but not a leader, the emergency room nurse is a leader but not a manager, and the head of pediatrics is both.

Organizations need both management and leadership to be effective. For example, leadership is necessary to create and direct change and to help the organization get through tough times.[6] Management is necessary to achieve coordination and systematic results and to handle administrative activities during times of stability and predictability. Management in conjunction with leadership can help achieve planned orderly change, and leadership in conjunction with management can keep the organization properly aligned with its environment. In addition, managers and leaders play a major role in establishing the moral climate of the organization and determining the role of ethics in its culture.[7]

Early Approaches to Leadership

LEARNING OBJECTIVE

Trace the early approaches to leadership.

Although leaders and leadership have profoundly influenced the course of human events, careful scientific study of them began only about a century ago. Early studies focused on the traits, or personal characteristics, of leaders.[8] Later research shifted to examine actual leader behaviors.

Trait Approaches to Leadership

The **trait approach** to leadership attempted to identify stable and enduring character traits that differentiated effective leaders from nonleaders.

Lincoln, Napoleon, Joan of Arc, Hitler, and Gandhi are names that most of us know quite well. Early researchers believed notable leaders such as these had some unique set of qualities or traits that distinguished them from their peers. Moreover, these traits were presumed to be relatively stable and enduring. Following this **trait approach,** these researchers focused on identifying leadership traits, developing methods for measuring them, and using the methods to select leaders.

Hundreds of studies guided by this research agenda were conducted during the first several decades of the twentieth century. The earliest writers believed important leadership traits include intelligence, dominance, self-confidence, energy, activity, and task-relevant knowledge. The results of subsequent studies gave rise to a long list of additional traits. Unfortunately, the list quickly became so long that it lost any semblance of practical value. In addition, the results of many studies were inconsistent.

For example, one early argument was that effective leaders such as Lincoln tended to be taller than ineffective leaders. Critics were quick to point out that Hitler and Napoleon, both effective leaders in their own way, were not tall. Some writers have even tried to relate leadership to such traits as body shape, astrological sign, or handwriting patterns. The trait approach also had a significant theoretical problem in that it could neither specify nor prove how presumed leadership traits are connected to leadership per se. For these and other reasons, the trait approach was all but abandoned several decades ago.

In recent years, however, the trait approach has received renewed interest. For example, some researchers have sought to reintroduce a limited set of traits into the leadership literature. These traits include drive, motivation, honesty and integrity, self-confidence, cognitive ability, knowledge of the business, and charisma (discussed in Chapter 11).[9] Some people even believe biological factors may play a role in leadership. Although it is too early to know whether these traits have validity from a leadership perspective, it does appear that a serious, scientific assessment of appropriate traits may further our understanding of the leadership phenomenon.

Similarly, other work has also started examining the role of gender and other diversity factors in leadership. For example, do women and men tend to lead differently? Some early research suggests that there are indeed fundamental differences in leadership as practiced by women and men.[10] Given that most leadership theories and research studies have focused on male leaders, developing a better understanding of how females lead is clearly an important next step. Similarly, are there differences in the leadership styles exhibited by individuals of different ethnicity, or between younger and older leaders? Again, few answers exist for these questions, but researchers are beginning to address them.

The role of national culture may also be important. For instance, there may be important leadership differences in different cultures.[11] U.S. business leaders often talk about growth, profits, strategy, and competition. But Japanese leaders are more prone to stress group cohesiveness and identity. And Kim Sang Phi, chair of South Korea's Samsung group, is fond of talking about management morality and etiquette.[12] The World View box explores how leadership at Samsung has emulated both Japanese and American styles to bring the company to the forefront of the electronics industry. Thus, as they have with gender, ethnicity, and age, researchers need to focus on cultural differences in terms of leadership traits, roles, and behaviors.

WORLD VIEW

New Leadership Styles Propel Samsung Ahead

For decades the Japanese firms Fujitsu, Hitachi, Matsushita, NEC, Sony, and Toshiba have dominated the international electronics industry, but recently they have been experiencing slower sales and lower profits at home. A former "copycat" of the Japanese firms, Korean-based Samsung Electronics, is taking over their position, rapidly becoming Korea's first multinational powerhouse. "Five years ago, we had to buy chips from Sony or Matsushita, so we were always behind," says Chin Dae Je, head of Samsung's digital media division. "Now, we can be number one. There's no doubt in my mind."

Samsung is following the same path to success that the Japanese employed after World War II: imitating market leaders and perfecting their processes. The Japanese adopted practices from American manufacturing; now they find themselves being emulated, and bettered, by companies from Pacific Rim rival nations Taiwan, Malaysia, Singapore, and Korea. Samsung's products already are the leaders in Russia and China, and the firm is now turning its attention to the largest market in the world: the United States. It is significant that Samsung CEO Yun John Yong speaks Japanese, having spent part of his career in Japan, and two of his three top executives were educated in the United States and are fluent in English.

How have Samsung managers led their company to the vanguard of the electronics industry? Heavy investments in R&D led to innovations that have propelled Samsung to rank fifth in the world in the number of patents held. The firm has adopted a Western-style

> *"We used to benchmark [foreign firms] for the phone business. Now, we have nobody to benchmark against."*—*Lee Sang Chul, CEO of KT*

corporate governance, with open books and non-Koreans on its board of directors. The most radical change, however, has occurred within the firm's culture, which has changed from a top-down, bureaucratic style to one that is aggressive, flexible, and results oriented. Yun believes in pay for performance and has even fired low-performing managers, both of which are highly unusual practices in Korea.

Samsung is not the only Korean firm following this strategy. Lee Sang Chul, CEO of KT, formerly Korea Telecom, says, "We used to benchmark BT (which is English), NTT (Japanese), and AT&T for the phone business. Now, we have nobody to benchmark against." As success follows success for Korean companies, will we soon see American companies "copycatting" them?

References: "Watch Out Japan, Korea Is Gaining," *BusinessWeek*, May 9, 2002; William J. Holstein, "Samsung's Golden Touch," *Fortune*, April 1, 2002, pp. 89–94; "South Korea: High-Speed Profits Ahead," *BusinessWeek*, March 18, 2002 (quotation); Anthony Paul, "The Pyongyang Paradox," *Fortune*, May 28, 2001.

Behavioral Approaches to Leadership

The **behavioral approach to leadership** tried to identify behaviors that differentiate effective leaders from nonleaders.

In the late 1940s, most researchers began to shift away from the trait approach and look at leadership as an observable process or activity. The goal of the so-called **behavioral approach** was to determine what behaviors are associated with effective leadership.[13] The researchers assumed the behaviors of effective leaders differ somehow from the behaviors of less effective leaders and the behaviors of effective leaders would be the same across all situations. The behavioral approach to the study of leadership included the Michigan studies and the Ohio State studies.

The **Michigan leadership studies** defined job-centered and employee-centered leadership as opposite ends of a single leadership dimension.

The Michigan Studies

The **Michigan leadership studies** were a program of research conducted at the University of Michigan.[14] The goal of this work was to determine the pattern of leadership behaviors that results in effective group performance. From interviews with supervisors and subordinates of high- and low-productivity groups

Leader behaviors have long played a fundamental role in various leadership models and theories. Moreover, certain behaviors are especially common in different approaches to leadership. One such behavior, variously termed *employee-centered behavior, consideration behavior,* or *concern for people,* obviously relates to how leaders treat their subordinates. But as Charlie Brown will no doubt learn from Lucy, the effectiveness of consideration behavior by the leader may substantially diminish when others have to ask for it!

PEANUTS Reprinted by permission of United Feature Syndicate, Inc.

Job-centered leader behavior involves paying close attention to the work of subordinates, explaining work procedures, and demonstrating a strong interest in performance.

Employee-centered leader behavior involves attempting to build effective work groups with high performance goals.

The **Ohio State leadership studies** defined leader consideration and initiating-structure behaviors as independent dimensions of leadership.

Consideration behavior involves being concerned with subordinates' feelings and respecting subordinates' ideas.

Initiating-structure behavior involves clearly defining the leader-subordinate roles so that subordinates know what is expected of them.

in several organizations, the researchers collected and analyzed descriptions of supervisory behavior to determine how effective supervisors differed from ineffective ones. Two basic forms of leader behavior were identified—job-centered and employee-centered—as shown in the top portion of Figure 10.1.

The leader who exhibits **job-centered leader behavior** pays close attention to the work of subordinates, explains work procedures, and is interested mainly in performance. The leader's primary concern is efficient completion of the task. The leader who engages in **employee-centered leader behavior** attempts to build effective work groups with high performance goals. The leader's main concern is with high performance, but that is to be achieved by paying attention to the human aspects of the group. These two styles of leader behavior were presumed to be at opposite ends of a single dimension. Thus, the Michigan researchers suggested that any given leader can exhibit either job-centered or employee-centered leader behavior, but not both at the same time. Moreover, they suggested that employee-centered leader behavior is more likely to result in effective group performance than is job-centered leader behavior.

The Ohio State Studies   The **Ohio State leadership studies** were conducted about the same time as the Michigan studies (in the late 1940s and early 1950s).[15] During this program of research, behavioral scientists at Ohio State University developed a questionnaire, which they administered in both military and industrial settings, to assess subordinates' perceptions of their leaders' behavior. The Ohio State studies identified several forms of leader behavior but tended to focus on the two most significant ones: consideration and initiating-structure.

When engaging in **consideration behavior,** the leader is concerned with the subordinates' feelings and respects their ideas. The leader-subordinate relationship is characterized by mutual trust, respect, and two-way communication. When using **initiating-structure behavior,** on the other hand, the leader clearly defines the leader-subordinate roles so that subordinates know what is expected of them. The leader also establishes channels of communication and determines the methods for accomplishing the group's task.

Unlike the employee-centered and job-centered leader behaviors, consideration and initiating structure were not thought to be on the same continuum.

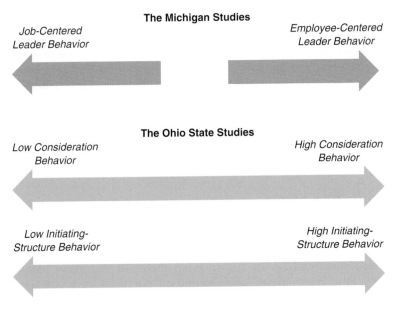

FIGURE 10.1

Early Behavioral Approaches to Leadership

Two of the first behavioral approaches to leadership were the Michigan and Ohio State studies. These results of the Michigan studies suggested there are two fundamental types of leader behavior, job centered and employee centered, that were presumed to be at opposite ends of a single continuum. The Ohio State studies also found two similar kinds of leadership behaviors, consideration and initiating-structure, but this research suggested these two types of behavior are actually independent dimensions.

Instead, as shown in the bottom portion of Figure 10.1, they were seen as independent dimensions of the leader's behavioral repertoire. As a result, a leader could exhibit high initiating-structure behavior and low consideration or low initiating-structure behavior and high consideration. A leader could also exhibit high or low levels of each behavior simultaneously. For example, a leader may clearly define subordinates' roles and expectations but exhibit little concern for their feelings. Alternatively, she or he may be concerned about subordinates' feelings but fail to define roles and expectations clearly. However, the leader may also demonstrate concern for performance expectations and employee welfare simultaneously.

The Ohio State researchers also investigated the stability of leader behaviors over time. They found that a given individual's leadership pattern appeared to change little as long as the situation remained fairly constant.[16] Another factor they looked at was the combinations of leader behaviors that were related to effectiveness. At first, they believed leaders who exhibit high levels of both behaviors would be most effective. An early study at International Harvester (now Navistar Corporation), however, found that employees of supervisors who ranked high on initiating-structure behavior were higher performers but also expressed lower levels of satisfaction. Conversely, employees of supervisors who ranked high on consideration had lower performance ratings but also had fewer absences from work.[17] Later research showed that these conclusions were misleading because the studies did not consider all the important variables. In other words, the situational context limits the extent to which consistent and uniform relationships exist between leader behaviors and subordinate responses. As a result, no simple explanations exist for what constitutes effective leader behavior because leader effectiveness varies from one situation to another.

The Michigan and Ohio State behavioral models attracted considerable attention from managers and behavioral scientists. Unfortunately, later research on each model revealed significant weaknesses. For example, the models were not always supported by research and were even found to be ineffective in some settings.[18] The behavioral approaches were valuable in that they identified several fundamental leader behaviors that are still used in most leadership theories today. Moreover, they moved leadership research away from the narrow trait theory. The Michigan and Ohio State studies were exploratory in nature and have given researchers several fundamental insights into basic leadership processes. However, in trying to precisely specify a set of leader behaviors effective in all situations, the studies overlooked the enormous complexities of individual behavior in organizational settings.

In the end, the studies' most basic shortcoming was that they failed to meet their primary goal: to identify universal leader-behavior and follower-response patterns and relationships. Managers and behavioral scientists thus realized that still different approaches were needed to accommodate the complexities of leadership. Consequently they began to focus on contingency theories to better explain leadership and its consequences. These theories assume that appropriate leader behavior varies across settings. Their focus is on better understanding how different situations call for different forms of leadership. As related at the beginning of this chapter, Andy Pearson at YUM! Brands clearly changed his behavior as a leader. We discuss the three major contingency theories next, beginning with the LPC theory.

The LPC Theory of Leadership

The **LPC theory of leadership** suggests that a leader's effectiveness depends on the situation.

The **LPC theory of leadership,** developed by Fred Fiedler, attempts to explain and reconcile both the leader's personality and the complexities of the situation. (This theory was originally called the "contingency theory of leadership." However, because this label has come to have generic connotations, new labels are being used to avoid confusion. *LPC* stands for "least-preferred coworker," a concept explained later in this section.) The LPC theory contends that a leader's effectiveness depends on the situation and, as a result, some leaders may be effective in one situation or organization but not in another. The theory also explains why this discrepancy may occur and identifies leader-situation matches that should result in effective performance.

The LPC theory suggests that the situation determines what constitutes effective leadership. These Native American elders have helped gain formal recognition for the Cowlitz tribe and have recruited more than 2,000 members. The leadership styles they used to accomplish this task were partially dictated by what they wanted to accomplish. Now the leadership style needed to lead the tribe in its formative stages may be different. Finally, when the tribe becomes mature and a fully functional entity, yet another style may be needed.

Task Versus Relationship Motivation

Fiedler and his associates maintain that leadership effectiveness depends on the match between the leader's personality and the situation. Fiedler devised special terms to describe a leader's basic personality traits in relation to leadership: *task motivation* versus *relationship motivation.* He also conceptualized the situational context in terms of its favorableness for the leader, ranging from highly favorable to highly unfavorable.

In some respects, the ideas of task and relationship motivation resemble the basic concepts identified in the behavioral approaches. Task motivation closely parallels job-centered and initiating-structure leader behavior, and relationship motivation is similar to employee-centered and consideration leader behavior. A major difference, however, is that Fiedler viewed task versus relationship motivation as being grounded in personality in a way that is basically constant for any given leader.

The **least-preferred coworker (LPC) scale** presumes to measure a leader's motivation.

The degree of task or relationship motivation in a given leader is measured by the **least-preferred coworker (LPC) scale.** The LPC instructions ask respondents (i.e., leaders) to think of all the individuals with whom they have worked and then select their least-preferred coworker. Respondents then describe this coworker by marking a series of sixteen scales anchored at each end by a positive or negative quality or attribute.[19] For example, three of the items Fiedler uses in the LPC are

Pleasant	8 7 6 5 4 3 2 1	Unpleasant
Inefficient	1 2 3 4 5 6 7 8	Efficient
Unfriendly	1 2 3 4 5 6 7 8	Friendly

The higher numbers on the scales are associated with a positive evaluation of the least-preferred coworker. (Note that the higher scale numbers are associated with the more favorable term and that some items reverse both the terms and the scale values. The latter feature forces the respondent to read the scales more carefully and provide more valid answers.) Respondents who describe their least-preferred coworker in relatively positive terms receive a high LPC score, whereas those who use relatively negative terms receive a low LPC score.

Fiedler assumed these descriptions actually say more about the leader than about the least-preferred coworker. He believed, for example, that everyone's least preferred coworker is likely to be equally "unpleasant" and that differences in descriptions actually reflect differences in personality traits among the leaders responding to the LPC scale. Fiedler contended that high-LPC leaders are basically more concerned with interpersonal relations and low-LPC leaders with task-relevant problems. Not surprisingly, controversy has always surrounded the LPC scale. Researchers have offered several interpretations of the LPC score, arguing that it may be an index of behavior, personality, or some other unknown factor. Indeed, the LPC measure and its interpretation have long been among the most debated aspects of this theory.

Situational Favorableness

Fiedler also identified three factors that determine the favorableness of the situation. In order of importance (from most to least important), these factors are leader-member relations, task structure, and leader position power.

Leader-member relations refers to the personal relationship between subordinates and their leader. It is based on the extent to which subordinates trust, respect, and have confidence in their leader, and vice versa. A high degree of mutual trust, respect, and confidence obviously indicates good leader-member relations, and a low degree indicates poor leader-member relations.

Task structure is the second most important determinant of situational favorableness. A structured task is routine, simple, easily understood, and unambiguous. The LPC theory presumes that structured tasks are more favorable because the leader need not be closely involved in defining activities and can devote time to other matters. On the other hand, an unstructured task is nonroutine, ambiguous, and complex. Fiedler argues that this task is more unfavorable because the leader must play a major role in guiding and directing subordinates' activities.

Finally, *leader position power* is the power inherent in the leader's role itself. If the leader has considerable power to assign work, reward and punish employees, and recommend them for promotion, position power is high and favorable. If the leader must have job assignments approved by someone else, does not control rewards and punishment, and has no voice in promotions, position power is low and unfavorable; that is, many decisions are beyond the leader's control.

Leader Motivation and Situational Favorableness   Fiedler and his associates conducted numerous studies examining the relationships among leader motivation, situational favorableness, and group performance. Table 10.2 summarizes the results of these studies.

To begin interpreting the results, let's first examine the situational favorableness dimensions shown in the table. The various combinations of these three dimensions result in eight different situations, as arrayed across the first three lines of the table. These situations, in turn, define a continuum ranging from very favorable to very unfavorable situations from the leader's perspective. Favorableness is noted in the fourth line of the table. For example, good relations, a structured task, and either high or low position power result in a very favorable situation for the leader; poor relations, an unstructured task, and either high or low position power create very unfavorable conditions for the leader.

The table also identifies the leadership approach intended to achieve high group performance in each of the eight situations. These linkages are shown in the bottom line of the table. A task-oriented leader is appropriate for very favorable as well as very unfavorable situations. For example, the LPC theory predicts that if leader-member relations are poor, the task is unstructured, and leader position power is low, a task-oriented leader will be effective. It also predicts that a task-oriented leader will be effective if leader-member relations are good, the task is structured, and leader position power is high. Finally, for situations of intermediate favorableness, the theory suggests that a person-oriented leader will be most likely to achieve high group performance.

Leader-Situation Match   What happens if a person-oriented leader faces a very favorable or very unfavorable situation, or a task-oriented leader faces a situation of intermediate favorableness? Fiedler considers these leader-situation combinations to be "mismatches." Recall that a basic premise of his theory is that leadership behavior is a personality trait. Thus, the mismatched leader cannot readily adapt to the situation and achieve effectiveness. Fiedler contends that when a leader's style and the situation do not match, the only available course of action is to change the situation through "job engineering."[20]

For example, Fiedler suggests that if a person-oriented leader ends up in a very unfavorable situation, she or he should attempt to remedy matters by spending

TABLE 10.2

The LPC Theory of Leadership

Leader-Member Relations	Good				Poor			
Task Structure	Structured		Unstructured		Structured		Unstructured	
Position Power	High	Low	High	Low	High	Low	High	Low
Situational Favorableness	Very favorable		Moderately favorable				Very unfavorable	
Recommended Leader Behavior	↓ Task-oriented behavior		↓ Person-oriented behavior				↓ Task-oriented behavior	

more time with subordinates to improve leader-member relations and laying down rules and procedures to provide more task structure. Fiedler and his associates have also developed a widely used training program for supervisors on how to assess situational favorableness and change the situation, if necessary, to achieve a better match.[21] Weyerhauser and Boeing are among the firms that have experimented with Fiedler's training program.

Evaluation and Implications

The validity of Fiedler's LPC theory has been heatedly debated because of the inconsistency of the research results. Apparent shortcomings of the theory are that the LPC measure lacks validity, research does not always support the theory, and Fiedler's assumptions about the inflexibility of leader behavior are unrealistic.[22] The theory itself, however, represents an important contribution because it returned the field to a study of the situation and explicitly considered the organizational context and its role in effective leadership.

The Path-Goal Theory of Leadership

LEARNING OBJECTIVE

Discuss the path-goal theory of leadership.

Another important contingency approach to leadership is the path-goal theory. Developed jointly by Martin Evans and Robert House, the path-goal theory focuses on the situation and leader behaviors rather than on fixed traits of the leader.[23] In contrast to the LPC theory, the path-goal theory suggests that leaders can readily adapt to different situations.

Basic Premises

The path-goal theory has its roots in the expectancy theory of motivation discussed in Chapter 4. Recall that expectancy theory says that a person's attitudes and behaviors can be predicted from the degree to which the person believes job performance will lead to various outcomes (expectancy) and the value of those outcomes (valences) to the individual. The **path-goal theory of leadership** argues that subordinates are motivated by their leader to the extent that the leader's behaviors influence their expectancies. In other words, the leader affects subordinates' performance by clarifying the behaviors (paths) that will lead to desired rewards (goals). Ideally, of course, getting a reward in an organization depends on effective performance. Path-goal theory also suggests that a leader may behave in different ways in different situations.

The **path-goal theory of leadership** suggests that effective leaders clarify the paths (behaviors) that will lead to desired rewards (goals).

Leader Behaviors   As Figure 10.2 shows, path-goal theory identifies four kinds of leader behavior: directive, supportive, participative, and achievement-oriented. With *directive leadership*, the leader lets subordinates know what is expected of them, gives specific guidance regarding how to accomplish tasks, schedules work to be done, and maintains definitive standards of performance for subordinates. A leader exhibiting *supportive leadership* is friendly and shows concern for subordinates' status, well-being, and needs. With *participative leadership*, the leader consults with subordinates about issues and takes their suggestions into account before making a decision. Finally, *achievement-oriented leadership* involves setting challenging goals, expecting subordinates to perform at their highest level, and showing strong confidence that subordinates will put forth effort and accomplish the goals. Unlike the LPC theory, path-goal theory assumes leaders can change their behavior and exhibit any or all of these leadership styles. The theory also predicts that

The path-goal theory of leadership encompasses four kinds of leader behavior. Andrea Jung, chair and CEO of Avon, uses each of these behaviors on a regular basis. For example, she occasionally uses directive behavior to set performance expectations and provide guidance. Jung demonstrates supportive behavior through her interest in those she works with. She frequently uses participative leadership by soliciting input from other executives in the firm. Finally, she uses achievement-oriented leadership by setting challenging goals and providing constant encouragement for everyone to work toward those goals.

the appropriate combination of leadership styles depends on situational factors.

Situational Factors   The path-goal theory proposes two types of situational factors that influence how leader behavior relates to subordinate satisfaction: the personal characteristics of subordinates and the characteristics of the environment (see Figure 10.2).

Two important personal characteristics of subordinates are locus of control and perceived ability. Locus of control, discussed in Chapter 3, refers to the extent to which individuals believe that what happens to them results from their own behavior or from external causes. Research indicates that individuals who attribute outcomes to their own behavior may be more satisfied with a participative leader (since they believe their own efforts can make a difference), whereas individuals who attribute outcomes to external causes may respond more favorably to a directive leader (since they think their own actions are of little consequence). Perceived ability pertains to how people view their own ability with respect to the task. Employees who rate their own ability relatively high are less likely to feel a need for directive leadership (since they think they know how to do the job), whereas those who perceive their own ability as relatively low may prefer directive leadership (since they think they need someone to show them how to do the job).

Important environmental characteristics are task structure, the formal authority system, and the primary work group. The path-goal theory proposes that leader behavior will motivate subordinates if it helps them cope with environmental uncertainty created by those characteristics. In some cases, however, certain forms of leadership will be redundant, decreasing subordinate satisfaction. For example, when task structure is high, directive leadership is less necessary and therefore less effective; similarly, if the work group gives the individual plenty of social support, a supportive leader will not be especially attractive. Thus, the extent to which leader behavior matches the people and environment in the situation is presumed to influence subordinates' motivation to perform.

As another example, consider the success of Barbara Samson, founder of Intermedia, a Florida telephone company. To get her idea from the drawing board into the business world, Samson had to use directive leadership to organize her employees. However, she also had to use supportive leadership to help them get through the tough times during the early days of start-up. When she met with investors, she had to demonstrate achievement-oriented leadership to convey her goals and strategies. As her business has grown, she has increasingly used participative leadership to spread decision-making authority throughout the firm.[24]

FIGURE 10.2

The Path-Goal Theory of Leadership

The path-goal theory of leadership specifies four kinds of leader behavior: directive, supportive, participative, and achievement oriented. Leaders are advised to vary their behaviors in response to such situational factors as personal characteristics of subordinates and environmental characteristics.

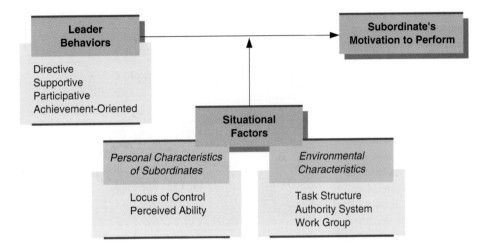

Leader Behaviors: Directive, Supportive, Participative, Achievement-Oriented → Subordinate's Motivation to Perform

Situational Factors

Personal Characteristics of Subordinates: Locus of Control, Perceived Ability

Environmental Characteristics: Task Structure, Authority System, Work Group

Evaluation and Implications

The path-goal theory was designed to provide a general framework for understanding how leader behavior and situational factors influence subordinate attitudes and behaviors. The intention of path-goal theorists, however, was to stimulate research on the theory's major propositions, not to offer definitive answers. Researchers hoped a more fully developed, formal theory of leadership would emerge from continued study. Further work actually has supported the theory's major predictions, but it has not validated the entire model. Moreover, many of the theory's predictions remain overly general and have not been fully refined and tested.

Vroom's Decision Tree Approach to Leadership

┌─ *LEARNING OBJECTIVE* ─┐

Describe Vroom's decision tree approach to leadership.
└────────────────────────┘

Vroom's decision tree approach to leadership attempts to prescribe how much participation to allow subordinates in making decisions.

The third major contemporary approach to leadership is **Vroom's decision tree approach.** The earliest version of this model was proposed by Victor Vroom and Philip Yetton and later revised and expanded by Vroom and Arthur Jago.[25] Most recently, Vroom has developed yet another refinement of the original model.[26] Like the path-goal theory, this approach attempts to prescribe a leadership style appropriate to a given situation. It also assumes the same leader may display different leadership styles. Vroom's approach, however, concerns only a single aspect of leader behavior: subordinate participation in decision making.

Basic Premises

Vroom's decision tree approach assumes the degree to which subordinates should be encouraged to participate in decision making depends on the characteristics of the situation. In other words, no one decision-making process is best for all situations. After evaluating a variety of problem attributes (characteristics of the problem or decision), the leader determines an appropriate decision style that specifies the amount of subordinate participation.

Vroom's current formulation suggests that managers should use one of two different decision trees.[27] To do so, the manager first assesses the situation in terms of several factors. This assessment involves determining whether the given factor is "high" or "low" for the decision to be made. For instance, the first factor is

Victor Vroom's decision tree approach to leadership suggests that leaders should vary the degree of participation they provide to subordinates in making decisions. In the wake of one financial scandal after another, some top managers have begun to systematically increase communication and participation throughout the ranks of their organizations. Steve Odland (standing), CEO of AutoZone, now insists that all top managers fully participate in discussions and decisions regarding the firm's finances. Indeed, he requires that each top manager certify the accuracy of his or her unit's financial performance before submitting the results to him.

decision significance. If the decision is extremely important and may have a major impact on the organization (e.g., choosing a location for a new plant), its significance is high. But if the decision is routine and its consequences not very important (e.g., selecting a logo for the firm's softball team uniforms), its significance is low. This assessment guides the manager through the paths of the decision tree to a recommended course of action. One decision tree is to be used when the manager is interested primarily in making the decision on the most timely basis possible; the other is to be used when time is less critical and the manager is interested mainly in helping subordinates improve and develop their own decision-making skills.

The two decision trees appear in Figures 10.3 and 10.4. The problem attributes (situational factors) are arranged along the top of the decision tree. To use the model, the decision maker starts at the left side of the diagram and assesses the first problem attribute (decision significance). The answer determines the path to the second node on the decision tree, where the next attribute (importance of commitment) is assessed. This process continues until a terminal node is reached. In this way, the manager identifies an effective decision-making style for the situation.

The various decision styles reflected at the ends of the tree branches represent different levels of subordinate participation that the manager should attempt to adopt in a given situation. The five styles are defined as follows:

- *Decide:* The manager makes the decision alone and then announces or "sells" it to the group.
- *Delegate:* The manager allows the group to define for itself the exact nature and parameters of the problem and then develop a solution.
- *Consult (individually):* The manager presents the program to group members individually, obtains their suggestions, and then makes the decision.
- *Consult (group):* The manager presents the problem to group members at a meeting, gets their suggestions, and then makes the decision.
- *Facilitate:* The manager presents the problem to the group at a meeting, defines the problem and its boundaries, and then facilitates group member discussion as members make the decision.

Vroom's decision tree approach represents a very focused but quite complex perspective on leadership. To compensate for this difficulty, Vroom has developed elaborate expert system software to help managers assess a situation accurately and quickly and then make an appropriate decision regarding employee participation.

Problem Statement	Decision Significance	Importance of Commitment	Leader Expertise	Likelihood of Commitment	Group Support	Group Expertise	Team Competence	
P R O B L E M S T A T E M E N T	H	H	H	H	-	-	-	Decide
				L	H	H	H	Delegate
							L	Consult (Group)
						L	-	Consult (Group)
					L	-	-	Consult (Group)
			L	H	H	H	H	Facilitate
							L	Consult (Individually)
						L	-	Consult (Individually)
					L	-	-	Consult (Individually)
				L	H	H	H	Facilitate
							L	Consult (Group)
						L	-	Consult (Group)
					L	-	-	Consult (Group)
		L	H	-	-	-	-	Decide
			L	-	H	H	H	Facilitate
							L	Consult (Individually)
						L	-	Consult (Individually)
					L	-	-	Consult (Individually)
	L	H	-	H	-	-	-	Decide
				L	-	-	H	Delegate
							L	Facilitate
		L	-	-	-	-	-	Decide

FIGURE 10.3

Vroom's Time-Driven Decision Tree

This matrix is recommended for situations in which time is of the highest importance in making a decision. The matrix operates like a funnel. You start at the left with a specific decision problem in mind. The column headings denote situational factors that may or may not be present in that problem. You progress by selecting High or Low (H or L) for each relevant situational factor. Proceed down from the funnel, judging only those situational factors for which a judgment is called for, until you reach the recommended process.

Reference: "Vroom's Time-Driven Tree" from *A Model of Leadership Style* by Victor H. Vroom. Copyright © 1998. Reprinted by permission of Victor H. Vroom.

Decision Significance	Importance of Commitment	Leader Expertise	Likelihood of Commitment	Group Support	Group Expertise	Team Competence	
H	H	-	H	H	H	H	Decide
						L	Facilitate
					L	-	Consult (Group)
				L	-	-	Consult (Group)
			L	H	H	H	Delegate
						L	Facilitate
					L	-	Facilitate
				L	-	-	Consult (Group)
	L	-	-	H	H	H	Delegate
						L	Facilitate
					L	-	Consult (Group)
				L	-	-	Consult (Group)
L	H	-	H	-	-	-	Decide
			L	-	-	-	Delegate
	L	-	-	-	-	-	Decide

FIGURE 10.4

Vroom's Development-Driven Decision Tree

This matrix is to be used when the leader is more interested in developing employees than in making the decision as quickly as possible. Just as with the time-driven tree shown in Figure 10.3, the leader assesses up to seven situational factors. These factors, in turn, funnel the leader to a recommended process for making the decision.

Reference: "Vroom's Development-Driven Decision Tree" from *A Model of Leadership Style* by Victor H. Vroom. Copyright © 1998. Reprinted by permission of Victor H. Vroom.

Many firms, including Halliburton Company, Litton Industries, and Borland International, have provided their managers with training in using the various versions of this model.

Evaluation and Implications

Because Vroom's current approach is relatively new, it has not been fully scientifically tested. The original model and its subsequent refinement, however, attracted a great deal of attention and were generally supported by research.[28] For example, there is some support for the idea that individuals who make decisions consistent with the model's predictions are more effective than those who make decisions inconsistent with it. The model therefore appears to be a tool managers can apply with some confidence in deciding how much subordinates should participate in the decision-making process.

Other Contemporary Approaches to Leadership

LEARNING OBJECTIVE

Discuss two other contemporary approaches to leadership.

Because leadership is such an important area, managers and researchers continue to study it. As a result, new ideas, theories, and perspectives are continuously evolving. Two of the better-known theories are the LMX model and the Hersey and Blanchard theory.

The Leader-Member Exchange Model

The **leader-member exchange (LMX) model of leadership** stresses the fact that leaders develop unique working relationships with each of their subordinates.

The **leader-member exchange (LMX) model** of leadership, conceived by George Graen and Fred Dansereau, stresses the importance of variable relationships between supervisors and each of their subordinates.[29] Each superior-subordinate pair is referred to as a *vertical dyad*. The model differs from earlier approaches in that it focuses on the differential relationship leaders often establish with different subordinates. Figure 10.5 shows the basic concepts of the leader-member exchange theory.

The model suggests that supervisors establish a special relationship with a small number of trusted subordinates referred to as the *in-group*. The in-group usually receives special duties requiring responsibility and autonomy; members may also receive special privileges. Subordinates who are not part of this group are called the *out-group*; they receive less of the supervisor's time and attention. Note in the figure that the leader has a dyadic, or one-to-one, relationship with each of the five subordinates.

Early in his or her interaction with a given subordinate, the supervisor initiates either an in-group or out-group relationship. It is not clear how a leader selects members of the in-group, but the decision may be based on personal compatibility and subordinates' competence. Research has confirmed the existence of in-groups and out-groups. In addition, studies generally have found that in-group members have a higher level of performance and satisfaction than out-group members.[30]

The Hersey and Blanchard Model

Another popular perspective among practicing managers is the Hersey and Blanchard model. Like some other leadership models not discussed here, this model

FIGURE 10.5

The Leader-Member Exchange (LMX) Model

The LMX model suggests that leaders form unique, independent relationships with each of their subordinates. As illustrated here, a key factor in this relationship is whether the individual subordinate is in the leader's out-group or in-group.

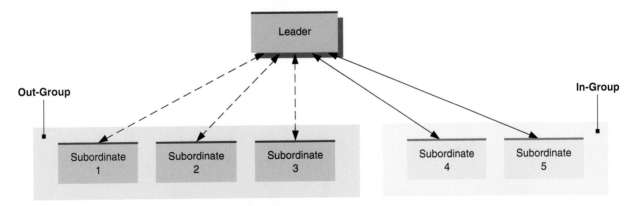

The **Hersey and Blanchard model** identifies different combinations of leadership presumed to work best with different levels of organizational maturity on the part of subordinates.

was developed as a consulting tool. The **Hersey and Blanchard model** is based on the notion that appropriate leader behavior depends on the readiness of the leader's subordinates.[31] In this instance, *readiness* refers to the subordinates' degree of motivation, competence, experience, and interest in accepting responsibility. Figure 10.6 shows the basic model.

The figure suggests that as subordinates' readiness increases, the leader's basic style should also change. When subordinate readiness is low, for example, the leader should rely on a "telling" style by providing direction and defining roles. When low to moderate readiness exists, the leader should use a "selling" style by offering direction and role definition accompanied by explanation and information. In a case of moderate-to-high subordinate readiness, the leader should use a "participating" style, allowing subordinates to share in decision making. Finally, when subordinate readiness is high, the leader is advised to use a "delegating" style by allowing them to work independently with little or no overseeing.

FIGURE 10.6

The Hersey and Blanchard Theory of Leadership

The Hershey and Blanchard theory suggests that leader behaviors should vary in response to the readiness of subordinates. This figure shows the nature of this variation. The curved line suggests that relationship leader behavior should start low, gradually increase, but then decrease again as subordinate readiness increases. Task behavior, however, shown by the straight line, should start high when subordinates lack readiness and then continuously diminish as they gain readiness.

Reference: The Situational Leadership Model is the registered trademark of the Center for Leadership Studies, Escondido, CA. Excerpt from P. Hersey and K. Blanchard, *Management of Organizational Behavior: Utilizing Human Resources,* 3rd ed. (Englewood Cliffs, NJ: Prentice-Hall, 1977), p. 165.

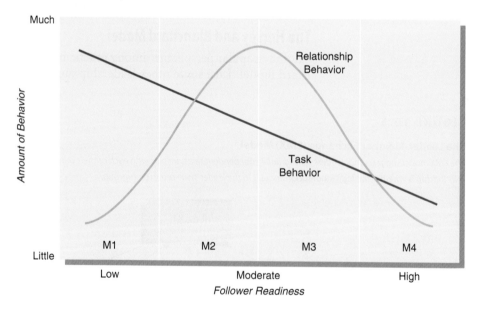

Synopsis

Leadership is both a process and a property. Leadership as a process is the use of noncoercive influence to direct and coordinate the activities of group members to meet goals. As a property, leadership is the set of characteristics attributed to those perceived to use such influence successfully. Leadership and management are related but distinct phenomena.

Early leadership research attempted primarily to identify important traits and behaviors of leaders. The Michigan and Ohio State studies each identified two kinds of leader behavior, one focusing on job factors and the other on people factors. The Michigan studies viewed these behaviors as points on a single continuum, whereas the Ohio State studies suggested they were separate dimensions.

Newer contingency theories of leadership attempt to identify appropriate leadership styles on the basis of the situation. Fiedler's LPC theory states that leadership effectiveness depends on a match between the leader's style (viewed as a trait of the leader) and the favorableness of the situation. Situation favorableness, in turn, is determined by task structure, leader-member relations, and leader position power. Leader behavior is presumed to reflect a constant personality trait and therefore cannot be easily changed.

The path-goal theory focuses on appropriate leader behavior for various situations. The path-goal theory suggests that directive, supportive, participative, or achievement-oriented leader behavior may be appropriate depending on the personal characteristics of subordinates and the characteristics of the environment. Unlike the LPC theory, this view presumes leaders can alter their behavior to best fit the situation.

Vroom's decision tree approach suggests appropriate decision-making styles based on situational characteristics. This approach focuses on deciding how much subordinates should participate in the decision-making process. Managers assess situational attributes and follow a series of paths through a decision tree that subsequently prescribes how they should make a particular decision.

Two recent perspectives not rooted in traditional leadership theories are the leader-member exchange (LMX) theory and the Hersey and Blanchard model. The LMX model focuses on specific relationships between a leader and individual subordinates. The Hersey and Blanchard model acknowledges that leader behavior toward a particular group needs to change as a function of subordinates' readiness.

Discussion Questions

1. How would you define *leadership*? Compare and contrast your definition with the one given in this chapter.

2. Cite examples of managers who are not leaders and leaders who are not managers. What makes them one and not the other? Cite examples of both formal and informal leaders.

3. What traits are presumed to characterize successful leaders? Do you think the trait approach has validity? Why or why not?

4. What other forms of leader behavior besides those cited in the chapter can you identify?

5. Critique Fiedler's LPC theory. Are other elements of the situation important? Do you think Fiedler's assertion about the inflexibility of leader behavior makes sense? Why or why not?

6. Do you agree or disagree with Fiedler's assertion that leadership motivation is basically a personality trait? Why?

7. Compare and contrast the LPC and path-goal theories of leadership. What are the strengths and weaknesses of each?

8. Of the three major leadership theories—the LPC theory, the path-goal theory, and Vroom's decision tree approach—which is the most comprehensive? Which is the narrowest? Which has the most practical value?

9. How realistic do you think it is for managers to attempt to use Vroom's decision tree approach as prescribed? Explain.

10. Which of the two contemporary theories of leadership—the LMX theory and the Hersey and Blanchard model—do you believe holds more promise? Why? Could either of these perspectives be integrated with any of the three major theories of leadership? If so, how?

Organizational Behavior Case for Discussion

How Do You Manage Magic?

According to science fiction writer Arthur C. Clarke, "Any significantly advanced technology is indistinguishable from magic." This statement aptly describes much of biotechnology. Manufacturing biotech pharmaceuticals is a complex, technical, and expensive process, with millions of pages of data, daily costs of $1 million, and an 80 percent failure rate. The entire process of getting a new product to market takes ten to twelve years, and numerous hurdles must be cleared along the way. The challenge for biotech managers, then, is how to manage complex processes as well as how to lead workers who are more knowledgeable and highly educated than their bosses.

The process begins with a test tube of cells being injected with a human gene. The gene creates a naturally occurring compound in the human body (interferon is one), but these cells have now been altered to make only that compound. The cells then reproduce and are moved into increasingly larger containers until the volume of the fluid is about 2,000 liters. The fluid is purified, yielding 2 liters of concentrated drug. All told, the procedure takes about five weeks, and if the batch has problems, they won't be discovered until the end. In spite of facilities more sterile than hospital operating rooms, bad batches can occur. The compounds are hundreds of times more complex than traditional drugs. For example, aspirin has a molecular weight (a crude measure of a compound's complexity) of about 180; biotech's average is 25,000.

The scientists who develop and manipulate this complicated process have M.D.s or Ph.D.s in subjects such as analytical chemistry, microbiology, or pharmacology. Biogen CEO James C. Mullen has a B.S. in chemical engineering and an M.B.A., has held engineering positions at pharmaceutical firms since 1980, and is an intellectual "heavyweight"; yet it's impossible for anyone to fully understand the firm's variety of specialized disciplines. Michael Gilman, Biogen's senior vice president of research, himself a research scientist, says, "I am completely ignorant about three-quarters of the stuff that goes on. And my colleagues on the senior management team? They are 98 percent ignorant."

Mullen is the right kind of person for the top job: open to debate, eager for input, yet decisive and tough-minded. He relies on objective data, asking, "Is this a fact, an opinion, or a guess?" "We're often making decisions in uncertainty," Mullen asserts. "If the organization is running correctly, the only decisions that get to my desk are the ones with high uncertainty." One development team couldn't answer Mullen's questions. Mullen says, "I was asking questions more from a commercial or a customer's point of view. I kept meeting resistance. Really, it was an attitude problem." Finally, in exasperation, Mullen demanded to see the raw data and analyzed it himself, finding trends the experts hadn't spotted. Mullen uses that experience as a lesson in how *not* to lead. He explains, "That group had the wrong values for this company. They no longer work at Biogen."

Another challenge is to focus on the end result while not losing track of the details. One team proposed a 180-day timetable for completing its FDA application; Mullen insisted it could be done in 90 days. According to Mullen, "Sometimes, you get more creativity when you're in a box than when you can do anything. In really difficult situations, sometimes you get the most interesting thinking." After Mullen pointed out to the scientists that an extra ninety days of drug sales might be worth $125 million, they completed the application in ninety-eight days. The ten-year development process is also a target. Mullen says, "People don't relate to ten-year product cycles. Half the people here haven't even worked for ten years. You have to break the time frames down so [that] a person can have an impact and see the impact."

Mullen wants more emphasis on the bottom line without sacrificing innovation. The CEO focuses intently on one thing at a time; he doesn't believe in multitasking. When teams are undisciplined, he ends the meeting by stating, "You aren't prepared. Call me when you're ready." Mullen reduced the number of people reporting to him from fifteen to nine to increase accountability. "The campfire culture doesn't work here anymore, with people sitting around telling each other what's going on," maintains Mullen, who is changing Biogen's culture. "We need to demand results."

Biogen's website's statement of corporate values claims, "Biogen's success is based on its people. Everyone here is a leader. The core of leadership is integrity and courage . . . These shared values describe how we aspire to lead and work together." Mullen's leadership at Biogen is moving the firm toward the accomplishment of that vision.

Case Questions

1. In what ways is James Mullen acting as a manager? In what ways is he acting as a leader? (Hint: For a good summary of the differences, see Table 10.1, "Distinctions Between Management and Leadership.")
2. Answer the following questions based on Fielder's LPC theory: Does Mullen seem to be motivated more by tasks or by relationships? Is the situation at Biogen more favorable or unfavorable? Considering the match or mismatch between leader motivation and situation favorableness, what outcomes would Fiedler predict?
3. Using the path-goal theory of leadership, explain whether you think Mullen is using the appropriate kind of leader behavior. Why or why not?

References: "Career Opportunities," "Our History," "Vision, Mission, Values," Biogen website, www.biogen.com on May 26, 2004; "Biogen Could Use This Shot in the Arm," *BusinessWeek*, May 16, 2002; "The Tech Outlook: Biotech," *BusinessWeek*, March 25, 2002; Charles Fishman, "Isolating the Leadership Gene," *Fast Company*, March 2002, pp. 83–90 (quotation, pp. 86–87).

Experiencing Organizational Behavior

Understanding Successful and Unsuccessful Leadership

Purpose: This exercise will help you better understand the behaviors of successful and unsuccessful leaders.

Format: You will be asked to identify contemporary examples of successful and unsuccessful leaders and then describe how these leaders differ.

Procedure:

1. With each student working alone, list the names of ten people you think of as leaders in public life. Note that the names should not be confined to "good" leaders but should also identify "strong" leaders.
2. Next, students will form small groups and compare their lists. This comparison should focus on common and unique names, as well as on the kinds of individuals listed (i.e., male or female, contemporary or historical, business or nonbusiness, and so on).

3. From all the lists, choose two leaders whom most people would consider very successful and two who would be deemed unsuccessful.
4. Identify similarities and differences between the two successful leaders and between the two unsuccessful leaders.
5. Relate the successes and failures to at least one theory or perspective discussed in the chapter.
6. Select one group member to report your findings to the rest of the class.

Follow-up Questions

1. What role does luck play in leadership?
2. Are there factors about the leaders you researched that might have predicted their success or failure before they achieved leadership roles?
3. What are some criteria of successful leadership?

Self-Assessment Exercise

Applying Vroom's Decision Tree Approach

This skill-builder will help you better understand your own leadership style regarding employee participation in decision making. Mentally play the role described in the following scenario; then make the comparisons suggested at the end of the exercise.

You are the southwestern U.S. branch manager of an international manufacturing and sales organi-

zation. The firm's management team is looking for ways to increase efficiency. As part of this effort, the company recently installed an integrated computer network linking sales representatives, customer service employees, and other sales support staff. Sales were expected to increase and sales expenses to drop as a result.

However, exactly the opposite has occurred: Sales have dropped a bit, and expenses are up. You have personally inspected the new system and believe the hardware is fine. However, you believe the software linking the various computers is less than ideal.

The subordinates you have quizzed about the system, on the other hand, think the entire system is fine. They attribute the problems to a number of factors, including inadequate training in how to use the system, a lack of incentive for using it, and generally poor morale. Whatever the reasons given, each worker queried had strong feelings about the issue.

Your boss has just called you and expressed concern about the problems. He has indicated he has confidence in your ability to solve the problem and will leave it in your hands. However, he wants a report on how you plan to proceed within one week.

First, think of how much participation you would normally allow your subordinates in making this decision. Next, apply Vroom's decision tree approach to the problem and see what it suggests regarding the optimal level of participation. Compare your usual approach with the recommended solution.

OB Online

1. Using your favorite search engine, do an Internet search using simply the word *leadership*. How many sites were identified? What conclusions can you draw based on this result?

2. Identify a historical figure whom you consider a highly effective leader. Use the Internet to find two or three sites that specifically address this individual as a leader.

3. Repeat the previous exercise for a contemporary figure.

4. Describe how a website might be created that would allow managers to input their situation and, using Vroom's tree diagram model, get advice on how much participation to allow their subordinates in making a decision. How popular do you think such a site would be? How much do you think managers might be willing to pay to use it?

Building Managerial Skills

Exercise Overview: Conceptual skills involve the manager's ability to think in the abstract. This exercise will enable you to apply your conceptual skills to better understand the distinction between leadership and management.

Exercise Task: Identify someone who currently occupies a management and/or leadership position. This individual can be a manager in a large business, the owner of a small business, the president of a campus organization, or any other similar position. Next, interview this individual and ask him or her the following questions:

1. Name three recent tasks or activities that were primarily managerial in nature, requiring little or no leadership.

2. Name three recent tasks or activities that primarily involved leadership, requiring little or no management.

3. Do you spend most of the time working as a manager or a leader?

4. How easy or difficult is it to differentiate activities based on their management versus leadership involvement?

After completing the interviews, the class breaks up into small groups. Discuss your results with your group. What have you learned about leadership from this activity?

TEST PREPPER

ACE self-test

You have read the chapter and studied the key terms, and the exam is any day now. Think you're ready to ace it? Take this sample test to gauge your comprehension of chapter material. You can check your answers at the back of the book. Want more test questions? Visit the student website at http://college.hmco.com/business/students/ (select Griffin/Moorhead, Fundamentals of Organizational Behavior 1e) and take the ACE quizzes for more practice.

1. **T F** Leadership was initially thought of as a process, but today it is studied primarily as a property.

2. **T F** Organizations are most effective once leadership has replaced traditional management.

3. **T F** Recently some researchers have reintroduced traits such as self-confidence and cognitive ability into the study of leadership.

4. **T F** A substantial amount of research and definitive conclusions have been reached regarding the differences between male and female leaders.

5. **T F** According to the University of Michigan leadership studies, an employee-centered leader attempts to build effective work groups with high performance goals.

6. **T F** A leader engaging in initiating-structure behavior is interested in forming new relationships with employees at work.

7. **T F** The major shortcoming of the behavioral theories of leadership is that they do not take into account important differences from situation to situation.

8. **T F** The LPC theory of leadership contends that a leader may be effective in one situation but not in another.

9. **T F** One element of situational favorableness in LPC theory is the potential performance of the group as a whole.

10. **T F** According to LPC theory, a task-oriented leader is most appropriate in highly favorable and highly unfavorable situations.

11. **T F** Fiedler suggested in his LPC theory that if a mismatch exists between the leader and the situation, the only thing that can be changed is the situation.

12. **T F** Path-goal theory is based in equity theory, the theory that emphasizes the universal desire to be treated fairly.

13. **T F** According to path-goal theory, subordinates who perceive their own ability as low prefer a nondirective leadership style so they can prove their worth to the leader.

14. **T F** Vroom's decision tree approach to leadership describes how leaders actually make decisions.

15. **T F** Recent developments in Vroom's decision tree approach to leadership are based on the question of whether time is a critical factor in the leader's decision-making process.

16. **T F** The basis of the leader-member exchange model of leadership is that leaders should treat all employees as similarly as possible.

17. **T F** According to the Hersey and Blanchard model of leadership, subordinates who are ready to perform the work should be led differently than those who are not ready to perform it.

18. An employee who follows a leader because he or she thinks the leader is intelligent subscribes to the _____ view of leadership.
    a. process

    b. property
    c. coercion
    d. influence
    e. behavioral

19. A person who adopts a trait approach to studying leadership would argue which of the following?
    a. Effective leaders build trust in their followers.
    b. Effective leaders clarify the tasks subordinates must accomplish.
    c. Effective leaders set effective goals.
    d. Effective leaders are taller than ineffective leaders.
    e. Effective leaders are successful because they are granted a position of authority.

20. According to the University of Michigan leadership studies, job-centered leaders do which of the following?
    a. Respect subordinates' ideas
    b. Build trust in subordinates
    c. Make sure employees' needs are met
    d. Explain work procedures
    e. Build effective work groups

21. According to the Ohio State University leadership studies, a leader engaged in initiating-structure behaviors may do all of the following except
    a. define the leader-subordinate roles.
    b. establish channels of communication.
    c. create a relationship of respect.
    d. determine methods of accomplishing the group's task.
    e. make sure subordinates know what is expected of them.

22. Unlike the researchers from the University of Michigan leadership studies, the Ohio State leadership researchers concluded that
    a. the most effective leaders also have the greatest number of subordinates.
    b. trait theories are as successful as behavioral theories in predicting leadership success.
    c. leaders of large companies are more effective than leaders of small companies.
    d. leaders usually come from inside the organization rather than from outside.
    e. leaders demonstrate concern for performance and concern for employee welfare simultaneously.

23. The basis of Fred Fiedler's LPC (least-preferred coworker) theory of leadership is that
    a. leaders are more effective with preferred coworkers.
    b. leaders are less effective with less-preferred coworkers.
    c. a leader's effectiveness depends on characteristics of the situation.
    d. a leader who engages in both employee-centered and job-centered behaviors is most effective.
    e. leaders must adapt their styles to meet certain conditions.

24. Which of the following factors does not affect the favorableness of the leader's situation as explained in Fiedler's LPC theory?
    a. Leadership motivation
    b. Leader-member relations
    c. Task structure
    d. Leader position power
    e. All of the above factors affect situational favorableness.

25. John is a leader whose primary motivation is to complete organizational tasks. In which of the following situations will John be

most effective?
    a. High least-preferred coworker
    b. Weak relationship motivation
    c. Strong job-centered motivation
    d. Moderate situational favorableness
    e. Poor situational favorableness

26. Michael attempts to motivate his employees by reinforcing their expectation that good job performance will lead to valuable outcomes. Michael's approach is consistent with which theory of leadership?
    a. Trait theory
    b. Behavioral theory
    c. LPC theory
    d. Directive theory
    e. Path-goal theory

27. According to research based on the path-goal theory, individuals who attribute outcomes to their own behaviors may be most satisfied with which style of leadership?
    a. Directive
    b. Supportive
    c. Participative
    d. Achievement oriented
    e. Ability-control oriented

28. Victor Vroom and Philip Yetton's decision tree approach to leadership focuses on which aspect of leader behavior?
    a. Subordinate participation in decision making
    b. Improving leader-member relations
    c. Enhancing position power
    d. Clarifying task structure
    e. Broadening leadership styles

29. Vroom recently elaborated his decision tree approach to leadership by suggesting managers should use one of two different decision trees. The appropriate decision tree to use depends primarily on the
    a. cost of the decision.

    b. number of employees involved in the decision.
    c. impact of the decision on organizational effectiveness.
    d. decisions made by direct competitors of the organization.
    e. amount of time the manager has to make the decision.

30. The possible decision styles in Vroom's approach to leadership range from
    a. deciding alone to facilitating the group as members make the decision.
    b. consulting with individuals to consulting with the group as a whole.
    c. delegating the decision to consulting with the group.
    d. consulting with the group to letting the group make its own decision.
    e. delegating the decision to deciding alone.

31. Harold receives special duties that require responsibility and autonomy from his work leader. According to the leader-member exchange model of leadership, Harold is in the
    a. leadership dyad.
    b. LPC group.
    c. consulting group.
    d. in-group.
    e. out-group.

32. If Maria were to follow the Hersey and Blanchard model of leadership, she would use a delegating style only when
    a. all other approaches fail.
    b. leaders form dyadic relationships with subordinates.
    c. subordinates are ready and willing to do the work.
    d. situations are highly unfavorable.
    e. situations are highly favorable.

CHAPTER 11

Leadership and Influence Processes

MANAGEMENT PREVIEW

As we learned in Chapter 10, leadership is a powerful, complex, and often abstract concept. This chapter explores many of the skills and personal resources that affect leaders and leadership. First, we revisit the role of influence in leadership. We then introduce two contemporary influence-based perspectives on leadership: transformational and charismatic leadership. Next, we discuss various substitutes for leadership that may exist in organizations. We then describe power and political behavior in organizations, influence-based phenomena that often involve leadership. Finally, we explore impression management, a related but distinct concept.

After you have studied this chapter, you should be able to:
- ☐ *Characterize leadership as influence.*
- ☐ *Discuss influence-based approaches to leadership.*
- ☐ *Describe key leadership substitutes.*
- ☐ *Explain power in organizations.*
- ☐ *Discuss power and organizational politics.*
- ☐ *Describe impression management.*

We start with a discussion of the challenges facing some of today's newest business leaders.

The twenty-first century has thus far been quite challenging for corporate leaders, especially for new leaders, who must learn to lead while facing a very tough business environment. ABC Entertainment, Kinko's, and Southwest Airlines are among the major businesses whose new CEOs have had to weather the current business climate.

Susan Lyne, president of ABC Entertainment, assumes responsibility for the network's television programming. She first worked in print publishing—the *Village Voice* and *Premiere*—and later managed ABC's TV miniseries division. Her top priority is "getting the younger creative people at the network to feel comfortable speaking up." Lyne wants to change the television giant, which she says is "quick to blame and slow to celebrate." Also on her agenda are increasing managers' entrepreneurial spirit and focusing on unfilled market niches when choosing new shows.

When entrepreneur-turned-CEO Gary Kusin became leader of Kinko's, he knew store employees had the best information about the state of the firm. He visited with 2,500 associates and learned that business customers were demanding more services, more technology, and closer working partnerships. He spent time listening and learning about his new firm, but he also brought renewed attention to efficiency and costs. He says, "As far as running a tight operation is concerned, it's always good to play very defensively. When things are good, people become lax. We've taken this opportunity to get buttoned down. Then, even if the economy lifts[,] … we will not lose that focus."

Southwest Airlines' James Parker has been with the airline since 1986, assuming the top position when Herb Kelleher stepped down. Three months after he became chief executive, the events of September 11 devastated the airlines. Unlike most of his competitors, Parker decided not to lay off any workers. He explains, "We have a lot of people who worked hard for more than thirty years so that they can have job security in hard times … Cutting jobs should be the last thing a company does rather than the first thing." Parker cut costs elsewhere, such as by delaying aircraft purchases, and spent time reassuring employees.

The job of CEO is ever varied, requiring leaders to utilize their skills with both people and processes. Leaders need to build on their own strengths, but they also must be adaptable to successfully face the challenges in a variety of situations.

"Cutting jobs should be the last thing a company does rather than the first thing."
—*James Parker, CEO of Southwest Airlines*

References: Alison Overholt, "New Leaders, New Agendas," *Fast Company*, May 2002, pp. 52–62 (quotation, p. 62); "Who's Smiling Through This Recession?" *BusinessWeek*, October 26, 2001; "ABC's Next Hit Could Co-Star the Internet," *BusinessWeek*, March 26, 2001.

The leaders just described are dealing with one of the most significant challenges any leader can face: the need to transform an organization from one thing into something different. To have any chance for success, they must rely on power and political processes to facilitate key changes. In her or his own way, each leader is also attempting to influence the organization in new and profound ways—and influence, as we will see, is the foundation of effective leadership.

Leadership as Influence

Characterize leadership as influence.

Recall that in Chapter 10, we defined *leadership* (from a process perspective) as the use of noncoercive influence to direct and coordinate the activities of group members to meet goals. We then described a number of leadership models and theories based variously on leadership traits, behaviors, and contingencies. Unfortunately, most of these models and theories essentially ignore the influence component of leadership. That is, they tend to focus on the characteristics of the leader (traits, behaviors, or both) and the responses from followers (satisfaction and/or performance, for instance) with little regard for how the leader actually exercises influence to bring about the desired responses from subordinates.

Influence should actually be considered the cornerstone of the process. Regardless of the leader's traits or behaviors, leadership matters only if influence actually occurs; that is, a person's ability to affect the behavior of others through influence is the ultimate determinant of whether she or he is really a leader. No one can truly be a leader without the ability to influence others. Furthermore, a person who has the ability to influence others clearly has the potential to become a leader.

Influence is the ability to affect the perceptions, attitudes, or behaviors of others.[1] If a person can make another person recognize that her working conditions are more hazardous than she currently believes them to be (change in perceptions), influence has occurred. If an individual can convince someone else that the organization is a much better place to work than he currently believes it to be (change in attitude), influence has occurred. Finally, if a person can get others to work harder or to file a grievance against their boss (change in behavior), influence has occurred.[2] Note, too, that influence can be used in ways that are beneficial or harmful. A person can be influenced to help clean up a city park on the weekend as part of a community service program, for example, or be influenced to use or sell drugs.

Influence is the ability to affect the perceptions, attitudes, or behaviors of others.

Influence-Based Approaches to Leadership

LEARNING OBJECTIVE

Discuss influence-based approaches to leadership.

In recent years, influence has become a more significant component of some leadership models and concepts.[3] The two contemporary approaches to leadership discussed in this section, for example, are tied directly or indirectly to influence. These approaches are transformational leadership and charismatic leadership.

Influence, the ability to affect the perceptions, attitudes, or behaviors of others, is a cornerstone of leadership. Childhood friends Rameck Hunt, Sampson Davis, and George Jenkins vowed to defy the limitations of their inner-city upbringing and became doctors together. Throughout the rigors of college and medical school, the friends pushed one another to do their best. And there is little doubt in any of their minds that their mutual influence was the catalyst for each one's success.

Transformational Leadership

Transformational leadership, a relative newcomer to the leadership literature, focuses on the basic distinction between leading for change and leading for stability.[4] According to this viewpoint, much of what a leader does occurs in the course of routine work-related transactions: assigning work, evaluating performance, making decisions, and so forth. Occasionally, however, the leader has to initiate and manage major change, such as managing a merger, creating a work group, or defining the organization's culture. The first set of issues involves transactional leadership, whereas the second entails transformational leadership.[5]

Recall from Chapter 10 the distinction between management and leadership. Transactional leadership is essentially the same as management in that it involves routine, regimented activities. Closer to the general notion of leadership, however, is **transformational leadership,** the set of abilities that allows the leader to recognize the need for change, create a vision to guide that change, and execute the change effectively. Only a leader with tremendous influence can hope to perform these functions successfully. Some experts believe change is such a vital organizational

Transformational leadership is the set of abilities that allows the leader to recognize the need for change, create a vision to guide that change, and execute the change effectively.

function that even successful firms need to change regularly to avoid complacency and stagnation; accordingly, leadership for change is also important.[6]

Moreover, some leaders can adopt either transformational or transactional perspectives, depending on their circumstances. Others are able to do one or the other, but not both. Ron Canion, the first CEO of Compaq Computer, was clearly an excellent transactional leader. He built the firm from a single new idea and managed it efficiently and profitably for several years. However, the environment changed to the point where Compaq needed to change as well, and Canion apparently was unable to recognize the need for change, let alone lead the firm through those changes. His replacement, Eckhard Pfeiffer, evidently excelled at transformational leadership, as he led the firm through several very successful new initiatives and transformations. However, when this work was done and Compaq needed to refocus on efficient and effective operations best directed by a transactional leader, Pfeiffer faltered, and he too was replaced. The next CEO, Michael Capellas, then successfully negotiated a merger between Compaq and Hewlett-Packard.

Charismatic Leadership

Charisma is a form of interpersonal attraction that inspires support and acceptance from others.

Charismatic leadership is a type of influence based on the leader's personal charisma.

Perspectives based on charismatic leadership, such as the trait theories discussed in Chapter 10, assume charisma is an individual characteristic of the leader. **Charisma** is a form of interpersonal attraction that inspires support and acceptance. **Charismatic leadership** is, accordingly, a type of influence based on the leader's personal charisma. All else being equal, then, someone with charisma is more likely to be able to influence others than someone without charisma. For example, a highly charismatic supervisor will be more successful in influencing subordinate behavior than a supervisor who lacks charisma. Thus, influence is again a fundamental element of this perspective.[7]

Robert House first proposed a theory of charismatic leadership based on research findings from a variety of social science disciplines.[8] His theory suggests that charismatic leaders are likely to have a lot of self-confidence, firm confidence in their beliefs and ideals, and a strong need to influence people. They also tend to communicate high expectations about follower performance and to express confidence in their followers. Gordon Bethune, CEO of Continental Airlines, is an excellent example of a charismatic leader. Bethune possesses a unique combination of executive skill, honesty, and playfulness. These qualities have attracted a group of individuals at Continental who are willing to follow his lead without question and to dedicate themselves to carrying out his decisions and policies with unceasing passion.[9]

Figure 11.1 portrays the three elements of charismatic leadership in organizations that most experts acknowledge today.[10] First, the charismatic leader envisions the future, sets high expectations, and models behaviors consistent with meeting those expectations. Next, the charismatic leader is able to energize others by demonstrating personal excitement, personal confidence, and patterns of success. Finally, the charismatic leader enables others by supporting them, empathizing with them, and expressing confidence in them.[11]

Charismatic leadership ideas are quite popular among managers today and are the subject of numerous books and articles. Unfortunately, few studies have specifically attempted to test the meaning and impact of charismatic leadership. Lingering ethical concerns about charismatic leadership also trouble some people: Some

FIGURE 11.1

The Charismatic Leader

The charismatic leader is characterized by three fundamental attributes. As illustrated here, these are behaviors resulting in envisioning, energizing, and enabling. Charismatic leaders can be a powerful force in any organizational setting.

Reference: Reprinted from David A. Nadler and Michael L. Tushman, "Beyond the Charismatic Leader: Leadership and Organizational Change," *California Management Review*, Vol. 32, No. 2. Copyright © 1990 by The Regents of the University of California. By permission of The Regents.

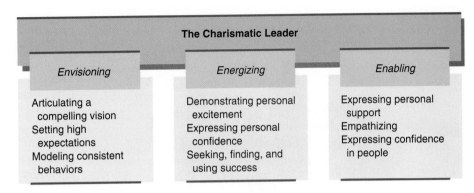

The Charismatic Leader

Envisioning
Articulating a compelling vision
Setting high expectations
Modeling consistent behaviors

Energizing
Demonstrating personal excitement
Expressing personal confidence
Seeking, finding, and using success

Enabling
Expressing personal support
Empathizing
Expressing confidence in people

charismatic leaders inspire such blind faith in their followers that they may engage in inappropriate, unethical, or even illegal behaviors merely because the leader instructed them to do so. Taking over a leadership role from someone with substantial personal charisma is also a challenge.

Leadership Substitutes: Can Leadership Be Irrelevant?

Leadership substitutes are individual, task, and organizational characteristics that tend to outweigh the leader's ability to affect subordinates' satisfaction and performance.

Another interesting twist on leadership is the premise that it may sometimes be unnecessary or irrelevant. An implicit assumption made by each leadership and influence perspective described thus far is that the leader and the follower can be differentiated; That is, one person, the leader, is trying to influence or control another, the follower. However, the concept of leadership substitutes points out that in some situations, leadership may not be necessary.

Leadership substitutes are individual, task, and organizational characteristics that tend to outweigh the leader's ability to affect subordinates' satisfaction and performance.[12] In other words, if certain factors are present, the employee will perform his or her job capably without the direction of a leader. Unlike traditional theories, which assume hierarchical leadership is always important, the premise of the leadership substitutes perspective is that leader behaviors are irrelevant in many situations.

Workplace Substitutes

Ability, experience, training, knowledge, need for independence, professional orientation, and indifference to organizational rewards are individual characteristics that may neutralize leader behaviors. For example, an employee who has the skills and abilities to perform her job and a high need for independence may not need, and may even resent, a leader who tries to provide direction and structure.

A task characterized by routine, a high degree of structure, frequent feedback, and intrinsic satisfaction may also render leader behavior irrelevant. Thus, if the task gives the subordinate enough intrinsic satisfaction, he may not need support from a leader.

Leadership substitutes allow people to perform effectively without the direction of a leader. The Dragon Slayers, shown here, are a volunteer group of high school girls who provide the only round-the-clock emergency care available for 3,000 people in a region of Alaska that is the size of Maryland. The girls voluntarily undergo 200 hours of medical training and respond to about 450 calls a year. And they do all this without supervision and without a formal leader; they simply know what to do and then get it done to help people and save lives.

Explicit plans and goals, rules and procedures, cohesive work groups, a rigid reward structure, and physical distance between supervisor and subordinate are organizational characteristics that may substitute for leadership. For example, if job goals are explicit and there are many rules and procedures for task performance, a leader providing directions may not be necessary. Preliminary research lends support for the concept of leadership substitutes, but additional research is needed to identify other potential substitutes and their impact on leadership effectiveness.[13]

Superleadership

A relatively new addition to the literature on leadership substitutes is the notion of superleadership. **Superleadership** occurs when a leader gradually turns over power, responsibility, and control to a self-managing work group. As we discussed more fully in Chapter 9, many firms today are making widespread use of work teams that function without a formal manager. A big challenge these firms face is what to do with the existing group leader. Al-

Superleadership occurs when a leader gradually and purposefully turns over power, responsibility, and control to a self-managing work group.

though some managers cannot handle this change and leave the firm, a superleader can alter his or her own personal style and become more of a coach or facilitator than a supervisor.

Power in Organizations

Influence is also closely related to the concept of power. Power is one of the most significant forces in organizations. Moreover, it can be an extremely important ingredient in organizational success—or organizational failure. In this section, we first describe the nature of power. Then we examine the types and uses of power.

The Nature of Power

Power is the potential ability of a person or group to exercise control over another person or group.

Power has been defined in dozens of ways; no one definition is generally accepted. Drawing from the more common meanings of the term, we define **power** as the potential ability of a person or group to exercise control over another person or group.[14] Power is distinguished from influence due to the element of control: The more powerful control the less powerful. Thus, power might be thought of as an extreme form of influence.

One obvious aspect of our definition is that it expresses power in terms of potential; that is, we may be able to control others but may choose not to exercise that control. Nevertheless, simply having the potential may be enough to influence others in some settings. Furthermore, power may reside in individuals (such as managers and informal leaders), in formal groups (such as departments and committees), and in informal groups (such as a clique of influential people). Finally, we should note the direct link between power and influence. If a person can convince another person to change his or her opinion on some issue, to engage in or refrain from some behavior, or to view circumstances in a certain way, that person has exercised influence—and used power.

Considerable differences of opinion exist about how thoroughly power pervades organizations. Some people argue that virtually all interpersonal relations are influenced by power; others believe exercise of power is confined to only certain situations. Whatever the case, power is undoubtedly a pervasive part of organizational life. It affects decisions ranging from the choice of strategies to the color of the new office carpeting. It makes or breaks careers. And it enhances or limits organizational effectiveness.

Types of Power

Within the broad framework of our definition, there obviously are many types of power. These types usually are described in terms of bases of power and position power versus personal power.

Bases of Power   The most widely used and recognized analysis of the bases of power is the classic framework developed by John R. P. French and Bertram Raven.[15] French and Raven identified five general bases of power in organizational settings: legitimate, reward, coercive, expert, and referent power.

Legitimate power is granted by virtue of one's position in the organization.	**Legitimate power,** essentially the same as authority, is granted by virtue of one's position in an organization. Managers have legitimate power over their subordinates. The organization specifies that it is legitimate for the designated individual to direct the activities of others. The bounds of this legitimacy are defined partly by the formal nature of the position involved and partly by informal norms and traditions. For example, it was once commonplace for managers to expect their secretaries not only to perform work-related activities such as typing and filing but also to run personal errands such as picking up laundry and buying gifts. In highly centralized, mechanistic, and bureaucratic organizations such as the military, the legitimate power inherent in each position is closely specified, widely known, and strictly followed. In less structured environments, such as research and development labs and software firms, the lines of legitimate power often are blurry. Employees may work for more than one boss at the same time, and leaders and subordinates may be on a nearly equal footing.
Reward power is the extent to which a person controls rewards that another person values.	**Reward power** is the extent to which a person controls rewards that another values. The most obvious examples of organizational rewards are pay, promotions, and work assignments. A manager who has almost total control over the pay subordinates receive, can make recommendations about promotions, and has considerable discretion to make job assignments has a high level of reward power. Reward power can extend beyond material rewards. As we noted in our discussions of motivation theory in Chapter 4, people work for a variety of reasons in addition to pay. For instance, some people may be motivated primarily by a desire for

Coercive power is the extent to which a person has the ability to punish or physically or psychologically harm another.

Expert power is the extent to which a person controls information that is valuable to others.

Referent power exists when one person wants to be like or imitates someone else.

Position power resides in the position regardless of who is filling it.

recognition and acceptance. To the extent that a manager's praise and acknowledgment satisfy those needs, that manager has even more reward power.

Coercive power exists when someone has the ability to punish or physically or psychologically harm another person. For example, some managers berate subordinates in front of everyone, belittling their efforts and generally making their lives miserable. Certain forms of coercion may be subtle. In some organizations, a particular division may be notorious as a resting place for people who have no future with the company. Threatening to transfer someone to a dead-end branch or some other undesirable location is thus a form of coercion. Clearly the more negative the sanctions a person can bring to bear on others, the stronger is her or his coercive power. At the same time, the use of coercive power carries a considerable cost in terms of employee resentment and hostility.

Control over expertise or, more precisely, over information is another source of power, referred to as **expert power.** For example, to the extent that an inventory manager has information that a sales representative needs, the inventory manager has expert power over the sales representative. The more important the information and the fewer the alternative sources for getting it, the greater the power. Expert power can reside in many niches in an organization; it transcends positions and jobs. Although legitimate, reward, and coercive power may not always correspond exactly to formal authority, they often do. Expert power, on the other hand, may be associated much less with formal authority. Upper-level managers usually decide on the organization's strategic agenda, but individuals at lower levels in the organization may have the expertise those managers need to do the tasks. A research scientist may have crucial information about a technical breakthrough of great importance to the organization and its strategic decisions. Likewise, an assistant may take on so many of the boss's routine activities that the manager loses track of such details and comes to depend on the assistant to keep things running smoothly. In other situations, lower-level participants are given power as a way to take advantage of their expertise.

Referent power is power through identification. If José is highly respected by Adam, José has referent power over Adam. Like expert power, referent power does not always correlate with formal organizational authority. In some ways, referent power is similar to the concept of charisma in that it often involves trust, similarity, acceptance, affection, willingness to follow, and emotional involvement. Referent power usually surfaces as imitation. For example, suppose a new department manager is the youngest person in the organization to have reached that rank. Further, it is widely believed that she is being groomed for the highest levels of the company. Other people in the department may begin to imitate her, thinking they too may be able to advance. They may begin dressing like her, working the same hours, and trying to pick up as many work-related pointers from her as possible.

Position Versus Personal Power   The French and Raven framework is only one approach to examining the origins of organizational power. Another approach categorizes power in organizations in terms of position or personal power.

Position power is power that resides in the position regardless of who holds it. Thus, legitimate, reward, and some aspects of coercive and expert power can all contribute to position power. Position power is thus similar to authority. In creating a position, the organization simultaneously establishes a sphere of power for the person filling that position. He or she will generally have the power to direct the activities of subordinates in performing their jobs, control some of their potential rewards, and have a say in their punishment and discipline. There are, however, limits to a manager's position power. A manager cannot order or control activities that fall outside his or her sphere of power—for instance, directing a subordinate to commit a crime, perform personal services, or take on tasks that clearly are not part of the subordinate's job.

Personal power resides in the person regardless of the position he or she holds.

Personal power is power that resides with an individual regardless of his or her position in the organization. Thus, the primary bases of personal power are referent and some traces of expert, coercive, and reward power. Charisma may also contribute to personal power. An individual usually exercises personal power through rational persuasion or by playing on followers' identification with him or her. An individual with personal power often can inspire greater loyalty and dedication in followers than someone who has only position power. The stronger influence stems from the fact that the followers are acting more from choice than from necessity (as dictated, for example, by their organizational responsibilities) and thus will respond more readily to requests and appeals. Of course, the influence of a leader who relies only on personal power is limited because followers may freely decide not to accept his or her directives or orders.

The distinctions between formal and informal leaders are also related to position and personal power. A formal leader will have, at minimum, position power, and an informal leader will have some degree of personal power. Just as a person may be both a formal and an informal leader, he or she can have both position and personal power simultaneously. Indeed, such a combination usually has the greatest potential influence on the actions of others. Figure 11.2 illustrates how personal and position power may interact to determine how much overall power a person has in a particular situation. An individual with both personal and position power will have the strongest overall power. Likewise, an individual with neither personal nor position power will have the weakest overall power. Finally, when either personal or position power is high but the other is low, the person will have a moderate level of overall power.

FIGURE 11.2

Position Power and Personal Power

Position power resides in a job, whereas personal power resides in an individual. When these two types of power are broken down into high and low levels and related to each other, the two-by-two matrix shown here is the result. For example, the upper-right cell suggests that a leader with high levels of both position and personal power will have the highest overall level of power. Other combinations result in differing levels of overall power.

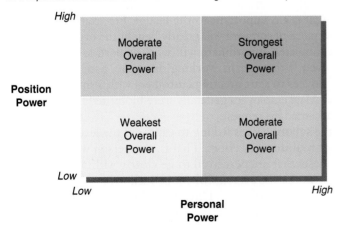

The Uses of Power in Organizations

Power can be used in many ways in an organization. Because of the potential for its misuse and concerns that it may engender, however, it is important that managers fully understand the dynamics of using power. Gary Yukl has presented a useful perspective for understanding how power may be wielded.[16] His perspective includes two closely related components. The first relates power bases, requests from individuals possessing power, and probable outcomes in the form of prescriptions for the manager. Table 11.1 indicates the three outcomes that may result when a leader tries to exert power. These outcomes depend on the leader's base of power, how that base is operationalized, and the subordinate's individual characteristics (for example, personality traits or past interactions with the leader).

TABLE 11.1

Uses and Outcomes of Power

Source of Leader Influence	Type of Outcome		
	Commitment	**Compliance**	**Resistance**
Referent Power	*Likely*	*Possible*	*Possible*
	If request is believed to be important to leader	If request is perceived to be unimportant to leader	If request is for something that will bring harm to leader
Expert Power	*Likely*	*Possible*	*Possible*
	If request is persuasive and subordinates share leader's task goals	If request is persuasive but subordinates are apathetic about leader's task goals	If leader is arrogant and insulting, or subordinates oppose task goals
Legitimate Power	*Possible*	*Likely*	*Possible*
	If request is polite and very appropriate	If request or order is seen as legitimate	If arrogant demands are made or request does not appear proper
Reward Power	*Possible*	*Likely*	*Possible*
	If used in a subtle, very personal way	If used in a mechanical, impersonal way	If used in a manipulative, arrogant way
Coercive Power	*Very Unlikely*	*Possible*	*Likely*
		If used in a helpful, nonpunitive way	If used in a hostile or manipulative way

Reference: From Dorwin P. Cartwright (ed.). *Studies in Social Power,* Copyright © 1959. Reprinted with permission from the Institute for Social Research, University of Michigan, Ann Arbor, Michigan.

Commitment will probably result from an attempt to exercise power if the subordinate accepts and identifies with the leader. Such an employee will be highly motivated by requests that seem important to the leader. For example, a leader might explain that a new piece of software will greatly benefit the organization if it is developed soon. A committed subordinate will work as hard as the leader to complete the project, even if that means working overtime. Sam Walton once asked all Wal-Mart employees to start greeting customers with a smile and an offer to help. Because Wal-Mart employees generally were motivated by and loyal to Walton, most of them accepted his request.

Compliance means the subordinate is willing to carry out the leader's wishes as long as doing so will not require extra effort. That is, the person will respond to normal, reasonable requests that are perceived to be clearly within the specified boundaries of the job. However, the person will not be inclined to do anything beyond the normal expectations for the job. Thus, the subordinate may work at a reasonable pace but refuse to work overtime, insisting that the job will still be there tomorrow. Many ordinary requests from a boss meet with compliant responses from subordinates.

Resistance occurs when the subordinate rejects or fights the leader's wishes. For example, suppose an unpopular leader asks employees to volunteer for a company-sponsored community activity project. The employees reject this request, largely because of their feelings about the leader. A resistant subordinate may even deliberately neglect the project to ensure that it is not done as the leader wants. When Frank Lorenzo, a very unpopular executive with employees, was CEO of Continental Airlines, some employees occasionally disobeyed his mandates as a form of protest against his leadership of the firm.

Table 11.2 suggests ways for leaders to use various kinds of power most effectively. By effective use of power, we mean using power in the manner that is most likely to engender commitment, or at the very least compliance, and least likely to

TABLE 11.2

Guidelines for Using Power

Basis of Power	Guidelines for Use
Referent Power	Treat subordinates fairly Defend subordinates' interests Be sensitive to subordinates' needs, feelings Select subordinates similar to oneself Engage in role modeling
Expert Power	Promote image of expertise Maintain credibility Act confident and decisive Keep informed Recognize employee concerns Avoid threatening subordinates' self-esteem
Legitimate Power	Be cordial and polite Be confident Be clear and follow up to verify understanding Make sure request is appropriate Explain reasons for request Follow proper channels Exercise power regularly Enforce compliance Be sensitive to subordinates' concerns
Reward Power	Verify compliance Make feasible, reasonable requests Make only ethical, proper requests Offer rewards desired by subordinates Offer only credible rewards
Coercive Power	Inform subordinates of rules and penalties Warn before punishing Administer punishment consistently and uniformly Understand the situation before acting Maintain credibility Fit punishment to the infraction Punish in private

Reference: Reprinted from Gary A. Yukl, *Leadership in Organization*, 5th ed., pp. 144–152. Copyright © 2002. Adapted by permission of Pearson Education, Inc., Upper Saddle River, NJ.

provoke resistance. For example, to suggest a somewhat mechanistic approach, managers may enhance their referent power by choosing subordinates with backgrounds similar to their own. They might, for instance, build a referent power base by hiring several subordinates who went to the same college they attended. A more subtle way to exercise referent power is through role modeling: The leader behaves as she or he wants subordinates to behave. As noted earlier, since subordinates relate to and identify with the leader with referent power, they may subsequently attempt to emulate that person's behavior.

In using expert power, managers can subtly make others aware of their education, experience, and accomplishments. To maintain credibility, a leader should not pretend to know things he or she really does not know. A leader whose pretensions are exposed will rapidly lose expert power. A confident and decisive leader demonstrates a firm grasp of situations and takes charge when circumstances dictate. Managers should also keep themselves informed about developments related to tasks that are valuable to the organization and relevant to their expertise.

A leader who recognizes employee concerns works to understand the underlying nature of these issues and takes appropriate steps to reassure subordinates. For example, if employees feel threatened by rumors that they will lose office space after an impending move, the leader might ask them about this concern and then find out just how much office space there will be and tell the subordinates. Finally, to avoid threatening the self-esteem of subordinates, a leader should be careful not to flaunt expertise or behave like a "know-it-all."

In general, a leader exercises legitimate power by formally requesting that subordinates do something. The leader should be especially careful to make requests diplomatically if the subordinate is sensitive about his or her relationship with the leader. This might be the case, for example, if the subordinate is older or more experienced than the leader. However, although the request should be polite, it should be made confidently. The leader is in charge and needs to convey his or her command of the situation. The request should also be clear. Thus, the leader may need to follow up to ascertain that the subordinate understood it properly. To ensure that a request is seen as appropriate and legitimate to the situation, the leader may need to explain the reasons for it. Often subordinates do not understand the rationale behind a request and consequently react negatively to it. It is important, too, to follow proper channels when dealing with subordinates.

Suppose a manager has asked a subordinate to spend his day finishing an important report. Later, while the manager is out of the office, her boss comes by and asks the subordinate to drop that project and work on something else. The subordinate will then be in the awkward position of having to decide which of two higher-ranking individuals to obey. Exercising authority regularly will reinforce its presence and legitimacy in the eyes of subordinates. Compliance with legitimate power should be the norm because if employees resist a request, the leader's power base may diminish. Finally, the leader exerting legitimate power should attempt to be responsive to subordinates' problems and concerns in the same ways we outlined for using expert power.

Reward power is, in some respects, the easiest base of power to use. Verifying compliance simply means leaders should find out whether subordinates have carried out their requests before giving rewards; otherwise, subordinates may not recognize a performance-reward linkage. The request to be rewarded must be both reasonable and feasible, because even the promise of a reward will not motivate a subordinate who thinks a request should not or cannot be carried out.

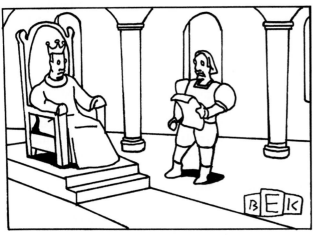

"You've got a power beheading at 8 A.M."

Managers can rely on several different types of power. Coercive power, however, should be used with caution. Otherwise, as shown here, it can be carried to excess!

The same can be said for a request that seems improper or unethical. Among other things, the employee may see a reward linked to an improper or unethical request as a bribe or other shady offering. Finally, if the leader promises a reward that subordinates know she or he cannot actually deliver, or if they have little use for a reward the manager can deliver, they will not be motivated to carry out the request. Further, they may grow skeptical of the leader's ability to deliver rewards that are worth something to them.

Coercion is certainly the most difficult form of power to exercise. Because coercive power is likely to cause resentment and erode referent power, it should be used infrequently, if at all. Compliance is about all one can expect from using coercive power, and that only if the power is used in a helpful, nonpunitive way—that is, if the sanction is mild and fits the situation and if the subordinate learns from it. In most cases, resistance is the most likely outcome, especially if coercive power is used in a hostile or manipulative way. Of course, if coercion is taken to the extreme—as shown in the cartoon—issues of compliance or resentment may become moot!

The first guideline for using coercive power—that subordinates should be fully informed about rules and the penalties for violating them—will prevent inadvertent violations of a rule, which pose an unpalatable dilemma for a leader. Overlooking an infraction on the grounds that the perpetrator was ignorant may undermine the rule or the leader's legitimate power, but carrying out the punishment probably will create resentment. One approach is to provide reasonable warning before inflicting punishment, responding to the first violation of a rule with a warning about the consequences of another violation. Of course, a serious infraction such as a theft or violence warrants immediate and severe punishment.

The disciplinary action needs to be administered consistently and uniformly because doing so shows that punishment is both impartial and clearly linked to the infraction. Leaders should obtain complete information about what happened before they punish, because punishing the wrong person or administering uncalled-for punishment can stir great resentment among subordinates. Credibility must be maintained because a leader who continually makes threats but fails to carry them out loses both respect and power. Similarly, if the leader uses threats that subordinates know are beyond his or her ability to impose, the attempted use of power will be fruitless. Obviously, too, the severity of the punishment generally should match the seriousness of the infraction. Finally, punishing someone in front of others adds humiliation to the penalty, which reflects poorly on the leader and makes those who must watch and listen uncomfortable as well.

Organizational politics are activities people carry out to acquire, enhance, and use power and other resources to obtain their desired outcomes.

Organizational Politics

A concept closely related to power in organizational settings is politics, or political behavior. **Organizational politics** consists of activities people perform to acquire, enhance, and use power and other resources to obtain their preferred outcomes in a situation of uncertainty or disagreement. Thus, political behavior is the general means by which people attempt to obtain and use power. Put simply, the goal of such behavior is to get one's own way about things. The Business of Ethics box illustrates how political behavior can translate into business practice—in this case, Boeing's questionable accounting practices.

The Pervasiveness of Political Behavior

One classic survey provides some interesting insights into how managers perceive political behavior in their organizations.[17] Roughly one-third of the 428 managers who responded to this survey believed political behavior influenced salary decisions in their organizations, whereas 28 percent believed it affected hiring decisions. Moreover, three-quarters of respondents also believed political behavior is more prevalent at higher levels of the organization than at lower levels. More than half believed politics is unfair, disruptive, and irrational, but also acknowledged that successful executives must be good politicians and that it is necessary to behave politically to get ahead. The survey results suggest that managers see political behavior as an undesirable but unavoidable facet of organizational life.

BUSINESS OF ETHICS

Five Years of Accounting Secrets at Boeing

The legality of an action is determined by interpretation of the language of a legal code. Whether that same action is socially responsible is determined by a different standard: The action should protect and contribute to the social environment. Thus, an action can be socially responsible but not legal, or legal but not socially responsible.

The latter applies to the actions of Boeing executives, which were publicly disclosed in May 2002. The firm began to experience cost overruns in 1996, as noted by auditors Deloitte Touche, because of faulty inventory scheduling, a high defect rate, and increased overtime pay. According to generally accepted accounting principles (GAAP), reporting of expenses may be spread over the life of a project under normal conditions, whereas expenses must be reported at occurrence if the conditions are considered abnormal. Deloitte Touche deemed Boeing's expenses abnormal; Boeing officials insisted these were normal costs and that normal costs fluctuate. Boeing's view prevailed, and the increased expenses were not made public until October 1997. This action was found to be legal, but many considered it unethical and socially irresponsible. The motive seems clear: Boeing was merging with rival McDonnell-Douglas and feared that disclosure would spoil the deal. Debra Smith, a former auditor, says, "Boeing basically decided in the short run that [underreporting expenses] was a lesser evil than losing

the merger." Boeing managers "were hoping against hope that none of the problems would bubble up before they got the deal done," says a Boeing ex-official.

Investors were hard hit by the announcement when it finally came, dropping Boeing's stock price 20 percent in one week and wiping out $10.7 billion in value. Also hurt

> *"[Boeing managers] were hoping against hope that none of the problems would bubble up before they got the deal done."—former Boeing official commenting on the company's proposed merger with rival McDonnell-Douglas*

were employees and suppliers due to the resulting layoffs and reduced spending. Customers suffered too when new planes were delivered late. Ultimately some customers defected to rivals, and several Boeing managers lost their jobs; CEO Phil Condit, however, retained his. The firm paid $92 million to settle a lawsuit without admitting guilt. The use of accounting technicalities to mask production inefficiencies continues at the firm, and an accurate picture of its financial state remains unclear. Fallout from the incident persists. When *BusinessWeek* published its investigative report in May 2002, the company's stock had declined yet again.

References: "Dow Jones Industrial Average," Dow Jones Index website, www.djindexes.com on May 27, 2002; "Boeing's Secret," *BusinessWeek*, May 20, 2002, pp. 110–120 (quotation, p. 110); "And Where Were the Auditors?" *BusinessWeek*, May 20, 2002, p. 120; Bethany McLean, "Markets Suffer Indigestion," *Fortune*, May 10, 2002, www. fortune.com on May 27, 2002.

Politics is often viewed as being synonymous with dirty tricks or backstabbing, and therefore as something distasteful and best left to others. The results of the survey just described, however, demonstrate that political behavior in organizations, like power, is pervasive. Thus, rather than ignoring or trying to eliminate political behavior, managers might more fruitfully consider when and how organizational politics can be used constructively.

Figure 11.3 presents an interesting model of the ethics of organizational politics.[18] In the model, a political behavior alternative (PBA) is a given course of action, largely political in character, in a particular situation. The model considers political behavior ethical and appropriate under two conditions: (1) if it respects the rights of all affected parties and (2) if it adheres to the canons of justice (that is, to a commonsense judgment of what is fair and equitable). Even if the political behavior does not meet these tests, it may be ethical and appropriate under certain circumstances. For example, politics may provide the only possible basis for deciding which employees to let go during a recessionary period of cutbacks. In all cases where nonpolitical alternatives exist, however, the model recommends rejecting political behavior that abrogates rights or justice.

To illustrate how the model works, consider Susan Jackson and Bill Thompson, both assistant professors of English. University regulations stipulate that only one of the assistant professors may be tenured; the other must be let go. (Some universities actually follow this practice.) Both Susan and Bill submit their credentials for review.

FIGURE 11.3

A Model of Ethical and Political Behavior

Political behavior can serve both ethical and unethical purposes. This model helps illustrate circumstances in which political behavior is most and least likely to have ethical consequences. By following the paths through the model, a leader concerned about the ethics of an impending behavior can gain insights into whether ethical considerations are really a central part of the behavior.

Reference: Gerald F. Cavanaugh, Dennis J. Moberg, and Manuel Velasques, "The Ethics of Organizational Politics," *Academy of Management Review*, July 1981, p. 368. Copyright © 1981 by Academy of Management. Reproduced with permission of Academy of Management in the format Textbook via Copyright Clearance Center.

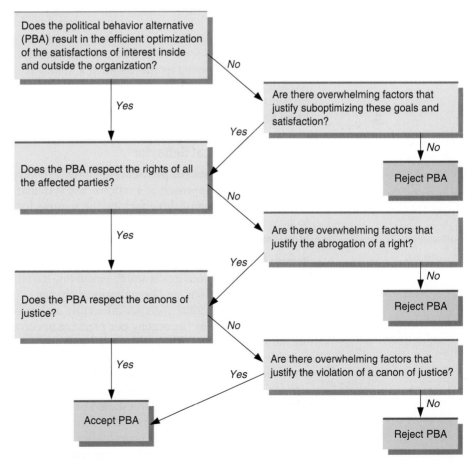

By most objective criteria, such as number of publications and teaching evaluations, the two faculty members' qualifications are roughly the same. Because he fears termination, Bill begins an active political campaign to support a tenure decision favoring him. He continually reminds the tenured faculty of his intangible contributions, such as his friendship with influential campus administrators. Susan, on the other hand, decides to say nothing and let her qualifications speak for themselves. The department ultimately votes to give Bill tenure and let Susan go.

Was Bill's behavior ethical? Assuming that his comments about himself were accurate and that he said nothing to disparage Susan, his behavior did not affect her rights; that is, she had an equal opportunity to advance her own cause but chose not to do so. Bill's efforts did not directly hurt Susan but only helped him. On the other hand, it might be argued that Bill's actions violated the canons of justice because clearly defined data on which to base the decision were available. Thus, one could argue that Bill's calculated introduction of additional information into the decision was unjust.

This model has not been tested empirically. Indeed, its very nature may make it impossible to test. Further, as the preceding example demonstrates, it is often difficult to give an unequivocal *yes* or *no* answer to the question, even under the simplest circumstances. Thus, the model serves as a general framework for understanding the ethical implications of various courses of action managers might take.

How, then, should managers approach the phenomenon of political behavior? Trying to eliminate political behavior will seldom, if ever, work. In fact, such action may well increase political behavior because of the uncertainty and ambiguity it creates. At the other extreme, universal and freewheeling use of political behavior probably will lead to conflict, feuds, and turmoil. In most cases, a position somewhere in between is best: The manager does not attempt to eliminate political activity, recognizing its inevitability, and may try to use it effectively, perhaps following the ethical model just described. At the same time, the manager can take certain steps to minimize the potential dysfunctional consequences of abusive political behavior.

Managing Political Behavior

Managing organizational politics is not easy. The very nature of political behavior makes it tricky to approach in a rational and systematic way. Success will require a basic understanding of three factors: the reasons for political behavior, common techniques for using political behavior, and strategies for limiting the effects of political behavior.

Reasons for Political Behavior Political behavior occurs in organizations for five basic reasons: ambiguous goals, scarce resources, technology and environment, nonprogrammed decisions, and organizational change.

Most organizational goals are inherently ambiguous. Organizations frequently espouse goals such as "increasing our presence in certain new markets" or "increasing our market share." The ambiguity of such goals provides an opportunity for political behavior because people can view a wide range of behaviors as helping to meet the goal. In reality, of course, many of these behaviors may actually be designed for the personal gain of the individuals involved. For example, a top manager might argue that the corporation should pursue its goal of entry into a new market by buying out another firm instead of forming a new division. The manager may appear to have the good of the corporation in mind—but what if he owns some of the target firm's stock and stands to make money on a merger or an acquisition?

Whenever resources are scarce, some people will not get everything they think they deserve or need. Thus, they are likely to engage in political behavior as a means of inflating their share of the resources. In this way, a manager seeking a larger budget might present accurate but misleading or incomplete statistics to inflate the perceived importance of her department. Because no organization has unlimited resources, incentives for this kind of political behavior are always present.

Technology and environment may influence the overall design of the organization and its activities. The influence stems from the uncertainties associated with nonroutine technologies and dynamic, complex environments. These uncertainties favor the use of political behavior because in such an environment, it is imperative that an organization respond to change. An organization generally reacts with a wide range of responses, from purposeful activities to uncertainty to a purely political response. In the last case, a manager might use an environmental shift as an argument for restructuring his department to increase his own power base.

Political behavior is also likely to arise whenever many nonprogrammed decisions need to be made. Nonprogrammed-decision situations involve ambiguous circumstances that allow ample opportunity for political maneuvering. The two faculty members competing for one tenured position is an example. The nature of the decision allowed political behavior and, in fact, from Bill's point of view, the nonprogrammed decision demanded political action.

As we discuss in Chapter 15, changes in organizations occur regularly and can take many forms. Each such change introduces some uncertainty and ambiguity into the organizational system, at least until it has been completely institutionalized. The period during which this occurs usually affords much opportunity for political activity. For instance, a manager concerned about the consequences of a reorganization may resort to politics to protect the scope of her authority.

The Techniques of Political Behavior   Several techniques are used in practicing political behavior. Unfortunately, because these techniques have not been systematically studied, our understanding of them is based primarily on informal observation and inference.[19] Further, the participants themselves may not even be aware they are using particular techniques.

One technique of political behavior is to control as much information as possible. The more critical the information and the fewer people who have access to it, the larger the power base and influence of those who do. For example, suppose a top manager has a report compiled as a basis for future strategic plans. Rather than distributing the complete report to peers and subordinates, he shares only parts of it with the few managers who must have the information. Because no one but the manager has the complete picture, he has power and is engaging in politics to control decisions and activities according to his own ends.

Similarly, some people create or exploit situations to control lines of communication, particularly access to others in the organization. Secretaries frequently control access to their bosses. A secretary may put visitors in contact with the boss, send them away, delay the contact by ensuring that phone calls are not returned promptly, and so forth. People in these positions often find they can use this type of political behavior very effectively.

Using outside experts, such as consultants or advisers, can be an effective political technique. The manager who hires a consultant may select one whose views match her own. Because the consultant realizes the manager was responsible for selecting him, he feels a certain obligation to her. Although the consultant

There are numerous techniques available for individuals who wish to engage in political behavior. The government's "No Child Left Behind" campaign has spawned many benefits for education, but has also prompted some political behaviors. For instance, there are documented cases of teachers coaching their students during exams and of school districts not counting test scores of special-education students or of students who subsequently drop out of school.

truly attempts to be objective and unbiased, he may unconsciously recommend courses of action favored by the manager. Given the consultant's presumed expertise and neutrality, others in the organization accept his recommendations without challenge. By using an outside expert, the manager has ultimately gotten what she wants.

Controlling the agenda is another common political technique. Suppose a manager wants to prevent a committee from approving a certain proposal. He first tries to keep the decision off the agenda entirely, claiming it is not yet ready for consideration, or attempts to have it placed last on the agenda. As other issues are decided, he sides with the same set of managers on each decision, building up a certain assumption that they are a team. When the controversial item comes up, he can defeat it through a combination of collective fatigue, the desire to get the meeting over with, and the support of his carefully cultivated allies. This technique, then, involves group polarization. A less sophisticated tactic is to prolong discussion of prior agenda items so the group never reaches the controversial one. Or the manager may raise so many technical issues and new questions about the proposal that the committee decides to table it. In any of these cases, the manager will have used political behavior for his or her own ends.

Game playing is a complex technique that may take many forms. When playing games, managers simply work within the rules of the organization to increase the probability that their preferred outcomes will result. Suppose a manager is in a position to cast the deciding vote on an upcoming issue. She does not want to alienate either side by voting on it. One game she might play is to arrange to be called out of town on a crucial business trip when the vote is to take place. Assuming no one questions the need for the trip, she will successfully maintain her position of neutrality and avoid angering either opposing camp.

Another game would involve using any of the techniques of political behavior in a purely manipulative or deceitful way. For example, a manager who will soon be making recommendations about promotions tells each subordinate, in "strictest confidence," that he is a leading candidate and needs only to increase his performance to have the inside track. Here the manager is using his control over information to play games with his subordinates. A classic power struggle at W. R. Grace further illustrates manipulative practices. A senior executive once fired the CEO's son and then allegedly attempted to convince the board of directors to oust the CEO and give the senior executive his job. In response, the CEO fired his rival and then publicly announced that the individual had been forced out because he had sexually harassed Grace employees.[20]

The technique of building coalitions has as its general goal convincing others that everyone should work together to accomplish certain things. A manager who believes she does not control enough votes to pass an upcoming agenda item may visit with other managers before the meeting to urge them to side with her. If her preferences are in the best interests of the organization, this may be a laudable strategy for her to follow. But if she herself is the principal beneficiary, the technique is not desirable from the organization's perspective. At its extreme, coalition building, which is frequently used in political bodies, may take the form of blatant reciprocity. Suppose that in return for Roberta Kline's vote on an issue that concerns him, José Montemayor agrees to vote for a measure that does not affect his group at all but is crucial to Kline's group. Depending on the circumstances, this practice may benefit or hurt the organization as a whole.

The technique of controlling decision parameters can be used only in certain situations and requires much subtlety. Instead of trying to control the actual decision, the manager backs up one step and tries to control the criteria and tests on which the decision is based. This allows the manager to take a less active role in the actual decision but still achieve his or her preferred outcome. For example, suppose a district manager wants a proposed new factory to be constructed on a site in his region. If he tries to influence the decision directly, his arguments will be seen as biased and self-serving. Instead, he may take a very active role in defining the criteria on which the decision will be based, such as target population, access to rail transportation, tax rates, distance from other facilities, and the like. If he is a skillful negotiator, he may be able to influence the decision parameters such that his desired location subsequently appears to be the ideal site as determined by the criteria he has helped shape. Hence, he gets just what he wants without playing a prominent role in the actual decision.

Limiting the Effects of Political Behavior   Although it is virtually impossible to eliminate political activity in organizations, managers can limit its dysfunctional consequences. The techniques for checking political activity target both the reasons it occurs in the first place and the specific techniques people use for political gain.

Opening communication is one very effective technique for restraining the impact of political behavior. For instance, with open communication the basis for allocating scarce resources will be known to everyone. This knowledge, in turn, will tend to reduce the propensity to engage in political behavior to acquire those resources because people will already know how decisions will be made. Open communication also limits the ability of any single person to control information or lines of communication.

A related technique is to reduce uncertainty. Several of the reasons political behavior occurs—ambiguous goals, nonroutine technology, an unstable environment, and organizational change—and most of the political techniques themselves are associated with high levels of uncertainty. Political behavior can be limited if the manager can reduce uncertainty. Consider an organization about to transfer a major division from Florida to Michigan. Many people will resist the idea of moving north and may resort to political behavior to forestall their own transfer. However, the manager in charge of the move can announce who will stay and who will go at the same time news of the change spreads throughout the company, thereby curtailing political behavior related to the move.

The adage "forewarned is forearmed" sums up the final technique for controlling political activity. Simply being aware of the causes and techniques of political behavior can help a manager check their effects. Suppose a manager anticipates that several impending organizational changes will increase the level of political activity. As a result of this awareness, the manager quickly infers that a particular subordinate is lobbying for the use of a certain consultant only because the subordinate thinks the consultant's recommendations will be in line with his own. Attempts to control the agenda, engage in game playing, build a certain image, and control decision parameters often are transparent to the knowledgeable observer. Recognizing such behaviors for what they are, an astute manager may be able to take appropriate steps to limit their impact.

Impression Management

┌─ *LEARNING OBJECTIVE* ─┐

*Describe impression
management.*

Impression management is
a direct and intentional effort to enhance one's own
image in the eyes of others.

Impression management is a subtle form of political behavior that deserves special mention. **Impression management** is a person's direct, intentional effort to enhance his or her image in the eyes of others. People engage in impression management for a variety of reasons. For one thing, they may do so to further their own careers. They think that by making themselves look good, they are more likely to receive rewards, attractive job assignments, and promotions. They may also engage in impression management to boost their self-esteem. When people have a solid image in an organization, others make them aware of it through their compliments, respect, and so forth. Another reason people use impression management is to acquire more power and hence more control.

People attempt to manage how others perceive them through a variety of mechanisms. Appearance is one of the first things people think of. Hence, a person motivated by impression management will pay close attention to choice of attire, selection of language, and use of manners and body posture. People engaged in impression management may also jockey to be associated only with successful projects. By being assigned to high-profile projects led by highly successful managers, a person can begin to link his or her own name with such projects in the minds of others.

Sometimes people too strongly motivated by impression management become obsessed by it and resort to dishonest or unethical means. For example, some people have been known to take credit for others' work in an effort to make themselves look better. People have also been known to exaggerate or even falsify their personal accomplishments to enhance their image.

Synopsis

Influence can be defined as the ability to affect the perceptions, attitudes, or behaviors of others. Influence is a cornerstone of leadership. Whereas the basic leadership models discussed in Chapter 10 acknowledge influence, they do not directly include it as part of the leadership process.

In recent years, new leadership approaches have attempted to consider the use of influence more directly. Transformational leadership, one such approach, is the set of abilities that allow a leader to recognize the need for change, create a vision to guide that change, and execute the change effectively. Another influence-based approach to leadership considers charismatic leadership. Charisma, the basis of this

approach, is a form of interpersonal attraction that inspires support and acceptance.

Leadership substitutes are individual, task, and organizational characteristics that tend to outweigh a leader's ability to affect subordinates' satisfaction and performance. Superleadership, a special type of leadership substitute, occurs when a leader gradually and purposefully turns over power, responsibility, and control to a self-managing work group.

Power is the potential ability of a person or group to exercise control over another person or group. The five bases of power are legitimate power (granted by virtue of one's position in the organization), reward power (control of rewards valued by others), coercive power (the ability to punish or harm), expert power (control over information valuable to the organization), and referent power (power through personal identification). Position power is tied to a position regardless of the individual who holds it. Personal power resides in a person regardless of position. Attempts to use power can result in commitment, compliance, or resistance.

Organizational politics is activities people perform to acquire, enhance, and use power and other resources to obtain their preferred outcomes in a situation of uncertainty or disagreement. Research indicates that most

managers do not advocate use of political behavior but acknowledge that it is a necessity of organizational life. Because managers cannot eliminate political activity, they must learn to cope with it. Understanding how to manage political behavior requires understanding why it occurs, what techniques it employs, and the strategies for limiting its effects.

Impression management is a direct, intentional effort to enhance one's image in the eyes of others. People engage in impression management for a variety of reasons and use a number of methods to influence how others see them.

Discussion Questions

1. Can a person without influence be a leader? Does having influence automatically make someone a leader?

2. Do all organizations need transformational leaders? Do all organizations need transactional leaders? Why are some leaders able to assume both roles, whereas others can perform only one?

3. Who are some of the more charismatic leaders today?

4. What might happen if two people, each with significant, equal power, attempt to influence each other?

5. Cite examples based on a professor-student relationship to illustrate each of the five bases of organizational power.

6. Is there a logical sequence in the use of power bases that a manager might follow? For instance, should the use of legitimate power usually precede the use of reward power, or vice versa?

7. Cite examples in which you have been committed, compliant, or resistant as a result of efforts to

influence you. Think of times when your attempts to influence others led to commitment, compliance, or resistance.

8. Do you agree or disagree with the assertion that political behavior is inevitable in organizational settings?

9. The term *politics* is generally associated with governmental bodies. Why do you think it has also come to be associated with the behavior in organizations described in the chapter?

10. Recall examples of how you have either used or observed others using the techniques of political behavior identified in the chapter. What other techniques can you suggest?

11. Have you ever engaged in impression management? Do you think impression management is acceptable behavior as long as it doesn't get out of hand, or is it misleading and therefore always inappropriate?

Organizational Behavior Case for Discussion

A Corporate Marriage Made in Heaven (Not!)

Enron was 2002's biggest business story, but the Hewlett-Packard–Compaq merger was a close runner-up. The story, which has been compared to both a soap opera and a prizefight, began with the appointment in 1999 of Carly Fiorina to the chief executive spot at HP. Fiorina took charge of a company that had

degenerated from the once-great computer giant envisioned by founders William Hewlett and David Packard into an unfocused, tradition-bound, and ailing jumble of unrelated business segments. A slowing economy had stalled profits in 2000, and in July 2001, Fiorina announced that she and Compaq CEO

Michael Capellas wanted a merger to give the combined firm a strong position in both PCs and PC peripherals. Howard Schultz, an HP customer and chairman of Starbucks, believed the merger would be beneficial. At the time, he said, "It's clear to me the best model in an industry that is rapidly consolidating is for this to happen."

The board agreed, but David W. Packard and Walter Hewlett, sons of HP's founders and individuals held in high regard by HP employees and investors, publicly opposed it; together they controlled 18 percent of the company's voting shares. Refuting their position, HP board member Tom Perkins said, "If Walter Hewlett wins this battle, HP will be another Polaroid or Xerox: conservative, risk averse, too reliant on its technology. This is really a proxy battle for the heart and soul of Hewlett-Packard."

The fight quickly became personal and emotional. Hewlett, who serves on HP's board, initially voted in favor of the merger, along with the rest of the board. However, on November 6, 2001, Hewlett told reporters he would vote against the merger, giving Fiorina thirty minutes' notice of his decision. In January 2002, HP ran print ads claiming that "Bill and Dave" would have approved the merger and sent a letter to stockholders calling Hewlett "an academic and a musician," implying that he doesn't understand business. In response, Packard printed a retort in *The Wall Street Journal* that concluded, "There is now a real danger that HP will die of a broken heart." Hewlett threatened to resign from the board if the merger was completed; Fiorina threatened to resign as CEO if it was blocked.

The conflict highlighted perceptions and prejudices. Walter Hewlett is soft-spoken, but he also earned three graduate degrees from Stanford, competes in marathons and long-distance bicycle races, and plays ten instruments. While appearing in court, Hewlett was described as "rumpled," "off-guard," and "uncomfortable." In contrast, the words "cool," "assertive," and "professional" were used to describe Fiorina. She has excellent business skills and experience, but because she is female, she might be perceived as ineffectual in a tough battle. "I think she's judged by a much harsher and colder metric than a male CEO would be," says Donna Hoffman, a Vanderbilt University management professor. However, according to Jeffrey Christian, Fiorina's executive recruiter, "She has proven [that] a woman can take the heat, stand up

to major conflict, and not give up[,] no matter what the odds." Nancy Rothbard, a management professor at the University of Pennsylvania, agrees, noting, "[Fiorina] demonstrates that there are a lot of styles out there. That's great for women. It makes a nice contrast to some of our stereotypical notions of women in leadership roles."

The fighting was followed by a too-close-to-call proxy vote; thus, even small investors got personalized attention through numerous mailings, emails, and phone calls. "Enough is enough already," protested an owner with less than two-tenths of 1 percent share of HP. In a scene reminiscent of the Bush-Gore presidential race, it took six weeks for all of the mailed-in votes to be counted; in the meantime, each side claimed victory. In the end, the merger was approved by a 51.4 percent majority. Many of those opposing the deal were HP employees—75 percent of shares in employee retirement accounts voted *No*.

The legacy of the fighting is a divided firm as Fiorina and Capellas work to merge two giants with very different cultures and history. HP employees fear the inevitable layoffs, in which 15,000 to 24,000 employees are likely to lose their jobs. At the April 2002 annual stockholders' meeting, Fiorina said, "I hope we can put the rancor of this campaign behind us and find common ground," but Hewlett later received standing ovations whereas Fiorina was booed. Hewlett lost his position on the board and sued the company, claiming that managers "coerced and enticed" Deutsche Bank, a major stockholder, to cast its votes in favor of the merger because Deutsche is providing a $4 billion loan to HP to help pay for the merger. According to *BusinessWeek* writer Peter Burrows, "If [HP] can't get the details right, the honeymoon could be painfully short." It's not yet clear if the divided firm can heal itself. After the eight-month battle, HP survives but remains in danger of dying of a broken heart.

Case Questions

1. Based on information from the case, what types of power are demonstrated by Carly Fiorina? By William Hewlett?
2. Based on information from the case, describe as many instances of the use of political techniques as you can. Consider the actions of all involved parties in your answer.

3. In your opinion, what are the likely consequences of the political behavior demonstrated during the HP-Compaq merger?

References: "Biography: Carleton S. (Carly) Fiorina," Hewlett-Packard Company website, www.thenew.hp.com on May 28, 2004; "What's in Store for This Happy Couple?" *BusinessWeek*, May 20, 2002; Adam Lashinsky, "Hanging Chads: Take 2," *Fortune*, May 13, 2002; "Walter Hewlett's Last Stand?" *BusinessWeek*, April 25, 2002; David Kirkpatrick, "After the Accolades, Now What?" *Fortune*, April 15, 2002; "Hewlett's Challenge: Proving It," *BusinessWeek*, April 9, 2002; "Fiorina's Stereotype-Smashing Performance," *BusinessWeek*, April 3, 2002; "What Price Victory at Hewlett-Packard?" *BusinessWeek*, April 1, 2002; "Table: A Corporate Soap Opera," *BusinessWeek*, February 11, 2002 (quotation); Adam Lashinsky, "The Defiant Ones," *Fortune*, January 7, 2002.

Experiencing Organizational Behavior
Learning About Ethics and Power

Purpose: This exercise will help you appreciate some of the ambiguities involved in assessing the ethics of power and political behavior in organizations.

Format: First, you will identify examples of more and less ethical uses of power and political behavior. Then you will discuss, compare, and contrast your examples with those generated by classmates.

Procedure:

1. Write down three examples of situations in which you think it would be ethical to use power and political behavior. For example, you might think it is ethical to use them to save the job of a coworker who you think is a very good but misunderstood employee.

2. Write down three examples of situations in which you think it would be unethical to use power and political behavior. For instance, you might think it is unethical to use power and political behavior to gain a job for which you are really not qualified.

3. Form small groups of three or four members. Each group member will read his or her examples of ethical and unethical uses of power and political behavior.

4. Discuss the extent to which group members agree on the ethics for each situation. See if your group members can think of different situations in which the ethical context changes. For example, if everyone agrees that a given situation is ethical, see if the group can think of slightly different circumstances in which, in essentially the same situation, using power and political behavior would become more unethical.

Follow-up Questions

1. How realistic was this exercise? What did you learn from it?

2. Could you assess real-life situations relating to the ethics of political activity using this same process?

Self-Assessment Exercise
Are You a Charismatic Leader?

Introduction: Charismatic leaders articulate a vision, show concern for group members, communicate high expectations, and create high-performing organizations. This assessment exercise measures your charismatic potential.

Instructions: The following statements refer to the possible ways in which you might behave toward others when you are in a leadership role. Please read each statement carefully and decide to what extent it applies to you. Then put a check on the appropriate number.

To a very great extent	= 5
To a considerable extent	= 4
To a moderate extent	= 3
To a slight extent	= 2
To little or no extent	= 1

1. I pay close attention to what others say when they are talking.	1	2	3	4	5
2. I communicate clearly.	1	2	3	4	5
3. I am trustworthy.	1	2	3	4	5
4. I care about other people.	1	2	3	4	5

5. I do not put excessive energy
into avoiding failure.   1 2 3 4 5

6. I make the work of others
more meaningful.   1 2 3 4 5

7. I seem to focus on the key
issues in a situation.   1 2 3 4 5

8. I get across my meaning
effectively, often in unusual ways.   1 2 3 4 5

9. I can be relied on to follow
through on commitments.   1 2 3 4 5

10. I have a great deal of
self-respect.   1 2 3 4 5

11. I enjoy taking carefully
calculated risks.   1 2 3 4 5

12. I help others feel more
competent in what they do.   1 2 3 4 5

13. I have a clear set of priorities.   1 2 3 4 5

14. I am in touch with how
others feel.   1 2 3 4 5

15. I rarely change once I have
taken a clear position.   1 2 3 4 5

16. I focus on strengths, of myself
and of others.   1 2 3 4 5

17. I seem most alive when deeply
involved in some project.   1 2 3 4 5

18. I show others that they are all
part of the same group.   1 2 3 4 5

19. I get others to focus on the
issues I see as important.   1 2 3 4 5

20. I communicate feelings as
well as ideas.   1 2 3 4 5

21. I let others know where I stand.   1 2 3 4 5

22. I seem to know just how I "fit"
into a group.   1 2 3 4 5

23. I learn from mistakes and do
not treat errors as disasters but
rather as learning experiences.   1 2 3 4 5

24. I am fun to be around.   1 2 3 4 5

For interpretation, see the Interpretation Guide in the *Instructor's Resource Manual.*

The questionnaire measures six facets of charismatic leadership. Your score can range from 4 to 20 for each section. Each question is stated as a measure of the extent to which you engage in the behavior—or elicit the feelings. The higher your score, the more you demonstrate charismatic leader behaviors.

Index 1: Management of Attention (1, 7, 13, 19).
Your score: ____. You pay especially close attention to people with whom you are communicating. You are also "focused in" on the key issues under discussion and help others to see clearly these key points. You have clear ideas about the relative importance or priorities of different issues under discussion.

Index 2: Management of Meaning (2, 8, 14, 20).
Your score: ____. This set of items centers on your communication skills, specifically your ability to get the meaning of a message across, even if this means devising some quite innovative approach.

Index 3: Management of Trust (3, 9, 15, 21).
Your score: ____. The key factor is your perceived trustworthiness as shown by your willingness to follow through on promises, to avoid "flip-flop" shifts in position, and to take clear positions.

Index 4: Management of Self (4, 10, 16, 22).
Your score: ____. This index concerns your general attitudes toward yourself and others—that is, your overall concern for others and their feelings as well as for "taking care of" feelings about yourself in a positive sense (e.g., self-regard).

Index 5: Management of Risk (5, 11, 17, 23).
Your score: ____. Effective charismatic leaders are deeply involved in what they do and do not spend excessive amounts of time or energy on plans to "protect" themselves against failure. These leaders are willing to take risks, not on a hit-or-miss basis, but after careful estimation of the odds of success or failure.

Index 6: Management of Feelings (6, 12, 18, 24).
Your score: ____. Charismatic leaders seem to consistently generate a set of positive feelings in others. Others feel that their work becomes more meaningful and that they are the "masters" of their own behavior—that is, they feel competent. They feel a sense of community, a "we-ness" with their colleagues and coworkers.

Reference: Marshall Sashkin and William C. Morris, *Experiential Exercises in Management Book*, p. 132. Copyright © 1987, Addison-Wesley Publishing Company, Inc. Reprinted by permission of Addison-Wesley Longman, Inc.

OB Online

1. Use a search engine to identify websites that deal with power and politics. What conclusions can you draw from your findings?
2. Identify a leader whose behavior you would consider transformational. Then use the Internet to find articles and/or other material that either support or refute your belief.
3. Think of three individuals who are both leaders and have their own websites. Review the sites to see what role, if any, impression management plays in how others perceive these individuals.
4. Describe how the Internet and related forms of information technology might serve as substitutes for leadership.

Building Managerial Skills

Exercise Overview: Diagnostic skills help a manager visualize appropriate responses to a situation. One situation managers often face is whether to use power to solve a problem. This exercise will help you develop your diagnostic skills as they relate to using different types of power in various situations.

Exercise Background: Several methods have been identified for using power. These include the following:

1. *Legitimate request:* The manager requests that the subordinate comply because the subordinate recognizes that the organization has given the manager the right to make the request. Most day-to-day interactions between manager and subordinate are of this type.
2. *Instrumental compliance:* A subordinate complies to get the reward the manager controls. Suppose a manager asks a subordinate to do something outside the range of her normal duties, such as working extra hours on the weekend, terminating a relationship with a long-standing buyer, or delivering bad news. The subordinate complies and, as a direct result, reaps praise and a bonus from the manager. The next time the subordinate is asked to perform a similar activity, she will recognize that compliance could help her get more rewards. Hence, the basis of instrumental compliance is clarifying important performance-reward contingencies.
3. *Coercion:* The manager suggests or implies that the subordinate will be punished, fired, or reprimanded if he does not do something.

4. *Rational persuasion:* The manager convinces the subordinate that compliance is in the subordinate's best interest. For example, a manager might argue that the subordinate should accept a transfer because it would be good for the subordinate's career. In some ways, rational persuasion is like reward power except the manager does not really control the reward.
5. *Personal identification:* A manager who recognizes that she has referent power over a subordinate can shape the subordinate's behavior by engaging in desired behaviors. The manager consciously becomes a model for the subordinate and exploits personal identification.
6. *Inspirational appeal:* A manager induces a subordinate to do something consistent with a set of higher ideals or values through inspirational appeal. For example, a plea for loyalty represents an inspirational appeal.

Exercise Task: With these ideas in mind, do the following:

1. Relate each use of power just listed to the five types of power identified in the chapter. That is, indicate which type or types of power are most closely associated with each use of power, which type or types may be related to each use of power, and which type or types are unrelated to each use of power.
2. Is a manager more likely to use multiple forms of power at the same time or use a single type of power?
3. Identify other methods of using power. What are some pitfalls associated with using power?

TEST PREPPER

ACE self-test

You have read the chapter and studied the key terms, and the exam is any day now. Think you're ready to ace it? Take this sample test to gauge your comprehension of chapter material. You can check your answers at the back of the book. Want more test questions? Visit the student website at http://college.hmco.com/business/students/ (select Griffin/Moorhead, Fundamentals of Organizational Behavior 1e) and take the ACE quizzes for more practice.

1. T F A main component of transformational leadership is creating a vision to guide change.

2. T F Charismatic leadership is the same as leading for stability.

3. T F Highly routine tasks can make leadership irrelevant.

4. T F A person truly has power only if he or she exercises it to control another person.

5. T F Legitimate power is the same as authority, granted by virtue of one's position in the organization.

6. T F A person who has coercive power controls rewards valued by others in the organization.

7. T F Managers at the top of the organization necessarily have more power than those at lower levels.

8. T F Jamie has always been able to influence others, from her early days with the company as an entry-level employee to her current position as a senior manager. This suggests Jamie has personal power.

9. T F If subordinates do not accept or identify with the leader, the best response the leader can expect to his or her requests is compliance.

10. T F To effectively use legitimate power, a leader may need to explain the reasons for his or her requests.

11. T F Punishing an employee in front of others is an effective way to use coercive power.

12. T F Most managers who responded to a survey on political behavior believe such behaviors are more prevalent at lower levels in the organization than at higher levels.

13. T F The model of political behavior presented in the text considers behaviors ethical as long as the rights of others are respected, regardless of whether the behaviors are considered fair.

14. T F The most effective strategy to manage political behaviors is to try to eliminate them.

15. T F There is enough money in the budget to implement only one new project. If two or more new projects have been proposed, political behaviors should be anticipated.

16. T F Political behaviors are more likely to arise when programmed decisions, rather than nonprogrammed decisions, need to be made.

17. T F One common political behavior technique is to control as much information as possible.

18. T F To control the agenda, a common political technique, a manager may try to stall discussion of an issue by constantly raising and pursuing minor points to meaningless ends.

19. T F Open communication is a very effective technique for restraining the impact of political behavior.

20. T F A direct, intentional effort to enhance one's image in the eyes of others is known as impression management.

21. The cornerstone of the leadership process is
   a. coercion.
   b. power.
   c. authority.
   d. responsibility.
   e. influence.

22. Leading for stability is _____ leadership; leading for change is _____ leadership.
   a. powerful; influential
   b. authoritative; responsible
   c. charismatic; coercive
   d. transactional; transformational
   e. process; property

23. As a leader, Elaine inspires interpersonal attraction, support, and acceptance. Elaine can be described as
   a. transformational.
   b. transactional.
   c. charismatic.
   d. focused on initiating structure.
   e. job centered.

24. Most experts acknowledge all of the following as elements of charismatic leadership except
   a. envisioning the future.
   b. empathizing with others.
   c. energizing others.
   d. setting high expectations.
   e. Charismatic leaders do all of the above.

25. All employees in Timothy's accounting firm are certified public accountants (CPAs) and have master's degrees. What is the likely effect of this situation on leadership in the firm?
   a. Leadership will be more necessary than ever.

   b. The most effective leader will come from outside the firm.

   c. The leadership role will likely rotate among the employees.

   d. Leaders will be effective only if they focus on job-centered behaviors.

   e. Leadership behaviors are likely to be neutralized by the employees' professional orientation.

26. As a leader, Rebecca has gradually turned over power, responsibility, and control to her self-managing group. Rebecca has engaged in
   a. consideration behaviors.
   b. superleadership.
   c. initiating-structure behaviors.
   d. transactional leadership.
   e. leadership neutralizers.

27. A person who occupies the position of chief executive officer (CEO) in the organization necessarily has the same level of _____ power.
   a. legitimate   d. expert
   b. personal   e. referent
   c. coercive

28. Because their work outcomes are so ambiguous, many workers seek approval and praise from Teresa. Teresa has _____ power.
   a. legitimate   d. position
   b. reward   e. referent
   c. coercive

29. Sandra is one of the few employees in the organization who has access to the master password list. If Carlos forgets his password, he must go to Sandra to retrieve it. Sandra has _____ power.
   a. legitimate   d. expert
   b. reward   e. referent
   c. coercive

30. Which of the following is least related to personal power?
   a. Referent   d. Reward
   b. Expert   e. Legitimate
   c. Coercive

31. A formal leader, at a minimum, will have
   a. personal power.
   b. position power.
   c. referent power.
   d. expert power.
   e. charisma.

32. A subordinate who accepts and identifies with a leader is likely to respond to the leader's influence attempts in which of the following ways?

   a. Resistance   d. Expertise
   b. Compliance   e. Reverence
   c. Commitment

33. Ted is willing to carry out his manager's wishes as long as doing so will not require extra effort. Ted's response is one of
   a. resistance.   d. expertise.
   b. compliance.   e. reverence.
   c. commitment.

34. Subtly making others aware of one's education, experience, and accomplishments is one way to exercise which form of power?
   a. Referent   d. Reward
   b. Legitimate   e. Coercive
   c. Expert

35. In general, a leader exercises legitimate power by
   a. formally requesting that subordinates do something.
   b. distributing rewards.
   c. clarifying punishments for noncompliance.
   d. sharing information.
   e. building subordinates' confidence.

36. The form of power that should be used least frequently is
   a. referent.   d. expert.
   b. legitimate.   e. coercive.
   c. reward.

37. Making sure subordinates are fully informed about rules and the penalties for violating them, and then administering discipline consistently and uniformly are recommendations for using _____ power.
   a. reward   d. coercive
   b. legitimate   e. referent
   c. expert

38. According to the model of political behavior, a given course of action is considered ethical as long as it
   a. helps more people than it hurts.
   b. respects the rights of others and is fair.
   c. makes money for the organization and threatens no relationships.
   d. is legal and is hidden from the public view.
   e. cannot be proven and harms no one.

39. Which of the following is not a basic reason political behaviors exist in organizations?
   a. Ambiguous goals
   b. Scarce resources
   c. Organizational change
   d. Charismatic leaders
   e. Nonprogrammed decisions

CHAPTER 12

Decision Making and Negotiation

MANAGEMENT PREVIEW

Making decisions is the most basic of all management activities. Some decisions involve major events, such as buying another company or launching an expensive new product line, and will have a dramatic impact on the firm's future growth, profits, and even survival. Others, such as choosing the colors of the new office carpet or deciding when to re-order office supplies, are much less significant. However, all decisions are important on some level; thus, managers need to understand how decisions are made.

This chapter explores decision making in detail. We start by examining the nature of decision making. Next, we describe several approaches to understanding the decision-making process. We then discuss two related behavioral aspects of decision making. Next, we explore several important issues in group decision making. Finally, we examine negotiation, a common management activity closely related to decision making.

After you have studied this chapter, you should be able to:
- ☐ *Describe the nature of decision making.*
- ☐ *Discuss the decision-making process for a variety of perspectives.*
- ☐ *Explain related behavioral aspects of decision making.*
- ☐ *Describe group decision making in organizations.*
- ☐ *Discuss negotiation in organizations.*

We begin by describing how effective decision making has been a boon to both MTV and its parent company, Viacom.

When Bill Roedy became president of MTV's Networks International division, he probably didn't count on singing *Madame Butterfly* arias alone and unaccompanied in front of dozens of Chinese executives and his boss. But Roedy, a fifty-three-year-old West Point graduate, was willing to do it, so intent is he on doing whatever it takes to cultivate long-term relationships with potential partners. Listeners took Roedy's opera performance as a sign of his understanding of Chinese customs, which can include impromptu classical singing at business dinners. Roedy was persuading Chinese cable TV operators to carry MTV, and the performance must have been effective because today MTV is watched in 60 million Chinese homes on more than forty cable systems.

In addition to his vocal talents, Roedy's decision-making skills are paying off for MTV. Early on, it was decided that programming in other countries should consist primarily of local performers (currently 70 percent local, 30 percent American). This move was part marketing genius—allowing MTV to attract both conservative and adventurous listeners—and part brilliant negotiation strategy. "We've had very little resistance once we explain that we're not in the business of exporting American culture," says Roedy. The mix allows MTV's parent company, Viacom, to obtain the rights to the best international performers for introduction to the American market. To overcome regulatory opposition, Roedy has dined with former Israeli prime minister Shimon Peres, Chinese president Jiang Zemin, and even Cuban leader Fidel Castro.

A key decision was to focus on regions with high numbers of teens and in high-growth television ownership, such as India, Brazil, and China. MTV is currently viewed by 84.6 million households in North America, 124.1 million in Europe, 28.1 million in Latin America, and 137.9 million in Asia. "Everyone who has a TV knows there's something called MTV," claims Chantara Kapahi, a student at Jai Hind College in Bombay, India. The decision to focus on countries with an increased standard of living pays a double bonus: As consumer buying power increases, local businesses are more willing and able to pay for MTV advertisements. In countries where public sentiment or government policy makes it difficult for American companies to compete, such as Italy and Brazil, MTV partners with a local cable provider.

Viacom cleverly decided to move into many aspects of the media and entertainment industry, leading to name recognition and other synergies. Among other holdings, Viacom owns CBS, UPN, Paramount, MTV, Nickelodeon, BET, VH1, CNN, CMT, Comedy Central, Showtime, Blockbuster, and the Simon and Schuster publishing house. Viacom plans to use MTV to break ground in new regional markets and then follow up with its other cable offerings. "Let's face it, the way people know Viacom is through MTV," says Viacom chief operating officer and president Mel Karmazin. Sound choices have put the firm on the path to success. Its latest achievement was a broadcast of the May 2004 China Central TV–MTV Mandarin Music awards. The show reached an estimated 500 million households in China and another 400 million around the world, making it one of the most-watched broadcasts ever.

"We've had very little resistance once we explain that we're not in the business of exporting American culture."—Bill Roedy, MTV Networks International president

References: "Businesses," "Viacom Chairman Sumner Redstone Meets with China's President Jiang Zemin in Beijing, to Reaffirm Viacom's Commitment to China," Viacom website, www.viacom.com on May 13, 2002; John Simmons, "Come Se Dice Must-See TV?" *Fortune*, April 15, 2002; "Viacom: A Survivor—and Much More," *BusinessWeek*, April 3, 2002; "How MTV Conquered Italy," *BusinessWeek*, February 18, 2002, p. 84; "MTV's World," *BusinessWeek*, February 18, 2002, pp. 81–84 (quotation, p. 82).

The individual at the top of an organization, such as Bill Roedy at MTV, is paid to make both tough and easy decisions. Regardless of which decisions are made, though, it is almost certain that some observers will criticize and others will applaud. Indeed, in the rough-and-tumble world of business, few simple or easy decisions exist. Some managers claim to focus on the company's long-term success and make decisions accordingly. Others clearly focus on the here-and-now. Some decisions deal with employees, some with investors, and some with dollars and cents. All decisions, however, require careful thought and consideration. This chapter describes many different perspectives on decision making.

The Nature of Decision Making

Decision making is the process of choosing from among several alternatives.

A **programmed decision** is a decision that recurs often enough for a decision rule to be developed.

A **decision rule** is a statement that tells a decision maker which alternative to choose based on the characteristics of the decision situation.

Decision making is the process of choosing one alternative from among several. In football, for example, the quarterback can run any of perhaps a hundred plays. With the goal of scoring a touchdown always in mind, he chooses the play that seems to promise the best outcome. His choice is based on his understanding of the game situation, the likelihood of various outcomes, and his preference for each outcome.

Figure 12.1 shows the basic elements of decision making. A decision maker's actions are guided by a goal. Each of several alternative courses of action is linked with various outcomes. Information is available on the alternatives, on the likelihood that each outcome will occur, and on the value of each outcome relative to the goal. The decision maker chooses one alternative on the basis of his or her evaluation of the information.

Decisions made in organizations can be classified according to frequency and to information conditions. In a decision-making context, frequency means how often a particular decision situation recurs and information conditions describe how much information is available about the likelihood of various outcomes.

Types of Decisions

The frequency of recurrence determines whether a decision is programmed or nonprogrammed. A **programmed decision** recurs often enough for a decision rule to be developed. A **decision rule** tells decision makers which alternative to choose once they have predetermined information about the decision situation. The appropriate decision rule is used whenever the same situation is encountered.

FIGURE 12.1

Elements of Decision Making

A decision maker has a goal, evaluates the outcomes of alternative courses of action in terms of the goal, and selects one alternative to implement.

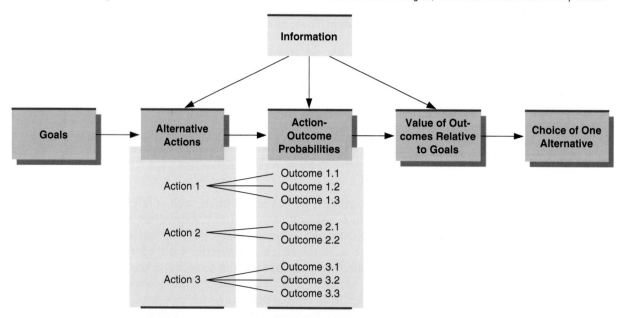

Programmed decisions are usually highly structured; that is, the goals are clear and well known, the decision-making procedure is already established, and the sources and channels of information are clearly defined.[1]

Airlines use established procedures when an airplane breaks down and cannot be used on a particular flight. Passengers may not view the issue as a programmed decision because they experience this situation relatively infrequently. However, the airlines know that equipment problems that render a plane unfit for service arise regularly. Each airline has its own set of clear-cut procedures to use in the event of equipment problems. A given flight may be delayed, canceled, or continued on a different plane, depending on the nature of the problem and other circumstances (such as the number of passengers booked, the next scheduled flight for the same destination, and so forth).

When a problem or decision situation has not been encountered before, however, a decision maker cannot rely on previously established decision rules. Such a decision is called a **nonprogrammed decision,** and it requires problem solving. **Problem solving** is a special form of decision making in which the issue is unique; it requires developing and evaluating alternatives without the aid of a decision rule. Nonprogrammed decisions are poorly structured because information is ambiguous, there is no clear procedure for making the decision, and the goals are often vague. Many of the decisions that had to be made by government, military, and business leaders in the wake of the events of September 11, 2001, were clearly of this type.

Table 12.1 summarizes the characteristics of programmed and nonprogrammed decisions. Note that programmed decisions are more common at the lower levels of the organization, whereas a primary responsibility of top management is to make the difficult, nonprogrammed decisions that determine the organization's long-term effectiveness. By definition, the strategic decisions for which top management is responsible are poorly structured and nonroutine, and have far-reaching consequences.[2] Programmed decisions, then, can be made according to previously tested rules and procedures. Nonprogrammed decisions generally require that the decision maker exercise judgment and creativity. In other words, all problems require a decision, but not all decisions require problem solving.

A **nonprogrammed decision** is a decision that recurs infrequently and for which there is no previously established decision rule.

Problem solving is a form of decision making in which the issue is unique, requiring that alternatives be developed and evaluated without the aid of a decision rule.

TABLE 12.1

Characteristics of Programmed and Nonprogrammed Decisions

Characteristics	Programmed Decisions	Nonprogrammed Decisions
Type of Decision	Well structured	Poorly structured
Frequency	Repetitive and routine	New and unusual
Goals	Clear, specific	Vague
Information	Readily available	Not available, unclear channels
Consequences	Minor	Major
Organizational Level	Lower levels	Upper levels
Time for Solution	Short	Relatively long
Basis for Solution	Decision rules, set procedures	Judgment and creativity

Information Required for Decision Making

While decisions are made to bring about desired outcomes, the information available about those outcomes varies. The range of available information can be considered as a continuum whose endpoints represent complete certainty when all alternative outcomes are known and complete uncertainty when alternative outcomes are unknown. Points between the two extremes create risk: The decision maker has some information about the possible outcomes and may be able to estimate the probability of their occurrence.

Different information conditions present different challenges to the decision maker.[3] For example, suppose the marketing manager of PlayStation 2 is trying to determine whether to launch an expensive promotional effort for a new video game (see Figure 12.2). For simplicity, assume there are only two alternatives: to promote the game or not to promote it. Under a **condition of certainty,** the manager knows the outcomes of each alternative. If the new game is promoted heavily, the company will realize a $10 million profit. Without promotion, the company will realize only a $2 million profit. Here the decision is simple: Promote the game. (Note: These figures are created for the purposes of this example and are not actual profit figures for any company.)

> Under a **condition of certainty**, the manager knows the outcomes of each alternative.

FIGURE 12.2

Alternative Outcomes Under Different Information Conditions

This figure shows the three decision-making conditions of certainty, risk, and uncertainty for the decision about whether to promote a new video game to the market.

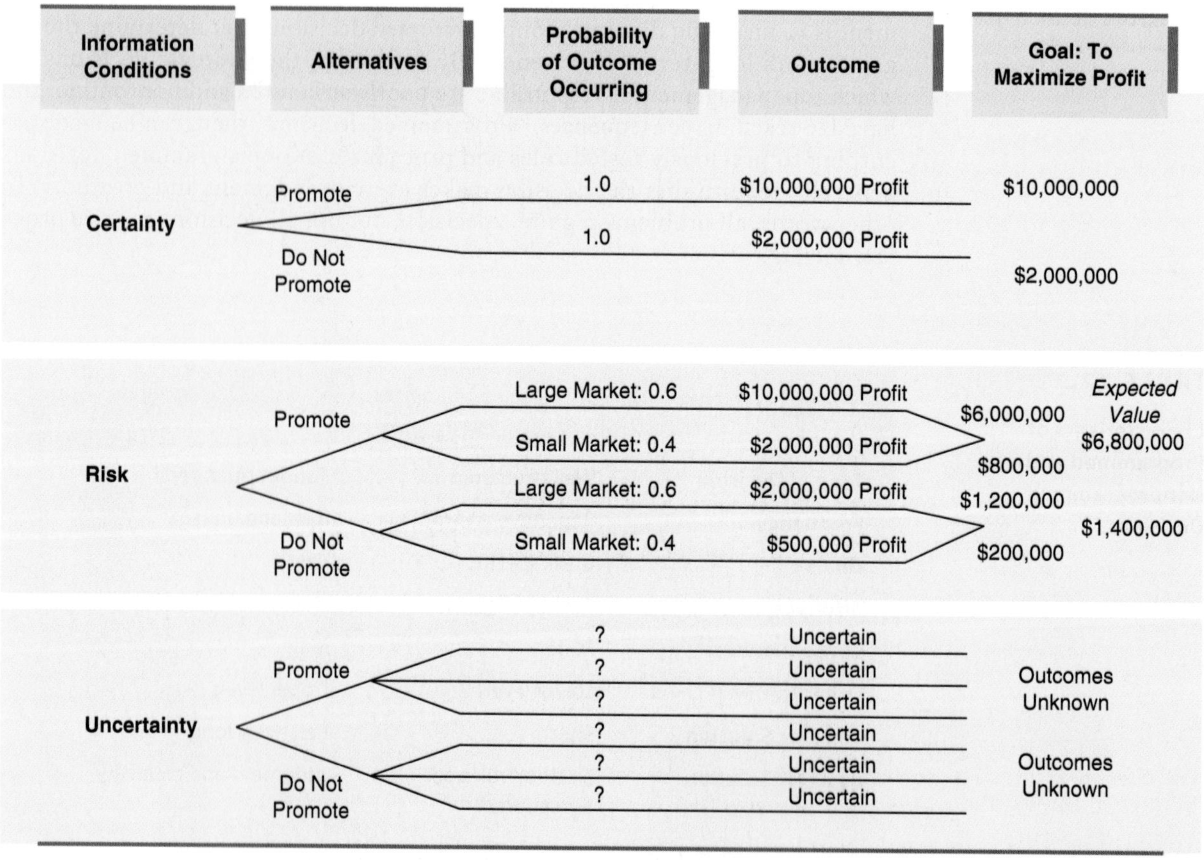

Information Conditions	Alternatives	Probability of Outcome Occurring	Outcome	Goal: To Maximize Profit
Certainty	Promote	1.0	$10,000,000 Profit	$10,000,000
	Do Not Promote	1.0	$2,000,000 Profit	$2,000,000
Risk	Promote	Large Market: 0.6	$10,000,000 Profit	$6,000,000 / $800,000 *Expected Value* $6,800,000
		Small Market: 0.4	$2,000,000 Profit	
	Do Not Promote	Large Market: 0.6	$2,000,000 Profit	$1,200,000 / $200,000 $1,400,000
		Small Market: 0.4	$500,000 Profit	
Uncertainty	Promote	?	Uncertain	Outcomes Unknown
		?	Uncertain	
		?	Uncertain	
	Do Not Promote	?	Uncertain	Outcomes Unknown
		?	Uncertain	
		?	Uncertain	

Under a **condition of risk**, the decision maker cannot know with certainty what the outcome of a given action will be but has enough information to estimate the probabilities of various outcomes.

Under a **condition of risk**, the decision maker cannot know with certainty what the outcome of a given action will be but has enough information to estimate the probabilities of various outcomes. Thus, working from information gathered by the market research department, the marketing manager in our example can estimate the likelihood of each outcome in a risk situation. In this case, the alternatives are defined by the size of the market. The probability for a large video game market is 0.6, and the probability for a small market is 0.4. The manager can calculate the expected value of the promotional effort based on these probabilities and the expected profits associated with each. To find the expected value of an alternative, the manager multiplies each outcome's value by the probability of its occurrence. The sum of these calculations for all possible outcomes represents that alternative's expected value. In this case, the expected value of alternative 1—to promote the new game—is as follows:

$$0.6 \times \$10,000,000 = \$6,000,000$$
$$+ \ 0.4 \times \$2,000,000 = \$800,000$$

Expected value of alternative 1 = $6,800,000

The expected value of alternative 2—not to promote the new game—is $1,400,000 (see Figure 12.2). The marketing manager should choose the first alternative, because its expected value is higher. The manager should recognize, however, that although the numbers look convincing, they are based on incomplete information and are only estimates of probability.

Under a **condition of uncertainty**, the decision maker lacks enough information to estimate the probabilities of possible outcomes.

The decision maker who lacks enough information to estimate the probabilities of outcomes (or perhaps even to identify the outcomes at all) faces a **condition of uncertainty.** In the PlayStation 2 example, this might be the case if sales of video games recently collapsed and it was not clear whether the precipitous drop was temporary or permanent, or when information to clarify the situation would be available. Under such circumstances, the decision maker may wait for more information to reduce uncertainty or rely on judgment, experience, and intuition to make the decision.

Decision making, however, is not always so easy to classify in terms of certainty, uncertainty, and risk. Some individuals are more likely than others to take risks, as we discussed in Chapter 3. In addition, as we saw in Chapter 2, it may be more common to take risks in some parts of the world than in others.

The Decision-Making Process

┌─*LEARNING OBJECTIVE*─┐
Discuss the decision-making process for a variety of perspectives.

Several approaches to decision making offer insights into the process by which managers arrive at decisions. The rational approach is appealing because of its logic and economy. Yet these very qualities raise questions about this approach because actual decision making often is not a wholly rational process. The behavioral approach, meanwhile, attempts to account for the limits on rationality in decision making. The practical approach combines features of the rational and behavioral approaches. Finally, the personal approach focuses on the decision-making processes individuals use in difficult situations.

The **rational decision-making approach** is a systematic, step-by-step process for making decisions.

The Rational Approach

The **rational decision-making approach** assumes managers follow a systematic, step-by-step process. It further assumes the organization is economically based and managed by decision makers who are entirely objective and have complete

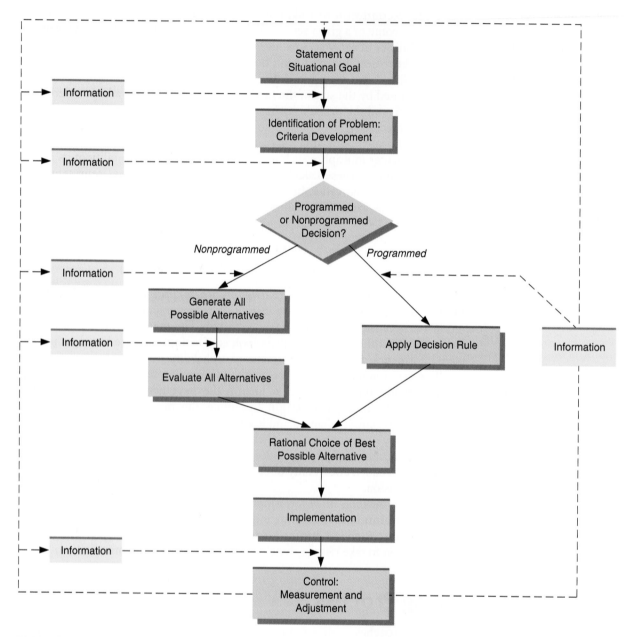

FIGURE 12.3

The Rational Decision-Making Process

The rational model follows a systematic, step-by-step approach from goals to implementation, measurement, and control.

information.[4] Figure 12.3 identifies the steps of the process, starting with stating a goal and running logically through the process until the best decision is made, implemented, and controlled.

State the Situational Goal   The rational decision-making process begins with the statement of a situational goal, that is, a goal for a particular situation. The goal of a marketing department, for example, may be to obtain a certain market share by the end of the year. (Some models of decision making do not start with a goal. We include it because it is the standard used to determine whether a decision is to be made.)

Identify the Problem   The purpose of problem identification is to gather information that bears on the goal. If a discrepancy exists between the goal and the actual state, action may be needed. In the marketing example, the group may gather information about the company's actual market share and compare it with the desired market share. A difference between the two represents a problem that necessitates a decision. Reliable information is very important in this step. Inaccurate information can lead to an unnecessary decision or no decision when one is required.

Determine the Decision Type   Next, the decision makers must determine if the problem represents a programmed or a nonprogrammed decision. If a programmed decision is needed, the appropriate decision rule is invoked, and the process moves on to the choice among alternatives. A programmed marketing decision may be called for if analysis reveals, for example, that competitors are outspending the company on print advertising. Because creating print advertising and buying space for it are well-established functions of the marketing group, the problem requires only a programmed decision.

Although it may seem simple to diagnose a situation as programmed, apply a decision rule, and arrive at a solution, mistakes can still occur. Choosing the wrong decision rule or assuming the problem calls for a programmed decision when it actually requires a nonprogrammed decision can result in a poor decision. The same caution applies to the determination that a nonprogrammed decision is called for. If the situation is wrongly diagnosed, the decision maker wastes time and resources seeking a new solution to an old problem, or "reinventing the wheel."

Generate Alternatives   The next step in making a nonprogrammed decision is to generate alternatives. The rational process assumes decision makers will generate all the possible alternative solutions to the problem. However, this assumption is unrealistic because even simple business problems can have scores of possible solutions. Decision makers may rely on education and experience as well as knowledge of the situation to generate alternatives. In addition, they may seek information from other people such as peers, subordinates, and supervisors. Decision makers may analyze the symptoms of the problem for clues or fall back on intuition or judgment to develop alternative solutions.[5] If the marketing department in our example determines that a nonprogrammed decision is required, it will need to generate alternatives for increasing market share.

Evaluate Alternatives   Evaluation involves assessing all possible alternatives in terms of predetermined decision criteria. The ultimate decision criterion is "Will this alternative bring us nearer to the goal?" In each case, the decision maker must examine each alternative for evidence that it will reduce the discrepancy between the desired state and the actual state. The evaluation process usually includes (1) describing the anticipated outcomes (benefits) of each alternative, (2) evaluating the anticipated costs of each alternative, and (3) estimating the uncertainties and risks associated with each alternative.[6] In most decision situations, the decision maker lacks perfect information regarding the outcomes of all alternatives. At one extreme, as shown earlier in Figure 12.2, outcomes may be known with certainty; at the other, the decision maker has no information whatsoever, so the outcomes are entirely uncertain. Risk, however, is the most common situation.

Choose an Alternative   Choosing an alternative is usually the most crucial step in the decision-making process. Choosing consists of selecting the alternative with the highest possible payoff based on the benefits, costs, risks, and uncertainties of all alternatives. In the PlayStation 2 promotion example, the decision maker evaluated the two alternatives by calculating their expected values. Following the rational approach, the manager would choose the alternative with the largest expected value.

Even with the rational approach, however, difficulties can arise in choosing an alternative. First, when two or more alternatives have equal payoffs, the decision maker must obtain more information or use some other criterion to make the choice. Second, when no single alternative will accomplish the objective, some combination of two or three alternatives may have to be implemented. Finally, if no alternative or combination of alternatives will solve the problem, the decision maker must obtain more information, generate more alternatives, or change the goals.[7]

An important part of the choice phase is the consideration of **contingency plans,** alternative actions that can be taken if the primary course of action is unexpectedly disrupted or rendered inappropriate.[8] Planning for contingencies is part of the transition between choosing the preferred alternative and implementing it. In developing contingency plans, the decision maker usually asks such questions as "What if something unexpected happens during the implementation of this alternative?" or "If the economy goes into a recession, will the choice of this alternative ruin the company?" or "How can we alter this plan if the economy suddenly rebounds and begins to grow?"

Contingency plans are alternative actions to take if the primary course of action is unexpectedly disrupted or rendered inappropriate.

Implement the Plan   Implementation puts the decision into action. It builds on the commitment and motivation of those who participated in the decision-making process (and may actually bolster individual commitment and motivation). To succeed, implementation requires the proper use of resources and good management skills. Following the decision to heavily promote the new PlayStation 2 game, for example, the marketing manager must implement the decision by assigning the project to a work group or task force. The success of this team depends on the leadership, the reward structure, the communications system, and group dynamics. Sometimes the decision maker begins to doubt a choice already made. This doubt is called *postdecision dissonance* or, more generally, **cognitive dissonance.**[9] To reduce the tension created by the dissonance, the decision maker may seek to rationalize the decision further with new information.

Cognitive dissonance is doubt about a choice that has already been made.

Control: Measure and Adjust   In the final stage of the rational decision-making process, the outcomes of the decision are measured and compared with the desired goal. If a discrepancy remains, the decision maker may restart the decision-making process by setting a new goal (or reiterating the existing one). The decision maker, dissatisfied with the previous decision, may modify the subsequent decision-making process to avoid another mistake. Changes can be made in any part of the process, as Figure 12.3 illustrates by the arrows leading from the control step to each of the other steps. Decision making therefore is a dynamic, self-correcting, and ongoing process in organizations.

Suppose a marketing department implements a new print advertising campaign. After implementation, it constantly monitors market research data and compares its new market share with the desired market share. If the advertising has the desired effect, no changes will be made in the promotion campaign. If, however, the data indicate no change in market share, additional decisions and imple-

The decision-making process is supposed to be logical and rational, but often it is affected by behavioral, practical, and personal considerations. Consider Gabrielle Melchionda, a Maine native whose skin care product business is booming. She was recently offered a lucrative contract to begin exporting her products to Turkey. But she turned it down when she learned the exporter also sold weapons. Had rational decision making prevailed, she would have jumped on the idea. But her own personal values kept her focused on what was important to her as a person—and it wasn't just the money!

mentation of a contingency plan may be necessary. In a classic example, when Nissan introduced its luxury car line Infiniti, it relied on a Zen-like series of ads that featured images of rocks, plants, and water—but no images of the car. At the same time, Toyota was featuring pictures of its new luxury car line, Lexus, which quickly established itself as a market leader. When Infiniti managers realized their mistake, they quickly pulled the old ads and started running new ones centered around images of the car.[10]

Strengths and Weaknesses of the Rational Approach The rational approach has several strengths. It forces the decision maker to consider a decision in a logical, sequential manner, and the in-depth analysis of alternatives enables the decision maker to choose on the basis of information rather than emotion or social pressure. However, the rigid assumptions of this approach are often unrealistic.[11] The amount of information available to managers is usually limited by either time or cost constraints, and most decision makers have limited ability to process information about the alternatives. In addition, not all alternatives lend themselves to quantification in terms that will allow for easy comparison. Finally, because they cannot predict the future, decision makers are unlikely to know all possible outcomes of each alternative.

The Behavioral Approach

Whereas the rational approach assumes managers operate logically and rationally, the behavioral approach acknowledges the importance of human behavior in the decision-making process. In particular, a crucial assumption of the behavioral approach is that decision makers operate with bounded rationality rather than with perfect rationality as assumed by the rational approach. **Bounded rationality** is the idea that although individuals may seek the best solution to a problem, the demands of processing all the information bearing on the problem, generating all possible solutions, and choosing the single best solution are beyond the capabilities of most decision makers. Thus, they accept less than ideal solutions based on a process that is neither exhaustive nor entirely rational. For example, one study found that under time pressure, groups usually eliminate all but the two most favorable alternatives and then process the remaining two in great detail.[12] Thus, decision makers operating with bounded rationality limit the inputs to the decision-making process and base decisions on judgment and personal biases as well as on logic.[13]

Bounded rationality is the idea that decision makers cannot deal with information about all aspects and alternatives pertaining to a problem and therefore choose to tackle some meaningful subset of it.

The **behavioral approach** uses rules of thumb, suboptimizing, and satisficing in making decisions.

The **behavioral approach** is characterized by (1) the use of procedures and rules of thumb, (2) suboptimizing, and (3) satisficing. Uncertainty in decision making can initially be reduced by relying on procedures and rules of thumb. If, for example, increasing print advertising has boosted a company's market share in the past, managers may use that linkage as a rule of thumb in decision making. When the previous month's market share drops below a certain level, the company might increase its print advertising expenditures by 25 percent during the following month.

Suboptimizing is knowingly accepting less than the
best possible outcome to
avoid unintended negative
effects on other aspects of
the organization.

Suboptimizing is knowingly accepting less than the best possible outcome. Frequently it is not feasible to make the ideal decision in a real-world situation given organizational constraints. The decision maker often must suboptimize to avoid unintended negative effects on other departments, product lines, or decisions.[14] An automobile manufacturer, for example, can cut costs dramatically and increase efficiency if it schedules the production of one model at a time. Thus, the production group's optimal decision is single-model scheduling. However, the marketing group, seeking to optimize its sales goals by offering a wide variety of models, may demand the opposite production schedule: short runs of entirely different models. The groups in the middle, design and scheduling, may suboptimize the benefits the production and marketing groups seek by planning long runs of slightly different models. This is the practice of large auto manufacturers such as General Motors and Ford, which make several body styles in numerous models on the same production line.

Satisficing is examining
alternatives only until a solution that meets minimal
requirements is found.

The final feature of the behavioral approach is **satisficing:** examining alternatives only until a solution that meets minimal requirements is found and then ceasing to look for a better one.[15] The search for alternatives is usually a sequential process guided by procedures and rules of thumb based on previous experiences with similar problems. The search often ends when the first minimally acceptable choice is encountered. The resulting choice may narrow the discrepancy between the desired and actual states, but it is not likely to be the optimal solution. As the process is repeated, incremental improvements slowly reduce the discrepancy between the actual and desired states.

The Practical Approach

The **practical approach to**
decision making combines
the steps of the rational approach with the conditions
in the behavioral approach
to create a more realistic approach for making decisions
in organizations.

Because of the unrealistic demands of the rational approach and the limited, short-run orientation of the behavioral approach, neither is entirely satisfactory. However, the worthwhile features of each can be combined into a **practical approach to decision making,** shown in Figure 12.4. The steps in this process are the same as in the rational approach; however, the conditions recognized by the behavioral approach are added to provide a more realistic process. For example, the practical approach suggests that rather than generating all alternatives, the decision maker should try to go beyond rules of thumb and satisficing limitations and generate as many alternatives as time, money, and other practicalities of the situation allow. In this synthesis of the other two approaches, the rational approach provides an analytical framework for making decisions, whereas the behavioral approach provides a moderating influence.

In practice, decision makers use some hybrid of the rational, behavioral, and practical approaches to make the tough day-to-day decisions in running organizations. Some decision makers use a methodical process of gathering as much information as possible, developing and evaluating alternatives, and seeking advice from knowledgeable people before making a decision. Others fly from one decision to another, making seemingly hasty decisions and barking out orders to subordinates. The second group would seem not to use much information or a rational approach to making decisions. Recent research, however, suggests that managers who make decisions very quickly probably are using just as much, or more, information and generating and evaluating as many alternatives as slower, more methodical decision makers.[16]

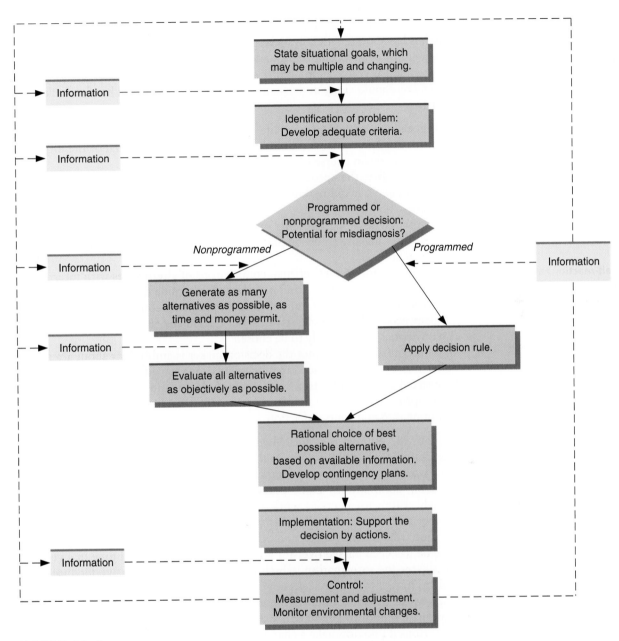

FIGURE 12.4

Practical Approaches to Decision Making with Behavioral Guidelines

The practical model applies some of the conditions recognized by the behavioral approach to the rational approach to decision making. Although similar to the rational model, the practical approach recognizes personal limitations at each point (or step) in the process.

The Personal Approach

Although the models just described have provided significant insight into decision making, they do not fully explain the processes people engage in when they are preoccupied and nervous about making a decision that has major implications for themselves, their organizations, or their families. In short, the models fail to capture all the conditions under which many decisions are made. One attempt to pro-

The **conflict model** deals with the personal conflicts people experience in particularly difficult decision situations.

vide a more realistic view of individual decision making is the model presented by Irving Janis and Leon Mann.[17] The Janis-Mann concept, called the **conflict model,** is based on research in social psychology and individual decision processes, and is a highly personal approach to decision making. Although the model may appear complex, if you examine it one step at a time and follow the example in this section, you should easily understand how it works. The model has five basic characteristics:

1. It deals only with important life decisions—marriage, schooling, career, and major organizational decisions—that commit the individual or the organization to a certain course of action following the decision.
2. It recognizes that procrastination and rationalization are mechanisms by which people avoid making difficult decisions and cope with the associated stress.
3. It explicitly acknowledges that some decisions probably will be wrong and that the fear of making an unsound decision can be a deterrent to making any decision at all.
4. It provides for **self-reactions,** comparisons of alternatives with internalized moral standards. Internalized moral standards guide decision making as much as economic and social outcomes do. A proposed course of action may offer many economic and social rewards, but if it violates the decision maker's moral convictions, it is unlikely to be chosen.
5. It recognizes that at times the decision maker is ambivalent about alternative courses of action; in such circumstances, it is very difficult to make a whole-hearted commitment to a single choice. Major life decisions seldom allow compromise, however; usually they are either-or decisions that require commitment to one course of action.

Self-reactions are comparisons of alternatives with internalized moral standards.

Figure 12.5 shows the Janis-Mann conflict model of decision making. A concrete example will help explain each step. Richard, a thirty-year-old engineer with a working wife and two young children, has been employed at a large manufacturing company for eight years. He keeps abreast of his career progress through visits with peers at work and in other companies, feedback from his manager and others regarding his work and future with the firm, the alumni magazine from his university, and other sources. At work one morning, Richard learns he has been passed over for a promotion for the second time in a year. He investigates the information, which can be considered negative feedback, and confirms it. As a result, he seeks out other information regarding his career at the company, the prospect of changing employers, and the possibility of going back to graduate school to get an MBA. At the same time, he asks himself, "Are the risks serious if I do not make a change?" If the answer is *no,* Richard will continue his present activities. In the model's terms, this option is called **unconflicted adherence.** If instead the answer is *yes* or *maybe,* Richard will move to the next question in the model.

Unconflicted adherence entails continuing with current activities if doing so does not entail serious risks.

The second step asks, "Are the risks serious if I *do* make a change?" If Richard goes on to this step, he will gather information about potential losses from making a change. He may, for example, find out whether he would lose health insurance and pension benefits if he changed jobs or went back to graduate school. If he believes changing presents no serious risks, Richard will make the change, called an **unconflicted change.** Otherwise, he will move on to the next step.

Unconflicted change involves making decisions in present activities if doing so presents no serious risks.

But suppose Richard has determined the risks are serious whether or not he makes a change. He believes he must make a change because he will not be pro-

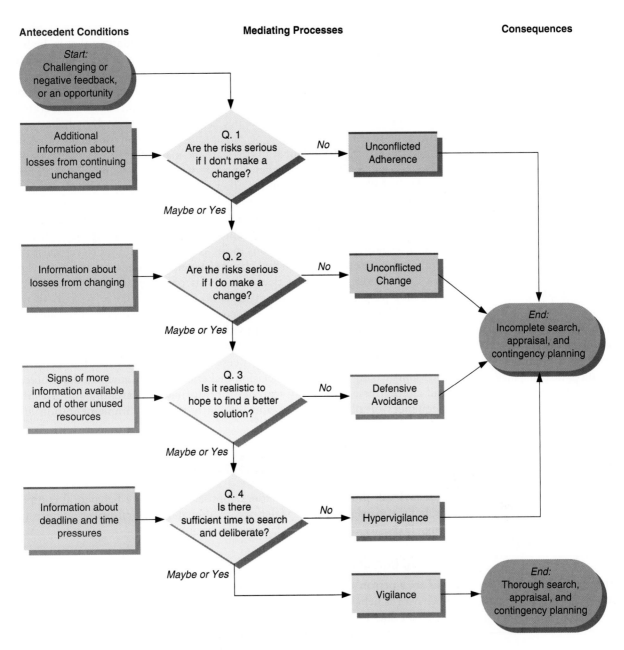

Antecedent Conditions   **Mediating Processes**   **Consequences**

FIGURE 12.5

Janis-Mann Conflict Model of Decision Making

A decision maker answering yes to all four questions will engage in vigilant information processing.

Reference: Adapted with the permission of The Free Press, a Division of Simon & Schuster Adult Publishing Group from *Decision Making: A Psychological Analysis of Conflict, Choice, and Commitment*, by Irving L. Janis and Leon Mann. Copyright © 1977 by the Free Press. All rights reserved.

moted further in his present company; yet serious risks are also associated with making a change—perhaps loss of benefits, uncertain promotion opportunities in another company, or lost income from going to graduate school for two years. In the third step, Richard wonders, "Is it realistic to hope to find a better solution?" He continues to look for information that can help him make the decision. If the

Defensive avoidance entails making no changes in present activities and avoiding further contact with associated issues because finding a better solution appears highly unlikely.

Hypervigilance is frantic, superficial pursuit of some satisficing strategy.

Vigilant information processing involves thoroughly investigating all possible alternatives, weighing their costs and benefits before making a decision, and developing contingency plans.

answer to this third question is *no*, Richard may give up hope of finding anything better and opt for what Janis and Mann call **defensive avoidance;** that is, he will make no change and avoid any further contact with the issue. A positive response, however, will move Richard onward to the next step.

At this point, Richard recognizes the serious risks involved but expects to find a solution, and asks himself, "Is there sufficient time to search and deliberate?" Richard now considers how quickly he needs to make a change. If he believes he has little time to deliberate, perhaps because of his age, he will experience what Janis and Mann call **hypervigilance.** In this state, he may suffer severe psychological stress and engage in frantic, superficial pursuit of some satisficing strategy. (This might also be called "panic"!) If, on the other hand, Richard believes he has two or three years to consider various alternatives, he will undertake vigilant information processing, in which he will thoroughly investigate all possible alternatives, weigh their costs and benefits before making a choice, and develop contingency plans.

Negative answers to the questions in the conflict model lead to responses of unconflicted adherence, unconflicted change, defensive avoidance, and hypervigilance. All are coping strategies that result in incomplete search, appraisal, and contingency planning. A decision maker who gives the same answer to all the questions will always engage in the same coping strategy. However, if the answers change as the situation alters, the individual's coping strategies may change as well. The decision maker who answers *yes* to each of the four questions is led to **vigilant information processing,** a process similar to that outlined in the rational decision-making model. The decision maker objectively analyzes the problem and all alternatives, thoroughly searches for information, carefully evaluates the consequences of all alternatives, and diligently plans for implementation and contingencies.

Related Behavioral Aspects of Decision Making

Ethics are an individual's personal beliefs about what is right and wrong behavior.

The behavioral, practical, and personal approaches all have behavioral components, but the manager must consider two additional behavioral aspects of decision making. These are ethics and escalation of commitment.

Ethics and Decision Making

Ethics are a person's beliefs about what constitutes right and wrong behavior. Ethical behavior is behavior that conforms to generally accepted social norms; unethical behavior does not conform to these norms. Some decisions managers make may have little or nothing to do with their own personal ethics, but many other decisions are influenced by managers' ethics. For example, decisions involving such disparate issues as hiring and firing employees, dealing with customers and suppliers, setting wages and assigning tasks, and maintaining one's expense account are all subject to ethical influences.

In general, ethical dilemmas for managers may center on direct personal gain, indirect personal gain, or simple personal preferences. Consider a top executive contemplating a decision about a potential takeover. Her stock option package may result in enormous personal gain if the decision goes one way, even though stockholders may benefit more if the decision goes the other way. An indirect personal gain may result when a decision does not directly add value to a manager's personal worth but does enhance her or his career. Or the manager may face a choice about relocating a company facility in which one of the options is closest to his residence.

Ethics and decision making have become very visibly linked in recent times. Indeed, so critical are ethics today that some MBA programs have started screening potential students on the basis of their integrity. In the words of Rosemarie Martinelli, director of MBA admissions at the Wharton School, "Everyone has ethics on the mind right now."

Managers should carefully and deliberately consider the ethical context of every one of their decisions. The goal, of course, is for the manager to make the decision that is in the best interest of the firm as opposed to the best interest of the manager. Doing so requires personal honesty and integrity. Managers also find it helpful to discuss potential ethical dilemmas with colleagues. Peers can often provide an objective view of a situation that may help a manager avoid unintentionally making an unethical decision. One recent situation concerning ethical decision making—Imclone's decision to present a cancer-fighting drug, Erbitux, for FDA approval—is discussed in the Business of Ethics box.

Escalation of Commitment

Escalation of commitment is the tendency to persist in an ineffective course of action when evidence reveals that the project cannot succeed.

Sometimes people continue trying to implement a decision despite clear and convincing evidence that substantial problems exist. **Escalation of commitment** is the tendency to persist in an ineffective course of action when evidence indicates the project is doomed to failure. A good example is the decision by the government of British Columbia to hold a World's Fair in Vancouver. Originally the organizers expected the project to break even financially so the province would not have to increase taxes to pay for it. However, as work progressed, it became clear that expenses were far greater than projected. However, organizers considered it too late to call off the event, despite the huge losses that obviously would occur. Eventually the province conducted a $300 million lottery to try to cover the costs.[18] Similar examples abound in stock market investments, in political and military situations, and in organizations developing any type of new project.

There are several possible reasons for escalation of commitment.[19] Some projects require much front-end investment and offer little return until the end, requiring the investor to stay in all the way to get any payoff. These "all-or-nothing" projects require unflagging commitment. Furthermore, investors' or project leaders' egos often become so involved with the project that it consumes their identities. Failure or cancellation seems to threaten their reason for existence. They therefore continue to push the project as potentially successful despite strong evidence to the contrary. At other times, the social structure, group norms, and group cohesiveness support a project so strongly that cancellation is impossible. Organizational inertia also may force an organization to maintain a failing project. Thus, escalation of commitment is a phenomenon that has a strong foundation.

How can an individual or organization recognize that a project needs to be stopped before it results in throwing good money after bad? Several suggestions have been made; some are easy to put to use, and others are more difficult. Having good information about a project is always a first step in preventing the escalation problem. Usually it is possible to schedule regular sessions to discuss the project, its progress, the assumptions on which it was originally based, the current validity

BUSINESS OF ETHICS

How Fast Is Too Fast?

On one side are ill patients desperate for a wonder drug. On the other side are pharmaceutical companies, from tiny biotechnology start-ups to giant multinational corporations, eager to find blockbuster drugs. In the middle is the Food and Drug Administration (FDA), charged with ensuring drug safety but also aware of the urgent need for quick action. This mix stirs up plenty of potential for trouble.

Consider Erbitux, a cancer-fighting drug under development by small Imclone, Inc., working in partnership with giant Bristol-Myers Squibb. The drug showed promise in clinical trials, so much promise that the FDA gave it fast-track status to hasten its final approval. Dr. Robert J. Mayer, an oncologist, says, "There is no doubt that the compound works. We have had people who benefited quite dramatically."

In December 2001, however, the FDA rejected the Erbitux application, and the blaming started. Imclone and Bristol managers claim the rejection was unexpected. Industry observers note that sometimes the federal agency has abruptly changed the rules for approval, causing expensive delays. The approval process itself is cumbersome and complex, and requires input from many different constituencies. Drug approval decisions are poorly structured and nonprogrammed, with both sides facing significant uncertainties.

On their side, FDA officials claim Imclone managers received warnings but did not heed them. Imclone managers seemed to be in a hurry and failed to send complete data to the FDA. Imclone was not profitable, and financial pressure may have caused management to push too hard for quick approval of the drug. FDA officials emphasize

"A lot of biotech companies get into survival mode instead of success mode."—Richard B. Brewer, CEO of Scios, Inc.

that the decision stakes in such a situation are high, with many lives at risk, and an incorrect decision can be lethal.

Richard B. Brewer, CEO of small drug manufacturer Scios, Inc., understands the ethical issues all too well—his company had a heart medication rejected by the FDA in 2003—but he believes it's up to Imclone executives to ensure that the process stays on track. "A lot of biotech companies get into survival mode instead of success mode. They forget that the FDA is not here to get your drug approved. It's here to protect patients." Hopefully the two sides can come to an agreement soon because those cancer patients are waiting for a resolution.

References: Andrew Serwer, "Bristol's Bad Medicine," *Fortune*, April 29, 2002; Andrew Serwer, "The Socialite Scientist," *Fortune*, April 15, 2002; "The Trials of Erbitux," *Fortune*, April 15, 2002; "Where Imclone Went Wrong," *BusinessWeek*, February 18, 2002, pp. 68–71 (quotation, p. 68).

of these assumptions, and any problems with the project. An objective review is necessary to maintain control.

Some organizations have begun to make separate teams responsible for the development and implementation of a project to reduce ego involvement. Often, however, the people who initiate a project are those who know the most about it, and their expertise can be valuable in the implementation process. Experts suggest that a general strategy for avoiding the escalation problem is to try to create an "experimenting organization" in which every program and project is reviewed regularly and managers are evaluated on their contribution to the total organization rather than to specific projects.[20]

Group Decision Making

People in organizations work in a variety of groups: formal or informal, permanent or temporary. Most of these groups make decisions that affect the welfare of the organization and its people. In this section, we discuss several issues surrounding how groups make decisions, including group polarization, groupthink, and group problem solving.

Group Polarization

Members' attitudes and opinions with respect to an issue or a solution may change during group discussion. Some studies of this tendency show the change to be a fairly consistent movement toward a riskier solution, called "risky shift."[21] Other studies and analyses have revealed that the group-induced shift is not always toward more risk; the group is just as likely to move toward a more conservative view.[22] Generally, **group polarization** occurs when the average of the group members' postdiscussion attitudes tends to be more extreme than the average prediscussion attitudes.[23]

Several features of group discussion contribute to polarization. When individuals discover during group discussion that others share their opinions, they may become more confident about their opinions, resulting in a more extreme view. Persuasive arguments can also encourage polarization. If members who strongly support a particular position are able to express themselves cogently in the discussion, less avid supporters may become convinced that the position is correct. In addition, members may believe that because the group is deciding, they are not individually responsible for the decision or its outcomes. This diffusion of responsibility may enable them to accept and support a decision more radical than those they would make as individuals.

Polarization can profoundly affect group decision making. If group members are known to lean toward a particular decision before a discussion, their postdecision position will likely be even more extreme. Understanding this phenomenon may be useful for an individual who seeks to affect their decision.

> **Group polarization** is the tendency for a group's average postdiscussion attitudes to be more extreme than its average prediscussion attitudes.

Groupthink

As discussed in Chapters 8 and 9, highly cohesive groups and teams are often very successful at meeting their goals, although they sometimes have serious difficulties as well. One problem that can occur is groupthink. According to Irving L. Janis, **groupthink** is "a mode of thinking that people engage in when they are deeply involved in a cohesive in-group, when the members' strivings for unanimity override their motivation to realistically appraise alternative courses of action."[24] When groupthink occurs, then, the group unknowingly makes unanimity rather than the best decision its goal. Individual members may perceive that raising objections is not appropriate. Groupthink can occur in many decision-making situations in organizations. The current trend toward increasing use of teams in organizations may increase instances of groupthink because self-managing teams tend to be susceptible to this type of thought.[25]

> **Groupthink** is a mode of thinking that occurs when members of a group are deeply involved in a cohesive in-group and their desire for unanimity offsets their motivation to appraise alternative courses of action.

Symptoms of Groupthink   The three primary conditions that foster the development of groupthink are cohesiveness, the leader's promotion of his or her preferred solution, and insulation of the group from experts' opinions. Based on analysis of the disaster associated with the explosion of the space shuttle *Challenger*, the original set of groupthink symptoms was expanded to include (1) the effects of increased time pressure and (2) the role of the leader in not stimulating critical thinking in developing the symptoms of groupthink.[26] Figure 12.6 outlines the revised groupthink process.

A group that has succumbed to groupthink exhibits eight well-defined symptoms:

1. An *illusion of invulnerability*, shared by most or all members, that creates excessive optimism and encourages extreme risk taking

FIGURE 12.6

The Groupthink Process

Groupthink can occur when a highly cohesive group with a directive leader is under time pressure. It can result in a defective decision process and a low probability of successful outcomes.

Reference: Gregory Moorhead, Richard Ference, and Chris P. Neck, "Group Decision Fiascoes Continue: Space Shuttle Challenger and a Revised Groupthink Framework," *Human Relations*, vol. 44 (1991), pp. 539–550.

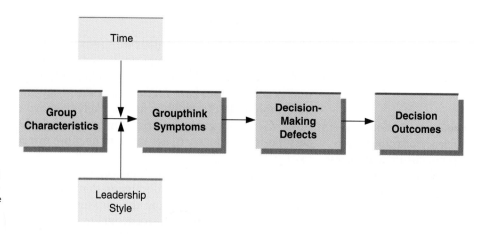

2. *Collective efforts to rationalize or discount warnings* that might lead members to reconsider assumptions before recommitting themselves to past policy decisions

3. An *unquestioned belief in the group's inherent morality*, inclining members to ignore the ethical and moral consequences of their decisions

4. *Stereotyped views of "enemy" leaders* as too evil to warrant genuine attempts to negotiate or as too weak or stupid to counter whatever risky attempts are made to defeat their purposes

5. *Direct pressure on a member* who expresses strong arguments against any of the group's stereotypes, illusions, or commitments, making clear that such dissent is contrary to what is expected of loyal members

6. *Self-censorship of deviations* from the apparent group consensus, reflecting each member's inclination to minimize the importance of his or her doubts and counterarguments

7. A *shared illusion of unanimity*, resulting partly from self-censorship of deviations, augmented by the false assumption that silence means consent[27]

8. *The emergence of self-appointed "mindguards,"* members who protect the group from adverse information that could shatter their shared complacency about the effectiveness and morality of their decisions[28]

Janis contends that the members of the group involved in the Watergate cover-up—Richard Nixon, H. R. Haldeman, John Ehrlichman, and John Dean—may have been victims of groupthink. Evidence of most of the groupthink symptoms appears in the unedited transcripts of the group's deliberations.[29]

Decision-Making Defects and Decision Quality   When groupthink dominates group deliberations, the likelihood that decision-making defects will occur increases. The group is less likely to survey a full range of alternatives and may focus on only a few, often one or two. In discussing a preferred alternative, the group may fail to examine it for obscure risks and drawbacks. Similarly, the group may not reexamine previously rejected alternatives for overlooked gains or some means of reducing apparent costs, even when it receives new information. The group may reject expert opinions that run counter to its own views and may choose to consider only information that supports its preferred solution. The decision to launch the space shuttle *Challenger* may have been a product of groupthink because due to the increased time pressure to make a decision and the leaders' style, negative information was ignored by the group that made the decision. Finally, the group may not

TABLE 12.2

Prescriptions for Preventing Groupthink

A. Leader prescriptions
  1. Assign everyone the role of critical evaluator.
  2. Be impartial; do not state preferences.
  3. Assign the devil's advocate role to at least one group member.
  4. Use outside experts to challenge the group.
  5. Be open to dissenting points of view.

B. Organizational prescriptions
  1. Set up several independent groups to study the same issue.
  2. Train managers and group leaders in groupthink prevention techniques.

C. Individual prescriptions
  1. Be a critical thinker.
  2. Discuss group deliberations with a trusted outsider; report back to the group.

D. Process prescriptions
  1. Periodically break the group into subgroups to discuss the issues.
  2. Take time to study external factors.
  3. Hold second-chance meetings to rethink issues before making a commitment.

consider any potential setbacks or countermoves by competing groups and therefore may fail to develop contingency plans. We should note that Janis contends these six defects may arise from other common problems as well, such as fatigue, prejudice, inaccurate information, information overload, or ignorance.[30]

Defects in decision making do not always lead to bad outcomes or defeats. Even if its own decision-making processes are flawed, one side can win a battle because of the poor decisions made by the other side's leaders. Nevertheless, decisions produced by defective processes are less likely to succeed.

Although the arguments for the existence of groupthink are convincing, the hypothesis has not been subjected to rigorous empirical examination. Research supports parts of the model but leaves some questions unanswered.[31]

Prevention of Groupthink   Several suggestions have been offered to help managers reduce the probability of groupthink in group decision making. Summarized in Table 12.2, these prescriptions fall into four categories based on whether they apply to the leader, the organization, the individual, or the process. All are designed to facilitate critical evaluation of alternatives and discourage single-minded pursuit of unanimity.

Participation

A major issue in group decision making is the degree to which employees should participate in the process. Early management theories, such as those of the scientific management school, advocated a clear separation between the duties of managers and workers: Management was to make the decisions, and employees were to implement them.[32] Other approaches have urged that employees be allowed to participate in decisions to increase their ego involvement, motivation, and satisfaction.[33] Numerous research studies have shown that whereas employees who seek responsibility and challenge on the job may find participation in the decision-making process both motivating and enriching, other employees may regard such participation as a waste of time and a management imposition.[34]

Whether employee participation in decision making is appropriate depends on the situation. In tasks that require an estimation, a prediction, or a judgment of accuracy—usually referred to as *judgmental tasks*—groups typically are superior to individuals simply because more people contribute to the decision-making process. However, one especially capable individual may make a better judgment than a group.

In problem-solving tasks, groups generally produce more and better solutions than do individuals. However, groups take far longer than individuals to develop solutions and make decisions. An individual or a very small group may be able to accomplish some things much faster than a large, unwieldy group or organization. In addition, individual decision making avoids the special problems of group decision making such as groupthink or group polarization. If the problem to be solved is fairly straightforward, it may be more appropriate to have a single capable individual concentrate on solving it. On the other hand, complex problems are more appropriate for groups. Such problems can often be divided into parts and the parts assigned to individuals or small groups that bring their results back to the larger group for discussion and decision making.

An additional advantage of group decision making is that it often creates greater interest in the task. Heightened interest may increase the time and effort given to the task, resulting in more ideas, a more thorough search for solutions, better evaluation of alternatives, and improved decision quality.

The Vroom decision tree approach to leadership (discussed in Chapter 10) is one popular way of determining the appropriate degree of subordinate participation.[35] The model includes decision styles that vary from "decide" (the leader alone makes the decision) to "delegate" (the group makes the decision, with each member having an equal say). The choice of style rests on seven considerations that concern the characteristics of the situation and the subordinates.

Participation in decision making is also related to organization structure. For example, decentralization involves delegating some decision-making authority throughout the organizational hierarchy. The more decentralized the organization, the more its employees tend to participate in decision making. Whether one views participation in decision making as pertaining to leadership, organization structure, or motivation, it remains an important aspect of organizations that continues to occupy managers and organizational scholars.[36]

Brainstorming is a popular technique used in group decision making when the objective is to identify a variety of different alternatives. This team, for example, is enthusiastically brainstorming in their effort to come up with some creative new ideas.

Group Problem Solving

A typical interacting group may have difficulty with any of several steps in the decision-making process. One common problem arises in the generation-of-alternatives phase: The search may be arbitrarily ended before all plausible alternatives have been identified. Several types of group interactions can have this effect. If members immediately express their reactions to the alternatives as they are first proposed, potential contributors may begin to censor their ideas to avoid embarrassing criticism from the group.

Less confident group members, intimidated by members who have more experience, higher status, or more power, may also censor their ideas for fear of embarrassment or sanctions. In addition, the group leader may limit idea generation by enforcing requirements concerning time, appropriateness, cost, feasibility, and the like.

To improve the generation of alternatives, managers may employ any of three techniques to stimulate the group's problem-solving capabilities: brainstorming, the nominal group technique, or the Delphi technique.

Brainstorming is a technique used in the idea generation phase of decision making that assists in developing numerous alternative courses of action.

Brainstorming   **Brainstorming** is most often used in the idea generation phase of decision making and is intended to solve problems that are new to the organization and have major consequences. In brainstorming, the group convenes specifically to generate alternatives. The members present ideas and clarify them with brief explanations. Each idea is recorded in full view of all members, usually on a flip chart. To avoid self-censoring, no attempts to evaluate the ideas are allowed. Group members are encouraged to offer any ideas that occur to them, even those that seem too risky or impossible to implement. (The absence of such ideas, in fact, is evidence that group members are engaging in self-censorship.) In a subsequent session, after the ideas have been recorded and distributed to members for review, the alternatives are evaluated.

The intent of brainstorming is to produce totally new ideas and solutions by stimulating the creativity of group members and encouraging them to build on the contributions of others. Brainstorming does not provide the resolution to the problem, an evaluation scheme, or the decision itself. Instead, it should produce a list of alternatives that is more innovative and comprehensive than one developed by the typical interacting group.

In the **nominal group technique,** group members follow a generate-discussion-vote cycle until they reach an appropriate decision.

The Nominal Group Technique   The nominal group technique is another means of improving group decision making. Whereas brainstorming is used primarily to generate alternatives, this technique may be used in other phases of decision making, such as identification of the problem and of appropriate criteria for evaluating alternatives. To use the **nominal group technique,** a group of individuals convenes to address an issue. The issue is described to the group, and each individual writes a list of ideas; no discussion among members is permitted. Following the five-to-ten-minute idea generation period, individual members take turns reporting their ideas, one at a time, to the group. The ideas are recorded on a flip chart, and members are encouraged to add to the list by building on the ideas of others. After all ideas have been presented, the members may discuss them and continue to build on them or proceed to the next phase. This part of the process can also be carried out without a face-to-face meeting or by mail, telephone, or computer. A meeting, however, helps members develop a group feeling and puts interpersonal pressure on the members to do their best in developing their lists.

After the discussion, members privately vote on or rank the ideas or report their preferences in some other agreed-on way. Reporting is private to reduce feelings of intimidation. After voting, the group may discuss the results and continue to generate and discuss ideas. The generation-discussion-vote cycle can continue until an appropriate decision is reached.

The nominal group technique has two principal advantages. It helps overcome the negative effects of power and status differences among group members, and it can be used to explore problems to generate alternatives or to evaluate them. Its primary disadvantage lies in its structured nature, which may limit creativity.

The **Delphi technique** is a method of systematically gathering judgments of experts for use in developing forecasts.

The Delphi Technique   The **Delphi technique** was originally developed by Rand Corporation as a method to systematically gather the judgments of experts for use in developing forecasts. It is designed for groups that do not meet face to face. For instance, the product development manager of a major toy manufacturer might use the Delphi technique to probe the views of industry experts to forecast developments in the dynamic toy market.

The manager who wants the input of a group is the central figure in the process. After recruiting participants, the manager develops a questionnaire for them to complete. The questionnaire is relatively simple, containing straightforward questions that deal with the issue, trends in the area, new technological developments, and other factors that interest the manager. The manager summarizes the responses and reports back to the experts with another questionnaire. This cycle may be repeated as many times as necessary to generate the information the manager needs.

The Delphi technique is useful when experts are physically dispersed, anonymity is desired, or the participants are known to have trouble communicating with one another because of extreme differences of opinion. This method also avoids the intimidation problems that may exist in decision-making groups. On the other hand, the technique eliminates the often fruitful results of direct interaction among group members.

Negotiation in Organizations

LEARNING OBJECTIVE

Discuss negotiation in organizations.

During **negotiation**, two or more parties (people or groups) reach agreement despite having different preferences.

One special way decisions are made in organizations is through negotiation. **Negotiation** is the process in which two or more parties (people or groups) reach agreement even though they have different preferences. In its simplest form, the parties may be two individuals trying to decide who will pay for lunch. A somewhat more complex form occurs when two people, such as an employee and a manager, sit down to decide on personal performance goals for the next year against which the employee's performance will be measured. Even more complex are negotiations that take place between labor unions and a company's management or between two companies as they negotiate the terms of a joint venture. The key issues in such negotiations are that at least two parties are involved, their preferences differ, and they need to reach agreement.

Approaches to Negotiation

Interest in negotiation has grown steadily in recent years.[37] Four primary approaches to negotiation have dominated this study: individual differences, situational characteristics, game theory, and cognitive approaches. The following sections briefly describe each approach.

Individual Differences   Early psychological approaches concentrated on the personality traits of the negotiators.[38] Traits investigated have included demographic characteristics and personality variables. Demographic characteristics have included age, gender, and race, among others. Personality variables have included risk taking, locus of control, tolerance for ambiguity, self-esteem, authoritarianism, and Machiavellianism. The assumption of this type of research was that the key to successful negotiation is selecting the right person to do the negotiating, one who has the appropriate demographic characteristics or personality. This assumption seemed to make sense because negotiation is such a personal and interactive process. However,

Stu's Views   © 2002 Stu All Rights Reserved www.stus.com

Negotiation can take place in many different settings. A key to any successful negotiation, however, is careful preparation. For instance, this antelope probably made a mistake by not learning more about the likely behavior of lions.

© Stu Rees

the research rarely showed the positive results expected because situational variables negated the effects of the individual differences.[39]

Situational Characteristics   Situational characteristics are the context within which negotiation takes place. They include such things as the types of communication between negotiators, the potential outcomes of the negotiation, the relative power of the parties (both positional and personal), the time frame available for negotiation, the number of people representing each side, and the presence of other parties. Some of this research has contributed to our understanding of the negotiation process. However, the shortcomings of the situational approach are similar to those of the individual characteristics approach. Many situational characteristics are external to the negotiators and beyond their control. Often the negotiators cannot change their relative power positions or the setting within which the negotiation occurs. Hence, although we have learned a lot from research on situational issues, we still need to learn much more about the process.

Game Theory   Game theory was developed by economists using mathematical models to predict the outcomes of negotiation situations (as illustrated in the Academy Award–winning movie *A Beautiful Mind*). It requires that every alternative and outcome be analyzed with probabilities and numerical outcomes reflecting the preferences for each outcome. In addition, the order in which different parties can make choices and every possible move are predicted, along with associated preferences for outcomes. The outcomes of this approach are exactly what negotiators want: a predictive model of how negotiation should be conducted. One major drawback is that it requires the ability to describe all possible options and outcomes for every possible move in every situation before the negotiation starts—an often tedious process, if possible at all. Another problem is that this theory assumes negotiators are rational at all times. Other research on negotiation has shown that negotiators often do not act rationally. Therefore, this approach, although elegant in its prescriptions, is usually unworkable in a real negotiation situation.

Cognitive Approaches   The fourth approach to negotiation consists of several cognitive approaches, which recognize that negotiators often depart from perfect rationality during negotiation; they try to predict how and when negotiators will make these departures. Howard Raiffa's decision analytic approach focuses on providing advice to negotiators actively involved in negotiation.[40] K. H. Bazerman and M. A. Neale have added to Raiffa's work by specifying eight ways in which negotiators systematically deviate from rationality.[41] The types of deviations they describe include escalation of commitment to a previously selected course of action, overreliance on readily available information, assuming the negotiations can produce fixed-sum outcomes, and anchoring negotiations in irrelevant information. These cognitive approaches have advanced the study of negotiation a long way beyond the early individual and situational approaches.

Negotiators can use them to attempt to predict in advance how the negotiation might take place.

Win-Win Negotiation

In addition to the approaches to negotiation previously described, a group of approaches proposed by consultants and advisers aims to give negotiators a specific model to use in carrying out difficult negotiations. One of the best of these models is the "Win-Win Negotiator" developed by Ross Reck and his associates.[42] The Win-Win approach does not treat negotiation as a game resulting in winners and losers. Instead, it approaches negotiation as an opportunity for both sides to be winners, to get what they want out of the agreement. The focus is on both parties reaching agreement such that both are committed to fulfilling their own end of the agreement and to returning for more agreements in the future. In other words, both parties want to have their needs satisfied. In addition, this approach does not advocate either a "tough guy" or a "nice guy" approach to negotiation, both of which are popular in the literature. It assumes both parties work together to find ways to satisfy each other at the same time.

> The **PRAM model** guides the negotiator through the four steps of planning for agreement, building relationships, reaching agreements, and maintaining relationships.

The Win-Win approach is a four-step approach illustrated in the **PRAM model** shown in Figure 12.7. The PRAM four-step approach proposes that proper planning, building relationships, getting agreements, and maintaining the relationships are the key steps to successful negotiation.

Planning requires that each negotiator set his or her own goals, anticipate the goals of the other, determine areas of probable agreement, and develop strategies for reconciling areas of probable disagreement. Developing Win-Win *relationships* requires that negotiators plan activities that enable positive personal relationships to develop, cultivate a sense of mutual trust, and allow relationships to evolve fully before discussing business in earnest. The development of trust between the parties is probably the single most important key to success in negotiation. Forming Win-Win *agreements* requires that each party confirm the other's goals, verify areas of agreement, propose and consider positive solutions to reconcile areas of disagreement, and jointly resolve any remaining differences. The key in reaching agreement is to realize that both parties share many of the goals. The number of areas of disagreement is usually small. Finally, Win-Win *maintenance* entails providing meaningful feedback based on performance, each party holding up his or her end of the agreement, keeping in contact, and reaffirming trust between the parties. The assumption is that both parties want to keep the relationship going so that future mutually beneficial transactions can occur. Both parties must uphold their ends of the agreement and do what they said they would do. Finally, keeping in touch is as easy as making a telephone call or meeting for lunch.

In summary, the PRAM model provides straightforward advice for conducting negotiations. The four steps are easy to remember and carry out as long as tactics employed by other parties do not distract the negotiator. The focus is on planning, agreeing on goals, trust, and keeping commitments.

FIGURE 12.7

The Pram Model of Negotiation

The PRAM model shows the four steps in setting up negotiation so that both parties win.

Reference: From *Win-Win Negotiator* by Ross R. Reck and Brian G. Long. Reprinted with permission of Simon & Schuster Adult Publishing Group, Copyright © 1985, 1987 by Brian G. Long and Ross R. Reck.

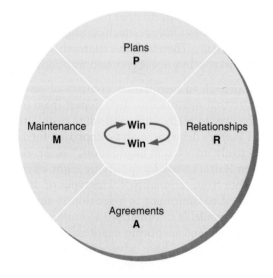

Synopsis

Decision making is the process of choosing one alternative from among several. The basic elements of decision making include choosing a goal; considering alternative courses of action; assessing potential outcomes of the alternatives, each with its own value relative to the goal; and choosing one alternative based on an evaluation of the outcomes. Information is available regarding the alternatives, outcomes, and values.

Programmed decisions are well-structured, recurring decisions made according to set decision rules. Nonprogrammed decisions involve nonroutine, poorly structured situations with unclear sources of information; these decisions cannot be made according to existing decision rules. Decision making may also be classified according to the information available. The classifications—certainty, risk, and uncertainty—reflect the amount of information available regarding the outcomes of alternatives.

The rational approach views decision making as a completely rational process in which goals are established, a problem is identified, alternatives are generated and evaluated, a choice is made and implemented, and control is exercised. The use of procedures and rules of thumb, suboptimizing, and satisficing characterize the behavioral model. The rational and behavioral views can be combined into a practical model. The Janis-Mann conflict model recognizes the personal anxiety individuals face when they must make important decisions.

Two related behavioral aspects of decision making are ethics and escalation of commitment. Ethics play an important role in both individual and managerial decisions. Escalation of commitment to an ineffective course of action occurs in many decision situations often caused by psychological, social, ego, and organizational factors. Group decision making involves problems as well as benefits. One possible problem is group polarization, the shift of members' attitudes and opinions to a more extreme position following group discussion. Another difficulty is groupthink, a mode of thinking in which the urge toward unanimity overrides critical appraisal of alternatives. Yet another concern involves employee participation in decision making. The appropriate degree of participation depends on the characteristics of the situation. Brainstorming, the nominal group technique, and the Dephi technique are three popular methods for managing group problem solving.

Negotiation is the process through which two or more parties (people or groups) reach agreement even though they have different preferences. Research on negotiation has examined individual differences, situational characteristics, game theory, and cognitive approaches. The Win-Win approach provides a simple four-step model to successful negotiation: planning, relationships, agreement, and maintenance.

Discussion Questions

1. Some have argued that people, not organizations, make decisions and that the study of "organizational" decision making is therefore pointless. Do you agree with this argument? Why or why not?

2. What information did you use in deciding to enter the school you now attend?

3. When your alarm goes off each morning, you have a decision to make: whether to get up and go to school or work or to stay in bed and sleep longer. Is this a programmed or nonprogrammed decision? Why?

4. Describe at least three points in the decision-making process at which information plays an important role.

5. How does the role of information in the rational model of decision making differ from its role in the behavioral model?

6. Why does it make sense to consider several different models of decision making?

7. Think of a time when you satisficed when making a decision. Recall a time when you suboptimized during decision making. How might your decision have differed had you used a different approach in each case?

8. Describe a situation in which you experienced escalation of commitment to an ineffective course of action. What did you do about it? Do you wish you had handled it differently? Why or why not?

9. How are group polarization and groupthink similar? How do they differ?

10. Describe a situation in which you negotiated an agreement, perhaps when buying a car or a house. How did the negotiation process compare with the PRAM approach? How did it differ? Were you satisfied with the result of the negotiation?

Organizational Behavior Case for Discussion

The Most Stressful Conditions

How can effective choices be made when there is no time, when your employees, your company, and your community are in imminent danger? Decision making under these conditions takes on a different character, as shown in the response of Sidley Austin Brown & Wood to the tragic events of September 11, 2001.

The giant law firm was formed in May 2001 when Brown & Wood merged its Wall Street financial law offices with those of Chicago-based Sidley & Austin, corporate law specialists, creating the nation's fourth-largest practice, with 1,400 lawyers worldwide. Many of the firm's lawyers are headquartered in New York City, with 600 formerly housed at 1 World Trade Center on floors 52 to 57 and another 100 seven miles away in midtown Manhattan. On September 11, the first plane struck overhead. Workers noticed the explosion's tremors and the smell of jet fuel. Director of Administration John Connelly asked workers to evacuate, helping the frightened, confused employees to the stairs. Being unaware of the extent of the danger, Connelly and others went from floor to floor to ensure that everyone was safely out, then left the building just as it collapsed. Only one company employee perished in the attack.

In the aftermath, with damaged facilities and workers in shock, Sidley Austin employees faced the most trying circumstances of their careers. When their attempts to contact the midtown building failed because cell phone towers had been destroyed, many employees walked to the site. At the midtown location, partner Alan S. Weil anticipated the need for additional office space and called his landlord, who granted immediate leases on two floors and also got another law firm to give up two newly leased floors. By the end of the day, hundreds of desks, computers, and cell phones were arriving, and contractors were installing computer cables. "It's just amazing what you can get in New York overnight," says partner Thomas R. Smith, Jr. According to *New York Times* writer John Schwartz, "The normal rules of business engagement—deliberate negotiation, adversarial wrangling

and jockeying for advantage—were swept away. The infamously in-your-face New York attitude was nowhere to be found."

The partnership's directors were supposed to meet in Los Angeles on September 12 but were stranded elsewhere as airlines ceased operations. The executives used conference calls to begin "issue-spotting," according to Thomas Cole, partner. He explained, "The lawyers who assembled that day and in the days thereafter were people who had spent their entire working lives engaged in solving complex problems for clients. . . . But that was under normal conditions. Would we succeed under the most stressful conditions . . . ?" Issues involving people, insurance, and communications were complex; for example, the people issue covered such items as payroll continuity, trauma counseling, and safety and security. The organization pulled together; staffers from the Chicago headquarters drove all night to assist. When the firm's backup data tapes needed transport from a New Jersey warehouse to Chicago, the storage companies offered to have their employees drive overnight because no planes were flying. Dennis J. O'Donovan, head of the firm's technology section, says, "[Disaster recovery seminars] always prepare you for the worst—people not being available, people not being cooperative; the opposite has happened."

On September 17, firm employees met, and partner Charles W. Douglas told the crowd, "The assets of the law firm are not the desks in the offices, the woodwork that's on the walls or the paintings that are hung in the corridors. The assets of the law firm are its people." Smith agreed: "Being able to keep the business going is great, but it's the people that count." Employees and partners at Sidley Austin have taken on the added work with few complaints; many say that work is therapeutic. The lawyers have completed many financial deals on time, believing it's their patriotic duty to continue working as before. Employees claim the tragedy drew them closer together, creating intimate friendships. Others still suffer from stress, and some may choose paid disability leave. Nancy L. Karen, chief information officer, says the firm has learned a lot about crisis conditions. "We ought to be able to recover in less than a day next time," she says, adding with a nervous laugh, "God forbid!" Perhaps Thomas Cole best sums up the firm's response: "I have been asked . . . if the disaster has been a setback to the full realization of the anticipated benefits of our merger. I answer that because of the way we have risen to this challenge together, the most important yet most elusive goal in any merger integration, namely the creation of a true partnership, occurred overnight."

Case Questions

1. Using the rational approach to decision making, describe the ways in which these crisis conditions affected each step of the decision-making process.

2. Based on your answer to question 1, what are some potential problems firms should be aware of when they must make decisions during a crisis? What are some steps firms can take to avoid those problems or to minimize their negative impact?

3. Due to the extraordinary circumstances in New York City during and just after September 11, many individuals and firms changed their behavior, acting more altruistically and ethically. In your opinion, why did this occur? Do you think the change is likely to endure for a long time, or is it only temporary?

References: "About Sidley," "Our Offices," "Our Practices," Sidley Austin Brown & Wood website, www.sidley.com on May 25, 2002; Thomas Cole, "Our Test," *American Lawyer*, November 2001; John Schwartz, "Rebuilding a Day at a Time: Law Firm Pushes 2 Steps Forward for Every Step Back, Rebuilds a Day at a Time," *New York Times*, December 14, 2001; John Schwartz, "Up from the Ashes: *N.Y. Times* Profile of Sidley Austin Brown & Wood's Response to the World Trade Center Tragedy," *New York Times*, September 16, 2001 (quotation).

Experiencing Organizational Behavior

Programmed and Nonprogrammed Decisions

Purpose: This exercise will allow you to take part in making a hypothetical decision and help you understand the difference between programmed and nonprogrammed decisions.

Format: You will be asked to perform a task both individually and as a member of a group.

Procedure: A list of typical organizational decisions follows. Your task is to determine whether they are programmed or nonprogrammed. Number your paper, and write *P* for programmed or *N* for nonprogrammed next to each number.

Your instructor will divide the class into groups of four to seven. All groups should have approximately the same number of members. Your task as a group is to make the determinations just outlined. In arriving at your decisions, do not use techniques such as voting or negotiating ("Okay, I'll give in on this one if you'll give in on that one.") The group should discuss the difference between programmed and nonprogrammed decisions and each decision situation until all members at least partly agree with the decision.

Decision List

1. Hiring a specialist for the research staff in a highly technical field

2. Assigning workers to daily tasks

3. Determining the size of dividend to be paid to shareholders in the ninth consecutive year of strong earnings growth

4. Deciding whether to officially excuse an employee's absence for medical reasons

5. Selecting the location for another branch of a 150-branch bank in a large city

6. Approving the appointment of a new law school graduate to the corporate legal staff

7. Making annual assignments of graduate assistants to faculty

8. Approving an employee's request to attend a local seminar in his or her special area of expertise

9. Selecting the appropriate outlets for print advertisements for a new college textbook

10. Determining the location for a new fast-food restaurant in a small but growing town on the major interstate highway between two very large metropolitan areas

Follow-up Questions

1. To what extent did group members disagree about which decisions were programmed and which were nonprogrammed?

2. What primary factors did the group discuss in making each decision?

3. Were there any differences between the members' individual lists and the group lists? If so, discuss the reasons for the differences.

Self-Assessment Exercise

Rational Versus Practical Approaches to Decision Making

Managers need to recognize and understand the different models they use to make decisions. They also need to understand to what extent they tend to be relatively autocratic or relatively participative in making decisions. To develop your skills in these areas, perform the following activity.

First, assume you are the manager of a firm that is rapidly growing. Recent sales figures strongly suggest the need for a new plant to produce more of your firm's products. Key issues include where the plant might be built and how large it might be (for example, a small, less expensive plant to meet current needs that could be expanded in the future versus a large, more expensive plant that may have excess capacity today but could better meet long-term needs).

Using the rational approach diagrammed in Figure 12.3, trace the process the manager might use to make the decision. Note the kinds of information it may require and the extent to which other people may need to participate in making a decision at each point.

Next, go back and look at various steps in the process where behavioral processes might intervene and affect the overall process. Will bounded rationality come into play? What about satisficing?

Finally, use the practical approach shown in Figure 12.4 and trace through the process again. Again note where other input may be needed. Try to identify points in the process where the rational and practical approaches are likely to result in the same outcome and points where differences are most likely to occur.

OB Online

1. Assume you need to make decisions about where to locate a new plant. The options have been narrowed down to Madison, Wisconsin; Columbia, Missouri; and Bryan, Texas. You now need to find information about tax rates, unemployment statistics, and airport access for each community. Use the Internet to search for this information.

2. In what ways do you think the emergence of the Internet has affected how managers make decisions? Give concrete examples to support your ideas.

3. Describe ways in which information technology might be used to manage brainstorming, the nominal group technique, and the Delphi technique more efficiently than using these techniques in more traditional ways.

4. Pair up with a classmate and conduct a hypothetical negotiation via email. Then discuss the pros and cons of electronic negotiation versus face-to-face negotiation based on your experience.

Building Managerial Skills

Exercise Overview: Interpersonal skills involve the manager's ability to understand and motivate individuals and groups. This exercise will allow you to practice your interpersonal skills in a role-playing exercise.

Exercise Background: You supervise a group of six employees who work in an indoor facility in a relatively isolated location. The company you work for recently adopted an ambiguous policy regarding

smoking. Essentially the policy states that all company work sites are to be smoke free unless employees at a specific site choose differently and at the discretion of the site supervisor.

Four members of the work group you supervise are smokers. They have come to you with the argument that since they constitute the majority, they should be allowed to smoke at work. The other two members, both nonsmokers, have heard about this request and have also discussed the situation with you. They argue that the health-related consequences of secondary smoke should outweigh the preferences of the majority.

To compound the problem, your boss wrote the new policy and is quite defensive about it; numerous individuals have already criticized the policy. You know your boss will get very angry with you if you also raise concerns about the policy. Finally, you are personally indifferent to the issue. You do not smoke yourself, but your spouse smokes. Secondary smoke does not bother you, and you do not have strong opinions about it. Still, you have to make a decision about what to do. You see that your choices are to (1) mandate a smoke-free environment, (2) allow smoking in the facility, or (3) ask your boss to clarify the policy.

Exercise Task: Based on the background previously presented, assume you are the supervisor and do the following:

1. Assume you have chosen option 1. Write an outline that you will use to announce your decision to the four smokers.
2. Assume you have chosen option 2. Write an outline that you will use to announce your decision to the two nonsmokers.
3. Assume you have chosen option 3. Write an outline that you will use when you meet with your boss.
4. Are there other alternatives?
5. What would you do if you were actually the group supervisor?

TEST PREPPER

ACE self-test

You have read the chapter and studied the key terms, and the exam is any day now. Think you're ready to ace it? Take this sample test to gauge your comprehension of chapter material. You can check your answers at the back of the book. Want more test questions? Visit the student website at http://college.hmco.com/business/students/ (select Griffin/Moorhead, Fundamentals of Organizational Behavior 1e) and take the ACE quizzes for more practice.

1. **T F** A decision rule tells a decision maker to consider multiple alternatives before making a decision.

2. **T F** The choice of what to do when the organization faces a major lawsuit is a nonprogrammed decision.

3. **T F** Managers prefer to operate in conditions of uncertainty rather than in conditions of risk.

4. **T F** Evaluating alternatives in the rational decision-making process involves describing anticipated outcomes, evaluating the expected costs of the alternatives, and estimating the risks associated with each alternative.

5. **T F** A contingency plan is a plan developed for temporary employees.

6. **T F** One strength of the rational decision-making model is that it forces the decision maker to consider a decision in a logical, sequential manner.

7. **T F** Managers who satisfice in making decisions attempt to maximize the satisfaction of their employees.

8. **T F** According to the Janis-Mann conflict model, decision makers who believe they have little time to deliberate over a decision experience hypervigilance.

9. **T F** A group whose members lean toward a particular decision before a discussion is likely to make an even more extreme decision following a discussion.

10. **T F** Self-censorship of deviations from the apparent group consensus is a symptom of groupthink.

11. **T F** The basic rule in the brainstorming technique is to evaluate alternatives as quickly as possible to generate more useful alternatives later.

12. **T F** The nominal group technique is used specifically to help newly formed groups determine their purpose.

13. **T F** The Delphi technique is a way to systematically gather the judgments of experts.

14. **T F** Picking the right person to do the negotiating, as suggested by early psychological approaches, has proven widely successful.

15. **T F** Game theory teaches managers the tricks and tips of how to win in negotiations.

16. **T F** In a Win-Win negotiation, managers are encouraged to adopt either a "tough" style or a "nice" style.

17. **T F** The PRAM model of negotiation assumes that negotiators want to keep the relationship going to enable future mutually beneficial transactions.

18. Each time inventory levels drop to a certain point, Rachel orders replacement items. Rachel is making a(n) _____ decision.
    a. programmed
    b. nonprogrammed
    c. artificial
    d. planning
    e. leadership

19. _____ decisions require the decision maker to exercise judgment and creativity.
    a. Programmed
    b. Nonprogrammed
    c. Artificial
    d. Planning
    e. Leadership

20. Jennifer believes there is a 60 percent chance she can successfully market a new athletic shoe by pricing it at $90 but an 80 percent chance by pricing it at $75. Jennifer's decision of which price to choose occurs in a condition of
    a. certainty.
    b. risk.
    c. uncertainty.
    d. rationality.
    e. irrationality.

21. The first step in the rational decision making-model is
    a. identify the problem.
    b. determine the decision type.
    c. generate alternatives.
    d. evaluate alternatives.
    e. state the situational goal.

22. Managers in Pentry Corporation have adopted a clear strategy to compete in a given market. However, they also have a secondary plan ready to implement should their intended strategy fail. This secondary plan is called a(n)
    a. programmed plan.
    b. nonprogrammed plan.
    c. rational plan.
    d. contingency plan.
    e. uncertainty plan.

23. What typically happens when decision makers experience cognitive dissonance?
    a. They immediately reverse their decision.
    b. They ignore it and move on to the next decision.
    c. They postpone future decisions.

d. They attempt to identify decision rules for future decisions.

e. They seek to rationalize the decision further with new information.

24. One assumption in the rational decision-making model is that

a. decisions will be made in a condition of uncertainty.

b. decision makers, being human, have limits on their rationality.

c. decision makers can generate all possible alternative solutions to a problem.

d. political processes inhibit effective decision making.

e. all decisions are permanent and cannot be changed.

25. Jack needs a new computer for his office. Rather than compare all possible alternatives in terms of processing speed, memory capacity, and so on, he chooses the first computer he finds that falls within his budget. This is an example of

a. satisficing.

b. suboptimizing.

c. programming.

d. rules of thumb.

e. bounded rationality.

26. According to the Janis-Mann conflict model, a decision maker who believes serious risks will not occur if no change is made will

a. make small, gradual changes.

b. make a sudden, large-scale change.

c. seek as much information as possible before making a change.

d. adopt a general decision rule and apply it to all situations.

e. continue his or her present activities.

27. Vigilant information processing, as described in the Janis-Mann conflict model of decision making, is similar to

a. generating alternatives.

b. the rational decision-making model.

c. cognitive dissonance.

d. transformational leadership.

e. groupthink.

28. A person's beliefs about what constitutes right and wrong behavior are called

a. decision rules.

b. rational bounds.

c. decision vigilance.

d. conditions of certainty.

e. ethics.

29. Which of the following is not a potential cause of escalation of commitment?

a. New information that contradicts the decision

b. Personal egos

c. Organizational inertia

d. Social structures that strongly support the decision

e. High front-end investment

30. Individually, the members of Kimberly's task force have fairly moderate views about an issue, but when they get together and discuss the issue, each member's views are reinforced and validated. By the end of the discussion, Kimberly's task force makes a more extreme decision than the individual members' initial views would have predicted. This effect is called

a. irrational decision making.

b. group polarization.

c. escalation of commitment.

d. cognitive dissonance.

e. nonprogrammed decision making.

31. Which of the following is not a symptom of groupthink?

a. An illusion of invulnerability

b. Stereotyped views of the "enemy"

c. A shared illusion of unanimity

d. A formally appointed "devil's advocate"

e. Unquestioned belief in the group's inherent morality

32. Brainstorming may help generate numerous creative ideas and solutions, primarily because the group avoids self-censorship; in other words,

a. the group believes in its inherent morality.

b. the group views its decisions as unanimous.

c. the group has formally appointed a "devil's advocate."

d. no attempts to evaluate the ideas are made.

e. the group believes it is invulnerable to failure.

33. A Win-Win negotiation includes all of the following elements except

a. opportunities for both sides to successfully reach their objectives.

b. jointly resolving differences.

c. a "nice guy" approach.

d. setting personal goals and anticipating the goals of the other party.

e. cultivating a sense of mutual trust.

PART FOUR   VIDEO CASE

The Bakers' Best Story

In 1984, Michael Baker and his wife established Bakers' Best, a small take-out restaurant in a community near Boston. In its first year, the restaurant was simply a deli and grossed around $200,000. Today Bakers' Best is a well-known multipurpose restaurant serving the greater Boston area. It has 75 full-time and 50 part-time employees, brings in $7.5 million per year, and includes a café and restaurant along with a full-service catering department. How did Bakers' Best grow from a small start-up to a bustling midsize firm? Much of its success can be attributed to the management style and leadership skills of its founder, Michael Baker.

In building his restaurant, Baker decided early on to focus on his employees and to build a fun, caring workplace. He believed if his employees enjoyed their jobs and felt cared for, they would be more committed to serving a quality product and providing exemplary customer service. To maintain this environment, Baker frequently does things for his employees that most companies don't do. For example, during a recent Thanksgiving holiday, he called a number of his managers at home and personally thanked them for working so hard. He regularly buys tickets to Boston Red Sox games and distributes them to his staff, free of charge. Baker also models the behavior he wants his employees to demonstrate. For example, he walks through the kitchen daily to make sure the kitchen staff is using the best possible ingredients. "I've been here for about seven-and-a-half years, and he actually comes through the kitchen every single day, and he'll see the food and taste it, [and] make sure we're all using the best ingredients," comments Geoff Skillman, one of Baker's executive chefs.

Judging by the impressive growth of his business and employees' admiration for him, Baker's efforts are clearly paying off,. "Michael is a salt-of-the-earth kind of guy, and you look around—the food—the environment—it's all a reflection of him," says Ken Gasse, an assistant manager. "He's such a people person, and really cares a lot about you, about the job you're doing and about how we deal with our clients," remarks Pamela Shaw, director of catering. Baker's positive attributes have clearly rubbed off on his staff. In describing how he manages the restaurant's kitchen, executive chef Skillman explains, "We try to create a really nice work environment for our staff. It's very important that we have people who work here that don't have attitude problems or big chips on their shoulder." Skillman works hard to try to accommodate employees in terms of scheduling."We believe in the quality of life outside of work," he says. Along with maintaining a fun and caring workplace, Baker believes in compensating his employees fairly. The company pays well, offers a health insurance plan, and offers an IRA. Still, employee turnover is about 20 percent per year, largely due to the demanding nature of the work. This statistic is a daily reminder to Baker and his managers that the company must continually work hard to attract, motivate, and retain high-quality employees.

Looking back over the years, Baker is pleased with the way his restaurant has grown and the environment he has created for his employees. "It's exceeded anything we've expected," he says. "It's a team effort, and although that's said all the time, I think that if everyone's on the same page, and if [the employees] are looking to serve a quality product and make people feel comfortable in the store, that's what brings in business."

Case Questions

1. Do you believe Michael Baker is an effective or ineffective leader? Cite evidence from the case to support your claim.
2. Discuss several key traits of effective leaders. To what extent does Michael Baker demonstrate these traits?
3. In what ways does Michael Baker's leadership style influence his employees? Does he make effective use of power? Which types of power does he use and which types does he avoid to influence his employees?
4. Would you enjoy working at Bakers' Best? Why or why not?

Reference: Bakers' Best homepage, www.bakersbestcatering.com on June 25, 2004.

PART FIVE

Organizational Processes and Characteristics

CHAPTER 13

Organization Design

MANAGEMENT PREVIEW

Why is it that when some companies' products mature, the economy changes, or low-cost foreign competition enters the market, some companies die whereas others adjust and become stronger than ever? One key reason is organization design. Within the organization, the structure sets up a system to coordinate the efforts of individuals, work groups, and departments. It seems as though organizations are always restructuring, re-arranging the organization chart and having people report to different managers. What they are really doing is seeking the best way to design a system of task, reporting, and authority relationships that will lead to the efficient accomplishment of organizational goals. We begin this chapter with a description of the essential elements of organization structure. Next, we discuss decision making and authority. Then we examine and differentiate between the universal and contingency perspectives of organization design and discuss the factors that determine how an organization should be structured. Finally, we look at several commonly used organization designs.

After you have studied this chapter, you should be able to:
- [ ] *Describe the essential elements of organization structure.*
- [ ] *Explain three classic views of organization structure.*
- [ ] *Discuss the primary contingency approaches to organization design.*
- [ ] *Identify the factors and several popular approaches that determine how an organization should be designed.*

We begin with a look at some of the organizational challenges faced by AOL Time Warner following their merger.

Whether you call it *integration, synergy,* or *convergence,* the last being former Time Warner chairman Steve Case's favorite word, it is the driving force behind the organization structures of so-called "new economy" firms, based on the hypothetical benefits of owning a variety of related business units. Since the future of technology remains uncertain, it makes sense for firms to hedge their bets by owning many different technologies. Case, a visionary leader, says,

"We are moving into an era of convergence where the lines between industries will blur." However, it is clear that owning widely diversified businesses does not yet contribute to profitability, perhaps because an overly diversified corporate structure is difficult to manage.

Time Warner is still struggling with this issue today. The huge firm, with more than $40 billion in revenue in 2003, comprises dozens of major brands. An exhaustive, and exhausting, list of brands includes Internet businesses such as AOL, CompuServe, Road Runner, icq, Instant Messenger, Netscape, and Mapquest; cable networks HBO, Cinemax, CNN, the Cartoon Network, TNT, TBS Superstation, Turner Classic Movies, and the WB; movie studios Warner Brothers, Castle Rock Entertainment, and New Line Cinema; magazines such as *Time, People, Sports Illustrated, Fortune, InStyle, Money, Entertainment Weekly, marie claire, MAD* comics, and more than one hundred other specialty titles; the Time Warner cable provider and four local TV stations; the Atlanta Braves baseball team, the Atlanta Hawks basketball team, and the Atlanta Thrashers hockey team; several book publishers; the Looney Tunes animation studio; and Atlantic, Elektra, Rhino, and other recording companies.

Thus far, the much-hyped benefits of the merger between AOL and Time Warner have failed to materialize. According to Case, the slow start was to be expected:"I've always said this is a marathon, not a sprint." The firm is effectively cross-selling products, for example, by advertising its other products on its web portals and cable stations. But it could do more. Case maintains, "The merger was never about cross-divisional promotion. It was about cross-divisional innovation." The firm has taken the first step, adding divisions with responsibility for achieving synergies, but some obvious moves, such as offering movie sneak previews exclusively to AOL subscribers, have been widely discussed but never implemented.

The challenge for new Chairman and CEO Richard Parsons is to create an organization structure that will harness the power of these combined businesses, realizing synergies and sparking innovation while also maintaining control. Parsons, who assumed the CEO position in May 2002 and the Chairman position in 2003, began with a reorganization, asking some top executives who had previously reported to Case to report directly to him and changing other reporting relationships at the firm's top level. The changes will give more formal authority and public visibility to several top executives, mainly those in strategic planning, external communications, and technology development. Parsons also plans to concentrate on making each business unit successful on its own, downplaying the importance of convergence. According to a senior Time Warner executive, Parsons believes that "if we set convergence as a dramatic target, we set ourselves up for a fall because it's clearly going to take longer than we thought." The new CEO is also attempting to respond to investors, who are clamoring for a simplified, more easily understood structure.

The firm's missteps, along with the slump in the technology sector, have caused the company's stock price to fall, erasing more than $100 billion of shareholder value since the 2001 merger of AOL and Time Warner. Still, Case believes that a convergence strategy will ultimately yield the best results. He points out, "The Internet phenomenon, the trend toward more of a connected society, is unabated." Now it is up to Parsons to find a way to organize the entity to capture Case's vision and then to make that organization profitable.

"The merger was never about cross-divisional promotion. It was about cross-divisional innovation."—Steve Case, former Time Warner chairman

References: Jill Goldsmith, "TV, AOL, knock Time Warner Stock," *Daily Variety*, January 29, 2004, v 282 i23 pl(2); "AOL Time Warner 2002 Factbook," "Corporate Information: Timeline," "Overview," AOL Time Warner website, www.aoltimewarner.com on June 5, 2002; Martin Peers, "AOL CEO Parsons Reorganizes Reporting Lines for Senior Aides," *Wall Street Journal*, May 24, 2002, online.wsj.com on June 5, 2002; Marc Gunther and Stephanie N. Mehta, "Can Steve Case Make Sense of This Beast?" *Fortune*, May 13, 2002 (quotation), www.fortune.com on April 30, 2002; Martin Peers, "In New Turn, AOL Time Warner Will De-Emphasize 'Convergence,'" *Wall Street Journal*, May 13, 2002, online.wsj.com on June 5, 2002.

AOL Time Warner faces the task of developing an organization structure that allows the synergies it expected when the two companies merged, yet still enables management to have some control over operations. This is not unusual in business and industry today as companies struggle to remain competitive in a rapidly changing world. This chapter describes the essential elements of organization structure and several different ways they can be combined into an organization design that will help the organization achieve its objectives.

Essential Elements of Organization Structure

An **organization** is a group of people working together to attain common goals.

Organizational goals are objectives that management seeks to achieve in pursuing the firm's purpose.

In other chapters, we discuss key elements of the individual and the factors that tie the individual and the organization together. In a given organization, these factors must fit together within a common framework: the organization's structure. An **organization** is a group of people working together to achieve common goals. Top management determines the direction of the organization by defining its purpose, establishing goals to meet that purpose, and formulating strategies to achieve the goals. The definition of its purpose gives the organization reason to exist; in effect, it answers the question "What business are we in?" Establishing goals converts the defined purpose into specific, measurable performance targets. **Organizational goals** are objectives that management seeks to achieve in pursuing the firm's purpose. Finally, strategies are specific action plans that enable the organization to achieve its goals and thus its purpose. Pursuing a strategy involves developing an organization structure and the processes to do the organization's work.

Organization Structure

Organization structure is the system of task, reporting, and authority relationships within which the organization does its work.

Organization structure is the system of task, reporting, and authority relationships within which the work of the organization is done. Thus, structure defines the form and function of the organization's activities. Structure also defines how the parts of an organization fit together, as is evident from an organization chart.

The purpose of an organization's structure is to order and coordinate the actions of employees to achieve organizational goals. The premise of organized effort is that people can accomplish more by working together than they can separately. The work must be coordinated properly, however, to realize the potential gains of collective effort. Consider what might happen if the thousands of employees at Dell Computers worked without any kind of structure. Each person might try to build a computer that he or she thought would sell. No two computers would be alike, and each would take months or years to build. The costs of making the computers would be so high that no one would be able to afford them. To produce computers that are both competitive in the marketplace and profitable for the company, Dell must have a structure in which its employees and managers work together in a coordinated manner. Daimler-Chrysler faced similar coordination problems following its merger due to duplication of capabilities, facilities, and product lines, as discussed in the Mastering Change box.

An **organization chart** is a diagram showing all people, positions, reporting relationships, and lines of formal communication in the organization.

The structure of an organization is most often described in terms of its organization chart (see Figure 13.1 for an example). A complete **organization chart** shows all people, positions, reporting relationships, and lines of formal communication in the organization. For large organizations, several charts may be necessary to show all positions. For example, one chart may show top management, includ-

MASTERING CHANGE

DaimlerChrysler Revs Up

In 1999, German automaker Daimler, which manufactures Mercedes cars, merged with Chrysler, one of America's Big Three. The new firm, DaimlerChrysler, then purchased a 34 percent stake in Japan-based Mitsubishi Motors. Although the merger seemed like a brilliant move, combining powerhouses from three continents, the results have been weak thus far.

The German-born CEO, Jurgen Schrempp, is trying to combine the firm's disparate units into an integrated whole. "The chief executive should not be the one who just sort of guides the board on vision and strategy. You also have to know what you are talking about," Schrempp says. To advise him, Schrempp created a chairman's council of eleven outsiders, including IBM's Lou Gerstner. He also established an executive automotive committee whose members are the heads of Mercedes, Chrysler, and Mitsubishi; he hopes the group can improve coordination.

One problematic area is cost control. The merger resulted in duplication of capabilities, facilities, and product lines, consequently increasing expenses. Combined with the effect of slower sales and increased competition, the cost increase caused the firm to lose $589 million in 2001, compared with a 2000 gain of $7 billion. Three years after the merger, the firm is still seeking closer integration in some functions. Schrempp asks, "Why not combine parts departments, workshops and things like that?" Sharing components across the three major divisions could bring

significant savings; for example, using the Mercedes gearbox in Chrysler sedans could save as much as $100 million.

Another problem is the potential dilution of DaimlerChrysler's brands. For example, Schrempp wants to avoid the perception that a Mercedes is just an expensive Chrysler. Garel Rhys, professor at Cardiff Business School, warns, "[Mercedes] is not doing as well as it was. It is widening its share with cars that have lower margins."

A third problem is the need to jump-start synergy and creativity across the divisions. The new Crossfire roadster is a Chrysler brand, engineered by Mercedes, that shares components with both Mitsubishi and Mercedes. The innovative Pacifica station wagon/minivan hybrid was introduced in 2003, and Schrempp promises a pipeline of new designs through 2005. The changes seem to be working as DaimlerChrysler reported net income of almost $5 billion in 2002 and over $500 million in 2003.

References: Alex Taylor III, "Schrempp Shifts Gears," *Fortune*, March 18, 2002 (quotation), www.fortune.com on June 6, 2002; Christine Tierney and Joann Muller, "DaimlerChrysler's Foggy Forecast," *BusinessWeek*, February 14, 2002, www.businessweek.com on June 6, 2002; "DaimlerChrysler Chief Seeks Greater Brand Integration," as reported in the *Financial Times*, reprinted in Wall Street Journal Online, May 21, 2002, online.wsj.com on June 6, 2002; Joann Muller, "Daimler and Chrysler Have a Baby," *Business-Week*, January 14, 2002, www. businessweek.com on June 6, 2002. *Hoover's Online*, December 11, 2004, http://www.hoovers.com/daimlerchrysler/ —ID58357—/free-co-fin-factsheet.xhtml

ing the board of directors, the chief executive officer, the president, all vice presidents, and important headquarters staff units. Subsequent charts may show the structure of each department and staff unit. Figure 13.1 depicts two organization charts for a large firm; top management is shown in the upper portion of the figure and the manufacturing department in the lower portion. Notice that the structures of the different manufacturing groups are given in separate charts.

An organization's **configuration**, or shape, reflects the division of labor and the means of coordinating the divided tasks.

The **division of labor** is the way the organization's work is divided into different jobs to be done by different people.

An organization chart depicts reporting relationships and work group memberships, and shows how positions and small work groups are combined into departments, which together make up the organization's **configuration,** or shape. The configuration of organizations can be analyzed in terms of how the two basic requirements of structure—division of labor and coordination of the divided tasks—are fulfilled.

Division of Labor

Division of labor is the extent to which the organization's work is separated into different jobs to be done by different people. Division of labor is one of the seven

FIGURE 13.1

Examples of Organization Charts

These two charts show the similarities between a top management chart and a department chart. In each, managers have four other managers or work group reporting to them.

Top Management Chart

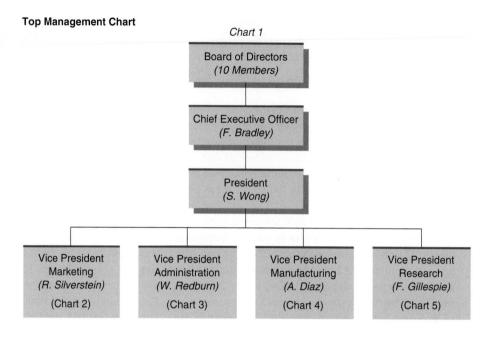

Chart 1

Department Chart

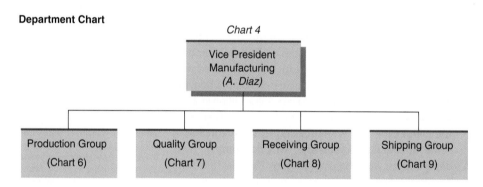

Chart 4

primary characteristics of structuring described by Max Weber,[1] but the concept can be traced back to the eighteenth-century economist Adam Smith. Division of labor grew more popular as large organizations became more prevalent in a manufacturing society. This trend has continued, and most research indicates that large organizations usually have more division of labor than smaller ones.[2] Division of labor has been found to have both advantages and disadvantages (see Table 13.1). Modern managers and organization theorists still struggle with the primary disadvantage: Division of labor often results in repetitive, boring jobs that undercut worker satisfaction, involvement, and commitment.[3] In addition, extreme division of labor may be incompatible with new, integrated computerized manufacturing technologies that require teams of highly skilled workers.[4] However, division of labor need not result in boredom. Visualized in terms of a small organization such as a basketball team, it can be quite dynamic. On a successful basketball team, each of five players—typically a center, a power forward, a small forward, a shooting guard, and a point guard—play different roles and do different tasks.

TABLE 13.1

Advantages and Disadvantages of Division of Labor

Advantages	Disadvantages
Efficient use of labor	Routine, repetitive jobs
Reduced training costs	Reduced job satisfaction
Increased standardization and uniformity of output	Decreased worker involvement and commitment
Increased expertise from repetition of tasks	Increased worker alienation
	Possible incompatibility with computerized manufacturing technologies

Coordinating the Divided Tasks

Departmentalization is the manner in which divided tasks are combined and allocated to work groups.

Three basic mechanisms are used to help coordinate the divided tasks: departmentalization, span of control, and administrative hierarchy. These mechanisms focus on grouping tasks in some meaningful manner, creating work groups of manageable size, and establishing a system of reporting relationships among supervisors and managers.

Departmentalization   **Departmentalization** is the manner in which divided tasks are combined and allocated to work groups. It is a consequence of the division of labor. Because employees engaged in specialized activities can lose sight of overall organizational goals, their work must be coordinated to ensure that it contributes to the organization's welfare.

There are many possible ways to departmentalize tasks. The five groupings most often used are business function, process, product or service, customer, and geography. The first two, function and process, derive from the internal operations of the organization; the others are based on external factors. Most organizations tend to use a combination of methods, and departmentalization often changes as organizations evolve.[5] Departmentalization by business functions is based on traditional business functions such as marketing, manufacturing, and human resource administration (see Figure 13.2, *part a*). In this configuration, employees most frequently associate with others engaged in the same function, which enhances communication and cooperation. In a functional group, employees who do similar work can learn from one another by sharing ideas about opportunities and problems they encounter on the job. Unfortunately, functional groups lack an automatic mechanism for coordinating the flow of work through the organization.[6] In other words, employees in a functional structure tend to associate little with those in other parts of

Larger and fancier hotels have many employees providing services to guests, including bellhops, reception desk personnel, concierge, floor attendants, room service providers, and many more. These tasks are separated and usually assigned to different functional departments. As a result, these employees usually work somewhat independently from those in other departments. However, some hotels are finding that the work of these employees often needs to be better coordinated to improve guest service. One way they are doing this is by equipping all these employees with tiny two-way radios to improve coordination among them. One added feature is the ability to tell one another the name of each guest as she or he enters the facility. This bellhop is able to tell the reception desk the names of arriving guests so they can be greeted by name as they approach the desk. Hotels are finding that high-end guests love this personal touch.

FIGURE 13.2

Departmentalization by Business Function, by Process, and by Product

These charts compare departmentalization by business function, by process, and by product. "Functions" are the basic business functions, whereas "processes" are the specific categories of jobs people perform.

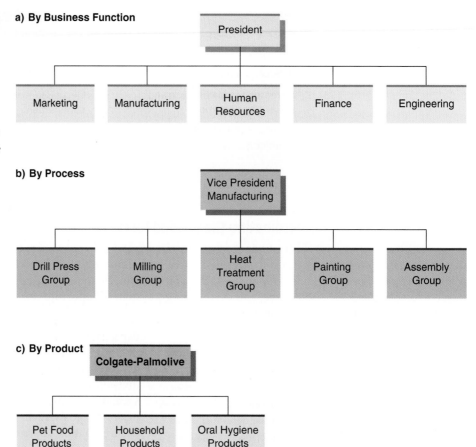

a) By Business Function

President

Marketing | Manufacturing | Human Resources | Finance | Engineering

b) By Process

Vice President Manufacturing

Drill Press Group | Milling Group | Heat Treatment Group | Painting Group | Assembly Group

c) By Product

Colgate-Palmolive

Pet Food Products | Household Products | Oral Hygiene Products

the organization. The result can be a narrow focus that limits the coordination of work among functional groups, such as when the engineering department fails to provide marketing with product information because it is too busy testing materials to think about sales.

Departmentalization by process is similar to functional departmentalization except the focus is much more on specific jobs grouped according to activity. Thus, as Figure 13.2, *part b*, illustrates, the firm's manufacturing jobs are divided into certain well-defined manufacturing processes: drilling, milling, heat treatment, painting, and assembly. Hospitals often use process departmentalization, grouping the professional employees such as therapists according to the types of treatment they provide. Process groupings encourage specialization and expertise among employees, who tend to concentrate on a single operation and share information with departmental colleagues. A process orientation may develop into an internal career path and managerial hierarchy within the department. For example, a specialist might become the "lead" person for that specialty, such as the lead welder or lead press operator. As in functional grouping, however, narrowness of focus can be a problem in a process group. Employees may become so absorbed in the requirements and execution of their operations that they disregard broader considerations such as overall product flow.[7]

Departmentalization by product or service occurs when employees who work on a particular product or service are members of the same department regardless of their business function or the process in which they engage. Figure 13.2, *part c*, shows a partial product structure of Colgate-Palmolive. Departmentalization according to product or service obviously enhances interaction and communication among employees who produce the same product or service and may reduce coordination problems. In this type of configuration, there may be less process specialization but more specialization in the unique aspects of the specific product or service. The disadvantage is that employees may become so interested in their particular product or service that they miss technological improvements or innovations developed in other departments.

Departmentalization by customer is often called "departmentalization by market." Many lending institutions in Texas, for example, have separate departments for retail, commercial, agriculture, and petroleum loans similar to those shown in Figure 13.3. When significant groups of customers differ substantially from one another, organizing along customer lines may be the most effective way to provide the best product or service possible. This is why hospital nurses are often grouped by the type of illness they handle; the various maladies demand different treatment and specialized knowledge.[8] Deutsche Bank recently changed its organization structure from a regional structure to one based on client groups.[9] With customer departmentalization, there is usually less process specialization because employees must remain flexible to do whatever is necessary to enhance the relationship with customers. This configuration offers the best coordination of work flow to the customer. However, it may isolate employees from others in their special areas of expertise. For example, if each of a company's three metallurgical specialists is assigned to a different market-based group, these individuals are unlikely to have many opportunities to discuss the latest technological advances in metallurgy.

With departmentalization by geography, groups are organized according to a region of the country or world. Sales or marketing groups are often arranged by

FIGURE 13.3

Departmentalization by Customer and by Geographic Region

Departmentalization by customer and by geographic region is often used in marketing or sales departments in order to focus on specific needs or locations of customers.

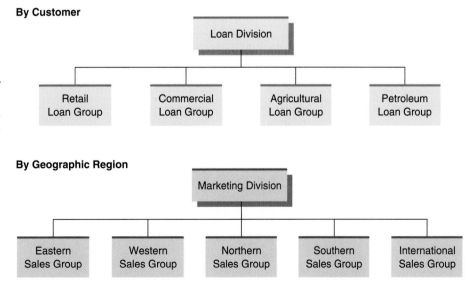

By Customer

Loan Division

- Retail Loan Group
- Commercial Loan Group
- Agricultural Loan Group
- Petroleum Loan Group

By Geographic Region

Marketing Division

- Eastern Sales Group
- Western Sales Group
- Northern Sales Group
- Southern Sales Group
- International Sales Group

geographic region. As Figure 13.3 illustrates, the marketing effort of a large multi-national corporation can be divided according to major geographical divisions. Using a geographically based configuration may result in significant cost savings and better market coverage. On the other hand, it may isolate work groups from activities in the organization's home office or in the technological community because the focus of the work group is solely on affairs within the region. Such a regional focus may foster loyalty to the work group that exceeds commitment to the larger organization. In addition, work-related communication and coordination among groups may be somewhat inefficient.

Many large organizations use a mixed departmentalization scheme. Such organizations may have separate operating divisions based on products, but within each division departments may be based on business function, process, customers, or geographic region (see Figure 13.4). Which methods work best depends on the organization's activities, communication needs, and coordination requirements. Another type of mixed structure often occurs in joint ventures, which are increasing in number.

The **span of control** is the number of people who report to a manager.

Span of Control   The second dimension of organizational configuration, **span of control** (or *span of management*), is the number of people reporting to a manager; thus, it defines the size of the organization's work groups. A manager who has a small span of control can maintain close control over workers and stay in contact with daily operations. If the span of control is large, close control is not possible. Figure 13.5 shows examples of large and small spans of control. Supervisors in the

FIGURE 13.4

Mixed Departmentalization

A mixed departmentalization scheme is often used in very large organizations with more complex structures. Headquarters is organized based on products. Industrial products and consumer products are departmentalized on the basis of function. The manufacturing department is based on process. Sales is based on customers. Marketing is based on geographical regions.

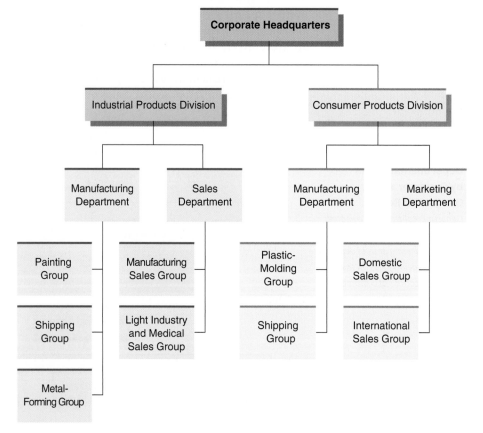

Large Span of Control

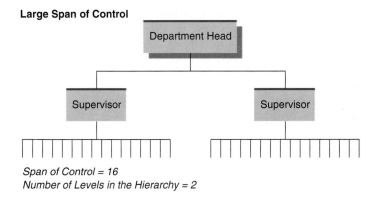

Span of Control = 16
Number of Levels in the Hierarchy = 2

Small Span of Control

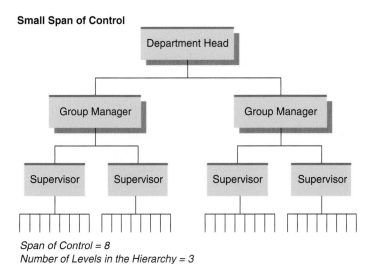

Span of Control = 8
Number of Levels in the Hierarchy = 3

FIGURE 13.5

Span of Control and Levels in the Administrative Hierarchy

These charts show how span of control and the number of levels in the administrative hierarchy are inversely related. The thirty-two first-level employees are in two groups of sixteen in the top chart and in four groups of eight at the bottom chart. Either may be appropriate depending on the work situation.

The **administrative hierarchy** is the system of reporting relationships in the organization, from the lowest to the highest managerial levels.

upper portion of the figure have a span of control of sixteen, whereas those in the lower portion have a span of control of eight.

A number of formulas and rules have been offered for determining the optimal span of control in an organization, but research on the topic has not conclusively identified a foolproof method.[10] Henry Mintzberg concluded that the optimal unit size, or span of control, depends on five conditions:

1. The coordination requirements within the unit, including factors such as the degree of job specialization
2. The similarity of tasks in the unit
3. The type of information available or needed by unit members
4. Differences in members' need for autonomy
5. The extent to which members need direct access to the supervisor[11]

For example, a span of control of sixteen (Figure 13.5) may be appropriate for a supervisor in a typical manufacturing plant in which experienced workers do repetitive production tasks. On the other hand, a span of control of eight or fewer (Figure 13.5) may be suitable in a job shop or custom-manufacturing facility in which workers do many different things and the tasks and problems that arise are new and unusual.[12]

Administrative Hierarchy   The **administrative hierarchy** is the system of reporting relationships in the organization, from the first level up through the president or CEO. It results from the need for supervisors and managers to coordinate the activities of employees. The size of the administrative hierarchy is inversely related to the span of control: Organizations with a small span of control have many managers in the hierarchy; those with a large span of control have a smaller administrative hierarchy. Companies often rearrange their administrative hierarchies to achieve more efficient operations. Using Figure 13.5 again, we can examine the effects of small and large spans of control on the number of hierarchical levels. The smaller span of control for the supervisors in the lower portion of the figure requires that there be four supervisors rather than two. Correspondingly, another management layer is needed to keep the department head's span of control at two. Thus, when the span of control is small, workers are under tighter supervision and more administrative levels exist. When the span of control is large, as in the upper portion of the figure, production workers are not closely supervised and fewer administrative levels exist. Because it measures the number of

Larry Scott took over as CEO of WTA Tour, Inc, the organization that runs professional women's tennis around the world, in 2003. With attendance dropping and tour revenues down 40 percent in 2003, Scott found an organization in complete disarray. He quickly took control and convinced the top players, like Maria Sarapova, to cooperate with sponsors, fans, and the media. He developed a program to restructure the budget, increase sponsor revenues, increase prize money, and beef up player relations. These changes have lead to an increase in the popularity of tennis, resulting in elevated revenues.

Authority is power that has been legitimized within a particular social context.

Responsibility is an obligation to do something with the expectation some act or output will result.

management personnel, or administrators, in the organization, the administrative hierarchy is sometimes called the *administrative component*, *administrative intensity*, or *administrative ratio.*

Authority, Responsibility, and Decision Making

In addition to dividing tasks, grouping them in departments, and determining reporting relationships, organization structure describes how decisions are made and the extent to which behaviors are specified.

Authority   **Authority** is power that has been legitimized within a specific social context and includes the legitimate right to use resources to accomplish expected outcomes. Authority to make decisions may be restricted to the top levels of the organization or dispersed throughout the organization. Authority originates in the owners of the organization, who establish a group of directors responsible for managing the organization's affairs. The directors, in turn, authorize various people in the organization to make decisions and use organizational resources. Thus, they delegate authority, or power in a social context, to others.

Responsibility   **Responsibility** is an obligation to do something with the expectation that some act or output will result. For example, a manager may expect an employee to write and present a proposal for a new program by a certain date; thus, the employee is responsible for preparing the proposal. Responsibility also derives from the organization's ownership. The owners hire or appoint a group, often a board of directors, to be responsible for managing the organization, making the decisions, and reaching the goals set by the owners. A downward chain of responsibility is then established. The board hires a chief executive officer (CEO) or president to be responsible for running the organization. The CEO or president hires more people and holds them responsible for accomplishing designated tasks that enable her or him to produce the results expected by the board and the owners. Jack Welch became famous for the way he ran GE for twenty years. During that time, he hired many managers and delegated responsibility for running various parts of the business. However, in the end, Welch was responsible for all of the organization's activities, including the degree to which business was conducted.

The chain extends throughout the organization because each manager has an obligation to fulfill: to appropriately employ organizational resources (people, money, and equipment) to meet the owners' expectations. Although managers seemingly pass responsibility on to others to achieve results, each manager is still held responsible for the outputs of those to whom he or she delegates tasks.

Authority is linked to responsibility because a manager responsible for accomplishing certain results must have the authority to use resources to achieve those results.[13] The relationship between responsibility and authority must be one of parity; that is, the authority over resources must be sufficient to enable the manager to meet the output expectations of others. One complaint often heard from employees is that they have too much responsibility but not enough authority to get the job done. This indicates a lack of parity between responsibility and authority. Managers are usually quite willing to hold individuals responsible for specific tasks but reluctant to delegate to them enough authority to do the job. In effect, managers try to rid themselves of responsibility for results (which they cannot do) but are loath to give away their cherished authority over resources. **Delegation** is the transfer to others of authority to make decisions and use organizational resources. Delegation of authority to make decisions to lower-level managers is common in organizations today. The important thing is to give lower-level managers authority to carry out the decisions they make. Managers typically have difficulty delegating successfully.

An Alternative View of Authority   So far we have described authority as a "top-down" function in organizations; that is, authority originates at the top and is delegated downward as the managers at the top consider appropriate. In author Chester Barnard's alternative perspective, authority is seen as originating in the individual, who can choose whether or not to follow a directive from above. The choice of whether to comply with a directive is based on the degree to which the individual understands it, feels able to carry it out, and believes it to be in the best interests of the organization and consistent with personal values.[14] This perspective has been called the **acceptance theory of authority** because it means the manager's authority depends on the subordinate's acceptance of the manager's right to give a directive and expect compliance.

Centralization   **Centralization** means decision-making authority is concentrated at the top of the organizational hierarchy. At the opposite end of the continuum is decentralization, in which decisions are made throughout the hierarchy. Increasingly, centralization is being discussed in terms of participation in decision making.[15] In decentralized organizations, lower-level employees participate in making decisions. Participative management has been described as a total management system in which people are involved in the organization's daily decision making and management. For many people, participation in decision making has become more than a simple aspect of organization structure; it has even been described as morally necessary. Caution is required, however, because if middle managers are to make effective decisions, as participative management requires, they must have sufficient information.[16] One highly touted benefit of the information age was that all employees throughout the organization would have more information and would therefore be able to participate more in decisions affecting their work, thus creating more decentralized organizations. However, some have suggested that this has had the opposite effect: enabling top managers to have more information about the organization's operations and to keep decisions to themselves, thus creating more highly centralized organizations.[17]

Formalization   **Formalization** is the degree to which rules and procedures shape employees' jobs and activities. The purpose of formalization is to predict and control how employees behave on the job.[18] Rules and procedures can be both explicit and implicit. Explicit rules are set down in job descriptions, policy and procedures manuals, or office memos. Implicit rules often develop as employees become accustomed to doing things in a certain way over a period of time. Though unwritten, these established ways of getting things done become standard operating procedures and have the same effect on employee behavior as written rules. We can

---

Delegation is the transfer to others of authority to make decisions and use organizational resources.

The **acceptance theory of authority** says that the authority of a manager depends on the subordinate's acceptance of the manager's right to give directives and expect compliance with them.

With **centralization**, decision-making authority is concentrated at the top of the organizational hierarchy.

Formalization is the degree to which rules and procedures shape the jobs and activities of employees.

assess formalization in organizations by looking at the proportion of jobs governed by rules and procedures and the extent to which those rules permit variation. More formalized organizations have a higher proportion of rule-bound jobs and less tolerance for rule violations. Increasing formalization may affect the design of jobs throughout the organization, as well as employee motivation and work group interactions.[19]

Organizations tend to add more rules and procedures as the need for control of operations increases. Some organizations have become so formalized that they have rules for how to make new rules! Other organizations are trying to become less formalized by reducing the number of rules and procedures employees must follow. Although rules exist in some form in almost every organization, how strictly they are enforced varies significantly from one organization to another and even within a single organization. Some managers argue that "a rule is a rule" and that all rules must be enforced to control employee behaviors and prevent chaos in the organization. Other managers act as though "all rules are made to be broken" and see rules as stumbling blocks on the way to effective action. Neither point of view is better for the organization; rather, a more balanced approach is recommended.

Classic Views of Structure: The Universal Approach

In the **universal approach** to organization design, prescriptions or propositions are designed to work in any circumstances.

Weber's **ideal bureaucracy** is characterized by a hierarchy of authority and a system of rules and procedures designed to create an optimally effective system for large organizations.

The earliest views of organization structure combined the essential elements of organization structure into recommendations on how to design organizations. In the **universal approach** to organization design, prescriptions or propositions are designed to work in any situation. Thus, a universal design prescribes the "one best way" to structure the jobs, authority, and reporting relationships of the organization, regardless of factors such as the organization's external environment, the industry, and the type of work to be done. These views have often been called *classical organization theory* and include Max Weber's concept of the ideal bureaucracy, the classic organizing principles of Henri Fayol, and the human organization view of Rensis Likert. Although all three are universal approaches, their concerns and structural prescriptions differ significantly.

Ideal Bureaucracy

Weber's **ideal bureaucracy,** presented in Chapter 1, was an organizational system characterized by a hierarchy of authority and a system of rules and procedures that, if followed, would create a maximally effective system for large organizations. Weber, writing at a time when organizations were inherently inefficient, claimed the bureaucratic form of administration is superior to other forms of management with respect to stability, control, and predictability of outcomes.[20] Weber's ideal bureaucracy had seven essential characteristics and utilized several of the essential elements of structure discussed in this chapter, including division of labor, hierarchy of authority, and rules and procedures. Weber intended these characteristics to ensure order and predictability in relationships among people and jobs in the bureaucracy. These same features, however, can lead to sluggishness, inefficiency, and red tape if any of the characteristics are carried to an extreme or are violated. Subsequent writers have claimed Weber's view of authority is too rigid and suggested that the bureaucratic organization may impede creativity and innovation and result in a lack of compassion for the individual.[21] In other words, the impersonality intended to foster objectivity in a bureaucracy may result in serious difficulties for both employees and the organization. However, some organizations retain some characteristics of a bureaucratic structure while remaining innovative and productive. Paul Adler has countered the currently popular movements of "bureaucracy busting" by noting that large-scale, complex organizations still need some of the basic characteristics Weber described—hierarchical structure, formalized procedures, and staff expertise—to avoid chaos and ensure efficiency, conformance quality, and timeliness.[22] The need for bureaucracy is not extinct. Bureaucracy, or at least some of its elements, is still critical for designing effective organizations.

The Classic Principles of Organizing

The **management functions** set forth by Henri Fayol include planning, organizing, command, coordination, and control.

Henri Fayol, a French engineer and chief executive officer of a mining company, presented a second classic view of organization structure at the beginning of the twentieth century. Drawing on his experience as a manager, Fayol was the first to classify the essential elements of management—now usually called **management functions**—as planning, organizing, command, coordination, and control.[23] In addition, he presented fourteen principles of organizing that he considered an indispensable code for managers. Fayol's principles have proved extraordinarily influential: They have served as the basis for the development of generally accepted means of organizing. For example, Fayol's *unity of command* principle means employees should receive directions from only one person, and *unity of direction* means tasks with the same objective should have a common supervisor. Combining these two principles with division of labor, authority, and responsibility results in a system of tasks and reporting and authority relationships that is the very essence of organizing. Fayol's principles thus provide the framework for the organization chart and the coordination of work. However, they have been criticized for ignoring the human element in organizations, their lack of operational specificity, and their lack of support by evidence other than Fayol's personal experiences.[24]

Human Organization

Rensis Likert's **human organization** approach is based on supportive relationships, participation, and overlapping work groups.

The **human organization,** developed by Rensis Likert, is based on supportive relationships, participation, and overlapping work groups, which is not surprising given Likert's criticisms of Fayol's classic principles of organizing for overlooking human factors.[25] The term *supportive relationships* suggests that in all organizational activities, individuals should be treated so that they experience feelings of support, self-worth, and importance. By *employee participation*, Likert meant the work group needs to be involved in decisions that affect it, thereby enhancing employees' sense of supportiveness and self-worth. The principle of *overlapping work groups* means work groups are linked, with managers serving as the "linking pins." Each manager (except the highest ranking) is a member of two groups: a work group that he or she supervises and a management group composed of the manager's peers and their supervisor. Coordination and communication strengthen when managers perform the linking function by sharing problems, decisions, and information both upward and downward in the groups to which they belong. The human organization concept rests on the assumption that people work best in highly cohesive groups oriented toward organizational goals. Management's function is to make sure the work groups are linked for effective coordination and communication.

Thus, the universal approaches to organizing embody the essential elements of organization structure. Each view, however, combined these key elements in different ways and with other management elements. These three classic views are typical of how the early writers attempted to prescribe a universal approach to organization structure that would be best in all situations.

Contingency Approaches to Organization Design

Under the **contingency approach** to organization design, the desired outcomes for the organization can be achieved in several ways.

A **strategy** is the plans and actions necessary to achieve organizational goals.

As noted earlier, most theories of organization design take either a universal or a contingency approach. A **contingency approach** suggests that organizational efficiency and effectiveness can be achieved in several ways. In this section we examine certain conditions, or contingency factors, and then attempt to specify how to combine the essential elements to maximize organizational effectiveness. The contingency factors include the strategy of the organization, its technology, the environment, the organization's size, and the social system within which the organization operates.

Strategy

A **strategy** consists of the plans and actions necessary to achieve organizational goals.[26] After studying the history of seventy companies, Alfred Chandler drew certain conclusions about the relationship between an organization's structure and its business strategy.[27] Chandler observed that a growth strategy to expand into a new product line is usually matched with some type of decentralization, necessary for dealing with the problems associated with the new line. Chandler's "structure follows strategy" concept seems to appeal to common sense. Management must decide what the organization is to do and what its goals are before deciding how to design the organization structure, which is how the organization will meet those goals. This perspective assumes a purposeful approach to designing the structure of the organization.

Structural Imperatives

Structural imperatives—size, technology, and environment—are the three primary determinants of organization structure.

The structural-imperatives approach to organization design probably has been the most discussed and researched contingency perspective of the last forty years. This perspective gradually emerged from a vast number of studies that sought to address the question "What are the compelling factors that determine how the organization must be structured to be effective?" As Figure 13.6 shows, the three factors that have been identified as **structural imperatives** are size, technology, and environment.

FIGURE 13.6

The Structural-Imperatives Approach

Organizational size, environment, and technology determine how an organization should be structured for greatest effectiveness.

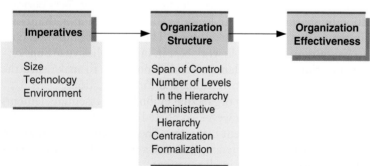

Size　The size of an organization can be gauged in many ways. Usually it is measured in terms of total number of employees, value of the organization's assets, total sales in the previous year (or number of clients served), or physical capacity. The method of measurement is very important, although the different measures are usually correlated.[28] Generally, larger organizations have a more complex structure than smaller ones in that large size is associated with greater specialization of labor, a larger span of control, more hierarchical levels, and greater formalization.[29]

Traditionally, as organizations have grown, several layers of advisory staff have been added to help coordinate the complexities inherent in any large organization. In contrast, a current trend is to cut staff throughout the organization. Known as **organizational downsizing,** this popular trend is aimed primarily at reducing the size of corporate staff and middle management to reduce costs. The results of downsizing have been mixed, with some observers noting that indiscriminate across-the-board cuts may leave the organization weak in certain key areas. However, positive results often include quicker decision making because fewer layers of management must approve every decision. One review of research on organizational downsizing found that it has both psychological and sociological impacts. This study suggested that in a downsizing environment, size affects organization design in very complex ways.[30]

Organizational downsizing aims to reduce the size of corporate staff and middle management to reduce costs.

Technology **Organizational technology** consists of the mechanical and intellectual processes that transform raw materials into products and services for customers. For example, the primary technology employed by major oil companies transforms crude oil (input) into gasoline, motor oil, heating oil, and other petroleum-based products (outputs). Prudential Insurance uses actuarial tables and information processing technologies to produce its insurance services. Of course, most organizations use multiple technologies. Oil companies use research and information processing technologies in their laboratories, where new petroleum products and processes are generated. Although many different ways to evaluate and measure technology are available, there is general agreement that technology is a very important determinant of organization design. Many early approaches focused on manufacturing technologies, while later perspectives examined service and knowledge technologies. The different perspectives on technology are somewhat similar in that most of them address the adaptability of the technological system to change.

Organizational technology refers to the mechanical and intellectual processes that transform inputs into outputs.

One major contribution of the study of organizational technology is the recognition that organizations have more than one important "technology" that enables them to accomplish their tasks. Instead of examining technology in isolation, some have recognized that size and technology are related in determining organization structure.[31] In smaller organizations, technology tends to have more direct effects on the structure. In large organizations, structure depends less on the operations technology and more on size considerations such as number of employees. In a large firm, each department or division may have a different technology that determines how that department or division should be structured. In short, in small organizations structure depends primarily on the technology, whereas in large organizations the need to coordinate complicated activities is the most important factor. Thus, both

Downsizing often has unintended consequences. Employees who survive the downsizing are usually required to pick up the work of those who left. This poor guy got a promotion and a new title, but he now has more jobs to do.

© 1998 Randy Glasbergen.
www.glasbergen.com

"I downsized our staff so effectively, they promoted me to Executive Vice President. They also made me custodian, receptionist and parking garage attendant."

organizational size and technology are important considerations in organization design.

Environment   The **organizational environment** includes all the elements—people, other organizations, economic factors, objects, and events—that lie outside the boundaries of the organization. The environment is composed of two layers: the general environment and the task environment. The **general environment** includes a broad set of dimensions and factors within which the organization operates, including political-legal, social, cultural, technological, economic, and international factors. The **task environment** includes specific organizations, groups, and individuals who influence the organization. People in the task environment include customers, donors, regulators, inspectors, and shareholders. Among the organizations in the task environment are competitors, legislatures, and regulatory agencies. Economic factors in the task environment might include interest rates, international trade factors, and the unemployment rate in a particular area. Objects in the task environment include such things as buildings, vehicles, and trees. Events that may affect organizations include weather, elections, or war. The difficulty for most managers is to determine how those changes affect the company.

The manager, then, faces an enormous, only vaguely specified environment that directly or indirectly affects the organization. Managing the organization within such an environment may seem an overwhelming task. The issue, then, is to determine which parts of the environment should receive the manager's attention. In the remainder of this section, we examine two perspectives on the organizational environment: the analysis of environmental components and environmental uncertainty. The environmental characteristic that brings together all of these different environmental influences and appears to have the greatest effect on the organization's design is uncertainty. **Environmental uncertainty** exists when managers have little information about environmental events and their impact on the organization.[32] Uncertainty results from complexity and dynamism in the environment. **Environmental complexity** is the number of environmental components that impinge on organizational decision making. **Environmental dynamism** is the degree to which these components change.[33] Environments that are both dynamic and complex are the most uncertain and require organization designs that can process a lot of uncertainty. At the other extreme, environments that are static and simple are the least uncertain and require organization designs that handle stability and predictability.

Organizations with international operations must contend with additional levels of complexity and dynamism, both within and across cultures. Many cultures have relatively stable environments. For example, the economies of Sweden and the United States are fairly stable. Although competitive forces within each country's economic system vary, each economy remains strong. In contrast, the environments of other countries are much more dynamic. For example, France's policies on socialism versus private enterprise tend to change dramatically with each election. At present, far-reaching changes in the economic and management philosophies of most Western European countries make their environments far more dynamic than that of the United States. Environments also vary widely in terms of their complexity. The Japanese culture, which is fairly stable, is also quite complex. Japanese managers are subject to an array of cultural norms and values that are far more encompassing and resistant to change than those U.S. managers face. India also has an extremely complex environment, which continues to be influenced by its traditional caste system.

The **organizational environment** is everything outside the boundaries of the organization, including people, other organizations, economic factors, objects, and events.

The **general environment** includes the broad set of dimensions and factors within which the organization operates, including political-legal, sociocultural, technological, economic, and international factors.

The **task environment** includes specific organizations, groups, and individuals who influence the organization.

Environmental uncertainty exists when managers have little information about environmental events and their impact on the organization.

Environmental complexity is the number of environmental components that impinge on organizational decision making.

Environmental dynamism is the degree to which environmental components that impinge on organizational decision making change.

Organization Designs

The previous section describes several factors that determine how organizations are structured. In this section, we examine several different organization designs created to help organizations adapt to the many contingency factors they face. These designs include mechanistic and organic structures, Mintzberg's designs, and matrix designs.

Mechanistic and Organic Designs

As we discussed in the previous section, most theorists assert that organizations need to be able to adapt to changes in technology. For example, if the rate of change in technology is slow, the most effective design is bureaucratic or "mechanistic." A **mechanistic structure** is primarily hierarchical in nature; interactions and communications are mostly vertical, instructions come from the boss, knowledge is concentrated at the top, and continued membership requires loyalty and obedience. If technology is changing rapidly, the organization needs a structure that allows more flexibility and faster decision making so it can react quickly to change. This design is called "organic." An **organic structure** resembles a network; interactions and communications are more lateral, knowledge resides wherever it is most useful to the organization, and membership requires a commitment to the organization's tasks. An organic organization is generally expected to react more quickly to changes in the environment.

A **mechanistic structure** is primarily hierarchical; interactions and communications typically are vertical, instructions come from the boss, knowledge is concentrated at the top, and loyalty and obedience are required to sustain membership.

An **organic structure** is set up like a network; interactions and communications are horizontal, knowledge resides wherever it is most useful to the organization, and membership requires a commitment to the organization's tasks.

Mintzberg's Designs

In this section, we describe the concrete organization designs proposed by Henry Mintzberg. The universe of possible designs is large, but fortunately we can divide designs into a few basic forms. Mintzberg proposed that the purpose of organizational design is to coordinate activities, and he suggested a range of coordinating mechanisms that are found in operating organizations.[34] In Mintzberg's view, organization structure reflects how tasks are divided and then coordinated. He described five major ways in which tasks are coordinated: by mutual adjustment, by direct supervision, and by standardization of worker (or input) skills, work processes, or outputs (see Figure 13.7). These five methods can exist side by side within an organization.

Coordination by mutual adjustment (mechanism 1 in Figure 13.7) simply means workers use informal communication to coordinate with one another, whereas coordination by direct supervision (mechanism 2) means a manager or supervisor coordinates the actions of workers. As noted, *standardization* may be used as a coordination mechanism in three different ways: (1) standardizing the *input skills* (mechanism 3)—the worker skills that are inputs to the work process; (2) standardizing the *work processes* themselves (mechanism 4 in Figure 13.7)—the methods workers use to transform inputs into outputs; and (3) standardizing the *outputs* (mechanism 5)—the products or services or the performance levels expected of workers. Standardization is usually developed by staff analysts and enforced by management such that skills, processes, and output meet predetermined standards.

Mintzberg pointed out that the five methods of coordination can be combined with the essential elements of structure to develop five structural forms: the simple structure, the machine bureaucracy, the professional bureaucracy, the divisionalized form, and the adhocracy. Mintzberg called these structures *pure* or *ideal* types of designs.

FIGURE 13.7

Mintzberg's Five Coordinating Mechanisms

Henry Mintzberg described five methods of coordinating the actions of organizational partici-pants. The dashed lines in each diagram show the five different means of coordination: (1) mutual adjustment, (2) direct supervision, and standardization of (3) input skills, (4) work processes, and (5) outputs.

Reference: Henry Mintzberg, *The Structuring of Organizations: A Synthesis of the Research.* ©1979, p. 4. Reprinted by permission of Pearson Education, Inc., Upper Saddle River, NJ.

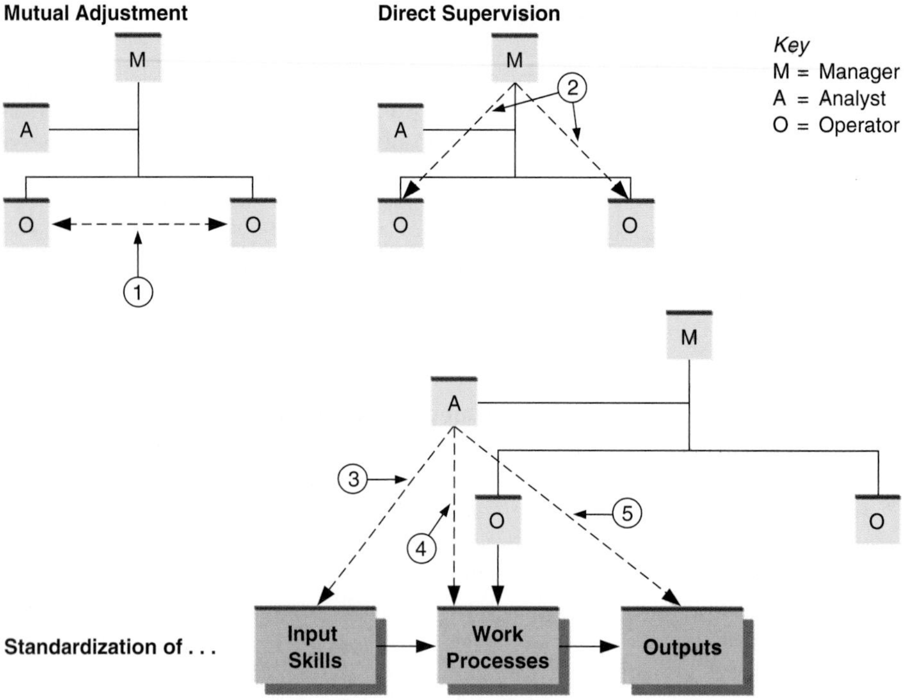

The **simple structure** has little specialization or formalization; power and decision making are concentrated in the chief executive.

In a **machine bureaucracy**, work is highly specialized and formalized, and decision making is usually concentrated at the top.

A **professional bureaucracy** is characterized by horizontal specialization by professional areas of expertise, little formalization, and decentralized decision making.

The **divisionalized form** is divided according to the different markets served; horizontal and vertical specialization exists between divisions and headquarters, decision making is divided between headquarters and divisions, and outputs are standardized.

Simple Structure   The **simple structure** characterizes relatively small, usually young organizations in a simple, dynamic environment. The organization has little specialization and formalization, and its overall structure is organic. Power and decision making are concentrated in the chief executive, often also the owner-manager, and the flow of authority is from the top down. The primary coordinating mechanism is direct supervision. The organization must adapt quickly to survive because of its dynamic and often hostile environment. Most small businesses—a car dealership, a locally owned retail clothing store, or a candy manufacturer with only regional distribution—have a simple structure.

Machine Bureaucracy   The **machine bureaucracy** is typical of large, well-established companies in simple, stable environments. Work is highly specialized and formalized, and decision making is usually concentrated at the top. Standardization of work processes is the primary coordinating mechanism. This highly bureaucratic structure does not have to adapt quickly to changes because the environment is both simple and stable. Examples include large mass production firms; some automobile companies; and providers of services to mass markets, such as insurance companies.

Professional Bureaucracy   Usually found in a complex and stable environment, the **professional bureaucracy** relies on standardization of skills as the primary means of coordination. There is much horizontal specialization by professional areas of expertise but little formalization. Decision making is decentralized and takes place where the expertise is. The only means of coordination available to the organization is standardization of skills—those of the professionally trained employees. Although it lacks centralization, the professional bureaucracy stabilizes and controls its tasks with rules and procedures developed in the relevant profession. Hospitals, universities, and consulting firms are examples.

Divisionalized Form   The **divisionalized form** is characteristic of old, very large firms operating in a relatively simple, stable environment with several diverse markets. It

This dog is wearing the latest in specialty doggy wear, Doggles, created by Roni and Ken DiLullo for their pet, MidKnight. Besides providing protection from sun, the anti-UVA doggie goggles can protect dogs' eyes from external materials following surgery or from harmful debris when searching building explosions or natural disasters. This small million-dollar company has a very simple structure composed of the DiLullos, who perform primarily marketing and distribution functions, while the product is manufactured in Asia.

resembles the machine bureaucracy except it is divided according to the various markets it serves. There is some horizontal and vertical specialization between the divisions (each defined by a market) and headquarters. Decision making is clearly split between headquarters and the divisions, and the primary means of coordination is standardization of outputs. The mechanism of control required by headquarters encourages the development of machine bureaucracies in the divisions. The classic example of the divisionalized form is General Motors, which, in a reorganization in the 1920s, adopted a design that created divisions for each major car model.[35] Although the divisions have been reorganized and the cars changed several times, the concept of the divisionalized organization is still very evident at GM.[36]

Adhocracy   The **adhocracy** is typically found in young organizations engaged in highly technical fields in which the environment is complex and dynamic. Decision making is spread throughout the organization, and power resides with experts. There is horizontal and vertical specialization but little formalization, resulting in a highly organic structure. Coordination is by mutual adjustment through frequent personal communication and liaison. Specialists are not grouped in functional units but instead are deployed into specialized market-oriented project teams. The typical adhocracy is usually established to foster innovation, something to which the other four types of structures are not particularly well suited. Most of the new start-up "dot-com" companies were most likely structured as adhocracies.

In an **adhocracy**, decision making is spread throughout the organization, power resides with the experts, horizontal and vertical specialization exists, and there is little formalization.

Mintzberg believed that fit among parts is the most important consideration in designing an organization. Not only must there be a fit among the structure, the structural imperatives (technology, size, and environment), and organizational strategy, but the components of structure (rules and procedures, decision making, specialization) must also fit together and be appropriate for the situation. Mintzberg suggested that an organization cannot function effectively when these characteristics are not combined properly.[37]

Matrix Organization Design

The **matrix design** com-bines two different designs to gain the benefits of each; typically combined are a product or project depart-mentalization scheme and a functional structure.

The **matrix design** attempts to combine two different designs to gain the benefits of each. The most common matrix form superimposes product or project depart-mentalization on a functional structure (see Figure 13.8). Each department and project has a manager; each employee, however, is a member of both a functional department and a project team. The dual role means the employee has two super-visors, the department manager and the project leader.

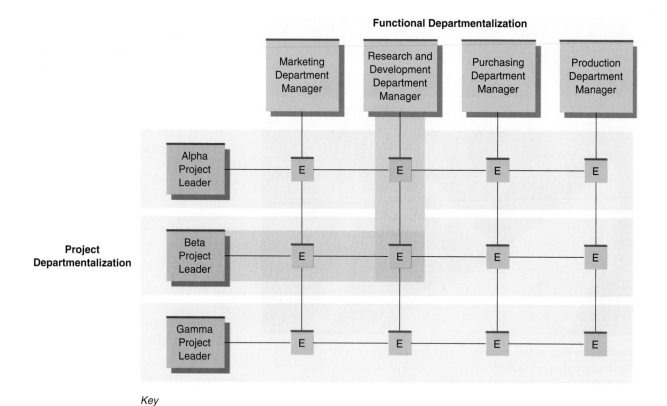

Key
E = Employee

FIGURE 13.8

A Matrix Organization Design

A matrix organization design superimposes two different types of departmentalization onto each other—for example, a functional structure and a project structure.

The matrix structure has the capacity for flexible and coordinated responses to internal and external pressures because members can be reassigned from one project to another as demands for their skills change. Engineers, for example, may work for a month on one project, be assigned to the functional home department for two weeks, and then be reassigned to another project for the next six months. The matrix form improves project coordination by assigning project responsibility to a single leader rather than dividing it among several functional department heads. Furthermore, it improves communication because employees can talk about the project with members of both the project team and the functional unit to which they belong. In this way, solutions to project problems may emerge from either group. Many different types of organizations have used the matrix form of organization, notably large-project manufacturing firms, banks, and hospitals.[38]

The matrix organizational form thus provides several benefits for the organization. It is not, however, trouble free. Typical problems can include role conflict among employees, power struggles over who has authority in various situations, and difficulty in tracing accountability.[39] In any case, it is a complex organizational system that must be carefully coordinated and managed to be effective.

Synopsis

The structure of an organization is the system of task, reporting, and authority relationships within which the organization does its work. The purpose of organization structure is to order and coordinate the actions of employees to achieve organizational goals. Every organization structure addresses two fundamental issues: dividing available labor according to the tasks to be performed and combining and coordinating divided tasks to ensure that tasks are accomplished. To achieve coordinated action, organizations typically create departments based on business function, process, product, customer, and geographic region, and design appropriate spans of control and an administrative hierarchy of reporting relationships in the organization. Decision-making authority, responsibility, and the degree of formal policies and procedures must also be established.

The classic views of organization design were universal approaches in that they attempted to prescribe a one-best-way to design an organization. Typical of these approaches were Weber's ideal bureaucracy, Fayol's classic principles of organizing, and Likert's human organization. Contingency approaches to organization design, on the other hand, propose that the best way to design the structure of the organization depends on a variety of factors. Important contingency approaches to organization design center on the organizational strategy, the size of the organization, the type of technology employed in transforming inputs into outputs, and uncertainty in the environment.

Organization designs can take many forms. A mechanistic structure relies on the administrative hierarchy for communication and directing activities. An organic design is structured like a network; communications and interactions are horizontal and diagonal across groups and teams throughout the organization.

Mintzberg's ideal types of organization design were derived from a framework of coordinating mechanisms. The five types are simple structure, machine bureaucracy, professional bureaucracy, divisionalized form, and adhocracy. Most organizations have some characteristics of each type, but one is likely to predominate. Mintzberg believed the most important consideration in designing an organization is the fit among its parts. The matrix design combines two types of structure (usually functional and project departmentalization) to gain the benefits of each. It usually results in a multiple command and authority system. Benefits of the matrix form include increased flexibility, cooperation, and communication and better use of skilled personnel. Typical problems are associated with the dual reporting system and the complex management system needed to coordinate work.

Discussion Questions

1. Define *organization structure* and explain its role in the process of managing the organization. What is the purpose of organization structure? What would an organization be like without a structure?

2. How is labor divided into departments in your college or university? In what other ways could your college or university be departmentalized?

3. How might centralization or decentralization affect the job characteristics specified in job design (discussed in Chapter 5)?

4. Why do employees typically want more authority and less responsibility?

5. What are the differences between universal approaches and contingency approaches to organization design?

6. Identify and describe some of the environmental and technological factors that affect your college or university. Give specific examples of how they affect you as a student.

7. How does organization design usually differ for large and small organizations?

8. What do you think are the purposes, goals, and strategies of your college or university? How are they reflected in its structure?

9. If you worked in a matrix-type organization, would you prefer to be a project leader, a functional department head, or a highly trained technical specialist? Why?

10. Discuss what you think the important design considerations will be for organization designers in the year 2020.

Organizational Behavior Case for Discussion
Restructuring at Cisco

Changing an organization's structure is a difficult, time-consuming, and expensive task. Therefore, organizations tend to maintain a structure for a considerable period of time, often for decades. Nevertheless, organization structure must also be somewhat flexible to allow the firm to adapt to internal and external changes. Some organizations, notably high-tech firms, compete in rapidly and radically changing industries. How, then, can a high-tech company structure itself to prepare for an uncertain future? Networking firm Cisco is one high-tech company that recently restructured its divisions. "We're building a base for the future," says Cisco CEO and president John Chambers. "If we do this right, it will position us to break away even faster [when the economy improves]."

Cisco is a provider of networking hardware, software, services, and support. It makes the big routers and servers that carry most Internet traffic; smaller routers and servers for local area networks; and components such as hubs, fiber optics, switches, and security software. The reorganization shifted the company from a customer orientation to a product orientation. It used to have three divisions: small businesses, large businesses, and service providers. That structure facilitated good relations with each customer segment. Often, however, a product developed for one customer group was not shared with the other groups, causing duplication of effort; at times, Cisco had as many as eight teams working to develop similar technology. The former structure also separated marketing from engineering. "What our [former] organizational structure had done is create a lot of overlap in technology developments," says chief marketing officer James Richardson.

Cisco's new organization structure has eleven divisions, each one concentrating on a specific set of related technologies such as access, core routing, storage, and wireless. Thus, duplication of effort is eliminated while engineering and marketing work more closely together to develop and sell a particular technology set. The reorganization was accomplished by reassigning personnel and promoting six managers to the senior vice president level. The restructuring followed layoffs that reduced the firm's workforce by about 17 percent, or 8,500 jobs, and resulted in fewer managers—twelve instead of fifteen—reporting directly to Chambers.

The publicly stated reasons for the shake-up were to provide better customer service, eliminate duplication, highlight the central role of technology, and strengthen the relationship between engineering and marketing. However, other explanations also exist, including the slowdown in high-tech industries. After years of strong growth, Cisco's sales dropped rapidly in 2001—for example, falling 25 percent in just one quarter. Chambers claims this "may be the fastest any industry our size has ever decelerated." U.S. markets for networking equipment are saturated, and customers are waiting for the next major breakthrough before making more purchases, asking, "How many times do I need another router?" Chambers claims the recent leveling off of high-tech sales aids the reorganization effort. "You make these transitions at times when you're stable," he says.

Another motivation for the changes was suggested by the departure of Kevin Kennedy, former head of the service provider division. This group contributed half of Cisco's revenues, but sales were slowing and technology stagnating. The official explanation is that Kennedy, in spite of efforts to keep him with the firm, left Cisco to "pursue other opportunities." But it is not clear whether Kennedy left for better career options, had a disagreement with Cisco leadership, or left involuntarily, a possible signal that Cisco is losing interest in the service provider segment. Richardson denies the loss of interest, asserting, "There's nothing to be read into that. The catalyst of all this is [Kennedy's] deciding to leave the company. As a result, [Chambers] said, 'If I'm going to change to a functional organization, I might as well do it now.'" Whatever Kennedy's motivation for quitting, Frank Dzubeck, industry observer, says, "Kevin [Kennedy] lost the fire in the belly and he literally wanted out. He's not the only one [who's] going to be going[,] either."

It is not yet certain whether the reorganization will be beneficial for Cisco. Tam Dell'Oro, a consultant, says it will. "When a company has tighter control [of its divisions], it knows more about what's happening in the business, and it may be able to move faster," she asserts. Others disagree. Technology researcher

Bill Lesieur says the shake-up "creates the perception that Cisco is not fully committed to [becoming] a top-three player" in the service provider segment. The CEO, however, denies that Cisco is giving up on any customers. "This should not be viewed as a shift in strategy," Chambers says.

Case Questions

1. How did Cisco's strategy affect decisions about its new organization structure?
2. How did Cisco's structural imperatives—size, technology, and environment—affect decisions about its new organization structure?
3. How would you resolve the "strategy versus structure" debate in Cisco's case? In other words,

which came first, its strategy or its structure? Provide specific details to support your answer.

References: "Chief Development Officer–Technology Groups," "Company Overview," "Mario Mazzola Gives Update on Cisco's Technology Organization," Cisco website, newsroom.cisco.com on June 13, 2002; Jim Duffy, "Shakeup at Cisco—Service Provider Business Lost in the Sauce in Enterprise-Heavy Reorganization," *Network World*, August 31, 2001, republished at www.tbri.com on June 13, 2002; Jim Duffy, "Cisco Restructures Around 11 Core Technologies," *Network World*, August 27, 2001, pp. 8–10 (see www.networkworld.com); David R. Baker, "Networking Company Streamlines, Consolidates in Major Restructuring," *San Francisco Chronicle*, August 24, 2001, p. B1 (quotation) (see www.sfchron.com); Scott Thurm, "Cisco Shake-Up Streamlines Operations—Three Units Are Eliminated in Effort to Centralize Engineering, Marketing," *Wall Street Journal*, August 24, 2001, p. A3 (see www.wsj.com); Stephen Lee, "Slumping Cisco Restructures," *Info World*, April 23, 2001, p. 10 (see www.infoworld.com).

Experiencing Organizational Behavior

Understanding Organization Structure in a Real-World Organization

Purpose: This exercise will help you understand how an organization is structured.

Format: You will interview at least five employees in different parts of either the college or university you attend or a small to medium-size organization and analyze its structure.

Procedure: If you use a local organization, your first task is to find one with fifty to five hundred employees. The organization should have more than two hierarchical levels, but should not be too complex to understand in a short period of study. You may want to check with your professor before contacting the company. Your initial contact should be with the highest-ranking manager, if possible. Be sure top management is aware of your project and gives its approval. If you use your local college or university, you could talk to professors, secretaries, and other administrative staff in the admissions office, student services department, athletic department, library, or many other areas. Be sure to represent a variety of jobs and levels in your interviews.

Using the material in this chapter, interview employees to obtain the following information on the structure of the organization:

1. The type of departmentalization (business function, process, product, customer, geographic region)
2. The typical span of control at each level of the organization

3. The number of levels in the hierarchy
4. The administrative ratio (ratio of managers to total employees and ratio of managers to production employees)
5. The degree of formalization (to what extent rules and procedures are written down in job descriptions, policy and procedures manuals, and memos)
6. The degree of decentralization (to what extent employees at all levels participate in making decisions)
7. What is the organization in business to do? What are its goals and its strategies for achieving them?
8. How large is the company? What is the total number of employees? How many work full time? How many work part time?
9. What are the most important components of the organization's environment?
10. Is the number of important environmental components large or small? How quickly or slowly do these components change?
11. Would you characterize the organization's environment as certain, uncertain, or somewhere in between? If in between, describe approximately how certain or uncertain.
12. What is the organization's dominant technology; that is, how does it transform inputs into outputs?
13. How rigidly does the company apply its rules and procedures? Is it flexible enough to respond to environmental changes?

14. How involved are employees in the daily decision making related to their jobs?
15. What methods are used to ensure control over employees' actions?

Interview three to five employees of the organization at different levels and in different departments. One should hold a top-level position. (Be sure to ask the questions in a way that is clear to the respondents; they may not be familiar with the terminology used in this chapter.)

Write a report describing the essential elements of structure and the technology, environment, and structure of the organization you studied. The report should discuss the extent to which the structure is appropriate for the organization's strategy, size, technology, and environment. If it does not seem appropriate,

explain the reasons. You may want to send a copy of your report to the cooperating company.

Follow-up Questions

1. Which aspects of organization structure were the hardest to obtain information about? Why?
2. If there were differences in the responses of the employees you interviewed, how do you account for them?
3. Which aspects of organizational strategy, size, environment, and technology were the most difficult to obtain information about? Why?
4. If you were president of the organization you analyzed, would you structure it in the same way? Why or why not? If not, how would you structure it?

Self-Assessment Exercise
Diagnosing Organization Structure

Introduction: You are probably involved with many different organizations—the place you work, a social or service club, a church, the college or university you attend. This assessment will help you diagnose the structure of one of those organizations.

Instructions: First, pick one of the organizations you belong to or know a lot about. Then read each of the following statements and determine the degree to which you agree or disagree with that statement about your organization by using the following scale. Then place the number of the response that best represents your organization in the space before each statement.

```
     5         4         3         2         1
  Strongly   Agree    Don't    Disagree  Strongly
   Agree               Know               Disagree
```

_____ 1. If people believe that they have the right approach to carrying out their job, they can usually go ahead without checking with their superior.
_____ 2. People in this organization don't always have to wait for orders from their superiors on important matters.
_____ 3. People in this organization share ideas with their superior.

_____ 4. Different individuals play important roles in making decisions.
_____ 5. People in this organization are likely to express their feelings openly on important matters.
_____ 6. People in this organization are encouraged to speak their minds on important matters, even if it means disagreeing with their superior.
_____ 7. Talking to other people about the problems someone might have in making decisions is an important part of the decision-making process.
_____ 8. Developing employees' talents and abilities is a major concern of this organization.
_____ 9. People are encouraged to make suggestions before decisions are made.
_____10. In this organization, most people can have their point of view heard.
_____11. Superiors often seek advice from subordinates before making decisions.
_____12. Subordinates play an active role in running this organization.
_____13. For many decisions, the rules and regulations are developed as we go along.
_____14. It is not always necessary to go through channels in dealing with important matters.

_____15. Employees do not consistently follow the same rules and regulations.

_____16. There are few rules and regulations for handling any kind of problem that may arise in making most decisions.

_____17. People from different departments are often put together in task forces to solve important problems.

_____18. For special problems, we usually set up a temporary task force until we meet our objectives.

_____19. Jobs in this organization are not clearly defined.

_____20. In this organization, adapting to changes in the environment is important.

_____ = Total Score

When you have finished, add up the numbers to get a total score. Your instructor can help you interpret your scores by referring to the *Instructor's Resource Manual.*

Reference: From Ricky W. Griffin, *Fundamentals of Management*, 4/e, which is adapted from Robert T. Keller, *Type of Management System.* Griffin copyright © 1996 by Houghton Mifflin Company. Keller copyright © 1988. Used by permission of Houghton Mifflin Company and Robert T. Keller.

OB Online

1. Some large, publicly traded organizations have a type of organization chart that at least shows the way their top level is structured. Using the Internet, look up the organization charts of several organizations. (You may have to go to documents that are reported to the Securities and Exchange Commission to find them.) Pick four companies in different industries for which you can find recent and well-defined organization charts.

2. Describe how each chart shows the essential elements of structure described in the chapter.

3. By reviewing the charts and reading the annual report for each company, what can you learn about decision making, authority, and responsibility?

Building Managerial Skills

Exercise Overview: Managers typically inherit an existing organization structure when they are promoted or hired into a position as manager. Often, however, after working with the existing structure for a while, they feel the need to rearrange the structure to increase the organization's productivity or performance. This exercise gives you the opportunity to restructure an existing organization.

Exercise Background: Recall the analysis you performed in the Experiencing Organizational Behavior exercise on page 363. In that exercise, you described the essential elements of structure of a local organization or a department at your college or university.

Exercise Task: Develop a different organization structure for that organization. You may utilize any or all of the factors described in the chapter. For example, you can alter the span of control, the administrative hierarchy, and the method of departmentalization, as well as the degree of formalization and centralization. You can even create some type of matrix organization. Remember, the key to structure is to develop a way to coordinate the divided tasks. You should draw a new organization chart and develop a rationale for your new design. Conclude by addressing the following questions:

1. How difficult was it to create a different way of structuring the organization?

2. What would it take to convince the current head of that organization to go along with your suggested changes?

TEST PREPPER

ACE self-test

You have read the chapter and studied the key terms, and the exam is any day now. Think you're ready to ace it? Take this sample test to gauge your comprehension of chapter material. You can check your answers at the back of the book. Want more test questions? Visit the student website at http://college.hmco.com/business/students/ (select Griffin/Moorhead, *Fundamentals of Organizational Behavior* 1e) and take the ACE quizzes for more practice.

1. T F Organization structure is a set of objectives that management seeks to achieve.

2. T F The primary disadvantage of division of labor is worker dissatisfaction.

3. T F A manufacturer that is divided into two divisions to produce the same product lines, but in commercial and residential versions, is departmentalized by product.

4. T F A manager who inspires the trust of his or her subordinates has a broader span of control than a manager who is not trusted.

5. T F When a manager has been given legitimate power within an organization, we say he or she has been granted authority.

6. T F According to the acceptance theory of authority, subordinates comply with managers once the managers have accepted them as valuable assets.

7. T F The more rules and regulations that shape employees' jobs, the more centralized the organization is.

8. T F According to Rensis Likert's human organization, managers should do their best to make organizations as impersonal as possible.

9. T F The three structural imperatives are size, technology, and environment.

10. T F Organizational downsizing usually involves reducing the size of middle management.

11. T F Technology has a more direct effect on the structures of small organizations than it does on the structures of large organizations.

12. T F Environmental complexity is the same as environmental uncertainty.

13. T F ImportBuyer, Inc., operates in a very rapidly changing environment. ImportBuyer, Inc., would be best off if it adopted a mechanistic structure.

14. T F One way to use standardization as a coordination mechanism is to make sure the methods workers use to transform inputs into outputs are standardized.

15. T F Mintzberg's simple structure was most appropriate for organizations in which employees have developed areas of expertise within a profession (e.g., doctor, lawyer, professor).

16. T F A firm that splits decision making between headquarters and several separate groups that produce their own products and/or services follows a divisionalized organizational structure.

17. T F The matrix form is flexible because employees can be assigned from one project to another as demand for their skills changes.

18. T F One problem in matrix organizations is the question of whether the department manager or the project team leader has final authority in various situations.

19. The key struggle Time Warner faces after merging the two companies and managing dozens of major brands is

   a. avoiding competition among suppliers and customers.

   b. harnessing the power of owning a variety of related business units while maintaining control.

   c. ensuring clear differences among the various business units for suppliers and customers.

   d. avoiding legislation that would break the large firm into several smaller businesses.

   e. creating a large enough asset base to cover current and future financial obligations.

20. The system of task, reporting, and authority relationships inside an organization is called organizational

   a. communication.   d. strategy.

   b. power.   e. culture.

   c. structure.

21. If you were interested in understanding the people, positions, reporting relationships, and formal communication lines of a business, you would look at the

   a. organization chart.

   b. balance sheet.

   c. income statement.

   d. division of labor.

   e. human resource plan.

22. After you have divided the work into smaller, more specialized jobs, your next task as a manager is to organize jobs into meaningful groups. This process is called
    a. socialization.
    b. integration.
    c. convergence.
    d. division of labor.
    e. departmentalization.

23. A local grocery store has a dairy section, a bakery, a meat/fish/poultry department, and a pharmacy. How is the store departmentalized?
    a. Process
    b. Function
    c. Customer
    d. Product
    e. Geography

24. The coordination requirements within a business unit, the similarity of the tasks within the unit, the type of information available to unit members, and the extent to which members need direct access to the supervisor all combine to influence a manager's appropriate
    a. span of control.
    b. administrative hierarchy.
    c. division of labor.
    d. departmentalization.
    e. organization structure.

25. If two organizations have the same number of employees, what would you expect the administrative hierarchy of the organization with a smaller average span of control to be?
    a. Smaller than the administrative hierarchy in the other organization
    b. Larger than the administrative hierarchy in the other organization
    c. The same size as the administrative hierarchy in the other organization
    d. Administrative hierarchy and span of control are not related, so it's impossible to tell.
    e. None of these is correct.

26. Which of the following is important for managers to remember when they delegate tasks?
    a. Managers should never delegate tasks for which they are responsible.
    b. Managers should never delegate tasks for which they have authority to complete.
    c. Lower-level managers can delegate responsibility but not authority.
    d. Managers should avoid delegating tasks they can complete themselves.
    e. The authority to complete the task must match the responsibility to complete the task.

27. Kristin thinks if an organization structure works well in one company, it ought to work well in any company. Kristin has adopted a _____ approach to organizational structure.
    a. universal
    b. contingency
    c. departmental
    d. strategic
    e. centralized

28. Which of the following describes current thinking on Max Weber's "ideal bureaucracy"?
    a. Most bureaucracies actually stimulate creativity and innovation.
    b. Bureaucracies are best for small, simple organizations.
    c. Bureaucracies have been deemed illegal because they discriminate against protected classes of employees.
    d. Some elements of bureaucracy are still critical for designing effective organizations.
    e. Bureaucracies are obsolete and no longer needed in modern organizations.

29. In which sequence should managers decide on the organization's strategy and structure?
    a. Strategy comes first, then structure.
    b. Structure comes first, then strategy.
    c. Strategy and structure should be determined simultaneously.
    d. Strategy comes first for small firms, but structure comes first for large firms.
    e. The sequence of strategy and structure is irrelevant.

30. Heather works in a company that operates in an environment where many components impinge on the organization's decision making. In addition, these components are changing rapidly. The combination of these factors leads to which of the following?
    a. Uncertainty
    b. Dynamism
    c. Complexity
    d. Contingency
    e. Universality

31. When an organization exists in a very stable environment, a(n) _____ structure is appropriate.
    a. organic
    b. mechanistic
    c. contingent
    d. universal
    e. dynamic

32. What does a professional bureaucracy rely on as a means of coordination?
    a. Centralized decision making
    b. Standardization of skills
    c. Rigid structure
    d. Departmentalization
    e. Divisions

CHAPTER 14

Organization Culture

MANAGEMENT PREVIEW

Many organizations attribute their success to a strong, deeply entrenched culture. Companies such as Sony, Microsoft, Nike, Intel, and many others are successful because they each have a culture that is unique and appropriate just for them. Organization culture, however, is often an elusive concept that can be easily misunderstood. In this chapter, we describe the organization cultures of several organizations and examine how organizations can develop their own cultures. We begin by exploring the nature and historical foundations of organization culture. Next, we describe the process of creating the culture. We then examine two basic approaches to describing the characteristics of organization culture and discuss two important issues in organization culture. Finally, we show how organization culture can be managed to enhance the organization's effectiveness.

After you have studied this chapter, you should be able to:

- [ ] *Define* organization culture *and explain how it affects employee behavior.*
- [ ] *Explain how to create an organization culture.*
- [ ] *Discuss two different approaches to describing culture in organizations.*
- [ ] *Identify important emerging issues in organization culture.*
- [ ] *Discuss the key elements of managing the organization culture.*

We begin by describing the unusual corporate culture at Microsoft.

Bill Gates and Paul Allen founded Microsoft in 1976. Their first blockbuster product, MS-DOS, was released in 1981. Windows was introduced to the public in 1985, and since then the company has saturated the PC software market with products covering the entire range of applications, from word processing to video editing to web surfing. The software giant has continued to grow internally and through acquisitions, and today employs almost 50,000 people worldwide.

Throughout the expansion, Microsoft's culture has remained recognizable and extremely effective. Its core values include an us-versus-them mentality, a fierce competitiveness, an ethic of hard work, and a strong bonding of coworkers. One former employee says, "By the time I was in my 20s, Microsoft was my whole identity." Another ex-employee, Scott Sandell, states, "Microsoft has a cult-like culture. It [either] assimilates you or spits you out." Marc Andreessen, formerly CEO of Netscape and cofounder of Loudcloud, believes a start-up's founder has a strong influence on the development of the organization's culture and employees' behavior. " These companies are like organisms. It's as if you took a DNA sample from the chief executive and blew it up to monstrous size. The founder and the company share all the same strengths and weaknesses," he explains. That certainly seems to be the case with Microsoft since employees have copied every detail of Gates's behavior, including his dress and speaking style. And the phenomenon extends beyond Microsoft.

In January 2000, Gates resigned as CEO and Steve Ballmer, who had been president, assumed the top role. At the time there was speculation that Microsoft might soften its competitive stance, lose its sharp focus on innovation, or even agree to split the firm to settle the Department of Justice's antitrust suit. None of those things happened; in fact, the company culture has remained very much the same, and business is being conducted as usual. If anything, Microsoft today is regarded as an even more unrepentant monopolist. This is not surprising given that Ballmer has worked at Microsoft since 1980 and is often described as Gates's "best friend."

In Microsoft's latest configuration, CEO Ballmer is in charge of strategy, marketing, and public relations while president Richard Belluzzo oversees finance, logistics, and other operations, leaving Gates the task of creating software architecture. Together the three decided the firm's old vision—a computer on every desk and in every home—had essentially been realized and a new vision was needed. The firm's new vision is to "empower people through great software—any time, any place, and on any device," and it seems to be working. *Fortune* writer Brent Schlender says, "A new cohesion of purpose and sense of inventiveness pervade the company." As the company's culture continues to strengthen, its challengers are disappearing or retreating. Microsoft seems destined to continue its domination of the high-tech industry.

"By the time I was in my 20s, Microsoft was my whole identity."—Former Microsoft employee

References: Jay Greene, "Ballmer's Microsoft," *BusinessWeek*, June 17, 2002, www.businessweek.com on June 18, 2002; Eryn Brown, "Just Another Product Launch," *Fortune*, November 12, 2001, www.fortune.com on June 18, 2002; Fred Vogelstein, "The Long Shadow of XP," *Fortune*, November 12, 2001 (quotation), www.fortune.com on June 18, 2002; Brent Schlender, "The Beast Is Back," *Fortune*, June 11, 2001, www.fortune.com on June 18, 2002; David Streitfeld, "Gates Leads Company Cult of Personality," *Arizona Republic* (Phoenix), May 8, 2000, pp. D1, D4 (see www.azcentral.com); *Webster's Revised Unabridged Dictionary*, Random House, 1998, www.dictionary.com on June 18, 2002.

Microsoft has developed a culture that reflects its founder's philosophy and is tailor made for the company. Bill Gates had the vision and set the expectations for Microsoft from the very start. All companies have some sort of culture, but it is not easy to create a winning culture such as Microsoft's. In this chapter we describe the organization cultures of several organizations and explain how a successful one can be created and managed.

The Nature of Organization Culture

┌─*LEARNING OBJECTIVE*─┐
Define organization culture and explain how it affects employee behavior.
└─────────────────────┘

Organization culture is the set of shared values, often taken for granted and communicated through stories and other symbolic means, that help the organization's people understand which actions are considered acceptable and which unacceptable. In some organizations, for example, it is unacceptable to blame customers when problems arise. Here the value "the customer is always right" tells managers

Organization culture is the set of values, often taken for granted and communicated through stories and other symbolic means, that helps the organization's employees understand which actions are considered acceptable and which unacceptable.

what actions are acceptable (not blaming the customer) and what actions are not acceptable (blaming the customer). In other organizations, the dominant values might support blaming customers for problems, penalizing employees who make mistakes, or treating employees as the firm's most valuable assets. In each case, values help members of an organization understand how they should act.

The values are often taken for granted; that is, they are basic assumptions made by the firm's employees rather than prescriptions written in a book or made explicit in a training program. It may be as difficult for an organization to articulate these basic assumptions as it is for people to express their personal beliefs and values. Several authors have argued that organization culture is a powerful influence on employees precisely because it is not explicit but instead becomes an implicit part of their values and beliefs.[1]

Even when firms can articulate and describe the basic values that make up their cultures, however, the values most strongly affect actions when organization members take them for granted. An organization's culture is not likely to influence behavior powerfully when employees must constantly refer to a handbook to remember what the culture is. When the culture becomes part of themselves—when they can ignore what the book says because they already have embraced the values it describes—the culture can have an important impact on their actions.

This definition also emphasizes the symbolic means through which the values in an organization's culture are communicated. Although, as we noted, companies can sometimes directly describe these values, their meaning is perhaps best communicated to employees through the use of stories, examples, and even what some authors call "myths" or "fairy tales." Stories typically reflect the important implications of values in a firm's culture. Often they develop a life of their own. As they are told and retold, shaped and reshaped, their relationship to what actually occurred becomes less important than the powerful impact they have on the way people behave every day. Nike uses a group of technical representatives called "Ekins" ("Nike" spelled backwards) who run a nine-day training session for large retailers, telling them stories about Nike's history and traditions, such as the stories about CEO Phil Knight selling shoes from the trunk of his car and cofounder Bill Bowerman using the family's waffle iron to create the first waffle-soled running shoe.[2]

Some organization stories have become famous. At E*Trade, CEO Christos M. Cotsakos has done many things that have become company legends because he does not follow the rules for the typical investment firm. To make people move faster, he organized a day of racing in Formula One cars at speeds of around 150 miles per hour. To create a looser atmosphere around the office, he has employees carry around rubber chickens or wear propeller beanies. To bond employees together, he organized gourmet-cooking classes.[3] These incidents and others are related to new employees and are spread throughout the company, thus affecting the behavior of many more people than those who actually took part in each event.

Historical Foundations

Although research on organization culture exploded on the scene in the early 1980s, its antecedents can be traced to the origins of social science. Understanding the contributions of other social science disciplines is particularly important in the case of organization culture, because many of the dilemmas and debates that continue in this area reflect differences in historical research traditions.

Anthropological Contributions   Anthropology is the study of human cultures.[4] Of all the social science disciplines, anthropology is most closely related to the study of

Students and the dean of Northwestern University's School of Management are celebrating the school's ranking of number one in the *BusinessWeek* rankings of top MBA programs. Kellogg attributes its lofty ranking to its "go-to-any-lengths" culture. Because new graduates are facing the most difficult job market in recent memory, deans work with students and use their personal contacts to help them find jobs. Students feel they are the deans' and the school's top priority.

culture and cultural phenomena. Anthropologists seek to understand how the values and beliefs that make up a society's culture affect the structure and functioning of that society. Whether the culture is that of a large, modern corporation or a primitive tribe in New Guinea, the questions asked are the same: How do people in this culture know what kinds of behavior are acceptable and what kinds are unacceptable? How is this knowledge understood? How is this knowledge communicated to new members? Through intense efforts to produce accurate descriptions, the values and beliefs that underlie actions in an organization become clear. However, these values can be fully understood only in the context of the organization in which they developed. In other words, communication of the values and beliefs of one organization is not transferable to those of other organizations; each culture is unique.

Sociological Contributions   Sociology is the study of people in social systems such as organizations and societies. Sociologists have long been interested in the causes and consequences of culture. In studying culture, sociologists have most often focused on informal social structure. Sociologists use systematic interviews, questionnaires, and other quantitative research methods rather than the intensive study and analysis anthropologists use. Practitioners of the sociological approach generally produce a fairly simple typology of cultural attributes and then show how the cultures of a relatively large number of firms can be analyzed with this typology. The major pieces of research on organization culture that later spawned widespread business interest— including Ouchi's *Theory Z*, Deal and Kennedy's *Corporate Cultures*, and Peters and Waterman's *In Search of Excellence*—used sociological methods.[5] Later in the chapter, we review some of this work in more detail.

Social Psychology Contributions   Social psychology is a branch of psychology that includes the study of groups and the influence of social factors on individuals. Social psychological theory, with its emphasis on the creation and manipulation of symbols, lends itself naturally to the analysis of organization culture. For example, research in social psychology suggests that people tend to use stories or information about a single event more than they use multiple observations to make judgments.[6] Thus, if your neighbor had trouble with a certain brand of automobile, you will probably conclude the brand is bad even though the carmaker can generate reams of statistical data to prove that the situation with your neighbor's car was a rarity.

The impact of stories on decision making suggests an important reason organization culture has such a powerful influence on the firm's people. Unlike other organizational phenomena, culture is best communicated through stories and examples, and these become the basis organization members use to make judgments.

If a story says that blaming customers is unacceptable, then blaming customers is unacceptable. This value is communicated much more effectively through the cultural story than through some statistical analysis of customer satisfaction.[7]

Economics Contributions   The influence of economics on the study of organization culture is substantial enough to warrant attention, although it has been less significant than the influence of anthropology and sociology. The economics approach attempts to link the cultural attributes of firms with their performance rather than simply describing the cultures of companies as the sociological and anthropological perspectives do. In *Theory Z*, for example, William Ouchi does not just say that Type Z companies differ from other kinds of companies; he asserts that Type Z firms outperform other firms.[8] When Thomas Peters and Robert Waterman say they are in search of excellence, they define *excellence*, in part, as consistently high financial performance.[9] These authors are using cultural explanations of financial success.

Researchers disagree about the extent to which culture affects organization performance. Several authors have investigated the conditions under which organization culture is linked with superior financial performance.[10] This research suggests that under some relatively narrow conditions, a link between culture and performance may exist. However, the fact that a firm has a culture does not mean it will perform well; indeed, a variety of cultural traits can actually hurt performance. Consider a firm whose culture includes values such as "customers are too ignorant to be of much help," "employees cannot be trusted," "innovation is not important," and "quality is too expensive." The firm may have a strong culture, but the culture may impair its performance. The relationship between culture and performance depends partly on the values expressed in the organization's culture.

Culture Versus Climate

During the past thirty years since the concept of organization culture has become widespread, managers have often asked about the similarities and differences between organization culture and organization climate. Managers and researchers alike have argued the two concepts are really the same, although their research bases differ. The two concepts are similar in that both concern the overall work atmosphere of an organization. In addition, both deal with the social context in organizations, and both are assumed to affect the behaviors of people who work in organizations.[11]

The two concepts differ in several significant ways, however. Much of the study of organization climate was based in psychology, whereas the study of organization culture was based in anthropology and sociology. **Organization climate** usually refers to current situations in an organization and the linkages among work groups, employees, and work performance. Climate, therefore, is usually more easily manipulated by management to directly affect employees' behavior. *Organization culture*, on the other hand, usually refers to the historical context within which a situation occurs and the impact of this context on the behavior of employees. Organization culture is generally considered much more difficult to alter in short-run situations because it has been defined over the course of years of history and tradition.

The two concepts also differ in their emphases. Organization culture is often described as the means through which employees learn and communicate what is acceptable and unacceptable in the organization, that is, its values and norms. Most descriptions of organization climate do not deal with values and norms. Therefore, descriptions of organization climate focus on the current atmosphere in a com-

Organization climate usually refers to current situations in the organization and the linkages among work groups, employees, and work performance.

pany, whereas organization culture is based on the firm's history and traditions, and emphasizes values and norms about employee behavior.

Creating the Organization Culture

LEARNING OBJECTIVE

Explain how to create an organization culture.

To the entrepreneur who starts a business, creating the company culture may seem secondary to the basic processes of creating a product or service and selling it to customers or clients. However, as the company grows and flourishes, it usually develops a culture that distinguishes it from other companies and is one of the reasons for its success. In other words, a company succeeds as a result of what the company does, its strategy, and how it does it—its culture. The culture is linked to the strategic values, whether one is starting up a new company or trying to change the culture of an existing company.[12] The process of creating an organization culture is really one of linking its strategic values with its cultural values, much as the structure of the organization is linked to its strategy, as we described in Chapter 13. Table 4.1 shows the process.

Establish Values

Strategic values are the basic beliefs about an organization's environment that shape its strategy.

The first two steps in the process involve establishing values. First, management must determine the strategic values of the organization. **Strategic values** are the basic beliefs about the organization's environment and its own capabilities that shape its strategy. They are developed following an environmental scanning process and a strategic analysis that evaluate economic, demographic, public policy, technological, and social trends to identify needs in the marketplace that the organization can meet. Strategic values, in effect, link the organization with its environment.

Cultural values are the values that employees need to have and act on for the organization to implement its strategic values.

The second set of required values is the organization's cultural values. **Cultural values** are the values employees need to have and to act on for the organization to carry out its strategic values. They should be grounded in the organization's beliefs about how and why the organization can succeed. Organizations that attempt to develop cultural values that are not linked to their strategic values may end up with an empty set of values that have little relationship to their business. In other words, employees need to value work behaviors that are consistent with and support the organization's strategic values: low-cost production, customer service, or technological innovation.

Create Vision

After developing its strategic and cultural values, the organization must establish a vision of its direction. This vision is a picture of what the organization will be like at some point in the future. It portrays how the strategic and cultural values will

TABLE 14.1

Creating Organizational Culture

Step 1—Formulate Strategic Values
Step 2—Develop Cultural Values
Step 3—Create Vision
Step 4—Initiate Implementation Strategies
Step 5—Reinforce Cultural Behaviors

combine to create the future. For example, an insurance company might establish a vision of "protecting the lifestyles of 2 million families by the year 2010." In effect, it synthesizes both the strategic and cultural values as it communicates a performance target to employees. The conventional wisdom has been that the vision statement is written first, but experience suggests the strategic and cultural values must be established first for the vision to be meaningful.

Initiate Implementation Strategies

The next step in creating the organization culture is to initiate implementation strategies. This step builds on the values and initiates the action to accomplish the vision. The strategies cover many factors, from developing the organization design to recruiting and training employees who share the values and will carry them out. Consider a bank that has the traditional orientation of handling customer loans, deposits, and savings. If the bank changes its orientation by placing more emphasis on customer service, it may have to recruit a different type of employee, one who is capable of building relationships. The bank will also have to commit to serious, long-term training of current employees to teach them the new service-oriented culture. The strategic and cultural values are the stimuli for the implementation practices.

Reinforce Cultural Behaviors

The final step is to reinforce the behaviors of employees as they act out the cultural values and implement the organization's strategies. Reinforcement can take many forms. First, the organization's formal reward system must reward desired behaviors in ways that employees value. Second, stories must be told throughout the organization about employees who engaged in behaviors that epitomize the cultural values. Third, the organization must engage in ceremonies and rituals that emphasize employees doing the things that are critical to carrying out the organization's vision. In effect, the organization must make a "big deal" out of employees doing the right things. For example, if parties are held only for retirement or to give out longevity and service pins, employees get the message that retirement and length of service are the only things that matter. On the other hand, holding a ceremony for a group of employees who provided exceptional customer service reinforces desirable employee behaviors. Reinforcement practices are the final link between the strategic and cultural values and the creation of the organization culture.

Describing Organization Culture

LEARNING OBJECTIVE

Discuss two different approaches to describing culture in organizations.

The descriptions of culture in this section provide valuable insights into the dimensions along which organization cultures vary. No single framework for describing the values in organization cultures has emerged; however, several frameworks have been suggested. Although these frameworks were developed in the 1980s, their ideas about organization culture are still influential today. Some of the "excellent" companies they described are not as highly lauded now, but the concepts remain in use in companies all over the world. Managers should evaluate the various parts of the frameworks described and use those that fit the strategic and cultural values of their own organizations.

The Ouchi Framework

One of the first researchers to focus explicitly on analyzing the cultures of a limited group of firms was William G. Ouchi. Ouchi analyzed the organization

The **Type Z firm** is committed to retaining employees; evaluates workers' performance based on both qualitative and quantitative information; emphasizes broad career paths; exercises control through informal, implicit mechanisms; requires that decision making occur in groups and be based on full information sharing and consensus; expects individuals to take responsibility for decisions; and emphasizes concern for people.

cultures of three groups of firms, which he characterized as (1) typical U.S. firms, (2) typical Japanese firms, and (3) **Type Z** U.S. firms.[13] Through his analysis, Ouchi developed a list of seven points on which these three types of firms can be compared. He argued that the cultures of typical Japanese firms and U.S. Type Z firms are very different from those of typical U.S. firms, and that these differences explain the success of many Japanese firms and U.S. Type Z firms and the difficulties typical U.S. firms face. Table 14.2 presents the seven points of comparison developed by Ouchi.

Commitment to Employees   According to Ouchi, typical Japanese and Type Z U.S. firms share the cultural value of trying to keep employees. Thus, both types of firms lay off employees only as a last resort. In Japan, the value of "keeping employees on" often takes the form of lifetime employment, although some Japanese companies are challenging this value in response to the economic troubles of the past few years. In U.S. Type Z companies, this cultural value is manifested in a commitment to what Ouchi called "long-term employment." Under the Japanese system of lifetime employment, employees usually cannot be fired. Under the U.S. system, workers and managers can be fired, but only if they are not performing acceptably. Ouchi suggested that typical U.S. firms do not have the same cultural commitment to employees that Japanese firms and U.S. Type Z firms do.

Evaluation   Ouchi observed that in Japanese and Type Z U.S. companies, appropriate evaluation of workers and managers is thought to take a very long time—up to ten years—and requires the use of qualitative as well as quantitative information about performance. For this reason, promotion in these firms is relatively slow, and promotion decisions are made only after interviews with many people who have had contact with the person being evaluated. In typical U.S. firms, on the other hand, the cultural value suggests that evaluation can and should be done rapidly and should emphasize quantitative measures of performance.

Careers   Ouchi next observed that the careers most valued in Japanese and Type Z U.S. firms span multiple functions. In Japan, this value has led to very broad career paths, which may lead to employees gaining experience in six or seven distinct

TABLE 14.2

The Ouchi Framework

Cultural Value	Expression in Japanese Companies	Expression in Type Z U.S. Companies	Expression in Typical U.S. Companies
Commitment to Employees	Lifetime employment	Long-term employment	Short-term employment
Evaluation	Slow and qualitative	Slow and qualitative	Fast and quantitative
Careers	Very broad	Moderately broad	Narrow
Control	Implicit and informal	Implicit and informal	Explicit and formal
Decision Making	Group and consensus	Group and consensus	Individual
Responsibility	Group	Individual	Individual
Concern for People	Holistic	Holistic	Narrow

business functions. The career paths in Type Z U.S. firms are somewhat narrower. However, the career path valued in typical U.S. firms is considerably narrower. Ouchi's research indicated that most U.S. managers perform only one or two different business functions in their careers.

Control   All organizations must exert some level of control to achieve coordinated action. Most Japanese and Type Z U.S. firms assume control is exercised through informal, implicit mechanisms, is more social in nature, and derives from the organization culture's shared norms and values. In contrast, typical U.S. firms expect guidance to come through explicit directions in the form of job descriptions, delineation of authority, and various rules and procedures.

Decision Making   Japanese and Type Z U.S. firms have a strong cultural expectation that decision making occurs in groups and is based on principles of full information sharing and consensus. In most typical U.S. firms, individual decision making is considered appropriate.

Responsibility   Closely linked to the issue of group versus individual decision making are ideas about responsibility. Here, however, the parallels between Japanese firms and Type Z U.S. firms break down. Ouchi showed that in Japan, strong cultural norms support collective responsibility; that is, the group as a whole, rather than a single person, is held responsible for decisions made by the group. In both Type Z U.S. firms and typical U.S. firms, individuals expect to take responsibility for decisions. Linking individual responsibility with individual decision making, as typical U.S. firms do, is logically consistent. Similarly, group decision making and group responsibility, the situation in Japanese firms, seem to go together.

How do Type Z U.S. firms combine the cultural values of group decision making and individual responsibility? Ouchi suggested that the answer depends on a cultural view we have already discussed: slow, qualitative evaluation. The first time a manager uses a group to make a decision, it is not possible to tell whether the outcomes associated with that decision resulted from the manager's influence or from the quality of the group. However, if a manager works with many groups over time, and if these groups consistently do well for the organization, it is likely that the manager is skilled at getting the most out of the groups. This manager can be held responsible for the outcomes of group decision-making processes. Similarly, managers who consistently fail to work effectively with the groups assigned to them can be held responsible for the lack of results from the group decision-making process.

Concern for People   The last cultural value examined by Ouchi deals with a concern for people. Not surprisingly, in Japanese firms and Type Z firms, the cultural value that dominates is a holistic concern for workers and managers. Holistic concern extends beyond concern for a person simply as a worker or manager to concern about that person's home life, hobbies, personal beliefs, hopes, fears, and aspirations. In typical U.S. firms, the concern for people is a narrow one that focuses on the workplace. A culture that emphasizes a strong concern for people, rather than one that emphasizes a work or task orientation, can decrease worker turnover.[14]

Type Z and Performance   Ouchi argued that the cultures of Japanese and Type Z firms help them outperform typical U.S. firms. Toyota imported the management style and culture that succeeded in Japan into its manufacturing facilities in North America. Toyota's success has often been attributed to the ability of Japanese and

Type Z firms to systematically invest in their employees and operations over long periods, resulting in steady and significant improvements in long-term performance.

The Peters and Waterman Approach

In their bestseller *In Search of Excellence*, Tom Peters and Robert Waterman focused even more explicitly than Ouchi on the relationship between organization culture and performance. Peters and Waterman chose a sample of highly successful U.S. firms and sought to describe the management practices that led to their success.[15] Their analysis rapidly turned to the cultural values that led to successful management practices. These "excellent" values appear in Table 14.3.

Bias for Action   According to Peters and Waterman, successful firms have a bias for action. Managers in these firms are expected to make decisions even if all the facts are not in. Peters and Waterman argued that for many important decisions, all the facts will never be in. Delaying decision making in these situations is tantamount to never making a decision. Meanwhile other firms probably will have captured whatever business initiative existed. On average, according to these authors, organizations with cultural values that include a bias for action outperform firms without such values.

Stay Close to the Customer   Peters and Waterman believe that firms whose organization cultures value customers over everything else outperform firms without this value. The customer is a source of information about current products, a source of ideas about future products, and the ultimate source of a firm's current and future financial performance. Focusing on the customer, meeting the customer's needs, and pampering the customer when necessary all lead to superior performance.

Autonomy and Entrepreneurship   Peters and Waterman maintained that successful firms fight the lack of innovation and the bureaucracy usually associated with large size. They do this by breaking the company into smaller, more manageable pieces and then encouraging independent, innovative activities within smaller business segments. Stories often exist in these organizations about the junior engineer who takes a risk and influences major product decisions or of the junior manager who, dissatisfied with the slow pace of a product's development, implements a new and highly successful marketing plan.

Productivity Through People   Like Ouchi, Peters and Waterman believed successful firms recognize that their most important assets are their people—both workers and managers—and that the organization's purpose is to let its people flourish. It is a basic value of the organization culture: a belief that treating people with respect and dignity is not only appropriate but also essential to success.

TABLE 14.3

The Peters and Waterman Framework

Attributes of an Excellent Firm	
1. Bias for action	5. Hands-on management
2. Stay close to the customer	6. Stick to the knitting
3. Autonomy and entrepreneurship	7. Simple form, lean staff
4. Productivity through people	8. Simultaneously loose and tight organization

Hands-on Management   Peters and Waterman noted that the firms they studied insisted that senior managers stay in touch with the firms' essential business. It is an expectation, reflecting a deeply embedded cultural norm, that managers should manage not from behind the closed doors of their offices but by "wandering around" the plant, the design facility, the research and development department, and so on.

Stick to the Knitting   Another cultural value characteristic of excellent firms is their reluctance to engage in business outside their areas of expertise. These firms reject the concept of diversification, the practice of buying and operating businesses in unrelated industries. This notion is currently referred to as relying on the company's "core competencies," or what the company does best.

Simple Form, Lean Staff   According to Peters and Waterman, successful firms tend to have few administrative layers and relatively small corporate staff groups. In excellently managed companies, importance is measured not only by the number of people who report to a manager but also by the manager's impact on the organization's performance. The cultural values in these firms tell managers that their staffs' performance rather than their size is important.

Simultaneously Loose and Tight Organization   The final attribute of organization culture identified by Peters and Waterman appears contradictory. How can a firm be simultaneously loosely and tightly organized? The resolution of this apparent paradox is found in the firms' values. The firms are tightly organized because all their members understand and believe in the firms' values. This common cultural bond is a strong glue that holds the firms together. At the same time, however, the firms are loosely organized because they tend to have less administrative overhead, fewer staff members, and fewer rules and regulations. The result is increased innovation and risk taking and faster response times.

Emerging Issues in Organization Culture

As the implementation of organization culture continues, it inevitably changes and develops new perspectives. Many new ideas about productive environments build on the views of Ouchi, Peters and Waterman, and others. Typical of these approaches are the total quality management movement, worker participation, and team-based management, which were discussed in earlier chapters. Two other movements are briefly discussed in this section: innovation and procedural justice.

Innovation

Innovation is the process of creating and doing new things that are introduced into the marketplace as products, processes, or services.

Innovation is the process of creating and doing new things that are introduced into the marketplace as products, processes, or services. Innovation involves every aspect of the organization, from research through development, manufacturing, and marketing. One of the organization's biggest challenges is to bring innovative technology to the needs of the marketplace in the most cost-effective manner possible.[16] Note that innovation does not only involve the technology to create new products. True organizational innovation is pervasive throughout the organization. According to *Fortune* magazine, the most admired organizations are those that are the most innovative.[17] Those companies are innovative in every way: staffing, strategy, research, and business processes.

Radical innovation is a major breakthrough that changes or creates whole industries.

Types of Innovation   Innovation can be either radical, systems, or incremental. A **radical innovation** is a major breakthrough that changes or creates whole industries. Examples include xerography (which was invented by Chester Carlson in 1935 and became the hallmark of Xerox Corporation), steam engines, and the internal combustion engine (which paved the way for today's automobile industry). **Systems innovation** creates a new functionality by assembling parts in new ways. For example, the gasoline engine began as a radical innovation and became a systems innovation when it was combined with bicycle and carriage technology to create automobiles. **Incremental innovation** continues the technical improvements and extends the applications of radical and systems innovations. There are many more incremental innovations than there are radical and systems innovations. In fact, several incremental innovations are often necessary to make radical and systems innovations work properly. Incremental innovations force organizations to continuously improve their products and keep abreast or ahead of the competition.

New Ventures   New ventures based on innovations require entrepreneurship and good management to work. The profile of the entrepreneur typically includes a need for achievement, a desire to assume responsibility, a willingness to take risks, and a focus on concrete results. Entrepreneurship can occur inside or outside large organizations. Large organizations are often not receptive of typical entrepreneurial activities. Thus, for a large organization to be innovative and develop new ventures, it must actively encourage entrepreneurial activity within the organization. This form of activity, often called **intrapreneurship,** is usually most effective when it is a part of everyday life in the organization and occurs organization-wide rather than in the research and development department alone.

Ed Sabol and his son, Steve, developed NFL Films into a $50 million business by doing what they love: watching football and filming professional football. Based on Ed's passions for football and videotaping his son's football games, the company has become an innovator in the industry. Though surrounded by mountains of competition, it still innovates in the use of color and music, camera positioning, and narration. Another innovative tactic the company has employed is giving a $1,000 award to the most spectacular failure to stimulate ingenuity, innovation, and risk taking. Each cameraperson is his or her own director and selects the location of all shots, which further encourages creativity. As a result of this innovation and creativity, the company has earned 89 Emmy awards.

Systems innovation creates a new functionality by assembling parts in new ways.

Incremental innovation continues the technical improvements and extends the applications of radical and systems innovations.

Intrapreneurship is entrepreneurial activity that takes place within the context of a large corporation.

Corporate Research   The most common means of developing innovation in the traditional organization is through corporate research, or research and development. Corporate research is usually set up to support existing businesses, provide incremental innovations in the organization's businesses, and explore potential new technology bases. It often takes place in a laboratory, either on the site of the main corporate facility or some distance away from normal operations. Corporate researchers are responsible for keeping the company's products and processes technologically advanced. Product life cycles vary a great deal, depending on how fast products become obsolete and whether substitutes for the product are developed. The job of corporate research is to keep the company's products current. The corporate culture can be instrumental in fostering an environment in which creativity and innovation occur.

Procedural Justice

Another movement in management that may be viewed as a cultural issue is procedural justice. **Procedural justice** is the extent to which the dynamics of an organization's decision-making processes are judged to be fair by those most affected by them. Especially in the United States, employees are demanding more say in determining work rules and in matters pertaining to health and safety on the job and the provision of certain benefits for all employees. Furthermore, each generation of new employees may feel more entitled to having certain kinds of influence in the organization, especially on matters pertaining to their work. Employees who expect to have more input into decision making may or may not comply with decisions or directives from top management in which they have had little or no part.

The lack of procedural justice may lead to less compliant attitudes on the part of lower-level managers. This has been shown to occur in strategic decision making in multinational organizations. The exercise of procedural justice can be an effective way to engender compliance from subsidiary managers in large multinationals.[18] The extent to which this movement continues may depend on the overall cultural shifts in society and the extent to which employee empowerment becomes entrenched in organizations and in management practice.

Managing Organization Culture

The work of Ouchi, Peters and Waterman, and many others demonstrates two important facts. First, organization cultures differ among firms; second, these different organization cultures can affect a firm's performance. Based on these observations, managers have become more concerned about how to best manage the cultures of their organizations. The three elements of managing organization culture are (1) taking advantage of the existing culture, (2) teaching organization culture, and (3) changing the organization culture.

Taking Advantage of the Existing Culture

Most managers are not in a position to create an organization culture; rather, they work in organizations that already have cultural values. For these managers, the central issue in managing culture is how best to work with the existing cultural system. It may be easier and faster to alter employee behaviors within the existing culture than to change the established history, traditions, and values.[19]

To take advantage of an existing cultural system, managers must first be fully aware of the culture's values and what behaviors or actions those values support. Becoming fully aware of an organization's values usually is not easy, however; it involves more than reading a pamphlet about what the company believes in. Managers must develop a deep understanding of how organizational values operate in the firm, an understanding that usually comes only through experience.

This understanding, once achieved, can be used to evaluate the performances of others in the firm. Articulating organizational values can be useful in managing others' behaviors. For example, suppose a subordinate in a firm with a strong cultural value of "sticking to its knitting" develops a business strategy that involves moving into a new industry. Rather than attempting to argue that this business strategy is economically flawed or conceptually weak, the manager who understands the corporate culture can point to the company's organizational value: "In this firm, we believe in sticking to our knitting."

Senior managers who understand their organization's culture can communicate that understanding to lower-level individuals. Over time, as these lower-level

The culture can be taught in many different ways: by example, by telling stories about what has happened in the past, and by formal training programs. The Ritz-Carlton has long been known for its outstanding customer service; so much so that it has been referred to as cult-like. It has won the Malcolm Baldrige National Quality Award twice and ranked first in guest satisfaction among luxury hotels in the J.D. Power & Associates hotel survey in 2004. Prior to 2000 Ritz-Carlton relied on sharing its culture of service through personal examples and telling stories about what it means to provide Ritz-Carlton-like service. However, in 2000 the company created the Ritz-Carlton Leadership Center to teach its employees about what it means to deliver service the Ritz-Carlton way. The Center has also become popular among other companies who are now sending their own employees to learn the Ritz-Carlton way.

Socialization is the process through which individuals become social beings.

Organizational socialization is the process through which employees learn about the firm's culture and pass their knowledge and understanding on to others.

managers begin to understand and accept the firm's culture, they will require less direct supervision. Their understanding of corporate values will guide their decision making.

Teaching the Organization Culture: Socialization

Socialization is the process through which individuals become social beings.[20] As studied by psychologists, it is the process through which children learn to become adults in a society: how they learn what is acceptable and polite behavior and what is not, how they learn to communicate, how they learn to interact with others, and so on. In complex societies, the socialization process takes many years.

Organizational socialization is the process through which employees learn about their firm's culture and pass their knowledge and understanding on to others. Employees are socialized into organizations just as people are socialized into societies; that is, they come to know over time what is acceptable in the organization and what is not, how to communicate their feelings, and how to interact with others. They learn both through observation and through efforts by managers to communicate this information to them. Research on the process of socialization indicates that for many employees, socialization programs do not necessarily change their values but instead make employees more aware of the differences between personal and organization values, and help them develop ways to cope with the differences.[21]

A variety of organizational mechanisms can affect the socialization of workers in organizations. Probably the most important are the examples new employees see in the behavior of experienced people. Through observing examples, new employees develop a repertoire of stories they can use to guide their actions. When a decision needs to be made, new employees can ask, "What would my boss do in this situation?" This is not to suggest that formal training, corporate pamphlets, and corporate statements about organization culture are unimportant in the socialization process. However, these factors tend to support the socialization process based on people's close observations of the actions of others.

In some organizations, the culture described in pamphlets and presented in formal training sessions conflicts with the values of the organization as expressed in the actions of its people. For example, a firm may say that employees are its most important asset but treat employees badly. In this setting, new employees quickly learn the rhetoric of the pamphlets and formal training sessions has little to do with the real organization culture. Employees who are socialized into this system usually come to accept the actual cultural values rather than those formally espoused.

BUSINESS OF ETHICS

Working with Diversity

Wal-Mart: Most Admired and Facing A Discrimination Lawsuit?

In 2002, mega-retailer Wal-Mart rose to the top slot of the Fortune 500, the first service company ever to occupy that position. In 2004 Wal-Mart was named Number 1 in the Most Admired Company by *Fortune* for the second straight year. It wins such high acclaim because it is such a dominant force in the retailing industry and it is super-efficient in its operations from suppliers through distribution. The company is flying high, but one potentially disastrous cloud is looming on the horizon—accusations about a lack of diversity, and even deliberate discrimination, particularly against women.

Wal-Mart publicly and proudly claims a commitment to diversity. Its web site mentions "respect the individual" as one of the firm's basic beliefs and then expands further: "We have very different backgrounds, different colors and different beliefs, but we do believe that every individual deserves to be treated with respect and dignity." Wal-Mart's founder, Sam Walton, described how to build a successful business in his 1992 book, *Made in America*. Of Walton's ten rules, six directly relate to the importance of employees and include advice such as "celebrate success," "listen to everyone," "appreciate," and "treat employees as partners."

Nevertheless, despite Wal-Mart's hiring a staff that is 59 percent women, some female workers describe a hostile culture that includes sexual talk, unwanted sexual advances, and even the showing of pornographic videos in the employee lounge. These women also note that 72 percent of the sales staff is female, but only one-third of managers are, despite the company's promote-from-within policy. Wal-Mart's proportion of female managers is below that of other retailers—who average 56 percent—and even worse, is below the other retailers' levels of 25 years ago. As a result, Wal-Mart has been the subject of a number of discrimination lawsuits, and it has a history of aggressively fighting such suits by stonewalling or even

violating court orders. Equal Employment Opportunity Commission lawyer Mary Jo O'Neill says, "I have never seen this kind of blatant disregard for the law . . . Wal-Mart[,] . . . at the top, isn't committed to taking . . . federal employment laws seriously." Six women filed the initial lawsuit (Duke vs. Wal-Mart Stores, Inc.) that has now been certified as a class action suit covering more than six million women across the country and could cost the company millions in settlement, court, and attorney costs.

The company continues to deny that it mistreats workers and will fight the lawsuit. In its defense, Wal-Mart maintains that its size and geographic spread make it hard to closely supervise every one of its worldwide locations. Spokesman Jay Allen says, "When you have a million people, you're going to have a few people out there who don't do things right." Still, it is difficult for a company that purports to be "so centralized that it can keep tabs on every last light bulb in its more than 3,100 stores" to claim ignorance about its employment discrimination. It has clearly been working on improving its reputation with new advertisements, establishing offices of diversity and corporate compliance, and pushing diversity in its hiring and promotion policies. Overhauling its current culture may take more than that.

References: Lisa Takeuchi Cullen, "Wal-Mart's Gender Gap: What a Landmark Lawsuit Aims to Prove about How the No. 1 Retailer Pays its Female Workers,: *Time*, July 5, 2004, p. 44; Vicki M. Young, Katherine Bowers, Samantha Conti, "Saving Face at Wal-Mart," *WWD*, June 25, 2004, p. 11; "UFCW: Wal-Mart's 'Open Door' Slams Shut for Women Workers: Wal-Mart on Trial in the Largest Sex Discrimination Lawsuit in History," *PR Newswire*, June 22, 2004; Ann Harrington, "America's Most Admired Companies," *Fortune*, March 8, 2004, pp. 80–82; "3 Basic Beliefs," "Sam's Rules for Building a Business," Wal-Mart web site. www.walmartstores.com on June 21, 2002; Cait Murphy, "Wal-Mart Rules: Now That Wal-Mart Is America's Largest Corporation, the Service Economy Wears the Crown," *Fortune*, April 15, 2002. www.fortune.com on June 21, 2002; "More Jobs for Women," *Fortune*, February 4, 2002. www.fortune.com on June 21, 2002; "The 100 Best Companies to Work for in America," *Fortune*, February 4, 2002. www.fortune.com on June 21, 2002; Wendy Zellner, "How Well Does Wal-Mart Travel?" *BusinessWeek*, September 3, 2001. www.businessweek.com on June 21, 2002; Michelle Conlin, "Is Wal-Mart Hostile to Women?" *BusinessWeek*, July 16, 2001. www.businessweek.com on June 21, 2002.

Changing the Organization Culture

Much of our discussion to this point has assumed that an organization's culture enhances its performance. When this is the case, learning what an organization's cultural values are and using those values to help socialize new workers and managers is very important, for such actions help the organization succeed. However, as Ouchi's and Peters and Waterman's research indicates, not all firms have cultural values that are consistent with high performance. Ouchi found that Japanese firms and U.S. Type Z firms have performance-enhancing values. Peters and Waterman identified performance-enhancing values associated with successful companies. By implication, some firms not included in Peters and Waterman's study must have had performance-reducing values. What should a manager who works in a company with performance-reducing values do?

The answer to this question is, of course, that top managers in such firms should try to change their organization's culture. However, this is a difficult thing to do.[22] Organization culture resists change for the same reasons it is a powerful influence on behavior: It embodies the firm's basic values, is often taken for granted, and is typically communicated most effectively through stories or other symbols. When managers attempt to change organization culture, they are attempting to change people's basic assumptions about what is and is not appropriate behavior in the organization. Changing from a traditional organization to a team-based organization (discussed in Chapter 9) is one example of an organization culture change. Another is Boeing's decision in 1999 to change from a family culture to a performance culture.[23]

Despite these difficulties, some organizations have changed their cultures from performance reducing to performance enhancing.[24] This change process is described in more detail in Chapter 15. The earlier section on creating organization culture describes the importance of linking the strategic values and cultural values in creating a new organization culture. We briefly discuss other important elements of the cultural change process in the following sections.

Managing Symbols　Research suggests that organization culture is understood and communicated through the use of stories and other symbolic media. If this is correct, managers interested in changing cultures should attempt to substitute stories and myths that support new cultural values for those that support old ones. They can do so by creating situations that give rise to new stories.

Suppose an organization traditionally has held the value "employee opinions are not important." When management meets in this company, the ideas and opinions of lower-level people—when discussed at all—are normally rejected as foolish and irrelevant. The stories that support this cultural value tell about managers who tried to make a constructive point only to have that point lost in personal attacks from superiors.

An upper-level manager interested in creating a new story, one that shows lower-level managers that their ideas are valuable, might ask a subordinate to prepare to lead a discussion in a meeting

GRANTLAND®

SHOULD WE PUT YOUR DESK OVER THERE OR BY THE WINDOW?

WOW! I DIDN'T REALIZE MANAGERS RATED SUCH NICE DESKS!

YOU'RE ONLY A MANAGER? WELL, IN THAT CASE,

WHERE DO YOU WANT THE SAWHORSES?

The culture of the organization is oftern shared through stories and symbols about what is important and valued in the organization. In this cartoon the new manager is excited about the new desk by the window that is apparently a result of the new managerial position. But what message does it send to everyone else that the desk is just a couple of sawhorses?

and follow through by asking the subordinate to take the lead when the topic arises. The subordinate's success in the meeting will become a new story, one that may displace some of the many stories suggesting that the opinions of lower-level managers do not matter.

The Difficulty of Change   Changing a firm's culture is a long and difficult process. A primary problem is that upper-level managers, no matter how dedicated they are to implementing some new cultural value, may sometimes inadvertently revert to old patterns of behavior. This happens, for example, when a manager dedicated to implementing the value that lower-level employees' ideas are important vehemently attacks a subordinate's ideas.

This mistake generates a story that supports old values and beliefs. After such an incident, lower-level managers may believe the boss seems to want employee input and ideas, but nothing could be further from the truth. No matter what the boss says or how consistent his or her behavior is, some credibility has been lost, and cultural change has been made more difficult.

The Stability of Change   The process of changing a firm's culture starts with a need for change and moves through a transition period in which efforts are made to adopt new values and beliefs. In the long run, a firm that successfully changes its culture will find the new values and beliefs are as stable and influential as the old ones. Value systems tend to be self-reinforcing. Once they are in place, changing them requires an enormous effort. Thus, if a firm can change its culture from performance reducing to performance enhancing, the new values are likely to remain in place for a long time.

Synopsis

Organization culture is the set of shared values, often taken for granted and communicated through stories and other symbolic means, that help people in an organization understand which actions are considered acceptable and which unacceptable. Current research on organization culture reflects various research traditions. The most important contributions have come from anthropology, sociology, social psychology, and economics. Anthropologists have tended to focus on the organization cultures of one or two firms and have used detailed descriptions to help outsiders understand organization culture from the "natives' point of view." Sociologists typically have used survey methods to study the organization cultures of larger numbers of firms. Social psychology emphasizes the manipulation of symbols in organizations. The economics approach sees culture both as a tool used to manage and as a determinant of performance.

Creating organization culture is a five-step process. It starts with formulating first strategic values and then cultural values for the organization. Next, a vision for the organization is created, followed by the institution of implementation strategies. The final step is reinforcing the cultural behaviors of employees.

Although no single framework for describing organization culture has emerged, several have been suggested. The most popular efforts in this area have been Ouchi's comparison of U.S. and Japanese firms and Peters and Waterman's description of successful firms in the United States. Ouchi and Peters and Waterman suggested several important dimensions along which organization values vary, including treatment of employees, definitions of appropriate means for decision making, and assignment of responsibility for the results of decision making.

Emerging issues in the area of organization culture include innovation and procedural justice. Innovation is the process of creating and doing new things that are introduced into the marketplace as products, processes, or services. The organization culture can either help or hinder innovation. Procedural justice is the extent to which the dynamics of an organization's decision-making processes are judged to be fair by those most affected by them.

Managing the organization culture requires attention to three factors. First, managers can take advantage of cultural values that already exist and use their knowledge to help subordinates understand them. Second, employees need to be properly socialized, or trained, in the organization's cultural values, either through formal training or by experiencing and

observing the actions of higher-level managers. Third, managers can change the culture of the organization through managing the symbols, addressing the extreme difficulties of such a change, and relying on the durability of the new organization culture once the change has been implemented.

Discussion Questions

1. A sociologist or an anthropologist might suggest that the culture in U.S. firms simply reflects the dominant culture of the society as a whole. Therefore, to change the organization culture of a company, one must first deal with the inherent values and beliefs of the society. How would you respond to this claim?

2. Psychology has been defined as the study of individual behavior. Organizational psychology is the study of individual behavior in organizations. Many of the theories described in the early chapters of this book are based in organizational psychology. Why was this field not identified as a contributor to the study of organization culture along with anthropology, sociology, social psychology, and economics?

3. Describe the culture of an organization with which you are familiar—one in which you currently work, one in which you have worked, or one in which a friend or family member works. What values, beliefs, stories, and symbols are significant to employees of the organization?

4. Discuss the similarities and differences between the organization culture approaches of Ouchi and those of Peters and Waterman.

5. Describe how organizations use symbols and stories to communicate values and beliefs. Give some examples of how symbols and stories have been used in organizations with which you are familiar.

6. What is the role of leadership (discussed in Chapters 10 and 11) in developing, maintaining, and changing organization culture?

7. Review the characteristics of organization structure described in earlier chapters, and compare them with the elements of culture described by Ouchi and Peters and Waterman. Describe the similarities and differences, and explain how some characteristics of one may be related to characteristics of the other.

8. Discuss the role of organization rewards in developing, maintaining, and changing the organization culture.

9. Explain how culture and climate in organizations are similar and how they differ.

10. Describe how the culture of an organization can affect innovation.

Organizational Behavior Case for Discussion

Southwest Airlines: Flying High with Culture

It was a move that had been widely anticipated but dreaded: the resignation of a popular leader who had propelled his company to the forefront of its highly competitive industry. In June 2001, Southwest Airlines' founder, CEO, president, and chairman, seventy-year-old Herb Kelleher, stepped down, keeping only his chairman position. (Kelleher also maintains an active involvement in the firm by serving as a sort of "community ambassador.") In his place, Colleen Barrett assumed the roles of president and chief operating officer

while James A. Parker tackled the CEO job. Although observers had confidence in the abilities of both Parker and Barrett—they have almost sixty years of combined experience at Southwest and were handpicked by Kelleher—there was concern that Southwest might lose its culture along with its flamboyant founder.

But such fears proved to be unfounded. Kelleher says, "We wanted to be sure the culture of Southwest Airlines would continue." Southwest has a strong culture that produces loyal and motivated employees, leading to high organization performance. The airline has worked to nurture its culture since Kelleher's resignation, starting with the appointment of the two insiders to the top positions. After the September 11, 2001, terrorist attacks, many airlines laid off workers, but Southwest chose not to do so. However, workers insisted on helping the company maintain profitability: some volunteered to mow lawns, while others worked "off the clock." When asked how the firm achieves such unity, Barrett answers, "It's a matter of getting buy-in from each new hire; making [ours] a culture they want to be part of. We want [employees] to start thinking in terms of 'we' immediately. You have a lot of mentoring going on, a lot of coaching, and a lot of storytelling."

Another Southwest value is "doing your own thing," even if that means overturning conventional wisdom. Kelleher's vision for the firm was a no-frills operation, with repetitive, short-haul flights and no seat assignments or food service. Unlike other airlines, Southwest sells tickets only on its own website. Parker claims, "Independence is the way we do things. Customers are not surprised when we do something different. They expect that." He adds that other airlines have tried to mimic Southwest's culture and practices but have failed. He explains, "They want to be Southwest, but they also want to assign seats, or offer a first class or serve hot meals. We've been very disciplined about what we are, and we stick to it, evolving with our vision." Barrett advises cultural copycats, "[Don't] mimic anybody. If you want a culture that's similar [to ours,] . . . you have to hold people accountable to whatever you want your core values to be."

Parker and Barrett will work together to help maintain the company, and the culture, that Herb Kelleher built. When asked if filling Kelleher's shoes will be difficult, Barrett replies, "Herb is who Herb is. Anyone who would even think they were going to emulate that would be crazy." Parker also acknowledges his indebtedness to Kelleher: "One thing I'll always think about is 'What would Herb do?' . . . This is a superb company that has been successful. My challenge is just [not to] screw it up."

Case Questions

1. Using the Ouchi framework, describe the organization culture of Southwest Airlines. (Hint: Use Table 14.2 of the chapter.) Address each of the seven cultural values. Is Southwest Airlines more like a Type Z firm or like a typical U.S. firm. Why?
2. What are the advantages of Southwest Airlines' culture for the firm? What are the disadvantages? In your opinion, is there anything that managers at Southwest Airlines can do to lessen or eliminate the disadvantages?
3. What have managers at Southwest Airlines done to make sure the culture continues since Herb Kelleher's departure? Do you think that is enough? What more, if anything, could they do?

References: Erika Rasmusson, "Flying High," *Sales and Marketing Management*, December 2001, p. 55 (quotation); Shaun McKinnon, "New Faces, Old Methods," *Arizona Republic* (Phoenix), July 29, 2001, pp. D1, D11 (see www.azcentral.com; Wendy Zellner, "Southwest: After Kelleher, More Blue Skies," *BusinessWeek*, April 2, 2001, p. 45 (see www.businessweek.com).

Experiencing Organizational Behavior
Culture of the Classroom

Purpose: This exercise will help you appreciate the fascination as well as the difficulty of examining culture in organizations.

Format: The class will divide into groups of four to six. Each group will analyze the organization culture of a college class. Students in most classes that use this book will have taken many courses at the college they attend and therefore should have several classes in common.

Procedure:

1. Each group first decides which class it will analyze. (Each person in the group must have attended the class.)

2. Each group lists the cultural factors to be discussed. Items to be covered should include
   a. Stories about the professor
   b. Stories about the exams
   c. Stories about the grading
   d. Stories about other students
   e. The use of symbols that indicate the students' values
   f. The use of symbols that indicate the instructor's values
   g. Other characteristics of the class as suggested by the frameworks of Ouchi and Peters and Waterman

3. Students carefully analyze the stories and symbols to discover their underlying meanings. They should seek stories from other members of the group to ensure that all aspects of the class culture are covered. Students should take notes as these items are discussed

4. After twenty to thirty minutes of work in groups, the instructor will reconvene the entire class and ask each group to share its analysis with the rest of the class.

Follow-up Questions

1. What was the most difficult part of this exercise? Did other groups experience the same difficulty?

2. How did your group overcome this difficulty? How did other groups overcome it?

3. Do you believe your group's analysis accurately describes the culture of the class you selected? Could other students who analyzed the culture of the same class come up with a very different result? How could that happen?

4. If the instructor wanted to try to change the culture in the class you analyzed, what steps would you recommend he or she take?

Self-Assessment Exercise

Assessing Your Preference for Organization Culture

Instructions: Using the 1–5 scale shown below, rate the extent to which you agree or disagree with each statement.

5	4	3	2	1
Completely Disagree	Somewhat Disagree	Neutral	Somewhat Agree	Completely Agree

_____ 1. I want to work for a company that can guarantee me a job for the rest of my life.

_____ 2. I prefer to be evaluated very often on very measurable, or quantitative, factors.

_____ 3. I want a career in which I can stay in one area of the company and progress within that area.

_____ 4. I like a job where it is clear exactly what I am supposed to do and how to do it.

_____ 5. I want a job where I make the decisions without having to ask my work group or colleagues.

_____ 6. I want a job where I take personal and individual responsibility for work outcomes.

_____ 7. My ideal place to work would be where the only issue is whether I do my job and there is no concern for my personal life.

_____ = Total Score is the sum of your score on each of the seven items.

Interpretation: Total scores can range from 5 to 35 and are based on Ouchi's three types of firms. If your score is high (25–35), you prefer an organization culture that is most like the typical U.S. firms; if your score is low (5–15), you prefer an organization culture that is most like the Japanese companies; if your score is in the middle (15–25), you prefer an organization culture most like the Type Z U.S. firms.

Note: This brief instrument has not been scientifically validated and is to be used for classroom discussion purposes only.

OB Online

1. As you near graduation, you may become interested in interviewing for a job you can take after graduation. Pick several companies that appeal to you. Rank-order the companies in the sequence in which you would choose them (at least at this point). Then, starting from the top, search the Internet for articles on the management of each company, specifically for articles that describe something about the company's culture. Not all companies have articles describing their culture, so it may take several tries to find articles that do. Remember, an article that has a description of an organization's culture may not always use the word *culture*, so read carefully.

2. Describe the kinds of information you were able to locate. How much valuable information on culture did the articles provide?

3. What other information do you need to better understand the cultures of these companies?

4. Would you change your initial preference ranking based on the information you found? Why or why not?

Building Managerial Skills

Exercise Overview: Typically managers are promoted or selected to fill jobs in an organization with a given organization culture. As they begin to work, they must recognize the culture and either learn how to work within it or figure out how to change it. If the culture is a performance-reducing one, managers must figure out how to change it to a performance-enhancing culture. This exercise will give you a chance to develop your own ideas about changing organization culture.

Exercise Background: Assume you have just been appointed to head the legislative affairs committee of your local student government. As someone with a double major in business management and government, you are eager to take on this assignment and really make a difference. This committee has existed at your university for several years, but it has done little because members use the committee as a social group and regularly throw big parties. In all the years of its existence, the committee has done nothing to influence the local state legislature in relation to the issues important to university students, such as tuition. Since you know the issue of university tuition will come before the state legislature during the current legislative session, and you know many students could not afford a substantial raise in tuition, you are determined to use this committee to ensure that any tuition increase is as small as possible. However, you are worried that the party culture of the existing committee may make it difficult for you to use it to work for your issues. You also know you cannot "fire" any of the volunteers on the committee and can add only two people to the committee.

Exercise Task: Using this information as context, do the following:

1. Design a strategy for utilizing the existing culture of the committee to help you affect the legislature regarding tuition.

2. Assuming the existing culture is a performance-reducing culture, design a strategy for changing it to a performance-enhancing culture.

TEST PREPPER

ACE self-test

You have read the chapter and studied the key terms, and the exam is any day now. Think you're ready to ace it? Take this sample test to gauge your comprehension of chapter material. You can check your answers at the back of the book. Want more test questions? Visit the student website at http://college.hmco.com/business/students/ (select Griffin/Moorhead, Fundamentals of Organizational Behavior 1e) and take the ACE quizzes for more practice.

1. T F Microsoft's culture changed dramatically once Bill Gates resigned as chief executive officer.

2. T F Organization culture may be communicated through stories some authors call "myths" and "fairy tales."

3. T F The study of organization culture reflects the approaches of anthropology, sociology, social psychology, and economics.

4. T F An organization's history and traditions are apparent in its climate.

5. T F Basic beliefs about an organization's environment and its own capabilities form the organization's strategic values.

6. T F The formal reward system in an organization is probably not a good way to reinforce desired cultural behaviors.

7. T F In U.S. Type Z firms, individual managers are held responsible for decisions made by groups.

8. T F In their book *In Search of Excellence,* Peters and Waterman recommend valuing the customer over everything else.

9. T F Adding a digital camera to a cell phone is an example of a radical innovation.

10. T F The extent to which an organization's decision-making process is judged to be fair is becoming increasingly important to employees in the United States.

11. T F Most managers are in a position to create an organization's culture.

12. T F Socialization almost always changes the values of individual employees to match the organization's values.

13. T F All firms have cultural values that are consistent with high performance.

14. T F Changing a culture means changing stories and symbols, not changing people's basic assumptions about what is and what is not appropriate behavior in the organization.

15. T F One reason cultural values are difficult to change is that they are self-reinforcing.

16. When Bill Gates resigned as CEO of Microsoft and Steve Ballmer, who had been president, assumed the top role,
   a. the company's culture remained essentially the same.
   b. the company softened its aggressive, competitive stance.
   c. hundreds of employees resigned with Gates.
   d. the federal government dropped its antimonopoly lawsuit against Microsoft.
   e. Ballmer made it his primary goal to change the company's vision and mission statement.

17. The set of shared values that help people understand which actions are considered acceptable and which unacceptable is called organization
   a. strategy.   d. mission.
   b. structure.   e. human resource
   c. culture.   management.

18. An organization's culture
   a. is recorded in the company handbook.
   b. has only a weak influence on organizational members.
   c. can easily be copied from competitors.
   d. starts to develop only after the company earns a profit.
   e. is often taken for granted by organizational members.

19. Jim wants to communicate his company culture to a set of new employees. What approach would likely be most successful?
   a. Have new employees read the company history.
   b. Include a description of the culture in the new employee handbook.
   c. Let the new employees learn the culture on their own.
   d. Tell stories and give examples.
   e. Offer a course in social psychology.

20. The current atmosphere in Tiffany's company is rather unpleasant. Despite a history of strong collaboration, for the past week union members have refused to speak with management representatives. This situation reflects the organization's
   a. culture.   d. departmentalization.
   b. climate.   e. structure.
   c. strategy.

21. The basic beliefs about an organization's environment and its own capabilities are called
   a. cultural values.
   b. structural values.
   c. strategic values.
   d. organization climate.
   e. organizational myths.

22. Tim sees his small business becoming the leader in "providing affordable healthcare to the families of all military veterans by 2010." This represents the organization's
   a. culture.   d. strategy.
   b. vision.   e. values.
   c. climate.

23. All of the following will reinforce key cultural behaviors except
   a. formal rewards given for desired behaviors.
   b. stories told throughout the organization about employees who engaged in desired behaviors.
   c. treating all employees similarly regardless of their behaviors.
   d. ceremonies and rituals that emphasize the critical desired behaviors.
   e. All of the above will reinforce key cultural behaviors.

24. Japanese and Type Z U.S. firms have a strong cultural expectation that decision making will occur
   a. in groups.
   b. individually.
   c. by the senior manager.
   d. by the customer.
   e. by strategic partners.

25. Shannon often makes decisions before she has all the facts because she believes that for many important managerial decisions, all the facts will never be in. Which value of Peters and Waterman's approach does this demonstrate?
   a. Productivity through people
   b. Bias for action
   c. Autonomy and entrepreneurship
   d. Hands-on management
   e. Simultaneously loose and tight organization

26. Which of the following explains how managers simultaneously maintain tight and loose organizations?
   a. Competition is so fierce that employees know they must perform well.
   b. Higher pay will prevent employees from quitting.
   c. Human resource laws keep managers from making costly mistakes.
   d. Managers need to understand that most people are good self-managers.

   e. The organization's culture is a strong glue that holds the organization together.

27. Artificial hearts have been in use for more than twenty years, but newer models are self-adjusting. This improvement represents a(n)
   a. radical innovation.
   b. systems innovation.
   c. Type Z innovation.
   d. incremental innovation.
   e. new venture.

28. For managers to take advantage of an existing cultural system, they must first
   a. stick to their knitting.
   b. be fully aware of the culture's values and what behaviors those values support.
   c. maintain a simultaneously loose and tight organization.
   d. communicate their understanding of the culture to lower-level individuals.
   e. allow cultural values to guide their decisions.

29. The process through which employees learn about their firm's culture is called
   a. indoctrination.   d. articulation.
   b. intrapreneurship.   e. socialization.
   c. stratification.

30. What is the primary reason culture is so difficult to change?
   a. Culture is easy to change, but the process simply costs too much.
   b. Employees rarely want to change their organization's culture.
   c. Human resource management laws prevent significant cultural changes.
   d. Keeping culture stable almost always ensures better performance.
   e. People sometimes inadvertently revert to old patterns of behavior.

31. Once an organization successfully changes its culture and fully adopts new values, which of the following is likely to happen?
   a. Employees who previously left the organization will return.
   b. Competitors will change their cultures to match the new value system.
   c. Managers will focus on loosening organizational control.
   d. Performance is likely to decline.
   e. The new values will tend to be self-reinforcing.

CHAPTER 15

Organization Change and Development

MANAGEMENT PREVIEW

Companies constantly face pressures to change. Significant decreases in revenues and profits, forecasts of changing economic conditions, consumer purchasing patterns, technological and scientific factors, and competition, both foreign and domestic, can force top management to evaluate the organization and consider significant changes.

This chapter presents several perspectives on change in organizations. First, we examine the forces for change and discuss several approaches to planned organization change. Then we consider organization development processes and the resistance to change that usually occurs. We briefly cover several international and cross-cultural factors that affect organization change processes. Finally, we discuss how to manage organization change and development efforts.

After you have studied this chapter, you should be able to:
- [ ] *Summarize four dominant forces for change in organizations.*
- [ ] *Describe the process of planned organization change as a continuous process.*
- [ ] *Discuss several approaches to organization development.*
- [ ] *Explain organizational and individual sources of resistance to change.*
- [ ] *Identify six keys to managing successful organization change and development.*

We begin with a look at how one CEO has changed a small water company in France into a media and entertainment giant.

In 1996, when Jean-Marie Messier was named chairman of the French conglomerate Compagnie Générale des Eaux, the appointing board did not anticipate the wild ride of changes that were in store for the tradition-bound firm. CGE, which roughly translates as the "General Water Company," has a proud history. It was founded in 1853 by decree of Emperor Napoleon III, nephew of Napoleon I, to sell municipal water to Lyons. For more than one hundred years, the firm expanded slowly into other utilities, such as waste management and energy. It began to move into cable and other media ventures, and in 1988 changed its name to Vivendi to reflect its growing diversification.

Messier began with reorganization, creating two divisions—environment and communications—and selling all other assets. The CEO then made an aggressive series of acquisitions to move the company into the entertainment and consumer products industries, forming four divisions: music, publishing, TV and film, and Internet. The conglomerate soon had acquired more than three hundred companies and brands, artistic management and production enterprises, and entertainment products. Among the recognizable names on its roster were *American Pie, A Beautiful Mind,* Blink 182, Crash Bandicoot video games, Curious George children's books, *E. T.,* Elton John, Enrique Iglesias, George Strait, Houghton Mifflin Company (which publishes this textbook), the *Jerry Springer Show,* Jump Start educational software, *Jurassic Park, Law and Order,* Limp Bizkit, Mary J. Blige, MCA Records, Motown Records, mp3.com, tenor Placido Domingo, *Rolling Stone* magazine, the Sci-Fi Channel, Spencer Gifts, *The Mummy,* U2, Universal Studios and Theme Parks, the USA Network, and European web portal Vivazzi. Messier said, "For the first time in five years, we can now say that there are no parts missing in the strategy."

Some were skeptical of Vivendi's phenomenal growth during Messier's tenure as CEO. In spite of a $30.8 billion acquisition-related debt, synergies among units were slow to develop. European companies have a poor track record in American media. And the company's hands-off management style, promised as part of many of its acquisition deals, could lead to a problematic lack of corporate control. Messier tangled with the French government, refusing to pay particularly high telecom licensing fees. When Messier fired several low-performing but top-level managers, he was accused of ruining a French "national treasure" (Canal1, a French cable system). Messier also battled government labor regulations, including a mandatory 35-hour workweek.

Europeans resented what some regard as the "Americanization" of Messier and Vivendi. Ever since his public service days, when he championed privatization of French industries, Messier was accused of promoting "Anglo-Saxon capitalism." The contention is well founded. Vivendi shifted to American accounting principles to make the company more transparent and acceptable to American investors. Messier, who speaks perfect English, calls himself "the most un-French Frenchman you'll ever meet." When he received the French Legion of Honor, the typically elegant and dull event was transformed into a gaudy multimedia show. French society reacted with shock and outrage—exactly what Messier intended, his supporters said. Expressing a sentiment more American than French, Messier claimed, "It's rare to have a CEO who succeeds in expressing his personal emotions. That's the way I am, and it's too late to change myself." It is unclear how, or if, Messier will overcome his problems, which, according to *BusinessWeek* writer Ron Grover, include the fact that "he isn't American enough to satisfy U.S. investors[,] ... and he isn't French enough to satisfy the hometown crew, who worry that he has gone Hollywood."

In 2002, Messier was forced to step down as head of Vivendi as his strategy collapsed around him and Vivendi posted a net loss of $18.8 billion in that year. Without Messier, and after selling off many of the acquisitions he had made (including Houghton Mifflin), Vivendi posted a net loss of $1.41 billion in 2003. The company continues to change rapidly and is likely to continue to make changes for several more years.

"It's rare to have a CEO who succeeds in expressing his personal emotions. That's the way I am, and it's too late to change myself."—Jean-Marie Messier, former CEO of Vivendi

References: "2001—The Year in Brief," "Company Profile," "Executive Bio," "Our Leaders," "The Group History," "What We Do," Vivendi website, www.vivendiuniversal.com on June 22, 2002; Janet Guyon, "Getting Messier by the Minute," *Fortune*, June 10, 2002, www.fortune.com on June 22, 2002; Ron Glover, "A Loser's Race for Media Moguls," *BusinessWeek*, June 6, 2002, www.businessweek.com on June 22, 2002; Geoffrey Colvin, "Culture in Peril? Mais Oui!" *Fortune*, May 13, 2002, www.fortune.com on June 22, 2002; Richard Tomlinson, "The Nouveau CEO," *Fortune*, December 10, 2001, www.fortune.com on June 22, 2002; Devin Leonard, "Mr. Messier Is Ready for His Close-Up," *Fortune*, September 3, 2001 (quotation), www.fortune.com on June 22, 2002; "What Really Brought Messier Down," *BusinessWeek*, July 15, 2002, p. 106; "Vivendi Slowly Emerging from Two Years of Turmoil," *Amusement Business*, March 29, 2004, pp. 5–6.

J ean-Marie Messier made many changes at Vivendi that he thought were necessary given his vision of what the strategy for the company should be. This was not a turnaround situation for a company in trouble; rather, Messier's view of what the company should be to maximize shareholder wealth was the trigger for his changes. Undoubtedly, Messier saw opportunities in the environment that matched the capabilities of the organization and sought to exploit them. However, both the changes Messier made and the ways in which he made them met with great resistance. The situation at Vivendi illustrates many key issues regarding change in organizations.

Forces for Change

LEARNING OBJECTIVE

Summarize four dominant forces for change in organizations.

An organization faces pressures for change from numerous sources—far too many to cover in our discussion here. Moreover, it is difficult to predict what types of pressures for change will be most significant in the next decade because the complexity of events and the rapidity of change are increasing. In this section, we look at four broad categories of pressures most likely to have major effects on organizations: people, technology, information processing and communication, and competition. Table 15.1 gives examples of each category.

People

Approximately 56 million people were born between 1945 and 1960. These baby boomers differ significantly from previous generations with respect to education, expectations, and value systems.[1] As this group has aged, the median age of the U.S. population has gradually increased, passing 32 for the first time in 1988[2] and further increasing to 35.6 in 1999.[3] The special characteristics of baby boomers show up in distinct purchasing patterns that affect product and service innovation, technological change, and marketing and promotional activities.[4] Employment

TABLE 15.1

Pressures for Organization Change

Category	Examples	Type of Pressure for Change
People	Generation X Baby boomers Senior citizens Workforce diversity	Demands for different training, benefits, workplace arrangements, and compensation systems
Technology	Manufacturing in space Internet Artificial Intelligence	More education and training for workers at all levels, more new products, products move faster to market
Information Processing and Communication	Computer, satellite communications Videoconferencing	Faster reaction times, immediate responses to questions, new products, different office arrangements, telecommuting
Competition	Worldwide markets International trade agreements Emerging nations	Global competition, more competing products with more features and options, lower costs, higher quality

practices, compensation systems, promotion and managerial succession systems, and the entire concept of human resource management are also affected.

Other population-related pressures for change involve the generations that sandwich the baby boomers: the increasing numbers of senior citizens and those born after 1960. The parents of the baby boomers are living longer, healthier lives than previous generations, and today they expect to live the "good life" they missed when they were raising their children. The impact of the large number of senior citizens is already evident in part-time employment practices; in the marketing of everything from hamburgers to packaged tours of Asia; and in service areas such as health care, recreation, and financial services. The post-1960 generation of workers who are entering the job market also differ from the baby boomers. These changes in demographics extend to the composition of the workforce, family lifestyles, and purchasing patterns worldwide. The World View box depicts the makeover of Avon in response to changes in the population and workforce.

Technology

Not only is technology changing, but the rate of technological change is also increasing. In 1970, for example, all engineering students owned slide rules and used

WORLD VIEW

A Makeover at Avon

What could possibly be more dated than the 1950s version of the Avon Lady, perfectly dressed down to her white gloves, ringing doorbells on weekday mornings to sell lipstick and perfume to stay-at-home moms? "Dingdong. Avon calling." Yet today, thanks to savvy business moves by CEO Andrea Jung, the retailer is thriving, and so is the Avon Lady.

Today's Avon Lady is likely to be a young professional woman who supplements her income by selling products ranging from perfume and cosmetics to exercise equipment and vitamins to both men and women. She profits not only from sales but also from recruitment bonuses she earns for attracting new representatives, and she uses the Internet to find customers, place orders, and advertise. All of these changes were either introduced or advanced by Jung, who took the CEO role in 2000. Her other strategies for change include selling a new line of cosmetics in mall kiosks and at JCPenney under the brand name Becoming and focusing more on the international market, where 62 percent of the firm's sales occur.

Jung, the first woman to head Avon, has teamed with president Susan Kropf to improve back-office operations, reducing costs in R&D, purchasing, and logistics while also getting innovative products to market faster. Jung and Kropf agree that a female executive has only a minor advantage in the glamour industry. "You go home and try on a new mascara, and I guess a male CEO can't do that," Jung wryly notes. Kropf points out, "Maybe, on the periphery, there is a greater personal affinity for the products we sell. [But] in terms of leadership, the strategy, the disciplines, [and] the analytical rigor, it doesn't matter if you're a man, woman, dog, or cat. There is no gender consideration."

The two leaders do believe, however, that their gender allows them to relate well to the company's 500,000 representatives, the majority of whom are female. Jung asserts, "[Women] see that the glass ceiling has been broken at Avon."

References: "Let's Talk About Avon," Avon website, www.avoncompany. com on June 18, 2002; Diane Brady, "A Makeover Has Avon Looking Good," *BusinessWeek*, January 22, 2002, www.businessweek.com on June 18, 2002; Patricia O'Connell, "Meet the Avon Ladies-in-Chief," *BusinessWeek*, January 22, 2002, www.businessweek.com on June 18, 2002; Katrina Booker, "It Took a Lady to Save Avon," *Fortune*, October 15, 2001, pp. 202–208 (see www.fortune.com); Jennifer Pellet, "Ding-dong Avon Stalling?" *Chief Executive*, June 2000, pp. 26–31 (see www.chiefexecutive. net).

them in almost every class. By 1976, slide rules had given way to portable electronic calculators. In the mid-1980s, some universities began issuing microcomputers to entering students or assumed those students already owned one. In 1993, the Scholastic Aptitude Test (SAT), which many college-bound students take to get into college, allowed the use of calculators during the test. Today students cannot make it through college without owning or at least having ready access to a personal computer. At many universities, dorm rooms are wired for direct computer access for email and class assignments and for connection to the Internet. Now that buildings, hotels, and cafes are also wireless, anyone can hook up to the Internet just about anywhere. Technological development is increasing so rapidly in almost every field that it is quite difficult to predict which products will dominate ten years from now.

Interestingly, organization change is self-perpetuating. With the advances in information technology, organizations generate more information that circulates more quickly. Consequently employees can respond more rapidly to problems, enabling organizations to respond more quickly to demands from other organizations, customers, and competitors.[5]

Cell phone giants such as Nokia, Motorola, and Erikson have had a stranglehold on the worldwide cellular phone market. All three have major operations in China, manufacturing and selling in Asia as well as the rest of the world. That world is changing fast, however. The new competition may soon be from Chinese companies. More than thirty Chinese companies now manufacture cellular phones and work with software providers Microsoft and Qualcomm Inc. to develop much lower-priced handsets. Nokia and others had better watch out!

Information Processing and Communication

Advances in information processing and communication have paralleled each other. A new generation of computers, which will mark another major increase in processing power, is being designed. Satellite systems for data transmission are already in use. Today people carry their telephone, portable computer, music player, and pager all in one instrument.

In the future, people may not need offices as they work with computers and communicate through new data transmission devices. Workstations, both in and outside of offices, are more electronic than paper and pencil. For years the capability has existed to generate, manipulate, store, and transmit more data than managers could use, but the benefits were not fully realized. Now the time has come to utilize all of this information processing potential, and companies are making the most of it. Typically companies received orders by mail in the 1970s, by toll-free telephone numbers in the 1980s, by fax machine in the late 1980s and early 1990s, and by electronic data exchange in the mid-1990s. Orders used to take a week; now they are placed instantaneously, and companies must be able to respond immediately, because of advances in information processing and communication.[6]

Competition

Although competition is not a new force for change, competition today has some significant new twists. First, most markets are international because of decreasing transportation and communication costs and the increasing export orientation of business. The adoption of trade agreements such as the North American Free Trade Agreement (NAFTA) and the presence of the World Trade Organization (WTO) have changed the way business operates. Competition from industrialized countries such as Japan and Germany are taking a back seat to competition from the booming industries of developing nations. The Internet is creating new competitors overnight and in ways unimaginable just a decade ago. Companies in developing nations are offering different, newer, cheaper, or higher-quality products and services while enjoying the benefits of low labor costs, abundant supplies of raw materials, expertise in certain areas of production, and financial protection from their governments that may not be available to firms in older industrialized states.

Planned Organization Change

LEARNING OBJECTIVE

Describe the process of planned organization change as a continuous process.

External forces may impose change on an organization. Ideally, however, the organization will not only respond to change but will anticipate it, prepare for it through planning, and incorporate it in the organization strategy. Organization change can be viewed from a static point of view, such as that of Lewin (see the next section), or from a dynamic perspective.

Lewin's Process Model

Planned organization change requires a systematic process of movement from one condition to another. Kurt Lewin suggested that efforts to bring about planned change in organizations should approach change as a multistage process.[7] His model of planned change consists of three steps—unfreezing, change, and refreezing—as shown in Figure 15.1

Unfreezing is the process by which people become aware of the need for change. If people are satisfied with current practices and procedures, they may have little or no interest in making changes. The key factor in unfreezing is making employees understand the importance of a change and how it will affect their jobs. The employees who will be most affected by the change must be made aware of why it is needed, which in effect makes them dissatisfied enough with current operations to be motivated to change. **Change** itself is the movement from the old way of doing things to a new way. Change may entail installing new equipment, restructuring the organization, implementing a new performance appraisal system—anything that alters existing relationships or activities. **Refreezing** makes new behaviors relatively permanent and resistant to further change. Examples of refreezing techniques include repeating newly learned skills in a training session and role playing to teach how the new skill can be used in a real-life work situation. Refreezing is necessary because without it, the old ways of doing things may soon resurface while the new ways are forgotten. For example, many employees who attend special training sessions apply themselves diligently and resolve to change things in their organizations. When they return to the workplace, however, they find it easier to conform to the old ways than to make waves. There are usually few, if any, rewards for trying to

Unfreezing is the process of becoming aware of the need for change.

Change is the movement from an old way of doing things to a new way. This may be the adoption of any new idea, process, or procedure that requires organizational participants to alter how they do their jobs.

Refreezing is the process of making new behaviors relatively permanent and resistant to further change.

FIGURE 15.1

Lewin's Process of Organization Change

In Lewin's three-step model, change is a systematic process of transition from an old way of doing things to a new way. Inclusion of an unfreezing stage indicates the importance of preparing for the change. A refreezing stage reflects the importance of following up on the change to make it permanent..

change the organizational status quo; in fact, the personal sanctions against doing so may be difficult to tolerate. Learning theory and reinforcement theory (see Chapter 4) can play important roles in the refreezing phase.

The Continuous Change Process Model

Perhaps because Lewin's model is very simple and straightforward, virtually all models of organization change use his approach. However, it does not deal with several important issues. A more complex, and more helpful, approach is illustrated in Figure 15.2. This approach treats planned change from the perspective of top management and indicates that change is continuous. Although we discuss each step as if it were distinct from the others, it is important to note that as organization change becomes continuous, different steps probably occur simultaneously throughout the organization. The model incorporates Lewin's concept into the implementation phase.

In this approach, top management perceives that certain forces or trends call for change, and the issue is subjected to the organization's usual problem-solving and decision-making processes (see Chapter 12). Usually top management defines its goals in terms of what the organization or certain processes or outputs will be like after the change. Alternatives for change are generated and evaluated, and an acceptable one is selected.

A **change agent** is a person responsible for managing a change effort.

Early in the process, the organization may seek the assistance of a **change agent,** a person who will be responsible for managing the change effort. The change agent may also help management recognize and define the problem or the need for the change, and may be involved in generating and evaluating potential plans of action. The change agent may be a member of the organization, an outsider such as a consultant, or even someone from headquarters whom employees view as an outsider. An internal change agent is likely to know the organization's people, tasks, and political situations, which may be helpful in interpreting data and understanding the system; however, an insider may also be too close to the situation to view it objectively. (In addition, a regular employee would have to be removed from normal duties to concentrate on the transition.) An outsider, then, is often received better by all parties because of his or her assumed impartiality. Under the direction and management of the change agent, the organization implements the change through Lewin's unfreeze–change–refreeze process.

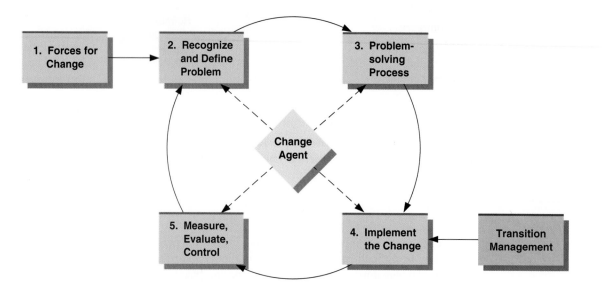

FIGURE 15.2

Continuous Change Process Model of Organization Change

The continuous change process model incorporates the forces for change, a problem-solving process, a change agent, and transition management. It takes a top management perspective and highlights the fact that in today's organizations change is a continuous process.

The final step is measurement, evaluation, and control. The change agent and the top management group assess the degree to which the change is having the desired effect; that is, they measure progress toward the goals of the change and make appropriate adjustments if necessary. The more closely the change agent is involved in the change process, the less distinct the steps become. The change agent becomes a "collaborator" or "helper" to the organization as she or he delves into defining and solving the problem with members of the organization. When this happens, the change agent may be working with many individuals, groups, and departments within the organization on different phases of the change process. When the change process is moving along from one stage to another, it may not be readily observable due to the total involvement of the change agent in every phase of the project. Throughout the process, however, the change agent brings in new ideas and viewpoints that help members look at old problems in new ways. Change often arises from the conflict that results when the change agent challenges the organization's assumptions and generally accepted patterns of operation.

Through the measurement, evaluation, and control phase, top management determines the effectiveness of the change process by evaluating various indicators of organizational productivity, effectiveness, and employee morale. It is hoped that the organization will be better after the change than before. However, the uncertainties and rapid change in all sectors of the environment make constant organization change a certainty for most organizations.

Transition management is the process of systematically planning, organizing, and implementing change.

Transition management is the process of systematically planning, organizing, and implementing change, from the disassembly of the current state to the realization of a fully functional future state within the organization.[8] Once change begins, the organization is in neither the old state nor the new state, yet business must go on. Transition management ensures that business continues while the change is under way; therefore, it must begin before the change occurs. The members of the regular management team must take on the role of transition managers and coordinate organizational activities with the change agent. An interim management structure or interim positions may be created to ensure continuity and control of the business during the transition. Communication about the changes to all involved, from employees to customers and suppliers, plays a key role in transition management.[9]

Organization Development

Organization development is the process of planned change and improvement of the organization through application of knowledge of the behavioral sciences.

Organization development is the process of planned change and improvement of an organization through the application of knowledge of the behavioral sciences. Three points in this definition make it simple to remember and use. First, organization development involves attempts to plan organization changes, which excludes spontaneous, haphazard initiatives. Second, the specific intention of organization development is to improve the organization. This point excludes changes that merely imitate those of another organization, are forced on the organization by external pressures, or are undertaken merely for the sake of changing. Third, the planned improvement must be based on knowledge of behavioral sciences such as organizational behavior, psychology, sociology, cultural anthropology, and related fields of study rather than on financial or technological considerations. The replacement of manual personnel records with a computerized system would not be considered an instance of organization development. Although such a change has behavioral effects, it is a technology-driven reform rather than a behavioral one. Likewise, alterations in recordkeeping to support new government-mandated reporting requirements are not a part of organization development because the change is obligatory and the result of an external force. The most basic types of organization development techniques are systemwide, task and technological, and group and individual.

Systemwide Organization Development

Structural change is a systemwide organization development involving a major restructuring of the organization or instituting programs such as quality of work life.

The most comprehensive type of organization change involves a major reorientation or reorganization, usually referred to as a **structural change** or a systemwide rearrangement of task division and authority and reporting relationships. A structural change affects performance appraisal and rewards, decision making, and communication and information processing systems. Reengineering and rethinking the organization are two contemporary approaches to systemwide structural change. Reengineering can be a difficult process, but it has great potential for organizational improvement. It requires that managers challenge long-held assumptions about everything they do, and set outrageous goals and expect they will be met.

An organization may change the way it divides tasks into jobs, combines jobs into departments and divisions, and arranges authority and reporting relationships among positions. It may move from functional departmentalization to a system based on products or geography, for example, or from a vertical, functional design to a matrix or a team-based design. Other changes may include dividing large groups into smaller ones or merging small groups into larger ones. In addition, the degree to which rules and procedures are written down and enforced, as well as the locus of decision-making authority, may be altered. Supervisors may become "coaches" or "facilitators" in a team-based organization.

No systemwide structural change is simple.[10] A company president cannot simply issue a memo notifying personnel that on a certain date they will report to a different supervisor and be responsible for new tasks, and expect everything to change overnight. Employees have months, years, and sometimes decades of experience in dealing with people and tasks in certain ways. When these patterns are disrupted, employees need time to learn the new tasks and settle into the new relationships. Moreover, they may resist the change for a number of reasons; we discuss resistance to change later in this chapter. Therefore, organizations must manage the change process.

Quality of work life is the extent to which workers can satisfy important personal needs through their experiences in the organization.

Another systemwide change is the introduction of quality-of-work-life programs. J. Lloyd Suttle defined **quality of work life** as the "degree to which members of a work organization are able to satisfy important personal needs through their experiences in the organization."[11] Quality-of-work-life programs focus strongly on providing a work environment conducive to satisfying individual needs. The emphasis on improving life at work developed during the 1970s, a period of increasing inflation and deepening recession. The development was rather surprising because an expanding economy and substantially increased resources are the conditions that usually induce top management to begin people-oriented programs. However, top management viewed improving life at work as a means of improving productivity.

Total quality management (TQM), discussed in several earlier chapters, can also be viewed as a systemwide organization development program. In fact, some might consider total quality management as a broad program that includes structural change as well as quality of work life. It differs from quality of work life in that it emphasizes satisfying customer needs by making quality-oriented changes rather than focusing on satisfying employee needs at work. Often, however, the employee programs are very similar to TQM.

The benefits gained from quality-of-work-life programs differ substantially, but generally they are of three types. A more positive attitude toward the work and the organization, or increased job satisfaction, is perhaps the most direct benefit.[12] Another is increased productivity, although it is often difficult to measure and separate the effects of the quality-of-work-life program from the effects of other organizational factors. A third benefit is increased organizational effectiveness as measured by the firm's profitability, goal accomplishment, shareholder wealth, or resource exchange. The third gain follows directly from the first two: If employees have more positive attitudes about the organization and their productivity increases, everything else being equal, the organization should be more effective.

Task and Technological Organization Development

Another way to bring about systemwide organization development is through changes in the tasks involved in doing the work, the technology, or both. The direct alteration of jobs is usually called *task redesign*. Changing how inputs are transformed into outputs is called *technological change* and also usually results in task changes. Strictly speaking, changing the technology is typically not part of organization development, whereas task redesign usually is.

The structural changes discussed in the preceding section are explicitly systemwide in scope. Those we examine in this section are more narrowly focused and may not seem to have the same far-reaching consequences. Nevertheless, their impact is felt throughout the organization. The discussion of task design in Chapter 5 focused on job definition and motivation, and gave little attention to implementing changes in jobs. Here we discuss task redesign as a mode of organization change.

TABLE 15.2

Integrated Framework for Implementation of Task Redesign in Organizations

Step 1: Recognition of a need for a change
Step 2: Selection of task redesign as a potential intervention
Step 3: Diagnosis of the work system and context
      a. Diagnosis of existing jobs
      b. Diagnosis of existing workforce
      c. Diagnosis of technology
      d. Diagnosis of organization design
      e. Diagnosis of leader behavior
      f.   Diagnosis of group and social processes
Step 4: Cost-benefit analysis of proposed changes
Step 5: Go/no-go decision
Step 6: Formulation of the strategy for redesign
Step 7: Implementation of the task changes
Step 8: Implementation of any supplemental changes
Step 9: Evaluation of the task redesign effort

Reference: Ricky W. Griffin, *Task Design: An Integrative Framework* (Glenview, Ill.: Scott, Foresman, 1982), p. 208. Used by permission.

Several approaches to introducing job changes in organizations have been proposed. Ricky Griffin proposed an integrative framework of nine steps that reflect the complexities of the interfaces between individual jobs and the total organization.[13] The process, shown in Table 15.2, includes the steps usually associated with change, such as recognizing the need for a change, selecting the appropriate intervention, and evaluating the change. Griffin's approach, however, inserts four additional steps into the standard sequence: diagnosis of the overall work system and context, including examination of the jobs, workforce, technology, organization design, leadership, and group dynamics; evaluating the costs and benefits of the change; formulating a redesign strategy; and implementing supplemental changes.

Diagnosis includes analysis of the total work environment within which the jobs exist. It is important to evaluate the organization structure, especially the work rules and decision-making authority within a department, when job changes are being considered.[14] For example, if jobs are to be redesigned to give employees more freedom in choosing work methods or scheduling work activities, diagnosis of the present system must determine whether the rules will allow that to happen. Diagnosis must also include evaluation of the work group and teams and intragroup dynamics (discussed in Chapters 8 and 9). Furthermore, it must determine whether workers have or can easily obtain the new skills to perform the redesigned task.

It is extremely important to recognize the full range of potential costs and benefits associated with a job redesign effort. Some are direct and quantifiable; others are indirect and not measurable. Redesign may involve unexpected costs or benefits; although these cannot be predicted with certainty, they can be weighed as possibilities. Factors such as short-term role ambiguity, role conflict, and role overload can be major stumbling blocks to a job redesign effort.

Group and Individual Organization Development

Groups and individuals can be involved in organization change in a vast number of ways. Retraining a single employee can be considered an organization change if the training affects the way she or he performs the job. In this section, we look at four popular types of people-oriented change techniques: training, management development programs, team building, and survey feedback.

Training   Training is generally designed to improve employees' job skills. Employees may be trained to run certain machines, taught new mathematical skills, or acquainted with personal growth and development methods. Stress management programs are becoming popular for helping employees, particularly executives, understand organizational stress and develop ways to cope with it. Training may also be used in conjunction with other, more comprehensive organization changes. For instance, if an organization is implementing a management-by-objectives program, training in establishing goals and reviewing goal-oriented performance is probably needed. One type of training that is becoming increasingly important is training people to work in other countries. Companies such as Motorola give extensive training programs to employees at all levels before they start an international assignment. Training includes intensive language courses, cultural courses, and courses for the employee's family.

Among the many training methods, the most common are lectures, discussions, lecture-discussion combinations, experiential methods, case studies, and films or videotapes. Training can take place in a standard classroom, either on company property or in a hotel, at a resort, or at a conference center. On-the-job training provides a different type of experience in which the trainee learns from a veteran worker. Most training programs use a combination of methods determined by the topic, the trainees, the trainer, and the organization.

A major problem of training programs is transferring employee learning to the workplace. Often an employee learns a new skill or a manager learns a new management technique but, on returning to the normal work situation, finds it easier to go back to the old way of doing things. As we discussed earlier, the process of refreezing is a vital part of the change process, and some way must be found to make the accomplishments of the training program permanent.

Management Development Programs   Management development programs, like employee training programs, attempt to foster certain skills, abilities, and perspectives. Often, when a highly qualified technical person is promoted to manager of a work group, he or she lacks training in how to manage or deal with people. In such cases, management development programs can be important to the organization, both for the new manager and for his or her subordinates.

Typically management development programs use the lecture-discussion method to some extent, but rely most heavily on participative methods such as case studies and role playing. Participative and experiential methods allow the manager to experience the problems of being a manager as well as the feelings of frustration, doubt, and success that are part of the job. The subject matter of this type of training program is problematic, however, in that management skills, including com-

Top Gun training for corporate execs? What can military pilots possibly have that highly paid corporate executives would pay for? Combat planning, preparedness, reaction to unforeseen emergencies, contingency planning, discipline, and knowing your competitors are among the lessons Afterburner Seminars is selling and delivering to top management of companies, including Dell, Charles Schwab, Ford Motor, IBM, and Pfizer.

munication, problem diagnosis, problem solving, and performance appraisal, are harder to identify or to transfer from a classroom to the workplace than the skills required, say, to run a machine. In addition, rapid changes in the external environment can make certain managerial skills obsolete in a very short time. As a result, some companies are approaching the development of their management teams as an ongoing, career-long process and requiring their managers to attend refresher courses periodically.

As corporate America invests hundreds of millions of dollars in management development, certain guiding principles are evolving. First, management development is a multifaceted, complex, and long-term process to which there is no quick or simple approach. Second, organizations should carefully and systematically identify their unique developmental needs and evaluate their programs accordingly. Third, management development objectives must be compatible with organizational objectives. Finally, the utility and value of management development remain more an article of faith than a proven fact.[15]

Team Building   When interaction among group members is critical to group success and effectiveness, team development, or team building, may be useful. Team building emphasizes members working together in a spirit of cooperation and generally has one or more of the following goals:

1. To set team goals and priorities
2. To analyze or allocate the way work is performed
3. To examine how a group is working in terms of processes such as norms, decision making, and communications
4. To examine relationships among the people doing the work[16]

Team building should not be thought of as a one-time experience, perhaps something undertaken on a retreat from the workplace; rather, it is a continuing process. It may take weeks, months, or years for a group to learn to pull together and function as a team. Team development can be a way to train the group to solve its own problems in the future. So far, research on the effectiveness of team building as an organization development tool is mixed and inconclusive. For more details on developing teams in organizations, refer to Chapter 9.

Survey Feedback   Survey feedback techniques can form the basis for a change process. In this process, data are gathered, analyzed, summarized, and returned to those who generated them to identify, discuss, and solve problems. A survey feedback process is often set in motion either by the organization's top management or by a consultant to management. By providing information about employees' beliefs and attitudes, a survey can help management diagnose and solve the organization's problems. A consultant or change agent usually coordinates the process and is responsible for data gathering, analysis, and summary. The three-stage process appears in Figure 15.3.[17]

The use of survey feedback techniques in an organization development process differs from their use in traditional attitude surveys. In an organization development process, data are (1) returned to employee groups at all levels in the organization and (2) used by all employees working together in their normal work groups to identify and solve problems. In traditional attitude surveys, top management reviews the data and may or may not initiate a new program to solve problems the survey has identified.

In the data-gathering stage, the change agent interviews selected personnel from appropriate levels to determine the key issues to be examined. Information

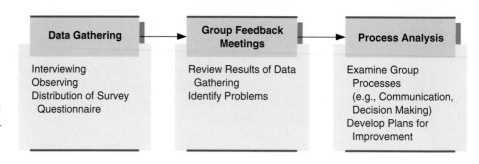

from these interviews is used to develop a survey questionnaire, which is distributed to a large sample of employees. The questionnaire may be a standardized instrument, an instrument developed specifically for the organization, or a combination of the two. The questionnaire data are analyzed and aggregated by group or department to ensure respondents remain anonymous.[18] Then the change agent prepares a summary of the results for the group feedback sessions. From this point on, the consultant is involved in the process as a resource person and expert.

The feedback meetings generally involve only two or three levels of management. Meetings are usually held serially, first with a meeting of the top management group, followed by meetings of employees throughout the organization. The group manager rather than the change agent typically leads sessions to transfer "ownership" of the data from the change agent to the work group. The feedback consists primarily of profiles of the group's attitudes toward the organization, the work, the leadership, and other topics on the questionnaire. During the feedback sessions, participants discuss reasons for the scores and the problems the data reveal.

In the process analysis stage, the group examines the process of making decisions, communicating, and accomplishing work, usually with the help of the consultant. Unfortunately, groups often overlook this stage as they become absorbed in the survey data and the problems revealed during the feedback sessions. Occasionally group managers simply fail to hold feedback and process analysis sessions. Change agents should ensure that managers hold these sessions and that they are rewarded for doing so. The process analysis stage is important because its purpose is to develop action plans to make improvements. Several sessions may be required to discuss the process issues fully and to settle on a strategy for improvements. Groups often find it useful to document the plans as they are discussed and to appoint a member to follow up on implementation. Generally the follow-up assesses whether communication and communication processes have actually been improved. A follow-up survey can be administered several months to a year later to assess how much these processes have changed since they were first reported.

The survey feedback method is probably one of the most widely used organization change and development interventions. If any of its stages are compromised or omitted, however, the technique becomes less useful. A primary responsibility of the consultant or change agent, then, is to ensure the method is fully and faithfully carried through.

Resistance to Change

Just as change is inevitable, so is resistance to change. Paradoxically, organizations both promote and resist change. As an agent for change, the organization asks prospective customers or clients to change their current purchasing habits by switching to the company's product or service, asks current customers to change by increasing their purchases, and asks suppliers to reduce the costs of raw materials. The organization resists change in that its structure and control systems protect the daily tasks of producing a product or service from uncertainties in the environment. The organization must have some elements of permanence to avoid mirroring the instability of the environment, yet it must also react to external shifts with internal change to maintain currency and relevance in the marketplace.

A commonly held view is that all resistance to change needs to be overcome, but that is not always the case. Resistance to change can be used for the benefit of the organization and need not be eliminated entirely. By revealing a legitimate concern that a proposed change may harm the organization or that other alternatives might be better, resistance may alert the organization to reexamine the change.[19] For example, an organization may be considering acquiring a company in a completely different industry. Resistance to such a proposal may cause the organization to examine the advantages and disadvantages of the move more carefully. Without resistance, the decision may be made before the pros and cons have been sufficiently explored.

Resistance may come from the organization, the individual, or both. Determining the ultimate source is often difficult, however, because organizations are composed of individuals. Table 15.3 summarizes various types of organizational and individual sources of resistance.

Organizational Sources of Resistance

Daniel Katz and Robert Kahn have identified six major organizational sources of resistance: overdetermination, narrow focus of change, group inertia, threatened expertise, threatened power, and changes in resource allocation.[20] Of course, not every organization or every change situation displays all six sources.

Overdetermination   Organizations have several systems designed to maintain stability. For example, consider how organizations control employees' performance. Job candidates must have certain specific skills so they can do the job the organization needs them to do. New employees are given a job description, and the supervisor trains, coaches, and counsels the employee in job tasks. The new employee usually serves some type of probationary period that culminates in a performance review; thereafter, the employee's performance is regularly evaluated. Finally, rewards, punishment, and discipline are administered, depending on the level of performance. Such a system is said to be characterized by **overdetermination,** or **structural inertia,** in that one could probably have the same effect on employee performance with fewer procedures and safeguards.[21] In other words, the structure of the organization produces resistance to change because it was designed to maintain stability. Another important source of overdetermination is the organization culture. As discussed in Chapter 14, the culture of an organization can have powerful and long-lasting effects on employees' behavior.

Overdetermination, or **structural inertia**, occurs because several organizational systems and processes exist to make sure that workers do a specific job in a certain way. In order to change the way an employee does her or his job, we must change all of those systems or processes that determine how an employee does the job.

TABLE 15.3

Organizational and Individual Sources of Resistance

Organizational Sources	Examples
Overdetermination	Employment system, job descriptions, evaluation, and reward system, organization culture
Narrow Focus of Change	Structure changed with no concern given to other issues, e.g., jobs, people
Group Inertia	Group norms
Threatened Expertise	People move out of area of expertise
Threatened Power	Decentralized decision making
Resource Allocation	Increased use of part-time help

Individual Sources	Examples
Habit	Altered tasks
Security	Altered tasks or reporting relationships
Economic Factors	Changed pay and benefits
Fear of the Unknown	New job, new boss
Lack of Awareness	Isolated groups not heeding notices
Social Factors	Group norms

Narrow Focus of Change   Many efforts to create change in organizations adopt too narrow a focus. Any effort to force change in the tasks of individuals or groups must take into account the interdependencies among organizational elements such as people, structure, tasks, and the information system. For example, some attempts to redesign jobs fail because the organization structure within which the jobs must function is inappropriate for the redesigned jobs.[22]

Group Inertia   When an employee attempts to change his or her work behavior, the group may resist by refusing to change other behaviors that are necessary complements to the individual's changed behavior. In other words, group norms may act as a brake on individual attempts at behavior change.

Threatened Expertise   A change in the organization may threaten the specialized expertise that individuals and groups have developed over the years. A job redesign or a structural change may transfer responsibility for a specialized task from the current expert to someone else, threatening the specialist's expertise and building his or her resistance to the change.

Threatened Power   Any redistribution of decision-making authority, such as with reengineering or team-based management, may threaten an individual's power relationships with others. If an organization is decentralizing its decision making, managers who wielded their decision-making powers in return for special favors from others may resist the change because they do not want to lose their power base.

Resource Allocation   Groups that are satisfied with current resource allocation methods may resist any change they believe will threaten future allocations. Resources in this context can mean anything from monetary rewards and equipment to additional seasonal help to more computer time.

These six sources explain most types of organization-based resistance to change. All are based on people and social relationships. Many of these sources of resistance can be traced to groups or individuals who are afraid of losing something, such as resources, power, or a comfortable routine.

Individual Sources of Resistance

Individual sources of resistance to change are rooted in basic human characteristics such as needs and perceptions. Researchers have identified six reasons for individual resistance to change: habit, security, economic factors, fear of the unknown, lack of awareness, and social factors (see Table 15.3).[23]

Habit   It is easier to do a job the same way every day if the steps in the job are repeated over and over. Learning an entirely new set of steps makes the job more difficult. For the same amount of return (pay), most people prefer to do easier rather than harder work.

Security   Some employees like the comfort and security of doing things the same old way. They gain a feeling of constancy and safety from knowing that some things stay the same despite all the change going on around them. People who believe a change threatens their security are likely to resist the change.

Economic Factors   Change may threaten employees' steady paychecks. Workers may fear that change will make their jobs obsolete or reduce their opportunities for future pay increases.

Fear of the Unknown   Some people fear anything unfamiliar. Changes in reporting relationships and job duties create anxiety for such employees. Employees become familiar with their bosses and their jobs, and develop relationships with others within the organization, such as contact people for various situations. These relationships and contacts help facilitate their work. Any disruption of familiar patterns may create fear because it can cause delays and foster the belief that nothing is getting accomplished. The cartoon shows how people sometimes appear brave but, when alone, they worry about what the changes might bring.

This little guy brags to his coworkers that he is not worried about the reorganization when he really *is* worried about it. In any organization change, most people are concerned about how the changes will affect their jobs and their futures. Most people learn how to survive in the job and the work environment and fear the unknowns that changes might bring.

© Grantland

Lack of Awareness   Because of perceptual limitations such as lack of attention or selective attention, a person may fail to recognize a change in a rule or procedure and thus may not alter his or her behavior. People may pay attention only to things that support their point of view. As an example, employees in an isolated regional sales office may not notice—or may ignore—directives from headquarters regarding a change in reporting procedures for expense accounts, continuing the current practice as long as possible.

Social Factors   People may resist change for fear of what others will think. As mentioned before, a group can be a powerful motivator of behavior. Employees may believe change will hurt their image, result in ostracism from the group, or simply make them "different." For example, an employee who agrees to conform to work rules established by management may be ridiculed by others who openly disobey the rules.

Managing Successful Organization Change and Development

┌ *LEARNING OBJECTIVE* ┐

Identify six keys to managing successful organization change and development.

In conclusion, we offer six keys to managing change in organizations. These guidelines relate directly to the problems identified earlier and to our view of the organization as a comprehensive social system. Each can influence the elements of the social system and may help the organization avoid some of the major problems typical in managing change. Table 15.4 lists the six keys and their potential impacts.

Take a Holistic View

Managers must take a holistic view of the organization and the change project. A limited view can endanger the change effort because the subsystems of the organization are interdependent. A holistic view encompasses the culture and dominant coalition as well as the people, tasks, structure, and information subsystems.

TABLE 15.4

Keys to Managing Successful Organization Change and Development

Key	Impact
Take a holistic view of the organization.	Helps anticipate the effects of change on the social system and culture
Start small.	Works out details and shows the benefits of the change to those who might resist
Secure top management support.	Gets dominant coalition on the side of change; safeguards structural change, heads off problems of power and control
Encourage participation by those affected by the change.	Minimizes transition problems of control, resistance, and task redefinition
Foster open communication.	Minimizes transition problems of resistance and information and control systems
Reward those who contribute to change.	Minimizes transition problems of resistance and control systems

Start Small

Peter Senge claims that every truly successful, systemwide change in large organizations starts small.[24] He recommends that change start with one team, usually an executive team. One team can evaluate the change, make appropriate adjustments along the way, and, most important, show that the new system works and gets desired results. If the change makes sense, it begins to spread to other teams, groups, and divisions throughout the system. Senge described how at Shell and Ford, significant changes started small, with one or two parallel teams, and then spread as others recognized the benefits of the change. When others see the benefits, they automatically drop their inherent resistance and join in voluntarily, and often become committed to the success of the change effort.

Secure Top Management Support

The support of top management is essential to the success of any change effort. As the organization's probable dominant coalition, it is a powerful element of the social system, and its support is necessary to deal with control and power problems. For example, a manager who plans a change in the ways tasks are assigned and responsibility is delegated in his or her department must notify top management and gain its support. Complications may arise if disgruntled employees complain to high-level managers who were not notified of the change or do not support it. The employees' complaints may jeopardize the manager's plan—and perhaps her or his job.

Linda Dillman, Senior Vice President Information Systems Division and CIO, Wal-Mart Stores, Inc. has made many changes in her twelve years with Wal-Mart. The pressure is always on to use information technology to reduce costs. One of the ways she does that is by regularly asking her managers what they would change about the way they do their jobs in the Information Systems Division. These often take place in town hall style meetings. The results are approximately 300 changes per day in how the Information Systems Division does its work.

Encourage Participation

Problems related to resistance, control, and power can be overcome by broad participation in planning the change. Allowing people a voice in designing the change may give them a sense of power and control over their own destinies, which may help win their support during implementation.

Foster Open Communication

Open communication is an important factor in managing resistance to change and overcoming information and control problems during transitions. Employees typically recognize the uncertainties and ambiguities that arise during a transition and seek information about the change and their place in the new system. In the absence of information, the gap may be filled with inappropriate or false information, which may endanger the change process. Rumors tend to spread through the grapevine faster than accurate information can be disseminated through official channels. A manager should always be sensitive to the effects of uncertainty on employees, especially during a period of change; any news, even bad news, seems better than no news.

Reward Contributors

Although this last point is simple, it can easily be neglected. Employees who contribute to the change in any way need to be rewarded. Too often the only people acknowledged after a change effort are those who tried to stop it. Those who quickly grasp new work assignments, work harder to cover what otherwise may not get done during the transition, or help others adjust to changes deserve special credit: perhaps a mention in a news release or the internal company newspaper, special consideration in a performance appraisal, a merit raise, or a promotion. From a behavioral perspective, individuals need to benefit in some way if they are to willingly help change something that eliminates the old, comfortable way of doing the job.

In the current dynamic environment, managers must anticipate the need for change and satisfy it with more responsive and competitive organization systems. These six keys to managing organization change may also serve as general guidelines for managing organizational behavior because organizations must change or face elimination.

Synopsis

Change may be forced on an organization, or an organization may change in response to the environment or an internal need. Forces for change are interdependent and influence organizations in many ways. Currently the areas in which pressures for change seem most powerful involve people, technology, information and communication, and competition.

Planned organization change involves anticipating change and preparing for it. Lewin described organization change in terms of unfreezing, the change itself, and refreezing. In the continuous change process model, top management recognizes forces encouraging change, engages in a problem-solving process to design the change, and implements and evaluates the change.

Organization development is the process of planned change and improvement of the organization through application of knowledge of the behavioral sciences. It is based on a systematic change process and focuses on managing the culture of the organization. The most comprehensive change involves altering the organization structure through reorganization of departments, reporting relationships, or authority systems.

Quality-of-work-life programs focus on providing a work environment in which employees can satisfy individual needs. Task and technological changes alter the way the organization accomplishes its primary tasks. Along with the steps usually associated with change, task redesign entails diagnosis, cost-benefit analysis, formulation of a redesign strategy, and implementation of supplemental changes.

Frequently used group and individual approaches to organization change are training and management development programs, team building, and survey feedback techniques. Training programs are usually designed to improve employees' job skills, help employees adapt to other organization changes, or develop employees' awareness and understanding of problems such as workplace safety or stress. Management development programs attempt to foster in current or future managers the skills, abilities, and perspectives important to good management. Team-building programs are designed to help a work team or group develop into a mature, functioning team by helping it define its goals or priorities, analyze its tasks and the way they are performed, and examine relationships among the people doing the work. As used in the organization development process, survey feedback techniques involve gathering data, analyzing and summarizing them, and returning them to employees and groups for discussion and to identify and solve problems.

Resistance to change may arise from several organizational and individual sources. Resistance may indicate a legitimate concern that the change is not good for the organization and may warrant a reexamination of plans.

To manage change in organizations, managers should take a holistic view of the organization and start small. Top management support is needed, and those most affected by the change must participate. Open communication is important, and those who contribute to the change effort should be rewarded.

Discussion Questions

1. Is most organization change forced on the organization by external factors or fostered from within? Explain.

2. What broad category of pressures for organization change other than the four discussed in the chapter can you think of? Briefly describe it.

3. Which sources of resistance to change present the most problems for an internal change agent? For an external change agent?

4. Which stage of the Lewin model of change do you think is most often overlooked? Why?

5. What are the advantages and disadvantages of having an internal rather than an external change agent?

6. How does organization development differ from organization change?

7. How and why would organization development differ if the elements of the social system were not interdependent?

8. Do quality-of-work-life programs rely more on individual or organizational aspects of organizational behavior? Why?

9. Describe how the job of your professor could be redesigned. Include a discussion of other subsystems that would need to be changed as a result.

10. Which of the six keys for successfully managing an organizational change effort seem the most difficult to manage? Why?

Organizational Behavior Case for Discussion

Change of Direction at Schwab

Charles Schwab Company has long provided individual investors with an alternative to traditional investment firms. Unlike its Wall Street competitors, Schwab does not give investment advice; it merely facilitates trades chosen by the investors themselves. Schwab also has no investments of its own and does not employ any commissioned brokers, so there is no conflict of interest; the company is free to concentrate on each investor's needs. This unique philosophy has made Schwab a leader in its industry—that is, until now. Due to the bear market and a post-Enron loss of investor confidence, the number of daily trades executed by the firm was down 18 percent from the previous year, causing Schwab to lay off 6,000 workers in 2001. In the face of these challenges, Schwab, known as a company that thrives on change, is making an abrupt departure from business as usual.

Every investment firm has suffered in this age of lowered expectations and distrust, but Schwab has been hit especially hard. Other investment banks have institutional trades, merger and acquisition involvement, and other types of financial transactions to provide ongoing funds when one area dries up, but stock trades are Schwab's only business. Schwab's past success has led to another problem. As the company grew during the boom years, it added workers, bought servers, and opened more facilities, all of which led to higher costs. Unfortunately, the firm's greatest spending spree occurred just before the stock market bubble burst, leaving an unfavorable cost structure.

After having relinquished more and more leadership to co-CEO David Pottruck in the previous months, the crisis brought founder and co-CEO Charles Schwab back. One of Schwab's first moves was to return the company to making money the old-fashioned way: by raising prices and lowering costs. The firm is introducing higher fees for customers who do not trade very often so that high-volume customers will no longer have to subsidize them. "We feel very strongly about our heritage of helping people become investors and teaching people how to invest," Pottruck says, "but there is a tension in that, because it's also very expensive." The firm is also making its website more easily accessible, which should encourage customers to make more trades online rather than through a costly phone system.

Offering advice is perhaps the biggest change yet because it comes close to changing Charles Schwab's vision of an investment firm focused on the needs of clients, with no conflicts of interest. The company has developed a computerized stock analysis program that will compare each investor's risk profile and current holdings against a list of recommended stocks and then notify the customer of any suggested changes. Charles Schwab insists that the firm will still be differentiated from competitors because the advice will be free of bias. The program builds on the expertise of Schwab's financial advisers, so it will be a low-cost way to increase customer service. And customer service is sorely needed at discounter Schwab. One perplexing problem has been finding a way to keep customers who, although they started small with Schwab's discount trading system, have increased their wealth significantly. When they can pay for more sophisticated support, they often abandon Schwab and move up to a full-service investment firm.

Moreover, as Schwab shifts closer to the full-service sector of the industry, it will begin competing against heavyweights such as Merrill Lynch and Fidelity for a shrinking number of investors. As *Fortune* writer Fred Vogelstein explains, "It is true that Schwab's advantage is that it is building a new business rather than trying to dismantle an old one. That's the problem facing the full-service brokerages, which understand full well that their commission-based pay structure is ultimately untenable. Pottruck likens it to the choice between adding ten stories to a building or taking ten stories away. He believes adding is less risky to the underlying structure than taking away."

The change presents a new set of challenges for Schwab employees as well as for Charles Schwab and Pottruck. Maintaining a harmonious relationship has been problematic for the two CEOs in the past, with Pottruck threatening to quit if Schwab did not share more of the decision-making power. Pottruck changed his management style, too, shedding his aggressive, edgy, "East Coast" approach to appeal to Schwab's more laid-back West Coast workers. Still ahead for the firm is the task of inspiring workers to adapt to the changes while preserving Schwab's unique culture. Schwab chief information officer Dawn Lepore believes the company's vision of "no conflicts of interest" remains intact and inspiring to employees. "People will work for money, but they'll give a piece of their lives for meaning," she maintains.

Case Questions

1. What are the forces for change at Charles Schwab? (Hint: Use Table 15.1 on page 393 for ideas.) Name specific examples from the case that fit within each category.

2. What types of resistance to change is Schwab experiencing? (Hint: Use Table 15.3 on page 406.) Give specific examples. Consider the behavior of both Schwab employees and Schwab customers.

3. Based on your answers to questions 1 and 2, what are some actions Schwab leaders could undertake to attempt to either support the forces for change or overcome the resistance to change? Are those actions likely to be successful? Why or why not?

References: "June 2002 Monthly Report," Charles Schwab Company website, aboutschwab.com on June 20, 2002; Fred Vogelstein, "Can Schwab Get Its Mojo Back?" *Fortune*, September 17, 2001, pp. 93–98 (see www.fortune.com); Clinton Wilder, "Leaders of the Net Era," *InformationWeek*, November 27, 2000. pp. 44–56 (quotation) (see www.informationweek.com); Kathleen Melymuka, "Taking Stock," *Computerworld*, June 26, 2000, pp. 66–69 (see www.computerworld.com); Jerry Useem, "Internet Defense Strategy: Cannibalize Yourself," *Fortune*, September 6, 1999. pp. 121–134 (see www.fortune.com).

Experiencing Organizational Behavior

Planning a Change at the University

Purpose: This exercise will help you understand the complexities of change in organizations.

Format: Your task is to plan the implementation of a major change in an organization.

Procedure:

Part 1

The class will divide into five groups of approximately equal size. Your instructor will assign each group one of the following changes:

1. A change from the semester system to the quarter system (or the opposite, depending on the school's current system)
2. A requirement that all work—homework, examinations, term papers, problem sets—be done on computer and submitted via computers
3. A requirement that all students live on campus
4. A requirement that all students have reading, writing, and speaking fluency in at least three languages, including English and Japanese, to graduate
5. A requirement that all students room with someone in the same major

First, decide what individuals and groups must be involved in the change process. Then decide how the change will be implemented using Lewin's process of organization change (Figure 15.1) as a framework. Consider how to deal with resistance to change, using Tables 15.3 and 15.4 as guides. Decide whether a change agent (internal or external) should be used. Develop a realistic timetable for full implementation of the change. Is transition management appropriate?

Part 2

Using the same groups as in Part 1, your next task is to describe the techniques you would use to implement the change described in Part 1. You may use structural changes, task and technology methods, group and individual programs, or any combination of these. You may need to go to the library to gather more information on some techniques. You should also discuss how you would utilize the six keys to successful change management discussed at the end of the chapter.

Your instructor may make this exercise an in-class project, but it is also a good semester-ending project for groups to work on outside class. Either way, the exercise is most beneficial when groups report their implementation programs to the entire class. Each group should report on which change techniques are to be used, why they were selected, how they will be implemented, and how problems will be avoided.

Follow-up Questions

Part 1

1. How similar were the implementation steps for each change?
2. Were the plans for managing resistance to change realistic?
3. Do you think any of the changes could be successfully implemented at your school? Why or why not?

Part 2

1. Did various groups use the same technique in different ways or to accomplish different goals?
2. If you did outside research on organization development techniques for your project, did you find any techniques that seemed more applicable than those in this chapter? If so, describe one of these techniques.

Self-Assessment Exercise

Support for Change

Introduction: The following questions are designed to help people understand the level of support or opposition to change within an organization. Scores on this scale should be used for classroom discussion only.

Instructions: Think of an organization for which you have worked in the past or an organization to which you currently belong and consider the situation when a change was imposed at some point in the recent past. Then circle the number that best represents your feeling about each statement or question.

1. **Values and Vision**
   (Do people throughout the organization share values or vision?)

   1   2   3   4   5   6   7
   Low   High

2. **History of Change**
   (Does the organization have a good track record in handling change?)

   1   2   3   4   5   6   7
   Low   High

3. **Cooperation and Trust**
   (Do they seem high throughout the organization?)

   1   2   3   4   5   6   7
   Low   High

4. **Culture**
   (Is it one that supports risk taking and change?)

   1   2   3   4   5   6   7
   Low   High

5. **Resilience**
   (Can people handle more?)

   1   2   3   4   5   6   7
   Low   High

6. **Rewards**
   (Will this change be seen as beneficial?)

   1   2   3   4   5   6   7
   Low   High

7. **Respect and Face**
   (Will people be able to maintain dignity and self-respect?)

   1   2   3   4   5   6   7
   Low   High

8. **Status Quo**
   (Will this change be seen as mild?)

   1   2   3   4   5   6   7
   Low   High

A Guide to Scoring and explanation is available in the *Instructor's Resource Manual*.

Reference: From Rick Maurer, *Beyond the Wall of Resistance*, 1996 (Austin: Bard Press), pp. 104–105. Used by permission of Rick Maurer.

OB Online

1. Use any available search engine to look up two of the companies that are discussed in this chapter as being involved in making organizational changes (Vivendi, Avon, Schwab, Nokia, Motorola). Visit the companies' websites and utilize any of several databases that have magazine, newspaper, and journal articles.

2. Create an update report on these companies describing how well the changes have worked, whether the companies have continued the changes, and whether they have made even more changes.

Building Managerial Skills

Exercise Overview: Many organizations utilize surveys to assess the needs and concerns of their employees. On the basis of the results of such surveys, many companies make significant organizational changes. This exercise will help you understand more about organizational surveys.

Exercise Background: Your organization has a new CEO who has been brought in to make changes. Her first priority is to survey all employees to find out what they think about the company, what they want from the company, and what their needs and concerns are.

Exercise Task: You have been assigned to find several organizational surveys that your company could use.

Search the Internet for resources that might help you find several different surveys and other related resources. Describe the kinds of information you were able to locate and explain its likely value to you. Finally, respond to the following questions:

1. What information would you need in addition to that found on the Internet to actually use one of the surveys that you found?
2. How would the type of survey you use differ if you worked for a large, multinational company versus a small manufacturing company with employees at only one location?

TEST PREPPER

ACE self-test

You have read the chapter and studied the key terms, and the exam is any day now. Think you're ready to ace it? Take this sample test to gauge your comprehension of chapter material. You can check your answers at the back of the book. Want more test questions? Visit the student website at http://college.hmco.com/business/students/ (select Griffin/Moorhead, Fundamentals of Organizational Behavior 1e) and take the ACE quizzes for more practice.

1. **T F** The median age of the U.S. population has gradually increased because of the advancing age of the baby boomers.

2. **T F** Technology is changing, but the rate of technological change is decreasing.

3. **T F** Advances in information processing and communication have paralleled each other.

4. **T F** The best approach to change is to respond to external forces that impose change on the organization.

5. **T F** In Lewin's model of change, organizations first freeze, then unfreeze, then refreeze.

6. **T F** A change agent is usually a government employee charged with ensuring the change effort stays within the bounds of the law.

7. **T F** Organizational development consists primarily of spontaneous change efforts.

8. **T F** Structural changes are the most comprehensive type of organizational change.

9. **T F** Quality-of-work-life programs focus strongly on providing a work environment conducive to satisfying individual needs.

10. **T F** Task redesign and technological change are essentially identical.

11. **T F** When job changes are being considered, it is important to evaluate the organization structure in which the jobs exist.

12. **T F** Stress management programs are a popular people-oriented approach to organization development.

13. **T F** Management development programs have been scientifically proven to increase organizational effectiveness.

14. **T F** One common goal of team building is to set team goals and priorities.

15. **T F** Team building usually can be started and finished in a one-time experience undertaken at a retreat from the workplace.

16. **T F** The survey feedback technique involves holding feedback meetings, first with top managers, then with employees throughout the organization.

17. **T F** Resistance to change is inevitable, regardless of how well the change effort is planned and implemented.

18. **T F** The term *overdetermination* means the structure of the organization produces resistance to change because it was designed to maintain stability.

19. **T F** The ideal way to implement a change is to start big and get everyone on board at once rather than starting small and risking increased resistance.

20. **T F** Often the only people acknowledged after a change are those who tried to stop it.

21. The areas in which pressures for change appear most powerful involve all of the following except
    a. people.
    b. government.
    c. information processing.
    d. competition.
    e. technology.

22. Advances in which two areas of change are most closely related?
    a. People and government
    b. Information processing and communication
    c. Technology and competition
    d. Competition and people
    e. Government and information processing

23. Competition is not a new force for change, but it has some significant new twists, including all of the following except
    a. fixed currency exchange rates.
    b. international markets.
    c. trade agreements.
    d. booming industries of developing nations.
    e. the Internet.

24. After adopting a new strategy, managers at Forge, Inc., want to ensure that the new behaviors accompanying the change remain relatively permanent and resistant to further change. These managers will have to enter which step of Lewin's process model of change?
    a. Continuity   d. Unfreezing
    b. Freezing   e. Implementation
    c. Leading

25. What is one problem in using an internal change agent for overseeing the change effort?
    a. An internal agent is usually too expensive.

415

   b. An internal agent is less likely to become a collaborator than is an external agent.

   c. An internal agent is less likely to know the organization's tasks and political situations.

   d. An internal agent may be too close to the situation to view it objectively.

   e. An internal agent may abandon the change effort prematurely.

26. The final step of the continuous change process model is

   a. measurement, evaluation, and control.

   b. appointment of a change agent.

   c. implementation of the change.

   d. defining goals and objectives.

   e. recognition of the need for change.

27. Organization development is a specific process with three critical elements. Which of the following elements are not part of organizational development?

   a. Planned change

   b. Intended organizational improvement

   c. Focus on defeating the competition

   d. Application of knowledge from the behavioral sciences

   e. All of the above elements are part of organization development.

28. At Royce Company, managers want to improve employees' attitudes toward the organization to increasing productivity and organizational effectiveness. These managers ought to consider which form of organization development?

   a. Reengineering

   b. Structural change

   c. Task redesign

   d. Management development programs

   e. Quality-of-work-life programs

29. Training, management development programs, team building, and survey feedback are all

   a. organizationwide change efforts.

   b. people-oriented changes.

   c. task and technological changes.

   d. structural changes.

   e. All of the above are correct.

30. The use of survey feedback techniques in an organization development process differs from their use in traditional attitude surveys. What is one major difference?

   a. Respondents in traditional attitude surveys remain anonymous.

   b. Respondents in survey feedback techniques are paid for their participation.

   c. Responses in survey feedback techniques are summarized and then shared in group sessions.

   d. Most responses in traditional attitude surveys are eliminated because of errors.

   e. Change agents manage the traditional attitude survey process.

31. Which of the following should you know about resistance to change?

   a. Resistance is inevitable.

   b. Resistance can be used for the benefit of the organization.

   c. All resistance does not necessarily need to be overcome.

   d. Resistance may alert the organization to reexamine the change.

   e. All of the above are important to know about resistance to change.

32. Which of the following is not an organizational source of resistance?

   a. Overdetermination

   b. Group inertia

   c. Fear of the unknown

   d. Changes in resource allocation

   e. Narrow focus of change

33. Why do some employees lack awareness of a change?

   a. It doesn't support their point of view and they may not have even noticed it.

   b. It makes them fear the unknown.

   c. It goes against their established habits of doing things.

   d. It makes them feel insecure.

   e. It threatens their core expertise.

34. Which of the following is not a key to successfully managing change in organizations?

   a. Take a holistic view.

   b. Encourage participation.

   c. Secure top management support.

   d. Punish resistance to change.

   e. Foster open communication.

35. Peter Senge claims that every truly successful change in large organizations starts small. Why is starting small a good idea?

   a. The change can easily be abandoned.

   b. Multiple change efforts can be started simultaneously.

   c. Every person in the organization can take that small first step at the same time.

   d. Competitors won't be aware of the change effort until it's well along.

   e. When others see the benefits of the change, they automatically drop their resistance and join in voluntarily.

The process of creating a business organization is similar to planting a garden. The gardener must decide how to group the plants, where to put the pathways, and how to support the plants as they grow. The managers of a business organization must make similar decisions regarding how to organize the business. As with a garden, if a business isn't organized in a coherent manner, it will quickly get out of control and its productivity will greatly diminish.

One of the biggest challenges for most businesses is to decide the best way to organize. The four most common ways to organize is around function, product, customer served, or geographic location. In a functional structure, employees are organized by function, such as operations, marketing, and finance. This type of structure makes sense when a firm sells a uniform product or group of products. In a product structure, employees are organized by product. For example, a bakery that produces a variety of products might organize employees in areas such as bread production, cookie production, and pastry production. A customer structure is appropriate for a company that sells to distinct customer segments such as consumers, businesses, schools, and government. In this case, the firm would organize its employees around the customer groups they serve. Finally, a geographic location structure applies mainly to firms with multinational operations. For example, a firm may do business in the United States, Japan, and Europe, and organize its employees around the specific geographic location they serve.

An appropriate structure allows a firm to organize its employees in a way that allows them to be as efficient and effective as possible and stay focused on a specific outcome. An example of a firm that has benefited from this approach is General Mills. Like many companies with multiple brands, General Mills is organized along product lines. Its products are brands most people recognize, such as Yoplait, Pillsbury, Green Giant, and Betty Crocker. Individual employees are assigned to specific product divisions, such as the Yoplait or Betty Crocker division. Although this approach has worked well, General Mills has added a twist to its method of organizing by having employees work in different divisions occasionally. The company does this to keep employees fresh and to allow employees from one division to observe the innovations taking place in other divisions.

General Mills also encourages its employees to look for innovations in organization structure and design outside the firm. For example, in one General Mills cake factory, the operators have to periodically "change over" all their equipment to convert from making white cake mix to chocolate cake mix. (Can you imagine getting the chocolate cake mix out of all the pipes and other equipment?) The process routinely takes seven to eight hours. One employee said, "You know, I've seen the NASCAR events and I don't know how those people gas up, change tires, and give water to the driver in 30 seconds—if we could do that, then maybe we could figure out how to make our changeovers quicker." In response to this observation, the factory flew a number of its employees to NASCAR events to observe pit crews in action. Picking up on some of the practices the pit crews use, the operators of the cake factory were able to significantly cut down on changeover time. In fact, in one case, they reduced an 8-hour changeover to 20 minutes!

Like a garden, businesses must be organized and structured to allow them to reach their full potential. The key is to select an organization structure that is consistent with the business's needs, skills, and ultimate objectives.

Case Questions

1. Find an example of a company that is organized by (a) function, (b) customer served, and (c) geographic location. Explain why the structure each company employs does or does not make sense for that particular company.

2. According to the case, General Mills is organized around product. Do you think this is the best way for General Mills to organize? What would happen if General Mills decided to organize around function instead of product?

3. Over time, will an organization's structure stay the same, or is it likely to change? What factors cause an organization's structure to change?

4. Suppose a friend just started her own computer software firm but didn't know anything about how to "structure" her organization. If she asked you, "What is the most important thing I should be thinking about in selecting a structure for my organization," what would you tell her?

References: R. L. Daft, *Organization Theory and Design* (Cincinnati: South-Western, 2003); J. R. Galbraith, *Designing Organizations: An Executive Briefing on Strategy, Structure, and Process* (New York: Jossey-Bass, 1995).

ENDNOTES

Chapter 1

1. For a classic discussion of the meaning of *organizational behavior*, see Larry Cummings, "Toward Organizational Behavior," *Academy of Management Review*, January 1978, pp. 90–98.
2. Daniel A. Wren, *The Evolution of Management Thought*, 4th ed. (New York: Wiley, 1994), Chapters 1 and 2. See also Stephen J. Carroll and Dennis A. Gillen, "Are the Classical Management Functions Useful in Describing Managerial Work?" *Academy of Management Review*, January 1987, pp. 38–51; and Daniel A. Wren, "Management History: Issues and Ideas for Teaching and Research," *Journal of Management*, Summer 1987, pp. 339–350.
3. Frederick W. Taylor, *Principles of Scientific Management* (New York: Harper, 1911).
4. See "The Line Starts Here," *Wall Street Journal*, January 11, 1999, pp. R25–R28.
5. For critical analyses, see Charles D. Wrege and Amedeo G. Perroni, "Taylor's Pig-Tale: A Historical Analysis of Frederick W. Taylor's Pig-Iron Experiment," *Academy of Management Journal*, March 1974, pp. 6–27; and Charles D. Wrege and Ann Marie Stoka, "Cooke Creates a Classic: The Story Behind Taylor's Principles of Scientific Management," *Academy of Management Review*, October 1978, pp. 736–749. For a more favorable review, see Edwin A. Locke, "The Ideas of Frederick W. Taylor: An Evaluation," *Academy of Management Review*, January 1982, pp. 14–24. See Oliver E. Allen, "'This Great Mental Revolution,'" *Audacity*, Summer 1996, pp. 52–61, for a discussion of the practical value of Taylor's work.
6. Max Weber, *Theory of Social and Economic Organization*, trans. A. M. Henderson and T. Parsons (London: Oxford University Press, 1921).
7. Hugo Münsterberg, *Psychology and Industrial Efficiency* (Boston: Houghton Mifflin, 1913); Wren, *Evolution of Management Thought*. See also Frank J. Landy, "Hugo Münsterberg: Victim or Visionary?" *Journal of Applied Psychology*, vol. 77, no. 6 (1992), pp. 787–802; and Frank J. Landy, "Early Influences on the Development of Industrial and Organizational Psychology," *Journal of Applied Psychology*, vol. 82, no. 4 (1997), pp. 467–477.
8. Elton Mayo, *The Human Problems of Industrial Civilization* (New York: Macmillan, 1933); Fritz J. Roethlisberger and William J. Dickson, *Management and the Worker* (Cambridge, MA.: Harvard University Press, 1939).
9. Alex Carey, "The Hawthorne Studies: A Radical Criticism," *American Sociological Review*, June 1967, pp. 403–416; Lyle Yorks and David A. Whitsett, "Hawthorne, Topeka, and the Issue of Science Versus Advocacy in Organizational Behavior," *Academy of Management Review*, January 1985, pp. 21–30.
10. Douglas McGregor, *The Human Side of Enterprise* (New York: McGraw-Hill, 1960); Abraham Maslow, "A Theory of Human Motivation," *Psychological Review*, July 1943, pp. 370–396. See also Paul R. Lawrence, "Historical Development of Organizational Behavior," in Jay W. Lorsch, ed., *Handbook of Organizational Behavior* (Englewood Cliffs, NJ: Prentice Hall, 1987), pp. 1–9.
11. See "Conversation with Lyman W. Porter," *Organizational Dynamics*, Winter 1990, pp. 69–79.
12. Jeffrey Pfeiffer and John F. Veiga, "Putting People First for Organizational Success," *Academy of Management Executive*, vol. 13, no. 2 (1999), pp. 37–48. See also Richard Chase and Sriram Dasu, "Want to Perfect Your Company's Service? Use Behavioral Science," *Harvard Business Review*, June 2001, pp. 79–89.
13. See Fremont Kast and James Rosenzweig, eds., *Contingency Views of Organization and Management* (Chicago: Scientific Research Associates, 1973), for a classic overview and introduction.
14. James Terborg, "Interactional Psychology and Research on Human Behavior in Organizations," *Academy of Management Review*, October 1981, pp. 569–576; Benjamin Schneider, "Interactional Psychology and Organizational Behavior," in Larry Cummings and Barry Staw, eds., *Research in Organizational Behavior* (Greenwich, CT: JAI Press, 1983), vol. 5, pp. 1–32; Daniel B. Turban and Thomas L. Keon, "Organizational Attractiveness: An Interactionist Perspective," *Journal of Applied Psychology*, vol. 78, no. 2 (1993), pp. 184–193.
15. Henry Mintzberg, "Rounding Out the Manager's Job," *Sloan Management Review*, Fall 1994, pp. 11–26. See also "All in a Day's Work," *Harvard Business Review*, December 2001, pp. 55–60.
16. Brian Dumaine, "The New Non-Manager Managers," *Fortune*, February 22, 1993, pp. 80–84. See also "In Praise of Middle Managers," *Harvard Business Review*, September 2001, pp. 72–81.
17. Mauro F. Guillen, "The Age of Eclecticism: Current Organizational Trends and the Evolution of Managerial Models," *Sloan Management Review*, Fall 1994, pp. 75–86.
18. John P. Kotter, "What Effective General Managers Really Do," *Harvard Business Review*, March–April 1999, pp. 145–159. See also David H. Freedman, "Is Management Still a Science?" *Harvard Business Review*, November–December 1992, pp. 26–38.
19. For an overview of the management process, see Ricky W. Griffin, *Fundamentals of Management*, 4th ed. (Boston: Houghton Mifflin, 2006).
20. Henry Mintzberg, "The Manager's Job: Folklore and Fact," *Harvard Business Review*, July–August 1975, pp. 49–61.
21. Robert L. Katz, "The Skills of an Effective Administrator," *Harvard*

Business Review, September–October 1987, pp. 90–102.

22. Rahul Jacob, "The Struggle to Create an Organization for the 21st Century," *Fortune*, April 3, 1995, pp. 90–99; Susan Sonnesyn Brooks, "Managing a Horizontal Revolution," *HRMagazine*, June 1995, pp. 52–57.

23. For an overview, see Ricky W. Griffin and Michael W. Pustay, *International Business—A Managerial Perspective*, 4th ed. (Upper Saddle River, NJ: Prentice Hall, 2005).

24. David M. Messick and Max H. Bazerman, "Ethical Leadership and the Psychology of Decision Making," *Sloan Management Review*, Winter 1996, pp. 9–22.

Chapter 2

1. R. Roosevelt Thomas, Jr., "Redefining Diversity," *HRFOCUS*, April 1996, pp. 6–7.

2. Ibid.

3. Jeremy Kahn, "Diversity Trumps the Downturn," *Fortune*, July 9, 2001, pp. 114–116.

4. "America's 50 Best Companies for Minorities," *Fortune*, July 9, 2001, pp. 122–128.

5. "Diversity Today: Developing and Retaining the Best Corporate Talent," *Fortune*, June 21, 1999, pp. S2–S4.

6. Michael L. Wheeler, "Diversity: Making the Business Case," *Business-Week*, December 9, 1996, special advertising section.

7. Elaine Carter, Elaine Kepner, Malcolm Shaw, and William Brooks Woodson, "The Effective Management of Diversity," *S.A.M. Advanced Management Journal*, Autumn 1982, pp. 49–53.

8. Marilyn Loden and Judy B. Rosener, *Workforce America! Managing Employee Diversity as a Vital Resource* (Homewood, IL: Business One Irwin, 1991), pp. 58–62.

9. Ibid., p. 60.

10. Ibid., pp. 68–70.

11. Howard N. Fullerton, Jr., and Mitra Toossi, "Labor Force Projections to 2010: Steady Growth and Changing Composition," *Monthly Labor Review*, November 2001, pp. 21–38.

12. Ibid., p. 22.

13. Michael Crawford, "The New Office Etiquette," *Canadian Business*, May 1993, pp. 22–31.

14. Harish C. Jain and Anil Verma, "Managing Workforce Diversity for Competitiveness: The Canadian Experience," *International Journal of Manpower*, April–May 1996, pp. 14–30.

15. "Plenty of Muck, Not Much Money," *The Economist*, May 8, 1999, p. 52.

16. Barry Louis Rubin, "Europeans Value Diversity," *HRMagazine*, January 1991, pp. 38–41, 78.

17. Ron Corben, "Thailand Faces a Shrinking Work Force," *Journal of Commerce and Commercial Transactions*, December 26, 1996, p. 5a.

18. Martha Irvine, "EEOC Sues Illinois Company Over 'English-Only' Policy," *Legal Intelligence*, September 2, 1999, p. 4.

19. Wheeler, "Diversity: Making the Business Case."

20. Lennie Copeland, "Making the Most of Cultural Differences at the Workplace," *Personnel*, June 1988, pp. 52–60.

21. M. J. Gent, "Theory X in Antiquity, or the Bureaucratization of the Roman Army," *Business Horizons*, January–February 1984, pp. 53–54.

22. "Saybolt Inc. Pleads Guilty and Is Fined $1.5 Million for Bribery of Panamanian Officials, Reports U.S Attorney," *PR Newswire*, January 21, 1999.

23. Henry W. Lane and Joseph J. DiStefano, *International Management Behavior* (Ontario: Nelson, 1988).

24. Brian O'Reilly, "Your New Global Workforce," *Fortune*, December 14, 1992, pp. 58–66.

25. Christopher Knowlton, "What America Makes Best," *Fortune*, March 28, 1988, pp. 40–54.

26. Alex Taylor III, "Why GM Leads the Pack in Europe," *Fortune*, May 17, 1993, pp. 83–86.

27. Richard M. Steers and Edwin L. Miller, "Management in the 1990s: The International Challenge," *Academy of Management Executive*, February 1988, pp. 21–22.

28. Simcha Ronen and Oded Shenkar, "Clustering Countries on Attitudinal Dimension: A Review and Synthesis," *Academy of Management Review*, July 1985, pp. 435–454.

29. Nancy J. Adler, Robert Doktor, and Gordon Redding, "From the Atlantic to the Pacific Century," *Journal of Management*, Summer 1986, pp. 295–318.

30. Brian O'Reilly, "Japan's Uneasy U.S. Managers," *Fortune*, April 25, 1988, pp. 245–264.

31. "Learning to Accept Cultural Diversity," *Wall Street Journal*, September 12, 1990, pp. B1, B9.

32. Tamotsu Yamaguchi, "The Challenge of Internationalization," *Academy of Management Executive*, February 1988, pp. 33–36.

33. Geert Hofstede, *Culture's Consequences: International Differences in Work-Related Values* (Beverly Hills: Sage Publications, 1980).

34. Loden and Rosener, *Workforce America!*, p. 19.

35. Fullerton and Toossi, "Labor Force Projections to 2010," p. 36.

36. Sar A. Levitan, "Older Workers in Today's Economy," presentation at the Textbook Author's Conference, Washington, DC, October 21, 1992.

37. Beverly Hynes-Grace, "To Thrive, Not Merely Survive," presentation at the Textbook Author's Conference, Washington, DC, October 21, 1992.

38. Ibid.

39. Wheeler, "Diversity: Making the Business Case."

40. Charlene Marmer Soloman, "The Corporate Response to Workforce Diversity," *Personnel Journal*, August 1989, pp. 42–54.

41. Susan Faludi, *Backlash: The Undeclared War Against American Women* (New York: Doubleday, 1991).

42. Loden and Rosener, *Workforce America!*, pp. 85–86.

43. Richard L. Drach, "Making Reasonable Accommodations Under the ADA," *Employment Relations Today*, Summer 1992, pp. 167–175.

44. Toby B. Gooley, "Ready, Willing and Able!" *Traffic Management*, October 1993, pp. 63–67.

45. Thomas A. Stewart, "Gay in Corporate America," *Fortune*, December 16, 1991, pp. 42–56.

46. Ibid., p. 45.

47. Wheeler, "Diversity: Making the Business Case."

48. André Laurent, "The Cultural Diversity of Western Conceptions of Management," *International Studies of Management and Organization*, Spring–Summer 1983, pp. 75–96.

49. O'Reilly, "Your New Global Workforce"; Richard I. Kirkland, Jr., "Europe's New Managers," *Fortune*, September 29, 1986, pp. 56–60.

50. Bill Leonard, "Ways to Make Diversity Programs Work," *HRMagazine*, April 1991, pp. 37–39, 98.

51. Taylor H. Cox and Stacy Blake, "Managing Cultural Diversity: Implications for Organizational Competitiveness," *Academy of Management Executive*, August 1991, pp. 45–56.

52. Taylor H. Cox, "The Multicultural Organizational," *Academy of Management Executive*, May 1991, pp. 34–47.

53. Ibid., p. 42.

Chapter 3

1. Lynn McGarlane Shore and Lois Tetrick, "The Psychological Contract as an Explanatory Framework in the Employment Relationship," in C. L. Cooper and D. M. Rousseau, eds., *Trends in Organizational Behavior* (London: John Wiley & Sons Ltd., 1994).

2. Elizabeth Wolfe Morrison and Sandra L. Robinson, "When Employees Feel Betrayed: A Model of How Psychological Contract Violation Develops," *Academy of Management Review*, January 1997, pp. 226–256.

3. Lawrence Pervin, "Personality," in Mark Rosenzweig and Lyman Porter, eds., *Annual Review of Psychology*, Vol. 36 (Palo Alto, CA: Annual Reviews, 1985), pp. 83–114; S. R. Maddi, *Personality Theories: A Comparative Analysis*, 4th ed. (Homewood, IL: Dorsey, 1980).

4. L. R. Goldberg, "An Alternative 'Description of Personality': The Big Five Factor Structure," *Journal of Personality and Social Psychology*, vol. 59, no. 5,(1990), pp. 1216–1229.

5. Michael K. Mount, Murray R. Barrick, and J. Perkins Strauss, "Validity of Observer Ratings of the Big Five Personality Factors," *Journal of Applied Psychology*, vol. 79, no. 2 (1994), pp. 272–280; Tomothy A. Judge, Joseph J.

Martocchio, and Carl J. Thoreson, "Five-Factor Model of Personality and Employee Absence," *Journal of Applied Psychology*, vol. 82, no. 5 (1997), pp. 745–755.

6. J. B. Rotter, "Generalized Expectancies for Internal vs. External Control of Reinforcement," *Psychological Monographs*, vol. 80 (1966), pp. 1–28; see also Simon S. K. Lam and John Schaubroeck, "The Role of Locus of Control in Reactions to Being Promoted and to Being Passed Over: A Quasi Experiment," *Academy of Management Journal*, vol. 43, no. 1 (2000), pp. 66–78.

7. Marilyn E. Gist and Terence R. Mitchell, "Self-Efficacy: A Theoretical Analysis of Its Determinants and Malleability," *Academy of Management Review*, April 1992, pp. 183–211.

8. T. W. Adorno, E. Frenkel-Brunswick, D. J. Levinson, and R. N. Sanford, *The Authoritarian Personality* (New York: Harper & Row, 1950).

9. "The Rise and Fall of Dennis Kozlowski," *BusinessWeek*, December 23, 2002, pp. 64–77.

10. Jon L. Pierce, Donald G. Gardner, and Larry L. Cummings, "Organization-Based Self-Esteem: Construct Definition, Measurement, and Validation," *Academy of Management Journal*, vol. 32, no. 3, (1989), pp. 622–648.

11. Michael Harris Bond and Peter B. Smith, "Cross-Cultural Social and Organizational Psychology," in Janet Spence, ed., *Annual Review of Psychology*, vol. 47 (Palo Alto, CA: Annual Reviews, 1996), pp. 205–235.

12. See Daniel Goleman, *Emotional Intelligence: Why It Can Matter More Than IQ* (New York: Bantam Books, 1995).

13. Daniel Goleman, "Leadership That Gets Results," *Harvard Business Review*, March–April 2000, pp. 78–90.

14. Leon Festinger, *A Theory of Cognitive Dissonance* (Palo Alto, CA: Stanford University Press, 1957).

15. See John J. Clancy, "Is Loyalty Really Dead?" *Across the Board*, June 1999, pp. 15–19.

16. Patricia C. Smith, L. M. Kendall, and Charles Hulin, *The Measurement of Satisfaction in Work and Behavior* (Chicago: Rand-McNally, 1969).

17. "Companies Are Finding Real Payoffs in Aiding Employee Satisfaction," *Wall Street Journal*, October 11, 2000, p. B1.

18. James R. Lincoln, "Employee Work Attitudes and Management Practice in the U.S. and Japan: Evidence from a Large Comparative Study," *California Management Review*, Fall 1989, pp. 89–106.

19. For research work in this area, see Jennifer M. George and Gareth R. Jones, "The Experience of Mood and Turnover Intentions: Interactive Effects of Value Attainment, Job Satisfaction, and Positive Mood," *Journal of Applied Psychology*, vol. 81, no. 3 (1996), pp. 318–325; Larry J. Williams, Mark B. Gavin, and Margaret Williams, "Measurement and Nonmeasurement Processes with Negative Affectivity and Employee Attitudes," *Journal of Applied Psychology*, vol. 81, no. 1 (1996), pp. 88–101.

20. Kathleen Sutcliffe, "What Executives Notice: Accurate Perceptions in Top Management Teams," *Academy of Management Journal*, vol. 37, no. 5 (1994), pp. 1360–1378.

21. For a recent overview of the stress literature, see Frank Landy, James Campbell Quick, and Stanislav Kasl, "Work, Stress, and Well-Being," *International Journal of Stress Management*, vol. 1, no. 1 (1994), pp. 33–73.

22. Hans Selye, *The Stress of Life* (New York: McGraw-Hill, 1976).

23. M. Friedman and R. H. Rosenman, *Type A Behavior and Your Heart* (New York: Alfred A. Knopf, 1974).

24. "Work & Family," *BusinessWeek*, June 28, 1993, pp. 80–88.

25. Richard S. DeFrank, Robert Konopaske, and John M. Ivancevich, "Executive Travel Stress: Perils of the Road Warrior," *Academy of Management Executive*, vol. 14, no. 2 (2000), pp. 58–67.

26. "Breaking Point," *Newsweek*, March 6, 1995, pp. 56–62.

27. John M. Kelly, "Get a Grip on Stress," *HRMagazine*, February 1997, pp. 51–58.

28. See Richard W. Woodman, John E. Sawyer, and Ricky W. Griffin,

"Toward a Theory of Organizational Creativity," *Academy of Management Review*, April 1993, pp. 293–321.

29. John Simons, "The $10 Billion Pill," *Fortune*, January 20, 2003, pp. 58–68.

30. "That's It, I'm Outa Here," *BusinessWeek*, October 3, 2000, pp. 96–98.

31. See Anne O'Leary-Kelly, Ricky W. Griffin, and David J. Glew, "Organization-Motivated Aggression: A Research Framework," *Academy of Management Review*, January 1996, pp. 225–253.

32. See Philip M. Podsakoff, Scott B. MacKenzie, Julie Beth Paine, and Daniel G. G. Bacharah, "Organizational Citizenship Behaviors: A Critical Review of the Theoretical and Empirical Literature and Suggestions for Future Research," *Journal of Management*, vol. 26, no. 3 (2000), pp. 513–563, for recent findings regarding this behavior.

33. Dennis W. Organ, "Personality and Organizational Citizenship Behavior," *Journal of Management*, vol. 20, no.2 (1994), pp. 465–478; Mary Konovsky and S. Douglas Pugh, "Citizenship Behavior and Social Exchange," *Academy of Management Journal*, vol. 37, no. 3 (1994), pp. 656–669; Jacqueline A-M. Coyle-Shapiro, "A Psychological Contract Perspective on Organizational Citizenship," *Journal of Organizational Behavior*, vol. 23, no. 6, (2000), pp. 927–946.

Chapter 4

1. See Craig Pinder, *Work Motivation in Organizational Behavior* (Upper Saddle River, NJ: Prentice Hall, 1998).

2. Richard M. Steers, Gregory A. Bigley, and Lyman W. Porter, *Motivation and Leadership at Work*, 6th ed. (New York: McGraw-Hill, 1996). See also Ruth Kanfer, "Motivational Theory and Industrial and Organizational Psychology," in M. D. Dunnette and L. M. Hough, eds., *Handbook of Industrial and Organizational Psychology*, 2nd ed., Vol. 1 (Palo Alto, CA: Consulting Psychologists Press), pp. 75–170; and M. L. Ambrose, "Old Friends, New Faces: Motivation Research in the 1990s," *Journal of Management*, vol. 25, no. 2 (1999), pp. 110–131.

3. Roland E. Kidwell, Jr., and Nathan Bennett, "Employee Propensity to Withhold Effort: A Conceptual Model to Intersect Three Avenues of Research," *Academy of Management Review*, July 1993, pp. 429–456.

4. Jeffrey Pfeiffer, *The Human Equation* (Boston: Harvard Business School Press, 1998).

5. E. L. Deci and R. M. Ryan, "The 'What' and 'Why' of Goal Pursuits: Human Needs and the Self-Determination of Behavior," *Psychological Inquiry*, vol. 11, no. 4 (2000), pp. 227–269.

6. Frederick W. Taylor, *Principles of Scientific Management* (New York: Harper, 1911).

7. Elton Mayo, *The Social Problems of an Industrial Civilization* (Boston: Harvard University Press, 1945); Fritz J. Rothlisberger and W. J. Dickson, *Management and the Worker* (Boston: Harvard University Press, 1939).

8. Gerald R. Salancik and Jeffrey Pfeiffer, "An Examination of Need-Satisfaction Models of Job Attitudes," *Administrative Science Quarterly*, September 1977, pp. 427–456.

9. Abraham H. Maslow, "A Theory of Human Motivation," *Psychological Review*, vol. 50 (1943), pp. 370–396; Abraham H. Maslow, *Motivation and Personality* (New York: Harper & Row, 1954). Maslow's most famous work includes Abraham Maslow, Deborah C. Stephens, and Gary Heil, *Maslow on Management* (New York: Wiley, 1998); and Abraham Maslow and Richard Lowry, *Toward a Psychology of Being* (New York: Wiley, 1999).

10. See Nancy Adler, *International Dimensions of Organizational Behavior*, 3rd ed. (Boston: PWS-Kent, 1997).

11. Mahmond A. Wahba and Lawrence G. Bridwell, "Maslow Reconsidered: A Review of Research on the Need Hierarchy Theory," *Organizational Behavior and Human Performance*, April 1976, pp. 212–240.

12. Clayton P. Alderfer, *Existence, Relatedness, and Growth* (New York: Free Press, 1972).

13. Ibid.

14. Frederick Herzberg, Bernard Mausner, and Barbara Synderman, *The Motivation to Work* (New York: Wiley,

1959); Frederick Herzberg, "One More Time: How Do You Motivate Employees?" *Harvard Business Review*, January–February 1968, pp. 53–62.

15. Herzberg, Mausner, and Synderman, *The Motivation to Work*.

16. Ibid.

17. Quoted in "Can Trees and Jogging Trails Lure Techies to Kansas?" *Wall Street Journal*, October 21, 1998, p. B1.

18. Herzberg, "One More Time"; Ricky W. Griffin, *Task Design: An Integrative Approach* (Glenview, IL: Scott, Foresman, 1982).

19. Pinder, *Work Motivation in Organizational Behavior*.

20. Frederick Herzberg, *Work and the Nature of Man* (Cleveland: World, 1966); Valerie M. Bookman, "The Herzberg Controversy," *Personnel Psychology*, Summer 1971, pp. 155–189; Benedict Grigaliunas and Frederick Herzberg, "Relevance in the Test of Motivation-Hygiene Theory," *Journal of Applied Psychology*, February 1971, pp. 73–79.

21. Marvin Dunnette, John Campbell, and Milton Hakel, "Factors Contributing to Job Satisfaction and Job Dissatisfaction in Six Occupational Groups," *Organizational Behavior and Human Performance*, May 1967, pp. 143–174; Charles L. Hulin and Patricia Smith, "An Empirical Investigation of Two Implications of the Two-Factor Theory of Job Satisfaction," *Journal of Applied Psychology*, October 1967, pp. 396–402.

22. Adler, *International Dimensions of Organizational Behavior*.

23. David McClelland, *The Achieving Society* (Princeton, NJ: Nostrand, 1961). See also David C. McClelland, *Human Motivation* (Cambridge, UK: Cambridge University Press, 1988).

24. Michael J. Stahl, "Achievement, Power, and Managerial Motivation: Selecting Managerial Talent with the Job Choice Exercise," *Personnel Psychology*, Winter 1983, pp. 775–790.

25. Stanley Schachter, *The Psychology of Affiliation* (Palo Alto, CA: Stanford University Press, 1959).

26. David McClelland and David H. Burnham, "Power Is the Great Motivator," *Harvard Business Review*, March–April 1976, pp. 100–110.

27. Pinder, *Work Motivation in Organizational Behavior*; McClelland and Burnham, "Power Is the Great Motivator."

28. J. Stacy Adams, "Toward an Understanding of Inequity," *Journal of Abnormal and Social Psychology*, November 1963, pp. 422–436. See also Richard T. Mowday, "Equity Theory Predictions of Behavior in Organizations," in Richard M. Steers and Lyman W. Porter, eds., *Motivation and Work Behavior*, 4th ed. (New York: McGraw-Hill, 1987), pp. 89–110.

29. Priti Pradham Shah, "Who Are Employees' Social Referents? Using a Network Perspective to Determine Referent Others," *Academy of Management Journal*, vol. 41, no. 3 (1998), pp. 249–268.

30. J. Stacy Adams, "Inequity in Social Exchange," in L. Berkowitz, ed., *Advances in Experimental Social Psychology*, Vol. 2 (New York: Academic Press, 1965), pp. 267–299.

31. Craig Pinder, *Work Motivation in Organizational Behavior* (Upper Saddle River, N.J.: Prentice Hall, 1998).

32. See Kerry Sauler and Arthur Bedeian, "Equity Sensitivity: Construction of a Measure and Examination of Its Psychometric Properties," *Journal of Management*, vol. 26, no. 5 (2000), pp. 885–910; Mark Bing and Susan Burroughs, "The Predictive and Interactive Effects of Equity Sensitivity in Teamwork-Oriented Organizations," *Journal of Organizational Behavior*, vol. 22, no. 3, (2001), pp. 271–290.

33. Victor Vroom, *Work and Motivation* (New York: Wiley, 1964).

34. Lyman W. Porter and Edward E. Lawler, *Managerial Attitudes and Performance* (Homewood, IL: Dorsey Press, 1968).

35. For reviews, see Terence R. Mitchell, "Expectancy Models of Job Satisfaction, Occupational Preference, and Effort: A Theoretical, Methodological, and Empirical Appraisal," *Psychological Bulletin*, vol. 81 (1974), pp. 1096–1112; and John P. Campbell and Robert D. Pritchard, "Motivation Theory in Industrial and Organizational Psychology," in Marvin D. Dunnette, ed., *Handbook of Industrial and Organizational Psychology*

(Chicago: Rand McNally, 1976), pp. 63–130.

36. Pinder, *Work Motivation and Organizational Behavior*.

37. Ibid.

38. Campbell and Pritchard, "Motivation Theory in Industrial and Organizational Psychology."

39. Adler, *International Dimensions of Organizational Behavior*.

40. David A. Nadler and Edward E. Lawler, "Motivation: A Diagnostic Approach," in J. Richard Hackman, Edward E. Lawler, and Lyman W. Porter, eds., *Perspectives on Behavior in Organizations*, 2nd ed. (New York: McGraw-Hill, 1983), pp. 67–78.

41. Ivan P. Pavlov, *Conditional Reflexes* (New York: Oxford University Press, 1927).

42. Albert Bandura, "Social Cognitive Theory: An Agentic Perspective," *Annual Review of Psychology*, vol. 52 (2001), pp. 1–26.

43. B. F. Skinner, *Science and Human Behavior* (New York: Macmillian, 1953); B. F. Skinner, *Beyond Freedom and Dignity* (New York: Knopf, 1972).

44. Fred Luthans and Robert Kreitner, *Organizational Behavior Modification and Beyond* (Glenview, IL: Scott, Foresman, 1985).

45. "Workers: Risks and Rewards," *Time*, April 15, 1991, pp. 42–43.

46. See Richard Arvey and John M. Ivancevich, "Punishment in Organizations: A Review, Propositions, and Research Suggestions," *Academy of Management Review*, April 1980, pp. 123–132, for a review of the literature on punishment.

47. Fred Luthans and Robert Kreitner, *Organizational Behavior Modification* (Glenview, IL: Scott, Foresman, 1975); Luthans and Kreitner, *Organizational Behavior Modification and Beyond*.

48. Alexander D. Stajkovic, "A Meta-Analysis of the Effects of Organizational Behavior Modification on Task Performance, 1975–95," *Academy of Management Journal*, vol. 40, no. 5 (1997), pp. 1122–1149.

49. "At Emery Air Freight: Positive Reinforcement Boosts Performance," *Organizational Dynamics*, Winter 1973, pp. 41–50; W. Clay Hamner and Ellen

P. Hamner, "Organizational Behavior Modification on the Bottom Line," *Organizational Dynamics*, Spring 1976, pp. 3–21.

50. Hamner and Hamner, "Organizational Behavior Modification on the Bottom Line."

51. Edwin Locke, "The Myths of Behavior Mod in Organizations," *Academy of Management Review*, vol. 2, no. 2, (1977), pp. 543–553.

Chapter 5

1. Ricky W. Griffin and Gary C. McMahan, "Motivation Through Job Design," in Jerald Greenberg, ed., *Organizational Behavior: State of the Science* (New York: Lawrence Erlbaum and Associates, 1994), pp. 23–44.

2. Frederick W. Taylor, *The Principles of Scientific Management* (New York: Harper & Row, 1911).

3. C. R. Walker and R. Guest, *The Man on the Assembly Line* (Cambridge, MA: Harvard University Press, 1952).

4. Jia Lin Xie and Gary Johns, "Job Scope and Stress: Can Job Scope Be Too High?" *Academy of Management Journal*, vol. 38, no. 5 (1995), pp. 1288–1309.

5. Ricky W. Griffin, *Task Design: An Integrative Approach* (Glenview, IL: Scott, Foresman, 1982).

6. "These Six Growth Jobs Are Dull, Dead-End, Sometimes Dangerous," *Wall Street Journal*, December 1, 1994, pp. A1, A8, A9.

7. H. Conant and M. Kilbridge, "An Interdisciplinary Analysis of Job Enlargement: Technology, Cost, Behavioral Implications," *Industrial and Labor Relations Review*, vol. 18, no. 7 (1965), pp. 377–395.

8. Frederick Herzberg, "One More Time: How Do You Motivate Employees?" *Harvard Business Review*, January–February 1968, pp. 53–62; Frederick Herzberg, "The Wise Old Turk," *Harvard Business Review*, September–October 1974, pp. 70–80.

9. R. N. Ford, "Job Enrichment Lessons from AT&T," *Harvard Business Review*, January–February 1973, pp. 96–106.

10. E. D. Weed, "Job Enrichment 'Cleans Up' at Texas Instruments," in J. R. Maher, ed., *New Perspectives in Job*

Enrichment (New York: Van Nostrand, 1971).

11. Griffin, *Task Design;* Griffin and McMahan, "Motivation Through Job Design."

12. J. Richard Hackman and Greg Oldham, "Motivation Through the Design of Work: Test of a Theory," *Organizational Behavior and Human Performance*, vol. 16 (1976), pp. 250–279. See also Michael A. Campion and Paul W. Thayer, "Job Design: Approaches, Outcomes, and Trade-Offs," *Organizational Dynamics*, Winter 1987, pp. 66–78.

13. J. Richard Hackman, "Work Design," in J. Richard Hackman and J. L. Suttle, eds., *Improving Life at Work: Behavioral Science Approaches to Organizational Change* (Santa Monica, CA: Goodyear, 1977).

14. Griffin, *Task Design.*

15. Ibid. See also Karlene H. Roberts and William Glick, "The Job Characteristics Approach to Task Design: A Critical Review," *Journal of Applied Psychology*, vol. 66 (1981), pp. 193–217; and Ricky W. Griffin, "Toward an Integrated Theory of Task Design," in Larry L. Cummings and Barry M. Staw, eds., *Research in Organizational Behavior*, Vol. 9 (Greenwich, CT: JAI Press, 1987), pp. 79–120.

16. Ricky W. Griffin, M. Ann Welsh, and Gregory Moorhead, "Perceived Task Characteristics and Employee Performance: A Literature Review," *Academy of Management Review*, October 1981, pp. 655–664.

17. For a recent discussion of these issues, see Timothy Butler and James Waldroop, "Job Sculpting," *Harvard Business Review*, September–October 1999, pp. 144–152.

18. David J. Glew, Anne M. O'Leary-Kelly, Ricky W. Griffin, and David D. Van Fleet, "Participation in Organizations: A Preview of the Issues and Proposed Framework for Future Analysis," *Journal of Management*, vol. 21, no. 3 (1995), pp. 395–421; for a recent update, see Russ Forrester, "Empowerment: Rejuvenating a Potent Idea," *Academy of Management Executive*, vol. 14, no. 1 (2002), pp. 67–78.

19. John A. Wagner III, "Participation's Effects of Performance and Satisfaction: A Reconsideration of Research Evidence," *Academy of Management Review*, vol. 19, no. 2 (1994), pp. 312–330.

20. Quoted in "Herb Kelleher Has One Main Strategy: Treat Employees Well," *Wall Street Journal*, August 31, 1999, p. B1.

21. "9 to 5 Isn't Working Anymore," *BusinessWeek*, September 20, 1999, pp. 94–98.

22. A. R. Cohen and H. Gadon, *Alternative Work Schedules: Integrating Individual and Organizational Needs* (Reading, MA: Addison-Wesley, 1978).

23. See Barbara Rau and MaryAnne Hyland, "Role Conflict and Flexible Work Arrangements: The Effects on Applicant Attraction," *Personnel Psychology*, vol. 55, no. 1 (2002), pp. 111–136.

24. For a recent analysis, see Sumita Raghuram, Raghu Garud, Batia Wiesenfeld, and Vipin Gupta, "Factors Contributing to Virtual Work Adjustment," *Journal of Management*, vol. 27 (2001), pp. 383–405.

Chapter 6

1. Jon R. Katzenbach and Jason A. Santamaria, "Firing Up the Front Line," *Harvard Business Review*, May–June 1999, pp. 107–117.

2. A. Bandura, *Social Learning Theory* (Englewood Cliffs, NJ: Prentice-Hall, 1977).

3. See Edwin A. Locke, "Toward a Theory of Task Performance and Incentives," *Organizational Behavior and Human Performance*, vol. 3 (1968), pp. 157–189.

4. Gary P. Latham and Gary Yukl, "A Review of Research on the Application of Goal Setting in Organizations," *Academy of Management Journal*, vol. 18, no. 4 (1975), pp. 824–845.

5. Gary P. Latham and J. J. Baldes, "The Practical Significance of Locke's Theory of Goal Setting," *Journal of Applied Psychology*, vol. 60, no. 1 (1975), pp. 187–191.

6. Gary P. Latham, "The Importance of Understanding and Changing Employee Outcome Expectancies for Gaining Commitment to an Organiza-

tional Goal," *Personnel Psychology*, vol. 54, no. 3 (2001), pp. 707–720.

7. H. John Bernardin and Richard W. Beatty, *Performance Appraisal: Assessing Human Behavior at Work* (Boston: Kent, 1984).

8. See Bruce Pfau and Ira Kay, "Does 360-Degree Feedback Negatively Affect Company Performance?" *HRMagazine*, June 2002, pp. 54–59.

9. Joan Brett and Leanne Atwater, "360° Feedback: Accuracy, Reactions, and Perceptions of Usefulness," *Journal of Applied Psychology*, vol. 86, no. 5 (2001), pp. 930–942; Terry Beehr, Lana Ivanitskaya, Curtiss Hansen, Dmitry Slovich, and David Gudanowski, "Evaluation of 360-Degree Feedback Ratings: Relationships with Each Other and with Performance and Selection Predictors," *Journal of Organizational Behavior*, vol. 22 (2001), pp. 775–788.

10. Vanessa Urch Druskat and Steven B. Wolff, "Effects and Timing of Developmental Peer Appraisals in Self-Managing Work Groups," *Journal of Applied Psychology*, vol. 84, no. 1 (1999), pp. 58–74.

11. See Edward E. Lawler, *Pay and Organization Development* (Reading, MA: Addison-Wesley, 1981).

12. Brian Boyd and Alain Salamin, "Strategic Reward Systems: A Contingency Model of Pay System Design," *Strategic Management Journal*, vol. 22 (2001), pp. 777–792.

13. Alfred Rappaport, "New Thinking on How to Link Executive Pay with Performance," *Harvard Business Review*, March–April 1999, pp. 91–99.

14. Steve Bates, "Piecing Together Executive Compensation," *HRMagazine*, May 2002, pp. 60–69.

15. "Rich Benefit Plan Gives GM Competitors Cost Edge," *Wall Street Journal*, March 21, 1996, pp. B1, B4.

16. "Painless Perks," *Forbes*, September 6, 1999, p. 138. See also "Does Rank Have Too Much Privilege?" *Wall Street Journal*, February 26, 2002, pp. B1, B4.

17. John R. Deckop, Robert Mangel, and Carol C. Cirka, "Getting More Than You Pay For: Organizational Citizenship Behavior and Pay-for-Performance Plans," *Academy of*

Management Journal, vol. 42, no. 4 (1999), pp. 420–428.

18. Charlotte Garvey, "Steering Teams with the Right Pay," *HRMagazine*, May 2002, pp. 70–80.

19. Andrea Poe, "Selection Savvy," *HRMagazine*, April 2002, pp. 77–80.

20. Ricky W. Griffin and Michael W. Pustay, *International Business—A Managerial Perspective*, 4th ed. (Upper Saddle River, NJ: Prentice Hall, 2005).

Chapter 7

1. Otis W. Baskin and Craig E. Aronoff, *Interpersonal Communication in Organizations* (Santa Monica, CA: Goodyear, 1980), p. 2.

2. "How Merrill Lynch Moves Its Stock Deals All Around the World," *Wall Street Journal*, November 9, 1987, pp. 1, 8.

3. Jeanne D. Maes, Teresa G. Weldy, and Marjorie L. Icenogle, "A Managerial Perspective: Oral Communication Competency Is Most Important for Business Students in the Workplace," *Journal of Business Communication*, January 1997, pp. 67–80.

4. Melinda Knight, "Writing and Other Communication Standards in Undergraduate Business Education: A Study of Current Program Requirements, Practices, and Trends," *Business Communication Quarterly*, March 1999, p. 10.

5. Robert Nurden, "Graduates Must Master the Lost Art of Communication," *The European*, March 20, 1997, p. 24.

6. Silvan S. Tompkins and Robert McCarter, "What and Where Are the Primary Affects? Some Evidence for a Theory," *Perceptual and Motor Skills*, February 1964, pp. 119–158.

7. See Everett M. Rogers and Rekha Agarwala-Rogers, *Communication in Organizations* (New York: Free Press, 1976), for a brief review of the background and development of the source-message-channel-receiver model of communication.

8. Charles A. O'Reilly III, "Variations in Decision Makers' Use of Information Sources: The Impact of Quality and Accessibility of Information," *Academy of Management Journal*, December 1982, pp. 756–771.

9. See Jerry C. Wofford, Edwin A. Gerloff, and Robert C. Cummins, *Organizational Communication* (New York: McGraw-Hill, 1977), for a discussion of channel noise.

10. Donald R. Hollis, "The Shape of Things to Come: The Role of IT," *Management Review*, June 1996, p. 62.

11. Kym France, "Computer Commuting Benefits Companies," *Arizona Republic*, August 16, 1993, pp. E1, E4.

12. Paul S. Goodman and Eric D. Darr, "Exchanging Best Practices Through Computer-Aided Systems," *Academy of Management Executive*, May 1996, pp. 7–18.

13. Jenny C. McCune, "The Intranet: Beyond E-Mail," *Management Review*, November 1996, pp. 23–27.

14. See Daniel Katz and Robert L. Kahn, *The Social Psychology of Organizations*, 2nd ed. (New York: Wiley, 1978), for more about the role of organizational communication networks.

15. For good discussions of small-group communication networks and research on this subject, see Wofford, Gerloff, and Cummins, *Organizational Communication*; and Marvin E. Shaw, *Group Dynamics: The Psychology of Small Group Behavior*, 3rd ed. (New York: McGraw-Hill, 1981), pp. 150–161.

16. See R. Wayne Pace, *Organizational Communication: Foundations for Human Resource Development* (Englewood Cliffs, NJ: Prentice-Hall, 1983), for further discussion of the development of communication networks.

17. David Krackhardt and Lyman W. Porter, "The Snowball Effect: Turnover Embedded in Communication Networks," *Journal of Applied Psychology*, February 1986, pp. 50–55.

18. "Has Coke Been Playing Accounting Games?" *BusinessWeek*, May 13, 2002, pp. 98–99.

19. See "E-mail's Limits Create Confusion, Hurt Feelings," *USA Today*, February 5, 2002, pp. 1B, 2B.

20. "Talk of Chapter 11 Bruises Kmart Stock," *USA Today*, January 3, 2002, p. 1B.

21. Thomas J. Peters and Robert H. Waterman, Jr., *In Search of Excellence: Lessons from America's Best-Run Companies* (New York: Harper & Row, 1982), p. 121.

22. Shari Caudron, "Monsanto Responds to Diversity," *Personnel Journal*, November 1990, pp. 72–78; "Trading Places at Monsanto," *Training and Development Journal*, April 1993, pp. 45–49.

Chapter 8

1. Marvin E. Shaw, *Group Dynamics: The Psychology of Small Group Behavior*, 3rd ed. (New York: McGraw-Hill, 1981), p. 11.

2. Francis J. Yammarino and Alan J. Dubinsky, "Salesperson Performance and Managerially Controllable Factors: An Investigation of Individual and Work Group Effects," *Journal of Management*, vol. 16 (1990), pp. 87–106.

3. Rob Cross and Laurence Prusak, "The People Who Make Organizations Go—or Stop," *Harvard Business Review*, June 2002, pp. 104–114.

4. William L. Sparks, Dominic J. Monetta, and L. M. Simmons, Jr., "Affinity Groups: Developing Complex Adaptive Organizations," (working paper, The PAM Institute, Washington, DC, 1999).

5. Shawn Tully, "The Vatican's Finances," *Fortune*, December 21, 1987, pp. 28–40.

6. Bernard M. Bass and Edward C. Ryterband, *Organizational Psychology*, 2nd ed. (Boston: Allyn & Bacon, 1979), pp. 252–254. See also Scott Lester, Bruce Meglino, and M. Audrey Korsgaard, "The Antecedents and Consequences of Group Potency: A Longitudinal Investigation of Newly Formed Work Groups," *Academy of Management Journal*, vol. 45, no. 2 (2002), pp. 352–368.

7. Susan Long, "Early Integration in Groups: A Group to Join and a Group to Create," *Human Relations*, April 1984, pp. 311–332.

8. For example, see Mary Waller, Jeffrey Conte, Cristina Gibson, and Mason Carpenter, "The Effect of Individual Perceptions of Deadlines on Team Performance," *Academy of Management Review*, vol. 26, no. 4 (2001), pp. 586–600.

9. Steven L. Obert, "Developmental Patterns of Organizational Task

Groups: A Preliminary Study," *Human Relations*, January 1983, pp. 37–52.

10. Bass and Ryterband, *Organizational Psychology*, pp. 252–254.

11. Bernard M. Bass, "The Leaderless Group Discussion," *Psychological Bulletin*, September 1954, pp. 465–492.

12. Jill Lieber, "Time to Heal the Wounds," *Sports Illustrated*, November 2, 1987, pp. 86–91.

13. Connie J. G. Gersick, "Marking Time: Predictable Transitions in Task Groups," *Academy of Management Journal*, vol. 32 (1989), pp. 274–309.

14. James H. Davis, *Group Performance* (Reading, MA: Addison-Wesley, 1964), pp. 82–86.

15. Shaw, *Group Dynamics*.

16. Charles A. O'Reilly III, David F. Caldwell, and William P. Barnett, "Work Group Demography, Social Integration, and Turnover," *Administrative Science Quarterly*, March 1989, pp. 21–37.

17. See Sheila Simsarian Webber and Lisa Donahue, "Impact of Highly and Less Job-Related Diversity on Work Group Cohesion and Performance: A Meta-Analysis," *Journal of Management*, vol. 27 (2001), pp. 141–162.

18. Nancy Adler, *International Dimensions of Organizational Behavior*, 3rd ed. (Boston: PWS-Kent, 1997), pp. 132–133.

19. Shaw, *Group Dynamics*, pp. 173–177.

20. See Jennifer Chatman and Francis Flynn, "The Influence of Demographic Heterogeneity on the Emergence and Consequences of Cooperative Norms in Work Teams," *Academy of Management Journal*, vol. 44, no. 5 (2001), pp. 956–974.

21. Daniel C. Feldman, "The Development and Enforcement of Group Norms," *Academy of Management Review*, January 1984, pp. 47–53.

22. William E. Piper, Myriam Marrache, Renee Lacroix, Astrid M. Richardson, and Barry D. Jones, "Cohesion as a Basic Bond in Groups," *Human Relations*, February 1983, pp. 93–108.

23. Robert T. Keller, "Predictors of the Performance of Project Groups in R & D Organizations," *Academy of*

Management Journal, December 1986, pp. 715–726.

24. Irving L. Janis, *Groupthink*, 2nd ed. (Boston: Houghton Mifflin, 1982), p. 9.

25. Blake E. Ashforth and Fred Mael, "Social Identity Theory and the Organization," *Academy of Management Review*, January 1989, pp. 20–39.

26. "Now That It's Cruising, Can Ford Keep Its Foot to the Gas?" *BusinessWeek*, February 11, 1985, pp. 48–52; Reed E. Nelson, "The Strength of Strong Ties: Social Networks and Intergroup Conflict in Organizations," *Academy of Management Journal*, June 1989, pp. 377–401, reprinted by permission.

27. See Stephen P. Robbins, *Managing Organizational Conflict* (Englewood Cliffs, NJ: Prentice-Hall, 1974), for a classic review.

28. Charles R. Schwenk, "Conflict in Organizational Decision Making: An Exploratory Study of Its Effects in For-Profit and Not-for-Profit Organizations," *Management Science*, April 1990, pp. 436–448.

29. Robbins, *Managing Organizational Conflict*.

30. Kenneth Thomas, "Conflict and Conflict Management," in Marvin Dunnette, ed., *Handbook of Industrial and Organizational Psychology* (Chicago: Rand McNally, 1976), pp. 889–935.

31. Alfie Kohn, "How to Succeed Without Even Vying," *Psychology Today*, September 1986, pp. 22–28.

32. See Carsten K. W. De Dreu and Annelies E. M. Van Vianen, "Managing Relationship Conflict and the Effectiveness of Organizational Teams," *Journal of Organizational Behavior*, vol. 22 (2001), pp. 309–328.

33. Patrick Nugent, "Managing Conflict: Third-Party Interventions for Managers," *Academy of Management Executive*, vol. 16, no. 1 (2002), pp. 139–148.

Chapter 9

1. Eric L. Trist and K. W. Bamforth, "Some Social and Psychological Consequences of the Longwall Method of Goal-Getting," *Human Relations*, February 1951, pp. 3–38; Jack D.

Orsburn, Linda Moran, and Ed Musselwhite, with John Zenger, *Self-Directed Work Teams: The New American Challenge* (Homewood, IL: Business One Irwin, 1990).

2. See Jon R. Katzenbach and Douglas K. Smith, *The Wisdom of Teams: Creating the High-Performance Organization* (Boston: Harvard Business School Press, 1993), p. 45.

3. See Ruth Wageman, "How Leaders Foster Self-Managing Team Effectiveness: Design Choices Versus Hands-on Coaching," *Organization Science*, vol. 12, no. 5 (2001), pp. 559–577.

4. See Michelle Marks, John Mathieu, and Stephen Zaccaro, "A Temporally Based Framework and Taxonomy of Team Processes," *Academy of Management Review*, vol. 26, no. 3 (2001), pp. 356–376.

5. Michele Williams, "In Whom We Trust: Group Membership as an Affective Context for Trust Development," *Academy of Management Review*, vol. 26, no. 3 (2001), pp. 377–396.

6. Katzenbach and Smith, *The Wisdom of Teams*, p. 3.

7. See Michelle Marks, Mark Sabella, C. Shawn Burke, and Stephen Zaccaro, "The Impact of Cross-Training on Team Effectiveness," *Journal of Applied Psychology*, vol. 87, no. 1 (2002), pp. 3–13.

8. Orsburn, Moran, Musselwhite, and Zenger, *Self-Directed Work Teams*, p. 15.

9. Manz and Sims, *Business Without Bosses*, pp. 10–11.

10. See Deborah Ancona, Henrik Bresman, and Katrin Kaeufer, "The Competitive Advantage of X-Teams," *Sloan Management Review*, Spring 2002, pp. 33–42.

11. Katzenbach and Smith, *The Wisdom of Teams*, pp. 184–189.

12. Manz and Sims, *Business Without Bosses*, pp. 74–76.

13. Jason Colquitt, Raymond Noe, and Christine Jackson, "Justice in Teams: Antecedents and Consequences of Procedural Justice Climate," *Personnel Psychology*, vol. 55 (2002), pp. 83–95.

14. Nigel Nicholson, ed., *Encyclopedic Dictionary of Organizational Behavior*

(Cambridge, MA: Blackwell, 1995), p. 463.

15. Brian Dumaine, "The Trouble with Teams," *Fortune*, September 5, 1994.

16. Ibid.

17. Ibid.

18. Ibid.

19. Ellen Hart, "Top Teams," *Management Review*, February 1996, pp. 43–47.

20. Dan Dimancescu and Kemp Dwenger, "Smoothing the Product Development Path," *Management Review*, January 1996, pp. 36–41.

21. Ibid.

22. Manz and Sims, *Business Without Bosses*, pp. 27–28.

23. Ibid., pp. 29–31.

24. Ibid., p. 130.

25. Ibid., p. 200.

26. Ibid., p. 200

Chapter 10

1. Ralph M. Stogdill, *Handbook of Leadership* (New York: Free Press, 1974). See also Bernard Bass, *Bass and Stogdill's Handbook of Leadership*, 3rd ed. (Riverside, NJ: Free Press, 1990); and "In Search of Leadership," *BusinessWeek*, November 15, 1999, pp. 172–176.

2. See Gary Yukl and David D. Van Fleet, "Theory and Research on Leadership in Organizations," in M. D. Dunnette and L. M. Hough, eds., *Handbook of Industrial and Organizational Psychology*, Vol. 3 (Palo Alto, CA: Consulting Psychologists Press, 1992), pp. 148–197.

3. Arthur G. Jago, "Leadership: Perspectives in Theory and Research," *Management Science*, March 1982, pp. 315–336.

4. Melvin Sorcher and James Brant, "Are You Picking the Right Leaders?" *Harvard Business Review*, February 2002, pp. 78–85.

5. See John P. Kotter, "What Leaders Really Do," *Harvard Business Review*, May-June 1990, pp. 103–111. See also Abraham Zaleznik, "Managers and Leaders: Are They Different?" *Harvard Business Review*, March-April 1992, pp. 126–135; and John Kotter, "What Leaders Really Do," *Harvard Business Review*, December 2001, pp. 85–94.

6. Ronald Heifetz and Marty Linsky, "A Survival Guide for Leaders," *Harvard Business Review*, June 2002, pp. 65–74.

7. Frederick Reichheld, "Lead for Loyalty," *Harvard Business Review*, July-August 2001, pp. 76–83.

8. David D. Van Fleet and Gary A. Yukl, "A Century of Leadership Research," in D. A. Wren and J. A. Pearce II, eds., *Papers Dedicated to the Development of Modern Management* (Chicago: The Academy of Management, 1986), pp. 12–23.

9. Shelly A. Kirkpatrick and Edwin A. Locke, "Leadership: Do Traits Matter?" *Academy of Management Executive*, May 1991, pp. 48–60. See also Robert J. Sternberg, "Managerial Intelligence: Why IQ Isn't Enough," *Journal of Management*, vol. 23, no. 3 (1997), pp. 475–493.

10. Russell L. Kent and Sherry E. Moss, "Effects of Sex and Gender Role on Leader Emergence," *Academy of Management Journal*, vol. 37, no. 5 (1994), pp. 1335–1346.

11. For example, see Sheila Puffer, "Understanding the Bear: A Portrait of Russian Business Leaders," *Academy of Management Executive*, vol. 8, no. 1 (1994), pp. 41–49.

12. "Korea's Samsung Plans Very Rapid Expansion into Autos, Other Lines," *Wall Street Journal*, March 2, 1995, pp. A1, A14.

13. Philip M. Podsakoff, Scott B. MacKenzie, Mike Ahearne, and William H. Bommer, "Searching for a Needle in a Haystack: Trying to Identify the Illusive Moderators of Leadership Behaviors," *Journal of Management*, vol. 21, no. 3 (1995), pp. 422–470.

14. Rensis Likert, *New Patterns of Management* (New York: McGraw-Hill, 1961).

15. Edwin Fleishman, E. F. Harris, and H. E. Burtt, *Leadership and Supervision in Industry* (Columbus, OH: Bureau of Educational Research, Ohio State University, 1955).

16. See Edwin A. Fleishman, "Twenty Years of Consideration and Structure," in Edward A. Fleishman and James G. Hunt, eds., *Current Developments in the Study of Leadership* (Carbondale, IL:

Southern Illinois University Press, 1973), pp. 1–40.

17. Fleishman, Harris, and Burtt, *Leadership and Supervision in Industry*.

18. See Gary A. Yukl, *Leadership in Organizations*, 3rd ed. (Englewood Cliffs, NJ: Prentice-Hall, 1994).

19. From Fred E. Fiedler, *A Theory of Leadership Effectiveness* (New York: McGraw-Hill, 1967). Reprinted by permission of the author.

20. See Fred E. Fiedler, "Engineering the Job to Fit the Manager," *Harvard Business Review*, September–October 1965, pp. 115–122.

21. See Fred E. Fiedler, Martin M. Chemers, and Linda Mahar, *Improving Leadership Effectiveness: The Leader Match Concept* (New York: Wiley, 1976).

22. Chester A. Schriesheim, Bennett J. Tepper, and Linda A. Tetrault, "Least Preferred Co-Worker Score, Situational Control, and Leadership Effectiveness: A Meta-Analysis of Contingency Model Performance Predictions," *Journal of Applied Psychology*, vol. 79, no. 4 (1994), pp. 561–573.

23. Martin G. Evans, "The Effects of Supervisory Behavior on the Path-Goal Relationship," *Organizational Behavior and Human Performance*, May 1970, pp. 277–298; Robert J. House, "A Path-Goal Theory of Leadership Effectiveness," *Administrative Science Quarterly*, September 1971, pp. 321–339; Robert J. House and Terence R. Mitchell, "Path-Goal Theory of Leadership," *Journal of Contemporary Business*, Autumn 1974, pp. 81–98.

24. "Woman with a Mission," *Forbes*, September 25, 1995, pp. 172–173.

25. Victor H. Vroom and Philip H. Yetton, *Leadership and Decision Making* (Pittsburgh: University of Pittsburgh Press, 1973); Victor H. Vroom and Arthur G. Jago, *The New Leadership* (Englewood Cliffs, NJ: Prentice-Hall, 1988).

26. Victor Vroom, "Leadership and the Decision-Making Process," *Organizational Dynamics*, Spring 2000.

27. Vroom and Jago, *The New Leadership*.

28. Madeline E. Heilman, Harvey A. Hornstein, Jack H. Cage, and Judith

K. Herschlag, "Reaction to Prescribed Leader Behavior as a Function of Role Perspective: The Case of the Vroom-Yetton Model," *Journal of Applied Psychology*, February 1984, pp. 50–60; R. H. George Field, "A Test of the Vroom-Yetton Normative Model of Leadership," *Journal of Applied Psychology*, February 1982, pp. 523–532.

29. George Graen and J. F. Cashman, "A Role-Making Model of Leadership in Formal Organizations: A Developmental Approach," in J. G. Hunt and L. L. Larson, eds., *Leadership Frontiers* (Kent, OH: Kent State University Press, 1975), pp. 143–165; Fred Dansereau, George Graen, and W. J. Haga, "A Vertical Dyad Linkage Approach to Leadership Within Formal Organizations: A Longitudinal Investigation of the Role-Making Process," *Organizational Behavior and Human Performance*, vol. 15 (1975), pp. 46–78.

30. Charlotte R. Gerstner and David V. Day, "Meta-Analytic Review of Leader-Member Exchange Theory: Correlates and Construct Issues," *Journal of Applied Psychology*, vol. 82, no. 6 (1997), pp. 827–844; John Maslyn and Mary Uhl-Bien, "Leader-Member Exchange and Its Dimensions: Effects of Self-Effort and Others' Effort on Relationship Quality," *Journal of Applied Psychology*, vol. 86, no. 4 (2001), pp. 697–708.

31. Paul Hersey and Kenneth H. Blanchard, *Management of Organizational Behavior: Utilizing Human Resources*, 3rd ed. (Englewood Cliffs, NJ: Prentice-Hall, 1977).

Chapter 11

1. Robert W. Allen and Lyman W. Porter, eds., *Organizational Influence Processes* (Glenview, IL: Scott, Foresman, 1983).

2. Alan L. Frohman, "The Power of Personal Initiative," *Organizational Dynamics*, Winter 1997, pp. 39–48. See also James H. Dulebohn and Gerald R. Ferris, "The Role of Influence Tactics in Perceptions of Performance Evaluations' Fairness," *Academy of Management Journal*, vol. 42, no. 3 (1999), pp. 288–303.

3. Gary Williams and Robert Miller, "Change the Way You Persuade,"

Harvard Business Review, May 2002, pp. 65–75.

4. James MacGregor Burns, *Leadership* (New York: Harper & Row, 1978); Karl W. Kuhnert and Philip Lewis, "Transactional and Transformational Leadership: A Constructive/Developmental Analysis," *Academy of Management Review*, October 1987, pp. 648–657; Nick Turner, Julian Barling, Olga Epitropaki, Vicky Butcher, and Caroline Milner, "Transformational Leadership and Moral Reasoning," *Journal of Applied Psychology*, vol. 87, no. 3, 2003, pp. 304–311.

5. Francis J. Yammarino and Alan J. Dubinsky, "Transformational Leadership Theory: Using Levels of Analysis to Determine Boundary Conditions," *Personnel Psychology*, vol. 47 (1994), pp. 787–800.

6. Vicki Goodwin, J. C. Wofford, and J. Lee Whittington, "A Theoretical and Empirical Extension to the Transformational Leadership Construct," *Journal of Organizational Behavior*, vol. 22 (2001), pp. 759–774.

7. Juan-Carlos Pastor, James Meindl, and Margarita Mayo, "A Network Effects Model of Charisma Attributions," *Academy of Management Journal*, vol. 45, no. 2 (2002), pp. 410–420.

8. See Robert J. House, "A 1976 Theory of Charismatic Leadership," in J. G. Hunt and L. L. Larson, eds., *Leadership: The Cutting Edge* (Carbondale, IL: Southern Illinois University Press, 1977), pp. 189–207. See also Jay A. Conger and Rabindra N. Kanungo, "Toward a Behavioral Theory of Charismatic Leadership in Organizational Settings," *Academy of Management Review*, October 1987, pp. 637–647.

9. "Play Hard, Fly Right," *Time*, Bonus Section: "Inside Business," June 2002, pp. Y15–Y22.

10. David A. Nadler and Michael L. Tushman, "Beyond the Charismatic Leader: Leadership and Organizational Change," *California Management Review*, Winter 1990, pp. 77–97.

11. David A. Waldman and Francis J. Yammarino, "CEO Charismatic Leadership: Levels-of-Management and Levels-of-Analysis Effects," *Academy of Management Review*, vol. 24, no. 2 (1999), pp. 266–285.

12. See Steven Kerr and John M. Jermier, "Substitutes for Leadership: Their Meaning and Measurement," *Organizational Behavior and Human Performance*, vol. 22 (1978), pp. 375–403; and Charles C. Manz and Henry P. Sims, Jr., "Leading Workers to Lead Themselves: The External Leadership of Self-Managing Work Teams," *Administrative Science Quarterly*, March 1987, pp. 106–129.

13. Jon P. Howell, David E. Bowen, Peter W. Dorfman, Steven Kerr, and Philip Podsakoff, "Substitutes for Leadership: Effective Alternatives to Ineffective Leadership," *Organizational Dynamics*, Summer 1990, pp. 20–38. See also Philip M. Podsakoff, Scott B. Mackenzie, and William H. Bommer, "Transformational Leader Behaviors and Substitutes for Leadership as Determinants of Employee Satisfaction, Commitment, Trust, and Organizational Citizenship Behaviors," *Journal of Management*, vol. 22, no. 2 (1996), pp. 259–298.

14. For reviews of the meaning of *power*, see Henry Mintzberg, *Power in and Around Organizations* (Englewood Cliffs, NJ: Prentice Hall, 1983); Jeffrey Pfeiffer, *Power in Organizations* (Marshfield, MA: Pitman Publishing, 1981); John Kenneth Galbraith, *The Anatomy of Power* (Boston: Houghton Mifflin, 1983); and Gary A. Yukl, *Leadership in Organizations*, 3rd ed. (Englewood Cliffs, NJ: Prentice Hall, 1994).

15. John R. P. French and Bertram Raven, "The Bases of Social Power," in Darwin Cartwright, ed., *Studies in Social Power* (Ann Arbor, MI: University of Michigan Press, 1959), pp. 150–167. See also Philip M. Podsakoff and Chester A. Schriesheim, "Field Studies of French and Raven's Bases of Power: Critique, Reanalysis, and Suggestions for Future Research," *Psychological Bulletin*, vol. 97 (1985), pp. 387–411.

16. Yukl, *Leadership in Organizations*, Chapter X.

17. Victor Murray and Jeffrey Gandz, "Games Executives Play: Politics at Work," *Business Horizons*, December 1980, pp. 11–23. See also Jeffrey Gandz and Victor Murray, "The Experience of Workplace Politics," *Acad-*

emy of Management Journal, June 1980, pp. 237–251.

18. Gerald F. Cavanaugh, Dennis J. Moberg, and Manuel Valasquez, "The Ethics of Organizational Politics," *Academy of Management Review*, July 1981, pp. 363–374.

19. Pfeiffer, *Power in Organizations*; Mintzberg, *Power in and Around Organizations*.

20. "How the 2 Top Officials of Grace Wound Up in a Very Dirty War," *Wall Street Journal*, May 18, 1995, pp. Al, A8.

Chapter 12

1. Herbert Simon, *The New Science of Management Decision* (New York: Harper & Row, 1960), p. 1.

2. Nandini Rajagopalan, Abdul M. A. Rasheed, and Deepak K. Datta, "Strategic Decision Processes: Critical Review and Future Directions," *Journal of Management*, Summer 1993, pp. 349–384.

3. See George P. Huber, *Managerial Decision Making* (Glenview, IL: Scott, Foresman, 1980), pp. 90–115, for a discussion of decision making under conditions of certainty, risk, and uncertainty.

4. See David Garvin and Michael Roberto, "What You Don't Know About Making Decisions," *Harvard Business Review*, September 2001, pp. 108–115.

5. "'90s Style Brainstorming," *Forbes ASAP*, October 25, 1993, pp. 44–61.

6. Henry Mintzberg, Duru Raisinghani, and Andre Thoret, "The Structure of 'Unstructured' Decision Processes," *Administrative Science Quarterly*, June 1976, pp. 246–275; Milan Zeleny, "Descriptive Decision Making and Its Application," *Applications of Management Science*, vol. 1 (1981), pp. 327–388.

7. See E. Frank Harrison, *The Managerial Decision-Making Process*, 5th ed. (Boston: Houghton Mifflin, 1999), pp. 55–60, for more on choice processes.

8. Ari Ginsberg and N. Ventrakaman, "Contingency Perspectives of Organizational Strategy: A Critical Review of the Empirical Research," *Academy of Management Review*, July 1985, pp. 412–434; Donald C. Hambrick and David Lei, "To-

ward an Empirical Prioritization of Contingency Variables for Business Strategy," *Academy of Management Journal*, December 1985, pp. 763–788.

9. Leon Festinger, *A Theory of Cognitive Dissonance* (Palo Alto, CA: Stanford University Press, 1957).

10. Patricia Sellers, "The Dumbest Marketing Ploys," *Fortune*, October 5, 1992, pp. 88–94.

11. See Harrison, *The Managerial Decision-Making Process*, pp. 74–100, for more on the rational approach to decision making.

12. Craig D. Parks and Rebecca Cowlin, "Group Discussion as Affected by Number of Alternatives and by a Time Limit," *Organizational Behavior and Human Decision Processes*, vol. 62, no. 3 (1995), pp. 267–275.

13. See James G. March and Herbert A. Simon, *Organizations* (New York: Wiley, 1958), for more on the concept of bounded rationality.

14. Herbert A. Simon, *Administrative Behavior: A Study of Decision Making Processes in Administrative Organizations*, 3rd ed. (New York: Free Press, 1976).

15. Richard M. Cyert and James G. March, *A Behavioral Theory of the Firm* (Englewood Cliffs, NJ: Prentice Hall, 1963), p. 113; Simon, *Administrative Behavior*.

16. Kathleen M. Eisenhardt, "Making Fast Strategic Decisions in High-Velocity Environments," *Academy of Management Journal*, September 1989, pp. 543–576.

17. Irving L. Janis and Leon Mann, *Decision Making: A Psychological Analysis of Conflict, Choice, and Commitment* (New York: Free Press, 1977).

18. Jerry Ross and Barry M. Staw, "Expo 86: An Escalation Prototype," *Administrative Science Quarterly*, June 1986, pp. 274–297.

19. Barry M. Staw, "Escalation of Commitment to a Course of Action," *Academy of Management Review*, October 1981, pp. 577–587.

20. Barry M. Staw and Jerry Ross, "Good Money After Bad," *Psychology Today*, February 1988, pp. 30–33.

21. M. A. Wallach, N. Kogan, and D. J. Bem, "Group Influence on Indi-

vidual Risk Taking," *Journal of Abnormal and Social Psychology*, August 1962, pp. 75–86; James A. F. Stoner, "Risky and Cautious Shifts in Group Decisions: The Influence of Widely Held Values," *Journal of Experimental Social Psychology*, October 1968, pp. 442–459.

22. Dorwin Cartwright, "Risk Taking by Individuals and Groups: An Assessment of Research Employing Choice Dilemmas," *Journal of Personality and Social Psychology*, December 1971, pp. 361–378.

23. S. Moscovici and M. Zavalloni, "The Group as a Polarizer of Attitudes," *Journal of Personality and Social Psychology*, June 1969, pp. 125–135.

24. Irving L. Janis, *Groupthink*, 2nd ed. (Boston: Houghton Mifflin, 1982), p. 9.

25. Gregory Moorhead, Christopher P. Neck, and Mindy West, "The Tendency Toward Defective Decision Making Within Self-Managing Teams: Relevance of Groupthink for the 21st Century," *Organizational Behavior and Human Decision Processes*, February–March 1998, pp. 327–351.

26. Gregory Moorhead, Richard Ference, and Chris P. Neck, "Group Decision Fiascoes Continue: Space Shuttle *Challenger* and a Revised Groupthink Framework," *Human Relations*, vol. 44 (1991), pp. 539–550.

27. See Robert Cross and Susan Brodt, "How Assumptions of Consensus Undermine Decision Making," *Sloan Management Review*, Winter 2001, pp. 86–95.

28. Irving L. Janis, *Victims of Groupthink* (Boston: Houghton Mifflin, 1972), pp. 197–198.

29. Janis, *Groupthink*.

30. Ibid., pp. 193–197; Gregory Moorhead, "Groupthink: Hypothesis in Need of Testing," *Group & Organization Studies*, December 1982, pp. 429–444.

31. Gregory Moorhead and John R. Montanari, "Empirical Analysis of the Groupthink Phenomenon," *Human Relations*, May 1986, pp. 399–410; John R. Montanari and Gregory Moorhead, "Development of the Groupthink Assessment Inventory," *Educational and Psychological Measurement*, Spring 1989, pp. 209–219.

32. Frederick W. Taylor, *The Principles of Scientific Management* (New York: Harper & Row, 1911).

33. Chris Argyris, *Personality and Organization* (New York: Harper & Row, 1957); Rensis Likert, *New Patterns of Management* (New York: McGraw-Hill, 1961).

34. Lester Coch and John R. P. French, "Overcoming Resistance to Change," *Human Relations*, vol. 1 (1948), pp. 512–532; N. C. Morse and E. Reimer, "The Experimental Change of a Major Organizational Variable," *Journal of Abnormal and Social Psychology*, January 1956, pp. 120–129.

35. Victor Vroom, "Leadership and the Decision-Making Process," *Organizational Dynamics*, Spring 2000.

36. For a recent example, see Carsten K. W. De Dreu and Michael West, "Minority Dissent and Team Innovation: The Importance of Participation in Decision Making," *Journal of Applied Psychology*, vol. 86, no. 6 (2001), pp. 1191–1201.

37. See Kimberly Wade-Benzoni, Andrew Hoffman, Leigh Thompson, Don Moore, James Gillespie, and Max Bazerman, "Barriers to Resolution in Ideologically Based Negotiations: The Role of Values and Institutions," *Academy of Management Review*, vol. 27, no. 1 (2002), pp. 41–57.

38. J. Z. Rubin and B. R. Brown, *The Social Psychology of Bargaining and Negotiation* (New York: Academic Press, 1975).

39. R. J. Lewicki and J. A. Litterer, *Negotiation* (Homewood, IL: Irwin, 1985).

40. Howard Raiffa, *The Art and Science of Negotiation* (Cambridge, MA: Belknap, 1982).

41. K. H. Bazerman and M. A. Neale, *Negotiating Rationally* (New York: Free Press, 1992).

42. Ross R. Reck and Brian G. Long, *The Win-Win Negotiator* (Escondido, CA: Blanchard Training and Development, 1985).

Chapter 13

1. Max Weber, *The Theory of Social and Economic Organization*, trans. A. M. Henderson and Talcott Parsons (New York: Free Press, 1947).

2. Nancy M. Carter and Thomas L. Keon, "The Rise and Fall of the Division of Labour, the Past 25 Years," *Organization Studies*, 1986, pp. 54–57.

3. Glenn R. Carroll, "The Specialist Strategy," *California Management Review*, Spring 1984, pp. 126–137.

4. "Management Discovers the Human Side of Automation," *Business-Week*, September 29, 1986, pp. 70–75.

5. See Robert H. Miles, *Macro Organizational Behavior* (Santa Monica, CA: Goodyear, 1980), pp. 28–34, for a discussion of departmentalization schemes.

6. Henry Mintzberg, *The Structuring of Organizations* (Englewood Cliffs, NJ: Prentice Hall, 1979), p. 125.

7. Miles, *Macro Organizational Behavior*, pp. 122–133.

8. Peggy Leatt and Rodney Schneck, "Criteria for Grouping Nursing Subunits in Hospitals," *Academy of Management Review*, March 1984, pp. 150–165.

9. "Speech by Rolf E. Breuer at the General Meeting of Deutsche Bank AG, May 22, 2002 (quotation)" "Fact Sheets," "Organizational Structure," Deutsche Bank website, group.deutsche-bank.de on June 7, 2002; Marcus Walker, "Lean New Guard at Deutsche Bank Sets Global Agenda—But Cultural Rifts Prevent More Aggressive Cost Cuts—The Traditionalists Haven't Gone Quietly," *Wall Street Journal*, February 14, 2002, www.wsj.com on April 4, 2002.

10. Lyndall F. Urwick, "The Manager's Span of Control," *Harvard Business Review*, May–June 1956, pp. 39–47; Dan R. Dalton, William D. Tudor, Michael J. Spendolini, Gordon J. Fielding, and Lyman W. Porter, "Organization Structure and Performance: A Critical Review," *Academy of Management Review*, January 1980, pp. 49–64.

11. Mintzberg, *The Structuring of Organizations*, pp. 133–147.

12. See David Van Fleet, "Span of Management Research and Issues," *Academy of Management Journal*, September 1983, pp. 546–552, for an example of research on span of control.

13. John B. Miner, *Theories of Organizational Structure and Process* (Hinsdale, IL: Dryden Press, 1982), p. 360.

14. Chester Barnard, *The Functions of the Executive* (Cambridge, MA: Harvard University Press, 1938), pp. 161–184.

15. See John Child, *Organization: A Guide to Problems and Practice*, 2nd ed. (New York: Harper & Row, 1984), pp. 145–153, for a detailed discussion of centralization.

16. Leonard W. Johnson and Alan L. Frohman, "Identifying and Closing the Gap in the Middle of Organizations," *Academy of Management Executive*, May 1989, pp. 107–114.

17. Michael Schrage, "I Know What You Mean, and I Can't Do Anything About It," *Fortune*, April 2, 2001, p. 186.

18. Mintzberg, *The Structuring of Organizations*, pp. 83–84.

19. For more discussion of the impact of formalization on other organizational characteristics, see Gregory Moorhead, "Organizational Analysis: An Integration of the Macro and Micro Approaches," *Journal of Management Studies*, April 1981, pp. 191–218; J. Daniel Sherman and Howard L. Smith, "The Influence of Organizational Structure on Intrinsic Versus Extrinsic Motivation," *Academy of Management Journal*, December 1984, pp. 877–885; John A. Pearce II and Fred R. David, "A Social Network Approach to Organizational Design-Performance," *Academy of Management Review*, July 1983, pp. 436–444; and Eileen Farihurst, "Organizational Rules and the Accomplishment of Nursing Work on Geriatric Wards," *Journal of Management Studies*, July 1983, pp. 315–332.

20. Weber, *The Theory of Social and Economic Organization*.

21. For more discussion of these alternative views, see Miner, *Theories of Organizational Structure and Process*, p. 386.

22. Paul S. Adler, "Building Better Bureaucracies," *Academy of Management Executive*, November 1999, pp. 36–46.

23. This summary of the classic principles of organizing is based on Henri Fayol, *General and Industrial*

Management, trans. Constance Storrs (London: Pittman, 1949); Miner, *Theories of Organizational Structure and Process*, pp. 358–381; and the discussions in Arthur Bedeian, *Organizations: Theory and Analysis*, 2nd ed. (Hinsdale, IL: Dryden Press, 1984), pp. 58–59.

24. Miner, *Theories of Organizational Structure and Process*, pp. 358–381.

25. See Rensis Likert, *New Patterns of Management* (New York: McGraw-Hill, 1961); and Rensis Likert, *The Human Organization: Its Management and Value* (New York: McGraw-Hill, 1967), for a complete discussion of the human organization.

26. John R. Montanari, Cyril P. Morgan, and Jeffrey Bracker, *Strategic Management* (Hinsdale, Ill.: Dryden Press, 1990), p. 114.

27. Alfred D. Chandler, *Strategy and Structure: Chapters in the History of the American Industrial Enterprise* (Cambridge, MA: MIT Press, 1962).

28. John R. Kimberly, "Organizational Size and the Structuralist Perspective: A Review, Critique, and Proposal," *Administrative Science Quarterly*, December 1976, pp. 571–597.

29. Peter M. Blau and Richard A. Schoenherr, *The Structure of Organizations* (New York: Basic Books, 1971).

30. Robert I. Sutton and Thomas D'Anno, "Decreasing Organizational Size: Untangling the Effects of Money and People," *Academy of Management Review*, May 1989, pp. 194–212.

31. David J. Hickson, Derek S. Pugh, and Diana C. Pheysey, "Operations Technology and Organization Structure: An Empirical Reappraisal," *Administrative Science Quarterly*, September 1969, pp. 378–397.

32. Richard L. Daft, *Organization Theory and Design*, 2nd ed. (St. Paul, MN: West, 1986), p. 55.

33. Robert B. Duncan, "Characteristics of Organizational Environments and Perceived Uncertainty," *Administrative Science Quarterly*, September 1972, pp. 313–327.

34. Henry Mintzberg, *The Structuring of Organizations: A Synthesis of the Research* (Englewood Cliffs, NJ: Prentice Hall, 1979).

35. See Harold C. Livesay, *American Made: Men Who Shaped the American Economy* (Boston: Little, Brown, 1979), pp. 215–239, for a discussion of Alfred Sloan and the development of the divisionalized structure at General Motors.

36. Anne B. Fisher, "GM Is Tougher Than You Think," *Fortune*, November 10, 1986, pp. 56–64.

37. Henry Mintzberg, "Organization Design: Fashion or Fit," *Harvard Business Review*, January–February 1981, pp. 103–116.

38. Lawton R. Burns, "Matrix Management in Hospitals: Testing Theories of Matrix Structure and Development," *Administrative Science Quarterly*, September 1989, pp. 355–358.

39. Ibid., pp. 129–154.

Chapter 14

1. See M. Polanyi, *Personal Knowledge* (Chicago: University of Chicago Press, 1958); E. Goffman, *The Presentation of Self in Everyday Life* (New York: Doubleday, 1959); and P. L. Berger and T. Luckman, *The Social Construction of Reality* (Garden City, NY: Anchor Books, 1967).

2. Eric Ransdell, "The Nike Story? Just Tell It!" *Fast Company*, January-February 2000, pp. 44–46 (quotation, p. 46); Claude Solnik, "Co-Founder of Nike Dies Christmas Eve," *Footwear News*, January 3, 2000, p. 2; Rosemary Feitelberg, "Bowerman's Legacy Runs On," *WWD*, December 30, 1999, p. 8.

3. Louise Lee, "Tricks of E*Trade," *BusinessWeek E.Biz*, February 7, 2000, pp. EB18–EB31.

4. A. L. Kroeber and C. Kluckhohn, "Culture: A Critical Review of Concepts and Definitions," in *Papers of the Peabody Museum of American Archaeology and Ethnology*, vol. 47, no. 1 (Cambridge, MA: Harvard University Press, 1952).

5. W. G. Ouchi, *Theory Z: How American Business Can Meet the Japanese Challenger* (Reading, MA.: Addison-Wesley, 1981); T. E. Deal and A. A. Kennedy, *Corporate Cultures: The Rites and Rituals of Corporate Life* (Reading, MA: Addison-Wesley, 1982); Thomas J. Peters and Robert H. Waterman, Jr., *In Search of Excellence: Lessons from America's Best-Run Companies* (New York: Harper & Row, 1982).

6. E. Borgida and R. E. Nisbett, "The Differential Impact of Abstract vs. Concrete Information on Decisions," *Journal of Applied Social Psychology*, July-September 1977, pp. 258–271.

7. J. Martin and M. Power, "Truth or Corporate Propaganda: The Value of a Good War Story," in Louis R. Pondy, Peter J. Frost, Gareth Morgan, and Thomas C. Dandridge, eds., *Organizational Dymbolism* (Greenwich. Conn.: JAI Pres, 1983), pp. 93–108.

8. W. G. Ouchi, "Markets, Bureaucracies, and Clans," *Administrative Science Quarterly*, March 1980, pp. 129–141; A. Wilkins and W. G. Ouchi, "Efficient Cultures: Exploring the Relationship Between Culture and Organizational Performance," *Administrative Science Quarterly*, September 1983, pp. 468–481.

9. Peters and Waterman, *In Search of Excellence*.

10. J. B. Barney, "Organizational Culture: Can It Be a Source of Sustained Competitive Advantage?" *Academy of Management Review*, July 1986, pp. 656–665.

11. Daniel R. Denison, "What Is the Difference Between Organizational Culture and Organizational Climate? A Native's Point of View on a Decade of Paradigm Wars," *Academy of Management Review*, July 1996, pp. 619–654.

12. Richard L. Osborne, "Strategic Values: The Corporate Performance Engine," *Business Horizons*, September–October 1996, pp. 41–47.

13. Ouchi, *Theory Z*.

14. John E. Sheridan, "Organizational Culture and Employee Retention," *Academy of Management Journal*, December 1992, pp. 1036–1056; Lisa A. Mainiero, "Is Your Corporate Culture Costing You?" *Academy of Management Executive*, November 1993, pp. 84–85.

15. Peters and Waterman, *In Search of Excellence*.

16. Watts S. Humphrey, *Managing for Innovation: Leading Technical People* (Englewood Cliffs, NJ: Prentice Hall, 1987).

17. Brian O'Reilly, "Secrets of the Most Admired Corporations: New Ideas and New Products," *Fortune*,

March 3, 1997, pp. 60–64.

18. W. Chan Kim and Renee A. Mauborgne, "Procedural Justice, Attitudes, and Subsidiary Top Management Compliance with Multinationals' Corporate Strategic Decisions," *Academy of Management Journal*, June 1993, pp. 502–526.

19. See Warren Wilhelm, "Changing Corporate Culture—or Corporate Behavior? How to Change Your Company," *Academy of Management Executive*, November 1992, pp. 72–77.

20. *Socialization* has also been defined as "the process by which culture is transmitted from one generation to the next." See J. W. M. Whiting, "Socialization: Anthropological Aspects," in D. Sils, ed., *International Encyclopedia of the Social Sciences*, Vol. 14 (New York: Free Press, 1968), p. 545.

21. J. E. Hebden, "Adopting an Organization's Culture: The Socialization of Graduate Trainees, " *Organizational Dynamics*, Summer 1986, pp. 54–72.

22. J. B. Barney, "Organizational Culture: Can It Be a Source of Sustained Competitive Advantage?" *Academy of Management Review*, July 1986, pp. 656–665.

23. Bellamy Pailthorp, "Safe Landing for Boeing," *U.S. News & World Report*, September 13, 1999, p. 43; Janet Rae-Dupree, "Can Boeing Get Lean Enough?" *BusinessWeek*, August 30, 1999, p. 182; Aaron Bernstein, "Boeing's Unions Are Worried About Job Security—The CEO's," *BusinessWeek*, July 5, 1999, p. 30; Kenneth Labich, "Boeing Finally Hatches a Plan," *Fortune*, March 1, 1999, pp. 101–106 (quotation, p. 102).

24. James R. Norman, "A New Teledyne," *Forbes*, September 27, 1993, pp. 44–45.

Chapter 15

1. "Baby Boomers Push for Power," *BusinessWeek*, July 2, 1984, pp. 52–56.

2. "Americans' Median Age Passes 32," *Arizona Republic*, April 6, 1988, pp. A1, A5.

3. "Population Estimates Program," Population Division, U.S. Census Bureau, Washington, DC.

4. Geoffrey Colvin, "What the Baby Boomers Will Buy Next," *Fortune*, October 15, 1984, pp. 28–34.

5. Peter Nulty, "How Personal Computers Change Managers' Lives," *Fortune*, September 3, 1984, pp. 38–48.

6. Thomas A. Stewart, "Welcome to the Revolution," *Fortune*, December 13, 1993, pp. 66–80.

7. Kurt Lewin, *Field Theory in Social Science* (New York: Harper & Row, 1951).

8. Linda S. Ackerman, "Transition Management: An In-Depth Look at Managing Complex Change," *Organizational Dynamics*, Summer 1982, pp. 46–66; David A. Nadler, "Managing Transitions to Uncertain Future States," *Organizational Dynamics*, Summer 1982, pp. 37–45.

9. Noel M. Tichy and David O. Ulrich, "The Leadership Challenge—A Call for the Transformational Leader," *Sloan Management Review*, Fall 1984, pp. 59–68.

10. Danny Miller and Peter H. Friesen, "Structural Change and Performance: Quantum Versus Piecemeal-Incremental Approaches," *Academy of Management Journal*, December 1982, pp. 867–892.

11. J. Lloyd Suttle, "Improving Life at Work—Problems and Prospects," in J. Richard Hackman and J. Lloyd Suttle, eds., *Improving Life at Work: Behavioral Science Approaches to Organizational Change* (Santa Monica, CA: Goodyear, 1977), p. 4.

12. Daniel A. Ondrack and Martin G. Evans, "Job Enrichment and Job Satisfaction in Greenfield and Redesign QWL Sites," *Group & Organization Studies*, March 1987, pp. 5–22.

13. Ricky W. Griffin, *Task Design: An Integrative Framework* (Glenview, IL: Scott, Foresman, 1982).

14. Gregory Moorhead, "Organizational Analysis: An Integration of the Macro and Micro Approaches," *Journal of Management Studies*, April 1981, pp. 191–218.

15. Kenneth N. Wexley and Timothy T. Baldwin, "Management Development," *1986 Yearly Review of Management of the Journal of Management*, in

Journal of Management, Summer 1986, pp. 277–294.

16. Richard Beckhard, "Optimizing Team-Building Efforts," *Journal of Contemporary Business*, Summer 1972, pp. 23–27, 30–32.

17. Michael Beer, *Organization Change and Development* (Santa Monica, CA: Goodyear, 1980).

18. Jerome L. Franklin, "Improving the Effectiveness of Survey Feedback," *Personnel*, May-June 1978, pp. 11–17.

19. Paul R. Lawrence, "How to Deal with Resistance to Change," *Harvard Business Review*, May–June 1954, reprinted in Gene W. Dalton, Paul R. Lawrence, and Larry E. Greiner, eds., *Organizational Change and Development* (Homewood, IL: Irwin, 1970), pp. 181–197.

20. Daniel Katz and Robert L. Kahn, *The Social Psychology of Organizations*, 2nd ed. (New York: Wiley, 1978), pp. 36–68.

21. See Michael T. Hannah and John Freeman, "Structural Inertia and Organizational Change," *American Sociological Review*, April 1984, pp. 149–164, for an in-depth discussion of structural inertia.

22. Moorhead, "Organizational Analysis: An Integration of the Macro and Micro Approaches."

23. G. Zaltman and R. Duncan, *Strategies for Planned Change* (New York: Wiley, 1977); David A. Nadler, "Concepts for the Management of Organizational Change," in J. Richard Hackman, Edward E. Lawler III, and Lyman W. Porter, eds., *Perspectives on Behavior in Organizations*, 2nd ed. (New York: McGraw-Hill, 1983), pp. 551–561.

24. Alan M. Webber, "Learning for a Change," *Fast Company*, May 1999, pp. 178–188.

ANSWERS TO TEST PREPPERS

Chapter 1
1. T	9. F	17. b	25. a
2. F	10. T	18. d	26. c
3. F	11. F	19. a	27. e
4. F	12. T	20. e	28. b
5. F	13. F	21. b	29. a
6. T	14. T	22. c	30. c
7. T	15. d	23. e	
8. T	16. e	24. b	

Chapter 2
1. T	10. F	19. b	28. d
2. T	11. F	20. a	29. e
3. F	12. F	21. d	30. a
4. F	13. F	22. c	
5. F	14. T	23. c	
6. F	15. T	24. b	
7. F	16. F	25. e	
8. T	17. a	26. c	
9. F	18. d	27. d	

Chapter 3
1. F	9. T	17. c	25. d
2. T	10. F	18. d	26. a
3. F	11. F	19. a	27. b
4. F	12. T	20. b	28. e
5. T	13. T	21. b	29. b
6. T	14. T	22. e	30. d
7. T	15. T	23. d	31. c
8. T	16. d	24. d	32. e

Chapter 4
1. F	9. T	17. F	25. b
2. T	10. T	18. d	26. c
3. T	11. F	19. c	27. a
4. F	12. T	20. d	28. b
5. T	13. T	21. b	29. d
6. F	14. T	22. c	30. e
7. T	15. T	23. d	31. d
8. F	16. F	24. d	

Chapter 5
1. T	9. T	17. F	25. e
2. F	10. F	18. a	26. b
3. F	11. F	19. d	27. b
4. T	12. T	20. b	28. c
5. F	13. F	21. c	29. d
6. T	14. T	22. a	30. c
7. T	15. T	23. b	31. e
8. F	16. T	24. e	

Chapter 6
1. T	10. T	19. c	28. c
2. F	11. T	20. d	29. a
3. F	12. T	21. e	30. b
4. T	13. F	22. e	31. e
5. F	14. T	23. e	32. c
6. T	15. F	24. d	33. e
7. T	16. T	25. c	
8. F	17. a	26. b	
9. T	18. b	27. a	

Chapter 7
1. F	10. F	19. e	28. e
2. F	11. T	20. a	29. b
3. F	12. T	21. e	30. e
4. T	13. T	22. d	31. b
5. F	14. F	23. b	32. b
6. T	15. T	24. e	33. e
7. F	16. F	25. c	34. d
8. F	17. d	26. c	
9. T	18. e	27. c	

Chapter 8
1. F	10. T	19. b	28. c
2. F	11. T	20. a	29. b
3. T	12. F	21. b	30. b
4. F	13. F	22. c	31. c
5. T	14. T	23. a	32. e
6. T	15. T	24. e	33. b
7. T	16. T	25. d	
8. T	17. F	26. b	
9. F	18. T	27. e	

Chapter 9
1. F	9. T	17. T	25. d
2. T	10. T	18. a	26. e
3. F	11. F	19. c	27. a
4. F	12. F	20. a	28. a
5. T	13. T	21. c	29. d
6. F	14. F	22. e	30. b
7. F	15. T	23. d	31. d
8. F	16. F	24. b	

Chapter 10
1. F	9. F	17. T	25. e
2. F	10. T	18. b	26. e
3. T	11. T	19. d	27. c
4. F	12. F	20. d	28. a
5. T	13. F	21. c	29. e
6. F	14. F	22. e	30. a
7. T	15. T	23. c	31. d
8. T	16. F	24. a	32. c

Chapter 11
1. T	11. F	21. e	31. b
2. F	12. F	22. d	32. c
3. T	13. F	23. c	33. b
4. F	14. F	24. e	34. c
5. T	15. T	25. e	35. a
6. F	16. F	26. b	36. e
7. F	17. T	27. a	37. d
8. T	18. T	28. b	38. b
9. T	19. T	29. d	39. d
10. T	20. T	30. e	

Chapter 12
1. F	10. T	19. b	28. e
2. T	11. F	20. b	29. a
3. F	12. F	21. e	30. b
4. T	13. T	22. d	31. d
5. F	14. F	23. e	32. d
6. T	15. F	24. c	33. c
7. F	16. F	25. a	
8. T	17. T	26. e	
9. T	18. a	27. b	

Chapter 13
1. F	9. T	17. T	25. b
2. T	10. T	18. T	26. e
3. F	11. T	19. b	27. a
4. F	12. F	20. c	28. d
5. T	13. F	21. a	29. a
6. F	14. T	22. e	30. a
7. F	15. F	23. d	31. b
8. F	16. T	24. a	32. b

Chapter 14
1. F	9. F	17. c	25. b
2. T	10. T	18. e	26. e
3. T	11. F	19. d	27. d
4. T	12. F	20. b	28. b
5. T	13. F	21. c	29. e
6. F	14. F	22. b	30. e
7. F	15. T	23. c	31. e
8. T	16. a	24. a	

Chapter 15
1. T	10. F	19. F	28. e
2. F	11. T	20. T	29. b
3. T	12. T	21. b	30. c
4. F	13. F	22. b	31. e
5. F	14. T	23. a	32. c
6. F	15. F	24. b	33. a
7. F	16. T	25. d	34. d
8. T	17. T	26. a	35. e
9. T	18. T	27. c	

INDEX